Finland

Lapland
p235

Oulu, Kainuu
& Koillismaa
p215

West
Coast
p194

The Lakeland
p150

Karelia
p173

Åland
Archipelago
p114

Tampere, Pirkanmaa

Turku
South
p...

D1292230

Mara Vorhees, Catherine Le Nevez, Virginia Maxwell

Contents

PLAN YOUR TRIP

Welcome to Finland 4
Finland Map 6
Finland's Top 15 8
Need to Know 16
What's New 18
If You Like 19
Month by Month 22
Itineraries 25
The Great Outdoors 28
Travel with Children 36
Regions at a Glance 38

TUOMIOKIRKKO P49, HELSINKI

URHO KEKKONEN NATIONAL PARK P263

ON THE ROAD

HELSINKI 42

TURKU & THE SOUTH COAST 82
Turku 84
Naantali 91
Turku Archipelago 93
Pargas 94
Nagu 94
Korpo 95
Houtskär 96
Iniö 96
Kustavi 97
The South Coast: West of Helsinki 97
Kimito Island & Archipelago National Park 97
Hanko 99
Raseborg 102
Fiskars 104
Lohja 104
The South Coast: East of Helsinki 105
Porvoo 106
Loviisa 108
Kotka 109
Hamina 112

ÅLAND ARCHIPELAGO 114
Fasta Åland 117
Mariehamn 117
Jomala 122
Hammarland 122
Eckerö 123
Geta 124
Saltvik 125
Sund 125

Vårdö 126
Finström 127
Lemland 127
Lumparland 128
Northern & Southern Archipelagos 128
Northern Archipelago . . . 129
Southern Archipelago . . . 130

TAMPERE, PIRKANMAA & HÄME 132
Tampere 133
Pirkanmaa 140
Ruovesi 141
Helvetinjärvi National Park 141
Keuruu 141
Mänttä 142
Häme 143
Iittala 143
Hämeenlinna 143
Lahti 146

THE LAKELAND . . . 150
Savonlinna 151
Punkaharju 155
The Seal Lakes 157
Sulkava 158
Mikkeli 158
New Valamo 160
Jyväskylä 161
Around Jyväskylä 167
Kuopio 168

KARELIA 173
South Karelia 175
Lappeenranta 175

Contents

Imatra. 179
North Karelia. **181**
Joensuu. 181
Ilomantsi 184
Hattuvaara. 185
Lake Pielinen. **186**
Koli National Park 186
Paalasmaa Island. 188
Vuonislahti. 188
Lieksa. 188
Patvinsuo
National Park 189
Ruunaa
Recreation Area 190
Nurmijärvi District. 192
Nurmes 192

WEST COAST. **194**
Uusikaupunki 196
Rauma 197
Pori. 200
Around Pori. 203
Kristinestad. 204
Närpes. 205
Seinäjoki 205
Vaasa. 206
Around Vaasa 209
Jakobstad 210
Around Jakobstad 211
Kokkola 212
Kalajoki 213

**OULU, KAINUU
& KOILLISMAA** **215**
Oulu 217
Around Oulu 222
Kajaani. 222

Sotkamo 223
Kuhmo 224
Hossa 225
Kuusamo & Ruka 226
Juuma 232
Karhunkierros Trek &
Oulanka National Park . . . 232

LAPLAND. **235**
Southern Lapland. **238**
Kemi. 238
Tornio 240
Rovaniemi 241
Around Rovaniemi 249
Kemijärvi 250
Pyhä-Luosto 250
Fell Lapland. **252**
Ylläs 252
Levi 253
Muonio. 255
Hetta. 256
Pallas-Yllästunturi
National Park 257
Kilpisjärvi 258
Northern Lapland. **259**
Sodankylä 259
Saariselkä 261
Around Saariselkä 262
Saariselkä Wilderness
& Urho Kekkonen
National Park 263
Ivalo 265
Nellim. 266
Inari 266
Lemmenjoki
National Park 268
Inari to Norway. 270

UNDERSTAND

Finland
Today 274
History. 276
The Sámi 284
Finnish Lifestyle
& Culture. 286
Finnish Design 289
The Arts. 292
Food & Drink 295

SURVIVAL GUIDE

Directory A-Z. 298
Transport. 303
Language. 309
Index 314
Map Legend. 319

SPECIAL FEATURES

Sauna Culture. 56
The Finnish
Lakeland 162
Native Wildlife 228
Snow Sports 244

Welcome to Finland

Inspired design, technology and epicurean scenes meet epic stretches of wilderness here in Europe's deep north, where summer's endless light balances winter's eerie frozen magic.

Call of the Wild

The Finland you encounter will depend on the season of your visit, but whatever the month, there's something pure in the Finnish air and spirit that's vital and exciting. With towering forests speckled by picture-perfect lakes, as if an artist had flicked a blue-dipped paintbrush at the map, Suomi offers some of Europe's best hiking, kayaking and canoeing. A fabulous network of national parks has well-marked routes and regularly spaced huts for overnighting, and you can observe bears and elk deep in the forests on nature-watching trips.

Summer Days

Finland's short but sparkling sunny season sees the country burst into life. Finns seem to want to suck every last golden drop out of the summer in the hope that it will sustain them through the long, dark winter months, and there's an explosion of good cheer and optimism. With surprisingly high temperatures for these latitudes, summer is a time for music festivals, art exhibitions, lake cruises, midnight sunshine on convivial beer terraces, idyllic days at remote waterside cottages and bountiful market produce.

After the Snowfall

Winter has its own charm as snow blankets the pines and lakes freeze over. The best way to banish the frosty subzero temperatures is to get active. Skiing is great through to May. Other pursuits include chartering a team of dogs, a posse of reindeer, or a snowmobile for a trek across snowy solitudes, lit by a beautiful, pale winter sun; catching the aurora borealis (Northern Lights) after your wood-fired sauna; drilling a hole for ice fishing; and spending a night in a glittering, iridescent ice hotel.

City Lights

Finland isn't just vast expanses of pristine wilderness. Vibrant cities stock the country's southern areas, headlined by the capital, Helsinki, an electrifying urban space with world-renowned design and music scenes. Embraced by the Baltic, it's a spectacular ensemble of modern and stately architecture, island restaurants and stylish and quirky bars. And the 'new Suomi' epicurean scene is flourishing, with locally foraged flavours to the fore. Beyond Helsinki, Tampere and Turku in particular are lively, engaging cities with spirited university-student populations.

By Catherine Le Nevez, Writer

What captivates me most about Finland is its extremes. The country is a study in contrasts, from lush, berry-filled forests to snowy, frozen winterscapes, traditional Sámi handicrafts to experimental design, vast wilderness to vibrant cities, time-honoured industry to cutting-edge tech, searing summers to vivifying winters, steaming saunas to bracing lakes, midnight sunlight to enveloping darkness, and skies that transform from expansive blackness to light shows of unearthly neon greens, pinks, purples and reds as the aurora borealis dances overhead. Finland is a paradox of perpetual change and abiding timelessness. It's an extraordinary place.

For more about our writers, see p320

Above: Reindeer, Lapland

Finland

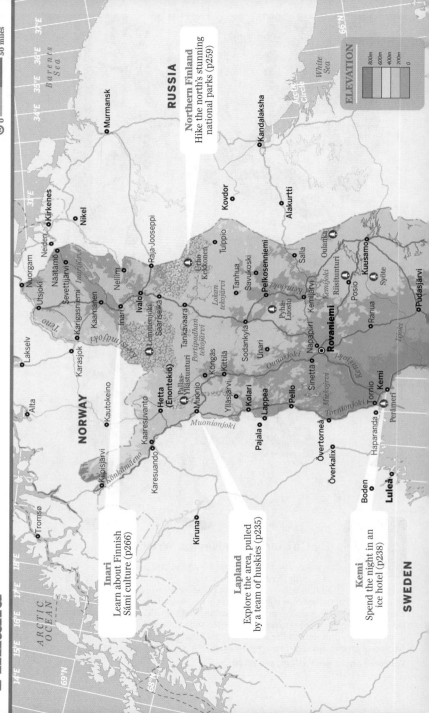

Inari
Learn about Finnish
Sámi culture (p266)

Lapland
Explore the area, pulled
by a team of huskies (p235)

Kemi
Spend the night in an
ice hotel (p238)

Northern Finland
Hike the north's stunning
national parks (p259)

ELEVATION

	800m
	600m
	400m
	200m
	0

Eastern Finland
See bears in
the wild (p188)

Karelia
Find a lonely lakeside
cottage (p173)

The Lakeland
Huge variety of
boating options (p150)

Savonlinna
Marvellous opera
festival in a castle (p151)

Helsinki
Browse world-famous
Finnish design shops (p42)

Hanko
Top beaches and romantic
Russian villas (p99)

Kuopio
Sweat it out
in a sauna (p168)

Tampere
Traditional produce at
the market hall (p132)

Rauma
Finland's finest
wooden Old Town (p197)

Turku
Investigate the city's
quirky bars (p84)

Åland
Cycle around this
scenic archipelago (p114)

Finland's
Top 15

Traditional Sauna

1 These days most Finns have saunas at home, but some public ones remain. They smell of old pine, tar shampoo and long tradition, with birch whisks and no-nonsense scrubdowns available as extras. Weathered Finnish faces cool down on the street outside, loins wrapped in a towel and hand wrapped around a cold beer. Helsinki and Tampere are the best places for this, while Kuopio's old-style smoke sauna (p169) takes a day to prepare and offers a more rural experience, with a lake to jump into right alongside.

Bottom left: A lakeside sauna, Tampere

Design Shopping, Helsinki

2 Functional, elegant, outrageous or wacky: the choice is yours. The capital's decidedly nonmainstream chic is best explored by browsing the vast variety of design shops that spatter its centre. Whether examining iconic 20th-century Finnish forms in the flagship emporia of brands such as Iittala, Marimekko and Artek, or tracking down the cutting-edge and just plain weird in the creative Punavuori (p45) backstreets in the heart of its Design District, you're sure to find something you didn't know you needed, but just can't do without. And yes, they can arrange shipping.

Bottom right: Classic Marimekko designs

JANNE SKINNARLA/PHOTOJANSKI/500PX ©

EQROY/SHUTTERSTOCK ©

2

MIKKO KARJALAINEN/ALAMY ©

National Park Hiking, Northern Finland

3 Finland's great swaths of protected forests and fells make it one of Europe's prime hiking destinations. Head to the Karhunkierros near Kuusamo for a striking terrain of hills and sharp ravines that is prettiest in autumn. The Urho Kekkonen National Park (p263) in Lapland is one of Europe's great wildernesses, while the spectacular gorge of the Kevo Strict Nature Reserve and the fell scenery of Pallas-Yllästunturi National Park (p257; pictured) are other northern options.

Bear-Watching, Eastern Finland

4 Old Honeypaws, the brown bear (*Ursus arctos*), is the national animal of Finland. Around 1000 of these powerful creatures live in the northeast, coming and going with impunity across the Finnish–Russian border. Operators (p189) run bear hides close to the frontier, where you can sit a silent night's vigil as bruins snuffle out elk carcasses and carefully hidden chunks of salmon. The best time to see them is between mid-April and August, with a slight gap in July when the bears have mating rather than meals in mind.

Cycling, Åland Archipelago

5 Paradisical Åland (p88) is best explored by bicycle – you'll appreciate its understated attractions all the more if you've used pedal power to reach them. Bridges and ferries link many of its 6000 islands, and well-signposted routes take you off 'main roads' down winding lanes and forestry tracks. En route you can pick wild strawberries, wander castle ruins (Kastelholms Slott p125; pictured), sunbathe on a slab of red granite, visit a medieval church, quench your thirst at a cider orchard, or climb a lookout tower to gaze at the glittering sea.

On the Water, Lakeland

6 The Lakeland (p150) seems to have more water than land, so it'd be a crime not to get out on it. You can take three days to paddle the family-friendly Oravareitti (Squirrel Route), or head out into Kolovesi and Linnansaari national parks to meet freshwater seals. Tired arms? Historic lake boats still ply what were once important transport arteries; depart from any town on short cruises, or make a day of it and go from Savonlinna right up to Kuopio or across Finland's largest lake, Saimaa, to Lappeenranta.

Right: Savonlinna, p151

RNDMS/SHUTTERSTOCK ©

Sledding & Snowmobiling, Lapland

7 Fizzing across Lapland (p235) behind a team of huskies under the low winter sun is tough to beat. Short jaunts are great, but overnight safaris give you time to feed and bond with your lovable dogs and try out a wood-fired sauna in the middle of the winter wilderness. It's no fairytale ride though; expect to eat some snow before you learn to control your team. If you're not a dog person, you can enjoy similar trips on a snowmobile or behind reindeer.

Music Festivals

8 Are you a chamber-music aficionado? Or do you like rock so raucous it makes your ears bleed? Whatever your pleasure, Finland has a music festival to suit. Savonlinna's castle is the dramatic setting for a month-long opera festival (p155); fiddlers gather at Kaustinen for full-scale folk; Pori, Espoo and Tampere attract thousands of jazz fans; Seinäjoki flashes sequins and high heels during its five-day tango festival; Turku's Ruisrock (p86; pictured) is one of several kicking rock festivals; and the Sibelius Festival in Lahti ushers in autumn with classical grace.

Summer Cottages

9 The symbol of the Finnish summer is a cosy cottage perched on a blue lake, with a little rowboat, a fishing pier and perhaps its own swimming beach. The simplest rustic cabins have outside loos and water drawn from a well, while the most modern designer bungalows have every creature comfort. Whether you're looking for a wilderness escape – picturesque Karelia (p173; pictured) offers some of Finland's most deeply forested corners – or somewhere for a big family party, you're bound to find the perfect place from the thousands of rental cottages on offer.

Sámi Culture, Inari

10 Finland's indigenous northerners have used technology to ease the arduous side of reindeer herding while maintaining an intimate knowledge of Lapland's natural world. Their capital, Inari, and the nearby Lemmenjoki National Park are the best places to begin to learn about Sámi culture and traditions. Start at the marvellous Siida museum (p266), with state-of-the-art exhibition halls and original buildings, including farmhouses, storage huts and a courthouse. Arrange wilderness excursions with Sámi guides, meet reindeer and browse high-quality handicrafts and music, the sale of which benefits local communities.

Bottom right: Sámi man in traditional dress

OLGA NEFFISTA/SHUTTERSTOCK ©

BLUEORANGE STUDIO/ALAMY ©

Bar Life

11 Rumours about Finnish beer prices are a little exaggerated, and there's a big social drinking scene that's great to take part in, particularly in student-filled Turku (p89). Finns lose that famous reserve after a *tuoppi* (half-litre glass) or three of beer and are keen to chat to visitors; it's a great way to meet locals. Finland's cities are full of original and off-beat bars and you'll soon find a favourite Suomi tipple, whether Finnish ciders, microbrewed beers, sweet-and-sour combinations, or unusual shots such as salty liquorice vodka or cloudberry liqueur.

Rauma Old Town

12 The largest wooden old town in the Nordic countries, Vanha Rauma (p197) deserves its Unesco World Heritage status. Its 600 houses might be museum pieces, but they also form a living centre: residents tend their flower boxes and chat to neighbours, while visitors meander in and out of the low-key cafes, shops, museums and artisans' workshops. Rauman giäl, an old sailors' lingo that mixes up a host of languages, is still spoken here, and the town's medieval lace-making heritage is celebrated during Pitsiviikko (Rauma Lace Week).

GEORGY GOLOVIN/ALAMY ©

HIVAKA/SHUTTERSTOCK ©

Icy Accommodation, Kemi

13 Even reading the words 'snow hotel' can shoot a shiver up your spine, but spending a night in one of these ethereally beautiful, extravagantly artistic icy buildings is a marvellous, though expensive, experience. There are several to choose from in Lapland, including Lumi-hotelli (p239; pictured) in Kemi. Heavy-duty sleeping bags ensure a relatively cosy slumber, and a morning sauna banishes any lingering chills. If you don't fancy spending the night inside, you can visit the complexes, maybe pausing for a well-chilled vodka cocktail in the bar.

Food Markets

14 Counters selling local cheeses, rough rye breads, handmade chocolates, Finnish sausages and smoked fish fill each town's indoor kauppahalli (covered market). Tampere's (p138) – try traditional *mustamakkara* (blood sausage) – is typical, with delicious aromas wafting between stalls. In summer the kauppatori (market square) in the towns burst with straight-from-the-garden fruit and vegetables such as juicy red strawberries or peas popped fresh from the pod. Autumn's approach is softened by piles of peppery chanterelles and glowing Lapland cloudberries (pictured), appearing in August like a magician's trick.

Seaside Hanko

15 Offering some of Finland's finest beaches, genteel Hanko (p99), the country's southernmost town, has a history intimately connected with Russia. The St Petersburg gentry for whom it was a favoured summering destination have left a noble legacy of lovely wooden villas, while the area saw heavy fighting in WWII when it was occupied by Russia and locals were forced to evacuate. Today the long sandy peninsula is all about yachts and sand castles, rather than gunboats and trenches, and makes a great place to relax.

Need to Know

For more information, see Survival Guide (p297)

Currency
Euro (€)

Language
Finnish, Swedish, Sámi languages

Visas
Generally not required for stays of up to 90 days; some nationalities will need a Schengen visa.

Money
Credit cards are widely accepted. ATMs are prevalent.

Mobile Phones
Purchasing a Finnish SIM card at any R-kioski shop for your own phone (provided it's unlocked) is cheapest. Top the credit up at the same outlets, online, or at ATMs. Roaming charges within the EU have been abolished.

Time
Eastern European Time (EET; UTC/GMT plus two hours)

When to Go

Warm to hot summers, cold winters
Mild summers, cold winters

Rovaniemi
● **GO** Dec–Apr, Jul–Sep

Oulu
GO Jun–Aug ●

Kuopio
● **GO** Jun–Aug

Tampere
● **GO** Jun–Aug, Dec

Helsinki
● **GO** May–Sep, Dec

High Season
(Jul)
➡ Attractions and lodgings are open.
➡ Hotels outside Helsinki are often substantially cheaper.
➡ Summer budget accommodation is open.
➡ Boat cruises running.
➡ Numerous festivals across country.

Shoulder
(Jun & Aug)
➡ Long days with decent temperatures.
➡ Most attractions are open.
➡ Not as crowded as July.
➡ Fewer insects up north.
➡ Country shuts down over midsummer weekend.

Low Season
(Sep–May)
➡ Outside cities, many attractions are closed.
➡ Hotels charge top rates, except on weekends.
➡ Aurora-spotting chances are highest in October, November and March.
➡ December to April is busy for winter sports.
➡ Short, cool or cold days.

Useful Websites

Metsähallitus (www.national parks.fi) Excellent resource, with detailed information on Finland's national parks and protected areas.

Finnish Tourist Board (www. visitfinland.com) Comprehensive official site.

Helsinki Times (www.helsinki times.fi) English-language newspaper.

This is Finland (https://finland. fi) Maintained by the Ministry of Foreign Affairs; informative and entertaining.

Lonely Planet (www.lonely planet.com/finland) Destination information, bookings, travel forum and more.

Finnish Camping Association (www.camping.fi) Book campsites online.

Important Numbers

Eliminate the initial zero from area/mobile codes if dialling from abroad.

Country code	☑358
International access code	☑00
General emergency	☑112

Exchange Rates

Australia	A$1	€0.65
Canada	C$1	€0.66
Japan	¥100	€0.74
New Zealand	NZ$1	€0.59
Norway	NKr10	€1.02
Russia	R100	€1.44
Sweden	Skr10	€1.02
UK	UK£1	€1.12
USA	US$1	€0.83

For current exchange rates, see www.xe.com.

Daily Costs

Budget:
Less than €120

➡ Dorm bed: €25–35

➡ Bike hire per day: €10–20

➡ Lunch buffet: €8–14

➡ Two-hour bus/train to next town: €8–30

Midrange:
€120–250

➡ Standard hotel double room: €80–130

➡ Two-course meal with wine: €50–80

➡ Car hire: €40–50 per day

➡ Museum entry: €5–10

Top end:
More than €250

➡ Room in boutique hotel: €150–300

➡ Upmarket degustation menu with wine: €100–350

➡ Taxi across town: €20–30

➡ Two-hour husky sled ride: €90–140

Opening Hours

Many attractions in Finland only open for a short summer season, typically mid-June to late August. Opening hours tend to shorten in winter in general.

Alko (state alcohol store) 9am–8pm Monday to Friday, to 6pm Saturday

Banks 9am–4.15pm Monday to Friday

Businesses & Shops 9am–6pm Monday to Friday, to 3pm Saturday

Nightclubs 10pm–4am Wednesday to Saturday

Pubs 11am–1am (often later on Friday and Saturday)

Restaurants 11am–10pm, lunch 11am–3pm. Last orders generally an hour before closing.

Arriving in Finland

Helsinki-Vantaa Airport Trains on the airport rail link (€5, 30 minutes, 5.05am to 12.05am) serve the city. Local buses (24 hours) and faster Finnair buses (5am to 1.10am) run into the city (30 to 50 minutes). Taxis cost €45 to €50 to the city centre (30 minutes). Cheaper shared airport taxis cost from €29.50 per person.

Tampere-Pirkkala Airport Bus 1A meets arriving flights (€5, 30 minutes to the city centre). Shared taxis cost €19 per person, standard taxis around €35 (25 minutes to the city centre).

Getting Around

You can set your watch by Finnish transport. For bus timetables, head to www. matkahuolto.fi, while for trains it's www.vr.fi. A useful combined journey planner for Finland's public-transport network is online at www.journey.fi.

Bus Around the same price as trains, but slower. Cover the whole country. Rarely need booking.

Car Hire widely available; week or weekend deals booked in advance are much better than sky-high day rates. Automatic transmission is rare; book well in advance and expect a hefty premium. Drive on the right.

Flights Generally expensive, but you can get some good deals on Lapland routes. Multitrip journeys are generally cheaper than one-way flights.

Train Generally modern and comfortable, with good coverage. Book busy routes in advance.

For much more on **getting around**, see p305

What's New

Hossa National Park

To commemorate Finland's centenary of independence in 2017, Hossa National Park became the country's 40th designated national park. Its 110 sq km take in lakes, forests, canyons and extraordinary 4000-year-old rock paintings. (p225)

Parliament House

After decamping to temporary accommodation during extensive renovations, the Finnish parliament returned to Helsinki's imposing Eduskunta (Parliament House) in 2017, with guided tours of the impressively overhauled building available. (p53)

Helsinki Airport Rail Link

Travelling from Helsinki's airport to the city centre is easier than ever thanks to the airport–city rail link, which cuts down the journey time to just 30 minutes (www.hsl.f).

City Bikes

Getting around the Finnish capital is a breeze thanks to its bike-share scheme. Launched in 2016, City Bikes has some 1500 bikes at 150 stations citywide (www.hsl.fi/citybikes).

Örö Fortress

In the Archipelago National Park, board a ferry to explore Örö Fortress' barracks, heavy artillery battery and fortifications on a previously closed military island that has opened to the public after more than a century. (p97)

Säynätsalon Kunnantalo Tours

Guided tours lead you through one of Alvar Aalto's most admired works, the Säynätsalon Kunnantalo (Säynätsalon Town Hall), conceived as a 'fortress of democracy' and constructed between 1949 and 1952. (p167)

Moomimuseo

The concert hall Tampere-talo is the new home of the wonderful Moomimuseo, with original drawings and delightful dioramas bringing the stories of Tove Jansson to life. (p134)

Regatta Spa

With 270-degree sea and sky views, the stunning new Regatta Spa opened in 2017 in Hanko, recalling the town's 19th-century spa-town heyday. (p100)

Santa's Seaside Office

In Lapland, Santa now has a new seaside office in Kemi, with activities such as elf sailor workshops. (p239)

Hotel Nestor & Back Pocket

Gorgeously restored, the former barn housing Hotel Nestor in the Turku Archipelago village of Korpo has a standout destination restaurant, Back Pocket, serving exquisitely presented contemporary Finnish cuisine. (p96)

For more recommendations and reviews, see lonelyplanet.com/finland

If You Like...

Offbeat Accommodation

With its dramatic landscapes and coastline and the country's design traditions and appreciation of the offbeat, you can stay in some truly unique properties here.

Lumihotelli On the Lapland coast, this romantic snow castle is Finland's most spectacular frozen hotel. (p239)

Lainio Snow Village Down vodkas from icy glasses in the igloo bar, then snuggle up atop your icy mattress here in western Lapland. (p253)

Arctic Snow Hotel In easy reach of Lapland's capital, this friendly place also has an ice restaurant. (p243)

Kylmäpihlajan Majakka Have an away-from-it-all experience in this lighthouse hotel on a west-coast island. (p199)

Little Tundra Guesthouse Yurt-like cabins furnished with beds, rugs and colourful textiles occupy an old railway workshop. (p147)

Wilderness Hotel Nellim Watch the aurora borealis from the warmth of your bed inside a translucent 'aurora bubble'. (p266)

Hotel Katajanokka On the Helsinki island of the same name, this former prison has been stunningly converted. (p59)

Art

From ancient rock art to cutting-edge contemporary art, Finland has a treasure trove of art in its cities, towns and even its remote wilderness.

Helsinki Outstanding galleries are headed up by the Ateneum and the contemporary Kiasma gallery. (p48)

Mänttä This small town has a great gallery, Gösta, with a striking modern annexe for contemporary works. (p142)

Tampere Stunning frescoes by Hugo Simberg adorn the interior of the cathedral. (p134)

Visavuori Visit the lakeside studio of sculptor Emil Wickström. (p142)

Vaasa This west-coast art hub has several excellent galleries, including the Kuntsi Museum of Modern Art. (p207)

Turku Modern art and traditional Finnish landscapes are displayed in Turku's turreted art museum. (p85)

Sodankylä View the work of Andreas Alariesto, who depicted traditional Sámi life in naive style. (p259)

Paateri See the home, workshop and masterwork wilderness church of Eva Ryynänen, Finland's most renowned wood sculptor. (p193)

Island-Hopping

Finland has tens of thousands of islands, ranging from suburbs of Helsinki to rocky islets in the middle of nowhere.

Ukko A Sámi sacred spot, this Lake Inari island can be visited on a boat trip. (p267)

Åland This archipelago between Finland and Sweden is ripe for exploration using local ferries or a sea kayak. (p114)

Helsinki Head out to one of the island restaurants in Helsinki harbour for a crayfish feast. (p69)

Kvarken This intriguing landscape of islands west of Vaasa is constantly changing. (p209)

Hailuoto Grab the ferry out to this island near Oulu for a peaceful northerly beach break. (p222)

Bengtskär Finland's southernmost inhabited island is famous for its staunch Baltic lighthouse. (p98)

Turku archipelago Freewheel around this complex of islands south of Turku by bike. (p93)

Paalasmaa In Lake Pielinen, this picturesque island rises 225m above sea level. (p188)

Ekenäs Archipelago National Park Maritime national parks dotted along Finland's coast include Ekenäs. (p105)

Wildlife

Finland's wilderness teems with wildlife and there are some superb opportunities to get up close to the creatures that inhabit the country's remoter reaches.

Bears, Kuusamo Observe these magnificent carnivores through long summer evenings from the comfort of a hide. (p227)

Elk, Kuhmo Increased fencing keeps these beasts off the main roads; try a safari to spot them. (p224)

Reindeer, Lapland There are numerous places where you can meet and feed them, or take a winter sled safari. (p242)

Wolverines, Lieksa With luck you'll spot this elusive predator on a trip out of Lieksa. (p189)

Seals, the Seal Lakes The rare Saimaa ringed seal is an inland variety, best seen by grabbing a canoe and exploring the Seal Lakes. (p157)

Traditional Architecture

Once upon a time, all towns in Finland were picturesque rows of painted wooden houses. Wars and a succession of great fires started by some unwary baker or smoker put paid to most of them, but some classic examples remain.

Porvoo Classic wooden warehouses and a noble Old Town less than an hour from Helsinki. (p106)

Rauma Vanha Rauma, the Old Town, is the most extensive and intriguing wooden district left in Finland. (p197)

Jakobstad An area of unspoiled wooden homes stretches north of the centre. (p210)

Top: Kamppi Chapel (p53), Helsinki

Bottom: Saimaa ringed seal (p157)

Turku Luostarinmäki is a historic quarter of the city that has been preserved in situ as a museum. (p84)

Naantali The quaint old cobbled streets here make for a very picturesque stroll. (p91)

Hanko Opulent wooden villas built for Russian aristocracy line the streets of this coastal town. (p99)

Petäjäveden Vanha Kirkko This Unesco-listed church is a magnificent example of 18th-century rustic Finnish architecture. (p168)

Kerimäki Enormous wooden church planned by a churchman who overestimated the size of his congregation. (p156)

Modern Architecture

Architecture and design are hallmarks of Finland, and continue to break new ground.

Jyväskylä University town central to Alvar Aalto's work; tour his centrepiece Säynätsalon Kunnantalo (town hall). (p161)

Seinäjoki Aalto was given licence to experiment as he redesigned the centre of this western Finnish town. (p205)

Villa Mairea This fabulous art-filled villa in Pori is an Aalto masterpiece. (p201)

Musiikkitalo Built from glass and copper, this music centre has become a Helsinki landmark. (p75)

Temppeliaukion Kirkko Helsinki's most striking church is bored into a hill of solid rock. (p54)

Kamppi Chapel Wood is used in the construction of this curvilinear chapel in Helsinki. (p53)

Sibeliustalo The spectacular wood-and-glass auditorium is the home of Lahti's symphony orchestra. (p146)

Finnish Food

Locally sourced, seasonal, sustainably farmed and foraged ingredients might be red-hot trends in many destinations today, but in Finland they have long been a way of life.

Smoked fish Head to any market in the country, such as Hakaniemi in Helsinki, for a huge array of salmon and other fish. (p71)

Lemin särä Majestic mutton roast, cooked on a birch tray, is a gastronomic highlight. (p177)

Ålandspannkaka Hit the Åland archipelago for semolina pudding with stewed prunes. (p114)

Kalakukko Tasty rye loaf stuffed with *muikku* (vendace, or whitefish; a small lake fish), a Kuopio speciality. (p168)

Game Dine on bear, elk or grouse by the Ruka ski slopes. (p231)

Comfort food Finnish staples such as herring, meatballs and liver in the unchanged '30s atmosphere of Sea Horse in Helsinki. (p68)

Mustamakkara This black sausage is a Tampere speciality and best accompanied by lingonberry jam. (p133)

Karjalanpiirakka Rice-filled pastry that has its origins in Karelia and is best tried with traditional egg-butter topping. (p173)

Reindeer Staple meat of Lapland that's found right across the region, including Rovaniemi. (p235)

Saunas

The sauna is where Finns go to sweat away their troubles, to socialise, or to contemplate the mysteries of life. It's worth seeking out traditional and/or unusual varieties – or rent a cabin by a lake and light a wood-burning sauna yourself.

Kuopio The sociable Jätkänkämppä smoke sauna is fired up here twice a week – a great chance to try this traditional type with its softer steam. (p169)

Tampere Over a century old, the venerable Rajaportin Sauna is a classic of its kind. (p135)

Helsinki Kotiharjun Sauna in working-class Kallio is a winner for its traditional atmosphere and optional scrubdown. (p54)

Ylläs The world's only sauna in a cable-car gondola takes a 20-minute, 4km circuit at Ylläs. (p252)

Month by Month

TOP EVENTS

Sled Safaris & Skiing, March to April

Savonlinna Opera Festival, July

Ruisrock, July

Ruska Hiking, September

Aurora-Watching, November

January

It's cold. Very cold and very dark. But this is the beginning of the active winter; there's enough snow for ice hotels, and sledding, snowmobiling and skiing are reliable.

🛏 Ice Hotels

It's a memorable experience to spend a night in one of these ethereally beautiful places, which are constructed each winter.

✨ Skábmagovat

In late January, this three-day film festival with an indigenous theme is held in Lapland in the Sámi capital of Inari. (p267)

February

Conditions are still cold, but skiing really kicks off at northern Finland's resorts and on its cross-country trails, with a peak holiday season around the middle of the month.

✨ Runeberg Day

This day, on 5 February, commemorates Finland's national poet, Johan Ludvig Runeberg (1804–77). Flags are at half mast and people eat jam-topped 'Runeberg tarts'.

March

Hours of light dramatically increase and temperatures begin to rise, making March an excellent time to take advantage of the hefty snow cover and indulge in some winter activities.

✨ Reindeer Racing

Held over the last weekend of March or first weekend of April, the King's Cup in Inari is the grand finale of Finnish Lapland's reindeer-racing season and a great spectacle. (p267)

🏃 Sled Safaris & Skiing

Whizzing across the snow pulled by a team of huskies or reindeer is a pretty spectacular way to see the northern wildernesses. Add snowmobiling or skiing to the mix and it's a top time to be at high latitude.

🏃 Tervahiihto

In Oulu's late February/early March snow, the Tervahiihto (Tar Ski Race) is a historic skiing race that's been running since 1889. (p218)

April

Easter is celebrated in a traditional fashion. Spring begins in southern Finland, but there's still solid snow cover in the north. It's a great month for outdoor activities in Lapland.

✨ Pääsiäinen (Easter)

On Easter Sunday people go to church, paint eggs and eat *mämmi* (pudding of rye and malt). The Sunday before, kids dress as witches and bless neighbouring houses in exchange for treats.

☆ April Jazz

Held in Espoo on the western outskirts of Helsinki in late April, this four-day jazz festival draws big-name artists and big crowds. (p58)

☆ Tampere Biennale

This five-day festival features new Finnish music and takes place in the buzzing city of Tampere in even-numbered years only. (p135)

May

A transitional month in the north, with snow beginning to disappear and signs of life emerging after the long winter. In the south, spring's in full flow. It's a quiet but rewarding time to visit.

☆ Vappu

Traditionally a festival of students and workers, Vappu (1 May) also marks the beginning of summer and is celebrated with sparkling wine and merry-making.

June

Midsummer weekend in late June is celebrated with great gusto, but it's typically a family-and-friends event. Lapland's a little muddy, but the rest of the country is warm and welcoming.

☆ Helsinki Day

Celebrations of the capital's anniversary, Helsinki Päivä, make for a busy time to be in town, with lots of events and activities around Esplanadin Puisto (Esplanade Park) on 12 June. (p58)

☆ Juhannus (Midsummer)

The most important annual event for Finns, Juhannus is held the weekend closest to 22 June. The country completely shuts down as people head to summer cottages to celebrate the longest day of the year with bonfires and dancing.

☆ Midnight Sun Film Festival

Round-the-clock screenings in Sodankylä while the never-setting sun circles around the sky outside bring a great atmosphere to this small Lapland town. (p259)

☆ Music Festivals

The glut of summer music festivals in Finland begins. Provinssirock (p206) is a big three-day rock fiesta in Seinäjoki and Kuopio Dance Festival (p169) is a major dance extravaganza in Kuopio.

July

Peak season sees long, long days and sunshine. Finland really comes to life, with festivals throughout, boat trips, activities, cheaper hotels and a celebratory feel. Insects in many areas are a nuisance.

☆ Savonlinna Opera Festival

A month of excellent performances in the romantic location of one of Europe's most picturesquely situated castles makes this Finland's biggest summer drawcard

for casual and devoted lovers of opera. (p155)

☆ Pori Jazz Festival

The nation's biggest jazz event packs out the port city of Pori on the west coast over a week in mid-July. More than 100 concerts, free jam sessions and dancing in the street make it hugely enjoyable. (p201)

☆ Ruisrock

Finland's oldest and possibly best rock festival takes place over two days in early July on an island just outside the southwestern city of Turku. Top Finnish and international acts take part. (p86)

☆ Tangomarkkinat

Finnish tango is an institution and the older generations converge on Seinäjoki in this massive celebration of singing and dancing in early July. (p206)

☆ Other Music Festivals

Kuhmon Kamarimusiikki (p225) in remote Kuhmo is an excellent fortnight of chamber music, with concerts featuring a large bunch of young and talented performers. The Hamina Tattoo (p113) has military music in even-numbered years.

☆ Wife-Carrying World Championships

Finland's, nay, the world's premier wife-carrying event is held in the village of Sonkajärvi. Victorious couples win the woman's weight in beer as well as significant kudos. (p168)

Jyväskylän Kesä

This multifaceted six-day festival makes sure the university town of Jyväskylä stays lively in summer. It's one of Finland's oldest arts festivals. (p164)

Sulkavan Suursoudut

This massive rowing festival in the Lakeland is all about participation...and downing lager. (p158)

Kotkan Meripäivät

The port of Kotka celebrates this maritime festival over three days in mid-July. It features music, sailing races and cruises. (p111)

Pitsiviikko

A week in late July sees the old wooden centre of Rauma come alive with music and cultural events. (p198)

August

Most Finns are back at work, so it's quieter than July but still with generally decent weather. It's a great time for hiking in Lapland or cycling in Åland.

☆ Air Guitar World Championships

Tune your imaginary instrument and get involved in this crazy rockstravaganza held in Oulu. It's all in the name of world peace. (p218)

Siirrettävien Saunojen

The mobile sauna building championships near Närpes offer a solid portion of off-beat Finnish humour and frivolity. (p206)

☆ Helsingin Juhlaviikot

Held over two weeks and three weekends from late August to early September, the all-arts Helsinki Festival keeps the capital pumping with loads of events. (p58)

☆ Ijahis Idja

Over a weekend usually in August in Inari, is this excellent music festival that features groups from all spectra of Sámi music. (p267)

September

Autumn colours are spectacular in northern forests, making it a great hiking month. Many attractions close.

🎋 Ruska Hiking

Ruska is the Finnish word for the autumn colours, and there's a mini high season in Kainuu, Koillismaa and Lapland as hikers take to the trails to enjoy nature's brief, brilliant artistic flourish.

☆ Sibelius Festival

Performances by the famous Lahti Symphony Orchestra, honouring composer Jean Sibelius, take to the stage in Lahti's impressive waterside auditorium. (p147)

October

Snow is already beginning to carpet the north, and it's generally a quiet time,

🍴 Baltic Herring Fair

Held in the first week of October on Helsinki's main market square, this traditional market has taken place since 1743. (p58)

November

November's bad for winter sports, as there's little light and not enough snow. It can be a good month to see the aurora borealis, though.

🎋 Aurora Watching

Whether you are blessed with seeing the aurora borealis (Northern Lights) is largely a matter of luck, but the further north you are, the better your chances. Dark, cloudless nights, patience and a viewing spot away from city lights are key.

December

The Christmas period is celebrated enthusiastically with the aromas of cinnamon, mulled drinks and festive traditions.

Itsenäisyyspäivä

Finland celebrates its independence, gained in 1917, on 6 December with torchlight processions, fireworks and concerts as well as cakes iced in blue and white, the colours of the country's flag.

Joulu (Christmas)

Pikkujoulu (little Christmas) parties, with plenty of *glögi* (hot punch) consumed, lead up to the main event, which features a family meal on Christmas Eve. Santa seems to be everywhere at once in Lapland, which sees reindeer and plenty of kitschy but fun Christmas spirit.

Itineraries

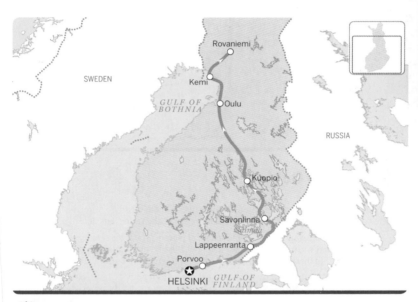

 Essential Suomi

This highlights tour of Finland covers some of the best places the country has to offer, with cities, castles, lakes, saunas and Santa on the menu.

Kick off in capital **Helsinki**, prowling the buzzing Design District and unwinding in excellent restaurants and bars. Hit Suomenlinna or an island restaurant to get a feel for the archipelago, and day trip to historic **Porvoo's** enchanting wooden buildings.

Next head to **Lappeenranta** on the shores of Finland's largest lake. Then – go by boat in summer – it's gorgeous **Savonlinna**, where the stunning castle hosts an opera festival.

From there, head to the heart of the Lakeland, **Kuopio**, another segment you can do on a lake boat. Try to time your visit to coincide with the convivial smoke sauna.

The high latitudes are in evidence once you get to **Oulu** – depending on the season, the sun barely sets or barely rises. It's one of Finland's liveliest towns, with a great summer marketplace.

In winter stop in **Kemi** to see the snow castle and take an icebreaker cruise. Finally head to **Rovaniemi**, capital of Lapland and a great base for outdoor activities. From there, explore the north or get the sleeper train or fly back to Helsinki.

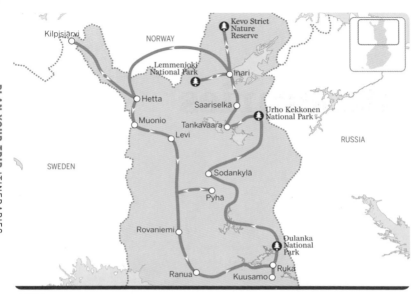

 10 DAYS ## Lapp Gold

Lapland's unique charms deserve plenty of time. This trip can be done in a week, but take two if you can, giving yourself time for some of the numerous activities on offer.

Rovaniemi is Lapland's capital and a logical place to start. It's also a good spot to hire a car. Santa Claus is the big crowd-puller here, but the real don't-miss attraction is the Arktikum museum. Further south, you can see some of the region's fauna at **Ranua's** zoo.

Cut eastward to **Ruka**, a lively winter ski resort and activity base. Here, there's walking to be done in **Oulanka National Park**, including the Karhunkierros, one of Finland's best treks. You can also canoe or go bear-watching from nearby **Kuusamo**.

From Ruka, head north via Kemijärvi to **Sodankylä**. Don't miss the wonderful old wooden church. Continue north through ever-more-sparsely populated territory; when you reach **Urho Kekkonen National Park** you're in one of Europe's great wildernesses. Take some time out for a hike across the fells, or try gold-panning at **Tankavaara's** Kultamuseo. **Saariselkä** is the best base to organise all sorts of summer and winter activities.

Inari, one of Lapland's most intriguing towns, is the capital of Finland's Sámi, a handicrafts centre and home to the memorable Siida museum, where you'll learn a lot about the Sámi and the wildlife of these northern latitudes. Next it's nearby **Lemmenjoki National Park**, where treks, river trips, gold-panning and more Sámi culture await. With time, head up to **Kevo Strict Nature Reserve** for a great three- to four-day trek.

Continue the loop towards northwest Finland, perhaps cutting through Norway and ending up at **Hetta**, another Sámi town and the trailhead for more excellent walking.

If you have time, take a detour up the 'arm' of Finland to remote **Kilpisjärvi**, in the shadow of fearsome Norwegian mountains and the smaller bulk of Saana Fell, a rewarding climb with some memorable views over three nations.

Then head to **Muonio**. In winter you should go husky sledding, but even in summer it's worth meeting the lovable dogs. Finally, return to Rovaniemi, stopping to ski or rent a summer cottage at built-up **Levi** or peaceful **Pyhä**.

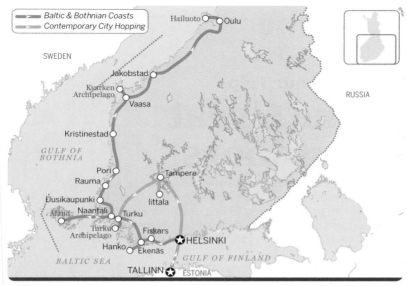

Contemporary City Hopping

10 DAYS

Finland's thriving design and music industries mean that its cities, though small, pack plenty of contemporary punch.

Take a few days to get to know **Helsinki**. Check out the Design Museum, then snoop around Punavuori's small studios and shops. See what's on at Kaapelitehdas and Korjaamo cultural centres, and pay Kiasma a visit. Fine-dining restaurants and quirky or just plain weird bars make evenings fly by.

Catch a ferry across to **Tallinn**, Estonia's capital. The traditional architecture of the Old Town meets the post-Soviet generation's creative energy in an intriguing mix.

Sail back to Helsinki and head to **Tampere**, a model of post-industrial regeneration. Take in the city's bohemian vibe and stunning lakescapes, and head for a half-day trip down to **Iittala** to see the home of one of Finland's iconic design brands.

Cut southwest down to **Turku**. The country's stateliest city has plenty going on, whether it's the Ruisrock festival or the latest exhibition in Ars Nova.

Head back to Helsinki along the coast. Thirsty for more? Sort out your visa and the city of St Petersburg is just a train ride away.

Baltic & Bothnian Coasts

10 DAYS

This trip takes you through Swedish- and Finnish-speaking communities and gives the chance to see picture-perfect towns, sparkling blue water and decent beaches.

Heading west from Helsinki, stop at the pretty ironworks village of **Fiskars**, near family-friendly, seaside **Ekenäs**. Then head on to the noble wooden villas of **Hanko**.

Turku has many drawcards, as does the surrounding **Turku Archipelago** and picturesque **Naantali**. Further offshore, **Åland** offers cycling and maritime history. To the north, **Uusikaupunki's** museum deserves a prize for ironic humour, while **Rauma** features charming wooden buildings. **Pori** hosts a pumping jazz festival.

The next coastline is 'Parallel Sweden': first stop **Kristinestad** with its Swedish-speaking majority. **Vaasa** has an excellent museum and kids' attractions. West of here, **Kvarken Archipelago** is an ever-changing landscape of land rising from the seabed.

Jakobstad's Old Town rivals Rauma's for beauty. Beyond here, beautiful coastline runs north to vibrant **Oulu**. Stop off at **Hailuoto** island for a stay by the beach; it's not often you can have a dip this far north.

Plan Your Trip

The Great Outdoors

Finland's beauty and appeal lie in its fantastic natural environment, with vast forests, long waterways, myriad lakes and Arctic northern wildernesses. Getting outdoors is the ultimate way to experience the country and Finland is remarkably well set up for all types of activities, from safari-style packages to map-and-compass DIY adventures.

Hiking Essentials

When to Hike
June to September is the main hiking season in Finland.

Where to Hike
There's a wide range of national parks with marked trails offering anything from short strolls to multiday treks.

What to Take
Insect repellent! There are literally clouds of biting insects, especially in July, and especially (but by no means only) in Lapland. You'll have to bring and carry all food when you walk in wilderness areas. Though there are plenty of huts to overnight in (sleeping bag and sleeping mat required), your own tent gives more flexibility and protection from mosquitoes.

How to Plan a Hike
Finland's protected areas are comprehensively covered in English by the website www.national parks.fi. It details walking routes, including all camping and other accommodation possibilities.

National Parks

Finland's excellent network of national parks and other protected areas is maintained by Metsähallitus (Finnish Forest & Park Service; www.nationalparks.fi). Currently there are 40 national parks that make up a total area of some 10,000 sq km (one million hectares). A similar amount of territory is protected under other categories, while further swaths of land are designated wilderness reserves. In total, around 9% of Finland's total area is in some way protected land.

The Metsähallitus website provides extensive information on all of these spots. The organisation also publishes individual leaflets on each park. Entry to all of Finland's national parks is free.

The largest and most pristine national parks are in northern Finland, particularly Lapland, where vast swaths of wilderness invite trekking, cross-country skiing, fishing and canoeing.

Many of the national parks have excellent networks of wilderness huts that provide cosy, free places to overnight on hiking routes.

Finland's National Parks

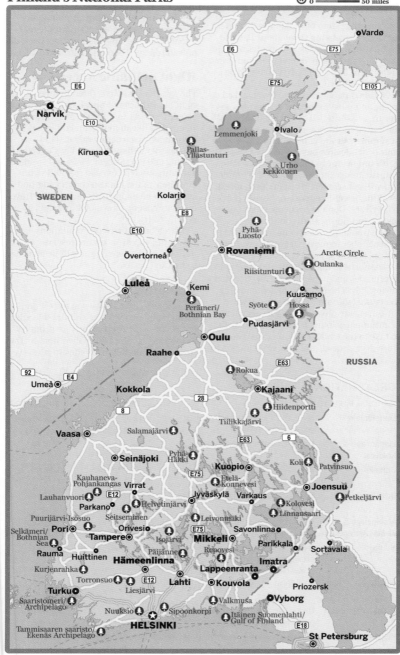

Hiking

The superb system of national parks offers memorable trekking throughout Finland in the summer months. The routes are supported by resources for camping and overnighting in huts, so it's easy to organise a multiday wilderness adventure.

National parks offer excellent marked trails, and most forest and wilderness areas are criss-crossed by locally used walking paths. Nights are short or non-existent in summer, so you can walk for as long as your heart desires or your feet permit.

It's important to remember what the Finnish landscape does and doesn't offer. You will get scented pine and birch forest, low hills, jewel-like lakes and brisk, powerful rivers. Don't expect epic mountainscapes and fjords; that's not Finland.

The trekking season runs from late May to September in most parts of the country. In Lapland the ground is not dry enough for comfortable hiking until mid-June, and mosquitoes and horseflies are an irritation during July. The first half of September is the *ruska* (autumn hiking) season, when the forests are alive with a glorious palette of autumnal colours; it's a very popular time to take to the trails. The insects have long since disappeared, and if there's a bit of a chill in the air in Lapland, it's all the better for ruddy-faced treks through the forests.

If heading off trekking on your own, always advise someone of your route and intended arrival time/date, or note these details in trekkers' books in huts and hostels.

Right of Public Access

The *jokamiehenoikeus* (literally 'everyman's right') is an ancient Finnish code that gives people the right to walk, ski or cycle anywhere they like in forests and other wilderness areas – even across private land – as long as they behave responsibly. Canoeing, rowing and kayaking on lakes and rivers is also unrestricted. You can rest and swim anywhere in the Finnish countryside, and camp for one night almost anywhere. Travel by motorboat or snowmobile, though, is heavily restricted.

Watch out for stricter regulations regarding access in nature reserves and national parks, where it might be confined to marked paths.

Camping

Everyman's right allows you to rest and camp temporarily in the countryside without permission, even on private property as long as you don't do so near homes. Try to camp on already-used sites to preserve

GREAT NATIONAL PARKS

NATIONAL PARK	FEATURES	ACTIVITIES	WHEN TO GO
Lemmenjoki	Broad rivers and old-growth forests; golden eagles, reindeer	Trekking, boating, gold panning	Aug–Sep
Linnansaari & Kolovesi	Luscious lakes and freshwater seals	Canoeing	May–Sep
Oulanka	Pine forests and river valleys; elk, white-tailed eagles; calypso flowers	Trekking the Bear's Ring, canoeing, rafting	late Jun–Sep
Urho Kekkonen	Fells, mires and old Sámi settlements; reindeer, flying squirrels	Trekking, cross-country skiing, fishing	Jul–Sep & Nov–Apr
Archipelago & Ekenäs Archipelago	Strings of islets and skerries (rocky islets); seals, eider ducks, greylag geese	Boating, fishing	May–Sep
Nuuksio	Forest within striking distance of Helsinki; elk, woodpeckers, red- and black-throated, yellow-billed and great northern divers	Nature trails	May–Oct
Patvinsuo	Broad boglands and old forest; bears, beavers, cranes	Hiking	Jun–Oct
Pallas-Yllästunturi	Undulating fells; bears, snow buntings, ptarmigans	Hiking, skiing	Jul–Sep & Nov–Apr
Hossa	Canyons, four-millennia-old rock paintings	Canoeing, hiking, scuba diving	May–Sep

the environment. Camping is not permitted in town parks or on beaches, and in national parks and reserves it may be restricted to certain designated areas.

Under the right of public access, you cannot make a campfire on private land unless you have the owner's permission. In national parks look for a designated campfire area *(nuotiopaikka)* and watch for fire warning signs – *metsäpalovaroitus* means the fire risk is very high. Felling trees or cutting brush to make a campfire is forbidden; use fallen wood instead.

Huts & Shelters

Metsähallitus operates a huge network of free, properly maintained wilderness huts across its swath of national parks and protected areas. Huts typically have sleeping platforms, cooking facilities, a pile of dry firewood and a compost toilet. You are required to leave the hut as it was – ie replenish the firewood from the woodshed and carry away your rubbish. The Finns' 'wilderness rule' states that the last person to arrive will be given the best place to sleep, but on busy treks in peak season it's good to have a tent, because someone usually ends up sleeping outside. You may also sleep sounder in a tent, as the huts tend to fill with mosquitoes as the evening goes on.

Some huts require advance booking, or have a separate, lockable section with sleeping mats that must be booked ahead. This is called a *varaustupa*.

Various other structures, including day huts and tepee-style *kotas* (Sámi huts) in Lapland, are designed for cooking and for temporary or emergency shelter from the weather. In a *laavu* (simple log shelter), you can pitch your tent inside or just roll out your sleeping bag.

It's a sociable scene in wilderness huts – take a bottle of something to join in the sharing culture.

The website www.nationalparks.fi has invaluable information on huts and hiking routes, and a 1:50,000 trekking map is recommended for finding wilderness huts. These are published by Karttakeskus (www.karttakauppa.fi) and are available from tourist offices, national park visitor centres or online. Karttakeskus also produces road maps, an annually updated road atlas and detailed maps of all the main walking areas and waterways. Waterproof plastic maps are also available.

NORDIC WALKING

Finland is proud of having invented the sport of Nordic walking, originally devised as a training method for cross-country skiers during the summer months. Basically it involves using two specially designed handheld poles while briskly walking. It may look a little weird at first, but involves the upper body in the activity and results in a 20% to 45% increase in energy consumption, and an increase in heart rate, substantially adding to the exercise value of the walk. Nordic blading is a speedier version, using poles while on in-line skates. Nordic skating is the on-ice equivalent.

Where to Trek

You can hike anywhere in Finland, but national parks and reserves have marked routes, designated campfire places, well-maintained wilderness huts and boardwalks over the boggy bits.

Lapland is the main trekking region, with huge national parks that have well-equipped huts and good, long hiking routes. There are other classic trekking areas in the Kainuu and Koillismaa regions, and in North Karelia, which has several long-distance forest trails.

Excellent trekking maps are available in Finland for most recommended routes.

Hetta–Pallastunturi One of western Lapland's best walks heads for 55km through light forest and up and down fells offering spectacular views through national park.

Karhunkierros (Bear's Ring) The most famous of all Finnish trekking routes, this trail in northern Finland covers 80km of rugged cliffs, gorges and forest.

Karhunpolku (Bear's Trail) This 133km marked hiking trail of medium difficulty leads north from Lieksa through a string of stunning national parks and nature reserves.

Kevo Route A fabulous point-to-point or loop walk of 64km to 78km through a memorable gorge in far-north Lapland.

UKK Route The nation's longest trekking route is this 400km route through northern Finland. It starts at Koli Hill, continues along the western side of Lake Pielinen and ends at Syöte.

Cycling

Riding a bike is one of the best ways to explore parts of Finland in summer. The terrain is largely flat, main roads are in good condition and traffic is generally light. Bicycle tours are further facilitated by the liberal camping regulations, excellent cabin accommodation at campgrounds, and the long hours of daylight in June and July.

The drawback is this: distances in Finland are vast. It's best to look at planning shorter explorations in particular areas, and combining cycling with bus and train trips – Finnish buses and trains are very bike-friendly.

Even if your time is limited, don't skip a few quick jaunts in the countryside. There are very good networks of cycling paths in and around most major cities and holiday destinations (for instance, the networks around Oulu and Turku).

Mountain biking on forest trails is popular in summer; in winter, try fat-biking – bikes with wide tyres especially adapted for the snow.

In most towns, bicycles can be hired from sports shops, tourist offices, campgrounds or hostels.

Transporting Your Bike

Bikes can be carried on long-distance buses for €3 to €12 (often free in practice) if there is space available (and there usually is).

Bikes can accompany passengers on most normal train journeys, with a surcharge of up to €5. Inter-City (IC) trains have spaces for bikes, which should be booked in advance. You'll have to take your bike to the appropriate space in the double-decker wagon. You can take your bike on regional trains that have a suitcase symbol on the timetable; put it in the luggage van.

Where to Cycle

You can cycle on all public roads except motorways. Many public roads in southern Finland have a dedicated cycling track running alongside.

Åland

The Åland islands are the most bicycle-friendly region in Finland, and the most popular region for bicycle tours. The flat, scenic terrain, manageable distances, network of ferries and general absence of traffic make the archipelago ideal.

Southern Finland

Southern Finland has more traffic than other parts of the country, but with careful planning you can find quiet roads that offer pleasant scenery. Around Turku, the Archipelago route offers excellent coastal scenery and island hopping.

Karelia & Northeastern Finland

Two themed routes cover the whole eastern frontier. The 1080km-long Runon ja Rajan tie (Poem and Border Route), from Hamina to Kuusamo, consists of secondary sealed roads and passes several typical Karelian villages. Some of the smallest and most remote villages along the easternmost roads have been lumped together to create the 266km Korpikylien tie (Road of Wilderness Villages). This route starts at Saramo village in northern Nurmes and ends at Hossa in central Finland.

A recommended loop takes you around Lake Pielinen, and may include a ferry trip across the lake. Another good loop is around Viinijärvi, west of Joensuu.

THE GREAT INDOORS: SAUNA

For centuries the sauna has been a place to meditate, warm up and even give birth, and most Finns still use it at least once a week. Saunas are usually taken in the nude (public saunas are nearly always sex-segregated) and Finns are quite strict about its nonsexual – even sacred – nature.

Shower first. Once inside (with a temperature of 80°C to 100°C; 176°F to 212°F), water is thrown onto the stove using a *kauhu* (ladle), producing *löyly* (steam). A *vihta* (whisk of birch twigs and leaves, known as a *vasta* in eastern Finland) is sometimes used to lightly strike the skin, improving circulation. Cool off with a cold shower or preferably by jumping into a lake. Repeat. The sauna beer afterwards is also traditional.

Western Finland

This flat region, known as Pohjanmaa, is generally good for cycling, except that distances are long. The scenery is mostly agricultural, with picturesque wooden barns amid fields of grain in this breadbasket of Finland. The 'Swedish Coast' around Vaasa and north to Kokkola is the most scenic part of this area.

Winter Sports

Winter is a wonderful time to get active in Finland. For most activities, the best time is in March and April, when you get a decent amount of light and temperatures are less harsh.

Sled Safari & Snowmobiling

Whether you head out for an hour, or on an epic week-long adventure, being whisked across the snow by an enthusiastic team of huskies or reindeer is an experience like no other. Lapland is the best place to do this, but it's also available further south in places such as Nurmes and Lieksa. Driving a sled takes a bit of practice, so expect sore arms and a few tumbles at first.

Similar excursions can be made on snowmobiles (Skidoos). Operators in the same locations offer these trips. You'll need a valid driving licence to use one.

Prices for both sled safaris and snowmobiling are normally based on two sharing, taking it in turns to drive. If you want one to yourself, count on a hefty supplement.

Downhill Skiing & Snowboarding

Finnish slopes are generally quite low and so are well suited to beginners and families. The best resorts are in Lapland, where the fells allow for longer runs. In central and southern Finland, ski runs are much shorter, averaging about 1km in length.

The ski season in Finland runs from late November to early May. It runs slightly longer in the north, where it's possible to ski from October to May. Beware of the busy Christmas, mid-February (or early March) and Easter holiday periods – they can get very crowded, and accommodation prices go through the roof.

FOREST FOOD

Except in strict nature reserves, it's permissible to pick berries and mushrooms – but not other kinds of plants – under Finland's right of public access. Finns do so with gusto, filling pails with blueberries, which come into season in late July, and delicious little wild strawberries. But there are more. Bearberries, cowberries (lingonberries), crowberries, cranberries, whortleberries and more are there to look out for. But the prize is the cloudberry, so appreciated by Finns that you may not have a chance to sample this orange, slightly sour, creamy berry in the wild. Edible mushrooms are numerous in Finnish forests, as are poisonous ones – make sure you have a mushroom guide or know your stuff.

You can hire all skiing or snowboarding equipment at major ski resorts for about €35/123 per day/week. A lift pass generally costs €42.50/204.50 per day/week (slightly less in the shoulder and off-peak seasons), although it is possible to pay separately for each ride. Skiing lessons are also available and start at around €60 for an hour's lesson for two.

The best resorts are Levi, Ruka, Pyhä-Luosto and Ylläs, but Syöte, Koli, Pallas, Ounasvaara and Saariselkä are also good.

Cross-Country Skiing

Cross-country skiing is one of Finland's simplest and most pleasant outdoor winter pursuits. It's the ideal way to explore the beautiful, silent winter countryside of lakes, fells, fields and forests, and is widely used by Finns for fitness and as a means of transport.

Practically every town and village has a network of ski tracks (*latu* or *ladut*) around the urban centre, in many cases illuminated (*valaistu*). The one drawback to using these tracks is that you'll need to bring your own equipment (or purchase some), as rentals often aren't possible.

Cross-country skiing at one of Finland's many ski resorts is an easier option. Tracks are much longer and also usually better maintained. Ski resorts offer excellent instruction and hire out equipment. The best cross-country skiing is in Lapland, where resorts offer hundreds of kilometres of trails. Keep in mind that there are few hours of daylight in northern Lapland during winter – if you're planning on a longer trek, spring is the best time. Cross-country skiing is best during January and February in southern Finland, and from December to April in the north.

Water Sports

Rowing, canoeing, rafting and fishing are popular summer water sports; in winter, there are numerous ice-fishing opportunities.

Rowing, Canoeing & Rafting

With 10% water coverage, Finland has always been a boating country, and until relatively recently boats were an important form of transport on the lakes and rivers. Every waterside town has a place (most frequently the campground) where you can hire a canoe, kayak or rowboat by the hour or day. Rental cottages often come with rowboat included that you can use free of charge to investigate the local lake and its islands.

Canoes and kayaks are suitable for longer adventures lasting several days or weeks. Route maps and guides may be pur-

chased at local or regional tourist offices and at Karttakeskus (www.karttakauppa. fi), which takes orders through its website. Canoe and kayak rentals cost €25 to €45 per day, and €90 to €200 per week; more if you need overland transport to the start or end point of your trip.

Where to Paddle

The sheltered bays and islands around the Turku archipelago and Åland in southwest Finland are good for canoeing in summer.

Finland's system of rivers, canals and linked waterways means there are some extensive canoeing routes. In the Lakeland, the Kolovesi and Linnansaari national parks have excellent waters for canoeing, and offer plenty of exploration opportunities. North Karelia, particularly around Lieksa and Ruunaa, also offers good paddling. Rivers further north are fast-flowing, with tricky rapids, making many of them suitable for experienced paddlers only.

Ivalojoki Route (easy) A 70km route along the Ivalojoki in northeast Lapland, starting at the village of Kuttura and finishing in Ivalo, passing through 30 rapids along the way.

Lakeland Trail (easy to medium) This 350km route travels through the heart of the lake district (Kangaslampi, Enonkoski, Savonranta, Kerimäki, Punkaharju, Savonlinna and Rantasalmi) and takes 14 to 18 days.

Oravareitti (easy to medium) In the heart of the Lakeland, the 'Squirrel Route' is a well-marked two- or three-day trip from Juva to Sulkava.

Oulankajoki and Kitkajoki (easy to difficult) A variety of choices on these neighbouring rivers in a spectacular wilderness area of northeast Finland.

Savonselkä Circuit (easy to difficult) The circuit, near Lahti, has three trails that are 360km, 220km and 180km in length. There are many sections that can be done as day trips and that are suitable for novice paddlers.

Seal Trail (easy) Explore the watery national parks of Kolovesi and Linnansaari, maybe spotting a rare ringed seal from your canoe.

Plenty of operators offer white-water rafting expeditions in canoes or rubber rafts. The Ruunaa area is one of the best of many choices for this adrenaline-packed activity.

ICE-FISHING

Nothing stops a Finn on a mission for fish – not even when the winter closes in, the lakes freeze over and the finny tribes below grow sluggish and hope for a breather from those pesky hooks.

No, the intrepid locals just walk or drive out to a likely spot on the ice, carve a hole using a hand drill, unfold the camp stool and drop in a line. And they wait, even if the temperature is around -30°C. Seriously warm clothes and your choice of a flask of coffee or a bottle of Koskenkorva vodka are welcome companions.

Many tour operators offering winter activities organise ice-fishing excursions.

Fishing

Finnish waters are teeming with fish, and with people trying to catch them – Finns must be among the Earth's most enthusiastic anglers. Commonly caught fish include salmon, trout, grayling, perch, pike, zander (pike-perch), whitefish and Arctic char.

With so many bodies of water there is no shortage of places to cast a line, and not even the lakes freezing over stops the Finns. Lapland has the greatest concentration of quality fishing spots, but the number of designated places in southern Finland is also increasing. Some of the most popular fishing areas are the spectacular salmon-rich Tenojoki in the furthest north, the Tornionjoki, the Kainuu region around Kajaani, Ruovesi, Hossa, Ruunaa, Lake Saimaa around Mikkeli, Lake Inari and the Kymijoki near Kotka, where the tsar used to catch his dinner.

Tourist offices can direct you to the best fishing spots in the area, and usually can provide some sort of regional fishing map and put you in touch with local guides. Fishing equipment of varying quality is widely available for hire from campgrounds and other accommodation providers in fishy areas.

The websites www.fishinginfinland.fi and www.fishing.fi have plenty of useful information in English on fishing throughout the country.

Permits

Several permits are required of foreigners (between the ages of 18 and 64) who wish to go fishing in Finland, but they are very easy to arrange. The website www.eraluvat.fi has all the details.

Simple angling with hook and line requires no permit. Neither does ice-fishing, unless you are doing these at rapids or other salmon waterways.

For other types of fishing, you will need a national fishing permit, known as the 'fisheries management fee'. A permit is €5/12/39 per day/week/year. They're payable online at www.eraluvat.fi, or at any bank or post office. In addition to this a local permit may be required. There are often automatic permit machines, while tourist offices, sports shops and campgrounds can also supply permits. The waters in Åland are regulated separately and require a dedicated regional permit. The Metsähallitus website (www.nationalparks.fi) details fishing restrictions in protected areas.

Birdwatching

Birdwatching is increasingly popular in Finland, in no small part because many bird species migrate to northern Finland in summer to take advantage of the almost continuous daylight for breeding and rearing their young. The best months for watching birds are May to June or mid-July, and late August to September or early October.

Liminganlahti (Liminka Bay), near Oulu, is a wetlands bird sanctuary and probably the best birdwatching spot in Finland. Other good areas include Puurijärvi-Isosuo National Park in Western Finland, Siikalahti in the Lakeland, Oulanka National Park near Kuusamo, the Porvoo area east of Helsinki and the Kemiö islands. Dave Gosney's *Finding Birds in South Finland* and *Finding Birds in Lapland* are field handbooks on birding sites with many practical tips. You can order them online at www.easy birder.co.uk.

Check out www.birdlife.fi for a good introduction and a few links for birdwatching in Finland.

Plan Your Trip
Travel with Children

Finland is incredibly child friendly, and is a terrific place to holiday with kids. Domestic tourism is largely dictated by children's needs, and child-friendly attractions abound in the height of summer, while winter brings its own snowy delights, including Santa.

Best Regions for Kids

Helsinki
Many attractions, with trams, boats, zoo, Suomenlinna fortress, Linnanmäki amusement park and Serena water park at Espoo. Most museums and galleries have child-friendly exhibits.

Åland Archipelago
Flat archipelago perfect for family cycling and gentle beaches; also has forts and castles both stone and bouncy.

The Lakeland
The castle at Savonlinna and scope for watery activities make this region one of the best for children.

West Coast
Water slides at Vaasa, sandy beaches at Yyteri and Kalajoki, and tranquil shores.

Turku & the South Coast
Moominworld at Naantali is a magnet for the young, who drag their parents here from all over the northern lands. Turku itself offers rope courses and skiing, while the Sirius Sport Resort in the southeast has flying, surfing and more.

Lapland
A winter wonderland with Kemi's snow castle, sled trips and children's ski runs. In summer there's gold-panning, meeting reindeer or huskies, and national parks. The region's most famous resident, Santa, is at Napapiiri year-round.

Finland for Kids

As it's such an outdoors-focused destination, planning a trip for kids could include splashing about on lakes and rivers, hikes in national parks, and cycling. In winter the reliable snow opens up a world of outdoor possibilities, and there's also the Santa Claus angle in Lapland. There are several standout theme parks across the country, and even potentially stuffy museums make the effort to engage kids, with simplified child-height information, hands-on activities and interactive displays or activity sheets in English.

Children's Highlights
Castles & Fortresses

➡ **Suomenlinna** (p46) The fortress island in Helsinki's harbour.

➡ **Raseborg** (p103) On its rocky perch near Ekenäs.

➡ **Savonlinna** (p152) This island castle is Finland's most impressive.

➡ **Turun Linna, Turku** (p84) Lords it over the medieval city of Turku.

➡ **Kastelholms Slott, Sund** (p125) One of Åland's mightiest sights.

Animals

➡ **Helsinki Zoo** (p65) Boat it over to the zoo.

➡ **Ranua Zoo** (p249) Learn about Arctic fauna in Lapland.

➡ **Aquariums** Admire the fish at aquariums in Kotka (p111), Helsinki (p65) or Tampere (p134).

➡ **Lapland** (p235) Meet the dogs at a husky kennel, or feed the reindeer at a farm.

➡ **Kuusamon Suurpetokeskus, Kuusamo** (p226) See the tame orphaned bears.

Theme Parks

➡ **Linnanmäki, Helsinki** (p65) Stomach-churning roller coasters, free-fall drops and more.

➡ **Serena Water Park, Espoo** (p65) Water slides galore near Helsinki.

➡ **Särkänniemi, Tampere** (p134) Dozens of rides, an observation tower, aquarium, farm zoo, planetarium and more.

➡ **Muumimaailma (Moominworld), Naantali** (p91) Enchanting Moomin-themed park.

➡ **Tropiclandia, Vaasa** (p207) Water slides and wave machines on Finland's west coast.

Museums

➡ **Outdoor museums** These exhibit traditional buildings and have plenty of demonstrations and activities in summer; there are good ones in Helsinki (p42) and Turku (p84) and at Turkansaari (p217) near Oulu.

➡ **Heureka, Vantaa** (p65) Hands-on science centre near Helsinki's airport.

➡ **Tietomaa, Oulu** (p217) Excellent science museum with a giant IMAX cinema screen.

➡ **Hiihtomuseo, Lahti** (p146) Ski museum with interactive exhibits.

➡ **Kierikkikeskus, near Oulu** (p222) Paddling in a Stone Age canoe is among the kid-friendly options here.

➡ **Vakoilumuseo, Tampere** (p134) Offbeat spy museum with lots of Bond-style gadgets.

Planning

For all-round information and advice, check out Lonely Planet's *Travel with Children*.

When to Go

Finnish children are on holidays from mid-June to early August, and many child-oriented activities are closed outside this period. This is when campgrounds are buzzing with Finnish families – and temperatures are usually reliably warm.

Winter is also a great time to take the family to Finland, especially to the north. December sees all sorts of Christmasy things spring up in Lapland, with Santas, elves and reindeer galore. But if your kids are older and you want to get active in the snow, March or April are the months to go: there's plenty of daylight, better snow and not such extreme cold.

Accommodation

Self-catering is huge in Finland, and the wide network of rental cabins, apartments and cottages – ranging from simple huts with bunks to luxurious bungalows with fully equipped kitchen and electric sauna – make excellent family bases. Campgrounds are also particularly good, with cabins, rowboats and bikes available for hire, and often a lake beach. There are always things to do and other children in these places, and larger ones offer activity programs.

Most Finnish hotels and hostels will put an extra bed in a room for little extra cost – and kids under 12 often sleep free. Many hotel rooms have sofas that can fold out into beds or family suites, and hostels often have connecting rooms. The Holiday Club (www.holidayclub.fi) chain of spa hotels is especially child-friendly. These and other resort hotels always have family-friendly restaurants with a menu for the kids, or deals where children eat free if accompanied by adults.

Practicalities

➡ Local tourist information booklets and websites highlight attractions with family appeal.

➡ Car-hire firms have child safety seats for hire, but it is essential that you book them in advance.

➡ High chairs and cots (cribs) are standard in many restaurants and hotels, but numbers may be limited.

➡ Entrance fees and transport tickets for children tend to be around 60% of the adult charge.

➡ Most museums in Helsinki are free for kids.

➡ Public breast feeding is normal practice.

Regions at a Glance

⚓ Helsinki

Design
Museums & Galleries
Food & Drink

Design
Finnish design is a byword for quality, but it's not just the reliable excellence of the big-name brands that impresses. Wander through Helsinki's backstreets to discover numerous small ateliers and shops displaying the quirky, the innovative, the what-were-they-thinking and the brilliant.

Food & Drink
Helsinki's fine-dining restaurants turn heads all over the north. Ally that with traditional places serving heart-warming wintry fare and a wonderful array of off-beat drinking options and you've got quite a package.

Museums & Galleries
Finns are enthusiastic museum-goers, and Helsinki has an enviable selection. There are so many that you'll have to rigorously prune most of them, but there are enough must-see galleries and exhibitions to keep you busy for several days.

p42

Turku & the South Coast

Architecture
Islands
Beaches

Architecture
This region holds the lion's share of Finland's historic buildings. Turku's castle and cathedral, old ironworks, Porvoo's wooden warehouses, Hanko's posh tsarist villas, and various fortresses and churches make this prime territory to explore the past.

Beaches
The sea might be a little chilly, but there's plenty of sand and sun. The area around Hanko has many choices, but you can find decent strands right across the region.

Islands
Zoom in on a map and prepare to be astounded by the quantity of small islands speckling Finland's Baltic coastline. Some you can explore by bike, others will need boat hire.

p82

Åland Archipelago

Cycling
Islands
Historic Sights

Cycling
Flat, sunny, light traffic: these islands are a cycling paradise. Campgrounds, farmstays and bike-friendly inter-island ferries make touring here a breeze.

Historic Sights
Åland has an intriguing history. As an important strategic point in the Baltic, it has a couple of major fortresses to explore, plus a grand post office. In the capital, Mariehamn, the museum-ship *Pommern* speaks of the islands' maritime heritage.

Islands
If you love islands you'll love Åland. The main ones are already tranquil, but get out to the eastern archipelago and you'll virtually have a rock in the Baltic to yourself. Grab a kayak and you literally will.

p114

Tampere, Pirkanmaa & Häme

Galleries
Beer
Boat Trips

Beer

Finland downs a lot of the stuff, but most Suomi beer is generic mass-produced lager. Small breweries and bars in this region buck the trend; sampling their ales and ciders is one of the area's highlights.

Boat Trips

Getting out on the water, whether for a short jaunt or town-to-town lake cruise, is one of the region's great summer pleasures.

Galleries

Finland's art has traditionally been linked with its nature, so it should be no surprise to find studios and galleries in small towns or by some lake in the middle of nowhere. The three main cities of the region back these up with a fistful of excellent museums.

p132

The Lakeland

Canoeing
Festivals
Cruises

Canoeing

There's no better way to appreciate the lakes and rivers that form this watery land than by grabbing a canoe or kayak. Explore national parks hoping to spot an inland seal, or canoe the family-friendly Squirrel Route.

Cruises

Why jump on a bus to get to the next town when you can make the journey on the deck of a historic lake boat and appreciate the scenery at a stately pace?

Festivals

Finland's festivals are a diverse bunch, and particularly in the Lakeland, where glorious castle opera takes the stage alongside rowboat regattas, car rallies, wife-carrying runs and more.

p150

Karelia

Hiking
Festivals
Food

Festivals

Karelia is the best place to explore Finnish Orthodox customs. Onion-domed churches and traditional festivals give the place a different feel from the predominantly Lutheran rest of the country.

Food

The savoury 'Karelian pie' is a rice-filled staple eaten widely across the country, but you'll find several intriguing variants here. Better yet is Lemi's speciality: birch-roasted mutton, a Finnish culinary highlight.

Hiking

Karelia has some excellent long-distance hiking routes that wind their way through some of Finland's deepest and most remote forests. There are hundreds of kilometres of marked trails to keep you busy.

p173

West Coast

Festivals
Architecture
Coastline

Architecture

Rauma, Jakobstad and Kokkola bring Finnish history alive with their rows of charming wooden buildings, some of the few to have survived the years and the fires.

Coastline

The Gulf of Bothnia isn't the likeliest of sun-and-sand destinations, but there are some great family beaches here. The rising landscapes of the Kvarken archipelago are another highlight.

Festivals

The west coast celebrates summer in style. Normally tranquil Seinäjoki kicks its heels up for contrasting tango and rock festivals, while Kaustinen becomes a folk-music mecca. Add Pori's jazz do and Rauma's bustling lace week and it's a busy season.

p194

Oulu, Kainuu & Koillismaa

Activities
Wildlife
Festivals

Lapland

Hiking
Activities
Sámi Culture

Activities

Central Finland is a fantastic area for getting active, particularly around Kuusamo and Ruka. In summer great hiking, canoeing and rafting is the draw; winter sees skiing, sled safaris and snowmobiling.

Festivals

Oulu raises the weirdness stakes with its air-guitar championships. A more stately counterpoint is Kuhmo's chamber-music festival.

Wildlife

Around Kuhmo and Kuusamo there are all sorts of impressive beasts to see if you creep out into the forest with a guide. Elk, flying squirrels, wolverines and bears are all viewable from the comfort and safety of a hide.

p215

Activities

Winter doesn't get much more wintry than Lapland, but that's no invitation to huddle indoors. There's a wealth of things to do, including skiing, safaris with huskies or reindeer, ice-fishing and snowmobiling.

Hiking

The big skies, clear air, splendid landscapes and enormous national parks make Lapland one of Europe's best hiking destinations. Networks of wilderness huts and campgrounds mean planning a walk is easy.

Sámi Culture

The northern part of Lapland is the homeland of various indigenous Sámi groups. Learning a little about their culture, art and reindeer herding is a highlight of any visit.

p235

On the Road

Lapland
p235

Oulu, Kainuu & Koillismaa
p215

West Coast
p194

The Lakeland
p150

Karelia
p173

Åland Archipelago
p114

Tampere, Pirkanmaa & Häme
p132

Turku & the South Coast
p82

Helsinki
p42

Helsinki

Includes ➡

Sights 48
Activities 54
Tours. 55
Festivals & Events 58
Sleeping. 58
Eating 64
Drinking & Nightlife . . .72
Entertainment. 75
Shopping 77

Best Places to Eat

➡ Grön (p70)
➡ Olo (p67)
➡ Vanha Kauppahalli (p67)
➡ Savoy (p69)
➡ Saaristo (p69)

Best Places to Stay

➡ Hotel Katajanokka (p59)
➡ Hotelli Krapi (p70)
➡ Klaus K (p62)

Why Go?

It's fitting that harbourside Helsinki, capital of a country with such watery geography, melds so graciously into the Baltic. Half the city seems liquid, and the writhings of the complex coastline include any number of bays, inlets and islands.

Though Helsinki seems like a younger sibling to other Nordic capitals, it's the one that went to art school, scorns pop music and works in a cutting-edge studio. The design scene here is legendary, whether you're browsing showroom brands or taking the backstreet hipster trail. The city's gourmet side is also flourishing, with new gastronomic eateries offering locally sourced tasting menus popping up at dizzying speed.

Nevertheless, much of what is lovable in Helsinki is older. Its understated yet glorious art nouveau buildings, the spacious elegance of its centenarian cafes, dozens of museums carefully preserving Finnish heritage, restaurants that have changed neither menu nor furnishings since the 1930s: all part of the city's quirky charm.

When to Go
Helsinki

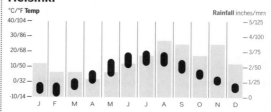

Jun Terraces are sprouting outside every cafe and the nights never seem to end.

Aug The city is functioning again after the July lull, but all of the summer activities are still on.

Dec Ice skate and absorb the Christmassy atmosphere before temperatures get too extreme.

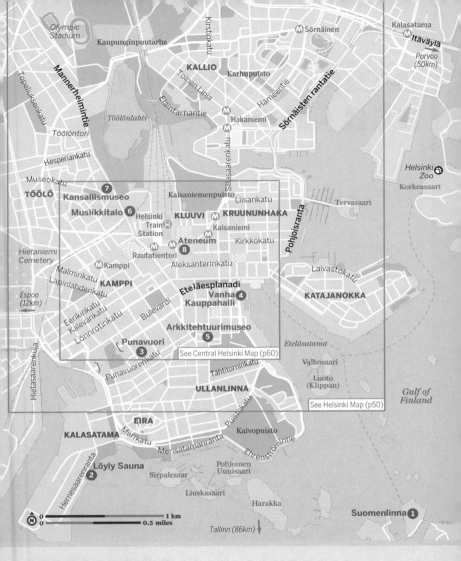

Helsinki Highlights

1 **Suomenlinna** (p46)
Packing a picnic and exploring the fortress island.

2 **Löyly Sauna** (p54)
Sweating your cares away, then jumping straight into the sea.

3 **Punavuori** (p45) Tracking down cutting-edge designs in boutiques and at the fabulous Design Museum.

4 **Vanha Kauppahalli** (p67)
Browsing the fresh produce, meats and seafood.

5 **Arkkitehtuurimuseo** (p51)
Discovering the city's striking diversity of architectural styles at the Museum of Finnish Architecture.

6 **Musiikkitalo** (p75)
Listening to a performance at the state-of-the-art, glass-and-copper Helsinki Music Centre.

7 **Kansallismuseo** (p53)
Getting a vivid introduction to Finland's history at the National Museum of Finland.

8 **Ateneum** (p48) Viewing Akseli Gallen-Kallela's triptych depicting a scene from the national epic *Kaleva*.

Neighbourhoods at a Glance

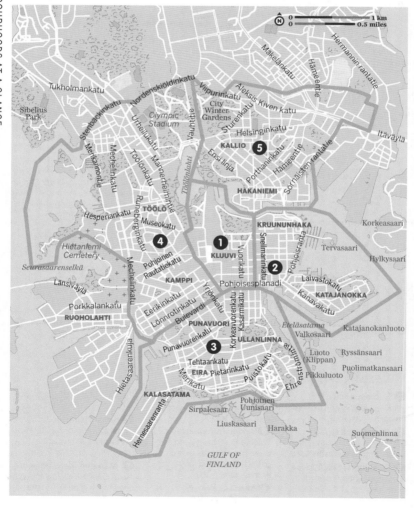

❶ City Centre (p48)

Helsinki's elegant city centre is graced with beautiful buildings in National Romantic style, Finland's distinctive interpretation of art nouveau.

While it's primarily a place of business and commerce, there are some standout attractions for visitors, including major museums and beautiful botanic gardens.

❷ Kruununhaka & Katajanokka (p49)

Waterfront wraps around this maritime neighbourhood, which spans the Kruununhaka area – home to Helsinki's main market square, the kauppatori, where boats depart for cruises in summer – and the adjacent genteel island of Katajanokka, which is linked by bridges to the mainland and awash with National Romantic art nouveau architecture.

❸ Punavuori & Ullanlinna (p51)

A trove of shops displaying furniture, art, fashion, accessories and homewares fill Helsinki's world-famous Design District, which centres on hip Punavuori.

To its south, the more residential area of Ullanlinna shelters some beautiful parks, while creative and recreational spaces continue to open in the southwest on and around the Hernesaari waterfront.

❹ Kamppi & Töölö (p53)

Abutting the city centre to the west, lively Kamppi is a busy transport hub and home to many outstanding museums and cultural institutions.

To its north, peaceful Töölö is a lovely, leafy area that stretches to Hietaranta, one of Helsinki's most popular beaches.

❺ Kallio (p54)

Traditionally a working-class neighbourhood, Kallio is rapidly gentrifying to become one of Helsinki's most up-and-coming areas.

Repurposed post-industrial venues here buzz with creative activity – from food labs to a cutting-edge distillery – with public art continuing to pop up throughout its streets, parks and squares.

⊙ TOP SIGHT
SUOMENLINNA

A Unesco World Heritage site, Suomenlinna (Sveaborg in Swedish), the 'fortress of Finland', was built by the Swedes in the mid-18th century and is spectacularly set over a series of car-free islands linked by bridges. Ferries from central Helsinki make the scenic journey to Suomenlinna, where you can explore museums, former bunkers and fortress walls, as well as Finland's only remaining WWII submarine.

Suomenlinna History

In the mid-18th century, Sweden was twitchy about a potential Russian invasion and decided to build a state-of-the-art offshore fortress near the eastern limits of its declining empire. At the time Helsinki wasn't a major town, and the bastion itself, Sveaborg, became one of Finland's largest settlements and a thriving community.

Despite Suomenlinna's meticulous planning and impressive military hardware, when the Russians finally came calling in 1808, the besieged commander, alarmed by Russian threats to bombard every last civilian to smithereens, tamely surrendered the fortress to spare the soldiers' families.

Once Finland was under Russian rule, the capital was moved from Turku to Helsinki, but the fortress was left to deteriorate. A wake-up call came with the Crimean War and rapid improvements were made...or so they said. As it turned out, British ships pounded the islands with 21,000 shots in a two-day bombardment, but Suomenlinna's guns were so out of condition they couldn't even fire far enough to reach the attacking ships.

The fortress nevertheless remained in Russian hands until independence. During the Finnish Civil War it served as a prison for communist prisoners. There's still an open prison on the islands today.

DON'T MISS

→ Suomenlinnan Kirkko

→ Ehrensvärd-Museo

→ Vesikko

→ Suomenlinna-Museo

→ Sotamuseo Maneesi

→ Lelumuseo

PRACTICALITIES

→ www.suomenlinna.fi

→ ⊠ ferry from kauppatori (market square)

Exploring Suomenlinna

From Suomenlinna's main quay, a blue-signposted walking path connects the key attractions.

You'll immediately see the distinctive church, **Suomenlinnan Kirkko** (www.helsinginkirkot.fi; ⊘noon-4pm Wed-Sun, plus Tue Jun-Aug). Built by the Russians in 1854, it served as a Russian Orthodox place of worship until the 1920s, when it became Lutheran. It doubles as a lighthouse – the beacon was originally gaslight, but is now electric and still in use.

Suomenlinna's most atmospheric area, **Kustaanmiekka**, is at the end of the blue trail. Exploring the old bunkers, crumbling fortress walls and cannon gives you an insight into this fortress. The monumental King's Gate was built in 1753–54 as a two-storey fortress wall that had a double drawbridge and a stairway added. In summer you can get a **water bus** (Map p60; www.jt-line.fi; return €7) to Helsinki from here, saving the walk back to the main quay.

At around 5.15pm it's worth finding a spot on Suomenlinna to watch the enormous Baltic ferries pass through the narrow gap between islands.

Suomenlinna Museums

On the main island, Susisaari, the **Ehrensvärd-Museo** (adult/child €5/2; ⊘10am-5pm Jun-Aug, 11am-4pm May & Sep) was once the home of Augustin Ehrensvärd, who designed the fortress. Outside is Ehrensvärd's elaborately martial tomb. Opposite, sailmakers and other workers have been building ships since the 1750s at the picturesque **Viaporin Telakka** shipyard, which is today used for the maintenance of wooden vessels.

Along the shore, the **Vesikko** (adult/child incl Suomenlinna-Museo €7/4; ⊘11am-6pm May-Sep) is the only WWII-era submarine remaining in Finland. It saw action against the Russians. It's fascinating to climb inside and see how it all worked (accompanied by sound effects). Needless to say, there's not much room to move. A combined ticket here is also valid at the **Suomenlinna-Museo** (adult/child incl Vesikko €7/4; ⊘10am-6pm May-Sep, 10.30am-4.30pm Oct-Apr), a two-level museum covering the history of the fortress, located by the bridge that links Susisaari and Iso Mustasaari.

On Iso Mustasaari is **Sotamuseo Maneesi** (www.sotamuseo.fi; adult/child €7/4; ⊘11am-6pm early May-Sep), which has a comprehensive overview of Finnish military hardware from bronze cannons to WWII artillery.

Nearby, inside a charming wooden building, the **Lelumuseo** (Toy Museum; www.lelumuseo.fi; adult/child €6/3; ⊘11am-6pm May-Sep) contains a delightful private collection of hundreds of dolls, teddy bears and wind-up toys.

RANTAKASARMI

At Suomenlinna's main quay, the pink Rantakasarmi (Jetty Barracks) is one of the best-preserved Russian-era buildings. Make it your first stop to view its small exhibition and visit the multilingual **tourist office** (☑029-533-8420; ⊘10am-6pm May-Sep, to 4pm Oct-Apr), with downloadable content for your phone.

Guided walking tours (☑029-533-8420; adult/child €11/4; ⊘up to 3 times daily Jun-Aug, 1.30pm Sat & Sun Sep-May) depart from the tourist office.

HOSTEL SUOMENLINNA

An excellent alternative to staying in central Helsinki, this **hostel** (☑09-684-7471; www.hostelhelsinki.fi; dm/s/d/tr from €25/56/72/100; ⊘reception 8am-3.30pm Mon-Sat, to noon Sun; @♠) is near the ferry pier. Once a Russian primary school then a barracks, the red-brick building's dorms occupy bright, high-ceilinged classrooms, while cosy private rooms upstairs have sloping ceilings. There's a kitchen (and supermarket nearby) and laundry.

History

Helsinki was founded in 1550 by King Gustav Vasa to rival the Hansa trading town of Tallinn. Earlier trials at Ekenäs were fruitless, so traders from there and a few other towns were shanghaied to newly founded Helsingfors (the Swedish name). For over 200 years it remained a backwater, though it was razed in 1713 to prevent the Russians occupying it. The inhabitants fled or were captured, and only returned after the Peace of Nystad in 1721.

Later the Swedes built the Sveaborg fortress (Suomenlinna; see p46) to protect this eastern part of their empire against further Russian attack. Following the war of 1808, however, the Russians succeeded in taking the fortress and a year later Russia annexed Finland as an autonomous grand duchy. A capital nearer Russia than Sweden was required and Helsinki was chosen in 1812: Turku lost its long-standing status as Finland's capital.

In the 19th and early 20th centuries, Helsinki grew rapidly. The city suffered heavy Russian bombing during WWII, but recovered and hosted the 1952 Summer Olympics. These days the capital is so much the centre of everything that goes on in Finland that its obscure market-town past is totally forgotten.

⊙ Sights

Helsinki has over 50 museums and galleries, including many special-interest museums that will appeal to enthusiasts. For a full list, check the tourist office website (www.visithelsinki.fi), or pick up its free *Museums* booklet.

ⓘ HELSINKI CARD

The **Helsinki Card** (www.helsinkicard.com; one/two/three day pass €46/56/66) gives you free public transport around the city and **local ferries** (Map p60; Kauppatori) to Suomenlinna, entry to 28 attractions in and around Helsinki and a 24-hour hop-on, hop-off bus tour.

The **Helsinki & Region Card** (one/two/three day pass €50/62/72) offers the same benefits and adds in free transport to/from the airport as well as greater Helsinki destinations, including the satellite city of Espoo.

Both cards are cheaper online; otherwise, get them at tourist offices, hotels or transport terminals. To make the cards worthwhile, you'd need to pack lots of sightseeing into a short time.

⊙ City Centre

★ Kajsaniemi   GARDENS

(Botanic Gardens; Map p50; www.luomus.fi; Kaisaniemenranta 2; gardens free, greenhouses adult/child €9/4.50; ⊙ gardens 9am-8pm, greenhouses 10am-5pm Mon-Wed, Fri & Sat, to 6pm Thu, to 4pm Sun) Rambling over 4 hectares in the city centre alongside the north harbour, Töölönlahti, Helsinki's botanic gardens are filled with plants from Finland and other countries on the same latitude, with some 3600 species all up. The gardens' 10 interconnected greenhouses shelter 800 species from all latitudes, and are a wonderfully warm refuge for visitors in the chillier months.

★ Kiasma   GALLERY

(Map p60; www.kiasma.fi; Mannerheiminaukio 2; adult/child €14/free, 1st Sun of month free; ⊙ 10am-5pm Tue & Sun, to 8.30pm Wed-Fri, to 6pm Sat) Now one in a series of elegant contemporary buildings in this part of town, curvaceous and quirky metallic Kiasma, designed by Steven Holl and finished in 1998, is a symbol of the city's modernisation. It exhibits an eclectic collection of Finnish and international contemporary art, including digital art, and has excellent facilities for kids. Its outstanding success is that it's been embraced by the people of Helsinki, with a theatre and a hugely popular glass-sided cafe and terrace.

★ Ateneum   GALLERY

(Map p60; www.ateneum.fi; Kaivokatu 2; adult/child €15/free; ⊙ 10am-6pm Tue & Fri, to 8pm Wed & Thu, to 5pm Sat & Sun) Occupying a palatial 1887 neo-Rennaissance building, Finland's premier art gallery offers a crash course in the nation's art. It houses Finnish paintings and sculptures from the 'golden age' of the late 19th century through to the 1950s, including works by Albert Edelfelt, Helene Schjerfbeck, the von Wright brothers and Pekka Halonen. Pride of place goes to the prolific Akseli Gallen-Kallela's triptych from the Finnish national epic, the *Kalevala,* depicting Väinämöinen's pursuit of the maiden Aino.

Esplanadin Puisto   PARK

(Esplanadi Park; Map p60) Locally known as 'Espa', oblong-shaped Esplanadi stretches for four blocks between the squares Erottaja to the west and the kauppatori to the east. Designed by architect CL Engel and opened in 1818, it's one of the city's most loved green spaces and fills with picnickers on sunny days. Elegant shops, cafes and restaurants

HELSINKI IN...

One Day

If you're arriving by rail, Helsinki's central **train station** gives an immediate feel for the city's stunning National Romantic art-nouveau architecture. From here it's just footsteps to **Kiasma** for contemporary art or to the nearby **Ateneum** to see the country's 'golden age'. Break for lunch at **Karl Fazer Café** (p64), a Helsinki institution.

After lunch, stroll through the city's central strip of green, **Esplanadin Puisto**, and visit central Finnish design shops. Continue through the beautiful botanic gardens, **Kajsaniemi**. In the evening, book ahead for a concert at the **Musiikkitalo** (p75).

Two Days

Get an early start to beat the crowds at Helsinki's Lutheran cathedral, **Tuomiokirkko**, then head to the resplendent Finnish Orthodox **Uspenskin Katedraali**, still topped by its distinctive gold onion domes. For lunch, make reservations ahead for Michelin-starred modern Finnish cuisine at **Olo** (p67).

Board a local ferry bound for **Suomenlinna** (p46) and spend the afternoon exploring its fortifications, bunkers and numerous museums. For dinner there's game platters and house-brewed beers at **Suomenlinnan Panimo** (p69).

Back on the mainland, take in a stunning panorama of Helsinki aboard the **Sky Wheel** (p55) Ferris wheel or finish with a swim at waterfront **Allas Sea Pool** (p55).

---

line the streets Pohjoisesplanadi (North Esplanadi) and Eteläesplanadi (South Esplanadi). At the park's eastern end is a bandstand out the front of grand cafe Kappeli (p72).

◎ Kruununhaka & Katajanokka

Kauppatori   SQUARE

(Map p50) The heart of central Helsinki is the harbourside kauppatori (market square), where cruises and ferries leave for archipelago islands. It's completely touristy these days, with reindeer souvenir stands having replaced most market stalls, but there are still some berries and flowers for sale, and adequate cheap food options.

Helsingin Kaupunginmuseo   MUSEUM

(Helsinki City Museum; Map p60; www.helsingin kaupunginmuseo.fi; Aleksanterinkatu 16; ⊙11am-7pm Mon-Fri, to 5pm Sat & Sun) **FREE** The Helsinki City Museum spreads over five buildings from different eras, including Sederholmin talo, Helsinki's oldest central building (dating from 1757 and built by a wealthy merchant). They're linked by a contemporary structure, along with four other museums at separate locations. The must-see of the bunch is the main museum. Its collection of 450,000 historical artefacts and over one million photographs is backed up by entertaining information piecing together Helsinki's transition from Swedish to Russian hands and into independence.

Tuomiokirkko   CHURCH

(Lutheran Cathedral; Map p60; www.helsinginseura kunnat.fi; Unioninkatu 29; ⊙9am-midnight Jun-Aug, to 6pm Sep-May) **FREE** One of CL Engel's finest creations, the chalk-white neoclassical Lutheran cathedral presides over Senaatin-tori. Created to serve as a reminder of God's supremacy, its high flight of stairs is now a popular meeting place. Zinc statues of the 12 apostles guard the city from the roof of the church. The spartan, almost mausoleum-like interior has little ornamentation under the lofty dome apart from an altar painting and three stern statues of Reformation heroes Luther, Melanchthon and Mikael Agricola.

Uspenskin Katedraali   CHURCH

(Uspenski Cathedral; Map p50; www.hos.fi/ uspenskin-katedraali; Kanavakatu 1; ⊙9.30am-4pm Tue-Fri, 10am-3pm Sat, noon-3pm Sun) **FREE** The eye-catching red-brick Uspenski Cathedral towers above Katajanokka island. Built as a Russian Orthodox church in 1868, it features classic golden onion domes and now serves the Finnish Orthodox congregation. The high, square interior has a lavish iconostasis with the Evangelists flanking panels depicting the Last Supper and the Ascension.

Tervasaari   ISLAND, PARK

(Tar Island; Map p50; Tervasaarenkannas) Reached by a causeway, Tar Island is now a landscaped park with spectacular views over Helsinki's skyline. Covering 2.86 hectares, it's planted with several different varieties

Helsinki

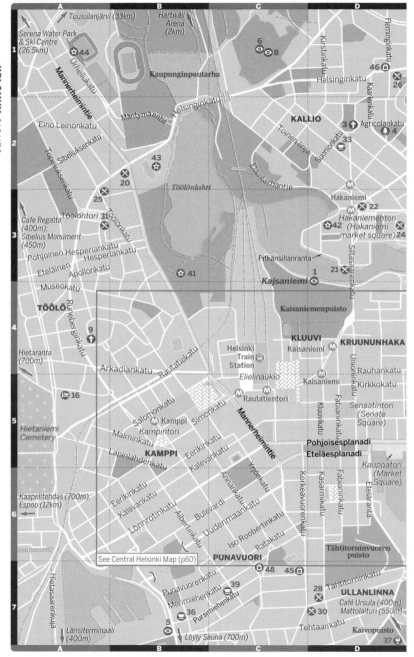

Tuusulanjärvi (33km)

Hartwall Arena (2km)

Serena Water Park & Ski Centre (26.5km)

44

Urheilukatu

Mannerheimintie

Kaupunginpuutarha

6 8

Kirstinkatu

Fleminginkatu

46

26

Helsinginkatu

Eino Leinonkatu

Mäntymäentie

Helsinginkatu

KALLIO

3 Agricolankatu

4

Kaarlenkatu

Toinen linja

Suonionkatu

33

Topeliuksenkatu

Sibeliuksenkatu

43

20

Töölönlahti

Eläintarhantie

Hakaniemi

22

Cafe Regatta (400m); Sibelius Monument (450m)

25

Töölöntori 31

Töölönkatu

Hakaniementori (Hakaniemi market square) 24

42

Siltasaarenkatu

Pohjoinen Hesperiankatu

Hesperiankatu

Pitkänsillanranta

21

Eteläinen

Apollonkatu

41

Kajsaniemi

1

Museokatu

TÖÖLÖ

Runeberginkatu

Kaisaniemenpuisto

9

Hietaranta (700m)

Helsinki Train Station

Kaisaniemi

KLUUVI

KRUUNUNHAKA

Arkadiankatu

Rautatiekatu

Elielinaukio

Kaisaniemi

Unioninkatu

Rauhankatu

Kirkkokatu

16

Rautatientori

Kluuvikatu

Fabianinkatu

Senaatintori (Senate Square)

Hietaniemi Cemetery

Salomonkatu

Kamppi

Kampintori

Simonkatu

Mannerheimintie

Pohjoisesplanadi

Eteläesplanadi

Malminkatu

Eerikinkatu

KAMPPI

Kalevankatu

Yrjönkatu

Kauppatori (Market Square)

Lapinlahdenkatu

Kaapelitehdas (700m); Espoo (12km)

Eerikinkatu

Kalevankatu

Lönnrotinkatu

Albertinkatu

Bulevardi

Annankatu

Uudenmaankatu

Iso Roobertinkatu

Ratakatu

Korkeavuorenkatu

Kasarmikatu

Fabianinkatu

Etelaranta

Tähtitorninvuoren puisto

See Central Helsinki Map (p60)

PUNAVUORI

48

45

28

Tähtitorninkatu

ULLANLINNA

Hietasaarenkuja

Punavuorenkatu

Merimiehenkatu

39

Pursimiehenkatu

Café Ursula (400m); Mattolaituri (550m)

30

36

5

Tehtaankatu

Länsiterminaali (400m)

Löyly Sauna (700m)

Kaivopuisto

37

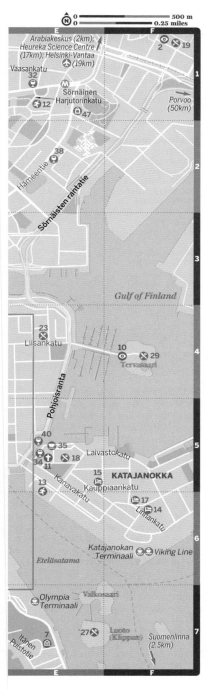

of roses, including the Karelian rose. There's a summer theatre with free performances (mostly in Finnish), a small kids' playground and the wonderful summer restaurant Savu (p64), specialising in smoked Finnish delicacies, situated in the last remaining wooden tar storehouse.

⊙ Punavuori & Ullanlinna

★ Design Museum MUSEUM

(Map p60; www.designmuseum.fi; Korkeavuorenkatu 23; combination ticket with Museum of Finnish Architecture adult/child €10/free; ⊙11am-6pm Jun-Aug, 11am-8pm Tue, to 6pm Wed-Sun Sep-May) An unmissable stop for Finnish design aficionados, Helsinki's Design Museum has a permanent collection that looks at the roots of Finnish design in the nation's traditions and nature. Changing exhibitions focus on contemporary design – everything from clothing to household furniture. From June to August, 30-minute tours in English take place at 2pm on Saturday and are included in admission. Combination tickets with the nearby Arkkitehtuurimuseo (architecture museum) are a great-value way to see the two museums.

Arkkitehtuurimuseo MUSEUM

(Museum of Finnish Architecture; Map p60; ☑045-7731-0474; www.mfa.fi; Kasarmikatu 24; adult/child €10/free, combination ticket with Design Museum €12/free; ⊙11am-6pm Tue & Thu-Sun, to 8pm Wed) Finland's architecture museum occupies a neo-Rennaissance building dating from 1899. Exhibitions are its key focus, including the fascinating *Decades of Finnish Architecture 1900–1970,* which runs until the end of 2020 and covers National Romanticism, classicism, functionalism and modernism, laying the groundwork for Finland's definitive 1970s works, as well as shorter retrospectives and thematic exhibitions. Permanent displays include architectural models, drawings and photographs. There's a library and an excellent bookshop.

Johanneksenkirkko CHURCH

(St John's Church; Map p60; www.helsinginkirkot.fi; Korkeavuorenkatu 12; ⊙10am-3pm Mon-Fri) Helsinki's largest church, with seating for 2600 worshippers, is the soaring neo-Gothic St John's Lutheran Church. Designed by architect Adolf Melander, it's topped by distinctive 74m-high twin spires. Construction began in 1888; it was consecrated in 1891. Excellent acoustics make it a memorable place for free organ concerts at 7pm on Wednesdays in

Helsinki

◉ Top Sights
1 Kajsaniemi..D3

◉ Sights
2 Helsinki Distillery Company...................F1
3 Kallion Kirkko.......................................D2
4 Karhupuisto...D2
5 Konepahalli..B7
6 Linnanmäki..C1
7 Mannerheim-Museo..............................E7
8 Sea Life..C1
9 Temppeliaukion Kirkko........................A4
10 Tervasaari..F4
11 Uspenskin Katedraali............................E5

⊕ Activities, Courses & Tours
12 Kotiharjun Sauna...................................E1
13 Sky Wheel...E5

⊜ Sleeping
14 Eurohostel...F6
15 Hellsten Helsinki Senate
   Apartments..E5
16 Hostel Domus Academica....................A5
17 Hotel Katajanokka................................F6

⊗ Eating
18 Bellevue..E5
19 B-Smokery...F1
20 Carelia...B2
21 Flying Dutch..D3
22 Hakaniemen Kauppahalli......................D3
23 Kolme Kruunua.....................................E4

24 Kuja...D3
25 Kuu..A3
26 Rupla...D1
27 Saaristo...E7
28 Saslik..D7
29 Savu..F4
30 Sea Horse..D7
   Teurastamo.................................(see 19)
31 Tin Tin Tango.......................................A3

◉ Drinking & Nightlife
32 Fairytale..E1
33 Good Life Coffee..................................D2
34 Holiday..E5
35 Johan & Nyström..................................E5
36 Kaffa Roastery......................................B7
37 Kaivohuone...D7
38 Kuudes Linja...E2
39 Kuuma...C7
40 Majakkalaiva Relandersgrund...............E5

⊕ Entertainment
41 Finlandia Talo.......................................B3
42 Juttutupa..D3
43 Oopperatalo..B2
44 Telia 5G Arena......................................A1

⊚ Shopping
45 Bisarri...C7
46 Fargo...D1
47 Fennica Records....................................E1
48 Roobertin Herkku.................................C7

August, as well as ticketed concerts throughout the year – check the program online.

Kaivopuisto PARK
(Puistokatu) On the waterfront, this sprawling park dating from 1834 is a favourite Helsinki idyll. There are expanses of lawns; numerous sculptures and winding paths; the waterside Mattolaituri (p73) cafe; the bar-club Kaivohuone (p73) – originally the park's spa, dating from 1838; and a small, domed observatory, **Ursa** (Kaivopuisto tähtitorni; ☑09-684-0400; www.ursa.fi; Kaivopuisto; adult/child €4/2; ⊙1-3pm Sun mid-Mar–mid-Jun, Aug & Sep, 7-9pm Tue-Sun mid-Oct–mid-Dec & mid-Jan–mid-Mar), dating from 1926. In winter, tobogganing down the slopes is a popular pastime for kids. Locals flock to the park on Vappu (p58) for picnics with sparkling wine.

Mannerheim-Museo MUSEUM
(Map p50; ☑09-635-443; www.mannerheim -museo.fi; Kalliolinnantie 14; adult/child €12/free; ⊙11am-4pm Fri-Sun) This fascinating museum by Kaivopuisto was the home of Baron Gustav Mannerheim, former president, commander

in chief of the Finnish army and Finnish Civil War victor. The great field marshal never owned the building; he rented it from chocolate magnate Karl Fazer until his death. The house tells of Mannerheim's intrepid life with hundreds of military medals and photographs from his Asian expedition. Entry includes an informative, compulsory one-hour guided tour (in English); the last is at 3pm.

Sinebrychoffin Taidemuseo GALLERY
(Sinebrychoff Art Museum; Map p60; www.sinebry choffintaidemuseo.fi; Bulevardi 40; house museum free, exhibitions adult/child €12/free; ⊙11am-6pm Tue, Thu & Fri, to 8pm Wed, 10am-5pm Sat & Sun) One of Helsinki's finest collections of classic European paintings is in these 1842-built former brewery offices, which also contained living quarters for the Sinebrychoff family of brewers. On the 2nd floor, the house museum of Paul and Fanny Sinebrychoff displays the main collection of old masters, furniture and other artefacts bequeathed to the Finnish government by Fanny Sinebrychoff in 1921. The Empire room is an impressive

re-creation that drips with chandeliers and opulence. Outstanding temporary exhibitions also take place here.

Konepahalli CULTURAL CENTRE
(Map p50; Telakkakatu 6) Steel girders and pulleys still line this cavernous brick hall dating from the early 20th century, which was formerly used for shipbuilding. Craft-beer bars, cafes and restaurants serving the likes of Vietnamese pho and Caribbean cuisine, Finnish design shops and a gym now fill the hall. Outside, the concrete courtyard has a beer garden that hosts live gigs in summer.

⊙ Kamppi & Töölö

Amos Andersonin Taidemuseo GALLERY
(Amos Anderson Art Museum; Map p60; www.amosanderson.fi; Yrjönkatu 27; adult/child €10/free; ☉10am-6pm Mon, Thu & Fri, to 8pm Wed, 11am-5pm Sat & Sun) This gallery occupies the 1913 apartment building built for publishing magnate Amos Anderson (1878–1961), one of the wealthiest Finns of his time. As well as housing modern art from his collection and temporary exhibitions that mix the old and cutting-edge contemporary, you can view the Empire-style interiors of Anderson's home as well as his private chapel. The museum is also opening a vast new space, the subterranean Amos Rex, 300m north on Lasipalatsinaukio in mid-2018.

Kamppi Chapel CHAPEL
(Map p60; www.helsinginseurakunnat.fi; Simonkatu 7; ☉8am-8pm Mon-Fri, 10am-6pm Sat & Sun) Built in 2012 by Helsinki architectural firm K2S, this exquisite, ultra-contemporary curvilinear chapel is constructed entirely from wood (wax-treated spruce outside, oiled alder planks inside, with pews crafted from ash) and offers a moment of quiet contemplation in cocoon-like surrounds. Its altar cross is the work of blacksmith Antti Nieminen. Known as the Chapel of Silence, the Lutheran chapel is ecumenical and welcomes everyone.

★**Tennispalatsi** CULTURAL CENTRE
(Tennis Palace; Map p60; Eteläinen Rautatiekatu) The 1938-completed Tennispalatsi (Tennis Palace) cultural and recreation centre was intended for the 1940 Summer Olympics, which were subsequently cancelled following the outbreak of WWII, although it went on to host basketball games during Helsinki's successful 1952 Summer Olympics. Today the building houses the superb **Helsinki Art Museum**

KUUSISAARI, THE ART ISLAND

The upmarket island of Kuusisaari has two excellent private galleries in elaborate villas: **Didrichsen Taidemuseo** (www.didrichsenmuseum.fi; Kuusilahdenkuja 1; adult/child €12/free; ☉11am-6pm Tue-Sun) and **Villa Gyllenberg** (www.gyllenbergs.fi; Kuusisaarenpolku 11; adult/child €10/free; ☉3-7pm Wed, 11am-3pm Sat, noon-4pm Sun), both showing the collections of their one-time owners. Both have a good permanent collection of golden-age Finnish art as well as local and international 20th-century art, supplemented by changing exhibitions. A combination ticket for the two galleries costs €18.

Bus 194 or 195 from Kamppi bus station or 50-minute summer ferries (p48) from the kauppatori will get you to the island. The galleries are under five minutes' stroll apart. It's also an easy walk from Seurasaari (p54), so there's plenty out here for a day trip.

(HAM; Map p60; www.hamhelsinki.fi; Eteläinen Rautatiekatu 8; adult/child €10/free; ☉11am-7pm Tue-Sun) and other venues, including a **cinema** (Map p60; www.finnkino.fi; Salomonkatu 15; tickets adult/child €11.50/9.20) and shops.

Parliament House NOTABLE BUILDING
(Eduskunta; Map p60; ☑09-432-2199; www.eduskunta.fi; Mannerheimintie 30) Finland's imposing parliament building was designed by Finnish architect Johan Sigfrid Sirén and inaugurated in 1931. Its pared-back neoclassicism combined with early 20th-century modernism gives it a serious, even somewhat mausoleum-like appearance. After lengthy renovations of its facade and interior (including a total replacement of its utilities) as part of Finland's centenary of independence commemorations, it reopened in 2017. It's possible to visit by guided tour (English tours are available); check the website for details.

★**Kansallismuseo** MUSEUM
(National Museum of Finland; Map p60; www.kansallismuseo.fi; Mannerheimintie 34; adult/child €10/free, 4-6pm Fri free; ☉11am-6pm Tue-Sun) Built in National Romantic art-nouveau style and opened in 1916, Finland's premier historical museum looks a bit like a Gothic church with its heavy stonework and tall square tower. A major overhaul is under way until 2019, but the museum will remain open

throughout. Already-completed sections include an exceptional prehistory exhibition and the Realm, covering the 13th to the 19th century. Also here is a fantastic hands-on area for kids, Workshop Vintti.

Temppeliaukion Kirkko CHURCH
(Map p50; ☎ 09-2340-6320; www.helsinginseura kunnat.fi; Lutherinkatu 3; adult/child €3/free; ⊙ 9.30am-5.30pm Mon-Thu & Sat, to 8pm Fri, noon-5pm Sun Jun-Aug, shorter hours Sep-May) Hewn into solid stone, the Temppeliaukio church, designed by Timo and Tuomo Suomalainen in 1969, feels close to a Finnish ideal of spirituality in nature – you could be in a rocky glade were it not for the stunning 24m-diameter roof covered in 22km of copper stripping. Its acoustics are exceptional; regular concerts take place here. Opening times vary depending on events, so phone or see its Facebook page. There are fewer groups midweek.

◉ Kallio

Kallion Kirkko CHURCH
(Kallio Church; Map p50; www.kallionseurakunta. fi; Itäinen Papinkatu 2; ⊙ 7am-2pm Mon-Fri, 9am-7pm Sat & Sun) FREE Designed by Lars Sonck and completed in 1912, this 65m-high Lutheran church is a Helsinki landmark and visible from all over the city. Built from grey granite and topped with a domed copper roof, it is a classic example of National Romantic art nouveau style. Acoustics are superb: check the website for details of regular organ concerts. The tower has seven bronze bells, four of which play a Sibelius composition every day at noon and 6pm.

Helsinki Distillery Company DISTILLERY
(Map p50; ☎ 020-719-1460; www.hdco.fi; Työpajankatu 2A, Teurastamo; tours €15; ⊙ tours in English 5pm Wed, bar 5pm-midnight Wed & Thu, to 2am Fri & Sat) At the former slaughterhouse Teurastamo (p71), Helsinki Distillery Company produces unique spirits including single-malt and rye whiskies, gin, akvavit, apple jack, sea buckthorn brandy and lingonberry liqueur, using Finnish ingredients. Tours lasting 25 minutes take you behind the scenes. Upstairs its raw concrete bar is a great place to sample its wares and hosts occasional live music.

🏃 Activities

⭐ Löyly Sauna SAUNA
(☎ 09-6128-6550; www.loylyhelsinki.fi; Hernesaarenranta 4; per 2hr incl towel €19; ⊙ 4-10pm Mon, 1-10pm Tue, Wed & Sun, 7.30am-9.30am & 1-10pm Thu, 1-11pm Fri, 7.30am-9.30am & 1-11pm Sat) ⚓ Built from striking natural timbers in 2016, with a pine exterior made from 4000 custom-cut planks and a Scandinavian birch interior, Löyly is entirely powered by water and wind. Its two electric saunas and traditional smoke sauna offer direct access to the Hernesaari waterfront (and winter ice hole). All saunas are mixed and swimsuits are required (swimsuit rental €6).

⭐ Kotiharjun Sauna SAUNA
(Map p50; www.kotiharjunsauna.fi; Harjutorinkatu 1; adult/child €13/7; ⊙ 2-9.30pm Tue-Sun) Helsinki's only original traditional public wood-fired sauna dates back to 1928. It's a classic experience, where you can also get a scrub down and massage (from €30). There are separate saunas for men and women; bring your own towel or rent one (€3). It's a 150m stroll southwest of the Sörnäinen metro station.

DON'T MISS

SEURASAARI OPEN-AIR MUSEUM

Situated 5.5km northwest of the city centre, this excellent island-set museum, **Seurasaaren Ulkomuseo** (Seurasaari Open-Air Museum; www.kansallismuseo.fi/en/seurasaari -openairmuseum; Seurasaari; adult/child €9/3; ⊙ 11am-5pm Jun-Aug, 9am-3pm Mon-Fri, 11am-5pm Sat & Sun mid-late May & early–mid-Sep), has a collection of 87 historic wooden buildings transferred here from around Finland. There's everything from haylofts to a mansion, parsonage and church, as well as the beautiful giant rowboats used to transport church-going communities. Prices and hours refer to entering the museum's buildings, where guides in traditional costume demonstrate folk dancing and crafts. Otherwise you're free to roam the picturesque wooded island, where there are several cafes.

Admission includes **guided tours** (3pm daily mid Jun–mid-Aug), in English. The island is also the venue for Helsinki's biggest midsummer bonfires (p58) and a popular area for picnicking. From central Helsinki, take bus 24.

★ **Allas Sea Pool** SWIMMING
(Map p60; www.allasseapool.fi; Katajanokanlaituri
2; day ticket adult/child €12/6, towel rental €5;
⊙6.15am-11pm Mon-Fri, 8am-11pm Sat & Sun)
Constructed from Finnish fir, this 2016-built
swimming complex sits right on the harbour against a spectacular city backdrop.
It incorporates a bracing Baltic seawater
pool, two freshwater pools (one for adults,
one for kids; both heated to 27°C; 80.6°F)
and three saunas (male, female and mixed).
Regular events include DJs or full-moon all-
night nude swimming. Its restaurant serves
Nordic cuisine.

★ **Sky Wheel** FERRIS WHEEL
(Map p50; www.skywheel.fi; Katajanokanlaituri 2;
adult/child €12/9; ⊙10am-9pm Mon-Fri, to 10pm
Sat, 11am-7pm Sun May-Oct, shorter hours Nov-Apr)
Rising above the harbour, this Ferris wheel
offers a fantastic panorama over central Helsinki during the 10-minute 'flight'. A truly
unique experience is the SkySauna gondola,
allowing you to sauna and sightsee simulta-
neously: one hour (up to four people €240
to €320) includes towels, drinks and use of a
ground-level Jacuzzi and lounge.

Yrjönkadun Uimahalli SWIMMING
(Map p60; www.hel.fi; Yrjönkatu 21B; adult/child
swimming €5.50/2.50, swimming plus sauna €14/7;
⊙men 6.30am-8pm Tue & Thu, 7am-8pm Sat, wom-
en noon-8pm Sun & Mon, 6.30am-8pm Wed & Fri,
closed Jun-Aug) For a sauna and swim, these
art-deco baths are a Helsinki institution – a
fusion of soaring Nordic elegance and Roman
tradition. There are separate hours for men
and women. Nudity is compulsory in the saunas; bathing suits are optional in the pool.

👉 **Tours**

Happy Guide Helsinki WALKING, CYCLING
(☑044-502-0066; www.happyguidehelsinki.
com; walking/bike tours from €20/55) Happy
Guide Helsinki runs a range of original,
light-hearted but informative cycling and
walking tours around the city. Just some
of its bike-tour options include berry picking or a sunset sauna tour; walking tours
range from an old-town tour to food tours
and craft-beer tours. Meeting points are con-
firmed when you book.

Natura Viva KAYAKING
(☑010-292-4030; www.naturaviva.fi; Harbonkatu
13, Vuosaari; 4½-hr tour €69, kayak hire per 2hr/day
€22/40; ⊙May-Sep) Located on the island of
Vuosaari, east of the city centre, Natura Viva

ARCHITECTURE TOURS

In July and August, Arkkitehtuurimuseo
offers excellent guided walking tours in
English. At 10am from Thursday to Monday, two-hour tours of Helsinki (adult/
child €10/5), start from **Senaatintori**
(Senate Sq; Map p60;) and finish at Helsinki's 1919-built National Romantic art
nouveau **train station** (Map p60; Rautatieasema; www.vr.fi; Kaivokatu 1).

runs daily three-hour paddling excursions
around the Helsinki archipelago. It's begin-
ner-friendly and pick-ups can be arranged
from the centre of town. You can rent kayaks
at the paddling centre here.

JL Runeberg CRUISE
(Map p60; ☑019-524-3331; www.msjlruneberg.fi;
Kauppatori; adult one way/return €29/39, bicycle
€5; ⊙Tue, Wed, Fri & Sat mid-May–early Sep, plus
Sun Jun-Aug & Mon Jul) This noble old steamship cruises from the kauppatori to Porvoo
in summer, and makes an excellent day trip,
with various lunch options available. The trip
takes 3½ hours each way, so you may prefer
to return by bus.

Royal Line CRUISE
(Map p60; ☑020-711-8333; www.royalline.fi; Kauppatori; 1½-hr cruise adult/child €23/free; ⊙late
Apr-late Oct) A great deal for families, Royal
Line offers free cruises for kids aged 12 and
under. It also offers bus-and-boat combinations (from €35). Check ahead for seasonal
schedules as they can vary.

Helsinki Sightseeing CRUISE
(Gray Line; Map p60; ☑09-2288-1600; www.
stromma.fi; Kauppatori; 1½-hr cruise adult/child
€25/13; ⊙late Apr-late Oct) In addition to its
90-minute islands-and-waterways sightseeing cruise, this company also runs evening
jazz cruises (from €31), dinner cruises
(from €60.50), and bus-and-boat combinations (from €41). Seasons vary, depending
on ice.

IHA Lines CRUISE
(Map p60; ☑09-6874-5050; www.ihalines.fi; Kauppatori; adult/child from €20/10; ⊙late Apr-late
Oct) IHA Lines runs cruises along two archipelago routes as well as lunch cruises (from
€34) and dinner cruises (from €46). Schedules vary seasonally, depending on weather
conditions.

Sauna Culture

Nothing is more integral to Finnish culture, psyche and well-being than the ritual of bathing in the sauna. From fire-heated chimney saunas in rustic summer cottages to modern electric saunas in most homes and apartments, the sauna is a place to cleanse the body and soul.

TBOTYAN/ISTOCK/GETTY IMAGES ©

KATI FINELL/SHUTTERSTOCK ©

1. Lakeside sauna
It's ideal to sauna near a body of water you can jump in. The hot-cold aspect is an integral part of the experience.

2. A sacred ritual
For hundreds of years, the sauna has been a place to meditate, warm up, bathe and even give birth in.

3. Log cabin sauna
It's common to seek out unusual locations to enjoy a sauna. There are over two million saunas in Finland.

4. *Vihta*
The *vihta* is traditional whisk made of fresh, leafy birch twigs, used to lightly strike the skin and improve circulation.

ANNE SAARINEN/ALAMY ©

✳️ Festivals & Events

Lux Helsinki
LIGHT SHOW

(www.luxhelsinki.fi; ⊘ early Jan) Some 15 installations create a route from the kauppatori to Kruununhaka during this four-day festival that brings light to the dark, chilly city in early January.

Helsinki Sauna Day
CULTURAL

(www.helsinkisaunaday.fi; ⊘ early Mar) For one day in early March, saunas all over the city that are normally private (in apartment blocks, government buildings, offices and hotels) open to the public free of charge.

Helsinki Beer Festival
FOOD & DRINK

(www.helsinkibeerfestival.fi; ⊘ early Apr) Finnish and guest international beers and ciders, along with DJs and bands, pull in the punters to this rollicking festival held at the Kaapelitehdas (p77) over two days. There are also food pairings, barbecues, brewing workshops, pouring workshops and various other events.

April Jazz Festival
MUSIC

(http://apriljazz.fi; ⊘ late Apr) Jazz, soul, funk, Latin and world music all feature in Espoo's week-long April Jazz Festival, which draws big crowds and international artists to various locations around this satellite city west of Helsinki.

Helsinki Coffee Festival
FOOD & DRINK

(⊘ late Apr) Helsinki's love of coffee is celebrated during the three-day Helsinki Coffee Festival at the Kaapelitehdas (p77), with roasting demonstrations, tastings, exhibitions, competitions and workshops on themes such as different brewing methods and cooking with coffee.

Vappu
CULTURAL

(May Day; ⊘ 1 May) Helsinki's student-graduation festival is celebrated by gathering around the Havis Amanda (Map p60) statue, which receives a white graduation cap, at 6pm on 30 April. The following day, May Day, is celebrated with plenty of sparkling wine, preferably outdoors, such as in the waterfront park Kaivopuisto (p52).

Helsinki Päivä
CULTURAL

(Helsinki Day; www.helsinkipaiva.fi; ⊘ 11 Jun-12 Jun) Celebrating the city's anniversary on 12 June, Helsinki Päivä (Helsinki Day) brings many free events to the city, with food stalls, concerts, theatre and dance performances, art exhibitions, workshops, cinema screenings, sports events and wellness activities.

Juhannus
CULTURAL

(Midsummer; ⊘ weekend closest to 22 Jun) Juhannus (Midsummer) is the most important annual event, celebrating the longest day of the year. The Seurasaaren Ulkomuseo (p54) on the island of Seurasaari sees the best celebration around Helsinki, with bonfires, midsummer poles and traditional activities.

Tuska Festival
MUSIC

(www.tuska-festival.fi; ⊘ late Jun/early Jul) Over four days in late June and/or early July, this huge festival in the suburb of Suvilahti, northeast of the centre, features one of Finland's all-time favourite music genres – metal – with local and international acts.

Helsingin Juhlaviikot
PERFORMING ARTS

(Helsinki Festival; www.helsinginjuhlaviikot.fi; ⊘ mid-Aug–early Sep) This three-week arts festival features chamber music, jazz, theatre, opera and more at venues throughout the city.

Helsinki Design Week
ART

(www.helsinkidesignweek.com; ⊘ mid-Sep) Spanning 10 days (rather than a week), the Nordic countries' largest design festival has 250-plus events, including workshops, talks, exhibitions, pop-up shops, product launches and parties citywide.

Baltic Herring Fair
FOOD & DRINK

(www.portofhelsinki.fi; Kauppatori; ⊘ early Oct) Delicious salted and marinated herring is traded at this fair on Helsinki's main market square, the kauppatori (p49), in the first week of October. It's been going since 1743.

🛏️ Sleeping

Helsinki is dominated by chain hotels, particularly Sokos and Scandic, but there are some boutique and designer gems too. Budget accommodation is in short supply.

From mid-May to mid-August bookings are strongly advisable, although July is a quieter time for business and high-end hotels.

Apartment rentals range from one-room studios to multi-room properties that are ideal for families. Often you'll get use of a sauna, parking area and other facilities.

🛏️ City Centre

⭐ Hotel Kämp
HOTEL €€€

(Map p60; ☎ 09-576-111; www.hotelkamp.com; Pohjoisesplanadi 29; d/ste from €272/593; 🅿️ ❄️ @ 🛜) A Helsinki emblem, this grand, stylish hotel is where the likes of Sibelius and Gallen-Kallela thrashed out their ideas. Its romantic marble lobby seduces you through to historic rooms furnished with antiques and then surprises in the marble bathrooms with trademark rubber ducks. Facilities include a day spa, saunas, an all-day brasserie serving sumptuous afternoon teas and two bars.

Hotelli Seurahuone HOTEL €€€
(Map p60; ☑020-048-106; www.hotelliseurahuone. fi; Kaivokatu 12; d/ste from €193/314; P🅿️❄️@🛜) Dating from 1833, this *seurahuone* (club room) was a meeting place for high society, where visiting officers, gentlemen and ladies came to stay, and a venue for concerts and dances in its ballroom. The building remains a classic, with period fittings and stately rooms, many with views over Rautatientori. Unusually for Finland, there's no sauna.

Hotel Carlton HOTEL €€€
(Map p60; ☑09-684-1320; www.carlton.fi; Kaisaniemenkatu 3; s/d from €139/165; ❄️🛜) Near the train station and very handy for trams and the metro, this friendly Best Western hotel has 21 rooms, all with decent-sized bathrooms (several with Jacuzzis) and, despite the busy road, minimal noise. It represents value for central Helsinki and has a bit of soul.

GLO Hotel Kluuvi HOTEL €€€
(Map p60; ☑010-344-4400; www.glohotels.fi; Kluuvikatu 4; s/ste from €155/340; ❄️🛜) On a pedestrian street in the heart of town, GLO Hotel Kluuvi has 184 rooms with clean, contemporary lines, including gleaming timber floors. The 'smart doubles' are compact, at 13 sq metres, but beds are comfortable – if there's not much price difference between those and the 'comfort double', go for the latter as you get quite a bit more space.

🛏️ **Kruununhaka & Katajanokka**

Eurohostel HOSTEL €
(Map p50; ☑09-622-0470; www.eurohostel.eu; Linnankatu 9; dm/s/d/tr from €29/39/46/60; @🛜) Close to the Viking Line ferry on Katajanokka, this busy hostel is easily reached on trams 4 and 5. All rooms share bathrooms. 'Eurohostel' rooms are more modern with TVs and parquet floors. Dorm rates mean sharing a twin – a good deal. Rates include a morning sauna; the cafe-bar serves breakfast (€10) and other meals. HI discount.

⭐ **Hotel Katajanokka** HOTEL €€
(Map p50; ☑09-686-450; www.hotelkatajanokka .fi; Merikasarminkatu 1A; d/f/ste from €108/130/185; P❄️@🛜) Set in a spectacularly refurbished 1888-built prison, which was in use until 2002, this fabulous hotel on Katajanokka island offers character in spades. Rooms stretch over two to three ex-cells, so they're anything but cramped. There's a 24-hour gym, a sauna, a good restaurant and an indoor and outdoor bar. Tram 4 stops right outside.

Hellsten Helsinki Senate Apartments APARTMENT €€
(Map p50; ☑09-5110-5243; http://hellstenhotels.fi; Kauppiaankatu 5; ⊙s/d/f from €112/122/162; P🛜) In a great location on Katajanokka, these spacious studio and one-bedroom apartments are split between a National Romantic art nouveau building from 1902 and modern building from 2001, and are equipped with kitchenettes. Singles only have a single bed, so solo travellers might want to upgrade to a double. One-bedroom executive apartments come with their own saunas.

🛏️ **Punavuori & Ullanlinna**

Hostel Diana Park HOSTEL €
(Map p60; ☑09-642-169; www.dianapark.fi; Uudenmaankatu 9; dm/s/d from €32/62/75; 🛜) More like a guesthouse, Helsinki's most characterful and laid-back hostel occupies the 3rd (top) floor of a walk-up building in a lively street of bars and restaurants. Its 50 beds are spread across 15 rooms; all share bathrooms but have in-room sinks. Private rooms offer more peace and there's a great lounge for socialising. Breakfast costs €7.

Hotel Indigo BOUTIQUE HOTEL €€
(Map p60; ☑020-048-105; www.ihg.com; Bulevardi 26; d/ste from €149/207; P❄️@🛜) Helsinki's

---

CAMPING IN THE CAPITAL

An 18-minute metro ride from the city centre (Rastila station), this year-round campground **Rastila Camping** (☑09-3107-8517; www.hel.fi; Karavaanikatu 4, Meri-Rastila; tent sites €17, plus per person €6, cabins €85-120, cottages €170-240, summer hostel dm/s/d €22/37/63; ⊙campground, cabins & cottages year-round, hostel mid-Jun–Jul; P🅿️@🛜) makes a good budget option. Though scarcely rural, it's green and well equipped, with a supermarket nearby. As well as grassy campsites, there are wooden cabins and more-upmarket log cottages, a bayside beach and facilities such as good showers, fast wi-fi, saunas and bike hire.

Central Helsinki

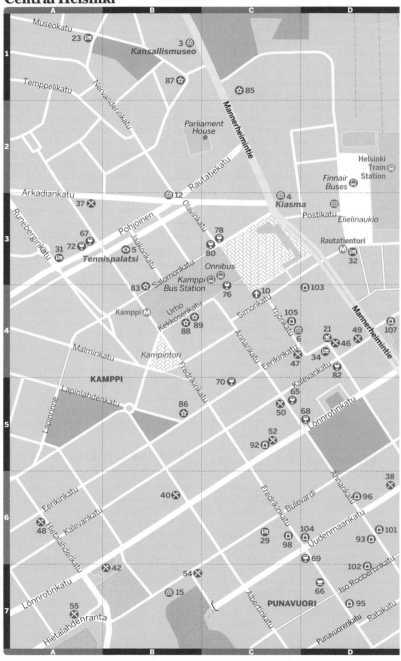

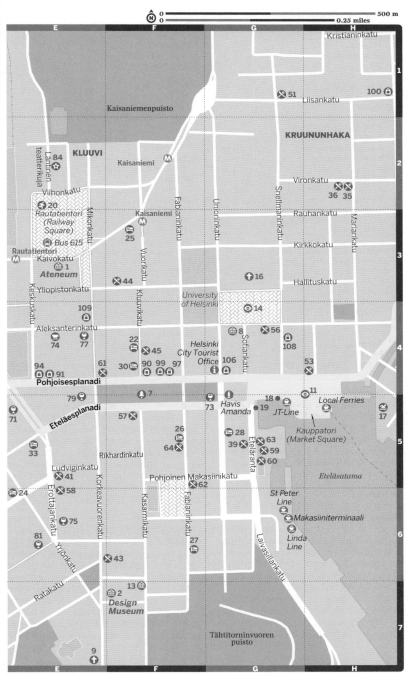

N

0 ─────────── 500 m
0 ─────────── 0.25 miles

Kristianinkatu

KRUUNUNHAKA

51 Liisankatu

100

Kaisaniemenpuisto

KLUUVI

84 Läntinen teatterikuja

Kaisaniemi

Vilhonkatu

Vironkatu
36 35

20 Rautatientori (Railway Square)

Kaisaniemi

Rauhankatu

Kirkkokatu

Bus 615

25

Shellmaninkatu

Marianankatu

Fabianinkatu

Unioninkatu

Rautatientori

Kaivokatu

1 Ateneum

Yliopistonkatu

44

16

Hallituskatu

Keskuskatu

Vuorikatu

University of Helsinki

14

109

Aleksanterinkatu

74 77

22

45

8 56

108

Kluuvikatu

Helsinki City Tourist Office

30 90 99 97

106

Sofiankatu

53

94
91

61

Pohjoisesplanadi

79

7

73

Havis Amanda

18
19

11

Local Ferries

JT-Line

17

71

Eteläesplanadi

57

Kauppatori (Market Square)

26

64

28

39 63
59
60

Etelälaituri

Rikhardinkatu

Etelätaranta

Eteläsatama

Ludviginkatu

41

33

Pohjoinen Makasiinikatu

62

St Peter Line

24

58

Makasiiniterminaali

75

Erottajankatu

Korkeavuorenkatu

Linda Line

81

Kasarmikatu

Fabianinkatu

27

Laivasillankatu

43

Yrjönkatu

13

2 Design Museum

Ratakatu

9

Tähtitorninvuoren puisto

Central Helsinki

◉ Top Sights
1 Ateneum..E3
2 Design Museum................................F7
3 Kansallismuseo...............................B1
4 Kiasma...C3
5 Tennispalatsi....................................B3

◎ Sights
6 Amos Andersonin Taidemuseo...........C4
7 Esplanadin Puisto F4
8 Helsingin Kaupunginmuseo.................G4
Helsinki Art Museum ....(see 5)
9 Johanneksenkirkko.............................. E7
10 Kamppi Chapel.................................C4
11 Kauppatori.......................................H4
12 Luonnontieteellinen Museo.................B3
13 Museum of Finnish Architecture...........F7
14 Senaatintori G4
15 Sinebrychoffin Taidemuseo B7
16 Tuomiokirkko....................................G3

⊕ Activities, Courses & Tours
17 Allas Sea Pool..................................H5
18 Helsinki Sightseeing G5
19 IHA Lines...G5
20 Jääpuisto...E2
JL Runeberg....................................(see 19)
Royal Line.......................................(see 18)
21 Yrjönkadun Uimahalli............................D4

🛏 Sleeping
22 GLO Hotel Kluuvi F4
23 Hellsten Helsinki Parliament................A1

24 Hostel Diana Park...................................E6
25 Hotel Carlton.....................................F3
26 Hotel F6...F5
27 Hotel Fabian.....................................F6
28 Hotel Haven.....................................G5
29 Hotel Indigo.....................................C6
30 Hotel Kämp.......................................F4
31 Hotelli Helka.....................................A3
32 Hotelli Seurahuone..........................D3
33 Klaus K..E5
34 Sokos Hotel Torni............................D4

⊗ Eating
35 Anton & Anton.................................H2
36 Ask..H2
37 Ateljé Finne......................................A3
38 Demo...D6
Emo...(see 30)
39 Goodwin..G5
40 Grön...B6
41 Grotesk..E5
42 Hietalahden Kauppahalli.....................B7
43 Juuri...F6
44 Kanniston Leipomo..........................F3
45 Karl Fazer Café.................................F4
46 KarlJohan...D4
47 Kitch...C4
48 Konstan Möljä...................................A6
49 Kosmos..D4
50 Lappi Ravintola................................C5
51 Mumin Kaffe.....................................G1
52 Naughty Brgr.....................................C5
53 Olo..H4

first branch of branded boutique chain Hotel Indigo opened in the Design District in 2016. Local artists designed and painted unique murals that splash colour across all 120 rooms. Suites have tubs with spa jets. Free bikes are available for guests; there's also a free on-site gym. Bröd, its restaurant, serves Nordic cuisine. Breakfast costs €15.

★ **Hotel F6**   BOUTIQUE HOTEL €€€

(Map p60; ☏ 09-6899-9666; www.hotelf6.fi; Fabianinkatu 6; s/d from €145/165; ✳ 🖛) ⦿ Stunningly designed, this 2016-opened hotel ranges around an internal courtyard (some rooms have direct access and patios); superior rooms come with French balconies. All 66 rooms are spacious (even the smallest are 27 sq metres) and stylishly furnished with cushion-strewn sofas. The courtyard's herb garden supplies the bar (great cocktails). Breakfast is organic, and wind and water powers all electricity.

★ **Hotel Haven**   HOTEL €€€

(Map p60; ☏ 09-681-930; www.hotelhaven. fi; Unioninkatu 17; s/d/ste from €192/229/349; 🅿 ✳ @ 🖛) Welcoming Hotel Haven has 137 elegant rooms. All grades feature excellent beds and linen, soft colour combinations, classy toiletries. Some face the street and are very spacious. Many higher-grade rooms offer a magnificent harbour view, as does the modern Finnish restaurant.

★ **Klaus K**   DESIGN HOTEL €€€

(Map p60; ☏ 020-770-4700; www.klauskhotel.com; Bulevardi 2; d/ste from €193/657; ✳ @ 🖛) Independent design hotel Klaus K has a theme of Finnish national epic *Kalevala* quotes throughout, and space-conscious architecture. Contemporary 'Sky Loft' rooms offer access to the roof terrace; some also come with balconies. The highlight is the fabulous all-organic breakfast spread (€25) with superfood juice shots and dishes sourced from small Finnish producers. Service is superb.

54	Saaga	B7
55	Salve	A7
56	Savotta	G4
57	Savoy	F5
58	Skiffer	E6
59	Soppakeittiö	G5
60	Story	G5
61	Strindberg	E4
62	The Cock	F5
63	Vanha Kauppahalli	G5
64	Zucchini	F5

Drinking & Nightlife

65	A21	C5
66	Andante	D7
	Ateljee Bar	(see 34)
67	Bäkkäri	A3
68	Bar Loose	D5
	Bier-Bier	(see 41)
69	Birri	D6
70	Corona Baari	C5
71	DTM	E5
72	Hercules	A3
73	Kappeli	G5
74	La Torrefazione	E4
75	Liberty or Death	E6
76	Maxine	C4
77	Raffaellon Terassi	E4
78	Steam Hellsinki	C3
79	Teatteri	E5
80	Teerenpeli	C3
81	TheRiff	E6
82	Vin-Vin	D4

Entertainment

83	FinnKino Tennispalatsi	B4
84	Kansallisteatteri	E2
85	Musiikkitalo	C1
86	Orion Theatre	B5
	Semifinal	(see 88)
87	Storyville	B1
88	Tavastia	B4
89	Tiketti	B4

Shopping

90	Aarikka	F4
91	Akateeminen Kirjakauppa	E4
92	Alnilam	C5
93	Art.fi	D6
94	Artek	E4
95	Awake	D7
96	Frank/ie	D6
97	Iittala	F4
98	Jukka Rintala	C6
99	Kalevala Koru	F4
100	Lasikammari	H1
101	Lokal	D6
102	Mafka & Alakoski	D7
103	Moomin Shop	D4
104	Nide	D6
105	Scandinavian Outdoor	C4
106	Schröder	G4
107	Stockmann	D4
108	Sweet Story	G4
109	Tre	E4

Hotel Fabian HOTEL €€€

(Map p60; ☑ 09-6128-2000; www.hotelfabian.com; Fabianinkatu 7; d €184-350; ❋ 🛜) In a central but quiet location, Fabian has elegant 'Comfort' (ie standard) rooms with a restrained modern design, higher-grade 'Style' rooms (some with French balconies) and top-range 'Lux' rooms equipped with kitchenettes. Staff are super-helpful. There's no restaurant, but a chef cooks breakfasts to order.

🛏 Kamppi & Töölö

Hostel Domus Academica HOSTEL €

(Map p50; ☑ 09-1311-4334; www.hostelacademica.fi; Hietaniemenkatu 14; dm/s/d/tr from €31/58/85/109; ⊙ Jun-Aug; 🅿@🛜🏊) Finnish students live well, so take advantage of this summer residence: a clean, busy, environmentally sound spot with a pool and sauna. Its 326 modern en suite rooms come with kitchenettes (crockery is in the common room) and Finnish textiles. Dorms sleep up to three. Breakfast costs €8.50. HI discount. Rates include a morning sauna.

★**Hotelli Helka** HOTEL €€

(Map p60; ☑09-613-580; www.hotelhelka.com; Pohjoinen Rautatiekatu 23; s/d/ste from €158/173/248; 🅿🛜) One of Helsinki's best midrange hotels, the Helka has friendly staff and excellent facilities, including parking if you can bag one of the 28 spots. Best are the rooms, with Alvar Aalto–designed furniture and a backlit print of a rural Suomi scene over the bed. Saunas are situated on the top floor, adjoining the rooftop terrace.

Hellsten Helsinki Parliament APARTMENT €€

(Map p60; ☑ 09-5110-5700; www.hellstenhotels.fi; Museokatu 18; apt €132-197; ⊙ reception 7am-10pm Mon-Fri; @🛜) A step up in style and comfort from many hotels, the apartments here have sleek modern furnishings and kitchenettes. It's in a peaceful, leafy local neighbourhood setting. There are another two apartment buildings at separate locations: one in Katajanokka (p59) and one at Espoo. Discounts are available for longer stays.

✗ Eating

Helsinki has an extensive range of restaurants, whether for Finnish classics, modern Suomi cuisine or international dishes. Cafes offer some of the cheapest lunchtime options and there are plenty of self-catering opportunities, including large seven-day supermarkets and, better yet, Helsinki's produce-laden outdoor markets in summer and wonderful market halls year-round.

✗ City Centre

Karl Fazer Café
CAFE €

(Map p60; www.fazer.fi; Kluuvikatu 3; dishes €4-12; ⏱7.30am-10pm Mon-Fri, 9am-10pm Sat, 10am-6pm Sun; 🛜🖋🍴) Founded in 1891 and fronted by a striking art deco facade, this cavernous cafe is the flagship for Fazer's chocolate empire. The glass cupola reflects sound, so locals say it's a bad place to gossip. It's ideal, however, for buying dazzling confectionery, fresh bread, salmon or shrimp sandwiches, or digging into towering sundaes or spectacular cakes. Gluten-free dishes are available.

Kanniston Leipomo
BAKERY €

(Map p60; www.kannistonleipomo.fi; Yliopistonkatu 7; pastries €2.50-4.50; ⏱7.30am-6pm Mon-Fri) Spectacular breads such as sourdough and rye are the hallmark of this fabulous Helsinki bakery chain, with half-a-dozen outlets around town. Alternatively, choose from savoury pastries such as a *karjalanpiirakka* (rice-filled rye Karelian pastry) or *lahapasteija* (cheese and sausage roll), or sweet options such as *korvapuusti* (cinnamon scroll) or *vadelmapulla* (raspberry bun). There's a handful of seats inside.

Strindberg
BISTRO €€

(Map p60; ☎09-6128-6900; www.strindberg.fi; Pohjoisesplanadi 33; mains €21-31.50; ⏱11am-10pm Mon-Sat) Strindberg has a casual ground-floor cafe and late-opening bar, but its finest dining is one flight up. In a light-filled room overlooking leafy Esplanadin Puisto (p48), it serves dishes such as seared scallops with tomato risotto and basil foam, lamb sirloin with smoked black salsify, and pan-fried liver with creamed chanterelles, followed by lush desserts like raspberry pavlova with mascarpone mousse.

Emo
EUROPEAN €€€

(Map p60; ☎010-505-0900; www.emo-ravintola.fi; Kluuvikatu 2; 3-course lunch menu €39, 4-/6-course dinner menus €54/69; ⏱11.30am-3pm & 5-10pm Mon-Fri, 2-10pm Sat, bar to midnight Mon-Sat) Popular with business diners, classy Emo serves dishes such as crab cakes with coriander and fennel, salt-baked trout with herb and juniper berry salad, halibut with wild garlic crème, and duck with red cabbage and apple in an elegant dining room decorated in sedate sage-green and oyster-grey hues. Astutely chosen wine pairings are available to complement each course.

✗ Kruununhaka & Katajanokka

Anton & Anton
DELI €

(Map p60; www.antonanton.fi; Mariankatu 18; dishes €3-6.50; ⏱8am-8pm Mon-Fri, to 6pm Sat) For gourmet picnic ingredients, this light-filled deli with black-and-white chequerboard tiles is a must. Fresh food changes with the seasons – there's a fantastic selection of Finnish cheeses, birch-smoked salmon, reindeer yoghurt, berries, locally baked breads, crisps, crackers, jams, chutneys and sweets such as *salmiakki* (salty Finnish liquorice). Ready-to-eat dishes include salads, sandwiches, wraps and savoury pastries and crêpes.

Mumin Kaffe
CAFE €

(Map p60; www.muminkaffe.com; Liisankatu 21; dishes €3.40-9.50; ⏱9am-7pm; 🛜🍴) A delight for families, this comic-adorned cafe is themed around the Moomins, the adorable creations of Helsinki-born author and illustrator Tove Jansson. Sandwiches, cakes, pastries and freshly squeezed juices are all served on authentic Moomin plates, cups and glasses. There's a kids' seating area for little diners and high chairs for infants. There's official Moomin merchandise, including books, for sale.

Savu
FINNISH €€

(Map p50; ☎09-7425-5574; www.ravintolasavu.fi; Tervasaari; mains €20-26, 3-course menus €41-54; ⏱noon-11pm Mon-Sat, 1-6pm Sun late May-Aug, 6-11pm Tue-Sat Sep) Dating from 1805, a rust-red wooden warehouse that once stored tar on Tervasaari (p49) now contains this delightful beam-ceilinged summer restaurant, which reflects its heritage in unique creations such as pine-tar-infused ice cream. Pine tar, birch and alder are all used to smoke meat, fish and vegetables at its smokery. Leafy trees and umbrellas shade the terrace.

Kolme Kruunua
FINNISH €€

(Map p50; ☎09-135-4172; www.kolmekruunua.fi; Liisankatu 5; mains €15-33; ⏱kitchen 4pm-midnight Mon-Sat, 2-11pm Sun) Well off the tourist trail, this unpretentious local in

HELSINKI FOR CHILDREN

Helsinki has a lot to offer kids, with summer boat trips, amusement parks and outdoor events year-round. Finland is a child-friendly society and just about every hotel and restaurant will be keen to help out with cots or high chairs. Family rooms are available even in business hotels.

Ferries & Cruises

Getting there is half the fun when it starts with a ferry ride.

➡ Activities on the island-set fortress of Suomenlinna (p46) include a nostalgic toy museum and crawling through the submarine. There's also a safe beach here.

➡ Encounter a host of animals at Helsinki's **zoo** (www.korkeasaari.fi; Mustikkamaanpolku 12, Korkeasaari; adult/child €16/8; ☺10am-8pm May-Aug, 10am-4pm Oct-Mar, 10am-6pm Sep & Apr), spread across the island of Korkeasaari.

➡ Kids under 12 creuise for free on Royal Line's (p55) sightseeing trips.

Museums

Most museums are free to under-18s.

➡ The pick of the museums for kids is the hands-on **Heureka** (www.heureka.fi; Tiedepuisto 1, Vantaa; adult/child €22/15; ☺10am-7pm Mon-Fri, to 6pm Sat & Sun) science centre, near the airport at Vantaa.

➡ Kiasma (p48) has loads of interaction, though check that special exhibits won't raise any 'adult themes'.

➡ Dinosaurs at Helsinki's Natural History Museum, the **Luonnontieteellinen Museo** (Map p60; www.luomus.fi; Pohjoinen Rautatiekatu 13; adult/child €13/6; ☺10am-5pm Tue, Wed & Fri-Sun, to 6pm Thu Jun-Aug, 9am-4pm Tue, Wed & Fri, to 8pm Thu, 10am-5pm Sat, 10am-4pm Sun Sep-May), are a hit with youngsters.

➡ Kansallismuseo (p53) brings history to lifeat its hands-on Workshop Vintti.

Amusements

➡ In Kallio, amusement park **Linnanmäki** (Map p50; www.linnanmaki.fi; Tivolikuja 1; single ride/day pass €8/39, combination ticket with Sea Life €47; ☺11am-10pm mid-Jun–Aug, hours vary late Apr–mid-Jun, Sep & Oct) ✿ has thrill-seeking rides.

➡ Kids can identify Helsinki landmarks on the high-flying Sky Wheel (p55).

Aquatic Fun

Opportunities to get into the water abound.

➡ Kallio's **Sea Life** (Map p50; ☎09-565-8200; www.visitsealife.com; Tivolitie 10; adult/child €16.50/13, combination ticket with Linnanmäki €47; ☺10am-8pm Jun–mid-Aug, hours vary mid-Aug–May) aquarium has walk-through tunnels for shark spotting.

➡ One of the superbly sited outdoor pools at Allas Sea Pool (p55) is dedicated for kids.

➡ Hietaranta has golden sands for building castles and safe beach swimming.

➡ Beautiful Kaivopuisto park (p52) has a great beach and good playground.

➡ In the satellite city of Espoo, **Serena water park** (☎09-887-0550; www.serena. fi; Tornimäentie 10, water park day/evening €26.50/22.50, ski park day ticket €29, ski/swim combination ticket €39; ☺11am-8pm late Jun–mid-Aug, noon-8pm most weekends late May-late Jun & mid-Aug–mid-Dec, hours vary mid-Dec–late May) is great fun, with plenty of water slides.

Winter Activities

➡ Come winter, the Serena offers skiing on gentle downhill runs.

➡ Wrap the kids up for ice skating at **Jääpuisto** (Ice Park; Map p60; ☎040-775-5791; www. icepark.fi; Rautatientori; adult/child €6/3, skate rental €6; ☺2-9pm Mon-Fri, 10am-9pm Sat & Sun Nov–Mar), while you stay snug in a nearby cafe.

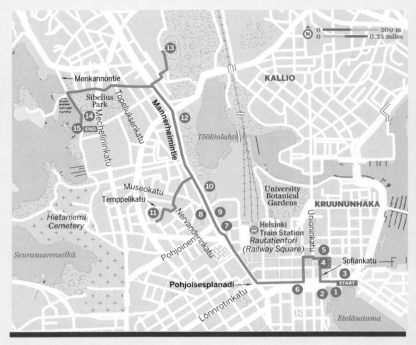

🏃 City Walk
Iconic Buildings & Monuments

START KAUPPATORI
END CAFE REGATTA
LENGTH 6.5KM; 4½ HOURS

The bustling **1 kauppatori** (market square; p49) is flanked by stately 19th-century buildings. The eagle-topped stone obelisk is the Keisarinnankivi (Empress' Stone), Helsinki's oldest monument, unveiled in 1835 in honour of a visit by Tsar Nicholas I and Tsarina Alexandra. **2 Havis Amanda** (p58), the female nude statue dipping in a fountain just west of the market, is regarded as the symbol of Helsinki. Across from the kauppatori is the **3 Presidentinlinna** (Presidential Palace), guarded by uniformed sentries. Head up Sofiankatu to **4 Senaatintori** (Senate Sq). Engel's stately neoclassical **5 Tuomiokirkko** (Lutheran Cathedral; p49) is the most prominent feature, topped by zinc statues of the 12 apostles on the roof. The main University of Helsinki building is on the west side and the magnificent National Library a little further north along Unioninkatu. Walking back to Pohjoisesplanadi, stroll through leafy **6 Esplanadin Puisto** (Esplanade Park; p48), or browse the design

shops. Turn right onto Mannerheimintie. An equestrian **7 statue of Marshal Mannerheim**, Finland's most revered military leader, dominates the square alongside the Kiasma museum.

Continue walking northwest. Monolithic **8 Parliament House** (opened 1931; p53) dominates this stretch. Opposite it is the striking modern glass-and-copper **9 Musiikkitalo** (p75), with concert halls and studios. Up on the right is one of Alvar Aalto's most famous works, angular **10 Finlandia Talo** (p76), a landmark concert hall completed in 1971 and subsequently expanded. At this point you can detour west through the leafy backstreets to the **11 Temppeliaukion Kirkko** (p54), an extraordinary church hewn from solid rock in 1969. A few blocks north, on Mannerheimintie, is the 1993 **12 Oopperatalo** (p76), home of the Finnish National Opera. Continue to the 1952 **13 Olympic Stadium** (undergoing major renovations until 2019). Finally head westward to take in the **14 Sibelius monument**. This striking sculpture was created in 1967 to honour Finland's most famous composer. Finish up at waterside **15 Cafe Regatta** (p69).

Kruununhaka offers no-frills Finnish dishes such as fried Baltic herring, sautéed reindeer or handmade malt pork sausages in a fabulously retro dining area – with stained-glass windows, jade-green carpeting and a curvilinear timber bar – that hasn't changed since the 1950s.

Bellevue
RUSSIAN €€

(Map p50; ☎09-179-560; http://restaurantbelle vue.com; Rahapajankatu 3; mains €20-30.50; ⏱11am-11pm Tue-Fri, 5-11pm Sat mid-Aug–mid-Jun, 5-11pm Tue-Sat mid-Jun–mid-Aug) Opened in 1917, Bellevue is Helsinki's oldest Russian restaurant. Along with its signature pot-roasted bear (€55), it offers more standard choices, from *zakuska* (mixed starters) and a range of blini (vendace roe, wild mushroom) to chicken Kiev and roast pheasant with beetroot troika, and cranberry soup for dessert. The atmosphere is elegant and old-fashioned.

Savotta
FINNISH €€

(Map p60; ☎09-7425-5588; www.ravintolasavotta. fi; Aleksanterinkatu 22; mains €22-38; ⏱11am-11pm Mon-Sat, 6-10pm Sun) Themey but good quality, this representation of a logger's mess hall fits a lot of specialities from around Finland into its short but authentic menu. Staff in traditional dress are happy to explain the dishes, which include excellent fish mixed starters and mains such as succulent slow-roasted lamb or Arctic char. Summer dining is a pleasure on the courtyard terrace.

★Olo
FINNISH €€€

(Map p60; ☎010-320-6250; www.olo-ravintola.fi; Pohjoisesplanadi 5; 4-course lunch menu €53, dinner tasting menus short/long from €79/109, with paired wines €173/255; ⏱6-11pm Tue-Sat Jun–mid-Aug, 11.30am-3pm & 6-11pm Tue-Fri, 6-11pm Sat mid-Aug–May) At the forefront of new Suomi cuisine, Michelin-starred Olo occupies a handsome 19th-century harbourside mansion. Its memorable degustation menus incorporate both the forage ethos and molecular gastronomy, and feature culinary jewels such as fennel-smoked salmon, herring with fermented cucumber, Åland lamb with blackcurrant leaves, juniper-marinated reindeer carpaccio, and Arctic crab with root celery. Book a few weeks ahead.

Ask
GASTRONOMY €€€

(Map p60; ☎040-581-8100; www.restaurantask. com; Vironkatu 8; 4-course lunch menu €49, tasting menu €98, with paired wines €178; ⏱6pm-midnight Wed & Thu, 11.30am-1pm & 6pm-midnight Fri & Sat) Small organic or biodynamic Finnish farms and foraged game, fish, forest mushrooms, herbs and berries provide the ingredients for Michelin-starred Ask's superb-value lunch menus and 16- to 20-course evening tasting menus. Delicious, exquisitely presented morsels might feature buckwheat and nettle, reindeer and hazelnut, pike-perch and tar butter, beetroot and wild duck or burbot and spruce. Book several weeks ahead.

✖ Punavuori & Ullanlinna

★Vanha Kauppahalli
MARKET €

(Map p60; www.vanhakauppahalli.fi; Eteläranta 1; ⏱8am-6pm Mon-Sat, plus 10am-5pm Sun Jun-Aug; ☑) 🖉 Alongside the harbour, this is Helsinki's iconic market hall. Built in 1888 it's still a traditional Finnish market, with wooden stalls selling local flavours such as liquorice, Finnish cheeses, smoked salmon and herring, berries, forest mushrooms and herbs. Its centrepiece is its superb cafe, Story. Look out too for soups from Soppakeittiö.

Story
CAFE €

(Map p60; www.restaurantstory.fi; Vanha Kauppahalli, Eteläranta; snacks €3.20-10, mains €12.80-17; ⏱kitchen 8am-3pm Mon-Fri, to 5pm Sat, bar to 6pm Mon-Sat; ☑) 🖉 At the heart of Helsinki's historic harbourside market hall Vanha Kauppahalli (p67), this sparkling cafe sources its produce from the surrounding stalls. Breakfast (oven-baked barley porridge, eggs Benedict) gives way to snacks (cinnamon buns, cakes) and hearty mains such as creamy salmon and fennel soup, aubergine ragout with couscous, and shrimp-laden *skagen* (Swedish-style open-faced sandwiches). Its outdoor terrace overlooks the water.

Soppakeittiö
SOUP €

(Map p60; www.sopakeittio.fi; Vanha Kauppahalli; soups €9-10; ⏱11am-5pm Mon-Sat; ☑) A great place to warm the cockles in winter, this soup stall inside the Vanha Kauppahalli is renowned for its bouillabaisse, which is almost always on the menu. Other options might include cauliflower and goat's cheese, smoked reindeer or potato and parsnip. There are also branches at the Hietalahden Kauppahalli (p69) in Kamppi, and Hakaniemen Kauppahalli (p71) in Kallio.

Skiffer
PIZZA €

(Map p60; www.skiffer.fi; Erottajankatu 11; pizzas €13-17.50; ⏱11am-9pm Mon & Tue, to 10pm Wed & Thu, 1-11pm Fri & Sat, 1-8pm Sun; 📶📼) Nautical-themed artworks brighten the low-lit interior of this out-of-the-ordinary pizza joint. Choices include the Hangö (juniper-berry-marinated herring and smoked whitefish) and Surf & Turf (crayfish and chorizo); smaller kids' pizzas are available for €10. It's a popular meeting spot, so be prepared to wait for a table.

Zucchini
VEGETARIAN €

(Map p60; Fabianinkatu 4; lunch mains €8-12; ⏱11am-4pm Mon-Fri; 🛪) 🌱 One of the city's original and most popular vegetarian cafes, Zucchini is a top-notch lunch spot; queues out the door aren't unusual. Steaming soups banish winter chills, while freshly baked quiche on the sunny terrace is a summer treat. Year-round you can choose soup or a salad/hot dish or both. At least one vegan dish features on the daily changing menu.

Saaga
FINNISH €€

(Map p60; ☑09-7425-5544; www.ravintolasaaga.fi; Bulevardi 34; mains €22-27, 3-course menus €49-65; ⏱6-11pm Mon-Fri late May-Aug, 6-11pm Mon-Sat Sep & Oct) Chandeliers made from reindeer antlers and split-log benches lined with reindeer furs adorn this rustic timber-lined Lappish restaurant. Specialities from Finland's far north include chargrilled whitefish with sour milk sauce and roast elk with juniper berry sauce, followed by desserts such as Lappish liquorice cake with birch ice cream and cloudberries.

Saslik
RUSSIAN €€

(Map p50; ☑09-7425-5500; www.ravintolasaslik.fi; Neitsytpolku 12; mains €24-37, 3-course menus €49-65; ⏱6-11pm Mon-Fri, noon-11pm Sat Sep-Jul, 6-11pm Tue-Sat Aug) Screened by tasselled curtains, Saslik's succession of aristocratic dining rooms have stained-glass windows, gilt-framed paintings of Russian hunting scenes and flowing tablecloths. *Borscht* (sour beetroot soup), lamb *pelmeni* (dumplings made from unleavened dough), blini with aubergine and black caviar, and potted-bear stroganoff are among its specialities, along with desserts such as baked Alaska. Traditional Russian musicians often perform.

Café Ursula
CAFE €€

(www.ursula.fi; Ehrenströmintie 3; lunch buffet €10.50, mains lunch €11-17, dinner €17.50-28.50; ⏱9am-9pm Mon & Tue, to 10pm Wed-Sat, to 8pm Sun; 🛪) Offering majestic views over the Helsinki archipelago, this upmarket cafe has marvellous outside summer seating. In winter you can sit in the modern interior and watch the ice on the sea. Along with daily specials, dishes range from elaborate open

sandwiches to portobello burgers with goat's cheese and sweet-potato fries to Russian-style bavette steaks and grilled Baltic herring.

Juuri
FINNISH €€

(Map p60; ☑09-635-732; www.juuri.fi; Korkeavuorenkatu 27; mains €18-25; ⏱11.30am-2.30pm & 5-11pm Mon-Fri, noon-11pm Sat, 4-11pm Sun) Creative takes on classic Finnish ingredients draw the crowds to this stylish modern restaurant, but the highlight here is sampling the 'sapas' – tapas with a Suomi twist (€7.80 per plate) – which is only served in the evenings. You might graze on rhubarb-marinated horse, juniper berry and pork croquettes, spruce-smoked salmon, or herring with horseradish crème.

Sea Horse
FINNISH €€

(Map p50; ☑09-628-169; www.seahorse.fi; Kapteeninkatu 11; lunch buffet €10.30, mains €25-38; ⏱10.30am-10pm Mon-Fri, noon-10pm Sat & Sun) A seahorse mural takes up an entire wall of this traditional Finnish restaurant dating from the 1930s. Locals gather in the gloriously unchanged interior to meet and drink over hefty dishes of Baltic herring, Finnish meatballs, liver and cabbage rolls.

The Cock
PUB FOOD €€

(Map p60; ☑09-6128-5100; www.thecock.fi; Fabianinkatu 17; mains lunch €12-22, dinner €22-28; ⏱kitchen 11am-11pm Mon-Fri, noon-11pm Sat, bar to late Mon-Sat; 🛜) The Cock combines a free-wheeling bar with ping-pong tables (hosting regular tournaments) and brilliant cocktails such as its house G&T (with pink grapefruit, lingonberry and Helsinki dry gin) and Blue Mule (blueberry-infused vodka, fresh mint, lime and ginger beer) with pub food spanning organic beef tartare with raw egg and bavette steak with Béarnaise sauce to white-wine-steamed mussels.

★ Demo
FINNISH €€€

(Map p60; ☑09-2289-0840; www.restaurantdemo.fi; Uudenmaankatu 9; 4-/5-/6-/7-course menus €62/75/92/102, with paired wines €110/138/170/185; ⏱4-11pm Tue-Sat) Book to get a table at this chic Michelin-starred spot, where young chefs wow with modern Finnish cuisine. Artfully presented, daily changing combinations are innovative (blackcurrant and liquorice-leaf marinated Åland lamb, spruce-smoked pumpkin with chanterelles, king crab with nettle pesto and vendace roe) and the slick contemporary decor appropriate: this is a place to be seen, not for quiet contemplation.

DON'T MISS

ISLAND DINING

By the main quay, the microbrewery **Suomenlinnan Panimo** (☑ 020-742-5307; www. panimoravintola.fi; Suomenlinna C1; mains €15-30; ☺ noon-10pm Mon-Sat, to 6pm Sun Jun-Aug, shorter hours Sep-May), is the best place to drink or dine on Suomenlinna. It brews three ciders and seven different beers, including a hefty porter, plus several seasonal varieties, and offers good food to accompany it, such as pike-perch with mustard tar sauce, or a game platter with bear salami, smoked reindeer and wild pheasant rillettes.

Most renowned of Helsinki's island restaurants is **Saaristo** (Map p50; ☑ 09-7425-5590; www.ravintolasaaristo.fi; mains €21-42, crayfish parties per person €67; ☺ by reservation 5-11pm Mon-Fri May-Sep), set in a spire-crowned art nouveau villa on Luoto (Swedish: Klippan), and famous for society weddings, refined Finnish cuisine and summer crayfish parties. It's reach by private boat from the pier south of the Olympia Terminaali (p80) ferry terminal; the fare of €6 per person return is automatically added to your bill.

★ **Savoy** FINNISH €€€
(Map p60; ☑ 09-6128-5300; www.ravintolasavoy. fi; Eteläesplanadi 14; 3-course lunch menu €63; ☺ 11.30am-3pm & 6pm-midnight Mon-Fri, 6pm-midnight Sat) Designed by Alvar and Aino Aalto in 1937, this is one of Helsinki's grandest dining rooms, with birch walls and ceilings and some of the city's finest views. The food is a modern Nordic tour de force, with the 'forage' ethos strewing flowers and berries across plates that bear the finest Finnish game, fish and meat.

Grotesk STEAK €€€
(Map p60; ☑ 010-470-2100; www.grotesk.fi; Ludviginkatu 10; mains €26-42; ☺ 5-9pm Tue-Thu, to 10pm Fri & Sat, bar to midnight; ☎) Elegant but reasonably informal, this former bank has a Finnish-baroque dining room where cured meat starters precede excellent meats grilled on a Spanish Josper (charcoal oven), accompanied by an especially good, fairly priced wine list. The attached bar is popular in summer when it migrates into the sheltered courtyard space with regular DJs.

Goodwin STEAK €€€
(Map p60; ☑ 050-419-8000; www.steak.fi; Eteläranta 14; mains €27-39; ☺ 11am-11pm; ☻) There's a lot to be said for doing one thing well, and Goodwin achieves it, with tenderised steaks cooked to order on a Josper. Kids' menus cost between €8.50 and €10.50. The split-level space is done out in stylish timbers; look for the lounging cow statue out the front.

✗ **Kamppi & Töölö**

★ **Cafe Regatta** CAFE €
(www.caferegatta.fi; Merikannontie 10; dishes €1.50-5; ☺ 8am-10.30pm) In a marvellous waterside location, this historic rust-red wooden cottage is scarcely bigger than a sauna, but has great outdoor seating. You can hire a canoe or paddleboards alongside, buy sausages and grill them over the open fire, or just kick back with a *korvapuusti* (cinnamon scroll). Expect to queue on sunny weekends. Cash only.

Hietalahden Kauppahalli MARKET €
(Map p60; www.hietalahdenkauppahalli.fi; Lönnrotinkatu 34; ☺ 8am-6pm Mon-Thu, to 10pm Fri & Sat, 10am-4pm Sun; ☒) ✿ Dating from 1903 and beautifully restored, this red-brick indoor market at Hietalahti has charming wooden food stalls and eateries, including enticing cafes with upstairs seating at each end. A flea market sets up here in the summer months.

Kitch CAFE €
(Map p60; www.kitch.fi; Yrjönkatu 30; mains €14.50-17, tapas €3.50-6; ☺ 11am-10pm Mon & Tue, to 11pm Wed-Sat mid-Aug–mid-Jun, 3-11pm Tue-Fri, noon-11pm Sat mid-Jun–mid-Aug; ☎☒) ✿ With big picture windows, this laid-back space is great for watching the world go by. Furnished with recycled materials, it offers generous tapas portions (such as roasted beetroot with goats' cheese), original salads (including a fantastic crab Caesar salad) and fat burgers. Produce is primarily sustainably sourced.

Tin Tin Tango CAFE €
(Map p50; www.tintintango.fi; Töölöntorinkatu 7; dishes €9-12; ☺ 7am-midnight Mon-Fri, 9am-midnight Sat, 10am-9pm Sun; ☎) This buzzy neighbourhood cafe decorated with prints from the quiffed Belgian's adventures has a bit of everything. There's a laundry and a sauna, as well as lunches, brunches and cosy tables where you can sip a drink or get to grips with delicious rolls absolutely stuffed full. The welcoming, low-key bohemian vibe is the real draw, though.

WORTH A TRIP

TUUSULANJÄRVI

The views from the narrow stretch of road running along Tuusulanjärvi (Tuusula Lake), 35km north of Helsinki, inspired some of Finland's greatest artists. Museums here include composer Sibelius' home, **Ainola** (www.ainola.fi; Ainolankatu, Järvenpää; adult/ child €8/2; ⊙10am-5pm Tue-Sun May-Sep); painter Pekka Halonen's studio and home, **Halosenniemi** (www.halosenniemi.fi; Halosenniementie 4-6, Järvenpää; adult/child €8/2; ⊙11am-6pm Tue-Sun May-Aug, noon-5pm Tue-Sun Sep-Apr); and the **Lottamuseo** (www. lottamuseo.com; Rantatie 39, Järvenpää; adult/child €6/1; ⊙9am-6pm Tue-Sun May-Sep, 10am-5pm Tue-Sun Oct-Apr), commemorating the Lotta women's voluntary defence force.

Mäntsälä-bound buses from Kamppi bus station travel here on weekdays. You could also make a bike tour of it, taking the train to Kerava and back from Järvenpää.

Belying its name, **Hotelli Krapi** (☑09-274-841; www.krapi.fi; Rantatie 2, Tuusula; s/d from €99/138; P✿), an historic red wooden estate 2km north of Tuusula at Tuusulanjärvi, shelters an excellent independent hotel in a former cowshed with countrified rooms, two restaurants, a traditional smoke sauna, summer theatre, golf course, Finnish cookery classes (five hours €145; English available) and resident ghost. Various activity packages are available; rates are cheapest in summer and on weekends.

Naughty Brgr
BURGERS €

(Map p60; www.naughtybrgr.com; Lönnrotinkatu 13; burgers €10-20; ⊙11am-10pm Tue-Sat, noon-7pm Sun; ✍) The open kitchen inside this cavernous space sizzles up monumental single-, double- and triple-patty burgers. Alongside meat options such as its signature Naughty Brgr (Finnish beef, blue cheese, bacon jam and aioli) are vegetarian burgers (such as roasted portobello, olive tapenade and lemon-truffle dressing) and a vegan burger (pulled oats, roast tomato, caramelised onion and coriander chipotle), plus rotating craft beers.

★Grön
BISTRO €€

(Map p60; ☑050-328-9181; www.restaurantgron. com; Albertinkatu 36; mains €23-26, 4-course menu €49; ⊙5-10pm Tue-Sat; ✿✍) ✪ Seasonal, often foraged ingredients are used in this exceptional bistro's plant, fish or meat starters and mains, and wild, plant or dairy desserts. Stunning plates might include pike-perch with charred leek parsley emulsion, nasturtium flowers, hazelnuts and burbot roe, followed by beef with sorrel and burnt-butter Béarnaise, and rose-oil-seasoned strawberries with strawberry granita, caramelised strawberry milk and rose petals.

★Kuu
FINNISH €€

(Map p50; ☑09-2709-0973; www.ravintolakuu. fi; Töölönkatu 27; mains €19-30, 2-/3-course lunch menus €24/28, 4-course dinner menus €47-51; ⊙11.30am-midnight Mon-Fri, 2pm-midnight Sat, 4-11pm Sun) Traditional Finnish fare is given a sharp, contemporary twist at Kuu, which creates dishes from local ingredients such as smoked reindeer heart with pickled forest mushrooms, poached pike-perch with Lappish fingerling potatoes, and liquorice ice cream with cloudberry soup. Wines aren't cheap, but there are some interesting choices. Its casual bistro sibling, KuuKuu, is located 800m south.

Kosmos
FINNISH €€

(Map p60; ☑09-647-255; www.kosmos.fi; Kalevankatu 3; mains €16-32; ⊙11.30am-11pm Mon-Fri, 4-11pm Sat, bar to 1am) Designed by Alvar Aalto, this 1924-opened restaurant is a Helsinki treasure, with a traditionally Finnish atmosphere and classic dishes such as reindeer, sweetbreads, kidneys and fish, along with amazing rye bread made from a 1940s starter. Service is impeccable.

Carelia
BRASSERIE €€

(Map p50; ☑09-2709-0976; www.ravintolacarelia. fi; Mannerheimintie 56; 2-/3-course lunch menu €23/29, mains €19-29; ⊙11am-10pm Mon-Thu, 11.30am-11pm Fri, 3-11pm Sat) In a former pharmacy, this striking spot opposite the Oopperatalo is ideal for a pre- or post-show drink or meal. Glamorously decorated in period style, with original timber cabinetry, it offers smart brasserie fare (pork fillet with beetroot and tar sauce, pike-perch and shellfish terrine, steak tartare with salted quail egg) and some intriguing pan-European wines by the glass.

Lappi Ravintola
FINNISH €€

(Map p60; ☑09-645-550; www.lappires.com; Annankatu 22; mains €23.50-39; ⊙4-10.30pm Mon-Sat) Log-cabin interior cladding, a stone fireplace, hefty timber tables and staff in traditional Sámi dress create an atmospheric backdrop for dining on authentic Lappish specialities such as a game platter for two (€68) with braised reindeer, roast elk, bear sausages, winter vegetables and creamy game sauce. Other dishes include smoked salmon soup and roast snow grouse with cranberries.

KarlJohan
FINNISH €€

(Map p60; ☑ 09-612-1121; www.ravintolakarljohan.fi; Yrjönkatu 21; mains €18-32; ⊙ 11am-3pm & 5-11pm Mon-Fri, 2-11pm Sat; ☜) Welcoming service and an elegant but relaxed atmosphere in a herringbone-floored dining room provide a fitting backdrop for carefully prepared Finnish cuisine, such as *vorschmack* (minced, salty beef and lamb, served with potatoes, pickles and sour cream) and blueberry parfait with mascarpone and rye biscuits. The central location is a plus point. Wines are rather pricey.

Salve
FINNISH €€

(Map p60; ☑ 010-766-4280; www.raflaamo.fi/fi/helsinki/salve; Hietalahdenranta 5C; mains €18-36; ⊙ 11am-11pm Mon-Sat, to 10pm Sun) Down by the water in the west of town, this 1897-founded establishment has long been a favourite of sailors, and has an appropriately high-seas decor, with paintings of noble ships on the walls. Great Finnish comfort food includes meatballs, fried Baltic herring and steaks in substantial quantities. The atmosphere is warm and the service kindly.

Ateljé Finne
FINNISH €€

(Map p60; ☑ 010-281-8242; www.ateljefinne.fi; Arkadiankatu 14; mains €23-26, 3-course menu €44; ⊙ 5-9.30pm Mon-Sat) Painted brick walls hung with original art make this bistro an intimate space for refined contemporary Finnish cooking. The short menu has just a handful of choices, but always includes a vegetable, meat and fish dish of the day, bookended by starters such as cold smoked herring croquettes or celeriac salad with roasted yeast, and desserts such as liquorice crème brûlée.

Konstan Mölja
FINNISH €€

(Map p60; ☑ 09-694-7504; www.konstanmolja.fi; Hietalahdenkatu 14; buffet €19; ⊙ 5-10pm Tue-Fri, 4-11pm Sat) The maritime interior of this old sailors' eatery – with fishing nets, hooks, brass clocks, lanterns and black-and-white photos – is an atmospheric setting for its great-value Finnish buffet for dinner. Though these days it sees plenty of tourists, it serves solid traditional fare (salmon soup, marinated herring, reindeer) with friendly explanations of what goes with what.

🍴 Kallio

Flying Dutch
GASTROPUB €

(Map p50; www.pikkudami.com; Pitkänsillanranta 2; mains €15-16.50; ⊙ kitchen noon-8pm Mon-Sat, to 7pm Sun, bar to midnight Mon-Sat, to 10pm Sun) Built in 1897 in the Netherlands, this timber boat makes a great stop for a craft beer or cider up on deck or dockside tables, but it's an even better bet for food, from salmon soup and *skagen* (prawn-topped toast) to burgers such as pulled duck with truffle-Champagne sauce, or goat's cheese with caramelised sweet potato, avocado and harissa mayo.

Kuja
BISTRO €

(Map p50; ☑ 040-046-1008; www.kujabarbistro.fi; Hakaniemenkatu 7; mains €13-23; ⊙ 10.30am-10pm Mon & Tue, to 11pm Wed & Thu, to midnight Fri, 11.30am-midnight Sat, 11.30am-9pm Sun; ☜☑) An upbeat young team helms this hip little bistro across from the waterfront. Burgers are a highlight, with choices including pulled pork (with noodles and chilli sauce), salmon (with pickled cucumber and slaw) and tofu (with roasted capsicums), with the option of gluten-free buns. There are gourmet salads, savoury crêpes, *flammkuchen* (thin-crusted Alsatian pizza) and over 30 craft beers.

Hakaniemen Kauppahalli
MARKET €

(Map p50; www.hakaniemenkauppahalli.fi; Hämeentie 1; ⊙ 8am-6pm Mon-Fri, to 4pm Sat; ☑) 🍴 This traditional-style Finnish food market hall sits right by the Hakaniemi metro station. With over 50 stalls, there's a great range of produce and a cafe, with textile outlets upstairs. An outdoor market sets up on the square in summer.

Rupla
CAFE €

(Map p50; www.rupla.fi; Helsinginkatu 16; snacks €2.50-5.50, weekday lunch buffet €9.50, weekend brunch €23; ⊙ 7.30am-8pm Mon-Fri, 11am-5pm Sat & Sun; ☜☑) Virtually everything, aside from the occasional fish dish, is vegetarian or vegan at this red-brick cafe, which has its own Helsinki-roasted coffee blends. Weekday lunch buffets and weekend brunch include dishes such as sweet potato hummus; green bean, chickpea and harissa spice-mix salad; cabbage, green apple and carrot slaw; and beluga red lentil stew.

Teurastamo
FOOD HALL €€

(Map p50; https://teurastamo.com; Työpajankatu 2; ⊙ 9am-9pm Mon & Tue, to 10pm Wed-Sat, to 8pm Sun) The former abattoir area between Sörnäinen and Kalasatama metro stations is an in place these days, with a range of locally sourcing eateries opening up in the casual post-industrial precinct. Choose from snacks including dim sum, smokehouse fare, pasta, artisan ice cream and more.

Drinking & Nightlife

Diverse drinking and nightlife in Helsinki ranges from cosy bars to specialist craft-beer and cocktail venues, and clubs with live music and DJs. In summer early-opening beer terraces sprout all over town. Some club nights have a minimum age of 20 or older; check event details on websites before you arrive.

City Centre

Kappeli BAR

(Map p60; www.kappeli.fi; Eteläesplanadi 1; ⊙10am-midnight; 🛜) Dating from 1867, this grand bar-cafe opens to an outdoor terrace seating 350 people and has regular jazz, blues and folk music in the nearby bandstand in Esplanadin Puisto (p48) from May to August. Locals and visitors alike flock here on a sunny day.

La Torrefazione COFFEE

(Map p60; www.latorre.fi; Aleksanterinkatu 50; ⊙7.30am-8pm Mon-Fri, 9am-7pm Sat, 10am-6.30pm Sun) One flight up from the street, this isn't a space to hang out with your laptop: La Torrefazione is so dedicated to its cause that it doesn't have wi-fi so you can focus solely on the coffee. It sources beans and creates roasting profiles for beans that are roasted in Helsinki, and prepares them using filter and drip brewing methods.

Teatteri BAR, CLUB

(Map p60; www.teatteri.fi; Pohjoisesplanadi 2; ⊙9am-1am Mon & Tue, to 2am Wed, to 4am Thu & Fri, 11am-4am Sat, noon-10pm Sun) Attracting an older, relaxed crowd, this stylish spot alongside Esplanadi has a lounge bar, a cocktail bar with drinks themed for countries around the world and a sophisticated, strobe-lit nightclub (10pm to 4am Thursday to Saturday). Its pavement terrace swells in summer.

Raffaellon Terassi BEER GARDEN

(Map p60; www.raflaamo.fi; Wanha Kauppakuja, Aleksanterinkatu 46; ⊙4pm-3am Wed-Sat May-Sep) In the covered Wanha Kauppakuja laneway, off Aleksanterinkatu, this terrace, or 'tunnel' (it's locally dubbed 'Mummotunneli'), has several bars that turn into a party scene once the restaurant terraces are done with serving food for the night. DJs and live bands rev the crowds up every night. On Friday and Saturday there's a €10 cover after 9pm.

Kruununhaka & Katajanokka

★**Holiday** BAR

(Map p50; http://holiday-bar.fi; Kanavaranta 7; ⊙4-11pm Tue-Thu, to 2am Fri, noon-2am Sat; 🛜) Even on the greyest Helsinki day, this colourful waterfront bar transports you to more tropical climes with vibrant rainforest wallpapers and plants such as palms, tropical-themed cocktails like frozen margaritas and mojitos (plus two dozen different gins) and a seafood menu that includes softshell crab. A small market often sets up out the front in summer, along with ping-pong tables.

Johan & Nyström COFFEE

(Map p50; www.johanochnystrom.fi; Kanavaranta 7C; ⊙8am-7pm Mon-Sat, 9am-6pm Sun; 🛜) 🖉 A red-brick split-level harbourside warehouse with outsized light fittings, low sofas and a waterside terrace is the atmospheric setting for this cafe run by boutique Swedish coffee roaster and tea merchant Johan & Nyström. Organic beans are all sourced from small-scale producers; choose from a huge variety of blends and brewing methods chalked on the blackboard.

Majakkalaiva Relandersgrund BAR

(Map p50; www.majakkalaiva.fi; Pohjoisranta; ⊙noon-2am) Built between 1886 and 1888, this elegant old lightship was sunk by the Russians in 1918 and subsequently raised and repaired. The deck provides a fabulous venue for a drink on a sunny afternoon.

Punavuori & Ullanlinna

★**Birri** MICROBREWERY

(Il Birrificio; Map p60; http://ilbirri.fi; Fredrikinkatu 22; ⊙11am-11pm Mon-Thu, to 1am Fri & Sat, to 4pm Sun) Birri brews three of its own beers on site at any one time, stocks a fantastic range of Finnish-only craft beers and also handcrafts its own seasonally changing sausages. The space is strikingly done out with Arctic-white metro tiles, exposed timber beams and gleaming silver kegs. Weekend brunch (11am to 1.30pm Saturday, to 2pm Sunday) is among Helsinki's best.

★**Kaffa Roastery** COFFEE

(Map p50; www.kaffaroastery.fi; Pursimiehenkatu 29A; ⊙7.45am-6pm Mon-Fri, 10am-5pm Sat; 🛜) Processing up to 4000kg of beans every week, this vast coffee roastery supplies cafes throughout Helsinki, Finland and beyond. You can watch the roasting in progress through the glass viewing windows while sipping Aeropress, syphon or V60 brews in its polished concrete surrounds.

Mattolaituri BAR
(☎ 045-119-6631; Ehrenströmintie 3A, Kaivopuisto; ☺9am-midnight May-Sep) In Kaivopuisto (p52) park, this summer beach bar overlooking the sand and glittering sea is an idyllic spot to lounge in a deck chair or umbrella-shaded sofa with a coffee, glass of wine or a cocktail. Live music plays most nights from 6pm from June to August. Michelin-starred restaurant Demo (p68) sets up an outdoor kitchen here from June to mid-August.

Kaivohuone BAR, CLUB
(Map p50; ☎ 020-775-9825; www.kaivohuone.fi; Iso Puistotie 1, Kaivopuisto; ☺bar noon-midnight May-Aug, club 10pm-4am Wed, Fri & Sat May-Aug; ☏) Built in 1838 as a spa in the Kaivopuisto (p52) park, this pavilion was later remodelled in art deco style and has been fabulously restored with dazzling chandeliers, and opens on to a vast terrace. Food is served until 4pm. DJs pack the club three nights weekly in summer. Minimum age is 20 on Wednesday and Friday, and 24 on Saturday.

Bier-Bier CRAFT BEER
(Map p60; www.bier-bier.fi; Erottajankatu 13; ☺4pm-midnight Mon-Thu, 2pm-2am Fri & Sat) Inside a glorious high-ceilinged, timber-panelled former bank dating from 1893, this jewel of a bar has a serious drinks list, with over 100 different beers categorised by taste and provenance, along with a stellar selection of 20 ciders and

20 astutely chosen wines. Expert staff can guide you through the offerings. The small, supremely elegant space creates an intimate atmosphere.

Liberty or Death COCKTAIL BAR
(Map p60; www.libertyordeath.bar; Erottajankatu 5; ☺6pm-1am Mon-Thu, to 2am Fri & Sat) Blacked-out windows make it easy to miss, but open the door and you'll find this small vintage-furnished speakeasy with exposed-brick walls lined with bookshelves. Made from rare spirits and seasonal fruit and herbs, each of its signature and classic cocktails, such as Hemingway's Moustache (Tullamore Dew, dry sherry, lavender and Galliano), comes with its own offbeat story.

Kuuma CAFE
(Map p50; Albertinkatu 6; ☺8am-5pm Tue-Fri, 10am-4pm Sat; ☏) With white tiles, turquoise flooring, birch and willow light fittings and hanging pot plants, this aptly named place (Kuuma means 'hot' in Finnish) is a Design District hot spot for superfood juices, loose-leaf teas, Amsterdam-roasted White Label Coffee and all-day breakfasts. Its attached shop sells locally made products, from clothing and cosmetics to homewares such as cushions and woolly blankets.

TheRiff BAR
(Map p60; www.theriff.fi; Iso Roobertinkatu 3; ☺2pm-3am) Signed guitars, drums and posters cover the walls of this rock and roll bar, which functions as a before- and after-party for gigs around town for musicians and their fans. A soundtrack of hard rock and metal keeps the crowds revved up. In summer the action spills out onto the terrace.

HELSINKI DRINKING & NIGHTLIFE

LGBT HELSINKI

Helsinki has a small but active scene with several dedicated venues and a host of gay-friendly spots. There's a list of gay-friendly places at www.visithelsinki.fi, and the tourist office (p79) stocks a couple of brochures on gay Helsinki. Every summer **Helsinki Pride** (https://helsinkipride.fi; ☺late Jun-early Jul) includes balls, karaoke and picnics.

DTM (Map p60; www.dtm.fi; Mannerheimintie 6B; ☺9pm-4am; ☏) Finland's most famous gay venue (Don't Tell Mama) now occupies smart premises in a very out-of-the-closet location on the city's main street.

Fairytale (Map p50; www.fairytale.fi; Helsinginkatu 7; ☺4pm-2am Mon-Fri, 2pm-2am Sat & Sun; ☏) This small, unassuming bar is frequented by both men and women.

Hercules (Map p60; www.hercules.fi; Pohjoinen Rautatiekatu 21; ☺9pm-4am) Set over three floors, this gay bar is aimed at men aged 30-plus (minimum age on Fridays and Saturdays is 24, and 20 on other days). There's a lounge bar, basement club and a busy disco with dance-floor classics and campy karaoke.

WORTH A TRIP

ESPOO: ART & NATURE

Espoo Museum of Modern Art (EMMA; www.emma.museum; Ahertajantie 5, Tapiola, Espoo; adult/child €12/free; ⊙11am-6pm Tue & Thu, to 7pm Wed & Fri, to 5pm Sat & Sun) In the commuter city of Espoo, this museum has a huge collection of mostly Finnish modern art, ranging from the early 20th century to the present. Works by acclaimed ceramicist Rut Bryk (1916–99) are a highlight. Sharing the same address and opening hours, and visitable with the same ticket, other museums on site (covering Espoo city, toys and horology) can round out a day trip. From Kamppi bus station, take bus 106 or 110 to the WeeGee-Talo stop.

Gallen-Kallelan Museo (www.gallen-kallela.fi; Gallen-Kallelantie 27, Espoo; adult/child €9/free; ⊙11am-6pm daily mid-May–Aug, 11am-4pm Tue-Sat, 11am-5pm Sun Sep–mid-May) Part castle, part studio, this was the home of Akseli Gallen-Kallela (1865–1931), one of Finland's most significant artists. Many of his works are displayed here, including his famed *Kalevala* illustrations. The tranquillity of the lakeside location is somewhat disturbed these days by the whoosh of the nearby Helsinki–Turku motorway, but it remains a worthwhile visit. From Helsinki, the fastest way to get here is to take bus 106 from Kamppi to Majurinkulma, from where it's a 1.2km walk east.

Nuuksio National Park (www.nationalparks.fi; Espoo) Close enough to Helsinki for a half-day trip, 35km northwest of the city, this 4500-hectare national park gives an immersive introduction to Finnish nature. An equidistant 4.6km walk north of its nature centre, **Haltia** (www.haltia.com; Nuuksiontie 84, Espoo; adult/child €12/5; ⊙10am-6pm May-Sep, 10am-5pm Tue-Sun Oct-Apr), are two trailheads, Haukkalampi and Kattila (3km apart), offering easy walking or cross-country ski trails through wooded Ice–Age–chiselled valleys that are a habitat for elk, lynx and nocturnal flying squirrels. There are campsites, cottages and huts available, which can be booked through Haltia.

Bus 245A runs to various stops around the park from Espoo Central train station, which is served by frequent trains from Helsinki's train station.

Andante
CAFE

(Map p60; Fredrikinkatu 20; ⊙noon-7pm Wed-Fri, 11am-6pm Sat & Sun; 🐾) Design District hang-out Andante is both a fragrant florist selling pot plants and bouquets of blooms and a cafe brewing organic, fair-trade coffee etched with intricate coffee art (oat milk available). There's also a wide range of Chinese teas, seasonal smoothies and juices, and snacks such as raw cakes with raspberry and goji berry or green tea and lingonberry.

 ## Kamppi & Töölö

★A21
COCKTAIL BAR

(Map p60; www.a21.fi; Annankatu 21; ⊙5pm-midnight Tue & Wed, to 1am Thu, to 2am Fri & Sat) At the cutting edge of Helsinki's cocktail scene, this constantly evolving bar revives classic cocktails from past eras, adapts international trends (such as boilermakers, blending craft beers with paired spirits) and crafts new concoctions using Nordic ingredients in cocktails such as Suomen Neito, made with foraged Finnish berries.

★Steam Hellsinki
COCKTAIL BAR

(Map p60; www.steamhellsinki.fi; Olavinkatu 1; ⊙4pm-4am Mon-Sat; 🐾) A wonderland of steampunk design – with futuristic-meets-19th-century industrial steam-powered machinery decor, including a giant Zeppelin floating above the gondola-shaped bar, mechanical cogs and pulleys, globes, lanterns, candelabras, Chesterfield sofas and a Zoltar fortune-telling machine – this extraordinary bar has dozens of varieties of gin and DJs spinning electro-swing.

Vin-Vin
WINE BAR

(Map p60; www.vin-vin.fi; Kalevankatu 6; ⊙4pm-midnight Mon-Fri, 2pm-2am Sat) Glistening mosaic tiles, chandeliers, fringed lamps and vintage velvet sofas make Vin-Vin a super-stylish spot for a glass and a cheese or charcuterie platter, but the natural wines sourced from small vineyards are the main event. Its beer-specialist sibling, Bier-Bier, is in Punavuori.

Ateljee Bar
BAR

(Map p60; www.raflaamo.fi; Sokos Hotel Torni, Yrjönkatu 26; ⊙2pm-1am Mon-Thu, to 2am Fri, noon-2am Sat, 2pm-midnight Sun; 🛜) An unrivalled panorama of Helsinki unfolds from this tiny 70m-high perch on the 14th floor of the Sokos Hotel Torni. Take the lift to the 12th floor, from where a narrow spiral staircase leads to the top. The bar has a capacity of just 30 people (with 12 more on the glassed-in summer terrace). Minimum age is 20.

Bar Loose
BAR, CLUB

(Map p60; www.barloose.com; Annankatu 21; ⊙8pm-4am Wed-Sat, 11pm-4am Sun; 🛜) The scarlet-coloured interior seems too stylish for a rock bar, but that's what Bar Loose is, with portraits of guitar heroes lining one wall and an eclectic crowd upstairs, served by two bars. Downstairs is a club area, with live music more nights than not and DJs spinning everything from metal to mod/retro classics. Drinks are decently priced.

Bäkkäri
BAR, CLUB

(Map p60; www.npg.fi/ravintolat/bakkari; Pohjoinen Rautatiekatu 21; ⊙6pm-4am) Central Bäkkäri is devoted to the heavier end of the metal spectrum, with lots of airplay for Finnish legends such as Nightwish, HIM, Children of Bodom and Apocalyptica. It's a classic after-party for bands. Outdoor tables are where the socialising goes on, while upstairs is a club space. Beer's cheap until 8pm.

Maxine
BAR, CLUB

(Map p60; www.maxine.fi; 6th fl, Kamppi Shopping Centre, Urho Kekkosenkatu 1A; ⊙10pm-4am Fri & Sat; 🛜) On the top of Kamppi shopping centre, this classy venue makes the most of the inspiring city views. It's divided into three sections, with a bar area – a great spot for a sundowner – and two dance floors, one of which is quieter. Over 24s only.

Teerenpeli
PUB

(Map p60; www.teerenpeli.com; Olavinkatu 2; ⊙noon-2am Mon-Thu, to 3am Fri & Sat, to midnight Sun; 🛜) In a long, split-level space with romantic low lighting and intimate tables, this excellent pub serves superb ales, stouts and berry ciders from its microbrewery in Lahti. The highish prices keep it fairly genteel. There's a minimum age limit of 20. It's right by Kamppi bus station.

Corona Baari
BAR

(Map p60; www.andorra.fi; Eerikinkatu 11-15; ⊙Corona 11am-2am Mon-Thu, to 3am Fri & Sat, noon-2am Sun, Kafe Mockba 6pm-2am Mon-Thu, to 3am Fri & Sat; 🛜) The offbeat film-making Kaurismäki brothers designed and once owned this drinking den. It has pool tables, no door person, an island bar and a relaxed mix of people. Other spaces here, largely used for private events, include USSR-styled Kafe Mockba, with a bubbling samovar and Soviet vinyl, and Dubrovnik Lounge & Lobby, which hosts cinema screenings and album launches.

🍷 Kallio

Kuudes Linja
CLUB

(Map p50; www.kuudeslinja.com; Hämeentie 13B; ⊙10pm-4am Wed, Fri & Sat, 11pm-4am Thu) Between Hakaniemi and Sörnäinen metro stations, this famed club is the place to find Helsinki's more experimental beats from top visiting DJs playing techno, industrial, post-rock and electro. There are also live gigs (invariably metal). Entry is free on Thursday and generally starts from €12 on other nights.

Good Life Coffee
CAFE

(Map p50; www.goodlifecoffee.fi; Kolmas Linja 17; ⊙8am-6pm Mon-Fri, 9am-4pm Sat; 🛜) Lime-green light fittings, geometric wallpaper, framed photography and art; and turntables spinning jazz make this a great neighbourhood hang-out. Aeropress coffee prepared from locally roasted beans is served alongside homemade cakes, pastries and cookies.

☆ Entertainment

Catching live music – from metal to opera – is a highlight of visiting Helsinki. The latest events are publicised in the free *Helsinki This Week* (http://helsinkithisweek.com). Tickets for big events can be purchased from Ticketmaster (www.ticketmaster.fi), Lippupiste (www.lippu.fi), LiveNation (www.live nation.fi) and Tiketti (www.tiketti.fi), which also has a booking office in Kamppi.

Booking agency **Tiketti** (Map p60; www. tiketti.fi; Urho Kekkosenkatu 4; ⊙11am-7pm Mon-Fri) sells tickets to a variety of live events throughout Helsinki.

★ Musiikkitalo
CONCERT VENUE

(Helsinki Music Centre; Map p60; ☎020-707-0400; www.musiikkitalo.fi; Mannerheimintie 13; tickets free-€30) Home to the Helsinki Philharmonic Orchestra, Finnish Radio Symphony Orchestra and Sibelius Academy, the glass-and copper-fronted Helsinki Music Centre, opened in 2011, hosts a diverse program of classical, jazz, folk, pop and rock. The 1704-capacity main auditorium has stunning acoustics. Buy tickets at the door or from www.ticketmaster.fi.

ARABIAKESKUS

Arabia refers to a district where the legendary Finnish **ceramics company** (www.arabia.fi; Hämeentie 135, Toukola; ⊘ noon-6pm Tue, Thu & Fri, to 8pm Wed, 10am-4pm Sat & Sun) has manufactured its products since 1873. The complex, 5km north of Helsinki, includes a design mall, with a large Arabia/Iittala outlet. Run by Helsinki's Design Museum (p51), the free Iittala & Arabia Design Centre museum tells of the brand's history. Take tram 6 or 8 to Arabiankatu stop.

Finlandia Talo   CONCERT VENUE
(Map p50; ☎09-40241; www.finlandiatalo.fi; Mannerheimintie 13) Designed by Alvar Aalto, this 1971-completed concert hall in angular white marble is one of Helsinki's landmark buildings. Alongside a varying program of music, it also mounts art exhibitions. Book tickets through www.lippu.fi. Hour-long guided tours (€15/10 per adult/child) take place in English; check the calendar online.

Tavastia   LIVE MUSIC
(Map p60; ☎09-7746-7420; www.tavastiaklubi.fi; Urho Kekkosenkatu 4; ⊘8pm-1am Sun-Thu, to 3am Fri, to 4am Sat) One of Helsinki's legendary rock venues, Tavastia attracts both up-and-coming local acts and bigger international groups, with a band virtually every night of the week. Most gigs start at 9pm; doors open two hours beforehand. Also check out what's on at its adjoining venue, **Semifinal** (Urho Kekkosenkatu 6), where new talent and young local bands take the stage.

Storyville   JAZZ
(Map p60; ☎050-363-2664; www.storyville.fi; Museokatu 8; ⊘jazz club 7pm-3am Thu, to 4am Fri & Sat, bar 7pm-2am Tue, to 3am Wed & Thu, to 4am Fri & Sat) Helsinki's number-one jazz club attracts a refined older crowd swinging to boogie woogie, trad jazz, Dixieland and New Orleans most nights. As well as the performance space, there's a stylish bar that has a cool outside summer terrace, restaurant and outdoor charcoal grill in the park opposite, where some summer concerts also take place.

Juttutupa   LIVE MUSIC
(Map p50; ☎020-742-4240; www.juttutupa.fi; Säästöpankinranta 6; ⊘bar 10.30am-midnight Mon & Tue, to 1am Wed & Thu, to 3am Fri, 11am-3am Sat, noon-11pm Sun) A block from Hakaniemi metro station, in an enormous granite building, Juttutupa is one of Helsinki's better bars for live music, focusing on contemporary jazz and rock fusion. All gigs are free. There's a great beer terrace and an on-site sauna.

Orion Theatre   CINEMA
(Map p60; ☎029-533-8000; www.kavi.fi; Eerikinkatu 15; tickets adult/child €6.50/3; ⊘screenings Tue-Sun) Opened in 1927, this gorgeous art deco cinema with chequerboard tiles has 216 plush red seats. It shows classics from the Finnish Film Archive through to new art-house releases, either in English or with English subtitles.

Kansallisteatteri   THEATRE
(Map p60; ☎010-733-1331; www.kansallisteatteri.fi; Läntinen teatterikuja 1) The Finnish National Theatre was founded in 1872 as the country's first Finnish-speaking theatre, but didn't move here until 1902. The beautiful art nouveau building was designed by architect Onni Törnqvist-Tarjanne, with a granite facade and interior of marble, soapstone and wood. Performances are usually in Finnish; book tickets online through www.lippu.fi.

Oopperatalo   OPERA, BALLET
(Opera House; Map p50; ☎09-4030-2211; www.oopperabaletti.fi; Helsinginkatu 58) From mid-August to May, opera, ballet and classical concerts are staged at Helsinki's opera house, set in landscaped parkland next to Töölönlahti bay. Designed by Eero Hyvämäki, Jukka Karhunen and Risto Parkkinen, the building was completed in 1993. Performances of the Finnish National Opera are subtitled in Finnish. Book tickets through www.kippu.fi.

Telia 5G Arena   SPECTATOR SPORT
(Map p50; www.sonerastadium.fi; Urheilukatu 5; tickets €12-15) Next to the Olympic Stadium, this 10,770-seat arena is the home ground of Helsinki's football team, HJK (Helsingin Jalkapalloklubi). The season runs from April to October. Book tickets online through www.lippu.fi.

Hartwall Arena   SPECTATOR SPORT
(☎020-41997; www.hartwall-arena.fi; Areenakuja 1, Pasila) The best place to see top-level hockey matches is at this arena 4km north of the city centre. It's the home of Helsinki's Jokerit ('Jesters') team, which plays in the international Kontinental Hockey League (KHL). Bus 69 from Kamppi bus station stops closest to the stadium at Vaihdemiehenkatu. Alternatively, it's a 1km walk east of Ilmala train station.

🔒 Shopping

Helsinki is a design epicentre, from fashion to furniture and homewares. Its hub is the Design District Helsinki (https://designdistrict.fi), spread out between chic Esplanadi to the east, retro-hipster Punavuori to the south and Kamppi to the west. Hundreds of shops, studios and galleries are mapped on its website; you can also pick up a map at the tourist office.

★ Tre   DESIGN
(Map p60; www.worldoftre.com; Mikonkatu 6; ⊙11am-7pm Mon-Fri, to 6pm Sat) If you only have time to visit one design store in Helsinki, this 2016-opened emporium is a brilliant bet. Showcasing the works of Finnish designers in fashion, jewellery and accessories, including umbrellas, furniture, ceramics, textiles, stationery and art, it also stocks a superb range of architecture and design books to fuel inspiration.

★ Artek   DESIGN
(Map p60; www.artek.fi; Keskuskatu 1B; ⊙10am-7pm Mon-Fri, to 6pm Sat) Originally founded by architects and designers Alvar Aalto and his wife Aino Aalto in 1935, this iconic Finnish company maintains the simple design principle of its founders. Textiles, lighting and furniture are among its homewares. Many items are only available at this 700-sq-metre, two-storey space.

Iittala   DESIGN
(Map p60; www.iittala.com; Pohjoisesplanadi 25; ⊙10am-8pm Mon-Fri, to 4pm Sat & Sun) Finland's famous glass manufacturer – established in 1881 in the southern Finnish town of the same name and later shaped by Alvar Aalto – has a central outlet here on Pohjoisesplanadi, and an outlet at Arabiakeskus (p80), 5km north of the city, which has a museum covering the brand. Along with glassware, it now creates ceramic, wood and textile designs.

Kalevala Koru   JEWELLERY
(Map p60; www.kalevalakoru.fi; Pohjoisesplanadi 25-27; ⊙10am-7pm Mon-Fri, to 5pm Sat) Gold, silver and bronze jewellery made by Kalevala Koru incorporates motifs based on Finnish history and legend.

Aarikka   DESIGN
(Map p60; www.aarikka.com; Pohjoisesplanadi 27; ⊙10am-7pm Mon-Fri, to 5pm Sat, noon-5pm Sun) Specialising in wood, Aarikka was founded in 1954 and, along with furniture and homewares, is known for its distinctive jewellery.

Akateeminen Kirjakauppa   BOOKS
(Map p60; www.akateeminen.com; Pohjoisesplanadi 39; ⊙9am-9pm Mon-Fri, to 7pm Sat, 11am-6pm Sun; 🖥) Finland's biggest bookshop has a huge travel section, maps, Finnish literature and an impressively large English section, including magazines and newspapers. It's worth visiting just to view the striking modernist building, designed by Alvar Aalto and completed in 1969. The cafe here is named Cafe Aalto.

Stockmann   DEPARTMENT STORE
(Map p60; www.info.stockmann.com; Aleksanterinkatu 52; ⊙9am-9pm Mon-Fri, to 7pm Sat, noon-6pm Sun; 🖥) Founded in 1862, Stockmann's 1930-built flagship store is Helsinki's biggest department store, spanning 50,000 sq metres. It carries luxury Finnish and international textiles, jewellery, fashion, cosmetics and much more, and has a large food hall.

★ Lasikammari   ANTIQUES
(Map p60; www.lasikammari.fi; Liisankatu 9; ⊙noon-5pm Tue, Wed & Thu, to 2pm Mon, Fri & Sat) Vintage Finnish glassware from renowned brands such as Iittala, Nuutajärvi and Riihimäki, and individual designers such as Alvar Aalto and Tapio Wirkkala, make this tiny shop a diamond find for collectors. Along with glass, you'll find vases, jugs, plates, bowls, light fittings and artistic sculptures. Prices are exceptionally reasonable; international shipping can be arranged.

Sweet Story   FOOD
(Map p60; www.sweetstory.fi; Katariinankatu 3; ⊙10am-6pm Tue-Fri, 11am-4pm Sat) 🍬 Handmade caramels, liquorices (including a

---

CABLE FACTORY

This sprawling site once manufactured sea cables and later became Nokia's main factory until the 1980s. It's now a cultural complex with design studios, galleries, expositions, and regular music, theatre and dance performances: **Kaapelitehdas** (Cable Factory; www.kaapelitehdas.fi; Tallberginkatu 1, Ruoholahti; ⊙11am-6pm Tue-Sun, hours vary). Also here are a photography museum, theatre museum and a hotel-and-restaurant museum. Tram 8 stops just 150m east of Kaapelitehdas at Länsisatamankatu, or take the metro to Ruoholahti and walk 600m west.

traditional Finnish variety with tar) and a rainbow of boiled sweets at this fantasy land are all organic and free from gluten, lactose and artificial colours and preservatives. Most are made at Sweet Story's own Helsinki workshop. There's also a handful of other specialities from Denmark, Lithuania and Austria.

Schröder
SPORTS & OUTDOORS

(Map p60; www.schroder.fi; Unioninkatu 23; ⊘10am-6pm Mon-Fri, to 4pm Sat) Opened in 1896, Helsinki's oldest angling shop was the world's first to sell prized Rapala fishing lures – after Fritz Schröder met with Finnish designer Lauri Rapala prior to the 1952 Summer Olympics, Schröder sold them to international visitors, making them a household name. Today it still sells Rapala and other tackle, along with fishing licences and permits.

Lokal
DESIGN

(Map p60; www.lokalhelsinki.com; Annankatu 9; ⊘11am-6pm Tue-Fri, 11am-4pm Sat, noon-4pm Sun) ✐ A Design District standout, this hybrid design shop-gallery has rotating exhibitions from Finnish-based artists and designers, including traditional woodcarver Aimo Katajamäki, ceramicist Kristina Riska, birch-bark painter and jeweller Janna Syvänoja, contemporary painter Visa Norros and industrial furniture designer Jouko Kärkkäinen. All pieces exhibited are for sale.

Awake
DESIGN

(Map p60; www.awake-collective.com; Fredrikinkatu 25; ⊘12.30-6.30pm Tue-Fri, 11am-4pm Sat) ✐ At this super-minimalist art gallery–concept store, changing displays of handmade, Finnish-only designs range from men's and women's fashion and accessories, including watches, jewellery, bags and shoes, to birch plywood furniture and homewares such as rugs, carpets, sheets and blankets. Everything is ecologically and sustainably produced.

Jukka Rintala
FASHION & ACCESSORIES

(Map p60; www.jukkarintala.fi; Fredrikinkatu 26; ⊘11am-6pm Mon-Fri, to 3pm Sat) Leading Finnish fashion designer Jukka Rintala is renowned for his women's evening wear, which is often worn at presidential functions and other high-profile events. In addition to his fashion creations, you'll also find prints of his artwork, jewellery pieces and wallpaper designs at this flagship boutique.

Frank/ie
DESIGN

(Map p60; www.frankie.fi; Annankatu 13; ⊘noon-6pm Tue-Fri, to 5pm Sat) In addition to creating the products stocked at this shop, the designers also take turns in staffing it. Look out for shoes and accessories by Kuula + Jylhä; men's, women's and kids' fashion made from recycled and surplus materials by Kiks; jewellery and casual women's wear by Jatuli; and women's fashion utilising mixed fabrics and monochrome colours by Miia Halmesmaa.

Art.fi
DESIGN, ANTIQUES

(Map p60; www.art.fi; Annankatu 8; ⊘noon-5pm Mon-Fri) At this treasure-filled shop specialising in 20th-century Finnish design (with occasional forays into 18th- and 19th-century folk art and antiques), items include Iittala glassware, Pape and Paavo Tynell lighting and Kukkapuro and Tapiovaara furniture, including chairs, tables, sofas and recliners, along with silverware, goldware and floor coverings.

Bisarri
ANTIQUES, DESIGN

(Map p50; www.bisarri.fi; Tarkk' Ampujankatu 5; ⊘noon-5.30pm Mon-Thu, to 3pm Sat) Vintage Finnish-designed glassware from Oivatoikka, Nanny Still and Tapio Wirkkala; ceramics from Birger Kaipiainen and Annikki Hovisaari; and kitchenware from Kaj Franck and Timo Sarpaneva are among the items displayed on the shelves at this small but well-organised shop. The emphasis is on pieces from the 1920s, '30s and '60s.

Mafka & Alakoski
DESIGN

(Map p60; ☑040-554-9939; www.mafka-alakoski.fi; Iso Roobertinkatu 19; ⊘11am-6pm Tue-Fri, to 4pm Sat) Hand-blown and sculpted glass vases, jewellery and kitchenware, such as glasses, cooking bowls, salad bowls, coasters and more, are created by Marja Hepo-aho and Kari Alakoski at their glass factory 70km north of Helsinki. They're beautifully displayed here in their Design District gallery-boutique.

Nide
BOOKS

(Map p60; www.nidekauppa.fi; Fredrikinkatu 35; ⊘10am-7pm Mon-Fri, to 5pm Sat) Glossy photo-filled books on Finnish design, architecture, art, fashion, music, photography and food are the big draw of this airy, light-filled bookshop framed by full-length windows. It also stocks other non-fiction titles such as philosophy books, fiction and periodicals.

Roobertin Herkku
FOOD

(Map p50; www.roobertinherkku.fi; Fredrikinkatu 19; ⊘10am-8pm Mon-Fri, to 6pm Sat, noon-6pm Sun) *Salmiakki* (salty Finnish liquorices) in over two dozen different sizes, shapes, textures and flavours are among the dazzling kaleidoscope of sweets at this colourful shop, which was reopened in 2014 by the granddaughter of the original 1963 founder. *Tervaleijona* (tar drops) are another Finnish speciality.

Scandinavian Outdoor SPORTS & OUTDOORS
(Map p60; www.scandinavianoutdoor.fi; Forum Shopping Centre, Yrjönkatu 29; ⊙10am-8pm Mon-Fri, to 6pm Sat, noon-6pm Sun) If you're heading into the Finnish wilderness, this vast three-level store in the Forum Shopping Centre has your needs covered.

Alnilam ART, ANTIQUES
(Map p60; www.alnilam.fi; Lönnrotinkatu 15; ⊙10am-5pm Mon-Fri, to 3pm Sat, closed early Jul-early Aug) Globes in a dizzying array of colours and sizes, maps, compasses, telescopes, kaleidoscopes, hot-air balloon sculptures, hourglasses, clocks and barometers, both new and antique, are among the exquisite items at this wanderlust-inspiring boutique.

Moomin Shop TOYS, BOOKS
(Map p60; www.moomin.com; Forum, Mannerheimintie 20; ⊙9am-9pm Mon-Fri, to 6pm Sat, noon-6pm Sun) All things Moomin are sold at this official shop, including author and illustrator Tove Jansson's classic books.

Fargo VINTAGE, MUSIC
(Map p50; www.fargoshop.fi; Fleminginkatu 20; ⊙3-7pm Tue-Thu, noon-4pm Fri & Sat) Vintage homewares from the 1950s, '60s and '70s, such as Finnish-designed lamps, chandeliers, crockery, vases, furniture and clocks, are scattered haphazardly. Music fans will love the racks of vinyl from the same era, as well as retro music and movie posters.

Fennica Records MUSIC
(Map p50; ☑09-685-1433; www.fennicakeskus.fi; Hämeentie 21; ⊙10am-6pm Mon-Fri, to 3pm Sat) Fennica stocks new and secondhand CDs and vinyl from Suomi pop to soul and jazz.

ⓘ Information

EMERGENCY
General emergency (☑112)

INTERNET ACCESS
Internet access at public libraries is free. Large parts of the city centre have free wi-fi, as do many restaurants, cafes and bars, and nearly all hotels.

Data is very cheap. If you have an unlocked smartphone, you can pick up a local SIM card for a few euros and charge it with a month's worth of data at a decent speed for under €20. Ask at R-kioski shops for the latest deals.

MEDICAL SERVICES
Haartman Hospital (☑09-3106-3231; www.hel.fi; Haartmaninkatu 4; ⊙24hr) For emergency medical assistance.
Töölön Terveysasema (Töölö Health Station; ☑09-3104-5588; www.hel.fi; Sibeliuksenkatu 14; ⊙8am-4pm Mon, Tue, Thu & Fri, to 6pm Wed) A medical centre for nonemergencies.

Pharmacy Yliopiston Apteekki has a late-opening branch in the **city centre** (www.yliopistonapteekki.fi; Mannerheimintie 5; ⊙10am-9pm) and a 24-hour branch in **Töölö** (www.yliopistonapteekki.fi; Mannerheimintie 96).

MONEY
Credit cards are widely accepted. ATMs (bearing the name 'Otto') are prevalent. There are currency-exchange counters at all transport terminals; visit www.forex.fi to locate others.

POST
Main Post Office (Map p60; www.posti.fi; Elielinaukio 2F; ⊙8am-8pm Mon-Fri, 10am-2pm Sat, noon-4pm Sun)

TOURIST INFORMATION
Between June and August, multilingual 'Helsinki Helpers' – easily spotted by their lime-green jackets – are a mine of tourist information.
Helsinki City Tourist Office (Map p60; ☑09-3101-3300; www.visithelsinki.fi; Pohjoisesplanadi 19; ⊙9am-6pm Mon-Sat, to 4pm Sun mid-May–mid-Sep, 9am-6pm Mon-Fri, 10am-4pm Sat & Sun mid-Sep–mid-May) Also has an office at the **airport** (Terminal 2, Helsinki-Vantaa Airport; ⊙10am-8pm May-Sep, 10am-6pm Mon-Sat, noon-6pm Sun Oct-Apr).
Strömma (www.stromma.fi; Pohjoisesplanadi 19; ⊙9am-6pm Mon-Sat, to 4pm Sun mid-May–mid-Sep, 9am-6pm Mon-Fri, 10am-4pm Sat & Sun mid-Sep–mid-May)

ⓘ Getting There & Away

Helsinki is easily accessed from Europe and beyond. There are direct flights from numerous destinations, while Baltic ferries are another good option.

Lockers are available at the bus and train stations, and there are lockers or left-luggage counters at ferry terminals. Prices per 24 hours range from €3 to €6, depending on size.

Flights, tours and rail tickets can be booked online at www.lonelyplanet.com/bookings.

AIR
Helsinki-Vantaa Airport (p303), 19km north of the city, is Finland's main air terminus. Direct flights serve many major European cities and

TO ST PETERSBURG & BEYOND

One of Russia's most beautiful cities feels tantalisingly close to Helsinki, but for most visits, including on the fast trains, you'll need a Russian visa. The exception to this is the overnight Helsinki–St Petersburg ferry run by **St Peter Line** (Map p60; ☑09-6187-2000; www.stpeterline.com; Makasiiniterminaali), which allows you a 72-hour visa-free stay in the city. A mandatory shuttle bus (for visa-free requirements) takes you from the harbour to the centre in St Petersburg.

Applying in your home country for a Russian visa is the easiest option. If you want to apply in Finland, it's simpler to do it via a travel agent such as **Russian Expert** (☑045-870-3450; www.russianexpert.fi; Töölönkatu 7; ⊗9.30am-5pm Mon-Fri), **Rustravel** (☑050-585-0955; www.rustravel.fi; Tehtaankatu 12; ⊗9am-5pm Mon-Fri), which is also helpful with visas for other former Soviet states, or **Venäjän Viisumikeskus** (☑010-235-0530; www.venajanviisumikeskus.fi; Urho Kekkosenkatu 2C; ⊗9am-5pm Mon-Fri). Visas start from €78 for the normal seven- to eight-working-day processing time, and from €218 for express processing (three to four working days). Prices depend on nationality.

In all cases, you'll need a passport with more than six months' validity, two free pages, a couple of photos and 'visa support', namely an invitation document, typically issued either by accommodation you've booked in Russia (even hostels) or by an authorised tour agent. Travel agencies can also organise this for you, and there are reliable set-ups that arrange visa support documents online, such as Way to Russia (http://waytorussia. net). These cost US$30. Once you've got the paperwork sorted, it's easy to jump on a train, bus or boat and head east.

several intercontinental destinations. **Finnair** (☑09-818-0800; www.finnair.fi) covers 18 Finnish cities, usually at least once per day.

BOAT

International ferries sail to Stockholm, Tallinn, St Petersburg and German destinations.

Ferry companies have detailed timetables and fares on their websites. Fares vary widely according to season. Purchase tickets online, at the terminal, or at ferry company offices. Book well in advance during high season (late June to mid-August) and on weekends. There are five main terminals:

Katajanokan Terminaali

On the island of Katajanokka, **Katajanokan Terminaali** (Map p50) is served by trams 4 and 5.

Viking Line (Map p50; ☑0600-41577; www.vikingline.com) runs car and passenger ferries to Stockholm (16½ hours, one daily) via Åland (11 hours), and Tallinn (2½ hours, two to three daily).

Makasiiniterminaali

Trams 1A and 2 serve **Makasiiniterminaali** (Map p60; Eteläranta 7).

Linda Line (p305) runs the fastest service between Helsinki and Tallinn, aboard small passenger-only hydrofoils (1½ hours, three daily).

St Peter Line runs to St Petersburg (14 hours, three weekly).

Olympia Terminaali

Trams 1A, 2 and 3 serve **Olympia Terminaali** (Map p50; Olympiaranta 1).

Tallink/Silja Line (p305) runs car and passenger services to/from Stockholm (16 hours, one daily) via Åland (11 hours).

Länsiterminaali (West Terminal)

Just southwest of the city centre, **Länsiterminaali** (Tyynenmerenkatu 8) is served by trams 6T and 9.

Tallink/Silja Line (p305) runs car and passenger services to/from Tallinn (two hours, eight daily).

Eckerö Line (p305) runs car and passenger ferries to/from Tallinn (two to 2½ hours, up to three daily).

Hansaterminaali

About 18km east of Helsinki, **Hansaterminaali** (Proviantkatu 5, Vuosaari) is served by bus 90A from Vuosaari metro station.

Finnlines (p304) runs car and passenger ferries between Helsinki and Travemünde, Germany (29 hours, six to seven per week).

BUS

Kamppi bus station (Map p60; www.matkahuolto.fi; Salomonkatu) has a terminal for local buses to Espoo in one wing, while longer-distance buses also depart from here. From Kamppi bus station, **Onnibus** (Map p60; www.onnibus.com) runs budget routes to several Finnish cities.

Destinations with several daily departures include the following:

Jyväskylä €30, 4½ hours, up to three hourly
Kuopio €34, six hours, hourly

Lappeenranta €30, 3½ hours, up to three hourly

Oulu €55, 9½ hours, up to 13 per day

Savonlinna €30, 5½ hours, nine daily

Tampere €25, 2½ hours, up to four hourly

Turku €28, 2½ hours, up to four hourly

Buses also run to St Petersburg (€35, nine hours, up to four daily); you must have a Russian visa.

CAR & MOTORCYCLE

Helsinki is easily accessible by car from Finnish destinations and neighbouring countries, including via car ferry.

Given the city's compact size and good public transport, a car is not necessary, but it can be handy if you're heading to outlying areas.

TRAIN

Helsinki's central **train station** (Rautatieasema; www.vr.fi; Kaivokatu 1) is linked to the metro (Rautatientori stop) and situated 500m east of Kamppi bus station.

The train is the fastest and cheapest way to get from Helsinki to major centres.

Destinations include the following:

Joensuu €44, 4½ hours, three daily

Kuopio €45, 4¼ hours, four daily

Lappeenranta €28, two hours, six daily

Oulu €56, six hours, four daily

Rovaniemi €80, eight hours, four daily

Tampere €21, 1½ hours, two hourly

Turku €20, two hours, hourly

There are also daily trains (buy tickets from the international counter) to the Russian cities of Vyborg, St Petersburg and Moscow; you'll need a Russian visa.

ⓘ Getting Around

TO/FROM THE AIRPORT

The airport-city rail link (www.hsl.fi, €5, 30 minutes, 5.05am to 12.05am) serves Helsinki's train station.

Bus 615 (Map p60; €3.20, 50 minutes, every 30 minutes, 24 hours) shuttles between Helsinki-Vantaa airport and the Rautatientori (Railway Sq), next to Helsinki's train station.

Faster **Finnair buses** (Map p60; www.finnair.com) head to and from Elielinaukio, outside Helsinki's train station (€6.30, 30 minutes, every 20 minutes, 5am to midnight). The last service leaves the airport at 1.10am.

Door-to-door **Yellow Line Airport Taxis** (☎0600-555-555; www.airporttaxi.fi; per two/four people €29.50/39.50) need to be booked the previous day before 6pm if you're leaving Helsinki. A regular **Taksi Helsinki** (☎010-00700; www.taksihelsinki.fi) should cost €45 to €50.

BICYCLE

With a flat inner city and well-marked cycling paths, Helsinki is ideal for cycling. Pick up the free *Ulkoilukartta* Helsinki cycling map at the tourist office, or view it online at www.ulkoilukartta.fi.

Launched in 2016, Helsinki's shared-bike scheme, City Bikes (www.hsl.fi/citybikes), has some 1500 bikes at 150 stations citywide. Bikes are free/€3.50/€7.50 per 30 minutes/two hours/four hours. Register online or pick up a bike at five locations – Hakaniemi metro station, Rautatientori bus station, Kiasma, Kaivopuisto or Unioninkatu – with just a credit card.

BUS, METRO & TRAIN

The city's public-transport system, HSL (www.hsl.fi), operates buses, metro and local trains, trams and local ferries.

➡ A one-hour flat-fare ticket for any HSL transport costs €3.20 when purchased on board, or €2.90 when purchased in advance. The ticket allows unlimited transfers, but must be validated at the machine on board on first use.

➡ A night ticket, for use between 2am and 4.30am, costs €5.

➡ For destinations further afield, including the airport, you'll need a more expensive regional ticket (€5 advance purchase; €5.50 on board a bus or tram; €8 for night tickets).

➡ Day or multiday tickets (€9/13.50/18 per 24/48/72 hours) are worthwhile; tickets up to seven days (€36) are available.

➡ Sales points at Kamppi bus station (p80) and the Rautatientori and Hakaniemi metro stations sell tickets and passes, as do many R-kioskis and tourist offices.

➡ The *Helsinki Route Map,* available at tourist offices, maps bus, metro and tram routes. Online, www.reittiopas.fi is a useful route planner.

CAR & MOTORCYCLE

Parking meters in the city centre cost up to €8 per hour, but most are free on Sundays. There are several well-indicated underground car parks.

Car-hire companies have offices in the city as well as at the airport:

Budget (☎010-436-2233; www.budget.fi; Malminkatu 24; ⊙8am-4pm Mon-Thu, to 6pm Fri) Near Kamppi bus station.

Europcar (☎040-306-2803; www.europcar.fi; Elielinaukio 5; ⊙7am-5pm Mon-Fri, 9am-2pm Sat) By the train station.

Lacara (☎09-719-062; http://lacara.net; Hämeentie 12; ⊙9am-4.30pm Mon-Fri) Low-cost local operator based in Kallio.

Sixt (☎020-112-2500; www.sixt.com; Työpajankatu 2; ⊙8am-4pm Mon-Thu, to 4.30pm Fri) Located in Kallio.

Turku &
the South Coast

Includes ➡

Turku 84
Naantali 91
Pargas 94
Nagu 94
Korpo 95
Houtskär 96
Iniö 96
West of Helsinki 97
Hanko 99
East of Helsinki 105
Porvoo 106

Best Places to Eat

➡ Smor (p88)
➡ Back Pocket (p96)
➡ Cafe Postres (p107)
➡ Vausti (p112)
➡ Uusi Kilta (p93)

Best Places to Stay

➡ Sea Hotel Mäntyniemi (p113)
➡ Hotel Bridget Inn (p92)
➡ Hotelli Onni (p107)
➡ Villa Maija (p101)
➡ Hotel Nestor (p96)

Why Go?

Anchoring the country's southwest is Finland's former capital, Turku. This striking seafaring city stretches along the broad Aurajoki from its Gothic cathedral to its medieval castle and vibrant harbour. Turku challenges Helsinki's cultural pre-eminence with cutting-edge galleries, museums and restaurants, and music festivals that electrify the summer air.

Throughout the south, the coastline is strung with characterful little towns. The Swedish and Russian empires fought for centuries over the area's ports, and today they're commandeered by castles and fortresses that seem at odds with the sunshine and sailing boats. Inland, charming *bruk* (ironworks) villages offer an insight into the area's industrial past.

Scattered offshore, islands provide yachting opportunities, sea-salt retreats and stepping stones across to Åland and Sweden. Most of the charming, history-steeped coastal towns offer summer cruises, guest-harbour facilities, and charter boats to discover your own island.

When to Go
Turku

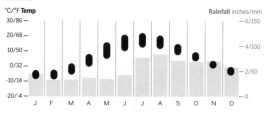

Jun Turku returns to the Middle Ages during its lively Medieval Market.

Jul Boats race in the Hanko Regatta, famous for its carnival atmosphere.

Aug Marching and military music take place at the week-long Hamina Tattoo.

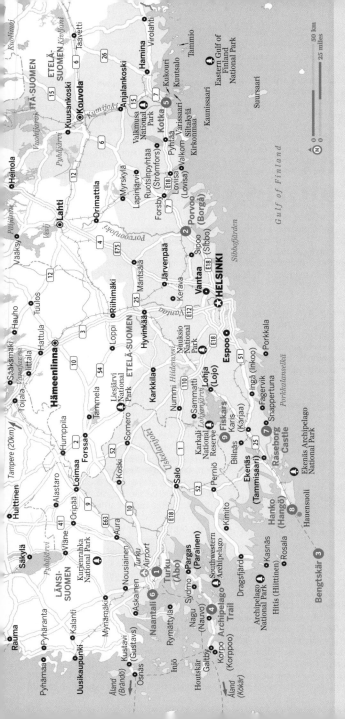

Turku & the South Coast Highlights

1 Aboa Vetus (p84)
Unearthing Turku's medieval history.

2 Vanha Porvoo (p106)
Strolling cobbled lanes lining the picturesque Old Town.

3 Bengtskär Lighthouse (p98) Climbing to the top of Finland's tallest lighthouse.

4 Archipelago Trail (p88)
Cycling and swimming in silent inlets.

5 Merikeskus Vellamo (p109) Exploring ice-breakers and discovering shipwrecks at Kotka's Maritime Centre.

6 Muumimaailma (p91)
Meeting famous cartoon characters at Naantali's endearing theme park, Moominworld.

7 Raseborg Castle (p103)
Stepping back 500 years to explore what remains of this medieval castle.

8 Rintama Museo (p102)
Learning about the Continuation War and finding hidden bunkers around Hanko.

9 Fiskars (p104) Admiring the village's neoclassical buildings.

TURKU

📷 02 / POP 187,600

Turku (Swedish: Åbo) is Finland's second city – or first, as it was the capital until 1812. The majestic Turun Linna (Turku Castle) and ancient Tuomiokirkko (cathedral) – both dating from the 13th century – are testament to the city's long and storied past.

Contemporary Turku is even more enticing, a hotbed of experimental art and vibrant music festivals, designer boutiques and innovative restaurants. University students populate the cafes and clubs, keeping the place buzzing.

Through the age-old network of bustling streets and squares, the Aurajoki river meanders picturesquely, heading out to sea. For nature-lovers, Turku is the gateway to the glorious Turku Archipelago. As one of the country's main ports of entry (as many visitors arrive by ferry from Sweden and Åland), it's a fabulous introduction to mainland Finland.

History

Archaeological finds in the Turku area date back to the Stone Age, but the city was founded when Catholic settlement began at Koroinen, near the present centre of Turku, in 1229. The consecration of a new church in 1300 and the construction of Turun Linna (Turku Castle) created an administrative and spiritual base for rule.

The original Swedish name, Åbo, comes from a settlement *(bo)* on a river *(å)*. The town was the second largest in Sweden, though much of it was levelled by fires, including the Great Fire of 1827. When the Russians took over, the city's long Swedish connection led them to make their new capital Helsinki, leaving Turku to concentrate on commerce. As such, the name Turku is an archaic Russian word for 'marketplace'. Today Turku's centre is still its kauppatori (market square), situated 3km northeast of the harbour.

◉ Sights

★**Turun Linna** CASTLE
(Turku Castle; 📷 02-262-0300; www.turku.fi/turun linna; Linnankatu 80; adult/child €10/5; ☉10am-6pm daily Jun-Aug, Tue-Sun Sep-May) Founded in 1280 at the mouth of the Aurajoki, mammoth Turku Castle is easily Finland's largest fortress. Highlights include two dungeons and sumptuous banqueting halls, as well as a fascinating **historical museum** of medieval Turku in the castle's Old Bailey. Models

depict the castle's growth from a simple island fortress to a Renaissance palace. Guided tours in English run four to six times daily from June to August.

★**Aboa Vetus & Ars Nova** MUSEUM, GALLERY
(Map p86; www.aboavetusarsnova.fi; Itäinen Rantakatu 4-6; adult/child €10/5.50; ☉11am-7pm) Art and archaeology unite here under one roof. **Aboa Vetus** (Old Turku) draws you underground to Turku's medieval streets, showcasing some of the 37,000 artefacts unearthed from the site (digs still continue). Back in the present, **Ars Nova** presents contemporary art exhibitions upstairs. English-language tours lasting 45 minutes take place daily from 11.30am in July and August.

★**Luostarinmäen Käsityöläismuseo** MUSEUM
(Luostarinmäki Handicrafts Museum; Map p86; 📷 02-262-0350; www.turku.fi/handicraftsmuseum; Vartiovuorenkatu 2; adult/child €6/4; ☉10am-6pm daily Jun-Aug, Tue-Sun May & Sep, 10am-4pm Tue-Sun late Nov–early Jan) When the savage Great Fire of 1827 swept through Turku, the lower-class quarter Luostarinmäki escaped the flames. Set along tiny lanes and around grassy yards, the 19th-century wooden workshops and houses now form the outdoor handicrafts museum, a national treasure since 1940. All the buildings are in their original locations, including 30 workshops (among them a silversmith, a watchmaker, a bakery, a pottery, a shoemaker, a printer and a cigar shop), where artisans in period costume ply their trades.

★**Turun Tuomiokirkko** CATHEDRAL
(Turku Cathedral; Map p86; 📷 040-341-7100; www.turunseurakunnat.fi; Tuomiokirkonkatu 1; cathedral free, museum adult/child €2/1; ☉cathedral & museum 9am-6pm) The 'mother church' of Finland's Lutheran faith, Turku Cathedral towers over the town. Consecrated in 1300, the colossal brick Gothic building was rebuilt many times over the centuries after damaging fires, but it still looks majestic and historic. Upstairs, a small **museum** traces the stages of the cathedral's construction, and contains medieval sculptures and religious paraphernalia. Free summer organ concerts (www.turkuorgan.fi) take place at 8pm Tuesday. English-language services are held at 4pm every Sunday except the last of the month year-round.

Forum Marinum MUSEUM
(www.forum-marinum.fi; Linnankatu 72; adult/child €9/5, incl ships €16/10; ☉11am-7pm May-Sep, to 6pm Tue-Sun Oct-Apr) Partly housed in an old

granary, this excellent maritime museum offers a comprehensive look at ships and shipping, from scale models to full-size vessels. Highlights include the museum's hydrocopter, WWII torpedoes and multimedia displays, plus a cabin from a luxury cruise liner (many of which were built in Turku). At the museum's cafe-restaurant, you'll find its namesake *Daphne*, a cute little boat that was home to author Göran Schild. Anchored outside is a small fleet of **museum ships** (adult/child €6/4; ⊙ 11am-7pm Jun-Aug).

Sibelius Museum MUSEUM
(Map p86; ☑ 02-215-4494; www.sibeliusmuseum.fi; Piispankatu 17; adult/child €4/free, concerts €10/6; ⊙ 11am-4pm Tue-Sun, plus 6-8pm Wed) Finland's most extensive musical museum displays some 350 instruments from accordions to Zimbabwean drums. A separate section is devoted to Finnish composer and bohemian carouser Jean Sibelius, with manuscripts and personal memorabilia. You can listen to Sibelius' music on scratchy records, or hear live jazz, folk and chamber music at Wednesday-evening concerts held from autumn to spring. The museum is a very cool, contemporary building by Woldemar Baeckman.

Turun Taidemuseo GALLERY
(Turku Art Museum; Map p86; www.turuntaidemuseo.fi; Aurakatu 26; adult/child €10/free, 4-7pm Fri free; ⊙ 11am-7pm Tue-Fri, to 5pm Sat & Sun) **FREE** Turku Art Museum is housed in a striking granite building with elaborately carved pilasters and conical turrets, perched on a hill on the north side of the river. Much of the art is modern, though the Victor Westerholm room offers traditional Finnish landscapes. Gunnar Berndtson's *Kesä* (Summer) is an idyllic depiction of sunny Suomi, while Akseli Gallen-Kallela's depictions of the epic *Kalevala* are compelling.

🏃 Activities

Archipelago cruises are popular in summer; most departures are from the quay at Martinsilta bridge (p91).

FlowPark ADVENTURE SPORTS
(☑ 040-086-4862; www.flowpark.fi; Skanssinkatu 10; all day/evening from €24/18; ⊙ noon-8pm Mon-Sat, to 6pm Sun Jun & Jul, 3-8pm Wed-Fri, noon-6pm Sat & Sun May, Sep & Oct) Swaying bridges, swings, jumps and cable slides reach heights of up to 20m at this state-of-the-art rope course; there's also a low-rope course for little would-be Tarzans and Janes. FlowPark is 4km southeast of the town centre; take bus 7, 7A or 12.

DON'T MISS

TAIDEKAPPELI

Like the bow of a ship on its end **Taidekappeli** (www.taidekappeli.fi; Seiskarinkatu 35; suggested donation €5; ⊙ 11am-4pm Mon-Fri, noon-3pm Sat & Sun May-Aug, 11am-3pm Tue-Fri, noon-3pm Sat & Sun Sep-Apr) perched on a rock and surrounded by forest on Hirvensalo island, 7km south of Turku centre. Looking at its oddly shaped, copper-clad exterior, you wouldn't know it's a chapel – St Henry's Ecumenical Art Chapel to be precise. But the timber interior feels holy indeed, with its high walls curving up to form a Reuleaux triangle, framing an altar of light. It's spectacular. Take bus 54 from Turku.

Jakke River Ferry CRUISE
(Map p86; http://jakkejokilautta.fi; day ticket adult/child €7/2, evening ticket €7-9; ⊙ 9am-5pm Mon-Thu, to 7pm Fri & Sat late Jun-Aug) Floating through the centre of town, this laid-back river ferry with an on-board bar makes seven stops, but it's also possible to hail it from the bank if there's room for it to dock. Tickets include travel on the little **Jokke tourist train** on the river's northern bank so that you can complete a circuit (around an hour all up).

Rosita CRUISE
(Map p86; ☑ 02-213-1500; www.rosita.fi; adult/child Vepsä €16/6, Bengskär €79/25; ⊙ 11am, 2pm & 5pm Jun-Aug) *Rosita* runs a one-hour cruise out to Vepsä island and occasional daylong adventures to the lighthouse island of Bengtskär (p98).

MS Rudolfina CRUISE
(Map p86; ☑ 040-846-3000; www.rudolfina.fi; Läntinen Rantakatu; cruises €29-37; ⊙ 1pm, 4pm & 7pm Tue-Sat, 2pm Sun Jun-Aug) Lunch and dinner harbour cruises provide glimpses of Turku Castle, Pikisaar island and Ruissalo island. The leisurely three-hour evening cruise also takes in Naantali Harbour and the Kultaranta (p91; president's summer residence).

SS Ukkopekka CRUISE
(Map p86; www.ukkopekka.fi; Naantali return adult/child €24/12, Loistokari €48-55; ⊙ Naantali 10am & 2pm Tue-Sat Jun-Aug, Loistokari 7pm Tue-Sat May-Sat) The historic SS *Ukkopekka* makes twice-daily cruises to Naantali, as well as evening dinner cruises, with dancing on the pier of the island of Loistokari.

Turku

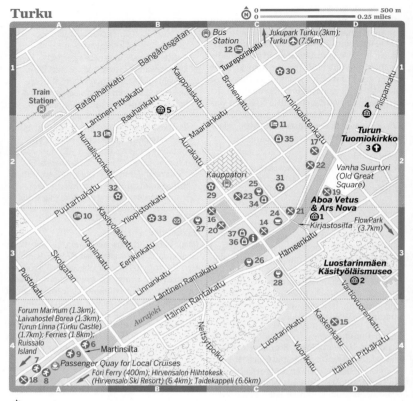

✈ Festivals & Events

Keskiaikaiset Markkinat CULTURAL
(Medieval Market; www.keskiaikaisetmarkkinat.fi)
Held over a variable long weekend in summer (usually late June), this lively four-day event brings a Middle Ages market back to the Vanha Suurtori (Old Great Sq) near Tuomiokirkko (Turku Cathedral).

Paavo Nurmi Marathon SPORTS
(http://paavonurmimarathon.fi; ⊙ late Jun/early Jul) Named for legendary Finnish distance runner Paavo Nurmi (aka the Flying Finn), this international marathon in loops through the town centre and Ruissalo island.

★ Ruisrock MUSIC
(www.ruisrock.fi; 1-/2-/3-day ticket €90/135/155; ⊙ Jul) Finland's oldest and largest annual rock festival – held since 1969 and attracting 100,000-strong crowds – takes over Ruissalo island for three days.

Turku Jazz MUSIC
(☎ 040-582-9366; www.turkujazz.fi; tickets €16-32, 1-/2-day pass €35/58.50; ⊙ early–mid-Aug) Hot bebop and smoking sax hits the city at three venues, including the main stage in the Panimoravintola Koulu (p89) courtyard.

Turun Musiikkijuhlat MUSIC
(Turku Music Festival; www.tmj.fi; tickets €11.50-43.50; ⊙ Aug) This two-week extravaganza offers an eclectic mix of classical and contemporary music and opera in amazing venues including Tuomiokirkko (Turku Cathedral; p84). Events range from free lunchtime concerts at local museums to orchestral extravaganzas at the concert hall.

🛏 Sleeping

★ Ruissalo Camping CAMPGROUND €
(☎ 02-262-5100; www.visitturku.fi/en/ruissalo-camping-_-0; Saaronniemi, Ruissalo; tent sites €18 plus per person €5, 2-/4-/6-person cabins €68/125/165; ⊙ May-Sep; P) On idyllic

Turku

⊚ Top Sights
1 Aboa Vetus & Ars Nova D3
2 Luostarinmäen Käsityöläismuseo D3
3 Turun Tuomiokirkko D2

◎ Sights
4 Sibelius Museum.................................... D1
5 Turun Taidemuseo..................................B1

✛ Activities, Courses & Tours
6 Jakke River Ferry................................... A4
7 MS Rudolfina A4
8 Rosita.. A4
9 SS Ukkopekka A4

🛌 Sleeping
10 Bridgettine Sisters' Guesthouse A3
11 Centro Hotel C2
12 Hotelli Helmi...C1
13 Park Hotel.. A2

✕ Eating
14 Blanko... C3
15 Kaskis..D4
16 Kauppahalli C3
17 Mami.. D2
18 Nerå A4

19 Pinella... D2
20 Sininen Juna Aschan Café.................... C3
21 Smor.. C3
22 Tårget D2
   Tintå..(see 14)
23 Viikinkiravintola Harald........................ C2

🍷 Drinking & Nightlife
24 CaféArt C3
25 Cosmic Comic Café............................... C2
26 Donna C3
27 Panimoravintola Koulu.......................... B3
   Tiirikkala...(see 22)
28 Uusi Apteekki C3

✪ Entertainment
29 Åbo Svenska Teater C2
30 Concert Hall...C1
31 Dynamo C2
32 Gong B2
33 Monk B3

🛍 Shopping
34 Casagrande C2
35 Kaisla C2
36 Klo Design C3
37 Kui Design C3

Ruissalo island, 10km west of the city centre, this sprawling campground has gently sloping grassy sites and a great choice of cabins, along with saunas, a cafe and Turku's closest beaches (including a naturist beach). Minigolf, ball courts, playgrounds and hiking trails will keep the troops entertained. Bus 8 runs from the kauppatori.

Laivahostel Borea HOSTEL €
(☎ 040-843-6611; www.msborea.fi; Linnankatu 72; dm/s/tw/d/tr/q from €30/51/82/92/112/135; P 🕏) Built in Sweden in 1960, the enormous passenger ship SS Bore is docked outside the Forum Marinum museum, just 500m northeast of the ferry terminal. It now contains an award-winning HI-affiliated hostel with 120 vintage en suite cabins. Most are squishy, but if you want room to spread out, higher-priced doubles have a lounge area. Rates include a morning sauna.

**Bridgettine Sisters'
Guesthouse** GUESTHOUSE €
(Map p86; ☎ 02-250-1910; www.kolumbus.fi/birgitta .turku; Ursininkatu 15A; s/d €45/65; P) Glowing white and run by nuns, this Catholic convent's guest wing is a haven of peace, with public areas silent after 10pm and a general respectful hush around the clock. Its small rooms are austere but spotless. Cash only.

Hotelli Helmi HOTEL €€
(Map p86; ☎ 020-786-2770; www.hotellihelmi.fi; Tuureporinkatu 11; s/d from €95/110; ✳ 🕏) Next door to the bus station, family-owned Helmi (literally, 'pearl') has 34 autumn-hued, soundproofed rooms with mini fridges, comfy mattresses and good-sized bathrooms.

Centro Hotel HOTEL €€
(Map p86; ☎ 02-211-8100; www.centrohotel.com; Yliopistonkatu 12; s/d from €96/119; P @ 🕏) The 62-room Centro Hotel is central (as you would guess), but its courtyard location cuts out street noise. Service is friendly and the blond-wood rooms are a good compromise between size and price. The breakfast buffet is worth getting out of bed for. Arrive early to nab one of the 14 parking spaces.

★ Park Hotel BOUTIQUE HOTEL €€€
(Map p86; ☎ 02-273-2555; www.parkhotelturku. fi; Rauhankatu 1; s/d/f €135/177/205; P 🕏) Overlooking a hilly park, this art-nouveau building was the home of a shipyard magnate. Nowadays it's a truly atmospheric place to stay, with classical music playing in the lift and a resident parrot in the lobby. Its 20 rooms are decorated in a lovably chintzy style. This is the antithesis of a chain hotel, thanks to the owners' wonderful hospitality.

CYCLING THE ARCHIPELAGO TRAIL

A popular way to the experience the Turku Archipelago is to cycle the **Archipelago Trail** (www.saaristonrengastie. fi), a 230km circular route that starts and ends in Turku. Cycling is on smooth country roads that provide glimpses of fields and farms, bridges and beaches, villages and sea. Stop for rest and recuperation in the villages or welcoming guesthouses along the way.

From mid-May to August, you can complete the entire route from Turku by hopping between the main islands and islets, which are linked by eight ferries and a dozen bridges. The further you travel, the more forward planning is required, as ferries run less frequently between the outer islands. Use Ferry.fi – or, http://lautta.net – to plan your route.

✖ Eating

Kauppahalli   MARKET €
(Map p86; www.kauppahalli.fi; Eerikinkatu 16; ⊙8am-6pm Mon-Fri, to 4pm Sat; 🖪) 🖉 Filled with speciality products, this historic covered market also contains the converted-train-carriage **Sininen Juna Aschan Café** (Map p86; http://aschan.fi; pastries & sandwiches €2.50-6; ⊙8am-6pm Mon-Fri, to 4pm Sat), run by top-quality Turku bakery chain Aschan.

Mami   BISTRO €€
(Map p86; 🖉02-231-1111; www.mami.fi; Linnankatu 3; lunch €9-10, mains €22-29; ⊙11am-10pm Tue-Fri, 1-10pm Sat) 🖉 Mami's riverside summer terrace is perfect for people-watching, though its abiding popularity means you'll have to fight for a table with half of Turku. Seasonal ingredients – chanterelles, perch, salmon, cockerel – from local, small-scale suppliers are prepared with care.

Tintå   BISTRO €€
(Map p86; 🖉02-230-7023; www.tinta.fi; Läntinen Rantakatu 9; mains lunch €7.50-14.50, dinner €17-32, pizza €13-16; ⊙11am-midnight Mon-Thu, to 2am Fri, noon-2am Sat, to 10pm Sun) With a cosy exposed-brick interior, this riverside wine bar is also a great bet for weekday lunches, gourmet pizzas and classy mains (like raspberry and rhubarb salmon or Moroccan-style lamb skewers). Grab a glass of wine and a seat on the summer terrace, and watch the world go by.

Blanko   BISTRO, BAR €€
(Map p86; 🖉02-233-3966; www.blanko.net; Aurakatu 1; lunch €9-12, mains €16-30, Sun brunch €18; ⊙11am-11pm Mon & Tue, to midnight Wed & Thu, to 3am Fri, noon-3am Sat, noon-6pm Sun) Look for the black-tile signage to find this hip venue. Inside it's all Scandi chic, with regular DJs, but the dining area is separate enough for you to concentrate on the food: stir-fries, salads and pasta, great lunch specials and the best Sunday brunch in town.

Nerå   EUROPEAN €€
(Map p86; 🖉020-741-5750; www.nera.fi; Läntinen Rantakatu 37; mains €18-29, pizza €14-17; ⊙11am-11pm Mon-Thu, noon-midnight Fri & Sat, 2-8pm Sun) This stylish place bustles with sophisticated people munching, sipping, chatting and laughing in the brick interior. The menu is one of contemporary classics – gourmet pizzas and burgers, fresh salads and tasty skewers – plus a good wine list.

Tårget   MODERN EUROPEAN €€
(Map p86; 🖉040-052-2707; http://matbar.fi; Linnankatu 3A; pizzas €14-17, mains €18-29; ⊙11am-10pm Mon-Fri, noon-11pm Sat, 1-7pm Sun, bar to 2am Fri & Sat) There's fancier fare on the menu, but the reason to come to Tårget is to try the exceptional pizzas with unusual topping combinations (goat cheese and strawberries, barbecue pork, crayfish and lemon crème fraîche etc). Great food, jovial atmosphere.

Pinella   INTERNATIONAL €€
(Map p86; 🖉02-445-6500; www.pinella.fi; Vanha Suurtori 2; mains lunch €9-22, dinner €16-27; ⊙11am-11pm Mon-Fri, noon-11pm Sat, noon-9pm Sun) Founded in 1848, this is one of Finland's oldest restaurants, but its menu is up to the minute: burgers in brioche buns or pulled pork in whisky barbecue sauce, and raspberry cake with liquorice ice cream for dessert. Upstairs the bar stays open to 1am on Friday and Saturday.

★Smor   GASTRONOMY €€€
(Map p86; 🖉02-536-9444; www.smor.fi; Läntinen Rantakatu 3; mains lunch €12-21, dinner €21-30, 4-course dinner menu €57; ⊙11am-11pm Mon-Fri, 4.30-10pm Sat) A vaulted cellar lit by flickering candles makes a romantic backdrop for appetising, organic, locally sourced food, such as roast lamb with orgánic currant sauce or the catch of the day with roasted hay sauce. Desserts are truly inspired: try quark mousse with wild blueberries and oat ice cream or caramelised yoghurt with thyme cookies and honey.

Kaskis
SCANDINAVIAN €€€

(Map p86; ☑ 044-723-0200; www.kaskis.fi; Kaskenkatu 6A; 4-/6-course menu €55/66; ⊗ 4pm & 7pm Tue-Sat, plus 10.30pm Fri & Sat) Foodies are buzzing about Kaskis, where there's no written menu – not only because it changes daily but also because there are no real decisions to make. You choose four courses or six, but the rest is up to the chefs. Rest assured: ingredients are fresh, seasonal and local, with a final result that shows off the versatility of the Finnish forests and sea.

Viikinkiravintola Harald
SCANDINAVIAN €€€

(Map p86; ☑ 044-766-8204; www.ravintolaharald.fi; Aurakatu 3; lunch €12.50, set menus from €39, mains €18-40; ⊗ noon-11pm Mon, to midnight Tue-Thu, to 1am Fri & Sat, 3-10pm Sun; ⊕) Subtlety is run through with a berserker's broadsword at this over-the-top Viking restaurant, which serves dishes like roast ox on a plank, 'witch of the north' reindeer or tar ice cream with cognac. Set menus are filling three-course samplers. It's not exactly gourmet, but it is great fun.

🍷 Drinking & Nightlife

⭐ Tiirikkala
COCKTAIL BAR

(Map p86; www.tiirikkala.fi; Linnankatu 3; ⊗ 11am-10pm Tue-Thu, to 2am Fri & Sat, noon-10pm Sun) Fresh from a cool, contemporary Nordic–style makeover, this gorgeous old wooden house opens to a street-level terrace and fabulous roof terrace. Unique cocktails and tasty tapas soothe the soul, as does the jazz and blues heading up the weekend live-music program. Weekend brunch is also a highlight.

CaféArt
CAFE

(Map p86; www.cafeart.fi; Läntinen Rantakatu 5; ⊗ 10am-7pm Mon-Fri, to 5pm Sat, 11am-5pm Sun) With freshly ground coffee, prize-winning baristas, a beautifully elegant interior and an artistic sensibility, CaféArt is an ideal place to get your caffeine fix, but be sure not to miss its cakes, which include sea buckthorn and carrot, apple and coffee, blueberry and white chocolate, and tangy lemon-meringue cheesecake. In summer, the terrace spills onto the riverbank, shaded by linden trees.

Uusi Apteekki
PUB

(Map p86; www.uusiapteekki.fi; Kaskenkatu 1; ⊗ 10am-2am) Lovely old fittings in this historic pharmacy include wooden dispensing drawers fashioned into tables where you can rest your pint.

Donna
BAR

(Map p86; www.donna.fi; Itäinen Rantakatu; ⊗ 11am-3am Apr-Sep) One of the most popular boat bars in Turku, Donna has a downstairs nightclub and open-air seating up on deck. It serves great cocktails and local Finnish beers, as well as pub food (like fried fish and grilled sausages) to soak them up.

Cosmic Comic Café
BAR

(Map p86; www.cosmic.fi; Kauppiaskatu 4; ⊗ 3pm-2am Mon-Thu, to 3am Fri & Sat) This fab late-night haunt is a fanboy's dream – comics paper the walls and you can browse its huge (mostly English-language) collection. Over 70 kinds of beer and 25 ciders rotate on the eclectic menu. Located inside the shopping mall.

Panimoravintola Koulu
MICROBREWERY

(School Brewery-Restaurant; Map p86; www.panimoravintolakoulu.fi; Eerikinkatu 18; ⊗ 11am-2am) In a former school, complete with maps on the wall, menu scrawled on a blackboard and playground-turned-summer beer garden, this fantastic brewpub only serves what it brews – around five lager-style beers that change with the seasons, and a couple of interesting ciders flavoured with tart cranberries and blackcurrants. The exception is the whisky collection, with 75 or so to sample.

☆ Entertainment

Monk
JAZZ

(Map p86; ☑ 02-251-2444; www.monk.fi; Humalistonkatu 3; ⊗ 10pm-4am Fri & Sat year-round, plus 9pm-1am Mon spring & autumn) Intimate venue for live jazz, funk and Latin.

Gong
LIVE MUSIC

(Map p86; ☑ 044-288-8888; www.gong.fi; Humalistonkatu 8A; cover €10-25; ⊗ 9pm-4am Wed, Fri & Sat) A great variety of Finnish bands play at this hot live-music venue. Also on site is the congenial Toby & Fellas, a convivial karaoke establishment.

Concert Hall
CONCERT VENUE

(Map p86; ☑ 02-262-0804; www.tfo.fi; Aninkaistenkatu 9; tickets from €23.50; ⊗ Sep-May) This music hall is the home of the illustrious Turku Philharmonic Orchestra. It's been playing since 1790, when the Musical Society of Turku was founded.

Åbo Svenska Teater
THEATRE

(Map p86; ☑ 02-277-7377; www.abosvenskateater.fi; Aurakatu 10; tickets €15-40) Founded in 1839, Finland's oldest theatre hosts performances in Swedish.

Dynamo LIVE MUSIC
(Map p86; ☑ 02-250-4904; www.dynamoklubi. com; Linnankatu 7; ☺ 9pm-4am Mon-Sat Jun-Aug, to 4am Tue-Sat Sep-May) Local DJs vie with national bands for a spot on the bill at this central venue. Great outdoor terrace.

🛍 Shopping

Kaisla CLOTHING
(Map p86; www.kaislamyymala.fi; Brahenkatu 7; ☺ 10am-6pm Mon-Fri, to 2pm Sat) Folks of all ages (and genders) can get outfitted at Kaisla. The signature item is the snuggly under-duds – perfect for cold Nordic nights. But shoppers will also find Finnish-designed sweaters and trousers that exude Scandi style.

Klo Design FASHION & ACCESSORIES
(Map p86; www.klodesign.fi; Läntinen Rantakatu 13A; ☺ 11am-6pm Mon-Fri, to 4pm Sat) Stylish and sweet, Klo does super-comfy clothing and accessories for women, especially dresses, tops and handbags, all with its signature bright colours and bold patterns.

Casagrande TOYS
(Map p86; www.casagrande.fi; Linnankatu 9/11; ☺ 10am-6pm Mon-Fri, to 3pm Sat) Over a century old, Casagrande is run by a family that loves to play. There are lots of old-fashioned wooden and plush toys, in addition to other childhood favourites.

Kui Design CHILDREN'S CLOTHING
(Map p86; www.kuidesign.fi; Läntinen Rantakatu 13A; ☺ 11am-6pm Mon-Fri, to 4pm Sat) Totally cute kids' clothes, plus bags, prints, postcards and other stuff with a Turku theme.

ℹ Information

Main Post Office (Map p86; Eerikinkatu 19; ☺ 8am-8pm Mon-Fri, 10am-2pm Sat)

Tourist Office (Map p86; ☑ 02-262-7444; www.visitturku.fi; Aurakatu 4; ☺ 8.30am-6pm Mon-Fri year-round, plus 9am-4pm Sat & Sun May-Sep, 10am-3pm Sat & Sun Oct-Mar; 🛜) Busy but helpful office with information on the entire region.

ℹ Getting There & Away

AIR
Turku Airport (p303) is 8.5km north of the city. Facilities are minimal and there are no ATMs – bring euros for the bus.
Airlines include the following:
AirBaltic (www.airbaltic.com) Serves Riga (Latvia).

Finnair (www.finnair.com) Regular flights to/ from Helsinki and Mariehamn; seasonal flights to Kittilä.

Nextjet (www.nextjet.se) Flies to Mariehamn.

SAS (www.flysas.com) Flights to/from Stockholm Arlanda (Sweden).

Wizz Air (http://wizzair.com) Seasonal flights to/from Gdańsk (Poland).

BOAT
Turku is a main gateway to Sweden and Åland. The harbour, about 3km southwest of the city centre, has terminals for **Tallink/Silja Line** (☑ 060-017-4552; www.tallinksilja.com; Linnankatu 91; ☺ 6.45am-8.15pm) and **Viking Line** (www.vikingline.fi; Ensimmäinen linja 6). Both companies sail to Stockholm, Sweden (10½ hours) via Åland (5½ hours). Book ahead during high season if you plan to take a car. Prices vary according to season and class:
Mariehamn Deck-class one-way tickets from €23/45 per passenger/car
Stockholm Cabin required; from €69/45 per passenger/car
Finnlink (www.finnlines.com) sails to Sweden from nearby Naantali, though this service doesn't take foot passengers. It's also possible to travel to Åland via the Turku Archipelago.

BUS
Long-distance buses use the **bus station** (Map p86; www.matkahuolto.fi; Aninkaistenkatu 20), while regional buses (including for Naantali) depart from the **kauppatori** (Map p86; www.foli. fi; single ride before/after 11pm €3/4, day pass €7.50).
Major intercity services:
Helsinki €25, 2½ hours, up to four hourly
Korpo €15.50, two hours, six daily (via Nagu; €11.80, 1¼ hours)
Pori €15, 2¼ hours, hourly (via Rauma; €10, 1½ hours)
Tampere €25, 2½ hours, hourly

TRAIN
Turku's train station is 400m northwest of the city centre; trains also stop at the ferry harbour.
Direct trains include the following:
Helsinki €20, two hours, hourly
Oulu €60 to €67, eight to 10 hours, two daily
Tampere €23, 1¾ hours, six daily

ℹ Getting Around

BICYCLE
Bike Rent (☑ 044-022-4161; www.polkupy oravuokraamo.fi; per day/week from €14/63, delivery €5; ☺ 9am-7pm) Offers good city-riding bikes, as well as tandems and kickbikes.

Tourist Office Rents seven-gear bikes and publishes an excellent free *pyörätiekartta* (bike-route map) of the city and surrounding towns.

BUS

Regional buses depart from the kauppatori (market square). Timetables are available from the tourist office, long-distance bus station and train station.

FERRY

Dating from 1904, the small **Föri ferry** (☉ 6.15am-11pm May-Sep, to 9pm Oct-Apr) (passengers and bicycles only) yo-yos across the river a few blocks southwest of the Martinsilta bridge. Journey time is around two minutes.

Local cruises depart from the **passenger quay** (Map p86).

NAANTALI

🗾 02 / POP 19,000

Most visitors to charming Naantali (Swedish: Nådendal) are summer day-trippers from Turku, 18km east. They come to meet their friends at Muumimaailma (Moominworld) or to browse the shops and galleries in the quaint Old Town. Even the Finnish president spends his summer holidays here – at the stately mansion overlooking the harbour at Kulturanta.

Out of season, Muumimaailma closes its gates and the Old Town acquires the melancholic air of an abandoned film set. But Naantali continues to work hard behind the scenes, with Finland's third-most-trafficked port, an oil refinery and an electricity plant.

◎ Sights

Surrounding the harbour, Naantali's photogenic Old Town is made up of narrow cobbled streets and wooden houses, many of which now house handicraft shops, art galleries, antiques shops and cafes.

Muumimaailma　　　AMUSEMENT PARK
(Moominworld; 🗾 02-511-1111; www.muumimaailma.fi; 1/2 days €28/38; ☉10am-6pm early Jun–mid-Aug, noon-6pm late Aug; 👶) Crossing the bridge from the Old Town to Kailo island takes you into the delightful world of the **Moomins** (p92). The focus is on hands-on activities and exploration, not rides. Kids love the costumed characters wandering through the Moominhouse, the Groke's Cave and Snork's Workshop (where they can help with inventions). Other Muumimaailma highlights include a swimming beach and Emma's Theatre. Your two-day ticket is also

good at Väski Adventure Island, which is a great stop for older kids.

Naantalin Kirkko　　　CHURCH
(Naantali Convent Church; www.naantalinseurakunta.fi; organ concerts €5-10; ☉10am-6pm Wed-Sun mid-May–end May, 10am-4pm Tue-Sun Jun–mid-Aug, noon-2pm Wed, 9am-noon Sun mid-Aug–mid-May) Medieval Naantali grew up around the Catholic Convent of the Order of St Birgitta, which was dissolved after the 1527 Reformation. Towering above the harbour, the massive 1462 Convent Church is all that remains. Archaeological digs have unearthed some 2000 pieces of jewellery, coins and relics now in the Naantali Museum. At 8pm on summer evenings a trumpeter plays vespers (evensong) from the belfry; there are also regular organ concerts.

Kultaranta　　　HISTORIC SITE
(🗾02-435-9800; tours from gate adult/child €13/5, from Naantali €19/7; ☉English tour 2pm Tue-Sun mid-Jun–late Aug) The Finnish president's summer residence is an elaborate stone castle on Luonnonmaa island, its tower visible from Naantali harbour. Designed by Lars Sonck, it was built in 1916 and is surrounded by beautiful, extensive rose gardens. Although the castle's interior is closed to the public, the grounds can be visited by guided tour. A bus takes visitors from Maariankatu, near the tourist office. Space is limited, so reserve your spot in advance at the tourist office (p93).

Naantali Museum　　　MUSEUM
(www.naantali.fi/museo; Katinhäntä 1; adult/child €5/3; ☉11am-6pm Tue-Sun mid-May–Aug) Housed in three Old Town wooden buildings dating from the 18th century, Naantali's museum traces the town's history from its convent roots, with plenty of artefacts to bring it to life. Exhibits cast light on disappearing trades such as needle making and goldsmithing.

🏃 Activities

Väski Adventure Island　　　ADVENTURE SPORTS
(🗾02-511-1111; www.vaski.fi; 1/2 days €24/43; ☉11am-6pm early Jun–mid-Aug) Older adventure-seekers will get their thrills at Väski, an island that features rock climbing, gold panning, ziplining and rope obstacle courses. Free shuttle boats depart every 30 minutes from Naantali, near the bridge to Muumimaailma, where you can also use your two-day ticket.

MOOMINMANIA

Beloved throughout Finland and beyond, the Moomins are an eccentric family of nature-loving, white-snouted, hippo-like trolls. Moominpappa, Moominmamma and their timid child, Moomintroll, are based closely on creator Tove Jansson's own bohemian family. Other characters include the eternal wanderer Snufkin; brutally honest Little My; the eerie Hatti-fatteners, who grow from seeds and are drawn to electrical storms; and the icy Groke, who leaves a frozen trail wherever she drifts.

Jansson's first published Moomin drawing appeared as a signature on her political cartoons. She wrote the first of her nine children's books, *Småtrollen och den stora översvämningen* (The Moomins and the Great Flood) during WWII, followed by several cartoon books based on her characters. Her comic strips debuted in the *London Evening News* in 1954, before being syndicated around the world: Canadian publisher Drawn & Quarterly recently republished them in six hardback editions. Adaptations have included a Japanese cartoon series, a film and an album; Moomintroll has even starred on the side of Finnair planes.

Moomin merchandise is everywhere in Finland, but the real deal is the **Moomin Shop**, which was set up by Jansson's heirs; branches include one in Naantali's **Old Town** (www.moominworld.fi; Mannerheiminkatu 3; ⊗10am-6pm Jun-Aug). For an up-close encounter, visit Naantali's **Muumimaailma** (p91) or Tampere's **Moomimuseo** (p134).

Naantalin Kylpylä SPA
(Naantali Spa; ☑02-445-5100; www.naantalispa.fi; Matkailijantie 2; pool adult/child from €20/8, manicure/pedicure/massage from €34/41/46; ⊗8am-8pm Mon-Sat, to 7pm Sun) Naantali's spa tradition began in 1723 with the discovery of the health-giving properties of the Viluluoto spring waters and peaked in the 19th century. Today the town's top-class spa hotel allows nonguests to access its impressive facilities, including several pools and a Turkish bath. Its massage and beauty treatments are popular – book ahead in summer.

MS Aavatar CRUISE
(☑020-435-9800; adult/child €12/5; ⊗7pm Wed & Sat Jul) Evening harbour cruises aboard the 1947-built schooner MS *Aavatar* sail from the Old Town pier.

🎆 Festivals & Events

Naantali Music Festival MUSIC
(www.naantalinmusiikkijuhlat.fi; ⊗Jun) This two-week event featuring first-rate classical music has been held for over 30 years. Events in the Convent Church are a real highlight and performers come from around the globe.

National Sleepyhead Day CULTURAL
(⊗Jul) According to tradition, the last family member asleep on 27 July gets awoken with a dousing of water. The city of Naantali takes it a step further by electing a celebrity 'Sleepyhead of the Year', who gets tossed into the sea. A carnival with dancing and games ensues.

🛏 Sleeping

Naantali Camping CAMPGROUND €
(☑02-435-0855; http://naantalicamping.sportum.info; Kopenkatu 20; tent sites €15 plus per person €6, 2-/4-/6-person cottages €130-180, without bathroom €60/80/100; ⊗Sat & Sun May, daily Jun-Aug) About 400m south of the harbour, this campground offers good facilities including a beachside sauna. Cabins range from basic to more luxurious with private sauna, bathroom and kitchen.

★Hotel Bridget Inn GUESTHOUSE €€
(☑02-533-4026; www.bridgetinn.fi; Kaivokatu 18; d €140-199; 🐾) Steeped in history, this dove-white 1880-built wooden inn (a one-time cafe frequented by former Finnish president PE 'Ukko-Pekka' Svinhufvud) has gorgeous period-furnished rooms in champagne and chocolate hues, some with patios or balconies. Two luxury suites feature private terraces and private saunas – worth a splurge!

Hotel Palo GUESTHOUSE €€
(☑040-558-3158; www.palo.fi; Luostarinkatu 12; d €127-147, f €198; ⊗8am-6pm; 🐾) Housed in a whitewashed wooden building, Hotel Palo is a quaint and comfortable family-run place. Furnished with wrought-iron beds and other antiques, the 14 rooms share access to garden-view balconies, as well as fridge and microwave. The excellent breakfasts (included in rates) are a hallmark.

Naantalin Kylpylä
SPA HOTEL €€€

(02-445-5100; www.naantalispa.fi; Matkailijantie 2; tw €168-188, d €188-218, ste from €244; @ 🛜 🐾) There's a large variety of rooms at this up-market spa complex, from spacious, contemporary hotel rooms to Moomin-themed family suites and luxurious apartments with private balconies. All guests have access to facilities at the spa, as well as two recommended restaurants.

✖ Eating

★ Uusi Kilta
SCANDINAVIAN €€

(02-435-1066; www.uusikilta.fi; Manner-heiminkatu 1; mains €18-33; ⊙ kitchen 10am-10pm May-Sep) Naantali's best restaurant has a sun-drenched terrace overlooking the pier and a superb, seafood-oriented menu. The selection changes seasonally, but you're likely to find Kilta's creamy fish soup (with pike-perch and salmon) any time of the year. Other favourites include smoked-reindeer pie with chanterelle cream and roasted Arctic char with crayfish and potato stew.

ℹ Information

Naantalin Matkailu (02-435-9800; www.visitnaantali.com; Kaivotori 2; ⊙9am-6pm Mon-Fri, 10am-4pm Sat & Sun Jun-Aug, 9am-4.30pm Mon-Fri Sep-May) Helpful harbour-front tourist office.

ℹ Getting There & Away

Naantali's bus station is 1km east of the harbour. Local buses 6 and 7 run to/from Turku's kauppatori (market square; €3.20, 30 minutes, four per hour).

SS Ukkopekka (p85) sails between Turku and Naantali in summer, arriving at the passenger quay on the south side of the harbour.

Finnlink (www.finnlines.com) car ferry runs between Naantali, Finland, and Kapellskär, Sweden, with a stop in Långnäs in Lumparland (either leg from €45 including passenger and vehicle). Långnäs is five hours from Naantali and 3½ hours from Kapellskär.

ℹ Getting Around

In summer the cute little tourist train **Minijuna Aikataulu** (adult/child return €7/5; ⊙ hourly 9.30am-6.30pm Mon-Sat, to 4.30pm Sun early Jun-early Aug) does a handy circuit between Naantalin Kylpylä and Naantalin Matkailu.

TURKU ARCHIPELAGO
02

An awesome 20,000 islands and skerries (rocky islets) make up the Turku Archipelago, one of Finland's most spectacular natural attractions. This is a majestic summertime playground – just a hop, a skip and a few ferry rides away from Turku. There are no big-ticket sights, just quiet settlements, abundant bird life and ever-changing views of sea and land. It's a magnificent environment for cycling, kayaking and island hopping.

Like much of Finland's south coast, the archipelago is primarily Swedish-speaking. The five largest inhabited islands – from east to west, Pargas, Nagu, Korpo, Houtskär and Iniö – are clustered in a tight crescent. Collectively they make up the municipality of Pargas (Finnish: Parainen).

The islands are home to a wide variety of music festivals; find a complete listing at Skärgårdens Musikfestivaler (www.festival net.info).

ℹ Information

Archipelago Booking (www.archipelagobooking.fi; Sähkömäki 1; ⊙8am-5pm Mon-Fri) A useful site, with an office in Nagu village centre.

Turun Saaristo (Turku Archipelago; 040-011-7123; www.visitarchipelago.com; Strandvägen 28; ⊙9am-5pm Mon-Wed, to 4pm Thu, to 3pm Fri) The archipelago's main tourist office is in Pargas centre.

ℹ Getting There & Around

Frequent, free ferries run continually between Pargas, Nagu and Korpo, with less frequent crossings from Korpo to Houtskär, and summer-only private ferries from Houtskär to Iniö. For details and timetables, consult FinFerries (www.finferries.fi).

Six buses travel daily to/from Turku as far as Korpo, with one bus continuing on to Houtskär (€17.80, 2¾ hours). Traveling in the other direction, there are five direct buses between Turku and Kustavi (€13.70, 1½ hours).

It's possible to island hop all the way to Åland with Åland's archipelago ferries, either from Galtby in Korpo via Kökar and Föglö, or from Osnäs near Kustavi via Brändö and Kumlinge. For details, see **Ålandstrafiken** (018-25600; www.alandstrafiken.ax).

Pargas

Once a Hanseatic League port, Pargas (Finnish: Parainen) is the de facto 'capital' of the archipelago. It still has a substantial port, and its limestone quarry – Finland's largest – is a major employer. Its quaint town centre and handful of interesting sights make it worth a quick stop before heading further into the archipelago.

As of 2009, the municipality of Pargas officially includes not only the island of Pargas but also the islands of Nagu, Korpo, Houtskär and Iniö.

Pargas Church   CHURCH
(Kyrkoesplanaden 4; ☉10am-5pm Jun-Aug) The Old Town of wooden houses is tucked behind Pargas Church, a beautiful early-14th-century building with whitewashed walls, medieval murals and brick Gothic supports.

Pargas Hembygdsmuseum   MUSEUM
(Local History Museum; ☏02-458-1452; www.pargashembygdsmuseum.fi; Storgårdsgatan 13; adult/child €3/free; ☉11am-4pm Tue-Sun Jun-Aug) When Lenin was on the lam from Russia to Stockholm in 1907, he stayed in Pargas under the pseudonym Mr Mueller. The outdoor local-history museum contains the house where he hid, along with cottages, crofts and a restored schoolhouse.

Solliden Camping   CAMPGROUND €
(☏040-540-9884; www.solliden.fi; Solstrand 7, Norrby; tent sites €15 plus per person €6, 3-person cottages €40, 4-person cottages with/without bathroom €90/65; ☉May-Sep) Pargas' waterside campground, 1.5km north of the town centre, is particularly lovely, with campsites and cottages surrounded by forest and sea. The rustic cottages have simple wooden interiors, with bunks and kitchenettes; some have fabulous sea views from the terrace. Bike rental, cafe, laundry and seaside sauna on site.

Sattmark   CAFE €
(☏044-970-2599; www.sattmark.fi; pastries €2-6; ☉10am-7pm Jun-Aug) Situated 10km southwest of Pargas along the road to Nagu, Sattmark is a charming 18th-century red wooden sailor's cottage with a cafe and a rustic handicrafts shop, plus nature trails criss-crossing the surrounding countryside.

Kamu   PIZZA, FINNISH €€
(☏050-452-4049; www.kamurestaurant.fi; Skräbbölevägen 2; lunch €10, pizza €12.50-17.50, mains €16-28; ☉11am-10pm Mon-Fri, noon-10pm Sat,

noon-6pm Sun) This is the liveliest eatery in town, with a stylish dining room, a sunny terrace and a full menu of pizza, fish and other favourites. Good selection of beer and cider.

❶ Information

Turun Saaristo (p93) Inside the Pargas library, the archipelago's main tourist office has information on all the islands. The website is also an excellent source of information.

❶ Getting There & Away
Regular buses run to/from Turku (€6.10, 35 minutes, six daily).

Nagu

The archipelago scenery really picks up once you reach Nagu (Finnish: Nauvo) – an idyllic island nestled between Pargas and Korpo. Its lively Swedish-style guest harbour has a string of shore-side huts selling souvenirs, designer sailor-wear and smoked salmon. Pleasant walking trails fan out around the harbour, leading to an atmospheric old church, a lively farmers market and several inviting beaches. One trail follows the shore of the Kyrkviken, the swampy inlet on the south side of the island, which is excellent for spotting wading birds.

Nagu is a highlight of the Turku Archipelago: it's a mandatory stop if you're riding the Archipelago Trail (p88), but it's also an ideal place to spend a few days relaxing and relishing fresh seafood, frigid dips and glorious sunsets. This is archipelago living at its best.

If you do it right, your meals will be a highlight of your visit to Nagu. There are several recommended restaurants in the village. Even better, local farmers and fishers sell fruit, vegetables and freshly smoked salmon from kiosks in the 'village centre', opposite the church.

Nagu kyrka   CHURCH
(Nagu Church; Kyrkvallen; ☉10am-5pm Jun-Aug) Lovely Nagu church dates from the 14th century. Look for the mysterious bogeyman sculpture and the primitive paintings on the walls, including the locally infamous Nagutrollet (Nagu troll).

Västergård   B&B €€
(☏040-586-1317; www.vastergard.fi; Gyttjavägen 29, Gyttja; s/d/ste €90/115/150; ℗) In a blissful spot 10km east of Nagu, this B&B has spacious rooms in a beautifully converted barn, with additional rooms (with shared bathroom) in

the main house. In true Scandinavian fashion, the rooms are filled with light, natural materials. There's a restaurant, a sauna and a hot tub, as well as bikes and kayaks for rent.

Hotel Stallbacken & Grännäs B&B
HOTEL, B&B €€

(☑ 040-486-6822; www.hotelstallbacken.fi; Grännäsintie 14, Grännäs; s/d B&B €100/110, hotel €110/145; 🔊) The forested hamlet of Grännäs is tucked just off the main road 3km south of Nagu. B&B guests get to share the adjoining hotel's facilities – private beach, summer evening restaurant, tennis court, sauna, and boat, bike and canoe rental.

Hotel Strandbo
HOTEL €€

(☑ 02-460-6200; www.strandbo.fi; Strandvägen 3; s/d/f from €95/125/190; @🔊) The pick of the 37 comfy guest rooms at this stately wooden seafront building are the light, airy bedrooms with balconies overlooking the waves. Accommodation is spread across four buildings. Downstairs, the restaurant offers a great lunch buffet and enticing outdoor seating.

Köpmans
SCANDINAVIAN, CAFE €€

(☑ 041-502-0290; www.kopmans.fi; Strandstigen 3; mains €14-26) With a quaint restaurant-cafe downstairs and four sweet guestrooms upstairs, this mustard-yellow clapboard house is delightful in every way. The restaurant highlights local ingredients, and offers wine and beer pairings. Don't miss the famous pike burger, served on archipelago bread with feta cheese, pickles and sea-buckthorn mustard. The 'secret garden' out the back is an exquisite place to dine.

Upstairs, rooms (doubles €125 to €135) exude a contemporary rusticity, with wooden interiors, old-fashioned furnishings, light colours and modern prints. Köpmans also organises guided treks and picnics around Nagu (€35 per person) and boat trips to the tiny island of Brännskär (€55 to €100 per person).

L'Escale
INTERNATIONAL €€

(☑ 040-744-1744; www.lescale.fi; Nagustrand 4; lunch buffet €12.50, mains €19-32; ⊘ 11.30am-10pm Mon-Thu, to 11pm Fri, noon-11pm Sat, to 8pm Sun; 🍴) The name might be French, but this renowned guest-harbour restaurant incorporates influences from further afield: sugar-salted salmon and potato-cucumber salad; crayfish soup with cayenne foam and puff pastry; slow-cooked pork with chilli-coriander glaze and apple slaw. There's fine dining upstairs, a casual bar downstairs and terraces on both levels that are heated in winter.

ⓘ Information

Archipelago Booking (p93) Assists with ferry bookings, concert tickets and accommodation options. Post office on site.

Harbour Info Point (☑ 040-011-7123; www.visitarchipelago.com; Strandstigen 2; ⊘ 11am-6pm Jun-Aug) Summertime information kiosk near the guest harbour.

Nauvo.net (www.nauvo.net) Links to accommodation, restaurants, ferry schedules and more.

ⓘ Getting There & Around

Buses run to/from Turku (€11.80, 1¼ hours, six to 10 daily), crossing with the free, year-round, round-the-clock car ferry.

If you want to explore some of the more obscure outcrops south of here, the **MS Eivor** (☑ 02-213-1500; www.rosita.fi) shuttles to islands including Nötö, Aspö, Jurmo and Utö.

Rent bikes at the **Strand Cafe** (☑ 045-321-3400; Gästhamn; €7.50/18 per half-day/day; ⊘ 8am-9pm Jun-Aug) or at **Hotel Strandbo** (€3/12 per hour/day).

Korpo

Korpo (Finnish: Korppoo) is the last of the 'inner islands' of the Turku Archipelago. That means it's the furthest island that you can reach without planning your trip around a ferry schedule. It does require two short trips on free inter-island shuttles, and it's still remote, wild and beautiful. As on the other islands of the archipelago, the main attractions in Korpo are pristine forests, hidden swimming beaches and welcoming island culture. There are a few sweet places to stay and one fantastic restaurant, making Korpo an ideal stop if you're riding the Archipelago Trail (p88) and an attractive destination in its own right.

Korpo is the gateway for shipping to Kökar on the Åland Archipelago's southern route. The main harbour is Galtby, 3km east of Korpo village.

Korpo kyrka
CHURCH

(Korpo Church of St Michael; www.korpo.net; Korppoontie 1; ⊘ 10am-5pm Jun-Aug) The centrepiece of Korpo village is its medieval church. Built in the late 13th century, it features naïve paintings on the ceiling and a statue of St George fighting a dragon.

Faffas B&B
B&B €

(☑ 040-522-4306; www.faffas.fi; Österretaisvägen 23; s/d €45/80, summer cottages per person €25) Overlooking fields and forests, this dignified century-old farmhouse now contains a B&B

with four charming guestrooms that share bathrooms. The simple rooms show off decorative paned windows, pine wainscotting and even an old tiled stove in the downstairs bedroom. In summer there are also three wooden cabins for rent, and a private swimming beach nearby. Cash only. Faffas is 7.2km east of Korpo village and 2km west of the ferry landing.

Hotel Nestor B&B €€
(☑ 040-060-1280; www.hotelnestor.fi; Österretaisvägen 45; s/d from €65/110; ☏) Owned and operated by a husband-wife, artist-designer team, this place exudes love, creativity and class. A barn has been renovated to accommodate seven light, airy rooms with pine floors, wrought-iron beds and muted walls. The scenic surroundings are as idyllic as it gets, with fields, forest and nearby seashore.

★ Back Pocket FUSION
(☑ 040-140-3113; www.hotelnestor.fi; Osterretaisvagen 45; ⊘6-10pm Mon-Sat Aug, Sat only Sep) Inside the exquisite restaurant at the Hotel Nestor, the dining room is a veritable gallery of old and new, creating an atmosphere that feels at once rustic and charming, as well as contemporary and cool. Chef William Hellgren sees each dish as an individual work of art – something to delight *all* the senses.

Buffalo Ravintola STEAK €€
(☑ 02-463-1600; www.ravintolabuffalo.com; Verkan guest harbour; lunch buffet €9-11, mains €19-30; ⊘8am-midnight Jul, 11am-10pm Mon-Fri, 8am-10am Sat & Sun Aug; ☏ ⊞) You guessed it: Buffalo specialises in steaks, but there are also salads, burgers and fish dishes. Its waterside terrace is a prime spot for lingering with a cold beer, and the bar kicks on after the kitchen closes.

❶ Information

Dag-15 (☑ 040-011-7123; www.dag15.com; Korppoontie 2; s/d €55/85) B&B, cafe and tourist-information centre all in one central location near the church.
Visit Korpo (www.visitkorppoo.com) In Finnish only.

❶ Getting There & Away

Regular buses link Korpo with Turku (€15.50, two hours, six to eight daily). Buses, cars and bicycles use the free ferry that crosses from Nagu pretty much constantly.

Ferries also run from Galtby harbour to Houtskär (free, 30 minutes, hourly) and to Kökar, Åland (passengers free, bicycle/car €6/34, 2¼ hours, up to three daily).

Houtskär

Houtskär is delightfully tranquil, if short on sights. The islanders (numbering around 600) are hardy, Swedish-speaking folk – fishers, sailors and nature-lovers. It's a fantastically remote and beautiful spot that they call home, characterised by red boathouses, blue waters and not much else.

Ferries arrive and depart from two ports, Mossala in the north and Kittius in the south, while the population is mostly congregated in the village of Näsby.

You can pitch camp or rent a cabin at **Mossala Skärgårdens Fritidscenter** (Mossala Island Resort; ☑ 050-347-7658; www.mossala-island-resort.com; Mossala, Houtskär; tent sites €20, cabins €65-85, 2-bedroom cottages €120-170) a resort surrounded by glorious forest, beach and sea. There are miles of hiking trails, as well as bicycles, stand-up paddle boards, Frisbee-golf and fishing. If your budget allows, consider a cottage with private sauna or the luxurious Scandinavian villa.

❶ Getting There & Away

Buses travel from Turku all the way to Houtskär (€17.80, three hours, one or two daily) via Pargas, Nagu and Korpo.

Stella and Mergus ferries run between Korpo and Kittius, Houtskär (free, 30 minutes, hourly). Fun fact: at 9.5km, this is the longest ferry route in the archipelago.

Iniö

Houtskär's tiny neighbour Iniö has more than 700km of shoreline, yet fewer than 300 residents. Its windswept landscape is strewn with pine forests, with violets and tufts of chives cropping up among the granite. It's a wild, remote island, with a hiking trail winding up to the highest point at Kasberget (40m), offering views of the surrounding islands.

The main population centre is Norrby, where you'll also find a few places to eat and the sweet stone **Iniö kyrka** (Church of Sofia Wilhelmina; ⊘10am-5pm Jun-Aug). This landmark was named after the newborn princess Sofia Wilhelmina when it was consecrated in 1801.

Aura ferries run between Kannvik harbour in the north and Heponiemi, Kustavi (six to eight daily). Antonia ferries link Norrby harbour in the south and Mossala, Houtskär (passenger/bicycle/car €10/15/40, one hour, three or four daily) from June to August. See www.finferries.fi for timetables.

Kustavi

The island village of Kustavi (Swedish: Gustavs) represents the final piece of the Archipelago Trail (p88) puzzle – or the first piece, depending on what direction you're travelling. About 70km west of Turku, it's connected to the mainland by bridges, making it one of the easier islands to access. And yet, with more than 2000 islands (and half as many residents), it's no less of a watery wonderland, with myriad beaches, boatyards and scenic seascapes.

Kustavi's wooden **church** (Kustavi Church; Kirkkotie; ⊙ noon-4pm mid-Jun–mid-Aug), built in 1783, features the cruciform shape and votive miniature ships common in coastal churches. There aren't too many other sights, but it's possible to charter a boat from Kustavi to **Isokari lighthouse** (www.isokari.fi) and to **Katanpää Fort Island** (http://katanpaa.fi). Enquire at the tourist office.

Pzéns   FINNISH €€
(☑ hotel 050-465-3387, restaurant 040-014-7148; www.peterzens.fi; Parattulanrantatie 16; mains €18-28; ⊙ 8am-9.30pm Jun & Jul, noon-6pm May & Aug) At the southern tip of the island, Pzéns (formerly Peterzéns) is the centre of the action, with guest harbour, hotel, restaurant and shop. In summer the restaurant bustles with a bountiful buffet, indoor art exhibits and outdoor seating on a picturesque wooden deck.

Pzéns also rents out its boathouses, refitted as delightful guest rooms with private bathrooms and terraces (single/double €80/98).

Kustavi Handicraft Village   ARTS & CRAFTS
(Kustavin Savipaja & Paratiisi Paja; www.kustavin savipaja.fi; Iniöntie 411; ⊙ 9am-8pm Jun-Aug; ⊕) Lots of arts and crafts, especially ceramics, soaps, candles and other household decorations. In summer there's an outdoor market with textiles and metals, as well as a petting zoo, a playground and other kid fun.

ⓘ Information

Tourist Office (☑ 02-842-6620; www.visitk-ustavi.fi; Keskustie 7; ⊙ 8.15am-4pm Mon-Sat Jun-Aug) Located inside the Kustavi municipal office.

ⓘ Getting There & Away

A free ferry, the MS *Aurora*, runs between Kustavi and Iniö (25 minutes, six to eight daily). Check the timetable at www.finferries.fi.

Travelling in the other direction, there are five direct buses to Turku (€13.70, 1½ hours).

If you're hopping across to the Åland Archipelago, head for the port of Osnäs (Finnish: Vuosnainen) on the island's western tip. From here, regular passenger ferries run to Långö on northern Brändö (passengers free, bicycle/car €6/22, 40 minutes). Book through Ålandstrafiken (p93).

THE SOUTH COAST: WEST OF HELSINKI

Driving west from Helsinki, you start to get a sense of the 'real' Finland. The region has a scattering of lakeside towns and coastal villages and the occasional industrial outpost – not to mention the many, many islands of Archipelago National Park.

Most places are accessible as day trips from Helsinki or Turku, but the seaside destinations merit longer stays, to give you an opportunity to explore the seemingly endless offshore islands.

Kimito Island & Archipelago National Park
☑ 02

Kimito (Finnish: Kemiö) is a sprawling coastal island – Finland's largest – located 65km southeast of Turku. Numerous inlets and waterways weave their way through the forested isle, which is dotted with seaside villages. It's worth taking your time exploring the island, as there are some fascinating sights along the way, including a historic church in Dragsfjärd and an art-filled manor house in Kimito.

But the main attraction is further south. You guessed it: more islands. Kimito is the main jumping-off point for Archipelago National Park, a scattering of spectacular islands that stretches south and west into the sea. Island attractions include Finland's tallest lighthouse, a century-old fortress island and a re-created Viking village. Cruises depart from Kasnäs, the harbour on the southern extreme of Kimito island.

⊙ Sights

Örö Fortress   ISLAND
(☑ 046-563-5207; www.visitoro.fi; return ferry adult/child €26/13) Örö was long a military island, first containing a defensive fortress built under Russian rule and later serving as training grounds for the Finnish military. The island's barracks, heavy artillery battery (complete with guns) and fortifications on

the northern tip were opened for exploration in 2015. The MS *Ejskär* makes the 1¼-hour trip between Örö and Kasnäs once or twice daily in summer and at weekends in September. Book ahead.

Because the island was closed for so many years, it's home to unique birds and butterflies, as well as rare plant species, such as pasque flower and sea kale. Birders will have a field day, as many migrating Arctic species stop here. The island is also a nesting place for the icterine warbler and the barred warbler (both can be seen in June).

There's a variety of accommodation, including a hostel (dorm beds/twins €35/110) in the old barracks, and a restaurant in the canteen.

Bengtskär Lighthouse   LIGHTHOUSE
(☑ 040-218-2960; www.bengtskar.fi; adult/child €8/4; ☉ 10am-7pm Jun-Aug) Towering 52m above the waves 25km offshore from Hanko, the Nordic countries' tallest lighthouse was built in 1906 to protect ships from the perilous archipelago waters. It was damaged extensively during the Continuation War by the departing Red Army but has been refurbished. There are historical exhibits downstairs and fabulous views from the top.

In the summer months, you can reach Bengtskär with Marine Lines (p100) from Hanko and with the **Rosala & Bengtskär Booking Office** (☑ 040-218-2960; www.rosala. net; adult/child €59/30; ☉ 11.30am-6.15pm Jun-Aug) from Kasnäs or Rosala. If you wish to spend the night, the lighthouse also contains simple but panoramic accommodation (single/double/family rooms €120/188/280).

Rosala Viking Centre   MUSEUM
(www.rosala.fi; Reimarsvägen 5, Rosala; adult/child €8/4; ☉ 10am-6pm Jun-Aug, noon-4pm Mon-Sat late May & early Sep) Rosala isn't just a museum but a Viking village, complete with homestead, chapel and moored Viking ship. An introductory video provides an informative overview of Viking history in the region, and then you're free to try on costumes, wield weapons, play musical instruments and explore the many buildings. Cafe on site.

Söderlångvik   HISTORIC BUILDING
(☑ 02-424-662; www.soderlangvik.fi; Amos Andersonvägen 2; adult/child €4/free; ☉ 11am-6pm mid-May–Aug, English tours 1pm) The beautiful manor house Söderlångvik belonged to local newspaper magnate and art collector Amos Anderson. There are paintings, furniture and special exhibitions, as well as extensive gardens and a cafe. It's signposted 6.3km southwest of Dragsfjärd.

Sagalunds Museum   MUSEUM
(☑ 02-421-738; www.sagalund.fi; Museotie 7; adult/child €7/1; ☉ 11am-5pm Jun-Aug) Near Kimito village, Sagalund is an open-air museum with more than 20 old buildings, including a traditional sauna and a blacksmith. English-speaking guides give 90-minute tours every hour.

Dragsfjärdin Kirkko   CHURCH
(Dragsfjärd church; Kappelimäentie 6, Dragsfjärd; ☉ 10am-5pm Jun-Aug) Dating from 1755, this yellow wooden church with marine-blue interior is a charmer. The church's oldest artefact is the crucifix, which dates from 1689.

🛏 Sleeping

Archipelago National Park contains some of Finland's most unusual lodgings, as you can spend the night in a lighthouse or in old army barracks (p97). If you prefer a more traditional hotel or hostel, you'll find that too (though the choice is limited).

Hostel Panget   HOSTEL €€
(☑ 044-238-7858; www.panget.fi; Täysihoitolantie 6, Kulla; s/d/tr/f €67/80/106/132) At the turn-off to Dragsfjärd, 1930s-built Hostel Panget retains the art deco detailing from its days as a boarding house. Its comfortable, old-fashioned rooms all have a private toilet; the four-person family rooms also have a private shower. Sociable common areas include a pub and a lounge with board games.

Hotel Kasnäs   SPA HOTEL €€
(☑ 02-521-0100; www.kasnas.com; Käsnäsintie 1294, Kasnäs; s/d/ste €92/132/216; @⃤) The end of the line (literally), on the island's southern tip, this modern complex sprawls over several buildings, offering affordable accommodation and a spot of pampering. Facilities and services include a 25m pool, various saunas, massages and a restaurant.

ⓘ Information

Blåmusslan (Blue Mussel Archipelago Nature Centre; ☑ 020-639-4620; www.nationalparks. fi/en/archipelagonaturecentre; Meripuiston-tie, Kasnäs; ☉ 10am-5pm mid-Jun–mid-Aug, 10am-3pm Tue-Fri, to 4pm Sat mid-Feb–late Apr & Oct–mid-Nov, 10am-4pm Mon-Sat late Apr–mid-Jun & mid-Aug–Sep) In Kasnäs, near the pier; organises tours to some Archipelago National Park islands. You'll also find info on nature trails in the area and several films in English (most around 10 minutes long).

Tourist Office (📞02-426-0170; www.visitkimitoon.fi; Engelsbyvägen 8, Kimito; ⊙noon-5pm Mon-Fri) Located in Villa Lande in Kimito village.

ⓘ Getting There & Away

Buses run from Dalsbruk (Taalintehdas) and Dragsfjärd to Turku (€17.30, 1½ hours, three daily). The trip to Helsinki (€30, three to four hours, three daily) requires a transfer at Salo.

From Dalsbruk, free ferries serve the southern archipelago islands in summer, such as Hitis (Hiittinen). Check timetables at Ferry.fi (http://lautta.net), which also has details of taxi boats.

Hanko

📍019 / POP 8800

On a long, sandy peninsula, Hanko (Swedish: Hangö) grew up as a well-to-do Russian spa town in the late 19th century. During this period entrepreneurs and industrialists built opulent seaside villas, with fabulous Victorian and art nouveau architectural detailing. These beauties are still a star attraction here, especially as many of them now house guesthouses and restaurants.

Summertime visitors flock to Hanko for sun and sand, and there are several attractive beaches. There's a party atmosphere throughout summer, especially around the huge Hanko Regatta in July. For island hoppers, Hanko's a good jumping-off point for the southern archipelago. Or you can stay on dry land and relish the fruits of the sea at the town's many excellent restaurants.

History

As the southernmost town in Finland, Hanko was a strategic anchorage well before its founding as a town in 1874. It was also a point of emigration: between 1881 and 1931 about 250,000 Finns left for the USA, Canada and Australia via these docks.

At the end of the Winter War, the March 1940 peace treaty with Russia required the ceding of Hanko as a naval base. Its inhabitants evacuated as the Russians moved in with a garrison of 30,000 and constructed a huge network of fortifications. Hanko was isolated from the Russian front lines and eventually abandoned in December 1941. Citizens returned to see their damaged town the following spring. Learn more about this little-known but fascinating history at the Rintama Museo (p102).

◉ Sights

Hanko is a treasure trove of interesting architecture, with notable buildings by Lars Sonck, Selim Lindqvist and other renowned architects. Appelgrenintie, east of East Harbour, is an impressive stretch, featuring many fine 20th-century villas. Pick up the brochure *An Architecture Walk in the Centre of Hanko* from the tourist office (p102).

Hauensuoli   HARBOUR

(Pike's Gut) This narrow strait between Tullisaari and Kobben is a protected natural harbour where ships from countries around the Baltic Sea once waited out storms. The sailors killed time by carving their initials or tales of bravery into the rocks, earning the area the nickname 'Guest Book of the Archipelago'. Some 600 carvings dating back to the 17th century remain. Hauensuoli can be reached by charter taxi boat or on a cruise (p100) from Hanko.

Water Tower   TOWER

(Map p100; Kirkkopuisto Park; €2; ⊙1-4pm Sat May, 1-4pm daily Jun & Aug, 1-6pm daily Jul) Zip up the lift to the top of the 50m-high water tower on Vartiovuori Hill for sweeping views across town and out to sea.

Neljän Tuulen Tupa   HISTORIC BUILDING

(House of the Four Winds; www.facebook.com/NeljanTuulenTupaHanko; ⊙10am-7pm daily mid-May–mid-Aug, Sat & Sun Sep) On Little Pine Island, 1.5km east of the town centre, is the House of the Four Winds, where locals snuck swigs of 'hard tea' during the Finnish Prohibition (1919–32). Disturbed by the merrymaking, Field Marshal CGE Mannerheim, who had his summer cottage nearby, bought the house in 1927, imported tea sets from France and personally ran the place until 1931. There's a beautiful cafe and summer terrace, with granite tables carved from the surrounding rocks.

🏃 Activities

As it has over 30km of beaches, swimming and sunbathing are two of the town's chief attractions. **Tennisranta** beach (Plagen) has some cute wooden changing boxes and a fantastic free water merry-go-round (move aside, kids!).

Some of Finland's best windsurfing is southwest of the guest harbour at **Tulliniemi** and 3km northeast of town at **Silversand**.

Hanko

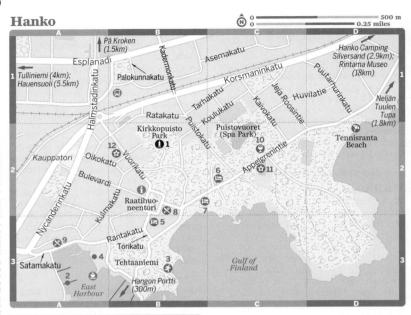

N 0 — 500 m
0 — 0.25 miles

Hanko

⊙ Sights
1 Water Tower B2

➕ Activities, Courses & Tours
2 Marine Lines A3
3 Regatta Spa B3
4 SunFun A3

🛏 Sleeping
5 Hotel Regatta.................................... B3
6 Villa Maija C2
7 Villa Tellina B2

🍴 Eating
8 Alan's Café B2
9 Origo A3

🍷 Drinking & Nightlife
10 Park Café.. C2

🎭 Entertainment
11 Casino.. C2
12 Kino Olympia..................................... B2

Regatta Spa   SPA
(Map p100; 📞 010-501-8430; www.regattaspa.fi;
Merikatu 2; ⊙ 10am-7pm Mon-Thu, 8am-7pm Fri
& Sat, 8am-6pm Sun) A throwback to Hanko's
heyday as a spa town, this gorgeous new facility boasts a massive glass-enclosed swimming
pool that offers 270-degree views of sea and

sky. There's a full spa menu, including facials,
massage and beauty treatments, as well as
the recommended restaurant Solsidan.

☞ Tours

SunFun   CRUISE
(Map p100; 📞 cruises 040-044-0802, rentals 040-
414-5681; www.sunfun.fi; East Harbour; boat trips
€25-35, bike rental per 2hr/day €10/16) A speedy
Kulkuri 34 takes passengers on trips to the
rock carvings in Hauensuoli (Pike's Gut)
strait (p99). Each trip goes twice a week.

Marine Lines   CRUISE
(Map p100; 📞 040-053-6930; www.marinelines.
fi; East Harbour; adult/child Bengtskär €60/25,
Russarö €37/20, Örö €75/30; ⊙ mid-Jun–mid-
Aug) The excellent options here include a
5½-hour cruise to the lighthouse island of
Bengtskär (p98); a 3½-hour cruise to Russarö, a former military base; and all-day trip
to Örö, another former military base that
opened to the public in 2015.

✨ Festivals & Events

Hanko Regatta   SAILING
(www.hangoregattan.fi; ⊙ 1st/2nd weekend Jul)
More than 200 boats compete in the Hanko
Regatta. The event attracts thousands of
spectators and has a high-spirited carnival
atmosphere.

🛏 Sleeping

Several of Hanko's Empire-era Russian-style villas operate as B&Bs. Don't expect luxury, but do come with a lively appreciation of history. You can book private accommodation (sometimes in villas) through the tourist office (p102).

Hanko Camping Silversand   CAMPGROUND €

(☑ 019-248-5500; www.silversand.fi; Aarne Karjalaisentie 13-15; tent sites €26.50 plus per person €5.80, s/d €64/83, cottages €79-129; ☉ 9am-9pm; 🛜) Situated 4km northeast of the town centre, this well-shaded campground stretches along a private beach. Its simple six-person huts are supplemented by newer, swisher four-person cottages. Ball courts, minigolf, rental bikes and a sauna are at your disposal.

Villa Tellina   VILLA €€

(Map p100; ☑ 019-248-6356; www.tellina.com; Appelgrenintie 2; per person with/without bathroom €60/50; 🅿🛜) Right by the beach, Tellina is a rambling, paint-peeling, pistachio-coloured villa that looks as though it's seen its share of hidden treasure and wild adventure. Rooms are basic but filled with light. There are additional rooms in two more villas across the street, if this one fills up.

★ Villa Maija   VILLA €€€

(Map p100; ☑ 050-505-2013; www.villamaija.fi; Appelgrenintie 7; s/d €135/175, without bathroom €100/130, f €200; 🅿🛜) Built in 1888, this is Hanko's best villa accommodation. Spread over three lovely buildings, the rooms are flawlessly restored and packed with character, featuring wooden floors and ceilings, decorative wainscotting, tile stoves and period chandeliers. Rooms vary widely in size and layout – some lack bathrooms and others sport balconies with wonderful sea views. There's a delightful garden.

Hotel Regatta   BOUTIQUE HOTEL €€€

(Map p100; ☑ 019-248-6491; www.hotelregatta.fi; Torikatu 2; s/d from €140/170; 🌐🛜) Designed by Finnish architect Lars Sonck, this landmark art nouveau hotel dates from 1898, but it was thoroughly updated this century. In an unbeatable beachfront location, its 49 rooms are uniquely decorated and come in a variety of sizes; the best have stunning sea views. Guests have access to all the facilities at the nearby Regatta Spa.

🍴 Eating

Alan's Café   CAFE €

(Map p100; www.facebook.com/Alans-Café-103343376402685; Raatihuoneentori 4; dishes €2-4; ☉ 10am-5pm Mon-Fri, to 4pm Sat, noon-4pm Sun May-Aug) Set in an old wooden villa, Alan's has house-baked treats to eat in the cosy interior or in the courtyard, shaded by a huge tree. Afterwards, browse the attached craft shop.

Hangon Portti   SEAFOOD €€

(☑ 010-05516; www.hangonportti.fi; Smultrongrundet; mains €15-32; ☉ noon-10pm Mon-Sat, 5-10pm Sun mid-Jun–Aug) You'll need to take a two-minute ferry journey from the East Harbour pier (p102) to this little whitewashed, wicker-furnished cottage, perched on a rugged granite island. Sailor's meatballs (with mashed potatoes and lingonberry jam), a smoked-and-glazed-pork 'captain's burger' with potato salad, and archipelago tapas are among the dishes on the menu.

Origo   SCANDINAVIAN €€

(Map p100; ☑ 019-248-5023; www.restaurant-origo.com; Satamakatu 7; lunch buffet €30.50, mains €18-32; ☉ 11am-10pm) 🍃 At the eatery-clad East Harbour, Origo distinguishes itself with geothermal heating, local, organic ingredients and a seasonal gourmet menu. Braised pork cheek cooked overnight is a treat, as is the salmon soup with dark bread. Vegetarians can choose from unusual dishes such as black-salsify pie.

På Kroken   SEAFOOD €€€

(☑ 040-358-1815; www.pakroken.fi; Tegelbruksvägen 12; mains cafe €10, restaurant €26-45; ☉ cafe 8am-6pm, restaurant noon-9pm) With its own smokehouse and boat-fresh lobster and shellfish, På Kroken's yacht-shaped buffet teems with choices. If the restaurant's beyond your budget, the adjoining cafe serves cheaper dishes, including fabulous salmon soup with dark archipelago bread. Stock up on picnic fare at its fish shop.

🍸 Drinking & Nightlife

Park Café   BAR

(Map p100; www.restaurangpark.fi; Appelgrenintie 11; ☉ 4pm-1am Mon-Fri, 2pm-1am Sat, 2-11pm Sun May-Sep) Surrounded by the greenery of Puistovuoret (Spa Park), this lovely clapboard cottage was recently restored to its Victorian grandeur. Tables set amid the trees make a perfect place for a summertime drink. There's occasional live music.

WORTH A TRIP

FRONT MUSEUM

Original trenches, bunkers and artillery guns remain at the site of some of the worst Winter War fighting, 19km northeast of Hanko. Also there's a poignant indoor museum, **Rintama Museo** (Front Museum; ☑ 019-244-3068; www.frontmuseum. fi; Rd 25, Lappohja; adult/child €5/2; ⊙11.30am-6.30pm mid-May–early Sep), with interesting exhibits and knowledgeable guides. It's worth driving 5km further east to Skogby, where there are still earth-covered bunkers in the forests near the road.

☆ Entertainment

Kino Olympia   CINEMA
(Map p100; www.kino-olympia.fi; Vuorikatu 11) A local treasure dating from 1919, the Olympia is Finland's southernmost cinema.

Casino   LIVE MUSIC
(Map p100; www.hangoncasino.fi; Appelgrenintie 9) An art nouveau beauty overlooking the beach, Hanko's twin-turreted, mint-green-and-white casino is an atmospheric setting for live music, drinking and dancing.

ℹ Information

Post Office (Tulliniementie 24)
Tourist Office (Map p100; ☑ 019-220-3411; www.hanko.fi; Raatihuoneentori 5; ⊙9am-6pm Mon-Fri, 10am-4pm Sat & Sun Jun-Aug, 9am-4pm Mon-Fri Sep-May) Helpful office with a large list of private accommodation.

ℹ Getting There & Away

Buses run to/from Helsinki (€25.20, 2½ hours, three daily) via Ekenäs (Raseborg; €8.40, 35 minutes, six daily). Services depart from the **bus station** (Map p100).

Trains go to Karis (Finnish: Karjaa) and connect to Helsinki (€23.80, 1¾ hours, hourly) or Turku (€26.80, two hours, eight daily).

ℹ Getting Around

Cruises to Hauensuoli (Pike's Gut) strait and day trips out to the islands in Archipelago National Park depart from the **passenger harbour** (Map p100). Rent bikes from **SunFun** (p100).

Raseborg

☑ 019 / POP 28,347
In 2009 Ekenäs merged with the nearby towns of Karis and Pohja to form the municipality of Raseborg, named after the nearby castle. Both names are still in use.

Ekenäs

Midway between Turku and Helsinki, the seaside resort of Ekenäs (Finnish: Tammisaari) is one of Finland's oldest towns. In 1546 King Gustav Vasa founded it as a trading port to rival Tallinn in Estonia, and the names of the streets in the Gamla Stan (Old Town) still reflect the crafts that were practised there. Nowadays the seaside village is an ideal base for exploring Ekenäs Archipelago National Park by boat or kayak, as well as the evocative ruins of Raseborg Castle in nearby Snappertuna.

⊙ Sights

Ekenäs' enchanting **Gamla Stan** is filled with 18th-century wooden buildings named after types of fish – a legacy of the area's fishing-village beginnings. The Gamla Stan still exhibits its origins as an artisan trade centre: its narrow streets bear the names of their industries, such as Hattmakaregatan (Hatters' St) and Linvävaregatan (Linen Weavers' St). Today most of the Old Town is residential, giving it an air of authenticity.

EKTA Museum   MUSEUM
(☑ 019-289-2512; www.ektamuseum.fi; Gustav Wasasgatan 11; €8; ⊙11am-5pm Wed-Sun Sep-Apr, plus Tue May-Aug) The highlight of the Ekenäs museum is the exhibit on the life and art of Finnish painter Helene Schjerfbeck, with a rotating display of 30 artworks. The Lindblad building re-creates a 1950s photographer's studio, while the Commoner's House displays the interiors and furnishings of a merchant's home.

Ekenäs Church   CHURCH
(Stora Kyrkogatan; ⊙11am-5pm late Jun-Aug) This Old Town church is the only baroque greystone church in Finland. The original church was constructed between 1651 and 1680, but it was destroyed by fire and rebuilt in 1841 in its current neoclassical style. The most valuable elements in the church are the altar paintings and their baroque frames.

🏃 Activities & Tours

Paddlingsfabriken   KAYAKING
(Paddle Factory; ☑ 040-041-1992; www.paddlings fabriken.fi) Paddlingsfabriken offers lessons and guided paddles, including an all-day safari from Raseborg Castle to Ekenäs and multiday trips to the outer island of Jussarö.

Guide-Matti
HIKING, BOATING

(www.guidematti.fi; hiking/boating per person from €50/70) Long-time guide Matti Piirainen leads walking tours of Ekenäs and Fiskars, as well as nature hikes in the surrounding Grabbskog forest. Matti can also take you out to explore the archipelago with boat trips to Jussarö island or Älgö island.

Saariston Laivaristeilyt
CRUISE

(Cruises in the Archipelago; ☑ 019-241-1850; www. surfnet.fi/saaristoristeilyt; cruises €20-30; ☺ daily Thu-Sun Jun & Aug, twice daily Wed-Sun Jul) Archipelago cruises aboard the 100-year-old former steamship MS *Sunnan II* depart from the passenger harbour and last two to four hours depending on the destination.

🛏 Sleeping

Ormnäs Camping
CAMPGROUND €

(☑ 019-241-4434; www.ek-camping.com; Ormnäsintie 1; tent sites €12 plus per person €4, 2-/4-person cottages from €40/55; ☺ May-Sep) A 1.4km stroll southeast of the town centre, this easygoing campground has its own picturesque slice of beach, complete with beach sauna. Bikes and rowing boats are available for rent.

Hotel Sea Front
HOTEL €€

(☑ 019-246-1500; www.hotelseafront.fi; Vitsippsgatan/Pojogatan 2; s/tw/d from €85/105/125; ☺ 7am-8pm; ℗ 🐾 🐕) About 1km north of the main harbour, this 20-room family-run place has a prime location overlooking Pråstviken inlet. It's right off Hwy 25 but otherwise rather intimate, with a private pier if you need to park your yacht. Rooms are straightforward and comfortable, with balconies on the bay side.

🍴 Eating

Café Gamla Stan
CAFE €

(Old Town Cafe; ☑ 050-556-1665; www.cafegamla stan.fi; Bastugatan 5; dishes €4.50-8; ☺ 11am-7pm mid-Apr-early Sep; ☑ 🐾) 🐾 Tables here sit amid a shady apple orchard where guests can enjoy fresh juices and home-baked goodness (quiches, pies, cakes and other sweet treats). There's also seating in the cosy cottage. There are regular concerts in the garden and handicrafts for sale in the shop.

Ravintola Albatros
SEAFOOD €€

(☑ 019-241-2848; www.albatros.fi; Norra Strandagatan; mains €16-41; ☺ kitchen 11am-midnight Apr-Aug) Sea views stream through the Albatross' huge windows to its cool, calm interior. The terrace is equally inviting, though the wind may blow

DON'T MISS

RASEBORG CASTLE RUINS

Looming on a high rock overlooking a grassy sward, the late-14th-century **Raseborg Castle** (Raasepori; ☑ 019-234-015; www.visitraseborg.com; Raseborgsslottsväg 110, Snappertuna; adult/child €5/1; ☺ 10am-5pm daily May-Aug, Sat & Sun Sep) was strategically crucial in the 15th century, when it protected the trading town of Tuna and exiled king of Sweden Karl Knutsson Bonde held his court here. The castle was abandoned in 1558 and lay deserted for more than 300 years. Nowadays the crumbling fortress is ripe for exploration, or you can sign up for a tour with Slottsknekten (www.slottsknekten.fi). The castle is in Snappertuna, 18km east of Ekenäs via Rd 25. Buses are limited to non-existent.

you down from the 2nd floor. Seafood is the speciality, including salmon soup and panfried archipelago pike-perch, but there are plenty of grilled meats and salads. Service is unhurried and exceedingly pleasant.

Knipan
FINNISH €€

(☑ 019-241-1169; www.knipan.fi; Strandallén; lunch buffet €15, mains €22-36; ☺ 11am-10pm Mon-Sat, noon-8pm Sun Jun-late Aug) In an 1867 building at the end of the pier, this venerable summer restaurant has the best views in town. Its brief menu of Finnish favourites is rather staid, and service can be slack. But the setting is incomparable.

ℹ Information

Naturum Visitor Centre (p105)

Tourist Office (☑ 019-289-2010; www.visit raseborg.com; Rådhustorget; ☺ 8.30am-6pm Mon-Fri, 10am-2pm Sat Jun-Aug, 8.30am-4pm Mon-Fri Sep-May) Located on the town square.

ℹ Getting There & Away

The bus and rail stations are side by side at the northern end of Flemingsgatan. Ekenäs is served by buses (not always direct), but trains are invariably quicker and cheaper. Trains from Helsinki and Turku go via Karis (Finnish: Karjaa), where a change is required; some connections from Ekenäs to Karis involve a railbus.

Train services include the following:

Hanko €5, 30 minutes, eight daily
Helsinki €17.50, 1½ hours, eight daily
Turku €17, 1½ hours, eight daily

❶ Getting Around

Bicycles are available for hire from **Ormnäs Camping** (p103) and the **Guest Harbour Café** (☑ 019-241-1790; Norra Strandgatan 6; pizzas €10-14; ☺ 8.30am-10pm Mon-Sat, 10am-10pm Sun Jun-Aug). A **taxi** (☑ 019-106-9191) is useful for getting to the Raseburg Castle Ruins (p103).

Fiskars

☑ 019 / POP 500

Fiskars is a charming factory village with a green river sliding between brick buildings, which now house studios and showrooms for cutting-edge design. Fiskars *bruk* (ironworks) began in 1649 with a single furnace and went on to make millions of horse ploughs. In 1822 Turku apothecary Johan Jacob Julin bought the factory and the company boomed, producing a huge range of farming and household items, including its iconic orange-handled scissors (since 1967).

Today more than 100 artisans, designers and artists live and/or work here, and craft shops, studios and galleries fill the village's neoclassical buildings. Strolling through the picturesque centre and shopping for Finnish designs are the twin draws here – pick up a free town map from the tourist office, which details Fiskars' historic buildings and the shops contained within.

◉ Sights & Activities

Fiskars Museum   MUSEUM
(☑ 019-237-013; www.fiskarsmuseum.fi; Peltorivi 13; adult/child €5/free; ☺ 11am-5pm Jun-Aug, 11am-4pm Wed-Sun Sep-May, closed Feb & Mar) Near the lake, Fiskars Museum details the evolution of the ironworks and the village that grew around it, with a different display of arts and crafts each season.

Fiskars Village Trail Center   MOUNTAIN BIKING
(Kuparivasarintie 6) Bike-rental centre that happens to have 60km of riding trails nearby.

🛏 Sleeping & Eating

Hotel Tegel   HOTEL €€
(☑ 050-441-9179; www.tegel.fi; Fiskarsintie 335; d €128-148) Housed in a handsome red-brick building that dates from 1888, Hotel Tegel contains 13 functional but attractive guestrooms (with additional rooms in a building across the street).

Restaurant Kuparipaja   FINNISH €€
(☑ 019-237-045; www.kuparipaja.fi; Kuparivasarintie 5; lunch buffet €25, dinner mains €17-29;

☺ 11am-8pm Mon-Fri, noon-8pm Sat, noon-6pm Sun) The terrace overhanging the river at the old copper forge is a mesmerising setting for a foray into Finnish gastronomy. Starters such as organic beef tartare (from a local cattle farm) are followed by mains like pike-perch loaf with fennel sauce and cauliflower, and topped off by such desserts as rhubarb with white chocolate.

🛍 Shopping

★Onoma   ARTS & CRAFTS
(☑ 019-277-7500; www.onoma.fi; Fiskarsintie 352; ☺ 10am-6pm) ✎ At this design shop in the distinctive clock-tower building, the sharp, stylish arts, crafts and homewares are produced by members of the Fiskars Cooperative of Artisans, Designers and Artists.

Fiskars Shop   HOMEWARES
(☺ 10am-6pm mid-May-Aug, 11am-5pm Sep-mid-May) You can buy the Fiskars company's distinctive scissors (and other handy stuff) at its shop in the clock-tower building, which also has a small exhibition on the firm's storied history.

Vanja Sea & Friends   CHILDREN'S CLOTHING
(www.vanjasea.com; Fiskarsintie 333; ☺ 11am-5pm Tue-Sun) Adorable knits, especially hats and sweaters for children, are on display at this little boutique. Take a peek at the art gallery upstairs too.

Kuura Cider   FOOD & DRINKS
(www.kuuracider.fi; Kuparivasarantie 7; ☺ 10am-6pm) At Kuura Cider, they're experts at finding ways to mix apples and alcohol. Concoctions for sale include Champagne-style apple cider and sweet apple liqueur.

❶ Information

Tourist Office (☑ 019-277-7504; www.fiskarsvillage.fi; Peltorivi 6; ☺ 8am-4pm Mon-Fri) Located near the car park and playground area.

❶ Getting There & Away

Bus services include Ekenäs (Raseborg; €7.40, 50 minutes, eight daily) and Helsinki (€18.70, 1¾ hours, three daily).

Lohja

☑ 019 / POP 47,500

The attractive town of Lohja (Swedish: Lojo) isn't on the sea coast, but it is on the coast of Lohjanjärvi – the biggest lake in these parts. The plethora of inlets and islets, and the easy

EKENÄS ARCHIPELAGO NATIONAL PARK

Almost 90% of the 5200-hectare **Ekenäs Archipelago National Park** is water, so to explore the 1300 islands you'll need to take a tour from Ekenäs harbour, such as an archipelago cruise with Saariston Laivaristeilyt (p103) or a kayaking tour with Paddlingsfabriken. You might also charter your own boat; the tourist office (p103) has a list of charter craft.

The most popular island is Älgö, with a 2km nature trail that takes in the island's observation tower. There's an old fisherman's home that's been converted to include a sauna and campsite facilities. There are also campgrounds on the islands of Fladalandet and Modermagan, but many other islands are off-limits to visitors, particularly the ecologically fragile outer islands. For information on the park and campground bookings, visit **Naturum Visitor Centre** (☑ 020-564-4613; www.outdoors.fi; Strandallén; ☺ 10am-3pm May & Jun, to 6pm Jul & Aug, 10am-3pm Sat & Sun Sep) in Ekenäs.

access from the capital, mean that most Helsinki residents seem to have a cottage here. The limestone-rich soil around the lake is ideal for growing apples, and orchards grace the shores. Lohja's wooded environs were also the stamping ground of Elias Lönnrot, compiler of the *Kalevala* epic.

The settlement itself is a hard-working mining town with a graceful medieval church and a small but interesting museum. It's worth a stop if you're in the area, but its main role for tourists is to keep the lake houses stocked with beer and supplies.

Pyhän Laurin Kirkko CHURCH
(St Lawrence Church; Kirkkokatu 1; ☺ 9am-4pm Jun-Sep, noon-3pm Oct-May) Dating from the 1480s, Lohja's medieval church contains incredible murals, mostly dating from the beginning of the 16th century. Starting from the right of the chancel, the murals depict the Creation and the story of the Garden of Eden. The narrative continues clockwise around the church, ending with the Last Judgment to the left of the chancel. Look out also for the 15th-century sculpture of St Lawrence on the southern wall.

Tytyrin Elämyskaivos MINE
(Tytyri Mine Experience; ☑ 044-369-1309; www.tytyrinkaivos.fi; Kuilukatu 42; adult/child €16/9; ☺ tours 5pm Tue-Fri, 2pm Sat & Sun Sep-May, 3 or 4 daily Jun-Aug) Learn all about the history and engineering of mining at this working limestone mine, 500m north of Lohja centre. A new state-of-the-art lift whisks visitors 110m underground. (It's not quite as exciting as the funicular that used to transport guests, but it's much faster.) Exhibits show off old mining equipment and underground art exhibits; the tour culminates in a hokey but fun sound-and-light

presentation over an awesome quarried cavern. Standard tours are in Finnish; book ahead for an English tour.

Kaljaasi BAR
(☑ 040-522-6612; www.facebook.com/KaljaasiLauttaravintola; ☺ noon-11pm Sun-Thu, to midnight Fri & Sat Jun-Aug) You can dock your boat right next to this serene summer bar floating on a platform in the middle of the lake. If you don't have your own boat, staff will collect you from Virkkala, 7km south of Lohja (€10 return).

Opus K PUB
(www.opusk.fi; Kauppakatu 6; ☺ 3-11pm Tue-Thu, 2pm-1.30am Fri, noon-1.30am Sat) Wonderfully cosy Opus K is lined floor to ceiling with books and new discoveries from obscure Finnish microbreweries.

❶ Information

Tourist Office (☑ 044-369-1309; www.visit lohja.fi; Laurinkatu 50; ☺ 9am-5pm Mon-Fri, 10am-3pm Sat) Offers information on cottages around the lake, as well as activities like canoeing, fishing and cross-country skiing.

❶ Getting There & Away

Bus services include the following:
Ekenäs (Raseborg) €12.20, 1½ hours, six daily
Hanko €16.20, 1½ to two hours, two daily
Helsinki €12.20, 1¼ hours, two or three hourly
Turku €22, 2½ hours, four daily; there's a transfer at Salo.

THE SOUTH COAST: EAST OF HELSINKI

Finland's fascinating past comes to life in the towns east of Helsinki, with intact ironworks, defensive fortifications, and museums exploring the country's seafaring history. The island-peppered coastline is enticing for exploration by boat. All of these places are relatively easy day-trip destinations from Helsinki: cruises from the capital to Porvoo and Loviisa are exceedingly pleasant ways to experience this part of the country.

The Russian influence is palpable all along this stretch of coast, as the 1743 Treaty of Åbo made much of this territory part of that eastern empire. Orthodox churches occupy prominent spots in most towns (alongside their Lutheran counterparts); other sites such as Hamina's town hall and Langikoski Fishing Lodge reflect this history of Russian rule. Nowadays the (relatively) open border means that Russians are again a prominent presence – now as tourists and investors rather than occupiers.

Porvoo

📓 019 / POP 50,000

Finland's second-oldest town is a popular day or weekend trip from Helsinki. Porvoo (Swedish: Borgå) officially became a town in 1380, but even before that it was an important trading post. Its historic centre includes oft-photographed riverside warehouses that once stored goods bound for destinations across Europe. Away from the river, the cobblestone streets are lined with charming wooden houses of every colour. Birthplace of national poet Johan Runeberg, the town is peppered with signs commemorating his whereabouts on various occasions.

Porvoo is home to a fantastic dining scene and a burgeoning arts movement. During the day these ancient streets are bustling with visitors, but spending a weeknight will mean you'll have the place more or less to yourself.

◎ Sights

★Vanha Porvoo   HISTORIC SITE

(Old Town; Map p108) One of Finland's most enticing old quarters, this tangle of cobbled alleys and wooden warehouses is entrancing. Once a vibrant port and market, Porvoo now has craft boutiques, galleries, souvenir stores and antique shops jostling for attention on the main roads, Välikatu and Kirkkokatu. The rows of **rust-red storehouses** along the Porvoonjoki are a local icon: cross the old bridge for the best photos. The relatively less-touristed area is east of the cathedral; Itäinen Pitkäkatu is one of the nicest streets.

★Tuomiokirkko   CATHEDRAL

(Map p108; www.porvoonseurakunnat.fi; ⊘10am-2pm Tue-Sat, 2-4pm Sun Oct-Apr, 10am-6pm Mon-Fri, to 2pm Sat, 2-5pm Sun May-Sep) Porvoo's historic stone-and-timber cathedral sits atop a hill overlooking the quaint Old Town. This is where Tsar Alexander I convened the first Diet of Finland in 1809, giving Finland religious freedom. Vandalised by fire in 2006, the church has been completely restored, so you can admire the ornate pulpit and tiered galleries. The magnificent exterior, with free-standing bell tower, remains the highlight.

Taidetehdas   GALLERY

(Art Factory; Map p108; www.taidetehdas.fi; Läntinen Aleksanterinkatu 1; ⊘10am-6pm Tue-Fri, 11am-4pm Sat & Sun) FREE This former tractor factory is now an exhibition space, with rotating exhibitions of contemporary art. The centrepiece is the permanent display of the Jäntti collection, featuring Finnish artworks from the second half of the 20th century.

Runebergin Koti   MUSEUM

(Runeberg House; Map p108; www.runeberg.net/runeberginkoti; Aleksanterinkatu 3; adult/child €8/1; ⊘10am-4pm May-Aug, noon-4pm Wed-Sun Sep-Apr) National poet JL Runeberg's former home has become a museum, with a period interior including stuffed foxes and muskets that demonstrate the poet's love of hunting.

Across the road, the **Walter Runeberg Sculpture Collection** (Map p108; Aleksanterinkatu 5; with Runebergin Koti free; ⊘10am-4pm May-Sep) has 150 sculptures by Walter Runeberg, the poet's son. It's only open May to September; admission is included with tickets to Runebergin Koti.

🛏 Sleeping

Porvoon Retkeilymaja   HOSTEL €

(📞019-523-0012; www.porvoohostel.fi; Linnankoskenkatu 1-3; s/d/tr/q €37/52/85/105; ⊘reception 7-10am & 4-11pm; 🅿🤶) Four blocks from the kauppatori, and set in a grassy garden, this historic wooden house holds a well-kept hostel. All rooms (for one to six people) have lockers, television and fridge, while bathrooms, showers and a common kitchen are in the corridor. There's also a great indoor pool and sauna complex over the road.

Ida-Maria   B&B €€

(Map p108; 📞045-851-2345; www.idamaria.fi; Jokikatu 10A; s/d/f without bathroom €65/85/125, apt €165; 🤶) The hospitable owner of this charming B&B does her utmost to make guests feel welcome. Housed in a wooden building on the main square, the rooms are imbued with historic character. All share a bathroom, but the ambience, sauna and appetising breakfast make this place a winner.

★ Hotelli Onni
BOUTIQUE HOTEL €€€

(Map p108; ☑ 044-534-8110; www.hotellonni.fi; Kirkkotori 3; r/ste €199/295; P ✳ 🗟) Opposite the cathedral, this gold-coloured wooden building is perfectly placed. The rooms are all unique, from the four-poster bed and slick design of the Funkishuone to the rustic single Talonpoikaishuone. Top of the line is the honeymoon suite, a small self-contained apartment with bathtub and complimentary Champagne. *Onni* means 'happiness' in Finnish; this place delivers.

Hotelli Pariisin Ville
BOUTIQUE HOTEL €€€

(Map p108; ☑ 019-580-131; www.pariisinville. fi; Jokikatu 43; r/superior r/ste €195/245/295; P ✳ 🗟) Named after sculptor Ville Vallgren, this plush place in the heart of the Old Town combines modern luxury and heritage atmosphere. Rooms named for former residents are supremely tasteful, with 2nd-floor rooms boasting their own mini saunas and views over the courtyard.

🍴 Eating & Drinking

★ Cafe Postres
DESSERTS €

(Map p108; www.cafepostres.fi; Gabriel Hagertinkuja; ⊙10am-6pm Mon-Fri, to 4pm Sat) Tantalise your sweet tooth at this delightful dessert cafe, brainchild of Michelin-starred chef Samuli Wirgentius. Take your pick from rich, creamy gelato and to-die-for desserts, or sample the savoury open-face *smørrebrød* sandwiches on house-made sourdough bread.

Helmi Tea & Coffee House
CAFE €

(Map p108; www.porvoonhelmet.net; Välikatu 7; cakes €3-7; ⊙11am-6pm Mon-Sat, to 4pm Sun) A kindly Russian grandmother would happily sip tea from the distinctive lilac-and-white cups in the courtyard of this Tsarist teahouse. It's famous for its Runeberg torte, but regular cakes and chocolates will also have you loosening your belt. It's closed Monday and Tuesday in winter.

Meat District
STEAK €€

(Map p108; ☑ 020-770-5390; www.meatdistrict. fi; Jokikatu 43; mains €18-25, prix fixe €59-79; ⊙5pm-midnight Mon-Fri, 2pm-midnight Sat, terrace noon-8pm Fri & Sat, to 4pm Sun) 🌱 When you go to a place called 'Meat District', you

---

RUNEBERG TORTE

A local speciality is Runeberg torte: an almond-rum cake topped with sugar icing and raspberry jam that was supposedly the favourite breakfast of national poet Johan Runeberg. Traditionally it's a treat eaten on the poet's birthday, but in Porvoo you can sample it on any day at the Helmi Tea & Coffee House.

---

probably expect high-quality, organic, grass-fed beef – and that's what you'll get here (the house speciality is the dry-aged beef for two; €84). What you might not expect is the fresh local produce and the made-from-scratch everything, which is what makes this place so special.

Fryysarinranta
SEAFOOD, STEAK €€

(Map p108; ☑ 040-073-2038; www.fryysarinranta. fi; Jokikatu 20; mains €23-28, lunch buffet €25; ⊙11am-11pm Jun-Aug) A delightful setting, delicious food and laid-back service (ahem) characterise this Old Town newcomer. Set in one of the iconic red wooden warehouses along the river, the restaurant has an tempting lunchtime fish buffet and an irresistible terrace.

Wanha Laamanni
FINNISH €€

(Map p108; ☑ 020-752-8355; www.wanhalaamanni. fi; Vuorikatu 17; mains €20-30, tasting menu €60; ⊙11am-11pm Mon-Sat, noon-8pm Sun) This rambling 18th-century log building has housed the renowned Wanha Laamanni for more than 30 years. The restaurant offers a classy menu of Finnish favourites and a six-course surprise menu. The setting is inviting, with a roaring fireplace inside and a sprawling terrace with views to the river.

★ Porvoon Paahtimo
CAFE, PUB

(Map p108; www.porvoonpaahtimo.fi; Mannerheiminkatu 2; ⊙10am-midnight Sun-Thu, to 3am Fri & Sat) On the main bridge, this atmospheric red-brick former storehouse is an ideal spot for drinks of any kind, whether house-roasted coffee or beers on tap. There's a terrace and boat deck.

ℹ️ Information

Tourist Office (Map p108; ☑ 040-489-9801; www.visitporvoo.fi; Läntinen Aleksanterinkatu 1; ⊙9am-6pm Mon-Fri, 11am-4pm Sat; 🗟) Offers maps and local information in the Taidetehdas (Art Factory) building across the river.

Porvoo

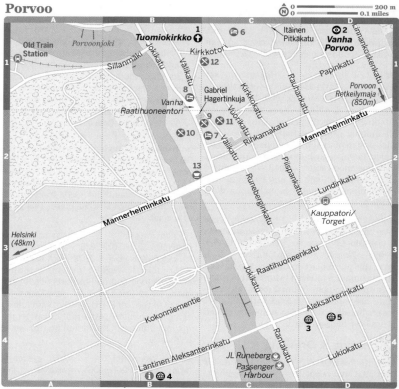

Porvoo

◉ Top Sights
1 Tuomiokirkko..B1
2 Vanha Porvoo D1

◉ Sights
3 Runebergin Koti...................................D4
4 Taidetehdas...B4
5 Walter Runeberg Sculpture
   Collection D4

🛏 Sleeping
6 Hotelli Onni...C1
7 Hotelli Pariisin Ville C2
8 Ida-Maria B1

✕ Eating
9 Cafe Postres C2
10 Fryysarinranta B2
11 Helmi Tea & Coffee House.................C2
   Meat District ....(see 9)
12 Wanha Laamanni C1

🍷 Drinking & Nightlife
13 Porvoon Paahtimo B2

❶ Getting There & Away

Buses travel between Porvoo **bus station** (Map p108; Kauppatori) and Helsinki's Kamppi every 30 minutes or so (€9 to €15, one hour). There are also frequent buses to/from towns further east.

The noble old steamship **JL Runeberg** (Map p108; ☏ 019-524-3331; www.msjlruneberg.fi; ⏱ Tue, Wed, Fri & Sat mid-May–early Sep, plus Sun Jun-Aug & Mon Jul) cruises from Helsinki's kauppatori to Porvoo's **passenger harbour** (Map p108) in summer (one way/return €27/39) and makes an excellent day trip, with various lunch options available. The trip takes 3½ hours each way, so you may prefer to return by bus.

Loviisa

☏ 019 / POP 15,300

Named for Swedish queen Lovisa Ulrika in 1752, Loviisa (Swedish: Lovisa) had its glory days as a Russian spa town in the 19th century. Like many of the towns along this stretch of coast, it was a pawn in Russo-Swedish conflicts, most devastatingly in 1855, when much of it burnt down. Only a vestige of the Old Town survives.

Today it's a sweet, sleepy summer resort – a popular stop for boaters and other holiday-makers, who explore the 18th-century sea fortress and wander among the boutiques and galleries in Laivasilta. Out of season, the place hibernates and little is open.

The street leading down to **Laivasilta Marina** is lined with picturesque red wood-en salt warehouses, now converted into restaurants, boutiques and art galleries, as well as the **Merenkulkumuseo** (Maritime Mu-seum; www.laivasilta.fi; Laivasilta 8; adult/child €3/free; ☉10am-5pm Sat & Sun May, daily Jun-Aug). From June to August, the place is buzzing with boaters and other visitors enjoying the atmospheric waterfront.

Svartholma Sea Fortress   FORTRESS
(https://visitsvartholm.fi; tours adult/child €6/3; ☉museum noon-6pm Wed-Sun mid-Jun–mid-Aug) **FREE** Situated 10km offshore from Loviisa, this four-bastion fortress was built in 1748 to protect against further Russian invasion after Swedish losses in eastern Finland. It lasted until the Crimean War (1853–56), when it was largely destroyed by the British. The reconstructed fortress is a fabulous place to explore, and you can learn more at the free museum. There's an on-site cafe.

A **waterbus** (☎050-010-2111; https://visit svartholm.fi; Laivasilta; ☉10.10am, 11.30am, 12.50pm, 2.10pm, 3.30pm & 4.50pm Wed-Sun mid-Jun–mid-Aug) runs from Laivasilta Marina (adult/child return €18/9, 35 minutes; cash only). Alternatively, the beautiful replica 19th-century yacht **Österstjernan** (☎040-012-0929; www.osterstjernan.fi; Laivasilta 8; return trip €35) makes occasional trips.

Sibelius Festival   MUSIC
(☎019-555-555; www.loviisansibeliuspaivat.fi; tick-ets €20-25) Loviisa's biggest annual event is in early September, when the Sibelius Festi-val features a long weekend of performances of the national composer's music.

Saltbodan   FINNISH €€
(http://saltbodan.fi; Laivasilta 4; mains lunch €12-16, dinner €15-24; ☉kitchen 10am-10pm May-Sep) While away a summer evening at this smart cafe-restaurant serving Finnish favourites in an atmospheric old storehouse on Laivasilta Marina. The place is famous for its salmon soup, fresh bread and homemade quiche.

Bistro Cantor   BISTRO €€
(☎040-135-5003; www.bistrocantor.fi; Mariankatu 1; mains €14-20; ☉11am-2pm & 5-9pm Mon-Thu, 11am-2pm & 5-10pm Fri, noon-10pm Sat, noon-4pm Sun) Just up the road from the marina, this art nouveau building is a classy backdrop for contemporary dishes like sage-stuffed chick-en breast wrapped in air-dried ham, and New York cheesecake with rhubarb coulis.

ⓘ Information

Tourist Office (☎040-555-3387; www.visitloviisa.fi; Mariankatu 12A; ☉10am-4pm Mon-Fri year-round, plus 10am-2pm Sat & Sun mid-Jun–Aug)

ⓘ Getting There & Around

Frequent buses serve the following destinations:

Helsinki €17.80, 1½ to two hours

Kotka €10, 50 minutes

Porvoo €10, 45 minutes

A **waterbus** (p109) runs from Laivasilta Marina to Svartholma Sea Fortress.

Rent bicycles from **Sunny Bikes** (☎019-50561; http://sunnybikes.fi; Brandensteininkatu 17; 12/24hr €8/12), inside the Dagerby Hotel.

Kotka

☑05 / POP 54,300

About 130km east of Helsinki, Kotka is Fin-land's only city set on an island. In Kotka's early days, the Kymijoki provided a critical transport route for logging and rich waters for fishing, so the city developed as a port. Nowadays it's one of Finland's most impor-tant industrial ports.

Celebrating these seafaring roots, Kotka boasts several superb sea-focused attrac-tions, most notably the Merikeskus Vellamo. The islands of the nearby archipelago, with their quaint villages and salty breezes, make for an appealing day trip. On dry land, Kotka has spruced up its city centre with parks and public art to make itself more of a holiday destination. But this hard-working port can't shake its inherent grittiness – which lends it an appealing authenticity.

◎ Sights

★**Merikeskus Vellamo**   MUSEUM
(Vellamo Maritime Centre; Map p110; ☎040-350-0497; www.merikeskusvellamo.fi; Torna-torintie 99; adult/child €10/free, Tarmo extra €5; ☉10am-5pm Tue-Sun, to 8pm Wed) In a tanker-sized, wave-shaped building with walls of

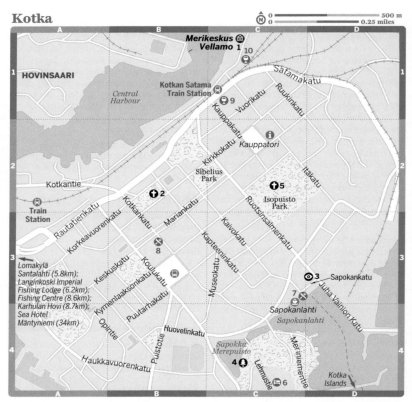

Kotka

◉ Top Sights
   1 Merikeskus Vellamo C1

◉ Sights
   2 Kotkan Kirkko B2
   3 Maretarium D3
   4 Sapokka Vesipuisto C4
   5 St Nicholas Orthodox Church C2

⊜ Sleeping
   6 Kesähotelli Katarina C4

⊗ Eating
     Laakonki .... (see 1)
   7 Tulikukko C3
   8 Vausti B3

⊖ Drinking & Nightlife
   9 Kairo C1
   10 Päätepysäkki C1

metal and printed glass, this state-of-the-art dockside museum recounts Finland's seafaring life. The star exhibit is the *Tarmo*, the world's third-oldest ice-breaker (1908), which ploughed Finnish waters until it was retired in 1970. There are also exhibitions on shipwrecks, navigation, fishing and logging. The boat hall contains many prizes, including an Olympic-winning 49er and a boat that belonged to the Moomins' creator, Tove Jansson. Look for the artifacts and dive simulation from the famous 'art wreck' *Vrouw Maria*, which was found in 1999.

Sapokka Vesipuisto   PARK
(Sapokka Water Garden; Map p110; www.kotka.fi/parks; Tallinnankatu 11) FREE Sapokanlahti is a natural inlet in central Kotka that provides the setting for the tranquil, award-winning Sapokka Water Garden. The centrepiece is the human-made waterfall, created with piped-in sea water that cascades over the rocks. This beauty

is surrounded by abundant native plants and flowers, with a dozen bronze animal sculptures frolicking nearby.

Maretarium
AQUARIUM

(Map p110; ☑ 040-311-0330; www.maretarium.fi; Sapokankatu 2; adult/child €12.50/6.50; ⊙ 10am-7pm Jun-Aug, noon-7pm Wed, 10am-5pm Thu-Sun Sep-May) Kotka's modern Maretarium has more than 20 giant fish tanks representing various bodies of water. The Baltic tank is the largest, with local sea life fed regularly by a diver (check the online calendar for weekly feeding times). Water is piped in from the sea to maintain the natural life cycle of the fish, so salmon spawn in autumn and freakish eelpout reproduce in winter.

Kotkan Saaret
ISLANDS

(Kotka Islands; ☑ 044-055-7499; www.kotkansaaret. fi) The smattering of islands off the coast of Kotka are former military outposts, some of which are now open to the public. Several boat trips depart from Sapokanlahti (Sapokka harbour; Map p110). From June to August, the MS *Klippan* (adult/child €8/4) runs hourly to Varissaari, where there are the remains of an 18th-century naval fortress. In July and August, the MS *Jaana* (adult/child €20/10) makes the 45-minute journey to the island of Rankki, returning 2½ hours later.

Accessible by free public ferry (from May to September), Kirkonmaa still contains a battery and military housing, set amid beautiful nature. All three islands have a summer cafe and other recreational facilities.

St Nicholas Orthodox Church
CHURCH

(Map p110; ⊙ noon-3pm Tue-Fri, to 6pm Sat & Sun Jun-Aug) Towering above Isopuisto Park, the 1801 church is Kotka's only building to survive the Crimean War. It's believed to be the work of architect Yakov Perrini, who designed the St Petersburg Admiralty.

Kotkan Kirkko
CHURCH

(Kotka Church; Map p110; ☑ 05-225-9250; Kirkkokatu 26; ⊙ noon-6pm Sun-Thu Jun-Aug) Kotkan Kirkko's distinctive steeple is visible throughout town. Inside the neo-Gothic church there's artful woodcarving, a resounding baroque-style organ and a beautiful altarpiece.

🏃 Activities

The Kymijoki is one of Finland's best fishing rivers – for detailed information, visit www. lohikeskuskotka.fi. The Fishing Centre (☑ 05-281-288; www.fishingcenter.fi; Kymijoentie

WORTH A TRIP

MALMGÅRD BREWERY

Situated 23km northwest of Loviisa, this 500-hectare estate, **Malmgård** (http:// malmgard.fi; Malmgård 53, Forsby; ⊙ bar & shop 10am-4pm Tue-Thu, to 6pm Fri, 11-4pm Sat & Sun), has been owned by the Creutz family since 1614 (current owner Count Johan Creutz is the 12th generation). Its brewery's all-organic beers and ciders are produced using local spring water and the estate's own hydro-power; you can see the brewing process in action through the viewing window in the bar.

55; fishing-gear rental per day from €20; ⊙ 11am-6.30pm Mon-Fri, to 3pm Sat) rents gear and sells permits (prices depend on where you plan to fish and what you plan to catch). Fishing trips to the nearby Kymijoki rapids or out to the Kuutsalo archipelago can be arranged. Langinkoski Imperial Fishing Lodge (p132) is popular for fly-fishing.

🎉 Festivals & Events

Kotkan Meripäivät
SAILING

(Kotka Maritime Festival; ☑ 040-635-1764; www. meripaivat.com; ⊙ mid-Jul) Kotka's seafaring heritage is celebrated with a regatta, concerts, markets and a huge wooden-boat show.

🛌 Sleeping

Lomakylä Santalahti
RESORT €

(Santalahti Holiday Resort; ☑ 05-260-5055; www. santalahti.fi; Santalahdentie 150, Mussalo; tent sites €19, cottage d/q €83/94, apt €190; 🛜 🏊) On the island of Mussalo, Santalahti has a huge range of cottages and shaded campsites. Shoreline and forest nature trails (each 2.5km long) weave through the property. Bikes and stand-up paddle boards are available for hire. Don't miss the unique 'cave sauna', a smoke sauna in a natural cave facing the glorious sea. Santalahti is 5km west of central Kotka. The resort offers a shuttle bus (adult/child €3.50/2.20), which runs into town up to three times a day in season.

Kesähotelli Katarina
HOSTEL €

(Katarina Summer Hotel; Map p110; ☑ 050-913-5763; www.kesahotellikatarina.net; Lehmustie 4; s/tw/f €50/70/80; ⊙ early Jun-early Aug) The hilltop location can be a tough walk, but rooms here are clean and bright with desk and TV. It's good-value accommodation in a town with limited choices.

WORTH A TRIP

LANGINKOSKI IMPERIAL FISHING LODGE

Situated 5km north of Kotka amid the salmon-rich Kymijoki's rapids, this rustic wooden **lodge** (☑05-211-1600; www. langinkoskimuseo.com; Keisarinmajantie 118; adult/child €6/3, nature reserve free; ⊙10am-4pm May & Sep, to 6pm Jun-Aug) was built in 1889 for Tsar Alexander III. Most of the furniture is original and rooms look much as they did when he was a frequent summertime visitor. The riverside forest setting is beautiful.From Kotka, take bus 12, 13, 14 or 15 to Karvuhuori and get off on Langinkoskentie, east of the bridge (€3.50, 15 minutes).

★**Karhulan Hovi**   HISTORIC HOTEL €€
(Karhula Manor Hotel; ☑044-055-7493; www.karhu lanhovi.fi; Ahlströmintie 26; d €119-179, without bathroom €79-99, ste from €260; 🛜) Surrounded by sprawling gardens that run down to the river, this magnificent 1891 French-style estate splits its 20 rooms between the period-furnished manor house, the guesthouse and the smaller garden cottage. Rooms are spacious and elegant, while the staff's friendly, attentive service guarantees that guests can fully appreciate their beautiful environs.

✖ Eating

Tulikukko   CAFE €
(Map p110; www.tulikukko.fi; Sapokankatu 3; dishes €3-10; ⊙7am-10pm Mon-Sat, 9am-9pm Sun) Pies, pastries, salads and sandwiches are all excellent at this waterside cafe, but the highlight is the dazzling array of cakes.

★**Vausti**   FINNISH €€
(Map p110; www.kotkanravintolat.fi; Keskuskatu 33; mains €16-32; ⊙11am-10pm Mon-Fri, 3-11pm Sat) Kotka's finest dining is at charcoal-hued Vausti, attached to Kotka's concert hall. The seasonal menu highlights local produce. Vegetarians are looked after with dishes such as grilled cauliflower 'steak' with cider sauce.

Laakonki   FINNISH €€
(Map p110; www.kotkanravintolat.fi; Tornatorintie 99; lunch weekday/weekend €12.50/19.50; ⊙10am-5pm Tue-Sun, to 8pm Wed) The cafe inside the Merikeskus Vellamo (p109) is excellent – worth a lunch stop even if you're not visiting the museum itself. The lunch buffet always includes two main courses, with plenty of accommodation for special diets.

🍷 Drinking & Nightlife

Päätepysäkki   BAR
(Map p110; www.facebook.com/paatepysakki; Tornatorintie 96; ⊙noon-8pm May-Sep) Kotka's quirkiest bar is this 1950s railway carriage attached to a steam locomotive, with great cocktails and beer on tap.

Kairo   PUB
(Map p110; www.ravintolakairo.fi; Satamakatu 7; ⊙5-10pm Tue-Thu, to 4am Fri & Sat) A legendary sailors' boozer, right down to the ships' flags and saucy paintings, with live music and a great terrace. The rules state that if someone asks you to dance, you can't turn them down!

ℹ Information

Tourist Office (Map p110; ☑040-135-6588; www.visitkotkahamina.fi; Keskuskatu 6; ⊙10am-6pm Mon-Fri year-round, plus 10am-3pm Sat Jun-late Aug)

ℹ Getting There & Away

BUS

Frequent services from the **bus station** (Map p110) include the following:
Hamina €6.80, 45 minutes
Helsinki €23, 2½ hours
Loviisa €10.70, 50 minutes
Porvoo €15, 1½ hours

TRAIN

Trains stop at both Kotka train station, 400m northwest of the city centre, and the more convenient **Kotkan Satama** (Kotka port) station, near the Merikeskus Vellamo museum. Trains run to Kouvola (€7, 45 minutes, six daily), which has connecting trains to all major Finnish cities.

Hamina

☑05 / POP 20,800

Located just 40km from the Russian border, Hamina has long been a military town. The town was founded in 1653 as a Swedish outpost, but it was largely destroyed during the Great Northern War. After Vyborg fell to Russia, Swedish king Frederick I began to rebuild the town in 1722, renaming it Fredrikshamn (as it's still known in Swedish today). At this time, construction began on the star-shaped fortifications and the circular Old Town, all designed by Axel Löwen. Alas, the fortress did not prevent Hamina's capture in 1743, and the town returned to Russian hands.

⊙ Sights & Activities

Hamina Bastioni RUINS
(Hamina Bastion; www.haminabastioni.fi) The ruins of the 18th-century Hamina Bastion include 3km of crumbling stone walls that would have made a star-shaped fortress. The bastion comes alive for the annual Hamina Tattoo (p113). At other times, it's an evocative and atmospheric spot, whispering of eras past. Pick up a free copy of *Walking in Old Hamina* from the tourist office.

**Orthodox Church of
Sts Peter & Paul** CHURCH
(Raatihuoneentori 2; ⊙noon-4pm Tue-Sun Jun-Aug) Topped by a classic onion dome, the 1837 Orthodox Church of Sts Peter & Paul is the work of architect Louis Visconti, who designed Napoleon's mausoleum.

Meriset BOATING
(📱040-090-2494; www.meriset.fi; Tullimakasiininranta; adult/child €25/10; ⊙mid-May–late Aug) Boats run from Tervasaari guest harbour to the old fishing village on the island of Tammio and further south to Ulko-Tammio, within the boundaries of the Eastern Gulf of Finland National Park.

✦ Festivals & Events

Hamina Tattoo MUSIC
(📱040-199-1426; www.visithamina.fi; tickets €25-55; ⊙late Jul/early Aug) Every even-numbered year, Hamina celebrates military music during the week-long Hamina Tattoo. Concerts are held at the Bastion, in Kesäpuisto Park and on 'Tattoo St' (Fredrikinkatu).

🛏 Sleeping & Eating

**Hamina Camping
Pitkät Hiekat** CAMPGROUND €
(📱040-151-3446; www.hamina-camping.fi; Vilniementie 375, Vilniemi; tent sites €14 plus per person €4, cottages €50-80; ⊙May-Sep) In Vilniemi, 7km south of Hamina, this beachside spot is surrounded by quiet forest, with free rowing boats, sauna and laundry. Cottages have kitchenettes but no bathrooms.

Spa Hotel Hamina HOTEL €€
(📱05-353-5555; www.spahotelhamina.fi; Sibeliuskatu 32; s/d/f €118/127/170; 🅿@🛜⊗) Conveniently located between the bus station

HIDDEN HAVEN
....
A little piece of Finnish paradise, **Sea Hotel Mäntyniemi** (📱05-353-3100; www.hotelmantyniemi.fi; Mäntyniementie 268, Siltakylä; s €79, d €89-98, f €126-136; 🛜⊗) is family-run haven sitting on a secluded forested island (linked by bridges) between Loviisa (35km) and Kotka (32km). The best of the 28 rooms have balconies overlooking the islet-strewn sea. Fantastic facilities include a traditional smoke sauna, an excellent restaurant, and free use of boats, bikes and fishing gear. You won't want to leave.

and the Old Town, this hotel has spa facilities including swimming pool, lap pool, hot tub, sauna and fitness centre. The 31 hardwood-floored rooms are plain but comfortable. Rates drop at weekends.

Konditoria A Huovila CAFE €
(📱05-344-0930; www.elisanet.fi/konditoria.huovila.oy; Fredrikinkatu 1; dishes €2-4.50; ⊙8am-5pm Mon-Fri, to 1pm Sat) Fêted for its berry pies, this traditional cafe has been a Hamina favourite since 1966.

Kamu! INTERNATIONAL €€
(📱044-728-0175; www.ravintolakamu.fi; Raatihuoneenkatu 12; mains €18-28; ⊙11am-9pm Mon-Thu, to 10pm Fri & Sat; 🛜) 🍴 The menu offers Finnish favourites with fortified flair, such as 'Löwen's flamed salmon' (smoked salmon; named after the general who started construction of the fortress) and 'gunpowder-cellar potshot steak' (beef tenderloin in horseradish-brandy sauce).

ℹ Information

Tourist Office (📱040-199-1330; www.visitkotkahamina.fi; Sibeliuskatu 32; ⊙9am-5pm Mon-Fri year-round, plus 10am-3pm Sat & Sun early Jun-late Aug) In the Spa Hotel Hamina.

ℹ Getting There & Away

Frequent local buses link Hamina with Kotka (€6.80, 45 minutes). Long-distances buses go to Helsinki (€25, 2½ hours, five daily).

If you have a Russian visa, you can catch a Sovavto (http://bus.sovavto.ru) bus to Vyborg (2½ hours, €15) or St Petersburg (6½ hours, €18).

Åland Archipelago

Includes ➡

Fasta Åland 117
Mariehamn 117
Hammarland 122
Eckerö 123
Geta 124
Sund 125
Vårdö 126
Lemland 127
Lumparland 128
Northern & Southern
Archipelagos 128

Why Go?

Glorious Åland Archipelago is a geopolitical anomaly: it is Finnish owned and Swedish speaking, but it has its own parliament, flies its own blue, gold and red flag, issues its own stamps and uses its own web suffix: 'dot ax'. Its 'special relationship' with the EU means it can sell duty free and make its own gambling laws.

Åland is the sunniest spot in northern Europe and its sweeping white-sand beaches and flat, scenic cycling routes attract crowds of holidaymakers during summer. Yet outside the lively capital, Mariehamn, a sleepy haze hangs over the islands' tiny villages: finding your own remote beach among the 6500 skerries (rocky islets) is surprisingly easy. A lattice of bridges and free cable ferries connects the central islands, while larger car ferries run to the archipelago's outer reaches.

Best Places to Eat

➡ Smakbyn (p126)
➡ Indigo (p120)
➡ Bodegan (p124)
➡ Café Kvarnen (p130)
➡ Pub Niska (p120)

Best Places to Stay

➡ Degersands Resort (p124)
➡ HavsVidden (p124)
➡ Sandösunds Camping (p126)
➡ Hotel Elvira (p124)
➡ Kvarnbo Gästhem (p125)

When to Go
Aland Archipelago

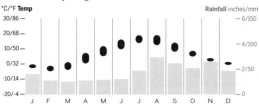

Jun Celebrate the barely-setting sun and dance around the decorated Midsummer poles.

Jul Experience Åland's most festive season, with music and cultural events all month long.

Sep Feast on the bounty of the island, especially at the Åland Skördefesten (Harvest Festival).

Åland Archipelago Highlights

❶ Ro-No Rent (p119)
Cycling the archipelago's flat, well-marked routes alongside green fields, red granite and sparkling seascapes.

❷ Bomarsund Fortress (p126) Running the ramparts of the cannonball-scarred ruins, then cooling off with a beach dip.

❸ Käringsund Harbour (p123) Hiking the trails, climbing the rocks or just enjoying a meal while overlooking this postcard-worthy scene in Eckerö.

❹ Pommern (p117)
Climbing aboard the four-masted barque moored outside Mariehamn's state-of-the-art maritime museum.

❺ Stallhagen Brewery (p128) Catching some rays and sipping a seasonal special on the terrace at this Finström gastropub.

❻ Kastelholms Slott (p125) Exploring this magnificent 14th-century castle and other historic buildings at the nearby

Jan Karlsgårdens open-air museum.

❼ Sjökvarteret (p118)
Admiring the handiwork of shipbuilders and artisans in Mariehamn's atmospheric maritime quarter.

❽ Sandösunds (p126)
Kayaking around Vårdö's islets of rustling birches and rippling bays.

❾ Smakbyn (p126)
Sampling Åland's bounty in Kastelholm near Sund, as prepared by culinary master Micke.

History

More than a hundred Bronze and Iron Age *fornminne* (burial sites) have been discovered across the Åland Archipelago, attesting to over 6000 years of human habitation. Though all are clearly signposted, most are in fairly nondescript fields. The discovery of fortress ruins confirms that the archipelago was an important harbour and trading centre during the Viking era.

During the Great Northern War of 1700–21 (dubbed the 'Great Wrath'), most Ålanders fled to Sweden. Further Russian incursions took place in the 1740s and 1809. When Finland gained independence in 1917, many Ålanders lobbied to be incorporated into Sweden, but Finland refused to give up the archipelago. The dispute concluded in 1921, when Åland was given its status as an autonomous, demilitarised and neutral municipality within Finland by a decision of the League of Nations. Åland joined the EU in 1995 but was granted a number of exemptions, including duty-free tax laws that allow ferry services to mainland Finland and Sweden to operate profitably.

Today peaceful Åland is divided into 16 municipalities, 10 on 'Fasta Åland' (the main group of larger islands). The other six municipalities cover the far-flung archipelago and its multitude of tiny islands.

🎉 Festivals & Events

Ålands Sjödagar CULTURAL
(www.alandssjodagar.ax; ⊙ mid-Jul) Åland's maritime history is celebrated at Sjökvarteret (p118) with boat races, folk music and short sailing tours on the schooner *Albanus*.

Viking Market CULTURAL
(www.fibula.ax; ⊙ late Jul) The best chance to see Åland's Viking heritage is at Saltvik's annual Viking Market, a three-day festival of feasting, drinking and costumed merrymaking in Kvarnbo. There's also the opportunity to sail on an authentic Viking ship.

Rockoff MUSIC
(www.rockoff.nu; 1-/9-day pass €30/90; ⊙ last week Jul) Nine days of Swedish pop and rock bands on the Mariehamn Torget (central square).

Skördefesten FOOD & DRINK
(Harvest Festival; ⊙ 3rd weekend Sep) Hosted by farms, restaurants and food producers around the island, this festival celebrates the local bounty with open farms and special restaurant menus.

ℹ️ Information

EMERGENCY

General emergency number ⌂ 112
Local police ⌂ 018-527-100
Medical services ⌂ 018-538-500

MONEY

The currency is the euro, but most places accept Swedish krona.

POST

Mail sent in Åland must have (highly collectable) Åland postage stamps.

TOURIST INFORMATION

Aland.ax (www.aland.ax) Official website of the government of Åland.

Aland.com (www.aland.com) Reams of information about local events, culture and more.

Ålandsresor (⌂ 018-28040; www.alandsresor. fi) Online booking for accommodation and tours.

Visit Åland (Ålands Turistinformation; Map p118; ⌂ 018-24000; www.visitaland.com; Storagatan 8; ⊙ 9am-6pm early Jun-Aug, to 4pm Apr, May & Sep, to 4pm Mon-Fri Oct-Mar; 🖥️) Helpful tourist office in Mariehamn.

ℹ️ Getting There & Away

AIR

Åland's **airport** (www.finavia.fi; Flygfältsvägen 67) is 4km northwest of Mariehamn. NextJet (www.nextjet.se) flies twice daily to/from Stockholm-Arlanda and once daily to/from Turku (both 30 minutes, from €95 return). Finnair (www.finnair.com) operates a flight between Mariehamn and Helsinki.

There are no regular buses from the airport. In the terminal there's a free hotline to order a taxi.

BOAT

Several car ferries serve the Åland mainland:

Eckerö Linjen (⌂ 018-28000; www.eckero linjen.ax) Branches at **Mariehamn** (Map p118; ⌂ 018-28000; www.eckerolinjen.ax; Torggatan 2; ⊙ 8.30am-5pm Mon-Fri) and **Eckerö** (⌂ 018-28300; www.eckerolinjen.ax; Berghamn). Sails from Eckerö to Grisslehamn, Sweden (adult/car €4.50/15, two hours).

Finnlink (www.finnlines.com) Serves Långnäs, Lumparland, from Naantali, Finland, and Kapellskär, Sweden.

Tallink/Silja Lines (Map p118; ⌂ 018-16179; www.tallinksilja.com; Västrahamnen; ⊙ 9.30am-5pm Mon-Fri) Runs direct services to Mariehamn from Turku (adult/car €11/23, five hours), Helsinki (€25/55, 12 hours) and Stockholm (€11/23, six hours). Ferries also run to Långnäs, Lumparland, from Stockholm (€23/45, 5½ hours) and Turku (€23/71, five hours).

Viking Line (Map p118; ⌂ 018-26211; www. vikingline.fi; Storagatan 3; ⊙ 9am-6pm Mon-Fri) Ferries to Mariehamn from Turku (adult/car €16/15, five hours), Helsinki (€30/36, 11 hours), Stockholm (€15/19, 5½ hours) and Kapellskär (€10/12, two hours). Ferries also link Långnäs,

Lumparland, with Turku (adult/car €29/40, five hours) and Stockholm (€29/10, 5½ hours).

It's also possible to reach the Northern and Southern Archipelagos from Fasta Åland. From Lumparland there are regular ferries to Föglö and on to Kumlinge or Kökar. From Vårdö, ferries run to Kumlinge and on to Brändö.

ℹ Getting Around

BICYCLE
Ro-No Rent (p119) has bicycles available near Mariehamn harbour. Many campgrounds and guest harbours also have bike hire.

Green-and-white signs trace cycling routes through the islands. Routes generally follow smaller, less busy roads; dedicated bicycle paths run parallel to some main roads.

BOAT
Three kinds of inter-island ferry serve the islands. For short trips, free vehicle ferries sail nonstop. There's also one private summer bicycle ferry running between Hammarland and Geta.

For longer routes – namely to the outer islands – ferries run to a schedule, which is available **online** (p121). These ferries are generally free for foot passengers, but you must buy tickets for bicycles or cars.

BUS
Five main bus lines depart from Mariehamn's **regional bus station** (p121).
Bus 1 Hammarland and Eckerö
Bus 2 Godby and Geta
Bus 3 Godby and Saltvik
Bus 4 Godby, Sund and Vårdö (Hummelvik)
Bus 5 Lemland and Lumparland (Långnäs)

Tickets from Mariehamn to the ferry ports cost around €4.50. Bicycles can be carried (space permitting) for €8.

FASTA ÅLAND

The core of the Åland Archipelago is a dozen or so larger islands that are connected by bridges. Known as Fasta Åland (Ahvenanmaa in Finnish), this 'mainland' comprises 70% of the archipelago's land area – including its only town. It's also home to 90% of Åland's population. Fasta Åland offers more historical sites, cultural attractions and recreational activities than any other island – as well as receiving the vast majority of tourists.

Åland's capital is Mariehamn, on the southern edge of the mainland. From this urban centre the islands stretch north, west and east, connected by bridges but still sprawling across the Archipelago Sea. This means that even the Fasta can feel like a remote island. If that's what you're going for, it's easy to find a quiet corner, surrounded by nature and sea but still within striking distance of the capital.

Mariehamn
🔊 018 / POP 11,470

The capital of Åland, Mariehamn was christened by Alexander II after the Empress Maria, and its broad streets lined with linden trees recall its Russian heritage. Nowadays it's a bustling, touristy place – home to parks, museums, minigolf, hotels, restaurants, bars, clubs, shops, galleries and more. During summer, visitors flood the bike paths, tour boats and pavement cafes. The calendar is packed with music festivals and cultural fairs, and folks stay out all night soaking up the midnight sun.

Of course, it's not all fun and games in the archipelago's only city. Two out of every five Ålanders live and work in Mariehamn, and Åland's parliament and government are also here. In summer, however, this workaday world fades into the background as holidaymakers take over the town.

⊙ Sights

★ **Sjöfartsmuseum** MUSEUM
(Maritime Museum; Map p118; www.sjofartsmuseum.ax; Hamngatan 2; adult/child incl Museumship Pommern €10/6; ⊙10am-5pm Jun-Aug, 11am-4pm Sep-May) Preserved boats make up most of the exhibitions at this state-of-the-art museum exploring Åland's marine heritage. In fact, the centrepiece is a reproduction of a ship, complete with mast, saloon, galley and cabins. The museum is a great place to discover your inner pirate, with plenty of ships in bottles, sea chests and accoutrements. Anchored outside is the **Museumship Pommern** (Map p118; Sjopromenaden; adult/child incl Sjöfartsmuseum €10/6; ⊙10am-5pm Jun-Aug, 11am-4pm Sep & May), a beautiful 1903-built four-masted merchant barque that plied the trade route between Australia and England. Also here is Mariehamn's top restaurant, Nautical (p120).

Sankt Göran's Kyrka CHURCH
(Map p118; www.mariehamn.evl.ax; Östra Esplanadgatan 6; ⊙10am-6pm Mon-Fri, to 3pm Sat mid-Jun–Aug) The copper-roofed Sankt Göran's Kyrka, built in 1927, is one of the island's few modern churches. Its art nouveau style was conceived by Lars Sonck, who grew up in Åland. Look for the art nouveau flourishes painted on the ceiling and brilliant stained

Mariehamn

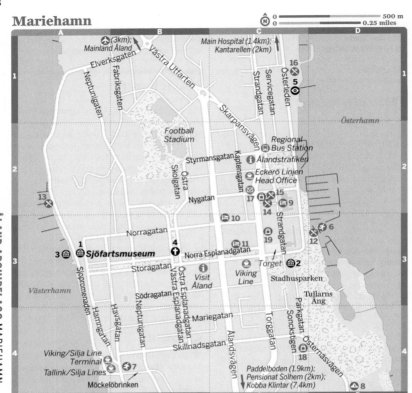

glass windows by Bruno Tuukkanen. The highlight of the interior is the glittering mosaic altarpiece, also by Tuukkanen.

Sjökvarteret
WATERFRONT, MUSEUM

(Maritime quarter; Map p118; ☑018-16033; www. sjokvarteret.com; Österleden 110; museum adult/ child €4/free; ⊙museum 10am-4pm Mon-Fri, 11am-3pm Sat & Sun mid-Jun–mid-Aug, 9.30am-4pm Tue-Thu May–mid-Jun) At the northern end of Österhamn, Sjökvarteret has long been devoted to boat building. You can stroll along the atmospheric quay, lined with traditional schooners, and perhaps see boats under construction. The **museum**, with exhibitions on shipbuilding (no English information), is located in a small timber boat shed. Don't miss the tiny reconstructed **seafarers' chapel** at the end of the pier.

Ålands Kulturhistoriska & Konstmuseum
MUSEUM, GALLERY

(Cultural History Museum & Art Museum of Åland; Map p118; www.museum.ax; Storagatan 1; adult/ child €8/5; ⊙10am-5pm May-Sep, 11am-5pm Tue-Sun Oct-Apr) After a recent renovation, these side-by-side museums offer an informative perspective on Åland's culture, past and present. The Konstmuseum showcases Åland art from the 20th and 21st centuries, with plenty of special exhibits. Kulturhistoriska focuses on the archipelago's historical development, from the arrival of the first seal hunters through the Age of Empire (Swedish and Russian) and its unique autonomous status in the last century. Artefacts exemplify the continuity and change of day-to-day life through the centuries.

🏃 Activities

Fiskelyckan
FISHING

(☑0457-342-0538; www.fiskelyckan.ax; per person half/full day €70/100) Åland native Bo-Erik Westberg specialises in pike, perch, trout and whitefish fishing, plus ice fishing in winter. Prices include all equipment, coffee and

Mariehamn

◎ Top Sights
1 Sjöfartsmuseum................................... A3

◎ Sights
2 Ålands Kulturhistoriska &
   Konstmuseum.................................... C3
3 Museumship Pommern........................ A3
4 Sankt Göran's Kyrka........................... B3
5 Sjökvarteret C1

◎ Activities, Courses & Tours
6 Ro-No Rent... D3
7 Ro-No Rent... B4

◎ Sleeping
8 Gröna Udden Camping........................ D4
9 Hotell Arkipelag.................................. C2
10 Hotell Pommern C3
11 Park Alandia Hotel C3

◎ Eating
12 Ångbåts Bryggan................................. D3
13 ÅSS Paviljongen................................... A2
14 Bagarstugan Cafe & Vin...................... C2
15 Indigo... C2
   Kvarter 5 ....(see 10)
   Nautical..(see 1)
16 Pub Niska...C1

◎ Drinking & Nightlife
   Dino's Bar & Grill...........................(see 15)

◎ Shopping
   Guldviva ....(see 5)
17 Jussis Keramik C2
18 Little BBQ's Junk Art........................... C4
   Salt...(see 5)
19 Torggatan 15 .... C3

snack. Day trips may also include a stop at Kobba Klintar lighthouse (p121). Westburg promises a 'generous' discount to families.

Paddelboden   WATER SPORTS
(Paddle Shop; ✎ 0457-343-3933; www.paddel boden.com; Lerviksmåbåtshamn; per 2hr/day single kayak €35/50, double €60/90, SUP €30/50; ☉ 10am-3pm mid-Jun–mid-Aug, plus by appointment) Rent a kayak or stand-up paddleboard to explore the southern coast. Paddelboden is 2.5km south of town.

Ro-No Rent   OUTDOORS
(Map p118; ✎ 018-12820; www.rono.ax; Österhamn; ☉ 9am-6pm Jun–mid-Aug, by arrangement Sep–May) Ro-No rents out a variety of bicycles (€10/50 per day/week), kayaks (€80/150), small boats (that don't require a licence; €100/200 for four hours/day) and mopeds (which do; €60/180 per day/week) from its outlet at Österhamn. The smaller outlet at Västerhamn just has bicycles.

🛏 Sleeping

Gröna Udden Camping   CAMPGROUND €
(Map p118; ✎ 018-528-700; www.gronaudden. com; Östernäsvägen; tent sites €10 plus per adult €10, 2-/4-/6-person cabins €105/140/180; ☉ early May-early Sep; ☀) By the seaside, 15 minutes' stroll south of the city centre, this campground is a family favourite, so you'll need to book its fully equipped spruce cabins ahead. Outdoor fun includes a safe swimming beach, a minigolf course (admission €5) and bike hire (€15). Linen costs €8.50 per person.

Park Alandia Hotel   HOTEL €€
(Map p118; ✎ 018-14130; www.parkalandiahotel. com; Norra Esplanadgatan 3; s/d €120/150; @🛜☀) Recently revamped, all rooms at this sophisticated spot on the main boulevard now feature big windows, sandy hues and hardwood floors. There's a swimming pool and sauna, and a recommended restaurant with an irresistible terrace. Bonus: guests can borrow bikes for free.

Pensionat Solhem   GUESTHOUSE €€
(✎ 018-16322; www.visitaland.com/solhem; Lökskärsvägen 18; s/d without bathroom €50/80; ☉ May-Oct; 🛜) Travellers love the Solhem's seaside location, just 3km south of the city centre. The living isn't fancy at this affordable spot, with small twin beds and shared bathrooms. But bicycles, rowing boats and a sauna are available for guests, and the cheerful staff keep the place running like clockwork.

Hotell Pommern   HOTEL €€€
(Map p118; ✎ 018-15555; www.alandhotels.fi; Norragatan 8-10; s/d/q €165/175/205, Moomin r €225; 🛜☀☀) Centrally located, the Pommern has stylish, modern rooms and up-to-snuff service. Rooms range from the simple but comfortable 'classic' to more spacious 'superior' and family rooms. Families might also want to request one of the Moomin rooms, which feature the lovable troll family on bedding, dishes and decor.

Hotell Arkipelag   HOTEL €€€
(Map p118; ✎ 018-24020; www.hotellarkipelag. com; Strandgatan 35; s/d €150/180, with sea view

SHIPWRECKED CHAMPAGNE

Divers exploring an 1840s shipwreck off the coast of Föglö in 2010 raised 162 bottles of Champagne, the world's oldest. Two bottles were auctioned in 2011 for the princely sum of €54,000; you can see a couple more in the Ålands Kulturhistoriska (p118), along with some other artefacts and a model of the shipwreck.

The divers also retrieved five bottles of 19th-century corked beer. The contents were analysed by the Technical Research Centre of Finland (VTT), and the master brewers at Stallhagen Brewery (p128) re-created the original recipe, which makes for a light but refreshing ale. You can sample it at the brewery.

€180/210; ❄ @ 🛜 ⛱) High-class Arkipelag is popular with business visitors, though water views from the balconies are tempting for anyone. Rooms are large, with wooden floors, modern furnishings and minimalist decor. Super facilities include indoor and outdoor pools, a freshly refurbished sauna, a nightclub, a casino, three restaurants and several bars.

✕ Eating & Drinking

★ Pub Niska
PIZZA €

(Map p118; ☎ 018-19151; www.pubniska.com; Sjökvarteret; pizza €11.50-12.50; ⊙ 11am-7pm Mon-Sat, 3-9pm Sun May & Sep, 11am-9pm Jun-Aug) 🍽 Star chef Michael 'Micke' Björklund of Smakbyn (p126) is the brains behind this *plåtbröd* (Åland-style pizza) restaurant in the maritime quarter. Toppings are diverse and delicious, including favourites like cold-smoked salmon and horseradish cream. In true locavore spirit, the cheese is from Åland's dairy. The atmospheric interior feels like the inside of a ship, but the place to be is the glorious sunny terrace.

Bagarstugan Cafe & Vin
CAFE €

(Map p118; www.bagarstugan.ax; Ekonomiegatan 2; mains €6-15; ⊙ 10am-6pm Mon-Fri, to 4pm Sat Jun-Aug, 10am-5pm Mon-Fri, 11am-4pm Sat Sep-May) 🍽 This sweet cafe is set in a cosy house crowded with bookshelves, chandeliers and tile stoves. It's a charming backdrop for homemade soups, salads, quiches, pies and cakes (scattered with flower petals and far too pretty to eat!) made from local, often organic produce. The courtyard is a delight in summer.

★ Indigo
FINNISH €€

(Map p118; ☎ 018-16550; www.indigo.ax; Nygatan 1; lunch €12-13, dinner mains €23-33, courtyard summer mains €18-22; ⊙ 11am-10pm Mon-Sat year-round, plus 2-10pm Sun May-Aug) The building might be historic brick and timber, but the menu is contemporary, with expertly cooked dishes like grilled Åland beef with Béarnaise sauce and homemade fries. There's a buzzing summer courtyard and a beautiful loft space. It's a stylish spot for a drink, with late-night hours for the bar.

Kvarter 5
FINNISH €€€

(Map p118; ☎ 018-1555; www.kvarter5.ax; Norragatan 10; lunch buffet €12, dinner mains €17-33, 3-course tasting menu €38; ⊙ 7am-10.30pm Mon-Sat, 7.30am-9pm Sun) This newish spot has received rave reviews for its sophisticated Nordic cuisine, featuring local ingredients and made-from-scratch everything. The location – inside the Hotell Pommern (p119) – detracts a bit from the atmosphere, but service and cuisine are spot on.

Nautical
FINNISH €€€

(Map p118; ☎ 018-19931; www.nautical.ax; Hamngätan 2; mains lunch €12-16, dinner €34-41, 6-course tasting menu €79; ⊙ 11am-11pm Mon-Fri, 5pm-midnight Sat; 🛜) Taking its cue from its maritime-museum (p117) location, this spiffy marine-blue restaurant overlooking the western harbour and *Pommern* is decked out with a ship's wheel and has a splendid umbrella-shaded summer terrace. Sea-inspired dishes range from salmon tartare with horseradish and fennel to pan-fried Åland perch with caraway foam; land-based options include red-wine-braised oxtail with forest mushrooms.

Ångbåts Bryggan
BRASSERIE €€€

(Map p118; ☎ 018-17613; www.brasserie.ax; Östra Hamnen; mains €24-34; ⊙ 5pm-1am) In a prime harbourside location, this is a semi-swanky place with glass walls and marvellous sea views. The grill gets a workout, with starters and mains that include beef, seafood and even tempting veggie dishes. House cocktails, live music and dancing guarantee a festive atmosphere.

ÅSS Paviljongen
FINNISH €€€

(Map p118; ☎ 018-19141; www.paviljongen.ax; Västerhamn; pizza €11-14, mains €28-32; ⊙ 11am-10pm Mon-Fri, noon-10pm Sat & Sun May-Aug) Listen to boat masts clinking in Åland's yacht-club marina while you dine on creatively prepared local fare: Åland cod with smoked shrimp and horseradish, Parmesan-baked fillet of perch with pickled zucchini and gnocchi, or grilled veal with chilli Béarnaise sauce. The pizza menu is not quite as interesting, but it's still good.

Dino's Bar & Grill　　　　　　BAR
(Map p118; www.dinosbar.com; Strandgatan 12; ☺ noon-2am Sun-Thu, to 4am Fri & Sat) Housed in a classic 19th-century wooden house, Dino's is a cosy restaurant as well as a convivial drinking establishment and excellent music venue. In summer the outdoor tables and balcony overflow with revellers. There's live music most nights in summer and at weekends in winter.

🛍 Shopping

Torggatan 15　　　　　　ARTS & CRAFTS
(Map p118; Torggatan 15) This charming old wooden house is packed with treasures that show off the creativity and industry of Åland's arty and crafty types. There's a handful of shops tucked into the various rooms – each one enticing in its own way.

Salt　　　　　　ARTS & CRAFTS
(Map p118; www.salt.ax; Sjökvarteret; ☺10am-6pm Mon-Fri, to 4pm Sat, 11am-3pm Sun Jun-early Aug) In a red-brown timber shed in the maritime quarter, you can browse the work of local artists and artisans, including textiles, ceramics, silverware and jewellery. It also sells local delicacies such as sea-buckthorn jam.

Jussis Keramik　　　　　　GLASS, CERAMICS
(Map p118; www.jussiskeramik.fi; Nygatan 1; ☺10am-5pm Mon-Fri, to 4pm Sat) Watch the glass-blowers at their craft in this workshop turning out ceramics and glassware in a wide variety of bright colours.

Guldviva　　　　　　JEWELLERY
(Map p118; www.guldviva.com; Sjökvarteret; ☺10am-5pm Mon-Fri, to 2pm Sat late Jun–mid-Aug) Brooches, cufflinks and necklaces based on the islands' flora and fauna. Some incorporate Åland's red rapakivi granite.

Little BBQ's Junk Art　　　　　　ART, HOMEWARES
(Map p118; https://thelittlebbq.wordpress.com; Krokviksgränd 2) The concept is simple: Johan 'Joppan' Karlsson takes junk – old tools, appliances, sheet metal and other discarded stuff – and turns it into art. His speciality is sculptures of creatures of all shapes and sizes, but he has also created a wide variety of unique interior-design pieces, such as chandeliers, lamps and candle holders.

WORTH A TRIP

KOBBA KLINTAR

Since 1862 a beacon has shone out from this island, **Kobba Klintar** (☎0457-344-7179; www.kobbaklintarsvanner.ax; €10), south of Mariehamn. Nowadays, the original pilot cottage is dwarfed by a bigger and better house with foghorn. There's no longer a pilot at this station, so the renovated buildings are used for art exhibitions, literary events and jazz concerts. There's a summertime cafe and plenty of picturesque picnicking spots on the island. Kobba Klintar makes for a fascinating history lesson and a lovely day out on the water. It's a 20-minute boat ride from Mariehamn. If you don't have your own boat, you can catch a ride from Fiskelyckan (p118) or Shipland (p122).

❶ Information

Ålandsresor (p116) Handles hotel, guesthouse and cottage bookings for the entire archipelago. Also books tours.
Ålandstrafiken (Transportation Office; Map p118; ☎018-25600; www.alandstrafiken.ax; Styrmansgatan 1; ☺10am-5pm Mon-Fri) Information on buses and ferries around Åland, and Archipelago Ticket bookings.
Main Hospital (Ålands centralsjukhus; ☎018-5355; www.ahs.ax; Doktorsvägen 1, Sjukhusvägen) Has an emergency ward.
Main Post Office (Map p118; Torggatan 4; ☺9am-5pm Mon-Fri, 10.30am-1.30pm Sat)
　The Tourist Office (p116) is very helpful with region-wide info.

❶ Getting There & Away

The airport (p116) is 4km northwest of the city centre.
　Viking (p116) and Tallink/Silja (p116) ferries dock at the ferry terminal (Map p118) at Västerhamn (West Harbour). The guest harbour for small boats is at Österhamn (East Harbour).
　Eckerö Linjen (p116) ferries sail from Eckerö to Grisslehamn, Sweden (adult/car €4.50/15, two hours); buy tickets at this office in Mariehamn.
　Island buses depart from the **bus station** (Map p118; Styrmansgatan) opposite the post office; enquire at Visit Åland (p116) for timetables.

❶ Getting Around

Mariehamn is very walkable (and even more bikeable), but you may want to hire a car to explore other parts of the archipelago. The friendly **RBS**

DON'T MISS

CYCLING THE MAIL ROAD

A good taster for cycling in the archipelago is the Mail Rd, a former postal route (p123) that crossed Åland between Stockholm and Turku. Today it's a signposted 65km cycling route from Storby in Eckerö to Hullvik in Vårdö. The route passes by some of the island's biggest sights, including Kastelholms Slott (p125) and Bomarsund (p126).

Allow a gentle two days – three if cycling with kids. There are accommodation and eating options along the way. Request the booklet Mail Road Across Åland from the Visit Åland (p116) tourist office in Mariehamn.

Biluthyrning (☑ 018-525-505; www.rundbergs. com; Strandgatan 1) is at the St1-garage petrol station opposite Mariebad; rates for small cars start at around €82 per day. Book well ahead in summer.

Ro-No Rent (p119) hires out bicycles, mopeds and other recreation gear.

For a taxi, call ☑ 018-26000. **Water taxis** (☑ 040-504-3601; www.shipland.ax) take passengers out to Kobba Klintar and nearby islands.

Jomala

POP 4650

The sprawling municipality of Jomala sits just above Mariehamn, spanning Fasta Åland from its east coast to its west. Its two main centres are Kyrkby in the east and small Gottby in the west, but the landscape is dotted with villages, guesthouses and museums.

Jomala's patron saint, St Olaf, has left his mark on this municipality – you'll see him on the Jomala coat of arms and inside his namesake church. The latter is said to be among the oldest churches in Finland, with many ancient sculptures and frescos to prove it.

Sankt Olof Kyrka   CHURCH
(www.jomala.evl.ax; Gottbyvägen 445, Kyrkby; ⊙9.30am-3.30pm Tue-Fri, 1-3.30pm Sun Jun-Aug) By some accounts, Sankt Olof Kyrka is the oldest church in Finland, existing (in some form) on this site since the beginning of the 13th century. Some of the original frescos depicting the story of the Prodigal Son are still visible in the tower arch. Don't miss the limestone sculptures and baptismal font, which date from the 1250s.

Önningebyn Museo   MUSEUM
(☑ 018-33710; www.onningeby.com; Önningebyvägen 31, Önningeby; adult/child €5/3; ⊙ noon-3pm Thu-Sat early Apr-May, 11am-6pm Tue-Sun Jun-Aug) In 1886 landscape painter Victor Westerholm invited fellow artists to his summer house in Önningeby, a tiny village in eastern Jomala. For almost 30 years artists gathered here at 'Önningeby Colony'. This interesting museum showcases their work (although there are no works by Westerholm himself) alongside memorabilia from the era. Other exhibits follow the work of contemporary artists. There's no signage in English, but the artwork is attractive in any language.

Djurviks Gästgård   GUESTHOUSE €
(☑ 018-32433; www.djurvik.ax; Gottbyvägen 420, Djurvik; s/d €50/60, 2-/4-person cabins €70/90; ⊙ May-Oct; ⌘) There's a lot to love about this waterside outpost, starting with the warm welcome you receive from hosts Harry and Birgitta. There's also the gorgeous setting – the guesthouse is surrounded by nature – as well as the endearing garden, rowing boats and kayaks, beach volleyball and boules, and, of course, the sauna. Take your pick from simple rooms or rustic cabins.

❶ Getting There & Away

From Mariehamn, catch bus 2, 3 or 4 to Kyrkby (€2.10, 10 minutes) or bus 5 to Önningeby (€2.10, 15 minutes).

Hammarland

POP 1520

Quiet Hammarland is a geographically prominent municipality, stretching from central Åland up to the northwestern corner. The main village is Kattby, which is where you'll find the ancient Sankta Catharina Kyrka. This is one of the archipelago's oldest inhabited areas, as evidenced by the Iron Age burial sites near the church. There's no reason to make a dedicated trip to Hammarland, but it's worth a stop if you're passing through en route to Eckerö or Geta.

Sankta Catharina Kyrka   CHURCH
(Prästgårdsgatan 41, Kattby; ⊙9am-4pm Mon-Fri Jun-early Aug) Sankta Catharina Kyrka was built in the 13th century, though a fire at the beginning of the 15th century led it to be rebuilt with fresh wall paintings. To the west of the church are more than 30 Iron Age burial sites.

Kattnäs Camping
CAMPGROUND €

([☑]018-37687; www.kattnas.ax; Kattnäsvägen 285; tent sites €4 plus per person €4, cabins €60; ☺May-Sep) This campground is surrounded by 3.2 hectares of grassy meadows, smooth granite rocks and fine sandy beaches – there's nothing but peace, tranquillity and more peace and tranquillity. (It also has a TV lounge and cafe in case you're missing civilisation.) A seaside sauna seals the deal. It's 3km south of the Eckerö–Mariehamn Rd.

🟆 Getting There & Away

Bus 1 from Mariehamn to Eckerö runs through Hammarland (€3.10, 35 minutes). From late June to late August the bicycle ferry **Silvana** ([☑]040-022 9149; www.alandstrafiken.ax) makes one daily trip between Skarpnåtö, Hammarland, and Hällö, Geta (adult/child €12/6). It departs Skarpnåtö at 11am and Hällö at 11.30am.

Eckerö

POP 930

On the far-western edge of mainland Åland, delightful Eckerö is the archipelago's closest point to mainland Sweden – just a two-hour ferry ride from Grisslehamn. While the island maintains an off-the-beaten-track atmosphere, it does contain a handful of excellent accommodation options and some offbeat but interesting sights. Eckerö is also home to Åland's loveliest stretch of sand at Degersand beach.

🔘 Sights

Käringsund Harbour
HARBOUR

About 2km north of Storby, Käringsund harbour is delightfully picturesque, with rustic red wooden boathouses reflected in the calm waters. A nature trail leads to a small beach; Käringsund Resort rents out canoes and rowing boats.

Ålands Jakt och Fiskemuseum
MUSEUM

(Åland Hunting & Fishing Museum; [☑]018-38299; www.jaktfiskemuseum.ax; adult/child €7/4; ☺10am-5pm Mon-Sat May–mid-Jun & late Aug, to 6pm daily mid-Jun–mid-Aug; [♿]) Overlooking Käringsund harbour, the Hunting & Fishing Museum addresses the role of these two activities in the history and culture of the Åland islands. Exhibits focus on seal hunting and seine (dragnet) fishing, as well as life in a traditional fishing village. Dinghies, seine boats and schooners are on display, as well as stuffed animals and birds.

Post och Tullhuset
HISTORIC BUILDING

(Post & Customs House; www.postochtullhuset.ax; Storby; museum €3; ☺main bldg 10am-5pm May-Aug, museum 10am-3pm May-Aug) Designed by German architect CL Engel, Storby's Post & Customs House is now a hub for local artists, with exhibitions, artisan shops and a terrific cafe (p124). The grand building was completed in 1828, during the era of Russian Tsar Alexander I, as a show of might to Sweden (as Åland was the Russian Empire's westernmost extremity at the time). It was a crucial point on the Sweden–Finland Mail Rd, detailed in the one-roomed mailboat museum.

Degersand
BEACH

Åland's rocky coastline doesn't often allow for good swimming beaches, but here's an exception – a long, pristine stretch of fine white sand that has been ranked as one of Europe's best unexplored beaches. Calm, shallow waters make it perfect for kids – or anyone who can stand the chilly temperatures.

🏃 Activities

Stall Rosenqvist
HORSE RIDING

([☑]0457-522-1617; www.rosenqvist.ax; Ollasgätan 35; 45/90min lesson €25/50, trail rides €70) Offers lessons and forest tours on Icelandic horses and Shetland ponies. Cash only.

Nimix
KAYAKING

([☑]050-66716; www.nimix.ax; single kayak per 2hr/day €30/50, tandem €50/90) Kayak-rental prices include spray deck, life vest, paddle and delivery to any location in Eckerö.

JaRo Guiding
FISHING, OUTDOORS

([☑]0457-342-7467; www.jaroguiding.com) Jakob Rosenqvist offers a variety of nature tours and fishing excursions, including birding, boat tours of the archipelago and snake walks.

Viltsafari
WILDLIFE

([☑]018-38151; www.granbergs.ax; Käringsund; tours adult/child €10/7; ☺3-6 tours 11am-4pm mid-Jun–early Aug) This fenced-in nature park is home to Finnish fauna like red and fallow deer, swans and wild boar, plus the odd ostrich. A safari 'train' departs from the entrance (near the Jakt och Fiskemuseum (p123)).

🛏 Sleeping

Käringsund Resort
CAMPGROUND €

([☑]018-38000; www.karingsund.ax; Käringsundsvägen 194; tent sites €18-24, cabins €68, bungalows €144-210; ☺mid-Mar–Oct; [☎]) This family resort packs the tents and campers into a wide green field by the seashore, with additional cabins and bungalows sleeping up to 10. Child-friendly entertainment ranges from minigolf and boules to pedal boats and more. There's a pizzeria, a tennis court and a sauna, as well as kayaks and bikes for hire.

★ Degersands Resort
CAMPGROUND, COTTAGE €€

(☑ 018-38004; www.degersand.ax; Degersandsvägen 311; tent sites €9 plus per person €6, 1-2 person/3-4 person cabins €145/170; 🕾) 🍴 Bang on Åland's most beautiful beach, this haven has stunning cottages in sleek Scandinavian blond wood with full kitchens, indoor and outdoor showers, and wraparound timber decks with barbecues. Awesome facilities include a traditional smoke sauna on the beach, and rowing-boat, kayak, fishing-gear and bike hire. Weekly discounts available. The excellent on-site Restaurant Q uses local, organic produce with delicious results.

Hotel Elvira
HOTEL €€

(☑ 0457-343-1530; www.elvira.ax; Sandmovägen 85, Storby; d from €115; 🕾) Fronting a small beach, this guesthouse is a charmer, with 20 individually decorated rooms, some with sea views. Sewing machines, typewriters and other antique items enhance the retro atmosphere, as do the animal hides and other recycled items. Excellent restaurant and sauna also on site. It's just up the road from the Post och Tullhuset (p123).

Gästgård Christiansund
GUESTHOUSE €€

(☑ 018-38679; gastgard.christiansund@gmail.com; Eckerövägen; d without bathroom €80, cabins €100; 🕾) The simple cabins here surround a wide expanse of greenery and trees leading down to a picturesque inlet. It's not great for swimming, but the public beach is only 400m away. Bikes available for hire. There are also cheaper doubles with shared bathroom in the main house. All prices include a scrumptious breakfast with homemade bread and fresh fruit.

✖️ Eating

Tsarevna
CAFE €

(http://tsarevna.ax; Sandmovägen 111; dishes €5-12; ⊙11am-5pm Tue-Sun May, 10am-6pm daily Jun-Aug) 🍴 With tables spilling into the courtyard of the historic Post och Tullhuset (p123), Tsarevna is much loved for its spectacular homemade cakes, well-stuffed sandwiches and bountiful organic salads with home-baked bread. Summertime weekend brunch is a local institution. Cash only.

★ Bodegan
SEAFOOD €€

(☑ 018-38530; www.karingsundsgasthamn.ax; Käringsund Harbour; mains lunch €15-16, dinner €18-25; ⊙11am-7pm mid-late Jun, 8am-10pm late Jun-mid-Aug; 🕾) Right on the pier, this delightful spot is perfect for a drink or a meal while watching the seagulls soar above the creaking red boathouses. The classic Nordic dishes are delectable: marinated salmon with dill potatoes; grilled tenderloin; or a plate of 'sea tapas', including smoked salmon, shrimp or whitefish, served with archipelago black bread.

❶ Information

Tourist Information Desk (☑ 018-39462; www.eckero.ax; ⊙10am-6pm Jun-Aug, to 5pm Sep-May) At Eckerö's ferry terminal.

❶ Getting There & Away

Eckerö Linjen (p116) ferries sail from Eckerö to Grisslehamn, Sweden (adult/car €4.50/15, two hours).

Williams Buss (bus 1) runs from Mariehamn to Eckerö about six times a day (€4.50, 50 minutes).

Geta
POP 510

Geta calls itself the 'top of Åland' – not only because it encompasses the archipelago's northern tip but also because it's home to one of the islands' highest peaks. As such, Geta is a popular destination for hiking, or just for taking in the panorama from the Soltuna Restaurang.

Getabergen
HIKING

The main attraction of Geta is Getabergen, a formidable peak of 98m. From Soltuna Restaurang a 5.5km trail leads to a spacious natural grotto called Djupviksgrottan. There's also the 1km Trollstigen (Troll Trail), which is perfect for nature-loving kids.

★ HavsVidden
RESORT €€€

(☑ 018-49408; www.havsvidden.com; Havsviddsvägen 90; tw with/without sea view €210/180, cliff houses from €350; 🕾❄🕾) At the far-northern tip of the island, HavsVidden is perched on the cliffs overlooking the wild Gulf of Bothnia. This is one of the most stunning – and remote – spots on Fasta Åland. The resort offers sweeping sea views all around – perhaps even from your private hot tub, if you spring for a luxurious cliff house.

Amenities are many, including a seaside spa and smoke sauna, a glass-enclosed pool, a brave-the-elements beach, hiking trails and bikes for hire. The resort's restaurant was recognised by White Guide Nordic as one of the country's best restaurants in 2017.

Soltuna Restaurang   CAFE €€
(☑018-49530; www.soltuna.ax; Getabergsvägen; breakfast €8, lunch buffet €15, mains €16-25; ☺11am-2pm Mon-Fri, to 8pm Sat & Sun) The food is tasty, the service is friendly...but the view! Soltuna claims to be Åland's highest restaurant, and it makes the most of its superior location, with a wide terrace and sweeping views of forest, sea and sky. It's all the better if you're feasting on a delicious cardamom pancake.

If you've made it this far, you might as well stay for a game of minigolf, or at least climb to the top of the observation tower. There are 10 cabins (doubles/triples/quads €40/47/57) on site. This is also the starting point for the Getabergen trails.

❶ Getting There & Away

Bus 2 runs from Mariehamn to Geta (€4.50, 45 minutes) Monday to Friday via Godby.

From late June to late August the bicycle ferry Silvana (p123) makes one daily trip between Skarpnåtö, Hammarland, and Hällö, Geta (adult/child €12/6). It departs Skarpnåtö at 11am and Hällö at 11.30am.

Saltvik

POP 1830

In the northeastern corner of Åland Fasta, the municipality of Saltvik is the island's highest ground, with the 'peak' of Orrdals Klint maxing out at 129m. It's also among Åland's earliest settled spots. Archaeological excavations have recently revealed farms and houses dating as far back as the 6th century. In particular, Vikings sharpened their swords in Saltvik for centuries: the main village, Kvarnbo, was likely their capital on Åland. The festive annual Viking Market (p116) celebrates this heritage.

Sankta Maria Kyrka   CHURCH
(Kvarnbo-Kyrkvägen, Kvarnbo; ☺10am-4pm Mon-Fri Jun-Aug) Kvarnbo's red-granite Sankta Maria Kyrka dates from the 13th century and contains a fine clover-shaped baptismal font and fragmentary frescos of the period. The island's largest Iron Age archaeological site surrounds the church.

❶ MONEY

Bring cash, as most of the islands in the outer archipelago don't have ATMs.

Kvarnbo Gästhem   GUESTHOUSE €€
(☑018-44015; www.kvarnbogasthem.com; Kyrkvägen 48, Kvarnbo; d/tr/q €96/109/124; ℗🛜) Kvarnbo Gästhem is housed in an elegant 19th-century home that's decked out with antique furnishings and many original architectural flourishes. Floral wallpaper, wide-plank wooden floors and frilly details adorn the charming guest rooms. The gorgeous dining room – centred on a grand fireplace – is the perfect setting for an elaborate breakfast spread (included in rates).

❶ Getting There & Away

Bus 3 runs from Mariehamn to Kvarnbo (€3.20, 35 minutes) and other villages in Saltvik.

Sund

POP 1030

Sund is situated 30km from Mariehamn, just east of the main island group. It's connected to Saltvik by bridge, but it's still a long haul from the capital. It's worth the trip, however, as Sund is home to Åland's highlight attractions: the muscular medieval castle Kastelholm and the battle-scarred ruins of the Russian stronghold at Bomarsund. In the midst of these historic sights is the island's most talked-about eatery, Smakbyn, which spearheaded the locavore movement on Åland. Midway between Kastelholm and Bomarsund is Sund's largest town, Finby, with all services.

❶ Sights

★**Kastelholms Slott**   CASTLE
(☑018-432-150; www.kastelholm.ax; adult/child €6/4.50; ☺10am-5pm mid-May–Jun & Aug–mid-Sep, to 6pm Jul) One of Åland's premier sights is this striking 14th-century castle on a picturesque inlet (signposted off Rd 2). The keep towers are 15m high in parts, with walls of 3m-thick red granite; it's easy to see how it would once have ruled over Åland. Exhibits showcase the castle's evolution and archaeological finds, including a medieval silver-coin hoard. English-language tours (included in admission) depart at 2pm Saturday and Sunday from June to early August and last around 45 minutes.

Fängelsemuseet Vita Björn MUSEUM
(Vita Björn Prison Museum; www.kastelholm.ax;
Slottsvägen, Kastelholm; €2; ⊙10am-5pm May–
mid-Sep) This building was a jail until 1975
and demonstrates how cells and conditions
evolved over the two centuries it was in use.
Although it looks like a cottage, the walls
and floor are of thick stone, so there was no
tunnelling out.

Jan Karlsgårdens Friluftsmuseum MUSEUM
(☑018-432-150; www.kastelholm.ax; Kastelholm;
⊙10am-5pm May–mid-Sep) **FREE** At this
sprawling open-air museum next to Kastelholms Slott, you can stroll around 20 traditional 18th- and 19th-century Ålandic buildings, including windmills and a smoke sauna. The museum shop's guidebook is useful
for background on each building.

★Bomarsund Fästningsruin RUINS
(Bomarsund Fortress Ruin; www.bomarsund.ax)
Following the war of 1808–09, Russia began building this major military structure
as its westernmost defence against the
Swedes. The fortress was still incomplete
when the Crimean War began in 1854, and
a French-British naval force bombarded it
heavily from the sea. Within four days the
Russians were forced to surrender it.

The evocative ruins stretch for a couple
of kilometres, straddling the road and overlooking the sea. Across the water on Prästö,
the small **Bomarsund Museum** (☑018-
44032; Prästö; admission by donation; ⊙10am-
5pm Mon-Fri Jun-Aug, plus 10am-5pm Sat & Sun
Jul) displays excavated artefacts.

Sankt Johannes Kyrka CHURCH
(Church of St John; Norra Sundsvägen; ⊙9am-4pm
Mon-Fri, noon-4pm Sun Jun-Aug) **FREE** North of
Kastelholm is Åland's biggest church, dedicated to John the Baptist. The structure dates
from the 13th century, and inside are some
original murals, as well as an enormous wood-
en crucifix made from local birch in 1250.

🍽 Sleeping & Eating

Puttes Camping CAMPGROUND €
(☑018-44040, 0457-313-4177; www.visitaland.
com/puttescamping; Bryggvägen 2, Bomarsund;
tent sites €12 plus per person €4, cabins without
bathroom €35-55, cottages €75; ⊙May-Aug)
Right on Bomarsund's doorstep, Puttes has
plenty of grassy sites and simple four-bed
cabins, plus a beach sauna, bike hire, rowing
boats and a canoe jetty. Its cafe does a brisk
trade in pancakes and other treats.

Kastelholms Gästhem B&B €€
(☑018-43841; Tosarbyvägen 47, Kastelholm; s/d
€91/98, without bathroom €64/86; ⊙May–
mid-Oct; ☞) The closest accommodation
to Kastelholms Slott is this pleasant little
guesthouse. Most of its spotless floral rooms
have private bathrooms, and there's access
to a self-catering kitchen and laundry. The
patios are perfect for evening lazing.

★Smakbyn FINNISH €€€
(☑018-43666; www.smakbyn.ax; Slottsvägen 134,
Kastelholm; lunch €10, light bites €15-19, evening
menu €36-44; ⊙11am-7pm Mon-Fri, 1-8pm Sat;
▣) ♪ The brainchild of award-winning
chef Michael 'Micke' Björklund, this 'taste
village' incorporates a farm shop, cookery
courses and a distillery (tours and tastings
available). The centrepiece is the airy open-
kitchen restaurant, where the cooks work
magic, using seasonal organic produce in
creative ways. The menu is always different
but usually features delicious local perch fillets and the beloved Hunter's sandwich.

ⓘ Getting There & Away

Bus 4 from Mariehamn to Vårdö serves Sund.
The bus goes via Kastelholm (€3.20, 30 min-
utes), Bomarsund (€4.40, 40 minutes) and
Prästö (€4.50, 45 minutes).

Vårdö

POP 430

Vårdö sprawls across the Archipelago Sea,
barely maintaining its connection to its
compatriots on Fasta Åland. This cluster of
isles – connected by bridges and ferries –
stretches up to the two islands of **Simskäla**
(Västra and Östra; West and East, respectively), with rustling silver birches, isolated
beaches and views over the countless skerries (rocky islets).

Vårdö is a handy stop if you're travelling to
the outer islands on the northern archipelago
route; ferries departing from Hummelvik.

★Sandösund Camping CAMPGROUND €
(☑018-47750; www.sandocamping.aland.fi;
Trollvägen 40, Vårdö; tent sites €2 plus per person
€5, s/d incl breakfast €90/110, 2-/4-person cabins
€44/52; ⊙May-Aug) On the northern coast of
Vårdö, this idyllic campground has peaceful
sites, spiffy townhouse rooms and well-kept
beachside log cabins. Excellent facilities include kayaks and bicycles, plus a 'floating
sauna', from where you can hop straight into
the water on the picture-perfect sound. The

on-site Sandösund Taverna is recommended for local food, including smoked fish from the surrounding waters.

ⓘ Getting There & Away

Bus 4 travels from Mariehamn to Vårdö (€4.50, one hour) and Hummelvik (€4.50, 1¼ hours), crossing on the short, free car ferry from Prästö.

Ferries depart from Hummelvik on the northern archipelago route, with stops at Enklinge, Kumlinge, Lappo and Torsholma.

Finström

POP 2530

Åland's central municipality fans out around Godby, the island's second-biggest 'town' – though with 800 people, it's scarcely a metropolis. While Finström itself is light on sights and activities, it's not a bad base for exploring Åland. The central location offers easy access to the historic sights in Saltvik, while Mariehamn is just a quick jaunt down Rte 2. Finström is interwoven with waterways, offering gorgeous scenery and the occasional swimming beach. And it doesn't hurt that the island's tastiest beer is brewed in the neighbourhood.

Höga C Observation Tower   TOWER
(www.facebook.com/cafeuffe; Sundsvägen; €2; ⊙10am-8pm Jun & Jul, 11am-7pm May & Aug, 11am-7pm Sat & Sun Sep) Above the tunnel before you cross the bridge to Sund, the 30m-high observation tower at **Café Uffe på Berget** (Sundsvägen; www.facebook.com/cafeuffe; lunch €9; ⊙10am-8pm Jun & Jul, 11am-7pm May & Aug, 11am-7pm Sat & Sun Sep) affords superb views of the archipelago and is a popular photo stop. Across the road is **Godby Arboretum**, a small nature park with native and exotic trees along a short, marked nature trail.

Sankt Mikael Kyrka   CHURCH
(Pålsböle; ⊙10am-4pm Mon-Fri May-Sep) Dating from the 1200s, Sankt Mikael Kyrka is the ancient place of worship in Pålsböle, a small village just 5km north of Godby. The church has a well-preserved interior featuring a wealth of medieval frescos and sculptures, most dating from the 15th century. Look for several depictions of St Michael himself, as well as the primitively carved triptych altarpiece.

Pensionat Stalldalen   GUESTHOUSE €€
(☑0457-345-4443; www.stalldalen.ax; Stornäsvägan 40; s/d/q €105/125/200; ☞) 🏊 In a gorgeous waterfront setting and surrounded

FOODIE BIKE TOUR

Here's a new concept: farm hopping by bicycle. Cycle the Åland countryside with **Mitt Åland** (www.mittaland.ax; per person €80-125), stopping to meet the livestock, sample the local bounty, marvel at the scenery and inhale the fresh air. Your guide will help you develop the itinerary, including destinations such as **Amalias Limonadfabrik** (☑0457-003-4000; www.amalias.net; Lemlandsvägen 1865; d without bathroom €75; ☞), Smakbyn (p126) and Stallhagen Brewery (p128).

by nature, this guesthouse offers 17 simple rooms that exemplify Scandinavian design, with subdued colours, natural materials and just a hint of whimsy. Featuring freshly squeezed juices and homemade bread, the breakfast is superb – not surprising, since the guesthouse is owned by the folks from the excellent Stallhagen Brewery (p128) nearby.

Godby Gästhem   B&B €€
(☑040-081-5268; www.godbygasthem.ax; von Knorringsvägen 13, Godby; s/d without bathroom €73/93; ⊙Jan-Oct; ☞) A lovely century-old farmhouse near Godby centre. The four spacious rooms have shiny wooden floors and flowing floral curtains. Breakfast is excellent, including fresh fruit and pastries. Spacious landscaped grounds, hire bicycles, a kitchen and an outdoor grill are all at your disposal.

ⓘ Getting There & Away

Rd 2 from Mariehamn takes you to Godby. Buses 2, 3 and 4 from Mariehamn all go via Godby (€2.80).

Lemland

POP 1990

When the occupying Russians needed a shipping route in the late 19th century, their prisoners of war dug the **Lemström Canal**. Today it remains one of Lemland's defining features. About 8km east of Mariehamn, the canal is a popular destination for bike rides from Åland's capital. Ambitious cyclists might venture further into Lemland to admire the 14th-century church **Sankta Birgitta Kyrka** (Norrbyvägen, Norrby; ⊙11am-4pm Mon-Fri Jun-early Aug), visit the home of a 19th-century

DON'T MISS

ÅLAND'S ARTISAN BREWERY

Sample unique brews and delicious food at this fabulous brewery, **Stallhagen Brewery** (☑018-48500; www.stallhagen. com; Getavägen 196; tour with tastings/dinner €36/72; ☺10.30am-10pm Mon-Fri, noon-11pm Sat, noon-10pm Sun), overlooking an idyllic lake and horse paddocks. Beers range from basic (pale ale or Baltic porter) to berry (blueberry ale or raspberry stout), with many options in between. Musical jam sessions often strike up on the terrace; the kitchen turns out limited-but-luscious gastropub fare (mains €10 to €16).

shipping magnate at **Skeppargården Pellas** (☑018-34420; www.skeppar gardenpellas.ax; Skepparvägen 30, Granboda; adult/child €5/free; ☺11am-4pm mid-Jun–late Aug) or buy a sparkling lemonade straight from the source at Amalia (p127).

❶ Getting There & Away

Bus 5 travels from Mariehamn past the Lemström Canal (€2.10, 10 minutes) and through Lemland (€3.10, 20 minutes).

Lumparland

POP 390

There aren't too many reasons to make the 30km drive to the eastern edge of Fasta Åland, where Lumparland juts into the sea, reaching out to its neighbours in the southern archipelago. But one compelling reason is to catch a ferry, either to nearby Föglö or out to Kökar. You can even ride a ferry all the way back to Turku or Naantali on the Finnish mainland.

But whatever their reason for being here, travellers will discover the charming old wooden church **Sankt Andreas Kyrka** (Lumpovägen, Lumparby; ☺10am-4pm early Jun–mid-Aug) (Åland's oldest, in fact) and a delightful, artsy summer cafe **Lumparby Ollas** (www. lumparbyollas.ax; Södra Lumparbyvägen 25; mains €5-8; ☺11am-6pm mid-May–mid-Sep). Enjoy.

❶ Getting There & Away

BOAT

Ferries from Långnäs:

Finnlink (p116) Ferries serve Naantali (adult and car €45, 3½ hours, up to two daily).

Tallink/Silja Lines (p116) Runs to Stockholm (adult/car €23/45, 5½ hours) and Turku (€23/71, five hours).

Viking Line (p116) Runs to Turku (adult/car €29/40, five hours) and Stockholm (€29/10, 5½ hours).

Three daily ferries run to Överö, Föglö (foot passengers free, bicycle/car €6/22), continuing to Kökar.

A dozen ferries make the one-hour trip between Svinö, Lumparland, and Degerby, Föglö (passengers free, bicycle/car €6/22).

BUS

From Mariehamn, take bus 5 to the ferry harbours Svinö (€3.80, 30 minutes) and Långnäs (€4.30, 40 minutes).

NORTHERN & SOUTHERN ARCHIPELAGOS

If you're feeling that Fasta Åland is too mainstream, then you're due for a trip to the remote outer islands of the archipelago. These tiny granite islets stretch out across the Archipelago Sea between Fasta and Finland. Strewn with silver-birch forests and connected by ferries (and the occasional bridge), the islands are criss-crossed by winding roads, cycling routes and walking trails – as well as many, many waterways. So no matter your mode of transport, the outer isles are ripe for exploration.

The thousands of islets in the outer archipelago fall into two geographic groups, served by two different ferry lines. The northern archipelago includes Kumlinge, Lappo, Brändö and Jurmo. The southern archipelago includes Föglö, Sottunga and Kökar.

❶ Getting There & Around

Fuel is limited, so fill up before hitting the outer islands.

The northern and southern archipelagos are served by the archipelago ferries:

Northern line (Norra linjen) Connects Hummelvik, Vårdö, with Kustavi, by way of Enklinge, Kumlinge and three islands of Brändö.

Southern line (Södra linjen) Connects Långnäs, Lumparland, and Korpo, by way of Föglö (Överö), Sottunga, Husö, Kyrkogårdsö and Kökar.

Cross line (Tvärgående linjen) Operates between Lumparland and Kumlinge; connects the northern and southern lines without requiring travel through Mainland Åland.

Föglö line (Föglölinjen) Operates the short passage between Svinö, Lumparland, and Degerby, Föglö.

Northern Archipelago

Kumlinge

POP 315

Kumlinge is little visited but much beloved for its peaceful forests, untrafficked walking trails and atmosphere of being undiscovered. There's not a great deal to see here – although the historic buildings are unique and certainly worthwhile. But you'll spend most of your time walking (or cycling) through the forest, climbing on the rocks and gazing out to sea. You're unlikely to meet other tourists, and the island's 315 residents certainly won't get in your way.

The top attraction in Kumlinge is the walking path from the guest harbour to the beautiful Sankta Anna Kyrka.

Kumlinge Apotek   HISTORIC BUILDING
(Kumlinga Pharmacy; www.facebook.com/pg/KumlingeApotek; ⊙9am-3pm Mon-Fri) FREE
It's worth a small purchase to glimpse the fantastic interior of this old-fashioned pharmacy. Inside a red house, the apothecary cabinets are lined with colourful bottles and labelled drawers, while a curious multiple-pendulum balance scale sits on the counter. The place is still in business.

Sankta Anna Kyrka   CHURCH
(☑040-031-1805; ⊙10am-noon & 2-6pm Mon-Sat Jun-Aug) Hidden away about 2km north of Kumlinge village, Sankta Anna Kyrka is an attractive, multicoloured fieldstone church. The interior contains incredible 500-year-old Franciscan-style paintings. The shrine to Mary on the altarpiece and the baptismal font likely date from the mid-13th century.

Hasslebo Gästhem   CAMPGROUND €
(☑0457-570-0834; www.hasslebo.com; tent sites €8 plus per person €4, s/d/f €50/60/100; ⊙Jun-Aug; 🐾) 🦴 About 3km outside Kumlinge village, Hasslebo Gästhem has an eco sensibility that's exemplified by bio-toilets, solar power and organic breakfasts (€9).

Kumlinge Stugor
& Restaurang Kastören   FINNISH €€
(☑040-052-9199; www.kumlingestugor.com; mains €12-28; ⊙8am-10pm May-Aug) The hotel facing the harbour in Kumlinge is a decent place to stay, but the highlight is the on-site Restaurang Kastören – a cosy place offering terrace seating, top-notch service and unexpectedly good food. If you wish to spend the night, there are 12 cabins with wonderful sea views (doubles €60). A hiking trail to the Sankta Anna Kyrka starts here.

ℹ Getting There & Away

Ferries on the route between Hummelvik, Värdö, and Torsholma, Brändö, stop at Kumlinge (passengers free, bicycle/car €6/34, 80 minutes).

Brändö

POP 465

It's a funny thing about Brändö, the northernmost municipality of the Åland Archipelago: it has more islands than people – way more. With a population hovering just under 500, Brändö is composed of some 1180 islands. The core group – Brändö, Torsholma, Åva and Jurmo – is connected by bridges and free ferries, with a signposted **bike route** traversing them as well. If you prefer to travel by boat, the winding waterways are brilliant for kayaking and sailing.

🛏 Sleeping

Brändö Stugby   CAMPGROUND €
(☑018-56221, 040-753-0514; www.facebook.com/BrandoStugby; tent sites €18, cabins €60-80; ⊙May–mid-Oct; 🐾) This splendidly located campground on Brändö has 10 simple cabins with kitchens, plus campsites, sauna and cafe. Hire a rowing boat to explore the surrounding seascape.

Pellas Gästhem   GUESTHOUSE €€
(☑040-832-4333; www.pellas.ax; Lappo; d/q €72/89; 🐾) In a former schoolhouse, Pellas promises a 'genuine archipelago experience', with fishing, rowing, exploring and picnicking. Accommodation is simple and clean; bathrooms are (mostly) shared. Breakfast and linens are extra.

Hotell Gullvivan   HOTEL €€
(☑018-56350; www.gullvivan.ax; Björnholma; s/d €75/110; 🐾) Every room at this modest hotel has a fantastic sea view. Some also have a kitchenette, which may come in handy, as there are few places to eat in the vicinity (aside from the mediocre on-site cafe). There's plenty to do, though, including fishing and minigolf. Gullvivan is on the island of Björnholma, which is just north of the main island of Brändö.

✗ Eating

★ Café Kvarnen
CAFE €€

(📞 040-506-4777; www.facebook.com/Djurmoturism; Jurmo; mains €13-27; ◎ noon-10pm Jun-Aug)
🍴 It's worth a special trip to tiny Jurmo to sample the organic steak at wonderful Café Kvarnen, near the pier. The steak is sourced from local long-haired highland cattle and seasoned with island herbs. Other delicacies include homemade sausages, burgers, locally caught fish and fantastic Åland pancakes.

Restaurang Galeasen
FINNISH €€

(📞 045-123-3413; www.lappo.net/galeasen; Lappo; mains €20-30; ◎ 12.30-10pm Jun-Aug) If you're on the island of Lappo, you'll likely to find your way to Restaurang Galeasen, a welcoming spot with a sunny terrace overlooking the guest harbour. Classic island fare like grilled whitefish and fried perch sits alongside Wiener schnitzel and escargots on the menu.

ℹ Information

Brändö Tourist Information (📞 040-720-2940; www.brando.ax)

ℹ Getting There & Around

Coming from Kustavi (passengers free, bicycle/car €6/22, 40 minutes) on the Finnish mainland, you'll arrive at Långö in the north of Brändö.

Three or four daily ferries from Hummelvik, Vårdö, stop at Lappo (passengers free, bicycle/car €6/34, two hours) and Torsholma (2½ hours).

The free ferry to Jurmo (10 minutes) departs every hour from Åva, north of Brändö.

Southern Archipelago

Föglö

POP 560

Föglö is a short, easy hop from Fasta Åland. With more than 500 residents, this is the largest outer-island municipality. The main attraction is the charming village of Degerby, which is blessed with some lovely art nouveau and empire-style architecture. Many islanders have made their living as civil servants rather than farmers, which explains the unique atmosphere.

A signposted bike route runs 16km from Degerby to Överö. For a shorter but no less scenic ride, pedal 4.5km to the 14th-century **Sankta Maria Magdalena Kyrka** (Kyrkvägen 106; ◎ 11am-4pm Mon-Sat mid-Jun–mid-Aug).

The other village of note is Överö, 16km away at the northern end of the island.

Museum
MUSEUM

(📞 018-50322; Föglövägen, Degerby; admission by donation; ◎ 9.45am-5.30pm Mon-Sat, 1-4.30pm Sun mid-Jun–mid-Aug) FREE Housed in a 19th-century warehouse, Degerby's little local museum contains the islanders' personal collections of biros, bottle tops and biscuit cutters. Check out the old pilot house nearby.

Coja Fishing
BOATING, FISHING

(📞 040-094-7502; www.coja.nu; trips per hour from €80, boat rental per day from €75; ◎ Jun-Aug) The conservation island of Björkör is close to Degerby harbour – Coja Fishing can take you there. Enquire also about cabins to rent.

Enighetens Gästhem
CAMPING, GUESTHOUSE €€

(📞 018-50310; www.enigheten.ax; Tingsvägen, Degerby; tent sites €10 plus per person €4, s/d/tr/q €80/110/120/150, s/d without bathroom €60/90; ◎ May-Sep; 🛜) The first guesthouse opened in this building in 1625, accommodating the many travellers en route from Stockholm, Sweden, to Åbo (Turku). The building has, thankfully, been updated since then, but it retains an old-fashioned charm. Creaky-floored rooms contain old stoves and period furniture, and a harmonium graces the sitting room. The restaurant serves excellent seafood and Stallhagen's Shipwreck Beer (among other things).

Restaurang Seagram
SEAFOOD €€€

(📞 018-51092; www.seagram.ax; Lotuddsvägen, Degerby; buffet €30; ◎ noon-8pm Mon-Fri, to 10pm Sat, 4-8pm Sun) Seagram is famous for its seafood buffet – a *smörgåsbord* of grilled and smoked fish, prawns, beef and game. Local produce and wild mushrooms and berries also play a prominent role. A wide terrace offers comfortable seating and a lovely panorama of sea and sky.

ℹ Information

Tourist Information Kiosk (📞 018-51037, 045-7342-7274; www.foglo.ax/turism; ◎ 10am-5.30pm Mon-Sat, 1-4.30pm Sun mid-Jun–mid-Aug) At Degerby ferry terminal.

ℹ Getting There & Away

A dozen ferries make the one-hour trip between Svinö, Lumparland, and Degerby (passengers free, bicycle/car €6/22).

Other ferries run from Långnäs, Lumparland, to Överö (passengers free, bicycle/car €6/22), some continuing to Kumlinge or Kökar.

Kökar

POP 240

Dangling off the southern end of the archipelago, Kökar is sea washed and windswept – a rocky island with few trees and a lovely desolate air. Most of the 240 inhabitants live in the quaint village of Karlby.

The islands' appealingly barren landscape attracted Bronze Age seal hunters and Hanseatic traders. Archaeologists have uncovered early settlements at Otterböte. Little remains now, but a tangle of atmospheric walking trails criss-crosses the area. Nearby, the Sankta Anne Kyrka sits on the ruins of an ancient Franciscan monastery – a site replete with historical and spiritual import.

Sankta Anne Kyrka   CHURCH

(Hamnö; ⊙ 9am-9pm May-Sep) Sankta Anne Kyrka was built on top of a medieval Franciscan monastery on the island of Hamnö, just west of Kökar. The monks' chapel and ruined walls make for a pensive evening stroll. Inside, look for the unusual votive featuring a Turkish pirate ship.

Kökar Hembygdsmuseum   MUSEUM

(Kökar Homestead Museum; ☑ 0457-524-4077; Hellsö; €2; ⊙ 11am-6pm late Jun–mid-Aug) In a former schoolhouse, Kökar Homestead Museum is a sweet little collection of local history in the village of Hellsö.

Sandvik Gästhamn
& Camping   CAMPGROUND €

(☑ 018-55911, 0457-342-9242; www.sandvik.ax; Överboda; tent sites €10 plus per person €3.50, 2-/4-person cabins €45/75; ⊙ May-Sep; 🛜 ⛵) Situated 3.5km southwest of Karlby, the fabulous Sandvik Gästhamn & Camping caters to your every need, with sheltered sites, kitchen and laundry facilities, sauna, barbecue, shop, bikes for hire and a good swimming beach.

❶ Getting There & Away

Up to three daily ferries (passengers free, bicycle/car €6/34, 2¼ hours) come to Kökar from Galtby, Korpo, in the Turku Archipelago. From Långnäs, Lumparland, there are up to five daily ferry connections (passengers free, bicycle/car €6/34, 2¼ hours).

ÅLAND ARCHIPELAGO SOUTHERN ARCHIPELAGO

Tampere, Pirkanmaa & Häme

Includes ➡

Tampere	133
Pirkanmaa	140
Ruovesi	141
Helvetinjärvi National Park	141
Keuruu	141
Mänttä	142
Häme	143
Iittala	143
Hämeenlinna	143
Lahti	146

Best Places to Eat

➡ Bistro Popot (p149)

➡ Piparkakkutalo (p145)

➡ Neljä Vuodenaikaa (p138)

➡ Bistro 14 (p137)

➡ Piemonte (p138)

Best Places to Stay

➡ Art Hotel Honkahovi (p142)

➡ Dream Hostel (p135)

➡ Ylä-Tuuhosen Maatila (p141)

➡ Lapland Hotel Tampere (p136)

➡ Little Tundra Guesthouse (p147)

Why Go?

Modern cities and traditional settlements exist side by side in this historically replete region. Here, you can explore Finland's rural past at ancient wooden churches, learn about its unsettled history at Hämeenlinna's castle and admire its rich industrial heritage at Tampere's handsome textile factories (most now museums). The other major town, Lahti, excels in two major 21st-century Finnish exports: technology and classical music. Smaller towns and a liberal scattering of villages and hamlets are home to picturesque churches, a much-loved artist's retreat and a world-renowned glass factory.

There are plenty of outdoor activities to keep you occupied too. Every town in the region sits on a magical stretch of water and one of Finland's essential summer experiences is taking a lake cruise. Hikers can head to the trails in Helvetinjärvi National Park and keen skiers can join the annual Finlandia Ski Marathon in Lahti.

When to Go
Tampere

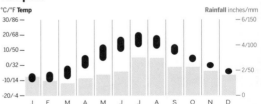

Jul Lake cruises and long evenings on summer terraces.

Sep Great hiking in national parks, and the Sibelius festival in Lahti.

Dec Christmas atmosphere and spectacular lights in Tampere.

Tampere, Pirkanmaa & Häme Highlights

① Serlachius Museum Gösta (p142) Admiring world-class art, architecture and landscape design in the attractive forest-edged art town of Mänttä.

② Tampere Absorbing the laid-back but culturally engaged vibe and checking out the vibrant local bar and restaurant scene in Finland's second-largest city.

③ Sibeliustalo (Sibelius Hall; p146) Attending a Sibelius performance at Lahti's architecturally significant and acoustically excellent harbourside concert hall.

④ Visavuori (p142) Exploring the wilderness atelier at this gallery and home of one of Finland's greatest sculptors, Emil Wickström.

⑤ Hattulan Pyhän Ristin (p143) Encountering extraordinary frescos in this 14th-century Gothic-style church in Hattula before wandering through the picture-perfect graveyard.

⑥ Hämeenlinna (p143) Visiting a sturdy 13th-century castle and authentically furnished 19th-century house in this museum-rich town.

TAMPERE

📞 03 / POP 228,907

Set between two vast lakes, scenic Tampere has a down-to-earth vitality and pronounced cultural focus. The Tammerkoski rapids churn through the centre, flanked by grassy banks contrasted with the red brick of the fabric mills that once drove the city's economy. Regenerated industrial buildings house quirky museums, enticing shops, pubs, cinemas and cafes.

History

In the Middle Ages the area was inhabited by the Pirkka, a devil-may-care guild of hunters, trappers and vigilant tax collectors. Modern Tampere was founded in 1779; during the 19th century its Tammerkoski rapids, which today supply abundant hydroelectric power, were a magnet for textile industries, and industrialists – including James Finlayson, a Scot – established huge mills here.

The 1917 Russian Revolution struck a chord with Tampere's large working-class population; the city became capital of the 'Reds' during the Finnish civil war and the scene of their biggest defeat. As the textile industry dwindled, the city was forced to reinvent itself; its urban renewal is one of Finland's success stories.

◉ Sights

★ Särkänniemi   AMUSEMENT PARK
(Map p136; www.sarkanniemi.fi; Laiturikatu 1; 1-day pass over 120cm/under 120cm €45/39; ⊙ rides mid-May–Aug, hours vary) This promontory-set amusement park complex offers dozens of rides, an observation tower, art gallery, aquarium, farm zoo and planetarium. A one-day pass gives you access to them all. Among the best rides are the Tornado roller coaster, super-fast High Voltage, speedboat rides on the lake and an Angry Birds area for younger kids. Opening times are complex; check the website. Indoor attractions stay open year-round. Take bus 20 (€3) from the train station or central square.

★ Amurin Työläismuseokortteli   MUSEUM
(Amuri Museum of Workers' Housing; Map p136; ☑ 03-5656-6690; www.museokortteli.fi; Satakunnankatu 49; adult/child €7/3, Fri 3-6pm free; ⊙ 10am-6pm Tue-Sun early May-early Sep) An entire block of wooden houses – including 32 apartments in five residential buildings, a bakery, a shoemaker, a public sauna, two general shops and a cafe – is preserved at the Amuri Museum of Workers' Housing, evoking life from 1882 to 1973. Interpretative panels (English translation available) outlining the fictional lives of residents give plenty of historical information and make for a visit that is as entertaining as it is educational. There's a good on-site cafe (soup lunch €7).

Moomimuseo   MUSEUM
(Moomin Museum; Map p136; ☑ 03-243-4941; www. muumimuseo.fi; Tampere Hall, Yliopistonkatu 55; adult/child €12/6; ⊙ 9am-7pm Tue-Fri, 11am-6pm Sat & Sun) Enter the world of Tove Jansson's enduringly popular Moomins (p92) at this impressive museum in Tampere-talo (p139). It contains original drawings and beautiful dioramas depicting scenes from these quirky stories (English explanations available).

Vakoilumuseo   MUSEUM
(Spy Museum; Map p136; ☑ 03-212-3007; www. vakoilumuseo.fi; Finlayson Centre, Satakunnankatu 18; adult/child €8/6; ⊙ 10am-6pm Mon-Sat, 11am-5pm Sun Jun-Aug, noon-6pm Mon-Sat, 11am-5pm Sun Sep-May; ⊕) The offbeat spy museum under the Finlayson Centre offers a small but well-assembled display of devices of international espionage, mainly from the Cold War era. As well as histories of famous Finnish and foreign spies, it has numerous Bond-style gadgets and some interactive displays. English translations are slightly unsatisfying. For €5 extra, kids aged 7+ can take a suitability test for KGB cadet school. Book ahead to take a lie detector test (€30) – excellent if you're travelling with teenagers!

Werstas   MUSEUM
(The Finnish Labour Museum; Map p136; www.tyo vaenmuseo.fi; Väinö Linnanaukio 8; admission charge for special exhibitions; ⊙ 11am-6pm Tue-Sun) FREE This worthwhile labour museum has a variety of changing exhibitions covering social history and labour industries. The permanent exhibition consists of three parts: a reconstruction of various historically typical Finnish workplaces – a shop and printing press; an in-depth focus on textiles; and a hall holding the enormous steam engine and wheel that powered the Finlayson factory in the 19th century.

★ Vapriikki   MUSEUM
(Map p136; www.vapriikki.fi; Alaverstaanraitti 5; adult/child €12/6, free Fri 3-6pm; ⊙ 10am-6pm Tue-Sun) This bright, modern glass-and-steel exhibition space in the renovated Tampella textile mill hosts regularly changing exhibitions on anything from bicycles to Buddhism. It also has a permanent display on Tampere's history, a beautiful mineral museum, a natural history museum and a small ice-hockey museum. There's also a museum of shoes – Tampere was known for its footwear industry – and a cafe (open 11am to 2pm Tuesday to Friday, noon to 3pm Saturday and Sunday).

★ Tuomiokirkko   CHURCH
(Map p136; ☑ 040-804-8765; www.tampereen seurakunnat.fi; Tuomiokirkonkatu 3; ⊙ 10am-5pm May-Aug, 11am-3pm Sep-Apr) FREE An iconic example of National Romantic art nouveau

architecture, Tampere's cathedral dates from 1907. Hugo Simberg created the frescoes and stained glass; you'll appreciate that they were controversial.

🏃 Activities

There are plenty of summer options on Tampere's two magnificent lakes. Trips on Näsijärvi leave from Mustalahti Quay (p140), while Laukontori Quay (p140) serves Pyhäjärvi. All cruises can be booked at the tourist office.

Suomen Hopealinja CRUISE
(Map p136; ☎010-422-5600; www.hopealinja.fi) Departing from Laukontori Quay (p140), the Finnish Silver Line operates short cruises on Pyhäjärvi between June and August and there's also a shuttle service (adult/child return €13/8) to nearby **Viikinsaari**, a pleasant picnic island.

Pyynikki WALKING
Rising between Tampere's two lakes, this forested ridge has fine views plus walking and cycling trails. It soars 85m above the lakeshores and claims to be the world's highest gravel ridge. A stone **observation tower** (www.munkkikahvila.net; Näkötornintie; adult/child €2/1; ☺9am-8pm, to 9pm Jun-Aug) holds a cafe serving freshly made doughnuts.

Rajaportin Sauna SAUNA
(☎050-310-2611; www.rajaportinsauna.fi; Pispalan Valtatie 9; adult/child €10/3, midweek €6/3; ☺6-10pm Mon & Wed, 3-9pm Fri, 2-10pm Sat) This traditional place is Finland's oldest operating public sauna. It's a chance to experience the softer steam from a traditionally heated sauna rather than the harsher electric ones. It's a couple of kilometres west of the city centre; buses 8, 11 and 13 head out there.

🎊 Festivals & Events

Tampere Film Festival FILM
(www.tamperefilmfestival.fi; ☺early Mar) A respected international festival of short films, held over five days in 10 venues across the city.

Tampere Biennale MUSIC
(www.tamperemusicfestivals.fi/biennale; ☺Apr) A festival of contemporary Finnish music, held in even-numbered years.

Tammerfest MUSIC
(www.tammerfest.fi; ☺mid-Jul) The city's premier rock-music festival is held over four days in summer. The main festival area is in the Ratinanniemi Festival Park, but there are also concerts across the city.

HIKING NORTH OF TAMPERE

The Pirkan Taival is a loose network of hiking trails totalling 330km in an area that stretches from Helvetinjärvi National Park (p141) westward to Seitseminen National Park and beyond. It's easy to work out your own route here; it's well marked, and regular signboards show distances. Scenery ranges from Finnish farmland to marshes, forests and gravel ridges. Huts and camping areas offer overnighting options. Trailheads reachable by bus from Tampere are Virrat, Ruovesi and Kuru. Buy a map at Tampere bookshops or the Seitseminen park visitor centre.

Tampere International Theatre Festival THEATRE
(www.teatterikesa.fi; ☺early Aug) Week-long showcase of international and Finnish theatre. Off-Tampere is a fringe festival held at the same time.

Tampere Jazz Happening MUSIC
(www.tamperemusicfestivals.fi/jazz/en; ☺Nov) International artists join local musicians from at this high-profile event. Gigs are held at The Old Customs House Hall, **Klubi** (Map p136; www.klubi.net; Tullikamarinaukio 2; ☺11am-6pm Mon-Tue, to 4am Wed-Sat) and Telakka (p139).

Tampereen Valoviikot LIGHT SHOW
(Tampere Festival of Light; www.valoviikot.fi; ☺late Oct–mid-Mar) The city's main streets are brightened by 40,000 coloured lights between sunset and 10.30pm (to 5am on Friday and Saturday) in winter. The central square becomes a Christmas market in December.

🛌 Sleeping

⭐**Dream Hostel** HOSTEL €
(Map p136; ☎045-236-0517; www.dreamhostel.fi; Åkerlundinkatu 2; dm €27-41, tw with shared bathroom from €53, s/d & tw from €65/72; ✳@🛜) 🌿 With its contemporary Nordic design, switched-on staff and good facilities, this hostel is consistently ranked Finland's best. Narrow dorms (unisex and female) have small under-bed lockers; bathrooms are barracks-like but clean. Facilities include a laundry and fully kitted-out self-catering kitchen (free tea and coffee). It's a 200m walk southeast of the train station in a quiet area. Breakfast costs €6.50.

Tampere

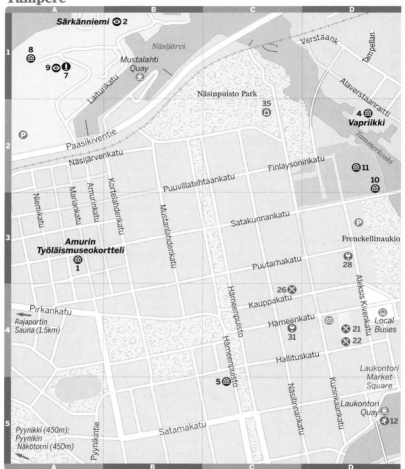

Scandic Tampere Station HOTEL €€
(Map p136; ☑03-339-8000; www.scandichotels.
com; Ratapihankatu 37; standard s/d €139/159,
superior s €160-220, superior d €180-240;
🅿✳@🛜🏊) As the name suggests, this
sleek, modern chain hotel is located right
by the train station. Spacious rooms are well
equipped; those in the superior category have
a kettle and some even have a sauna and balcony. Service is excellent. Parking costs €18.

Radisson Blu
Grand Hotel Tammer HISTORIC HOTEL €€
(Map p136; ☑020-123-4632; www.radissonblu.
com/hotel-tampere; Satakunnankatu 13; standard

s/d €140/160, superior d €180, ste €200-250;
🅿✳@🛜🏊) Constructed in 1929, this is one
of Finland's oldest hotels and enjoys a fine location beside the rapids. After the gloriously
old-fashioned elegance of the public areas,
the rooms are a little disappointing, though
they have the expected facilities and Nordic
comfort levels. Parking costs €18; a good
breakfast buffet and sauna are included.

★**Lapland Hotel Tampere** DESIGN HOTEL €€€
(Map p136; ☑03-383-000; www.laplandhotels.
com; Yliopistonkatu 44; s €180-210, d €200-230;
🅿✳@🛜) Part of the excellent portfolio of
contemporary hotels operated by the Lapland

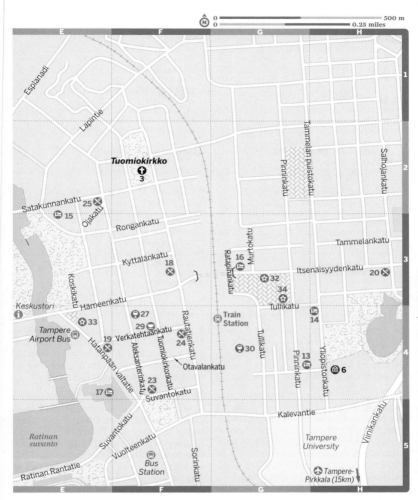

hotel group, this place has a chic ground-floor lounge bar, a sauna, well-equipped and extremely comfortable rooms and a restaurant where a generous and delicious buffet breakfast is served. Staff members are young and very helpful; on-site parking costs €18.

Sokos Hotel Ilves   HOTEL €€€
(Map p136; ☎020-123-4631; www.sokoshotels.fi; Hatanpään valtatie 1; r from €169; P❄@☎☰) This tower hotel was big news when it opened in the 1980s, and still keeps standards high. Very high: the view from upper-floor rooms is memorable, so ask for as lofty a chamber as you can get. Rooms are attractively furnished

with Finnish design classics; superiors are the same size but with even better views.

🍴 Eating

★Bistro 14   INTERNATIONAL €
(Map p136; ☎050-462-8204; http://bistro14.fi; Rautatienkatu 14; lunch buffet €7.50-9.70, 3-course dinner menu €33, mains €18; ⊙11am-9pm Wed-Thu, to 10pm Fri & Sat, to 3pm Sun Jun-Sep, 11am-3pm Mon & Tue, to 9pm Wed-Thu, to 10pm Fri & Sat, to 3pm Sun Oct-May; ☎🍴) With its sleek modern interior and talented French chef, this small place near the train station is garnering lots of local attention. The food is fresh

Tampere

◉ Top Sights
1 Amurin Työläismuseokortteli A3
2 Särkänniemi B1
3 Tuomiokirkko F2
4 Vapriikki D2

◉ Sights
5 Lenin Museo C5
6 Moomimuseo H4
7 Näsinneula Observation Tower A1
8 Sara Hildénin Taidemuseo A1
9 Särkänniemi Aquarium A1
10 Vakoilumuseo D2
11 Werstas D2

◉ Activities, Courses & Tours
12 Suomen Hopealinja D5

◉ Sleeping
13 Dream Hostel G4
14 Lapland Hotel Tampere H4
15 Radisson Blu Grand Hotel
     Tammer E3
16 Scandic Tampere Station G3
17 Sokos Hotel Ilves E4

◉ Eating
18 Bistro 14 .... F3
19 Bull E4
20 Hella & Huone H3
21 Kauppahalli D4
22 Neljä Vuodenaikaa D4
23 Piemonte F4
24 Ravintola C F4
25 Runo E2
26 Tiiliholvi C4

◉ Drinking & Nightlife
27 Café Europa F4
28 Deli 1909 & Wine Bar D3
29 Mokka Mestarit F4
30 Moro Sky Bar G4
31 Teerenpeli C4

◉ Entertainment
32 Klubi G3
33 Paapan Kapakka E4
     Tampere-Talo .... (see 6)
34 Telakka G3

◉ Shopping
     Taito Pirkanmaa .... (see 19)
35 Tallipiha C2

and light, with expertly balanced flavours and pretty presentation; diners who are gluten-free, lactose intolerant or vegetarian are catered for. The weekday lunch buffet is simply amazing value, as is the Sunday brunch (€12.50).

Kauppahalli   MARKET €
(Map p136; Hämeenkatu 19; ⊙8am-6pm Mon-Fri, to 3pm Sat; ☑) ✐ This intriguing indoor market is one of Finland's best, with picturesque wooden stalls serving a dazzling array of wonderful meats, fruit, baked goodies and fish. If hungry, you can snack on cheap *mustamakkara* (sausage made with cow's blood) with berry jam or sit down for a French feast at Neljä Vuodenaikaa.

Bull   BURGERS €
(Map p136; www.gastropub.net/bull; Hatanpään valtatie 4; burgers €14.50-18.50; ⊙10.30am-11pm Mon-Thu, to 1am Fri, 1pm-1am Sat, 1-11pm Sun; ☑) Patties made from 100% Black Angus beef are the centrepiece of many of Bull's towering burgers, including Dirty Harry (with blue cheese and red onion) and the Porn Master (with Thai spices).

Runo   CAFE €
(Map p136; www.kahvilaruno.fi; Ojakatu 3; pastries & buns €2.50; ⊙9am-8pm Mon-Sat, 10am-8pm Sun) Runo (Poem) is an tranquil cafe with armchairs, a large range of teas and excellent home-baked *pullat* (buns), croissants and biscuits. Slices of pizza and home-baked pies are popular orders at lunchtime.

★ Neljä Vuodenaikaa   BISTRO €€
(4 Saisons; Map p136; www.4vuodenaikaa.fi; Kauppahalli; soup €9.50, mains €18-22; ⊙8am-3.45pm Mon-Fri, to 3.30pm Sat) Tucked into the rear right-hand corner of the kauppahalli, the Four Seasons brings Gallic flair to the Finnish lunch hour with delicious plates such as bouillabaisse and *steak fritte* augmented by excellent daily specials and wines by the glass.

★ Piemonte   ITALIAN €€
(Map p136; ☑03-225-5505; www.piemonte.fi; Suvantokatu 9; mains €19-29; ⊙11am-9pm Mon, to 11pm Tue-Thu, to midnight Fri & Sat) The northwestern region of Italy is known for its excellent wine and food, and this laid-back wine bar pays it respect in both name and menu. A limited but delicious list of dishes includes a risotto, one or two pastas, a fish dish and one or two meat mains – the steak is particularly good. Excellent service and Italian wine list.

Tiiliholvi   FINNISH €€€
(Map p136; ☑020-766-9061; www.tiiliholvi.fi; Kauppakatu 10; mains €27-31, lunch buffet €28;

⊘11am-3pm & 5-11pm Mon-Fri, 3-11pm Sat) Set in the brick vaulted cellar of a Jugendstil (art nouveau) building, Tiiliholvi is into its fifth decade. It's still old-fashioned in feel, but the food isn't, and there are some excellent flavour combinations, along with beautiful presentation. If you're hungry, there are four- and six-course set menus (€58/69) on offer.

Hella & Huone
GASTRONOMY €€€

(Map p136; ☎010-322-3898; http://hellajahuone.fi; Salhojankatu 48; 6-/12-course menu €65/90, wine match €52/70; ⊘6-10pm Thu-Sat) Acclaimed chef Arto Rastas serves cutting-edge contemporary Nordic cuisine in this minimalistic space where black high-backed chairs provide a sharp contrast to the stark white tablecloths. Menus change with the season. Organic European drops dominate the wine list.

Ravintola C
FINNISH €€€

(Map p136; ☎010-617-9760; www.ravintola-c.fi; Rautatienkatu 20; mains €28, 6-course menu €68; ⊘5pm-midnight Tue-Sat; ☎) In a pristine, off-white dining room near the train station, this top Tampere restaurant creates innovative, beautifully presented modern dishes from a short menu with a focus on local ingredients and traditions. Meat tends to be slow-cooked and treated with respect, and there's always an interesting vegetarian main on offer.

🍷 Drinking & Nightlife

★ Mokka Mestarit
COFFEE

(Map p136; ☎03-253-0145; www.mokkamestarit.fi; Verkatehtaankatu 9; ⊘10am-6pm Mon-Fri, to 4pm Sat; ☎) 🍴 Espresso, cold-drip and Aeropress variations are on offer at this stylish cafe, along with hippie variations such as chai lattes and matcha bowls. It also has a huge range of tea and an array of panini and cakes to snack on – we love it.

★ Deli 1909 & Wine Bar
BAR

(Map p136; ☎050-441-1722; www.gastropub.net; Puutarhakatu 11; sandwiches €8.50; ⊘4-11pm Tue-Thu, 3pm-2am Fri & Sat) If only every Finnish town could have a bar like this one. Friendly staff, great music, highly drinkable beers on tap (try the Nordic Brewery's American Pale Ale), a good range of wine and a choose-your-own sandwich bar make for a great mix. Closes one hour earlier in winter.

Moro Sky Bar
BAR

(Map p136; www.sokoshotels.fi/en/tampere/solo -sokos-hotel-torni-tampere/restaurants; Ratapihankatu 43; ⊘11am-midnight Sun-Tue, to 2am Wed-Sat) Finland's highest bar sits on the 25th floor of the Solo Sokos Hotel Torni, Finland's tallest hotel, at 88m. Floor-to-ceiling glass windows offer a dizzying panorama of the city, as does the terrace. Local Olympians and other champion athletes are commemorated on its 'wall of heroes'. Craft beers are a speciality.

Café Europa
BAR

(Map p136; ☎010-05543; www.ravintola.fi/en/ravin tola/cafe-europa; Aleksanterinkatu 29; ⊘noon-midnight Mon & Tue, to 1am Wed & Thu, to 3am Fri & Sat, 1pm-midnight Sun; ☎) Horsehair couches, armchairs, mirrors, chandeliers and paintings endow this place with plenty of character, and there's a coveted summer pavement terrace too. It's a popular meeting spot for its board games, Belgian and German beers, huge salads and house-speciality hot breads (the kitchen closes at 9pm).

Teerenpeli
PUB

(Map p136; www.teerenpeli.com; Hämeenkatu 25; ⊘noon-midnight Sun-Thu, to 2am Fri, to 3am Sat) On the main street, this is a good place with excellent microbrewery beer and cider. It offers a relaxing, candlelit interior, a heated terrace and heaps of choice at the taps.

☆ Entertainment

★ Telakka
LIVE PERFORMANCE

(Map p136; ☎03-225-0700; www.telakka.eu; cnr Tullikamarinaukio & Tullikatu; cover €5-12; ⊘11am-midnight Mon-Thu, noon-3am Fri & Sat Jun-Aug, noon-3am Fri & Sat Sep-May) Comics and musicians regularly take the stage at this much-loved venue, which attracts arty, hip and fun-loving locals of every age. Drinkers and diners claim the tables in the front garden; the stage is inside. Always fun, it's irresistible during the Tampere Jazz Happening (p135).

Paapan Kapakka
JAZZ

(Pappa Music Pub; Map p136; ☎03-211-0037; www. paapankapakka.fi; Koskikatu 9; ⊘noon-midnight Sun-Mon, to 2am Tue-Thu, to 3am Fri & Sat) A bit of a Tampere institution, this offers live jazz, blues or swing every evening. The crowd is mostly 30-plus and really gets into it; this can be a special place on a good night.

Tampere-Talo
CONCERT VENUE

(Tampere Hall; Map p136; ☎03-243-4111; www.tam pere-talo.fi; Yliopistonkatu 55) Classical concerts are held in this modern hall. Performances by Tampere Filharmonia (www.tampere.fi/ filharmonia) are on Fridays from September to May. In addition to this it puts on regular chamber-music concerts and visiting opera and ballet performances.

GET YOUR KICKS ON RTE 66

Rte 66, starting northeast of Tampere and winding 75km north to Virrat, is one of Finland's oldest roads. When the song initially made famous by Nat King Cole was translated into Finnish, local rock star Jussi Raittinen adapted the lyrics to this highway in his song 'Valtatie 66'. It's a good drive, through young pine forest and lakescapes; the route is paralleled by the Poet's Way lake cruise. Good hiking and fishing opportunities exist; Ruovesi is the best-equipped base. Outside the June to high season, there's little going on.

Shopping

Taito Pirkanmaa   DESIGN
(Map p136; ☑ 03-225-1415; www.taitopirkanmaa.fi; Hatanpään valtatie 4A; ☺10am-6pm Mon-Fri, to 3pm Sat) ✎ Handcrafted Finnish products – clothing, textiles, confectionery, toys and jewellery included – are beautifully displayed at this corner boutique and make ideal gifts to take back home.

Tallipiha   ARTS & CRAFTS
(Map p136; www.tallipiha.fi; Kuninkaankatu 4; ☺10am-6pm Mon-Fri, to 5pm Sat, 11am-5pm Sun Jun-Aug) This restored collection of 19th-century stableyards and staff cottages houses artists and craftworkers who make handicrafts, chocolates, ceramics and shoes. The cafe and a shop open outside summer, but there's not much going on, except at Christmastime.

Information

Post Office (Map p136; www.posti.fi; Hämeenkatu 21; ☺9am-9pm Mon-Fri, to 7pm Sat, 11am-5pm Sun)
Visit Tampere (Map p136; ☑03-5656-6800; www.visittampere.fi; Hämeenkatu 14B; ☺10am-6pm Mon-Fri, to 3pm Sat & Sun Jun-Aug, 10am-5pm Mon-Fri, to 3pm Sat Sep-May; ☎)

Getting There & Away

AIR
Tampere-Pirkkala Airport (p303) is situated 17km southwest of the city. Airlines flying to/from Tampere:
AirBaltic Flies to Riga, Latvia.
Finnair Flies to Helsinki (though the train is more convenient), with connections to other Finnish cities.

Primera Air Nordic Flies to various destinations in Spain, Greece and Portugal.
Ryanair Flies to Bremen, Germany and Budapest, Hungary.
SAS Flies to Stockholm, Sweden.

BOAT
Boats from Mustalahti Quay head north to Virrat via Ruovesi. Cruises to Viikinsaari and to Hämeenlinna via Visavuori leave from Laukontori Quay.

BUS
From the **bus station** (Map p136; Hatanpään valtatie 7), express buses serve Helsinki (€25 to €27, 2¾ hours, up to four hourly) and Turku (€15 to €25, two hours, hourly). There are services to most other major towns in Finland.

TRAIN
Trains link Tampere's central **train station** (www.vr.fi; Rautatienkatu 25) with Helsinki (€21, 1½ to 1¾ hours, up to three hourly), Turku (€19 to €23, 1¾ hours, up to six daily) and other cities.

Getting Around

TO/FROM THE AIRPORT
Tampere-Pirkkala airport is 15km southwest; arriving flights are met by **bus** (Map p136; ☑0100-29400; www.paunu.fi; €4.70) 1A, which heads to the city centre (€5, 30 minutes). **Tokee** (☑0200-39000; www.airpro.fi) serves Ryanair flights, leaving from the train station forecourt about 2½ hours before take-off (€6).

Shared **airport taxis** (☑0100-4131; www.taksitampere.fi) must be booked in advance from the city to the airport (€19 per person). A regular cab will cost around €35.

BICYCLE
The summer-only **Citybike** (www.tamperecitybike.fi; ☺ mid-Jun–mid-Oct) scheme requires a €5 fee and a photo ID. Pay the fee and get the key from the tourist office and you'll have access to a whole network of bikes around town.

BUS
The local bus system is extensive. A one-day ticket costs adult/child €8/4 for inner-city zones and €16/8 to cover the complete network; single-trip tickets for short trips cost €3/1.50. Check route maps online at http://joukkoliikenne.tampere.fi. Buses depart from the stand near the Visit Tampere tourist office.

PIRKANMAA

Tampere is the geographic, cultural and economic centre of Pirkanmaa, a region of rolling green hills, picturesque lakes and rivers and small industrial towns.

Ruovesi

🔲 03 / POP 4532

Peaceful and pretty, Ruovesi is the main town on the Rte 66 stretch, with a couple of decent accommodation choices. Enjoying the lake is the only activity and cultural attractions are pretty well non-existent, but it makes a good base for exploring the area's attractions by car.

Haapasaaren Lomakylä　　CAMPGROUND €
(🔲 044-080-0290; www.haapasaari.fi; Haapasaarentie 5; tent sites €16.50 plus adult/child €5.50/2, cabins €40-75, 4-/8-person cottages €160/230; P 🛜 🐾) Connected to town by a causeway, this friendly and extremely well-kept campground on an islet north of town is a great choice. Surrounded by water, it offers grassed campsites, camp cabins with basic cooking facilities, and very comfortable self-contained cottages with sauna, barbecue and kitchen.

★ Ylä-Tuuhosen Maatila　　B&B €€
(🔲 050-553-4264; www.yla-tuuhonen.fi; Tanhuantie 105; s/d/q €75/100/160, cabins s €55-100, d €75-100; P 🛜) 🌿 A rustic, historic organic farm is run by generous-hearted owners, who offer three pretty rooms (sharing bathrooms) and an excellent communal kitchen and lounge. It also has boat and bike hire, and a lakeside smoke sauna. A variety of cabins are available too, plus evening meals (€20). Rates for subsequent nights drop by approximately 20%. Breakfast costs €8.

ℹ Information

Tourist Information (Wiljamakasiini; 🔲 044-787-1388; www.ruovesi.fi; Ruovedentie 5; ⊙11am-6pm early Jun–mid-Aug) Summer only.

ℹ Getting There & Away

At least one daily bus connects Ruovesi with Tampere (€15.50 to €18.80, 90 minutes), sometimes transferring at Orevesi. In summer, the **S/S Tarjanne** (🔲 010-422-5600; www.hopealinjat. fi/laivat/ss-tarjanne; ⊙ early Jun-early Aug), a historic steamship operated by the Hopealinjat company, cruises along the Poet's Way between Tampere and Virrat, stopping at Ruovesi en route.

Helvetinjärvi National Park

Northwest of Ruovesi, the main attraction of this **park** (www.nationalparks.fi) is narrow Helvetinkolu Gorge, gouged out by retreating glaciers at the end of the last Ice Age. The numerous trails include the 4km circular Helvetistä Itään Nature Trail into the gorge. There are designated campsites throughout the park, including one with a dry toilet at Helvetinkolu, near the Restaurant Helvetin Portti at the Kankimäki parking area. The park is signposted 7.5km west off Rte 66, about 9km north of Ruovesi.

Keuruu

🔲 014 / POP 9959

Nestled in a lovely location on the northern shore of Keurusselkä, Keuruu's major drawcard is its fascinating 18th-century wooden church. It and Petäjävesi, 28km east, make good pit stops en route between Jyväskylä and Mänttä.

Keuruun Vanha Kirkko　　CHURCH
(Keuru Old Church; 🔲 040-965-5597; Vanhankirkontie; adult/child €2/free; ⊙11am-4pm early Jun–mid-Aug, ask at tourist office rest of year) Keuruu's fascinating wooden church, built between 1756 and 1759, has superb portraits of Bible characters (although the artist didn't complete the set, due to a pay dispute), and its painted wooden ceiling depicts scenes from the Book of Revelations, with dark clouds across the firmament peopled by scattered cherubs, angels and devils. In true Lutheran fashion, there are no richly embroidered vestments or precious liturgical vessels in the rear sacristy – merely a nasty-looking set of stocks for miscreants.

M/S Elias Lönnrot　　CRUISE
(🔲 040-066-3689; adult/child return €15/7.50; ⊙mid-Jun–mid-Aug) This historic paddle steamer runs one-hour lake cruises between Ahtola Harbour in the centre of Keuruu and Hotel Keurusselkä near Valkealahti once or twice a week in summer. A one-way ticket costs adult/child €10/5. Check the schedule at www.visitkeuruu.fi.

ℹ Information

Tourist Information Office (🔲040-525-9548; www.keuruu.fi; Keuruuntie 7; ⊙10am-4.30pm Mon-Fri, to 2pm Sat) Close to Keuru Old Church.

ℹ Getting There & Away

Regular buses head to Jyväskylä (€12, one hour) via Petäjävesi (€6, 25 minutes) and to Mänttä (from €8, 30 to 40 minutes). All stop outside the Lähi-ABC petrol station on the main highway. Services are reduced on weekends.

Mänttä

📍 03 / POP 10,383

Set on a narrow isthmus between fast-flowing rapids, Mänttä grew around its paper mill, founded in the mid-19th century by the Serlachius dynasty. Progressive in outlook, the family endeavoured to build a model industrial community and endowed the town with noble buildings and art. In recent times, two impressive museums founded by the Serlachius family have led to Mänttä marketing itself as Finland's 'Art Town'. The Serlachius Museum Gösta attracts art-goers, and is the most persuasive reason to head here. Free bike and helmet hire at the Serlachius Museums encourages visitors to explore the town and travel between the museums. The best time to visit is between mid-June and August, during the Mänttä Art Festival.

◎ Sights

Free bike and helmet hire at the Serlachius Museums encourages visitors to explore the town and travel between the museums.

★ Serlachius Museum Gösta   GALLERY

(📍 03-488-6800; www.serlachius.fi; Joenniementie 47; adult/child incl entrance to Museum Gustaf €10/free; ⊙10am-6pm daily Jun-Aug, 11am-6pm Tue-Sun Sep-May) Once the private home of Gösta Serlachius, this world-class art gallery is one of Finland's premier cultural attractions. Situated 2km east of Mänttä's town centre in an exquisitely maintained

---

WORTH A TRIP

VISAVUORI

The residence of renowned sculptor Emil Wickström (1864–1942), **Visavuori** (📍 03-543-6528; www.visavuori.com; Visavuorentie 80; adult/child €8/2; ⊙10am-6pm daily Jun-Aug, to 4pm Tue-Sun Sep–mid-Dec & mid-Jan–May) consists of three buildings, the oldest of which is Wickström's 1902 house, built in Karelian and Finnish Romantic styles. This has an unusual octagonal lounge with a carved wooden ceiling. The fascinating studio next door (1903) is filled with dozens of models and sculptures; it also has a turret from which Wickström, a keen amateur astronomer, stargazed. The bronze foundry under the studio (Finland's first) is now a pleasant cafe.

---

garden, it comprises two buildings: a spectacular 2014 wooden pavilion designed by Spanish architectural firm MX_SI showcasing Finnish and international temporary exhibitions of contemporary art; and the original 1935 manor housing an excellent collection of Finnish golden-age works and European masterpieces, including works by Claude Monet, Jean-Baptiste Camille Corot and Camille Pissarro.

Serlachius Museum Gustaf   MUSEUM

(📍 03-488-6800; www.serlachius.fi; R Erik Serlachiuksenkatu 2; adult/child incl entrance to Museum Gösta €10/free; ⊙10am-6pm daily Jun-Aug, 11am-6pm Tue-Sun Sep-May) In the town centre, this elegant white 1930s modernist mansion was formerly the company HQ of the Serlachius family. Now a museum, it hosts a comprehensive display on the history of the paperworks and family, with audio exhibits on every conceivable aspect: you'd be here a week listening to them all.

★☆ Festivals & Events

Mänttä Art Festival   ART

(www.mantankuvataideviikot.fi; ⊙mid-Jun–Aug) Now in its second decade, this summer review of Finnish contemporary art is put together by a guest curator. It's staged in Pekilo, a former animal-feed refinery near the Mänttä mill chimney stack, and in various indoor and outdoor spots around town.

🛏 Sleeping & Eating

★ Art Hotel Honkahovi   BOUTIQUE HOTEL €€

(📍 03-474-7005; www.klubin.fi; Johtokunnantie 12; economy s/d €59/79, standard s/d €73/97, superior s/d €129/159; 🅿🖥) The prospect of spending a night in this wonderfully characterful hotel is reason enough for visiting Mänttä; when combined with a visit to the world-class Serlachius Museum Gösta, the prospect is even more enticing. A 1938 Moderne-style mansion, it offers three huge superior rooms overlooking the lake. These have their original (wonderful!) 1930s bathrooms, good beds, parquet floors and seating.

Hotel/Restaurant Mänttä Club   FINNISH €€

(📍 03-474-5900; www.klubin.fi; Tehtaankatu; set lunch €17.50; ⊙lunch 11am-3pm Mon-Fri) Popular with visiting businesspeople, this upmarket hotel near the Serlachius Museum Gustaf has a restaurant offering a well-priced three-course set lunch on weekdays.

ℹ Information

Tourist Information (📞 03-488-8555; www.
manttavilppula.fi; Seppälänpuistotie; ⊙10am-
5pm Mon-Fri, to 3pm Sat early Jun-Jul, to 5pm
Mon-Fri Aug, to 4pm Tue-Fri Sep-early Jun)

ℹ Getting There & Away

Several buses each weekday run to Jyväskylä
(€18 to €20, 1½ to two hours) via Keuruu and
Petäjävesi. There are also regular services to
Tampere (€17.30 to €20, 1½ to 1¾ hours). The
town appears as Mänttä-Vilppula on timetables.

The Serlachius Museums offer a shuttle bus
from Tampere's bus station at 10.50am on days
that the museums are open (one way/return
€25/15, child half-price, 90 minutes). It returns to
Tampere at 5.30pm. Advance bookings (📞 040-
166-3480; sales@serlachius.fi) are essential.

HÄME

This region of southern central Finland, also
known as Tavastia, has historically been an
important one. The castle at Hämeenlinna
was the middle of the line of three imposing
Swedish fortifications across the breadth of
Finland. Today this ancient stronghold contrasts with the modernity of Lahti, the region's other main city.

Iittala

📞 019

The little settlement of Iittala, just off the
E12 between Tampere and Hämeenlinna,
is world-famous for its glass factory, which
has been at the forefront of Finnish design
for decades. The factory complex includes a
glass museum, outlet shop and restaurant.

Suomen Lasimuseo   MUSEUM
(Finnish Glass Museum; 📞 019-758-4108; www.
suomenlasimuseo.fi; Könnölänmäentie 2C; adult/
child €6/3; ⊙11am-5pm Tue-Sun Jun-Aug, 11am-
5pm Sat & Sun Sep-May) Tracing the history of
Finland's glass industry, this museum has two
floors filled with thousands of glass items, including pieces from most of Iitalla's ranges.
There are also technical exhibits explaining
glass-making techniques and technologies.

Iittala Glass Factory   FACTORY
(📞 020-439-3512; Tehtaantie 3; ⊙10am-6pm Mon-
Fri Aug-late Jun) FREE Established in 1881, this
factory has huge kilns containing a total of 40
tonnes of molten glass kept at a temperature
of 1450°C (2642°F). On weekdays, you can
stand on an balcony above the factory floor

HATTULAN PYHÄN RISTIN

Dating from the early 1300s, **Hattulan
Pyhän Ristin** (Church of the Holy Cross;
Vanhankirkontie 41, Hattula; guided tour €6;
⊙11am-5pm mid-May–mid-Aug), a Gothic-style church in a walled churchyard,
has an interior filled with fabulous naive
frescoes created in the early 16th century. The interior also features a fine carved
and painted pulpit from 1550. A peaceful
grassed graveyard next to the church
slopes down to the water's edge.

to watch the master glass-blowers working in
front of one of the glowing steel kilns. To enjoy a guided tour (€40 per group) of the factory and Suomen Lasimuseo, book in advance.

ℹ Getting There & Away

Trains between Hämeenlinna (€2.60, 13 minutes, at least five daily) and Tampere (€4.60,
35 minutes) stop in Iittala, and buses also run
here weekdays from Hämeenlinna (€6.80, 35
minutes). Tampere–Hämeenlinna express buses
stop on the highway 2km from town.

Hämeenlinna

📞 03 / POP 67,706

Dominated by its namesake castle, Hämeenlinna (Swedish: Tavastehus) is Finland's oldest inland town, founded in 1649, though a
trading post had existed here since the 9th
century. The Swedes built the castle in the
13th century, and Hämeenlinna developed
into an administrative, educational and garrison town around it. The town is quiet but
picturesque, and its wealth of museums will
keep you busy for a day or two. It makes a
good stop between Helsinki and Tampere.

◎ Sights & Activities

★**Hämeenlinna**   CASTLE
(Häme Castle; Map p144; 📞 029-533-6932; www.
kansallismuseo.fi/en/hame-castle; adult/child
€9/4.50; ⊙10am-3.30pm Tue-Fri & 11am-4pm Sat
& Sun mid-Aug–mid-Dec & mid-Jan–Apr, 10am-4pm
Mon-Fri & 11am-4pm Sat & Sun May, daily 10am-
5pm Jun–mid-Aug) Hämeenlinna means Häme
Castle, so it's no surprise that this bulky twin-
towered red-brick fortress is the town's pride
and most significant attraction. Construction
was begun in the 1260s by the Swedes, who
wanted to establish a military redoubt against

Hämeenlinna

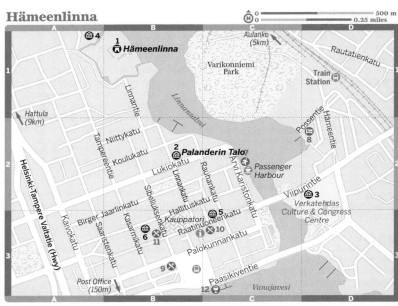

Hämeenlinna

◎ Top Sights
1 Hämeenlinna	B1
2 Palanderin Talo	B2

◎ Sights
3 Hämeenlinnan Taidemuseo	D2
4 Museo Militaria	A1
5 Museo Skogster	C3
6 Sibeliuksen syntymäkoti	B3

◉ Activities, Courses & Tours
7 Suomen Hopealinjat	C2

🛏 Sleeping
8 Sokos Hotel Vaakuna	D2

✖ Eating
9 Café Kukko	B3
10 Green Laurell	C3
11 Laurell	B3
Piparkakkutalo	(see 5)

🍷 Drinking & Nightlife
Albertin Kellari	(see 5)
12 Boat Bars	C3
Nooran Viinibaari	(see 5)

the power of Novgorod. It was originally built on an island, but the lake receded and necessitated the building of new walls. It never saw serious military action and, after the Russian takeover of 1809, was converted into a jail.

★ Palanderin Talo MUSEUM

(Map p144; ☏ 03-621-2967; www.hmlmuseo.fi; Linnankatu 16; adult/child €5/2; ⊙ noon-4pm Tue-Sun May-Aug, Sat & Sun Sep-Apr) Finland loves its house-museums and this is among the best, offering a wonderful insight into well-off 19th-century Finnish life, thanks to excellent English-speaking guided tours. There's splendid imperial and art nouveau furniture as well as delicate little touches like a double

-sided mirror to spy on street fashion, and a set of authentic children's drawings period.

Hämeenlinnan Taidemuseo GALLERY

(Hämeenlinna Art Museum; Map p144; ☏ 03-621-2669; www.hameenlinna.fi/taidemuseo; Viipurintie 2; adult/child €10/free; ⊙ 11am-6pm Tue-Thu, to 5pm Fri-Sun) Housed in a former granary designed by CL Engel, the town gallery holds an interesting collection of Finnish art from the 19th and 20th centuries. Notable is Gallen-Kallela's painting of the *Kalevala's* final scene, with the shaman Väinämöinen leaving Finland, representing the conquest of Christianity. The building opposite houses excellent temporary exhibitions.

Museo Militaria
MUSEUM

(Tykistömuseo, Military Museum; Map p144; ☎ 040-450-7479; www.museomilitaria.fi; Vanhankaupunginkatu 19; adult/child €8/4; ⊙ 11am-5pm Sep-May, 10am-5pm Jun-Aug) There are numerous museums devoted to Finnish involvement in WWII, but this takes the cake. It's huge. There are three floors packed with war memorabilia, including good information in English on the beginnings of the Winter War. Outside, and in a separate hall, is a collection of heavy artillery big enough to start a war.

Aulanko
PARK

(www.aulanko.fi) North of the town centre, this central-European-style park with ponds, swans, pavilions, a granite fortress and exotic trees was created early in the 20th century by Hugo Standertskjöld. Modern additions include a summer-only adventure park (www.hugopark.fi, admission €25) and a spa resort (www.cumulus.fi). Although the best way to explore it is on foot, the sealed one-way road loop is accessible by car. Bus 2 (€3.40, 15 minutes) gets you here from central Hämeenlinna, or it's a pleasant 5km bike ride.

Sibeliuksen syntymäkoti
MUSEUM

(Map p144; ☎ 03-621-2755; www.hmlmuseo.fi; Hallituskatu 11; adult/child €5/2; ⊙ 10am-4pm May-Aug, noon-4pm Tue-Sun Sep-Apr) Composer Johan Julius Christian (Jean) Sibelius was born in Hämeenlinna in 1865 and was schooled here, but the town makes surprisingly little fuss about it. His childhood home is a small museum containing photographs, letters, his upright piano and some family furniture. It's a likeable place, although uninformative about his later life. Concert performances on summer Sundays are free with an entry ticket.

Museo Skogster
MUSEUM

(Map p144; ☎ 03-621-2528; www.hmlmuseo.fi; Raatihuoneenkatu 8; ⊙ 11am-5pm Tue & Thu-Sun, to 7pm Wed) FREE The ground floor of this newly opened museum in the former Skogster Department Store has a small theatrette where an excellent short film about the history of Hämeenlinna is shown in a number of languages, including English. Entry to the museum's ground floor is free, but you'll need a ticket (adult/child €5/2) to visit the temporary exhibitions in the upstairs space.

Suomen Hopealinjat
CRUISE

(Finnish Silverline; Map p144; ☎ 010-422-5600; www.hopealinjat.fi) Suomen Hopealinja operates two-hour cruises around the harbour on the M/S *Silver Sky* (adult/child €20/12) and one 8½-hour cruise to Tampere via Visavuori between mid-May and August. Check the schedule and prices for the latter at the passenger harbour (p146).

🛏 Sleeping

There is a pronounced lack of accommodation in Hämeenlinna, with the only acceptable options being business hotels in the city centre and the Cumulus spa resort at Aulanko.

Sokos Hotel Vaakuna
HOTEL €€

(Map p144; ☎ 020-1234-636; www.sokoshotels.fi; Possentie 7; s/d from €116/131; 🅿 @ 🛜 🐾) Across the river from the town centre and very near the train station, this attractive hotel echoes Häme Castle with its design. Many of the rooms have great water views, as does the in-house French restaurant.

🍴 Eating

Café Kukko
CAFE €

(Map p144; ☎ 03-616-5670; www.cafekukko.fi; Palokunnankatu 11; sandwiches €4-6, buns & pastries €2.60; ⊙ 8am-8pm Mon-Fri, 10am-5pm Sat & Sun; 🛜) Every town needs a good cafe, and Kukko certainly fits the bill. Its bright, diner-style interior has a long counter with an espresso machine and displays of buns, brownies and pastries. A refrigerated cabinet is filled with healthy sandwiches (choose from salad, falafel or smoked salmon), making it as popular at lunch as it is at breakfast. Good coffee too.

Laurell
CAFE €

(Map p144; ☎ 03-467-7722; www.laurell.fi; Sibeliuksenkatu 7; pastries €2-3, sandwiches & baguettes €4-7; ⊙ 8.30am-6pm Mon-Fri, to 8pm Wed, to 5pm Sat, 11am-5pm Sun; 🛜) This spacious cafe on the market square is a Hämeenlinna stalwart and popular meeting place. Choose from the selection of both savoury and sweet. A more sandwichy Green Laurell (Map p144; Raatihuoneenkatu 11; lunches €5.50-9.50; ⊙ 7am-5pm Mon-Fri, 9am-2pm Sat; 🛜), is in the same building as the tourist office.

★ Piparkakkutalo
FINNISH €€

(Map p144; ☎ 03-648-040; www.ravintolapiparkakkutalo.fi; Kirkkorinne 2; mains €20-34; ⊙ 11am-10pm Tue-Thu, to 11pm Fri, noon-11pm Sat) This fairytale-style 'gingerbread house' was built in 1907 for merchant August Skogster, whose department store was next door, and it is now home to the town's best restaurant. The interior still has a warm, domestic feel. Food includes Finnish classics, a few vegetarian choices and burgers, all made using fresh local produce.

TAMPERE, PIRKANMAA & HÄME HÄMEENLINNA

🍷 Drinking & Nightlife

Nooran Viinibaari
WINE BAR

(Map p144; ☑040-487-8234; Raatihuoneenkatu 8; ⊗5-10pm Mon & Tue, to 11pm Wed & Thu, 3pm-midnight Fri & Sat, 3-9pm Sun) You'll feel as if you're enjoying a drink at a friend's house when at this wine bar next to the Skogster Museum. Featuring comfortable chairs, shelves of books and fresh flowers, it's a relaxing spot for a glass of wine and cheese platter.

Albertin Kellari
PUB

(Albert's Basement; Map p144; ☑03-633-5150; www.ravintolapiparkakkutalo.fi; Kirkkorinne 2; ⊗4pm-2am Wed & Thu, to 3am Fri & Sat) Head to this cosy basement pub under the Piparkakkutalo on Wednesdays and Thursdays for karaoke, and on weekends to hear live music.

Boat Bars
BAR

(Map p144; Paasikiventie; ⊗11am-2am mid-May–mid-Sep) In high summer, two adjacent boat bars offer relaxed lakeside drinking on floating wooden decks.

ℹ️ Information

Post Office (Hämeensaarentie 7; ⊗8am-9pm Mon-Fri, 10am-6pm Sat)

Tourist Office (Map p144; ☑03-621-3373; www.visithameenlinna.fi; Raatihuoneenkatu 11; ⊗9am-4pm Mon-Fri; 🛜)

ℹ️ Getting There & Away

Boats (p145) cruise to Tampere via Visavuori in summer. Services are limited, and depart from the passenger harbour.

Hourly buses between Helsinki (€17 to €20, 1½ to 1¾ hours) and Tampere (€12.60, 65 minutes) stop at the **bus station** (Map p144; Eteläkatu 1), as do regular buses to/from Lahti (€10 to €13.20, 75 minutes). From Turku, there are several buses daily (€15 to €21, 2¼ hours).

The train station is 1km from the town centre, across the bridge. Frequent trains between Helsinki (€15, one hour) and Tampere (€7 to €11, 40 to 60 minutes) stop here.

Lahti

☑03 / POP 119,368

The frighteningly high ski jumps at Lahti's sports centre are put to spectacular use during the annual Lahti Ski Games and have hosted plenty of international events over the years, including the 2017 FIS Nordic World Ski Championships. Of the other factors drawing visitors to this modern town 90km northeast of Helsinki, the architecturally significant Sibeliustalo (Sibelius Hall) and its world-class resident symphony orchestra are the most notable. There are also a number of well-presented museums and lake cruises. It's a pleasant place to visit, particularly as its eating and drinking options are more impressive than in most Finnish towns.

👁️ Sights & Activities

There's a winter ice-skating hall at the Lahden Urheilukeskus (Sports Centre) as well as a gym, an indoor swimming pool and 145km of cross-country ski tracks (great for summer biking and hiking too). In summer, the outdoor swimming pool, children's adventure playground and hiking trails are put to good use. In summer, **Päijänne Risteilyt Hilden Oy** (Map p148; ☑010-320-8820; www.paijanne-risteilythilden.fi; ⊗Jun-early Sep) runs a variety of cruises leaving from the harbour.

⭐ Sibeliustalo
ARCHITECTURE

(Sibelius Hall; Map p148; ☑600-393-949; www.sibeliustalo.fi; Ankkurikatu 7; tours per group Mon-Sat €100, Sun €200; ⊗box office noon-5pm Mon-Fri) Designed by acclaimed Finnish architects Hannu Tikka and Kimmo Lintula, the spectacular extension to Lahti's main concert venue opened in 2000 and is widely acknowledged as one of the most significant local architectural works of recent decades. Occupying a prime position on the harbour, the complex features a new timber-lined auditorium that is linked to an older building by a cathedral-like foyer with huge glass walls and tall pillars designed to resemble a Finnish forest.

Lahden Urheilukeskus
SPORTS CENTRE

(Lahti Sports Centre; Map p148; www.lahti.fi/palvelut/liikunta-ja-ulkoilu/urheilukeskus; Salpausselänkatu 8) Dominated by three imposing ski jumps, the biggest standing 73m high and stretching 116m, Lahti's Sports Centre is the city's major attraction. In summer, visitors can often see high-level jumpers training.

Hiihtomuseo
MUSEUM

(Ski Museum; Map p148; ☑050-398-5523; www.lahdenmuseot.fi; Sports Centre, Salpausselänkatu 8; adult/child €9/3; ⊗9am-5pm Tue-Fri, 11am-4pm Sat & Sun) As well as a refurbished 'Sense of Skiing' exhibition that documents the history of the city's snow sports, this popular museum has a hugely enjoyable 3D ski-jump simulator and an optical biathlon practice rifle that visitors can have fun with. If visiting in summer, consider taking the chairlift (€4) to the observation terrace at the top of the ski jump.

Ski-Jump Observation Terrace   VIEWPOINT
(adult/child €8/4; ⊙ 10am-5pm Mon-Fri, 11am-5pm Sat & Sun Jun-Aug) In summer you can take a chairlift (€4) up to this observation terrace at the top of the ski jumps at the Lahden Urheilukeskus; it's great if there's someone practising, and good for the views in any event.

Lahden Historiallinen Museo   MUSEUM
(Lahti Historical Museum; Map p148; ☑ 03-814-4536; www.lahdenmuseot.fi; Lahdenkatu 4; adult/child €9/3; ⊙ 9am-5pm Tue-Fri, 11am-4pm Sat & Sun) Occupying a handsome late-19th-century manor house, Lahti's historical museum stages hanging exhibitions illustrating aspects of the city's history, with a particular focus on the tradition of local furniture-making. The middle floor is mostly devoted to the collection of former diplomat Klaus Holma, which is a treasury of French and Italian religious art, rococo furniture and fine porcelain.

Ristinkirkko   CHURCH
(Church of the Cross; Map p148; Kirkkokatu 4; ⊙ 10am-3pm) Construction of this fourth and final church designed by Alvar Aalto was completed in 1978, two years after his death. Though showcasing his signature design style (light-saturated interior, windows overlooking greenery, lots of joinery, elegant lamps), its unusual features include a cross formed by glass bricks inserted into the exterior wall.

Hollolan Kirkko   CHURCH
(☑ 03-524-6611; Rantatie, Hollola; ⊙ 11am-6pm Jun-Aug, 10am-6pm Sun May, 11am-4pm Sun Sep-Apr) [FREE] On the shores of Vesijärvi, this large church 17km northwest of Lahti is an elegant late-15th-century structure with steep gables. Mounted above the double nave are 24 fine polychrome wooden sculptures of saints; also noteworthy are the 14th-century baptismal font and Pietà from an earlier, wooden church on the site. The church is marked 'Hollola kk' on signs and bus timetables.

⚜ Festivals & Events

Finlandia Ski Marathon   SPORTS
(Finlandia-hiihto; http://fhen.etaika.fi; ⊙ late Feb) Thousands of skiers of all ages attend this two-day mass ski event.

Ski Games   SPORTS
(www.lahtiskigames.com) Held in early March (usually on the first weekend), these games are the headline act in Lahti's program of winter sports events.

Sibelius Festival   MUSIC
(www.sinfonialahti.fi/sibelius; ⊙ Aug-Sep) Lahti's headline cultural festival presents performances by Sinfonia Lahti, the city's famous symphony orchestra. Performances are staged in the Sibeliustalo. Dates change each year.

🛏 Sleeping

⭐**Little Tundra Guesthouse**   GUESTHOUSE €€
(Map p148; ☑ 400-822-115; www.littletundra.fi; Moisionkatu 4B; s/d cabin €55/87, s/d apt €80/95; P 🛜) Plenty of ingenuity and flair have gone into the design of this welcoming guesthouse. Five yurt-like cabins furnished with colourful textiles have been inserted into an old railway workshop, offering an utterly unique sleeping experience. There's also a communal lounge with TV, a basic kitchenette, central heating and one shared bathroom. No breakfast.

Messilä Ski Centre   RESORT €€
(☑ 03-86011; www.messila.fi; Messiläntie 308; s/d €120/140, 3-/4-person cottages €180/220, log cabins €250-300; P 🛜) Various accommodation types are dotted around the 10 ski slopes here, managed as one estate. Packed in winter, it is quiet in summer, and visitors make use of the nearby Messilä golf course (check the website for packages). The two on-site restaurants are popular for après-ski socialising.

⭐**Solo Sokos Hotel
Lahden Seurahuone**   HOTEL €€€
(Map p148; ☑ 020-123-4655; www.sokoshotels.fi/en/lahti/sokos-hotel-lahden-seurahuone; Aleksanterinkatu 14; s €150-180, d €180-210; P ✴ 🛜) Located in the centre of town, this hotel is Lahti's best. It's also popular, so book in advance. Well-equipped rooms have double-glazed windows, comfortable beds and good-sized bathrooms. The buffet breakfast is excellent and the bar and bistro welcoming. Use of the sauna is free; parking costs €16.

🍴 Eating & Drinking

⭐**Kahvila Oskari**   CAFE €
(Map p148; ☑ 041-700-0735; www.kahvilaoskari.fi; Hämeenkatu 17; baked items from €3; ⊙ 9am-6pm Mon-Fri, 10am-5pm Sat) An intoxicating aroma of sugar and spices greets patrons as they enter this cute cafe in an old-timer house, making it almost obligatory to order a bun, brownie or indulgently rich slice of cake with your tea and coffee. In summer, the shady garden seating beckons; in cooler weather, a traditional stove inside keeps everyone toasty warm.

Lahti

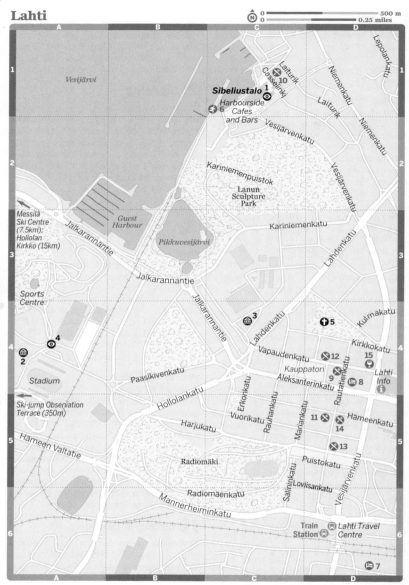

Vesijärvi

Messilä
Ski Centre
(7.5km);
Hollolan
Kirkko (15km)

Guest
Harbour

Pikkuvesijärvi

Jalkarannantie

Jalkarannantie

Jalkarannantie

Sports
Centre

Stadium

Ski-jump Observation
Terrace (350m)

Hämeen Valtatie

Paasikivenkatu

Hollolankatu

Harjukatu

Radiomäki

Radiomäenkatu

Mannerheiminkatu

Sibeliustalo

Harbourside
Cafes
and Bars

Vesijärvenkatu

Kariniemenpuistok

Lanun
Sculpture
Park

Kariniemenkatu

Lahdenkatu

Lahdenkatu

Vapaudenkatu

Kauppatori

Aleksanterinkatu

Erikonkatu

Vuorikatu

Rauhankatu

Mariankatu

Salininkatu

Loviisankatu

Puistokatu

Kulmakatu

Kirkkokatu

Rautatienkatu

Hämeenkatu

Vesijärvenkatu

Lahti
Info

Lepolankatu

Niemenkatu

Laiturik

Niemenkatu

Vesijärvenkatu

Laiturik
Casselinki

Train
Station

Lahti Travel
Centre

Mamma Maria   ITALIAN €

(Map p148; ☎03-751-6716; www.mammamaria.
fi; Vapaudenkatu 10; pizza €10-15, pasta €10-22;
⊙11am-10pm Mon-Thu, to 11pm Fri, noon-11pm
Sat, noon-9pm Sun) Family run, this bustling
trattoria takes its Italian heritage seriously.
It offers Italian beer and wine, an extensive pizza menu and an impressive range of
pasta, including *pasta fresca fatta a mano*
(handmade fresh pasta) dishes featuring
rich ragùs of boar, duck or reindeer.

Lahti

◎ **Top Sights**
1 Sibeliustalo................................C1

◎ **Sights**
2 Hiihtomuseo A4
3 Lahden Historiallinen Museo C4
4 Lahden Urheilukeskus A4
5 Ristinkirkko.............................D4

◉ **Activities, Courses & Tours**
6 Päijänne Risteilyt Hilden Oy..................C1

◎ **Sleeping**
7 Little Tundra Guesthouse D6

8 Solo Sokos Hotel Lahden
Seurahuone D4

◎ **Eating**
9 Bistro Popot D4
10 Casseli..C1
11 Kahvila Oskari D5
12 Mamma Maria D4
13 Roux...D5
14 Taivaanranta Grill & Distillery D5

◎ **Drinking & Nightlife**
15 Teerenpeli...D4

★ **Bistro Popot**   BISTRO €€

(Map p148; ☑010-279-2935; www.bistropopot.
fi; Rautatienkatu 26; starters €9-13, mains €16-29,
lunch buffet €10-13; ◐10.30am-9.30pm Fri & Sat,
to 10.30pm Fri & Sat; 🛜🍴) Chef Andrew Smith
learned his craft in the UK, France and Swit-
zerland before relocating to Finland and
wowing Lahti with his modern seasonally
driven cuisine. His menu roams Europe and
ventures occasionally into Asia – everything
is exquisitely presented and absolutely delicious. Service is friendly and assured, and
the wine list is excellent.

Taivaanranta Grill & Distillery   FINNISH €€

(Map p148; ☑042-492-5230; www.taivaanranta.
com; Rautatienkatu 13; mains €19-32; ◐11am-
11pm Mon-Tue, to midnight Wed-Fri, noon-midnight
Sat; 🛜) This good-natured place sits above
the distillery where Teerenpeli's well-regard-
ed single malt is produced, so it's no surprise that its whisky-and-mustard steak is
the most popular item on the menu. Other
choices are equally indulgent (try the escargot bruschetta or the lobster soup).

Casseli   FUSION €€

(Map p148; ☑010-422-5950; www.casseli.fi;
Borupinraitti 4; lunch mains €13-26, dinner mains
€18-33; ◐11am-3pm Mon, to 10pm Tue-Fri, noon-
10pm Sat; 🛜) One of a number of harbourside restaurants near Sibelius Hall, Casseli
boasts a large interior dining space and a
summertime deck. There's a popular weekday lunch buffet (€10.50) between 11am and
2pm. In the evening, the à la carte menu is
limited but competently executed.

Roux   FINNISH €€€

(Map p148; ☑010-279-2930; www.roux.fi; Rautatienkatu 7; mains €18-42, set menus €55-69;
◐4pm-midnight) Dishes at this endearingly
old-fashioned restaurant aren't as interesting

or impressive as its menu would suggest, but
it's still one of the city's best dining venues.
The owners and chef hail from Lapland, so
reindeer and other Sami delicacies are good
choices. The wine list and service levels are
impressive. It opens for Sunday brunch
(noon to 5pm) between September and May.

Teerenpeli   PUB

(Map p148; ☑042-492-5220; www.teerenpeli.com;
Vapaudenkatu 20; ◐noon-midnight Sun & Mon, to
2am Tue-Thu, to 3am Fri & Sat) A real Lahti success story, this pub has been serving its own
beers, ciders and single-malt whisky to loyal
regulars since 1994. It's got a welcoming interior and is always humming with chatter.
Those who choose to settle in for a long session can also order pub grub, including toasted sandwiches, salads and sausages.

ℹ Information

Lahti Info (Map p148; ☑300-472-222; www.
visitlahti.fi; Aleksanterinkatu 18; ◐10am-5pm
Mon-Fri, 9am-4pm Sat; 🛜) Centrally located
and extremely helpful.

The city offers free wi-fi through its Lahtifree
network. You'll be able to access this at most
cafes and shops in the centre.

ℹ Getting There & Away

Intercity buses depart from the **Lahti Travel
Centre** (Map p148; Mannerheiminkatu 15).
There are regular buses to Helsinki (from €10, 1½
hours), Tampere (€15 to €25.60, two hours) and
Hämeenlinna (€10 to €13.20, 75 minutes). There
are also hourly buses to Helsinki airport (from
€10, 75 minutes).

Numerous direct trains run daily to/from Helsinki (from €13, one hour) and Riihimäki, where
you can change for Tampere. There are also
services to/from Helsinki Airport (from €12.50,
55 minutes).

The Lakeland

Includes ➡

Savonlinna.......... 151
Punkaharju 155
The Seal Lakes 157
Sulkava............158
Mikkeli 158
New Valamo........160
Jyväskylä..........161
Around Jyväskylä....167
Kuopio 168

Best Places to Eat

➡ Pöllöwaari (p165)

➡ Figaro Winebistro (p165)

➡ Kahvila Nanda (p160)

Best Places to Stay

➡ Hotel Yöpuu (p164)

➡ Lossiranta Lodge (p153)

➡ Oravi Village (p157)

➡ Lomamokkila (p153)

➡ Scandic Hotel Kuopio (p171)

Why Go?

Most of Finland could be dubbed lakeland, but around here it seems there's more aqua than terra firma. Reflecting the sky and forests as clearly as a mirror, the sparkling, clean water leaves an indelible impression. When exploring the region, it's almost obligatory to get waterborne, whether it be while practising your paddling skills in a canoe or by hopping aboard a historic steamboat for leisurely progress down canals and across lakes.

On land, there's just as much to do. Architecture buffs from around the globe make the pilgrimage here to visit Alvar Aalto's buildings, opera aficionados arrive en masse to attend the world-famous Savonlinna Opera Festival and outdoor enthusiasts shoulder their packs and set out to hike through tranquil forests of spruce, birch and pine. And at the end of active days, there are always saunas to relax in.

When to Go
The Lakeland

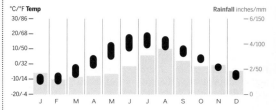

Feb Check out the ice sculptures in Savonlinna, and explore Linnansaari National Park on skates.

Jul Paddle the lakes and attend summer festivals, including the opera in Savonlinna.

Aug See all the highlights in decent weather but without the July crowds.

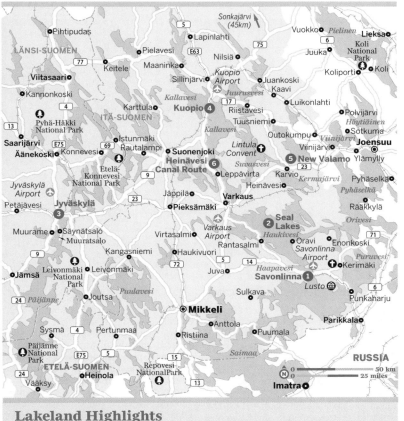

THE LAKELAND SAVONLINNA

Lakeland Highlights

❶ Savonlinna Opera Festival (p155) Attending an opera staged under the stars in the courtyard of a magnificent medieval castle.

❷ The Seal Lakes (p157) Seeking a glimpse of the rare Saimaa ringed seal while paddling around the lakes within the Linnansaari and Kolovesi national parks.

❸ The Alvar Aalto trail (p164) Joining international architecture buffs on an Aalto pilgrimage in and around Jyväskylä.

❹ Jätkänkämppä (p169) Sweating it out in Kuopio's sociable smoke sauna and then jumping into Lake Kallavesi whatever the weather.

❺ New Valamo (p160) Cruising the picturesque waters en route to Finland's only Orthodox monastery, Valamon Luostari.

❻ Heinävesi Canal Route (p169) Admiring some of the Lakeland's most magnificent scenery aboard the M/S *Puijo*.

Savonlinna

🎵 015 / POP 34,905

The historic frontier settlement of Savonlinna is one of Finland's prettiest towns and most compelling tourist destinations. Scattered across a garland of small islands strung between Haukivesi and Pihlajavesi lakes,

its major attraction is the visually dramatic Olavinlinna Castle, constructed in the 15th century and now the spectacular venue of July's world-famous Savonlinna Opera Festival (p155). In summer, when the lakes shimmer in the sun and operatic arias waft through the forest-scented air, the place is quite magical. In winter it's blanketed in fairy-tale-like

Savonlinna

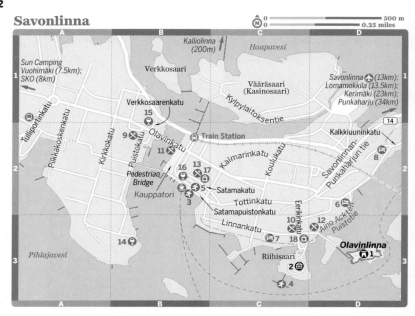

snow, and its friendly locals can be relied upon to offer visitors a warm welcome.

☉ Sights

★ Olavinlinna
CASTLE

(St Olaf's Castle; ☎ 029-533-6941; www.kansallis museo.fi; Olavinlinna; adult/child €9/4.50; ⊙ 11am-5.15pm Jun–mid-Aug, 10am-3.15pm mid-Aug–May, closed mid-Dec–early Jan) Built directly on rock in the middle of the lake (now accessed via bridges), this heavily restored 15th-century fortification was constructed as a military base on the Swedes' restless eastern border. The currents in the surrounding water ensure that it remains unfrozen in winter, which prevented enemy attacks over ice. To visit the castle's upper levels, including the towers and chapel, you must join an hour-long guided tour. Guides bring the castle to life with vivid accounts of its history.

Riihisaari
MUSEUM

(Lake Saimaa Nature & Culture Centre; ☎ 044-417-4466; www.savonlinna.fi/museo; adult/child €7/3, incl Olavinlinna €10/4.50; ⊙ 10am-5pm Tue-Sun Sep-Apr, 9am-5pm Mon-Fri & 10am-5pm Sat & Sun May, 10am-5pm daily Jun-Aug) On an island that was once a naval port, this museum housed in a handsome 16th-century granary recounts local history and the importance of water transport. It also has a number of exhibits about the history, flora and fauna of Lake Saimaa, including a 12-minute video about the underwater world of Torsti, an endangered ringed seal pup living in the lake. Exhibits on the ground floor are more interesting than those upstairs.

Outside, there's a group of historic watercraft to board (open mid-May to mid-September). These include the *SS Mikko*. Information about the town and region, including the Linnansaari National Park, is available from the ground-floor ticket office/information desk.

🏃 Activities

Numerous operators run tours allowing you to explore some of this Lakeland area – head to the Satamapuistonkatu (passenger harbour) to see what's on offer. Most offer one-hour cruises around town between June and August. You can also board one of the historic steamships operated by VIP Cruise for a 90-minute shoreline cruise.

VIP Cruise
CRUISE

(☎ 050-025-0075; www.vipcruise.info/en; Satamapuistonkatu; ⊙ Jun-Aug) Operates three historic steamships – S/S *Paul Wahl*, S/S *Punkaharju* and S/S *Savonlinna* – offering 90-minute sightseeing cruises on Lake Saimmaa (adult/child €20/10).

Savonlinna

◎ Top Sights
1 Olavinlinna...D3

◎ Sights
2 Riihisaari...C3

◔ Activities, Courses & Tours
3 Saimaan Laivamatkat Oy......................B2
4 SS Mikko...C3
5 VIP Cruise...B2

▣ Sleeping
6 Lossiranta Lodge....................................D2
7 Perhehotelli Hospitz C3
8 Tavis Inn D2

◎ Eating
9 Café Alegria B2
10 Kahvila Saima..C3
11 Kalastajan Koju B2
12 Linnakrouvi...D3
13 Majakka.. B2

◎ Drinking & Nightlife
14 Huvila.. B3
15 Olutravintola Sillansuu..........................B1
16 Waahto Bistro & Terrace..................... B2

◎ Shopping
17 Runo Design B2
18 Studio Marja Putus................................C3

SS Mikko CRUISE
(Map p152; ☎044-417-4466; adult/child €15/10; ◔Jul) Part of the watercraft collection of the Riihisaari, this 1914 wooden steam barge offers 90-minute cruises on the lake during July.

Saimaan Laivamatkat Oy CRUISE
(Map p152; ☎015-250-250; www.mspuijo.fi; Satamapuistonkatu; one-way €95, return by same-day car €130, return with/without overnight cabin €180/150; ◔mid-Jun–mid-Aug) Century-old M/S *Puijo* cruises from Savonlinna to Kuopio on Monday, Wednesday and Friday at 9am (10½ hours), returning on Tuesday, Thursday and Saturday. The boat passes through scenic waterways, canals and locks. You can book a return with or without an overnight cabin accommodation or opt for a same-day package with a return car transfer (minimum four passengers). On-board meals are available.

▣ Sleeping

SKO HOSTEL €
(☎015-572-910; www.sko.fi; Opistokatu 1; s €40-75, tw €50-100; ▣@☎) Six kilometres southwest of Savonlinna, this Christian college offers rooms in a variety of buildings in a peaceful location near a lake. Each building has a kitchen; some have good common areas. There's a big range: some cheaper rooms in Villa Tupala are brighter than pricier en suite rooms in Wanha Pappila, for example. Breakfast costs €6; lunch and dinner buffets €8 to €12. Bus 3 stops nearby. Signposted 'Kristillinen Opisto'.

Sun Camping Vuohimäki CAMPGROUND €
(☎045-255-0073; www.suncamping.fi; Pärnäläntie 21; tent sites €15 plus €5.50 per person, 4-person cottage €75-95, 4-person cottage with shared bathroom €65-90; ◔early Jun-late Aug; ▣☎▣) Located 7km southwest of town, this grassed and treed campground has good facilities but isn't

maintained as well as it should be. Nevertheless, its lovely setting ensures that it's usually solidly booked. It has an on-site sauna, a children's playground and a restaurant.

★Lomamokkila FARMSTAY €€
(☎015-523-117; www.lomamokkila.fi; Mikonkiventie 209; farmhouse s/d €105/110, guesthouse s €75-85, guesthouse d €80-90, cottages €55-180; ▣☎) ✦ This farmstay 12km northwest of Savonlinna is run by a genial Finnish family and incorporates a handsome century-old farmhouse, two guesthouses and lakeside cottages with sauna and their own jetty and rowboat (but no wi-fi). There are three pretty rooms in the main farmhouse and eight rooms in each guesthouse; the latter share a kitchen and lounge.

★Lossiranta Lodge BOUTIQUE HOTEL €€
(Map p152; ☎044-511-2323; www.lossiranta.net; Aino Acktén Puistotie; s €85-160, d €110-290, extra person €60; ▣☎) The dress-circle views of Olavinlinna Castle are one of many good reasons to stay at this boutique hotel on the lakeshore. There are five rooms sleeping between two and four, the best of which has its own wood sauna and outdoor hot tub. All are attractively decorated and most have kitchenettes. Staff are both friendly and helpful.

Tavis Inn GUESTHOUSE €€
(Map p152; ☎044-511-2323; www.lossiranta.net; Kalkkiuuninkatu; s €85-160, d €100-220, ste & apt €110-260, extra person €60; ▣☎) In a tranquil end-of-the-road spot that's a short lakeside stroll from Olavinlinna Castle, this annexe of Lossiranta Lodge (where you check in) offers two rooms, four suites and one apartment in a 1915 timber house; all are stylishly decorated. Some have kitchenettes. Bathrooms are small.

Perhehotelli Hospitz
HOTEL €€

(Map p152; ☑ 015-515-661; www.hospitz.com; Linnankatu 20; standard s €98-145, standard d €108-170, r with balcony €153-215; ⊙ Apr-Dec; 🅿 🛜) Endearingly old-fashioned, this hotel opened in the 1930s in an excellent location between the harbour and Olavinlinna. Common areas, including the grand breakfast room, retain many original fittings, and there's a wonderful lakeside terrace. Rooms are elegant, although beds are narrow and bathrooms small; the best have balconies with lake views. Service has a *Fawlty Towers*-esque flavour.

🍴 Eating

Kalliolinna
CAFE €

(https://lettukahvilakalliolinna.com; Sulosaari; crêpes from €4.50; ⊙ late May–mid-Aug) Hidden among the trees on a small island just north of the town centre, this ultra-friendly and quite delightful cafe serves a limited menu of coffee, tea and crêpes. Fillings for the freshly made crêpes are both sweet and savoury, and include delights such as cloudberry jam and cream. It's an easy walk from the kauppatori.

Café Alegria
CAFE €

(Map p152; ☑ 044-320-8001; www.cafealegria.net; Puistokatu 3; soup, roll & butter €6.80, sandwiches €6.50-8; ⊙ 10am-7pm Mon-Fri, to 3pm Sat; ☑) Tucked into the corner of an old timber hall that now functions as a community centre, Alegria offers comfortable indoor seating, a few tables on the rear grassed terrace, homemade soup, sandwiches and an array of delicious cakes. All can be enjoyed with fair-trade and organic tea and coffee. It's a great choice for a light lunch.

Kahvila Saima
CAFE €

(Map p152; ☑ 015-515-340; www.kahvilasaima.net; Linnankatu 11; dishes €7-17; ⊙ 9.30am-5pm Jun-Aug, 10.30am-4.30pm Wed-Sun Sep-May) Set inside a wooden villa with stained-glass windows, and opening to a wide terrace out the back, this charmingly old-fashioned cafe is adorned with striped wallpaper and serves home-style Finnish food, including good cakes and baked items. It stays open till 11.30pm on opera days.

Kalastajan Koju
SEAFOOD €€

(Map p152; www.kalastajankoju.com; Kauppatori; fried muikku €9.50, with dip, mayonnaise or remoulade €10.50, with potato & salad €16.90; ⊙ 11am-10pm Mon-Thu, to midnight Fri & Sat, to 9pm Sun) Owned by a fisherman who heads out on the lake each morning to catch the *muikku* (vendace, or whitefish, a common lake fish) that this place specialises in, Kalastajan

Koju is conveniently located on the water by the kauppatori and is particularly busy in summer. The menu also includes fish and chips, bratwurst and fried salmon.

Linnakrouvi
FINNISH €€

(Map p152; ☑ 015-576-9124; www.linnakrouvi.fi; Linnankatu 7; mains €18-33; ⊙ noon-10pm or later Mon-Sat, 3-10pm or later Sun late Jun–mid-Aug) Overlooking Olavinlinna Castle, this summer restaurant employs chefs from Helsinki and serves Savonlinna's most sophisticated food. Unsurprisingly it's hugely popular during the opera season. There's tiered outdoor seating, an attractive interior and a range of fare running from burgers to freshly caught and beautifully prepared fish from Lake Saimaa. There's a limited but impressive wine list.

Majakka
FINNISH €€

(Map p152; ☑ 015-206-2825; www.kattaasavon. fi; Satamakatu 11; mains €17-32, kids' menu €8; ⊙ 11am-10pm Mon-Thu, to 11pm Fri, noon-11pm Sat, noon-10pm Sun; ✳ 🛜 🚼) The name of this popular family bistro means 'lighthouse', reflecting its location overlooking the harbour. Steaks, burgers and locally caught fish are well-cooked, generously sized and fairly priced; the select-your-own appetiser plate is a nice touch. Service is brisk but friendly.

🍸 Drinking & Nightlife

⭐ Huvila
MICROBREWERY

(Map p152; ☑ 015-555-0555; www.panimoravintola huvila.fi; Puistokatu 4; mains €24-35, 3-course menu €45-50; ⊙ noon-10pm Jun-Aug; 🛜) Sitting across the harbour, Huvila is operated by the Waahto brewery and is a delightful destination in warm weather, when its lakeside deck is full of patrons relaxing over a pint or two of the house brew (try the Golden Ale). There's also an attractive dining area in the old timber house. Sadly the menu promises more than it delivers.

Olutravintola Sillansuu
PUB

(Map p152; Verkkosaarenkatu 1; ⊙ 2pm-2am Tue-Sat, to midnight Sun & Mon) Savonlinna's best pub is compact and cosy, offering an excellent variety of international bottled beers and a decent whisky selection. There's a downstairs area with a pool table; during the opera festival, amateur (and sometimes professional) arias are sung as the beer kegs empty.

Waahto Bistro & Terrace
BAR

(Map p152; ☑ 015-510-677; www.waahto.fi; Satamapuistonkatu 5; mains €19-34; ⊙ noon-10pm

SAVONLINNA OPERA FESTIVAL

This **festival** (Savonlinnan Oopperajuhlat; ☑ 015-476-750; www.operafestival.fi; Olavinkatu 27) enjoys an enviably dramatic setting in the covered courtyard of Olavinlinna Castle. Inaugurated in 1912, it stages four weeks of top-class opera performances between early July and early August each year. The atmosphere in town during the festival is reason enough to come: it's buzzing, with restaurants serving post-show midnight feasts, and animated discussions and impromptu arias on all sides. The festival's website details the program: there are rotating performances of four or five operas by the Savonlinna company, as well as at least one opera by an international guest company and a few concert performances. The castle walls are a magnificent backdrop to the set and add great atmosphere. There are tickets in various price bands. The top grades (€139 and up) are fine, but the penultimate grades (€85 to €112) put you in untiered seats, so it helps to be tall. The few cheap seats (€55) have a severely restricted view. Buy tickets up to a year in advance online.

Mon-Thu, to 11pm Fri & Sat, to 8pm Sun Jun-Aug, 4-10pm Tue-Sat Sep-May) By the kauppatori and harbour, this pub is owned by the local brewery and has a great summer terrace that's perfect for a sundowner. Come here for a drink rather than to eat, as the food is both pricey and disappointing.

🛍 Shopping

Runo Design　　　　　　　　　DESIGN
(Map p152; ☑ 050-3059-715; www.runodesign.fi; Satamakatu 11; ⊙10am-3pm Mon, to 4pm Tue-Fri) Everything in this gorgeous atelier has been handmade in Savonlinna. Textile designer Mervi Pesonen uses natural materials such as flax, wool, park skirt and cotton marshmallow to make stylish bags, cushions, throws and tea towels.

Studio Marja Putus　　　　　　CLOTHING
(Map p152; ☑ 040-526-5129; www.marjaputus.fi; Linnankatu 10; ⊙9am-5pm Mon-Fri, daily during Opera Festival) Artist and fashion designer Maria Putus makes and sells stylish outfits (many made using Marimekko fabric) at her atelier in a timber house in the historic precinct.

ℹ Information

Savonlinna has no official tourist office, but the ticket desk in the Riihisaari (p152) stocks maps and brochures about the city and region. Other information can be accessed via www.savonlinna.fi.

ℹ Getting There & Away

AIR

Savonlinna Airport (SVL; ☑ 020-708-8101; www.finavia.fi; Lentoasemantie 50) is 14km north of town, and is predominantly used by charter flights. Finnair flies here during the opera season.

BOAT

Boats connect Savonlinna's **passenger harbour** (Satamapuistonkatu; Map p152) with many lakeside towns; check www.oravivillage.com for seasonal schedules. The **M/S Puijo** (p153) cruises between Savonlinna and both Kuopio and Lappeenranta in summer.

BUS

Savonlinna is not on major bus routes, but buses link the **bus station** (Map p152; Tulliportinkatu 1) with Helsinki (€30, 5½ hours, up to nine daily), Mikkeli (€20, 1½ hours, up to 14 daily) and Jyväskylä (€30, 3½ hours, up to eight daily).

TRAIN

Punkaharju (€3, 30 minutes, at least four daily) is one of the few destinations that can be accessed via a direct service from Savonlinna. To get to Helsinki (€48, 4¼ hours, up to four daily) and Joensuu (€25, 2¼ hours, up to four daily), you'll need to change in Parikkala. The train station is in the town centre near the kauppatori. Buy your ticket at the machines – there's no ticket office.

ℹ Getting Around

Shared **taxis** (☑ 0500-250-099; www.jsturva taksit.fi) meet flights at Savonlinna airport.

There are car-hire agencies at the airport, and a **Hertz** (☑ 020-555-2750; www.hertz.fi; Rantakatu 2; ⊙7.30am-9pm Mon-Fri, 9am-9pm Sat & Sun) office in town. Book well ahead.

Several places hire bikes in summer, including **InterSport** (Olavinkatu 52; per day/week €20/70; ⊙9.30am-6pm Mon-Fri, to 5pm Sat, 11am-3pm Sun).

Punkaharju

☑ 015 / POP 3645
Punkaharju, the famous pine-covered esker (sand or gravel ridge) on the shore of Lake

KERIMÄKI

Kerimäki may be small (pop 5000), but its Lutheran church, **Kerimäen Iso Kirkko** (Kerimäki Church; www.kerimaenseurakunta.fi; ⊗10am-6pm late Jun & early Aug, to 7pm Jul, to 4pm early Jun & late Aug), certainly isn't. Built in 1847, the building was designed to accommodate 5000 and is commonly described as the world's largest wooden church. At the time of its construction, the town's population was 12,000, and the reverend wanted a church that could seat at least half of all residents. The building's scale is immense and the grand, light-drenched interior features stained-glass lamps and unusual wood panels painted to resemble marble.

Nineteenth-century worshippers arrived by water, crossing the lakes in a *kirkkovene* (church longboat). During services they were kept warm by eight huge stoves; these days the church is only open during the summer months.

A cafe and handicrafts shop are on the ground floor of the bell-tower structure in front of the church (proceeds go towards the maintenance, an onerous burden for a small parish).

Regular buses run between Savonlinna and Kerimäki (€6.10, 30 to 40 minutes); Sunday services are greatly reduced. Don't catch a train: Kerimäki station is miles from the village.

Saimaa, is touted in tourist brochures as 'Finland's national landscape'. The region was first declared a protected area by Tsar Alexander in 1803 and became a favoured summering spot for St Petersburg gentry. The unspoiled landscape is extremely picturesque and great for walking, cycling and cross-country skiing. It can be reached on an easy day trip from Savonlinna, but is also an appealing place to stay. For more information, go to www.visitpunkaharju.fi and www.nationalparks.fi/en/punkaharju.

◉ Sights & Activities

★**Lusto Suomen Metsämuseo**　　MUSEUM
(The Finnish Museum of Forestry; ☑015-345-100; www.lusto.fi; Lustontie 1; adult/child €10/5; ⊗10am-5pm Tue-Sun Jan-Apr & Oct-Dec, to 5pm daily May & Sep, to 7pm daily Jun-Aug) 'Lusto' is the Finnish word for a tree's annual growth ring, and this well-curated and cleverly presented museum is all about forests and the growth of the local timber industry. Displays (with English labels) cover everything from forest biodiversity, forest healers and forest myths, to the history of forest settlements and forestry technology. The huge hall filled with machinery features a tower of chainsaws and various interactive displays – everyone will enjoy testing their motor skills with a timber loader.

Punkaharju　　NATURAL FEATURE
(www.nationalparks.fi) During the Ice Age, formations similar to this 7km-long sand ridge were created all over Finland. Because it crosses a large lake, it's always been an important travel route. Short sections of the original unsealed road along the ridgetop remain – once part of a route to Russia connecting the Olavinlinna and Vyborg (Viipuri) castles. The national parks website carries information about hiking on the ridge.

🛏 Sleeping

Punkaharju Resort　　RESORT €
(Punkaharjun Lomakeskus; ☑029-007-4050; www.punkaharjuresort.fi; Tuunaansaarentie 4; tent & caravan sites €14 plus per adult/child €5/2.50, 2-person apt €125-190, 2-/4-person camping cottages €42/63; P🔊🐾) Near Retretti train station, this enormous lakeside resort has a whole town's worth of campsites, solid cabins, cottages and apartments. Facilities include a beach, restaurant, tennis court and minigolf course. It's great for kids, who'll want to spend most of their time in the popular waterpark next door.

Rantakatti　　FARMSTAY €€
(☑015-644-400; www.rantakatti.fi/en; Rantakatintie 22, Vaahersalo; s €70-80, d €90-110, villa €200, tent/caravan site €10/20 plus per person €3; ⊗May-Sep; P🔊) The highlight of this retreat in the forest is its wonderful lakeside location. It offers basic B&B rooms in three buildings and a self-contained villa sleeping up to eight; the villa has a private sauna. Rantakatti has a restaurant, plenty of animals for the children to visit and rowboats for hire (€5 per hour). It's popular with school groups.

Hotelli Punkaharju　　HOTEL €€€
(☑Mon-Fri 015-511-311; www.hotellipunkaharju.fi; Harjutie 596; s/d/ste €180/220/280, tw without bathroom €120; ⊗Jun-late Aug; P@🔊) Set among peaceful pine trees on the lake, this romantic 19th-century wooden hotel was once the gamekeeper's lodge for the Russian royal

hunting estates, and includes a majestic separate villa built for the tsarina. There's a variety of room types and prices, including summer-only cabins with shared bathroom facilities. Doubles are old-fashioned and cramped; opt for a superior instead.

❶ Getting There & Away

Trains between Savonlinna and Parikkala (€3.80, 55 minutes, five daily) stop at Retretti (€3, 20 minutes), Lusto (€3, 25 minutes) and Punkaharju (€3, 30 minutes).

The Seal Lakes

📄 015

Two primarily watery national parks in the Savonlinna area – Kolovesi and Linnansaari – offer fabulous lakescapes dotted with islands that are best explored by hiring a canoe or kayak. Several outfitters offer these services, and free camping spots dot the lakes' shores. It's the best part of the Lakeland to really get up close and personal with this region's natural beauty.

This is the habitat of the endangered freshwater Saimaa ringed seal. Separated from its Baltic cousins at the end of the last Ice Age, it was in imminent danger of extinction during the 20th century due to hunting and human interference. Though there remain only a precarious 300-odd of the greyish beasts, population levels are on the increase. Late May is the most likely time to see seals, as they are moulting and spend much time on rocks.

Linnansaari National Park

This scenic **national park** (http://www.national parks.fi/en/linnansaarinp) consists of Haukivesi Lake and hundreds of uninhabited islands; most visitors head to the largest island, Linnansaari, which has marked hiking trails. As well as the endangered Saimaa ringed seal, which features in the park's logo, rare birds, including ospreys, can also be seen. The best way to experience the park is to rent a kayak and spend a few days exploring. Kayaks, canoes, camping equipment, ice skates, snow shoes and ice-fishing sets can be hired from Oravi Village.

Sammakkoniemi　　CAMPGROUND, CABIN €
(📄 050-027-5458; http://oravivillage.com; tent sites €10, q hut €55; ☺May-Oct) Operated by Oravi Village, this summer-only campground on Linnansaari Island has simple sites, five huts and shared cooking and toilet facilities. It

also has a sauna (€25 per hour) and a kiosk-cafe (from late June to mid-August only). Camping is free outside high summer.

★ Oravi Village　　HOTEL €€
(📄 015-647-290; http://oravivillage.com; Kiramontie 15, Oravi; s/d from €65/75, villas from €400; P ❄ @ 🛜) Beautifully set by the river in Oravi, the eastern access point for Linnansaari National Park, this excellent facility offers comfortable accommodation and also provides everything necessary to get on the water (or ice). As well as upmarket holiday villas, it has a cracking modern hotel offering rooms with kitchen, drying cabinet and free sauna use. Breakfast costs an extra €10 to €14.

**Hotel & Spa Resort
Järvisydän**　　SPA HOTEL €€€
(📄 020-729-1760; www.jarvisydan.com; Porosalmentie 313, Porosalmi; s/d €170/200, ste €250-380; P @ 🛜 ❄) Located at Porosalmi, an embarkation point for Linnansaari National Park, this impressive medieval-themed holiday village offers a big variety of accommodation, including hotel rooms and self-contained villas; book well in advance for a villa. Good meals are available in the atmospheric restaurant: don't miss the unusual wine cellar.

❶ Getting There & Away

Buses run to Rantasalmi from Savonlinna (€10, 40 minutes). From Rantasalmi, it's 7km to the turn-off for Porosalmi (Varkaus-bound buses can drop you here), and a further 3km walk down to the accommodation complex.

The Savonlinna–Kuopio cruise operated by Saimann Laivamatkat Oy (p169) stops at Oravi.

Scheduled boat services run to Linnansaari from Oravi (adult/child €9.50/4.50, three daily late June to mid-August, 15 minutes).

Kolovesi National Park

Northeast of Linnansaari National Park, less-trafficked **Kolovesi** (http://www.national parks.fi/kolovesinp) covers several pine-forested islands. There are high hills, rocky cliffs and caves, and prehistoric rock paintings. Saimaa ringed seals, as well as otters and eagle owls, call Kolovesi home.

Hiking, fishing and berry picking are popular activities in the park, which is also a paradise for canoeing – the best way to explore the fantastic scenery. Motorboats are prohibited. There are several restricted areas, and the islands are out of bounds all winter to protect the seals, whose pups are born in February.

LOCAL KNOWLEDGE

CANOE TRIPS

Kolovesi Retkeily (☑040-558-9163; www.sealtrail.com) is an experienced tour operator, specialising in canoe rental, outfitting and multiday journeys for all abilities. It has a rental office in Oravi and another in Kirkkoranta, the major western entrance to Kolovesi National Park.

The gateway town is pleasant Enonkoski, with a bright stream and rapids dividing it in two. There's a **park information cabin** (☑020-639-5539; ◷10am-4pm Mon-Fri, to 3pm Sat & Sun mid-Jun–Jul, 10am-4pm Mon-Fri, to 3pm Sun early Aug) here. The park starts a further 12km north. A free ferry north of Enonkoski crosses the narrows between two lakes on Rd 471. You can head from Kolovesi to Oravi and then Linnansaari National Park by canoe. Kolovesi Retkeily specialises in canoe rental, outfitting and multiday journeys for all abilities.

ⓘ Getting There & Away

Three buses (€7.40, 40 minutes) travel between Savonlinna and Enonkoski, 15km south of the park, on weekdays. You'll need to take a taxi from Enonkoski to the park.

Sulkava

☑015 / POP 2846

Tiny, sedate and extremely scenic, this village 39km southwest of Savonlinna is known as the finishing point for the Oravereitti, Finland's most famous canoeing route. If visiting for the annual Sulkavan Suursoudut rowing festival, be sure to organise your accommodation well in advance.

Sulkavan Suursoudut   SPORTS
(Sulkava Rowing Race; www.suursoudut.fi; ◷Jul) This four-day rowing festival attracts huge crowds. Up to 10,000 competitors row wooden boats of various sizes around Partalansaari over a 70km two-day course or a 60km one-day course, then get thoroughly hammered. The highlights are the races involving *kirkkoveneet*, 15-person longboats traditionally used to get to church across the lakes. Boat-rental details and entry forms are on the website.

Sulkavan Oravanpesät   CAMPGROUND €
(☑040-093-8076; www.oravanpesat.fi; Kalajärventie 13; tent sites €12 plus per person €3, cabins €60-110; ◷May-Sep; ℗) At the halfway point of the Oravareitti (Squirrel Route), close to the

2km-long Kaitajärvi, is this friendly campground. It offers tent sites and six log cabins with shared bathroom and cooking facilities. There's also a much-appreciated smoke sauna. These folk can also hire canoes, kayaks and fishing gear, and arrange transport along the route. Meals can be pre-organised.

Ollinpolun Matkakoti   GUESTHOUSE €€
(☑050-593-9688; www.ollinpolunmatkakoti.fi; Ollinpolku 2; r per person €50; ℗ 🛜) Just up the hill from the bridge in the centre of Sulkava, the Ollinpolun Travel House offers simple, typically Finnish rooms. Breakfast is served at a nearby cafe. Open year-round.

Alina   CAFE
(☑044-417-5215; www.sulkava.fi; Alanteentie 28; ◷9am-4pm Tue-Fri, extended hours midsummer-Jul) Friendly cafe and shop that also offers limited tourist information.

ⓘ Information

Limited tourist information can be accessed at Alina cafe and shop. Information about accommodation and activities in the village and region can be accessed at www.sulkava.fi.

ⓘ Getting There & Away

There are five buses to/from Savonlinna Monday to Saturday (€8.20, 45 minutes). Weekday-only services to/from Mikkeli and Juva are predominantly geared towards school children.

Mikkeli

☑015 / POP 54,308

Set on the shores of Saimaa, Finland's largest lake, this sizeable provincial town is an important regional transport hub and military base, and was the headquarters of the Finnish army during WWII; visiting museums relating to those years are the main – in truth only – compelling reason to visit.

⊙ Sights & Activities

The Mikkeli area is excellent for fishing – the lakes teem with perch, salmon and trout, and ice-fishing is popular in winter. The tourist office (p160) can give advice as to how you can source permits, guides and equipment.

Kenkävero   HISTORIC SITE
(☑040-0162-270; www.kenkavero.fi; Pursialankatu 6; ◷10am-6pm Sun-Fri, to 4pm Sat) A picturesque 19th-century timber parsonage estate 1.3km southwest of the city centre on the shore of Lake Saimaa, Kenkävero is now Mikkeli's

CANOEING THE SQUIRREL ROUTE

The **Oravareitti** (Squirrel Route; www.oravareitti.fi) canoeing route is a Lakeland highlight. The 57km beginner- and family-friendly journey starts at Juva and traverses lakes, rivers and gentle rapids on the way to Sulkava. It's a very pretty trip: you feel miles away from the stresses of everyday life; information boards along the route describe local nature.

You can do the trip in two strenuous days; there's a good campground. But this means around six to nine hours of paddling each day, so you may want to do it in three, or even four days. This would mean taking a tent, which you can hire at Juva Camping. Another option is a drop-off further along the route, making for an easier first day. Late spring and early summer see the best water levels.

Getting Started

Hospitable **Juva Camping** (☎ 015-451-930; www.juvacamping.com; Poikolanniementie 68, Juva; tent/caravan €17, 2-/4-person cabins with shared bathroom €40/50, self-catering cottages €60-95; ☉ May-Sep; P 🖙 🐾) provides everything you need: it hires out two-person Canadian canoes (€40 per day) or single kayaks (€30 per day), supplies a waterproof route map, hires out tents and camping gear, and can arrange to pick you (or just the canoe) up at Sulkava (€20/60 for canoes/canoes plus passengers). It's just off the north–south highway between Mikkeli and Varkaus, 3km west of Juva and 63km from Savonlinna. Buses stop nearby.

The Route

There are regular rest stops with fireplaces and toilets. From Juva Camping it's an easy 8km paddle across Jukajärvi to the beginning of the river section, Polvijoki, where you must carry your canoe around the dam to the right. Passing through the small lakes Riemiö and Souru, you come to gentle 200m Voikoski rapids. Continue along the canal, carrying the canoe across the road at the end, before negotiating the Karijoki.

On Kaitajärvi, **Sulkavan Oravanpesät** is a friendly campground with tent sites, cabins and a much-appreciated smoke sauna. These folk also hire out canoes and kayaks, and arrange transport along the route. A kiosk sells drinks; meals can be pre-organised. This is approximately the halfway point. Next comes a series of rapids including Kissakoski and the strong currents of the Kyrsyänjoki. Continue through Rasakanjoki and Tikanjoki before coming to large Halmejärvi. The route continues on the western shore of Lohnajärvi to Lohnankoski. From here it's a leisurely paddle down Kuhajärvi, past a final set of rapids and into Sulkava. Pull in at Kulkemus Boat Centre on the right after the bridge. There's a summer cafe here and you can camp.

most popular tourist attraction. The parsonage building houses a restaurant (buffet lunch €29; open 11am to 3pm), and a variety of outbuildings are now home to handicrafts and design shops, the best of which is undoubtedly Myymälä. It also has a summer-only lakeside cafe, an artisan bakery and a gorgeous garden planted with over 500 plant species.

Jalkaväkimuseo MUSEUM
(Infantry Museum; ☎ 040-532-1397, 015-369-666; www.jalkavakimuseo.fi; Jääkärinkatu 6-8; adult/child €8/2; ☉ 11am-5pm Jun-Aug, to 4pm Wed-Sun Sep-May) The Jalkaväkimuseo is one of the largest military museums in Finland, with 10 exhibition rooms in two 19th-century timber army barracks. These are arranged chronologically and cover events in Finland between 1915 and 1951, featuring plenty of photographs, documents, military equipment and scale models. Book in advance to take a guided tour in Finnish, English or German (€40).

Päämajamuseo MUSEUM
(Headquarters Museum; ☎ 015-194-2427; www.mikkeli.fi/museot; Päämajankuja 1-3; adult/child €6/free; ☉ 10am-5pm daily May-Aug, Fri-Sun Sep-Apr) Päämajamuseo was Mannerheim's office and the base of the Finnish armed forces during WWII and evokes this period of Finland's history well.

🛏 Sleeping & Eating

Huoneistohotelli Marja HOSTEL €
(☎ 044-777-0676; www.huoneistohotellimarja.fi; Jääkärinkatu 8; dm €34, hostel s/d €45/62, guesthouse s/d €89/122; P 🖙 🐾) Owner Marja operates both a guesthouse and a hostel in characterful wooden 19th-century barracks buildings right by the Jalkaväkimuseo (Infantry Museum). The hostel is the better option of the two, with attractive single-sex dorms, private rooms, communal kitchen, clean shared bathrooms and laundry facilities. The

guesthouse has rooms with basic bathrooms and small kitchenettes and is overpriced.

Hotelli Uusikuu HOTEL **€**

(☑015-221-5420; www.uusikuu.fi; Raviradantie 13; r €59-79; ⊘9am-8pm Mon-Fri; P☎) This receptionless hotel in a green suburb just northwest of the city centre is quite a bargain. Rooms are clean, comfortable, modern and spacious; some have a fold-out bed and sleep up to four. Breakfast isn't available, but every room has its own kettle, fridge and microwave. Book online well in advance.

★Kahvila Nanda CAFE **€**

(☑044-304-7104; www.kahvilananda.fi; Savilahdenkatu 12; cakes €3-4, bocadillos €4.50; ⊘10am-4pm Mon-Fri) Bestowing new life on a previously derelict row of old timber houses, this chic cafe is a popular midweek lunch and coffee stop. Claim an armchair and settle down to enjoy the soup and salad buffet (€9.90) or choose from the enticing array of filled *bocadillos* (Spanish-style bread rolls) and cakes. The cute kiddies' play corner is a lovely touch.

Pruuvi MEDITERRANEAN **€€**

(☑015-206-3644; http://kattaasavon.fi/ravintolat/pruuvi-mikkeli; Raatihuoneenkatu 4; mains €19-35; ⊘11am-9.30pm Mon-Thu, 11am-11pm Fri, noon-11pm Sat, noon-3pm Sun; ☎) Having developed a loyal clientele since opening in the 1970s, Pruuvi works hard to keep its standards high and patrons happy. The à la carte menu includes stalwarts such as Caesar salad and steaks, and the weekday lunchtime buffet (€10.30) is both generous and inexpensive, offering soup, salad, one warm dish, dessert, water and coffee/tea. Good wine list too.

🛍 Shopping

★Taito Shop DESIGN

(☑0440-162-230; www.taitoshop.fi; Kenkävero, Pursialankatu 6; ⊘10am-6pm) Consider this a warning: once entered, this shop is almost certainly going to tempt you into extravagant expenditure. A showcase of top-quality Finnish design and handicrafts, it sells designer clothes (look out for the linen creations by Pirita Design), accessories, jewellery, bathwares, homewares, textiles, toys and gourmet foodstuffs, including bread bakes at the Kenkävero bakery.

❶ Information

Tourist Office (☑044-794-5669; www.visit mikkeli.fi; Maaherrankatu 22; ⊘10am-5pm Mon, 9am-5pm Tue-Fri; ☎) On Maaherrankatu, near the kauppatori.

❶ Getting There & Away

The train and bus stations are adjacent, a block east (downhill) from the kauppatori. Bus destinations include Helsinki (from €20, 3½ hours) and Savonlinna (€20, 1½ hours). Trains run to Helsinki (€36, 2¾ hours), Kuopio (€21, 1½ hours) and further north. For other cities, change at Pieksämäki or Kouvola.

New Valamo

The date when the Valamo community was initially established is disputed, but most historians cite the late 14th century. Originally located on Lake Ladoga, it survived the Russian Revolution's aftermath because the original monastery (now in Russian Karelia) fell just within newly independent Finland. This changed during the 1939-40 Winter War, when the region fell to the Soviets. Fortunately, Ladoga froze (a rare occurrence), allowing a hurried evacuation of 190 monks, icons and treasures. The evacuated monks set up a new community here in Heinävesi in 1940, and the original monastery became a Russian military base; it was only in 1989 that a monastic community was re-established there. With its idyllic setting on an island in Juojävi and its excellent facilities, the Heinävesi monastery is now one of Finland's most popular tourist attractions.

Valamon Luostari MONASTERY

(New Valamo, New Valaam; ☑017-570-111; www. valamo.fi; Valamontie 42, Heinävesi; ⊘9am-9pm) Finland's only Orthodox monastery is idyllically located on an island in Juojävi. Visitors are free to roam the site and enter the churches. The first church was made by connecting two sheds; the rustic architecture contrasts curiously with its gilded icons. The modern church has an onion-shaped dome and an incense-saturated interior featuring an elaborate iconostasis. Visitors can follow a 4.5km marked walking trail to a pilgrim's wooden cross located on the lake's edge.

There's a prayer service at noon on Saturday and liturgy at 9am on Sunday. Matins are held at 6am Monday to Saturday and vespers or a vigil at 6pm daily. **Guided tours** (adult/child €6/3; 75 minutes) of the monastery are offered between 10am and 5pm on Sundays and on other days in high summer.

The community encourages visitors, and is well geared to tourism, with a **cafeteria** (Valamon Luostari; buffet lunch adult/child €14/7; ⊘7.30am-6pm Mon-Thu, to 9pm Fri & Sat), huge gift shop, overnight **accommodation**

LINTULA CONVENT

Finland's only Orthodox convent, **Lintulan Luostari** (☑040-485-7603; www.lintulanluostari.fi; Honkasalontie 3, Palokki; ☺10am-6pm Jun-Aug) is particularly lovely in early summer, when the many flowers in its beautifully tended gardens bloom. The order was founded in Karelia in 1895 and its nuns relocated to this location near New Valamo after WWII. Visits outside summer are by appointment. When here, be sure to follow the walking trail from the car park past the small cemetery and down through the forest to the shed-like Chapel of St Paraskeva on the shore of Koskijärvi.

A souvenir shop near the convent's entrance sells handicrafts including handmade candles (the nuns supply all the Orthodox churches in Finland) and there's a simple cafe in the grounds offering tea, coffee and snacks.

Accommodation is offered in the on-site **Antonina Guesthouse** (☑040-485-7558; www.lintulanluostari.fi; s/d €27/46; ☺ Jun-Aug; [P]). It has simple but clean rooms, with separate bathrooms; it's open to men and women.

The convent is a worthwhile detour if you are on your way to or from New Valamo, which is 17km east. If you don't have a car, the only way to get here is on one of the overnight summer-only cruises from Savonlinna (adult return €130) and Kuoppio (adult return €120) operated by **Saimaan Laivamatkat Oy** (www.mspuijo.fi).

(☑017-570-1810; s/d without bathroom €45/66, hotel s/d €80/130; [P][☎][☺]) and a wine cellar where you can taste and purchase monastery-produced wine and whisky. Note that the monastery has a dress code: knees and shoulders must be covered.

ℹ Getting There & Away

Valamo is clearly signposted 4km north of the main Varkaus–Joensuu road. Two daily buses run here from Helsinki (€30, 6½ hours) via Mikkeli (€25, 2½ hours) and Joensuu (€15, one hour).

The most pleasant way to arrive in summer is on the M/S Puijo (p169) from Kuopio. The cruise uses a combination of the regular Kuopio–Savonlinna boat and road transport (adult return €80).

Jyväskylä

☑014 / POP 138,459

Vivacious and modern, western Lakeland's main town has a wonderful waterside location, an optimistic feel and an impeccable architectural pedigree. Thanks to the work of Alvar Aalto, who started his career here, Jyväskylä (yoo-vah-skoo-lah) is of global architectural interest. At the other end of the cultural spectrum, petrolheads the world round know it as a legendary World Rally Championships venue. The large student population and lively arts scenes give the town plenty of energy and nightlife.

◎ Sights

For architecture buffs the best visiting days are Tuesday to Friday, as many buildings are closed on weekends and the Alvar Aalto Museum is closed on Monday. Jyväskylä's museums are all free on Fridays between September and May.

Alvar Aalto Museo MUSEUM
(Map p166; ☑040-135-6210; www.alvaraalto.fi; Alvar Aallonkatu 7; adult/child €6/free; ☺11am-6pm Tue-Sun Sep-Jun, 10am-6pm Tue-Fri Jul-Aug) The town's most-famous son and the subject of this museum was a giant of 20th-century architecture. Schooled in Jyväskylä, Aalto opened his first offices here, designed many buildings in the town and later spent his summers in nearby Muuratsalo. Aalto devotees should start their pilgrimage at this informative museum in the university precinct, one of the last buildings he designed. Displays chronicle his life and work, focusing on his major buildings, as well as his furniture design and glassware.

Keski-Suomen Museo MUSEUM
(Museum of Central Finland; Map p166; www.jyvaskyla.fi/keskisuomenmuseo; Alvar Aallonkatu 7; adult/child €6/free; ☺11am-6pm Tue-Sun) Adjacent to the Alvar Aalto Museo and also designed by him, this museum building was temporarily closed for a major restoration when we last visited. When it reopens in 2019 it will continue to showcase the cultural history of Central Finland in temporary and permanent exhibitions.

🏃 Activities

An enjoyable 12km circuit can be walked or cycled around the lake, and can be cut in half

The Finnish Lakeland

Finland is called the Land of 1000 Lakes – a dramatic understatement, as there are nearly 188,000 lakes in this medium-sized country. For travellers, that means unlimited opportunities for swimming, canoeing, kayaking and cruising, not to mention lakeside sunset gazing.

VITALY TITOV/SHUTTERSTOCK ©

1. Linnansaari National Park (p157)
This stunningly scenic national park is made up of Haukivesi Lake and hundreds of uninhabited islands.

2. Olavinlinna (p152), Savonlinna
Currents in the lake surrounding this 15th-century military base prevent the water from freezing, which helps protect it from enemy attacks.

3. Kolovesi National Park (p157)
Hiking, fishing, berry-picking and canoeing are all popular ways to explore the park's brilliant scenery.

4. Harbour, Jyväskylä (p161)
One of the Lakeland region's premier towns is suitably situated lakeside.

4

MARIIA GOLOVIANKO/SHUTTERSTOCK ©

3

TIGLAT/SHUTTERSTOCK ©

using the road bridge. There are numerous boating options – check http://visitjyvaskyla.fi for information, or wander along the pleasant harbour area, where you'll also find boat bars, jet-ski hire, houseboats (www.houseboat.fi) and floating saunas for rent. Water craft can be hired from www.tavinsulka.com.

Päijänne Risteilyt Hilden
CRUISE

(Map p166; ☑ 010-320-8820; www.paijanne-risteilythilden.fi; ⊘ early Jun–mid-Aug) This cruise operator offers full-day or half-day cruises on the Keitele canal departing daily from the passenger harbour (p166) and costing between €40 and €60 for adults (half-price for kids). There's also a weekly Alvar Aalto architectural cruise in July and August, which visits the architect's Säynätsalo Town Hall and returns to Jyväskylä by bus (€33 per person; 4½ hours).

⚡ Festivals & Events

Jyväskylän Kesä
ART

(Jyväskylä Arts Festival; ☑ 050-464-6025; www.jyvaskylankesa.fi; ⊘ Jul) With a strong liberal and radical tradition, this is one of Finland's most important arts festivals. It offers an international program of concerts, exhibitions, theatre and dance.

Neste Oil Rally Finland
SPORTS

(www.nesteoilrallyfinland.fi; ⊘ early Aug) Many Finns regard the Finnish leg of the World Rally Championship as summer's most important event. It's perhaps the most spectacular of all the stages, and draws half a million spectators. Lasting four days, it involves big concerts and parties. Book tickets online and accommodation at least a year in advance.

🛌 Sleeping

Kesähotelli Harju
HOTEL €

(Map p166; ☑ 010-279-2004; www.hotelharju.fi; Sepänkatu 3; s €55-100, d €66-130, tr €81-159; ⊘ early Jun-early Aug; 🅿🛜) Five minutes uphill from the city centre, this summer hotel

has worn but light-filled student rooms with kitchenettes (no utensils) and basic bathrooms. Rates vary from good value to overpriced according to demand.

Hotelli Milton
HOTEL €€

(Map p166; ☑ 014-337-7900; www.hotellimilton.com; Hannikaisenkatu 29; s €70-85. d €90-120; 🅿🛜) Designed by Erkki Kantonen and Sakari Nironen and constructed in 1963, this architecturally notable building is one of the city's major landmarks. Family-run, it is extremely popular with visiting businesspeople – book ahead. Spacious rooms offer plenty of natural light; most have a balcony. It's very handy for the bus and train stations.

Hotelli Alba
HOTEL €€

(Map p166; ☑ 014-636-311; www.hotellialba.fi; Ahlmaninkatu 4; s/d/ste €101/124/178; 🅿✳@🛜🛁) Located within the university campus, this hotel on the lake shore has a bar-restaurant with a terrace cantilevered over the water (lunch buffet €16.80; mains €16 to €33). The rooms are light and comfortable, albeit with cramped bathrooms – the view from those facing the water is quite wonderful. Suites are much more spacious, and come with a sauna.

★ Hotel Yöpuu
BOUTIQUE HOTEL €€€

(Map p166; ☑ 014-333-900; www.hotelliyopuu.fi; Yliopistonkatu 23; standard s/d €145/168, superior s/d €159/189, ste €237; 🅿✳🛜🛁) Among Finland's most alluring boutique hotels, the Yöpuu has 26 rooms varying in size, decoration and facilities; those in the superior category are larger, with air-conditioning and tea/coffee facilities. Service is extremely professional, with personal touches including a welcome drink. There's a classy bar next to the highly recommended Pöllöwaari; an excellent buffet breakfast is served in the latter.

Verso Hotelli
HOTEL €€€

(Map p166; ☑ 014-333-999; www.hotelliverso.fi; Kauppakatu 35; ⊘ standard s/d €145/175, superior

---

ALVAR AALTO IN HIS ELEMENT

Jyväskylä's portfolio of Aalto-designed works include the main university campus (1953–70), Alvar Aalto Museo (1971–73; p114), Keski-Suomen Museo (1957–62; p114), the three buildings (1964–82) forming the town's Administrative and Cultural Centre (Map p166), the Workers' Club Building (1924–25; Map p166; Kauppakatu 30), the Vitatorni Apartment Tower (1962; Map p166; Viitaniementie 16) and a scattering of houses in the residential parts of town. For a handy map showing notable architectural works in the town, including all of Aalto's buildings, go to http://visitjyvaskyla.fi/filebank/1913-arkkitehtuurikartta_2014.pdf. Notable works outside town include the Säynätsalon Kunnantalo (1949–52; p118) and Muuratsalon Koetalo (1952–53; p118).

d 195-205; P✳🛜🐾) Located in adjoining buildings in the city centre, Jyväskylä's newest hotel has plenty of pizzazz. Standard rooms are comfortable and well equipped, but slightly cramped. Superior rooms are larger and have swish bathrooms (some with sauna); a few have windows onto the next-door shopping mall rather than outside. It also has a stylish foyer bar and a 1st-floor restaurant where excellent breakfasts are served.

✕ Eating

Jyväskylä is a university town, so it's not surprising that there are hipster-style cafes, bars selling pub grub, and vegan and vegetarian eateries here. For fine dining, head to Pöllöwaari, one of the region's most impressive restaurants.

★ Beans & More   VEGAN €
(Map p166; 📞 050-351-7731; www.beansandmore.fi; Asemakatu 11; dishes €10-15; ⊙ 10am-6pm Mon-Fri, 9am-5pm Sat; 🖉🐾) Artek furniture, a vaulted ceiling and artfully dangling light-fittings provide a stylish setting at this on-trend vegan cafe. The friendly staff serve up burgers, salads piled with kale and other goodies, sandwiches on gluten-free bread and vegetarian snack plates featuring seasonal produce. Coffee is made with oat, almond or soy milk, and there's a range of teas to choose from.

Katriinan Kasvisravintola   VEGETARIAN €
(Map p166; 📞 014-449-8880; www.maijasilvennoinen.fi; Kauppakatu 11; lunch €7-10; ⊙ 11am-2.30pm Mon-Fri; 🖉) A couple of blocks west of the Kirkkopuisto, this vegetarian and vegan lunch spot is great value. Seven euros gets you soup and salad bar, eight buys a hot dish instead of the soup, and 10 gets you the lot. The buffet changes daily – you might get pasta, ratatouille or curry – but it's good.

Ristorante Rosso   ITALIAN €
(Map p166; 📞 010-767-5441; Kauppakatu 19; pizzas €13-16, pastas €12-16; ⊙ 11am-9pm Mon & Tue, to 10pm Wed & Thu, to 11pm Fri & Sat, noon-9pm Sun) Billing itself as 'the familiar Italian', this branch of a popular Finnish chain serves up decent pizza and pasta in pleasant surroundings (we love the fresh herbs planted in the tomato-paste cans). It's located opposite the Kirkkopuisto and is a good choice for a cheap and *gustoso* (tasty) meal.

★ Figaro Winebistro   TAPAS €€
(Map p166; 📞 020-766-9811; www.figaro.fi; Asemakatu 2; lunch mains €15-18, tapas €3-9, dinner mains €16-28; ⊙ 11am-11pm Mon-Fri, 1-11pm Sat, 2-10pm Sun; 🛜) The three-course lunch menu (€25) at this this welcoming wine bar is an excellent deal, but most regulars head here after work or on weekends to graze on tapas and order drinks from the large and top-quality wine and beer list. It's so pleasant that many choose to stay on for a steak or burger dinner.

Kissanviikset   FINNISH €€
(Map p166; 📞 010-666-5150; www.kissanviikset.fi; Puistokatu 3; mains €21-35; ⊙ 11am-10pm Mon-Thu, to 10.30pm Fri, 1-10.30pm Sat, 1-8.30pm Sun) The 'cat's whiskers' is an enticing choice. The genteel but cosy upstairs dining room is complemented by an atmospheric cellar space when the restaurant is busy. Dishes are thoughtfully prepared; reindeer fillet and steaks with various sauces take pride of place.

★ Pöllöwaari   FINNISH €€€
(Map p166; 📞 014-333-900; www.ravintolapollowaari.fi; Yliopistonkatu 23; mains €22-29; ⊙ 11am-10.30pm Mon-Fri, 1-10.30pm Sat; 🛜) We're of the view that Hotel Yöpuu's fine-dining restaurant is the best in the region. Its menu places a laudable emphasis on seasonality, and the kitchen's execution is exemplary. Choose one of the set menus (€56 to €79, or €84 to €127 with wine matches) or order à la carte – the main courses are exceptionally well priced considering their quality. Excellent wine list

🍷 Drinking & Entertainment

★ Papu   CAFE
(Map p166; 📞 050-368-0340; www.paahtimopapu.fi; Yliopistonkatu 26D; ⊙ 10am-6pm Mon & Tue, to 9pm Wed-Fri, noon-6pm Sat) It would be easy to describe Papu as a hipster haunt, but this laid-back cafe doesn't lend itself to easy categorisation. Yes, its baristas have sleeve tattoos and a preference for pour-over coffee, but the loyal customer base is multi-aged and eclectic. The coffee is made with house-roasted organic beans, and there's also espresso tonic and iced chocolate on offer.

Sohwi   PUB
(Map p166; 📞 014-615-564; www.sohwi.fi; Vaasankatu 21; ⊙ 2pm-midnight Tue-Thu, to 2am Fri, noon-2am Sat, 2-10pm Sun & Mon; 🛜) A short walk from the city centre is this excellent bar with a spacious wooden terrace and plenty of lively student and academic discussion lubricated by a range of good bottled and draught beers. It also has a good menu of snacks and soak-it-all-up bar meals (pizza €15, burgers €12.50 to €17), including vegan options. Great stuff.

THE LAKELAND JYVÄSKYLÄ

Jyväskylä

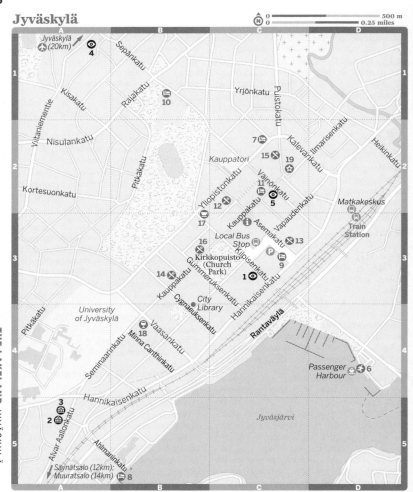

Poppari   LIVE MUSIC
(Map p166; http://ravintolapoppari.fi; Puistokatu 2; €5-12; ⊙4pm-3am Mon-Thu, to 4am Fri, 7pm-4am Sat; 🛜) This downstairs venue hosts live acts towards the end of each week. Expect tribute bands and soft rock. Check the website for details.

ⓘ Information

City Library (www.jyvaskyla.fi/kirjasto/eng; Vapaudenkatu 39-41; ⊙9am-8pm Mon-Fri, to 4pm Sat) Free wi-fi and internet terminals.

Tourist Office (Map p166; ☎014-266-0113; www.visitjyvaskyla.fi; Asemakatu 7; ⊙10am-5pm Mon-Fri, to 3pm Sat Jun-Aug, 10am-4pm Mon-Fri Sep-May) Helpful office where you can source plenty of information. Staff can arrange visits to the Muuratsalon Koetalo.

ⓘ Getting There & Away

The airport is at Tikkakoski, 23km northwest of the city centre. Finnair flies to/from Helsinki.

Päijänne Risteilyt Hilden (p164) boats travel between Jyväskylä's **passenger harbour** (Map p166; Satamakatu 8) and Lahti.

The bus and train stations share the **Matkakeskus** (Jyväskylä Travel Centre; Map p166; ⊙6am-10pm Mon-Sat, from 8am Sun). Daily express buses connect Jyväskylä to southern Finnish towns, including frequent departures to

Jyväskylä

◉ Sights
1 Administrative and Cultural Centre C3
2 Alvar Aalto Museo A5
3 Keski-Suomen Museo A5
4 Vitatorni Apartment Tower A1
5 Workers' Club Building C2

✪ Activities, Courses & Tours
6 Päijänne Risteilyt Hilden D4

🛌 Sleeping
7 Hotel Yöpuu C2
8 Hotelli Alba B5
9 Hotelli Milton C3
10 Kesähotelli Harju B1
11 Verso Hotelli C2

✖ Eating
12 Beans & More C2
13 Figaro Winebistro C3
14 Katriinan Kasvisravintola B3
15 Kissanviikset C2
Pöllöwaari .... (see 7)
16 Ristorante Rosso B3

🍷 Drinking & Nightlife
17 Papu B3
18 Sohwi B4

🎭 Entertainment
19 Poppari C2

Tampere (€20, 2¼ hours) and Helsinki (€25 to €30, 3½ to 4½ hours).

There are regular trains to/from Helsinki (from €32, 3½ hours), many of which travel via Tampere and Hämeenlinna.

ℹ Getting Around

TO/FROM THE AIRPORT
Karstulan Liikenne (☑ 014-461-179) offers transfers between the airport and the city centre (€8.80, 20 minutes). These must be booked in advance. A few buses between Jyväskylä and other towns stop at the airport en route (€8.80; check www.matkahuolto.fi for times). A taxi costs around €50.

BICYCLE
Jyväskylä is great to explore by bike. The visit jyvaskyla.fi website has a list of bike-hire operators, including **Polkupyörä Tori** (☑ 040-535-2010; www.polkupyoratori.fi; Minna Canthinkatu 22B; per day/week €10/40; ⊙ 9am-6pm Mon-Fri).

BUS
Local buses all leave from **Vapaudenkatu** (Map p166), near the tourist office. Tickets cost €3 to €8.20 depending on distance. Day tickets (€8 to €14) can be bought at the Linkki desk located in the same building as the tourist office – good value if you'll be making three or more journeys.

Around Jyväskylä

Säynätsalo

★ **Säynätsalon Kunnantalo**　　　　　　　NOTABLE BUILDING
(Säynätsalo Town Hall; ☑ 040-197-1091; www.aaltoinfo.com; Parviaisentie 9, Säynätsalo; tours €8; ⊙ tours noon-6pm Mon-Fri, 2-6pm Sat & Sun Jun-Sep) FREE One of Aalto's most admired

works, this town hall was conceived as a 'fortress of democracy' and constructed between 1949 and 1952. Its sturdy brick tower references the medieval town halls Aalto had admired in Italy, but the grassy inner courtyard bathes the interior with light and reflects a relationship with nature that is distinctively Nordic. Guided tours visit the council chamber, library and meeting rooms. The complex is remarkably intact and utterly magnificent.

To arrange overnight accommodation in the town hall building (single €85, two/- four-person apt €150/250) or to visit outside summer, email caretaker Harri Taskinen on harri.taskinen@hotmail.com.

Säynätsalo island is south of Jyväskylä. The most enjoyable way to reach it is to take the Alvar Aalto architectural cruise operated by Päijänne Risteilyt Hilden (p164) in July and August. At other times, drive or take bus 16, 16M or 21 (€4.70, 30 minutes, every 30 minutes) – get off at the SS-Kunnantalo stop.

Muuratsalo

Muuratsalon Koetalo　　　　　　　ARCHITECTURE
(Muuratsalo Experimental House; ☑ 014-266-7113; www.alvaraalto.fi; Melalammentie, Muuratsalo; adult/student €18/9; ⊙ 1.30pm Mon, Wed & Fri Jun, Jul & 1st half Sep, 1.30pm Mon-Fri Aug) Connected to Säynätsalo by bridges, peaceful Muuratsalo islet was the summer retreat of Alvar and Elissa Aalto. Aalto built his **Experimental House** on three hectares of forest on the shore of Päijänne, and it can now be visited by pre-arranged guided tours; book through the Alvar Aalto Museo (p161) or Jyväskylä tourist office. To get here, drive or take bus 16 (€4.70, 40 minutes) from Jyväskylä; the house is 500m on from the final stop.

After meeting your guide at the street gate, you'll walk past Aalto's beloved boat, *Nemo Propheta in Patria* (Nobody is a Prophet in their Homeland), which is now housed in a shelter on terra firma. Then on to the lakeside sauna and to the main event – the house itself. This is divided into two parts: the main building (1952) and a guestroom wing (1953). The latter isn't part of the tour as it is still used by members of the Aalto family. Aalto used the enclosed patio in front of the L-shaped main building to try out various types and patterns of bricks and tiles to see how they looked in different seasons and how they weathered – it's fascinating to see how he quality controlled materials before specifying their use. The interior of the house is extremely modest in scale and finish, and retains its original Artek furniture.

Petäjävesi

Petäjäveden Vanha Kirkko   CHURCH
(Petäjävesi Old Church; ☑ 040-582-2461; www.petajavesi.fi/kirkko; Vanhankirkontie, Petäjävesi; adult/child €6/4; ⊙ 10am-6pm Jun-Aug, reduced hours Sep, other times by appointment) This wonderfully gnarled Unesco-listed wooden church is located 35km west of Jyväskylä. Finished in 1765, it's a marvellous example of 18th-century rustic Finnish architecture, with crooked wooden pews, a pulpit held up by a rosy-cheeked St Christopher, and a fairytale shingle roof. Burials took place under the floorboards. Buses from Jyväskylä (€8, 35 minutes) stop here on their journey to/from Keuruu. If coming by car, walk across a road bridge to the church from the car park.

Kuopio

☑ 017 / POP 117,383
Kuopio is the quintessential summery lakeside town, offering pleasure cruises on the azure water, hikes in spruce forests, tasty local fish specialities and plenty of terraces and beer gardens where you can enjoy a drink. Those visitors who are more interested in cultural diversions than the great outdoors will enjoy visiting the town's portfolio of museums; note that museums are closed on Mondays.

⊙ Sights

Kuopio has several worthwhile museums; a combined ticket to the Kuopion Museo, Kuopion Taidemuseo and Kuopion Korttelimuseo costs €14 and is available at all three venues.

Puijo   HILL
Even small hills have cachet in flat Finland, and Kuopio was so proud of Puijo that it was crowned with a tower. Views from the top of **Puijon Torni** (Puijo Tower; ☑ 044-552-4887; www.puijo.com; Puijontie 135; adult/child €6/3; ⊙ 10am-9pm Mon-Sat, to 7pm Sun Jun-Aug, 11am-7pm Mon-Thu, to 9pm Fri & Sat, to 4pm Sun Sep-May) are very impressive; the vast perspectives of lakes and forests represent a sort of idealised Finnish vista. Atop is a revolving restaurant, a cafe and an open-air viewing deck. Surrounding it is one of the region's best-preserved spruce forests, with trails for walking, biking and cross-country skiing.

Kuopion Museo   MUSEUM
(Map p170; ☑ 017-182-603; www.kuopionmuseo.fi; Kauppakatu 23; adult/child €8/free; ⊙ 10am-5pm Tue-Sat) In a castle-like art nouveau mansion, this museum has a wide scope. The top two floors are devoted to cultural history, but the real highlight is the natural history display, which includes a wide variety of beautifully presented Finnish wildlife, including a mammoth and an ostrich wearing snowboots. The ground floor has temporary exhibitions. Pick up English explanations at the ticket desk.

Kuopion Korttelimuseo   MUSEUM
(Old Kuopio Museum; Map p170; ☑ 017-182-625; www.korttelimuseo.kuopio.fi; Kirkkokatu 22; adult/child €6/free; ⊙ 10am-5pm Tue-Sat mid-May–Aug,

---

SHE AIN'T HEAVY, SHE'S MY WIFE

What began as a heathenish medieval habit of pillaging neighbouring villages in search of nubile women has become one of Finland's oddest – and most publicised – events. Get to Sonkajärvi, in the northern Lakeland, for the **Wife-Carrying World Championships** (Eukonkanto; www.eukonkanto.fi) in early July. It's a race over a 253.5m obstacle course, where competitors must carry their 'wives' through water traps and over hurdles to achieve the fastest time. The winner gets the wife's weight in beer and the prestigious title of World Wife-Carrying Champion. To enter, men need only €50 and a consenting female. There's also a 40-plus and team competition, all accompanied by a weekend of drinking, dancing and typical Finnish frivolity.

10am-3pm Tue-Sat Sep–mid-May) This block of 11 wooden town houses dating from the 18th and 19th centuries includes several period-furnished homes representing family life between 1800 and 1930. **Apteekkimuseo** in building 11 contains old pharmacy paraphernalia, in another building it's fascinating to compare photos of Kuopio from different decades. Interpretative information is in English and Finnish. The museum's cafe serves delicious sweet and savoury dishes including a traditional *rahkapiirakka* (a local cheesecake-style pastry).

Suomen Ortodoksinen Kirkkomuseo
MUSEUM

(Orthodox Church Museum of Finland, RIISA; Map p170; ☑020-610-0206; www.riisa.fi; Karjalankatu 1; adult/child €10/free; ⊙noon-4pm Tue-Sat) Over 800 religious icons and 4000 textiles, along with documents, maps, drawings and photographs depicting Orthodox history in Finland, are displayed across nine rooms at this excellent museum. Many items were brought here from monasteries and churches now in Russian-occupied Karelia.

Kuopion Taidemuseo
GALLERY

(Map p170; www.taidemuseo.kuopio.fi; Kauppakatu 35; adult/child €6/free; ⊙10am-5pm Tue-Sat) Occupying an old bank building in the centre of town, this museum focuses on Finnish art created from the late 19th century to present times. Look out for paintings by local Juho Rissanen (1873–1950), whose realistic portraits of working Finns contrasted with the prevalent Romanticism. The museum's curatorial theme is nature and the environment, so many of the works focus on these subjects.

🏃 Activities

★ Jätkänkämppä
SAUNA

(☑030-60830; www.rauhalahti.fi/en/restaurants/jatkankamppa/public-traditional-finnish-evenings; Katiskaniementie 8; adult/child €14/7; ⊙4-10pm Tue & Thu Jun-Aug, 4-10pm Tue Sep-May) This giant *savusauna* (smoke sauna) is a memorable, sociable experience. It seats 60 and is mixed: you're given towels to wear. Bring a swimsuit for lake dipping – devoted locals and brave tourists do so even when it's covered with ice. Repeat the process several times. Then buy a beer and relax, looking out over the lake in Nordic peace.

Rauhalahti
OUTDOORS

(☑030-60830; www.rauhalahti.com; Katiskaniementie 8) This estate is full of activities for families, including boating, cycling, tennis and minigolf in summer, and skating, ice-fishing and snowmobiling in winter. You can hire bikes, rowboats, canoes and in-line skates. To get here, take bus 7 or 20 from the town centre (€3.30) or take a Koski-Laiva Oy cruise in summer. There's also a variety of **accommodation** (s/d from €105/120; P ☎ ☎ ☎) here.

Vesilento Taxi
SCENIC FLIGHTS

(Map p170; ☑050-572-6552; www.vesilentotaksi.fi; Kuopion Satama; ⊙Jun–mid-Aug) Runs quick jaunts over the town and lakes in a Cessna floatplane, departing from the *satama* (port). There's a minimum of three passengers for the standard 15-minute flight (€65 per person).

Cruises

Several different cruises depart from the town's passenger harbour daily during summer. Tickets are available at the Matkustajasatama (harbour) or directly on the boats.

Saimann Laivamatkat Oy
CRUISE

(Map p170; ☑015-250-250; www.mspuijo.fi) Operates the M/S *Puijo,* which sails along the Heinävesi Canal Route to/from Savonlinna (one way €95, 10½ hours) on Tuesdays, Thursdays and Saturdays, returning on Monday, Wednesday and Friday. Return same-day transport by car (€130, minimum four passengers) is offered.

Koski-Laiva Oy
CRUISE

(Map p170; ☑0400-207-245; www.koskilaiva.com; adult/child €16/8; ⊙mid-May–late Aug) Offers 90-minute or two-hour scenic cruises on M/S *Osmo* and M/S *Koski* between mid-May and August, as well as return trips to Rauhalahti between late June and early August; the latter is an excellent way to reach the famous smoke sauna there.

Roll Risteilyt
CRUISE

(Roll Cruises; Map p170; ☑017-266-2466; www.roll.fi; adult/child €18/9; ⊙Tue-Sat Jun & Aug, daily Jul) Runs regular 90-minute scenic cruises on M/S *Ukko and* M/S *Queen,* as well as a four-hour lunch cruise to the Alahovi Berry Wine Farm (adult/child €36/17).

🎊 Festivals & Events

Kupio Dance Festival
DANCE

(Kuopion Tanssii ja Soi; www.kuopiodancefestival.fi; ⊙mid-Jun) Open-air classical and modern dance performances are staged at this week-long festival, and there are also comedy and theatre gigs. There's a real buzz in town.

Kuopio

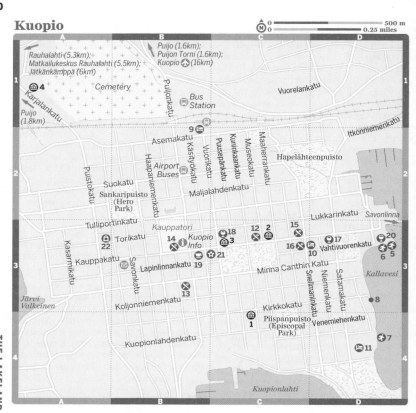

🛏 Sleeping

Matkailukeskus Rauhalahti CAMPGROUND €
(☎017-473-000; www.visitrauhalahti.fi; Rauhanka-tu 3; tent/caravan sites €15/23 plus per person €6, d/q camping cottages €35/65, q cottages €120-197; ⏰ mid-May–late Aug; P🐕🏊🐾) On a lake near the Rauhalahti hotel complex, this campground has top-notch facilities including a cafe, minigolf and croquet courses, volleyball and basketball courts, a children's playground, sauna (€18 for 50 minutes), excellent camp kitchen and good ablution blocks. Camping cabins are extremely basic; most standard cottages have a kitchen and sauna. Bus 16 (€3.30) will get you here.

Apartment Hotel Rauhalahti APARTMENT €€
(☎030-60830; www.rauhalahti.fi; Katiskaniementie 8; 1-/2-/4-person apt from €115/120/159; P🐕🏊🐾) Part of the Spa Hotel Rauhalahti complex, this has modern apartments with all the trimmings, including (for not much extra cash) a sauna. Guests have full use of the ho-tel's facilities.

Hotelli Jahtihovi HOTEL €€
(Map p170; ☎017-264-4400; www.jahtihovi.fi; Snellmaninkatu 23; standard s/d €89/119, superior s/d €109/129; P❄🐕🏊🐾) Located on a quiet street near the harbour, this independent, family-run hotel is a safe choice. Unrenovat-ed standard rooms have extremely cramped bathrooms and an ugly decor; the superiors are in a modern wing and are much better; all have air-conditioning and some have a kitchenette. Some car spaces are free; others cost €10. Prices drop by €20 on weekends.

Guest House Asema GUESTHOUSE €€
(Map p170; ☎044-788-1110; www.kuopionasema. fi; Asemakatu 1; s/d €64/84; P🐕) Let's get one thing straight: sleeping close to bus and train stations isn't lazy, it's practical. Operating out of the pleasant *grilli* (fast-food outlet) in the train station, Asema offers rooms in the

Kuopio

Sights
1 Kuopion Korttelimuseo C4
2 Kuopion Museo...C3
3 Kuopion Taidemuseo...............................C3
4 Suomen Ortodoksinen
   Kirkkomuseo..A1

Activities, Courses & Tours
5 Koski-Laiva Oy D3
6 Roll Risteilyt D3
7 Saimann Laivamatkat Oy D4
8 Vesilento Taxi D3

Sleeping
9 Guest House Asema B2
10 Hotelli Jahtihovi.......................................D3
11 Scandic Hotel Kuopio D4

Eating
12 Isä Camillo C3
13 Kummisetä B3
14 Kuopion Kauppahalli B3
15 Sampo..C3
16 Sorrento C3

Drinking & Nightlife
17 Helmi D3
18 Ilona C3
19 Kaneli...B3
20 Wanha Satama...D3

Entertainment
21 Henry's Pub C3

Shopping
22 Pikku Pietarin Torikuja..........................A3

building itself – well equipped with kettle and fridge. You'll breakfast in the *grilli*. The managers also offer cheaper accommodation in an apartment building opposite.

★ **Scandic Hotel Kuopio** HOTEL €€€
(Map p170; ☑ 017-195-111; www.scandichotels.fi; Satamakatu 1; s €220, standard/superior d €240/260, ste €300; P@🛜🏊🐕) Kuopio's best hotel has a tranquil lakeside location and a wealth of facilities, including a gym, sauna, hot tub, indoor swimming pool and kids' play room, plus free bike hire. The rooms have an attractive decor, but are on the small side. Superior rooms are worth the extra €20, as they have king-sized beds, kettles and balconies with lake views.

Eating

Kuopion Kauppahalli MARKET €
(Map p170; http://kuopionkauppahalli.fi; Kauppatori; ☺8am-5pm Mon-Fri, to 3pm Sat; 🍴) Beautifully restored, this classic Finnish indoor market hall at the southern end of the kauppatori was built in 1902 and has a distinctive yellow exterior. Inside, stalls sell produce including the local speciality *kalakukko*, a large rye loaf stuffed with whitefish and then baked. It's delicious hot or cold.

Sampo FINNISH €
(Map p170; ☑ 020-762-4818; www.ravintolamaailma.fi/ravintolat/sampo-kuopio; Kauppakatu 13; mains €12-20; ☺11am-midnight Mon-Sat, noon-10pm Sun) Have it stewed, fried, smoked or in a soup, but it's all about *muikku* (vendace or whitefish) here. This is one of Finland's most famous spots to try the small lakefish that

locals are so crazy about. The 70-year-old restaurant is cosy and classically Finnish.

Sorrento ITALIAN €
(Map p170; ☑ 045-896-6009; www.trattoriasorrento.fi; Snellmaninkatu 22; pizzas €12-18, pastas €13-18, mains €18-22; ☺10.30am-9pm Mon-Thu, to 10pm Fri, noon-10pm Sat; 🍴👪) Generous serves of pasta, decent pizzas and a genuine Southern Italian–style welcome are the hallmarks at this neighbourhood trattoria. At lunch, you can graze the salad buffet, choose a pasta or pizza and finish with a dessert and coffee for a mere €10. Amazing value! There's also a kids' menu (€8 to €12) and plenty of vegetarian and gluten-free choices.

Jätkänkämppä Restaurant FINNISH €€
(☑ 030-60830; www.rauhalahti.fi; Katiskaniementie 8; buffet adult/child €23/11.50, with sauna entry €35/17.50; ☺4-8pm Tue & Fri Jun-Aug, 4-8pm Tue Sep-May; 👪) Head to the loggers' cabin adjacent to the Jätkänkämppä (p169) smoke sauna at Spa Hotel Rauhalahti to enjoy a traditional Finnish buffet when the sauna is operating. You'll be serenaded with accordion entertainment and a lumberjack show.

Isä Camillo MEDITERRANEAN €€
(Map p170; ☑ 017-581-0450; www.isacamillo.net; Kauppakatu 25-27; mains €17-33; ☺11am-9pm Mon & Tue, to 10pm Wed & Thu, to midnight Fri, 2pm-midnight Sat) Set in a beautifully renovated former bank – look out for the old strongroom – this is an elegant but informal spot for a meal, offering Mediterranean-inspired dishes from a variety of countries as well as Finnish specialities such as reindeer roast. There's a good enclosed terrace at the side and a decent pub downstairs.

THE LAKELAND KUOPIO

Kummisetä FINNISH €€
(Map p170; ☑ 017-369-9880; www.kummiseta.com;
Minna Canthin Katu 44; mains €17-29; ⊙ 4-9pm Mon,
to 10pm Tue-Thu, 3-10.30pm Fri & Sat) The menu at
this old-fashioned eatery places an emphasis
on comfort food, offering excellent burgers,
steaks and ribs; the more-adventurous items
on offer aren't as successful. In summer, dining on the spacious two-level back terrace is a
pleasure, and there's live music on weekends.

Drinking & Entertainment

Wanha Satama PUB
(Map p170; ☑ 050-342-9276; www.wanhasatama.net;
Matkustajasatama; mains €15-26; ⊙ 11am-9pm Mon-
Thu, to 11pm Fri-Sun) In a blue-and-white timber
building right on the harbour, this popular
place has a rear deck and front terrace where
patrons can sit and watch the boats come and
go. It offers decent Finnish food and international favourites, including burgers, as well as
a semi-regular program of live music.

Kaneli CAFE
(Map p170; www.kahvilakaneli.net; Kauppakatu 22;
⊙ 10.30am-5.30pm Mon-Fri, 11am-4pm Sat, to 3pm
Sun; ☎) Just off the kauppatori, this friendly
cafe has a twee interior and great coffee. Enjoy
one with a pastry from the cafe's own bakery.

Helmi PUB
(Map p170; www.satamanhelmi.fi; Kauppakatu 2;
⊙ 11am-11pm Mon-Thu, to midnight Fri, noon-midnight Sat, noon-8pm Sun) This historic 19th-
century sailors' hang-out by the harbour is a
cosy, comfortable spot with a range of local
characters. It has a decent pool table and a
sociable beer garden. If hungry, you'll need
to rely on the house-made pizzas (from €9),
which would be publicly vilified if served up
in Italy.

Ilona CLUB
(Map p170; www.ravintola.fi/en/ravintola/viihdemaa
.ilma-ilona-kuopio; Vuorikatu 19; ⊙ 10pm-4am) The
city's largest nightclub has live-music space,
a quirky London-themed bar with a smoking
cabin done out like a red bus, and a separate
karaoke bar where enthusiastic punters belt
out Suomi hits. There's a fat list of English-
language songs if you don't fancy trying out
your Finnish vowels. Age limits apply on weekends (Friday/Saturday 20/22 years old).

Henry's Pub LIVE MUSIC
(Map p170; ☑ 010-271-4702; www.henryspub.net;
Kauppakatu 18; cover €5-8; ⊙ 9pm-4am Wed &

Thu, from 10pm Fri & Sat; ☎) Bands play here
several times a week, most at the heavier
end of the rock/metal spectrum.

Shopping

Pikku Pietarin Torikuja ARTS & CRAFTS
(Map p170; www.pikkupietarintorikuja.fi; Hatsalanka-
tu 24; ⊙ 10am-5pm Mon-Fri Sep-May, to 5pm Mon-Fri
& to 3pm Sat Jun-Aug) An atmospheric narrow
lane of renovated red wooden houses converted into quirky shops stocking jewellery, clothing, handicrafts and other items. Halfway
along is an excellent cafe (open from 8am)
with cosy upstairs seating and a great little
back deck for the summer sun.

ⓘ Information

Kuopio Info (Map p170; ☑ 017-182-584; www.
kuopio.fi; Apaja Shopping Centre, Kauppakatu 45;
⊙ 9am-4pm Mon-Fri) Underneath the kauppatori.
Information on local and regional attractions.

Main Post Office (Map p170; www.posti.fi;
Kauppakatu 40-42; ⊙ 8am-7pm Mon-Fri, 10am-
3pm Sat)

ⓘ Getting There & Away

Kuopio Airport (KUO; ☑ 020-708-7202; www.
finavia.fi; Lentokentäntie 275) is 14km northeast of Kuopio. Finnair (www.finnair.fi) operates
daily flights to/from Helsinki.

In summer, Saimann Laivamatkat Oy (p169)
operates regular cruises between Kuopio and
Savonlinna.

Bus services depart from Puijonkatu 45. Express services include the following:

Helsinki (from €10, 5½ hours, frequent) Some
require a change in Jyväskylä.

Savonlinna (€27.30, 2¾ hours, four daily)
Change in Varkaus.

Daily trains services include the following:

Helsinki (€41 to €45, 4½ hours, six daily)

Mikkeli (€18 to €21, 1¾ hours, four daily)

Change at Pieksämäki or Kouvola for other
destinations.

ⓘ Getting Around

Airport buses (Map p170; http://vilkku.kuopio.
fi/english) from Monday to Friday.

Secure 24-hour car parks under the kauppatori
charge €2 per hour or €13 per 24 hours. The car
park next to the harbour charges €1 per hour
between 8am and 8pm. You can hire cars at **Hertz**
(☑ 020-555-2670; www.hertz.fi; Asemakatu 1;
⊙ 8am-5pm Mon-Fri).

Karelia

Includes ➡

Lappeenranta	175
Imatra	179
Joensuu	181
Ilomantsi	184
Hattuvaara	185
Koli National Park	186
Lieksa	188
Ruunaa Recreation Area	190
Nurmijärvi District	192
Nurmes	192

Best Places to Eat

➡ Ravintola Nuotta (p180)

➡ Teatteri (p183)

➡ Parppeinpirtti (p185)

➡ Alamaja (p187)

➡ Säräpirtti Kippurasarvi (p179)

Best Places to Stay

➡ Salpalinjan Hovi (p177)

➡ Asko & Maija's Farmhouse (p178)

➡ Kestikievari Herranniemi (p188)

➡ Huhtiniemi Tourist Resort (p177)

Why Go?

If you're looking for wilderness, powerful history and even the Finnish soul, your search starts here.

Densely forested and gloriously remote, the region is a paradise for nature lovers. Bears and wolves roam freely across the Russian frontier, and animal hides allow visitors a close encounter. Opportunities to get active abound: the landscape is threaded by hiking routes, white-water rapids and waterways navigable by canoe, and lakes offer idyllic kayaking and boating. In winter, outdoor pursuits include fantastic skiing, dog-sledding, snowshoeing and ice fishing.

Karelia straddles both sides of the Finnish–Russian border, and has a distinct culture, language, religion, cuisine, music and architecture. In Finland's Karelian regions, lakeside Lappeenranta is still strongly connected to its sister cities that have been part of Russia since WWII. Once-battle-scarred Joensuu is now a vibrant university town, and Imatra still recalls its 18th-century golden age as a Russian aristocracy playground.

When to Go
Karelia

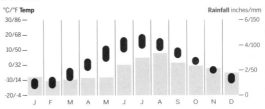

Mid-Apr The bear-watching season begins, when brown bears wake from their winter sleep.

Jul Joensuu's party atmosphere amps up during the international Ilosaari Rock Festival.

Dec Koli National Park's ski resort opens for business.

Karelia Highlights

1 Koli National Park (p186) Swooshing down the ski slopes in winter, or swooping above the tree line aboard the summer chairlift.

2 Rafting, Ruunaa (p190) Shooting Ruunaa's rapids on a rubber raft.

3 'Visa-free' trip to Russia (p181) Cruising from Lappeenranta to the Karelian town of Vyborg.

4 EU's Easternmost Point (p187) Ticking another 'superlative place' off your list beyond Hattuvaara at the EU's far-flung easternmost point.

5 Santa's Reindeers (p188) Walking with a reindeer in its natural habitat in the pristine Lake Pielinen region's Haapalahti.

6 Imatra Rapids (p179) Dangling upside down over torrents of water on a flying fox across Imatra's swirling rapids.

7 Paateri (p193) Being spellbound by the woodland chapel carved by artist Eva Ryynänen.

8 Erä Eero (p189) Spending the night in an animal hide near Lieksa, awaiting wolverines, lynx and bears.

9 Karhunpolku (Bear's Trail) (p191) Hiking among this poignant trail's WWII remains.

SOUTH KARELIA

Over the centuries the border has shuffled back and forth, and the South Karelian trade town of Vyborg (Finnish: Viipuri) and the Karelian Isthmus reaching to St Petersburg are now part of Russia, accessible from the former garrison town of Lappeenranta. The area was a favourite with Russian aristocracy, particularly Lappeenranta and the famous rapids at Imatra. Today Lappeenranta's fortress and Imatra's rapids remain the area's biggest draws. Both towns also have some great places to drink, dine or just stroll along the shores of Saimaa, Finland's largest lake.

Lappeenranta

☑ 05 / POP 73,101

On the banks of Lake Saimaa , Lappeenranta has encountered dramatic swings of fortune. Once famous for its scarlet-clad garrison, the 17th-century 'Cavalry City' was a humming trade port at the edge of the Swedish empire. In 1743 it came under Russian control, where it remained for the next 68 years, becoming an exclusive spa town. Much of the town was destroyed during the Winter and Continuation Wars, but its massive fortress and spa endure.

Russia still owns half of the 43km Saimaa Canal, which links Lappeenranta to the Gulf of Finland. It's currently 'leased' to Finland until 2063 – popular day trips run through its eight locks and across the Russian border.

◉ Sights

★ **Linnoitus**   FORTRESS
(Map p176; www.lappeenranta.fi; Kristiinankatu; fortress free, combined museum ticket adult/child €8/free; ⊙10am-6pm Mon-Fri, 11am-5pm Sat & Sun Jun-late Aug, 11am-5pm Tue-Sun late Aug-May) Standing guard above the harbour, this hulking hilltop fortification was begun by the Swedes and finished by the Russians in the late 18th century. Today it contains galleries, craft workshops and fascinating museums, including the history-focused **South Karelian Museum** (Etelä-Karjalan Museo) and **Cavalry Museum** (Ratsuväkimuseo; Kristaanankatu 2; combined Linnoitus museum ticket adult/child €8/free; ⊙10am-6pm Mon-Fri, 11am-5pm Sat & Sun), and the **Lappeenranta Art Museum** (Etelä-Karjalan Taidemuseo; combined fortress museum ticket adult/child €8/free; ⊙10am-6pm Mon-Fri, 11am-5pm Sat & Sun Jun-late Aug, 11am-5pm Tue-Sun late Aug-May). Its **Orthodox Church** (Map p176; www.2ort.fi; ⊙10am-5pm Tue-Sun Jun–mid-Aug), Finland's oldest church, was completed in 1785 by Russian soldiers. Pick up the tourist office's free walking guide *The Fortress of Lappeenranta,* or download its free app.

★ **Hiekkalinna**   PUBLIC ART
(Map p176; http://hiekkalinna.lappeenranta.fi; Satamatie 11; ⊙10am-9pm early Jun-Aug) FREE Every summer, around 30 sand artists from Finland and abroad gather to build the Hiekkalinna, a giant themed 'sandcastle' made from some three million kilograms of sand. Previous themes have included dinosaurs, a Wild West scene incorporating a gigantic steam train, and 'outer space' featuring ET and Darth Vader. Kids' entertainment here includes small carousel-style rides.

Karelia Aviation Museum   MUSEUM
(Karjala Nilmailu Museo; ☎050-370-2955; www.karjalanilmailumuseo.fi; Lentokentäntie 37; adult/child €4/free; ⊙by reservation noon-6pm Mon-Fri late May-Sep) Backing onto the runway of Lappeenranta airport (Finland's oldest still in operation), this extraordinary museum has three exhibition halls housed in hangars with helicopters, aeroplanes (including a supersonic MiG-21, a Saab 35 Draken and Saab 91 Safir, and a Nieuport 17 biplane), engines (among them a Fokker CX), scale models and other Finnish aviation memorabilia including air force medals. Reserve ahead to ensure someone's around to let you in.

Myllysaari   BEACH
(Map p176) On the lakeshore, this sandy beach has an outdoor swimming pool, beach volleyball, a water slide and kiosk, along with the Myllysaari **beach sauna** (Map p176; €8; ⊙women 4-8pm Wed & Fri, men 4-8pm Tue & Thu). Hardy souls can swim here in winter when two pools are cut into the ice.

Lappee Church   CHURCH
(Map p176; Kirkkokatu 11; ⊙10am-6pm Jun–mid-Aug) Diagonally across the park from its own bell tower, the adorable wooden Lappee Church was built in 1794 to an unusual 'double cruciform' floor plan, the only one of its kind in Finland. South of the church stretches the graveyard, with an evocative **war memorial**, which features poignant cubist and modernist sculptures commemorating Finns who died in the Winter and Continuation Wars.

Wolkoff Home Museum   MUSEUM
(Wolkoffin Talomuseo; Map p176; ☑05-616-2258; Kauppakatu 26; adult/child €8/free; ⊙10am-6pm Mon-Fri, 11am-5pm Sat & Sun early Jun-late

Lappeenranta

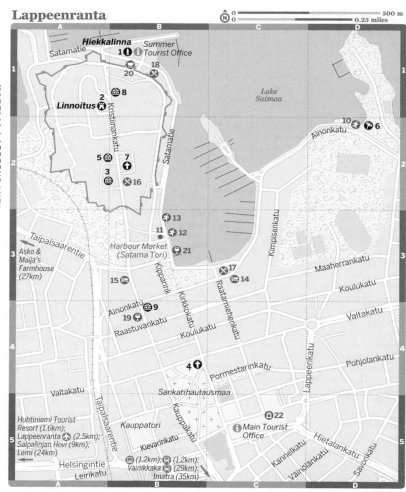

Aug, 11am-5pm Sat & Sun Mar-early Jun & late Aug-early Dec) Built in 1826, this lovingly preserved Russian home was owned by the merchant Wolkoff family from 1872 to 1986, and its 10 rooms have been maintained as they were in the late 1800s. The house is visitable only by 40-minute guided tours departing on the hour (English available).

🏃 Activities

Salpasafarit
OUTDOORS

(Map p176; ☎ 044-553-6384; www.salpasafarit. fi; Satamatie; hovercraft trips per 15min from €15; ⏱ hovercraft trips noon & 5pm Wed, Fri & Sat, rental office 11am-5pm Thu-Sat & by appointment) Activities operator Salpasafarit offers sports such as water-skiing (€30 per 15 minutes) and parasailing (€100 per 15 minutes) and runs ATV safaris (one hour €80). It also rents SUPs (€35 per two hours), fishing equipment (€20 per day) and bikes (€12/25 per two hours/day, electric bikes €20/30).

Saimaan Risteilyt
CRUISE

(Map p176; ☎ 045-673-8959; www.saimaanristeilyt. fi; adult/child €20/10; ⏱ up to three cruises daily late May-Oct) Popular two-hour trips aboard the M/S *SaimaaHoliday Margareta* cruise Lake Saimaa and the Saimaa Canal.

Lappeenranta

◎ **Top Sights**
  1 Hiekkalinna B1
  2 Linnoitus A1

◎ **Sights**
  3 Cavalry Museum A2
  4 Lappee Church B4
  5 Lappeenranta Art Museum A2
  6 Myllysaari D2
  7 Orthodox Church B2
  8 South Karelian Museum B1
  9 Wolkoff Home Museum B4

◎ **Activities, Courses & Tours**
  10 Myllysaari Beach Sauna D2
  11 Saimaan Matkaverkko B3
  12 Saimaan Risteilyt B3
  13 Salpasafarit B3

◎ **Sleeping**
  14 Lappeenrannan Kylpylä C3
  15 Scandic Hotel Patria B3

◎ **Eating**
  16 Kahvila Majurska B2
  17 Kasino C3
  18 Wanha Makasiini B1
    Wolkoff Restaurant & Wine
     Bar .... (see 9)

◎ **Drinking & Nightlife**
  19 Birra B4
  20 Lehmus Roastery B1
  21 Prinsessa Armaada B3

◎ **Shopping**
  22 IsoKristiina Shopping Centre C5

🎉 Festivals & Events

Lemin Musiikkijuhlat
MUSIC

(www.leminmusiikkijuhlat.fi; ⊙late Jul/early Aug) This four-day chamber-music festival takes place in late July or early August, mainly in churches throughout Lappeenranta, Imatra and Lemi. Many events are free.

🛏 Sleeping

Lappeenranta has several large chain hotels such as Cumulus and Sokos, a spa hotel and a great campground. **GoSaimaa** (☑05-667-788; www.gosaimaa.com) can book nearby lakeside cabins and cottages.

★Huhtiniemi
Tourist Resort
CAMPGROUND, COTTAGE €

(☑05-451-5555; www.huhtiniemi.com; Kuusimäenkatu 18; tent sites €14 plus per person €5, 2-/4-person cottages €40/50, apt €80-98; P🅿🛜) Situated 2km west of the centre, this 10-hectare lakeside campground has waterside sites, cottages and wi-fi–equipped apartments. In summer reservations are a must except for camping, which is first come, first served. Bus 5 from the city stops here, as do most intercity buses.

★Salpalinjan Hovi
BOUTIQUE HOTEL €€

(☑050-336-0986; www.salpalinjanhovi.com; Vanha Mikkelinte 125, Rutola; s/d/f from €89/99/144; P❄@🛜) Topped by a tin roof, this yellow-painted wooden schoolhouse dating from 1901 now has six rooms themed for different subjects once taught here: Languages and Literature, History, Science, Art, Music and Geography. All come with kitchens; there's a sauna, hot tub, ski storage and a courtyard barbecue area. It's a 400m stroll from a lakeside beach, 9km west of Lappeenranta.

Lappeenrannan Kylpylä
SPA HOTEL €€

(Map p176; ☑020-761-3761; www.kylpyla.info; Ainonkatu 17; s/d from €80/120; P❄🛜🅿) Bronze- and gold-toned, minibar-equipped rooms – some opening to balconies – range over the revamped 1970s spa hotel housing reception and the upper floors of the lakefront art nouveau Wanha Kylpylä (Old Spa) building across the street. Facilities include a gym, a couple of pools and a waterfall that delivers a pounding shoulder massage.

Scandic Hotel Patria
HOTEL €€

(Map p176; ☑05-677-511; www.scandichotels. com; Kauppakatu 21; d/f/ste from €122/158/219; P❄🛜) Definitely one of the best places to stay in Lappeenranta, the Patria is close to the harbour and fortress. The pick of its Scandi-chic rooms feature saunas and balconies with park views. There's also a communal hot tub, a gym and a kids' indoor play area. Its organic buffet includes gluten- and lactose-free options. Service is super-helpful.

🍴 Eating

Kahvila Majurska
CAFE €

(Map p176; www.majurska.com; Kristiinankatu 1; cakes and pastries €3-6; ⊙10am-8pm Mon-Sat, 11am-8pm Sun Jun-Aug, to 5pm Sep-May) If you can't border-hop to a genuine Russian teahouse, this is as close as you'll get in Finland. A former officer's club (check out the vintage furniture and august portrait of Mannerheim), it still serves tea from the samovar and does a range of homemade pastries and cakes.

Kasino
FINNISH €€

(Map p176; ☑040-716-8097; www.fazer.fi; Ainonkatu 10; lunch buffet €12.60, mains €14.50-23.50;

FARMHOUSES

If you're looking to get off the beaten track, meet locals and experience rural life, try a farm-stay in the countryside around Lappeenranta. Your double room, costing around €70, could be in a traditional 19th-century farmhouse, a former granary or perhaps a cosy log cabin in the grounds. Some places have animals for children to pet, and almost all offer outdoor activities, such as rowing, fishing, snowshoeing, snowmobiling or horse-drawn sleigh-riding.

A great option is the lakeside **Asko & Maija's Farmhouse** (☑ 040-507-5842; www.rantatupa.net; Suolahdentie 461, Taipalsaari; homestay per person €30, cottages per 2 days from €230; ☉ homestay Jun-Aug, cottages year-round; ℗), 30km northwest of Lappeenranta off Rd 408, with homestay accommodation in a traditional 1843-built log cabin and private timber cottages. Contact Lappeenranta's main tourist office to find others.

☉ 11am-3pm & 5-9pm Mon-Wed, 11am-3pm Thu & Fri, 11am-3pm & 5-11pm Sat Jun-Aug) Pork tenderloin with dill and sour cream sauce, crumbed white lake fish with salmon roe, and perch with cider sauce are among the options served at this venerable century-old wooden building. On sunny days, the best seats are on the floating terrace moored on the lake. Kid-pleasers include fish fingers.

Wanha Makasiini   BISTRO €€
(Map p176; ☑ 010-666-8611; www.ravintolawan hamakasiini.fi; Satamatie 4; pizzas €15-16, mains €18-38, 3-/5-course dinner menu €44/59, with wine €73-98; ☉ noon-11pm Tue-Sat, to 10pm Sun & Mon; ☑) High-quality dishes at this cosy spot in a red-brick former gunsmith's workshop range from fresh fish to house-made sausages and seasonal delicacies like chanterelle soup. Thin, crispy pizzas come with traditional toppings as well as local specialities like smoked *muikku* (vendace, or whitefish; a small lake fish) and pickled cucumber.

Wolkoff Restaurant & Wine Bar FINNISH €€€
(Map p176; ☑ 05-415-0320; www.wolkoff.fi; Kauppakatu 26; lunch buffet €15, mains €21-31, 3-course menu €43; ☉ 11am-2pm & 5-11pm Mon-Fri, 4.30-11pm Sat; ☎) This grand Old World restaurant utilises organic produce and seasonal ingredients to create gourmet Finnish cuisine with adventurous flavour combinations like reindeer tartare with fennel foam, pike perch with roast horseradish and lime slaw, and rhubarb, blueberry and rye crumble. The laden lunch buffet is a veritable bargain.

🍷 Drinking & Nightlife

★**Prinsessa Armaada**   BAR
(Map p176; ☑ 044-754-5504; www.prinsessaarmaa da.fi; Satamatori 10; ☉ 10am-2am mid-Apr–mid-Sep) Built in 1902, this tar steamship, which once transported timber to St Petersburg has operated as a bar since 1959 and has great

ciders and craft beers. Its cargo hold has a restaurant (reservations essential); up on deck is a 12-person sauna with its own mini-bar. There's regular live music.

★**Lehmus Roastery**   COFFEE
(Map p176; www.lehmusroastery.com; Satamatie 6; ☉ 10am-6pm Mon-Thu & Sat, 10am-8pm Fri, noon-6pm Sun; ☎) Crowned Finland's best coffee roastery at 2017's Suomen Paras Paahtimo awards, Lehmus occupies a red-brick former warehouse overlooking the lake. Behind the gleaming espresso machine, passionate staff roast four types of organic coffee, which they serve along with fresh pastries.

Birra   BAR
(Map p176; Kauppakatu 27; ☉ 2pm-1am Sun-Thu, to 2am Fri & Sat; ☎) One of the swankier bars in town, Birra has a shaded terrace, cosy booths and a great range of beer (over 100 by the bottle) and cider (20 varieties) with more rotating on the taps.

ℹ️ Information

Main Tourist Office (Map p176; ☑ 05-667-788; www.visitlappeenranta.fi; Brahenkatu 1; ☉ 10am-5pm Mon-Fri, to 4pm Sat; ☎) In the **IsoKristiina** (Map p176; www.isokristiina.fi; Brahenkatu 5; ☉ 7am-9pm Mon-Fri, 9am-9pm Sat, 9am-6pm Sun) shopping centre.

Summer Tourist Office (Map p176; ☑ 040-352-2178; www.visitlappeenranta.fi; Satamatie 11; ☉ 10am-8pm Jun-early Aug, to 6pm early Aug-late Aug) Located at the sandcastle Hiekkalinna (p175).

ℹ️ Getting There & Away

AIR

Lappeenranta airport (LPP; www.lppairport.fi; Lentokentäntie 21) is 2.5km west of the city centre. Finnair has year-round domestic flights; there are also seasonal flights to a handful of European destinations. Bus 4 (€3.20) links it with the bus station via the city centre. A **taxi** (☑ 020-060-400; www.taksisaimaa.fi) to the city centre costs around €9.

BUS

Lappeenranta's **bus station** (Ratakatu 23) is 1.2km south of the city centre; most intercity buses also stop on Valtakatu in the middle of town. Bus 9 (€3.20) runs between the bus station and the city centre.

Major **Matkahuolto** (www.matkahuolto.fi) services include the following:

Helsinki €30, 3½ hours, eight daily

Imatra €9.30, 35 minutes, two daily

Joensuu €30, 4½ hours, two daily

Mikkeli €20, 1¾ hours, three daily

Savonlinna €25, four hours, three daily

Onnibus (www.onnibus.com) has cheaper but less frequent services to destinations including Helsinki (€7, three hours, four daily), Imatra (€5, 30 minutes, one daily) and Joensuu (€10, three hours, one daily).

TRAIN

Intercity trains use **Lappeenranta train station** (Ratakatu 23), next to the bus station, 1.2km south of town. Services include Helsinki (€28, two hours, six daily), Imatra (€5, 25 minutes, eight daily) and Joensuu (€30, 2¼ hours, four daily).

International trains to/from Russia use **Vainikkala train station** (Rajamiehentie 147, Vainikkala), 29.5km south of Lappeenranta, linked by bus (€6.50, 40 minutes, up to 10 daily) from the bus station and Valtakatu in town. Trains run to Vyborg (€47, 25 minutes, two daily) and on to St Petersburg (€75, 1½ hours). Book through VR (Finnish Railways; www.vr.fi).

ⓘ Getting Around

Hire a bike from **Pyörä-Expert** (☑ 05-411-8710; www.pyoraexpert.com; Valtakatu 64; bike hire per day from €10; ⊙ 9am-6pm Mon-Fri, to 2pm Sat Jun-Aug, 10.30am-5pm Mon-Fri, to 2pm Sat Sep-May) or from **Salpasafarit** (p176), which also has electric bikes.

In summer you can rest your feet aboard the **street train** (per ride adult/child €5/2; ⊙ hourly noon-5pm Mon, 11am-5pm Tue-Sun early Jun-Aug), which links the market square, IsoKristiina shopping centre, Linnoitus, Hiekkalinna and Myllysaari beach.

Taxis can be useful for getting around this large town, especially in adverse weather.

Imatra

☑ 05 / POP 27,721

Imatra was once the darling of Russian aristocracy – one of the first tourists to the area was Catherine the Great who in 1772 gathered her entourage to view Imatra's thundering rapids. Although the rapids were harnessed for hydroelectricity in 1929, water pours forth again during dramatic daily summer shows.

The town has a number of dispersed, mostly modern 'centres' separated by kilometres of highway. Imatrankoski, the site of the rapids, is of most interest to visitors and has the majority of services. Boaties, beach goers and spa seekers may prefer the Imatran leisure area, 7km northwest of Imatrankoski.

⊙ Sights

★**Imatra Rapids**　　　　　　　　RIVER
(⊙ Rapids Show 6pm Jun-late Aug) **FREE** The 1929 construction of Imatra's hydroelectric complex (Finland's largest) dammed the river, but the watery wonder lives on with the spectacular 20-minute **Rapids Show**, when the dam is opened to a rousing *son et lumière*. If your inner daredevil wants to get involved, Imatra Express (p180) runs a flying fox over the gushing waters. Both attractions were closed in 2017 due to construction works, but are expected to reopen by summer 2018.

Kruununpuisto　　　　　　　　　PARK
(Crown Park; ⊙ 24 hr) Founded in 1842, Finland's oldest nature park is one of the 27 Finnish national landscapes selected in 1992 as part of the 75th anniversary of the country's independence, representing its unique culture and environment. The 5000-sq-metre park spans both sides of the Vuoksi river, and takes in the hydroelectric plant powered by the rapids, as well as imperial pavilions and statues.

> **WORTH A TRIP**
>
> ### LEMI
>
> This tiny village, 25km west of Lappeenranta, is synonymous with its signature dish *lemin särä* (roast mutton). Hailed as one of the seven wonders of Finland, it's cooked in a birch trough to infuse the meat with a sweet, woody flavour. Preparation takes nine hours, so you'll need to book at least two days in advance.
>
> The best place to sample it is the lakeshore restaurant **Säräpirtti Kippurasarvi** (☑ 05-414-6470; www.sarapirtti.fi; Rantatie 1; adult/child €33/16.50; ⊙ by reservation; ⊕), which serves nothing but *lemin särä* (the recipe for which dates back a thousand years), accompanied by soup, bread and homemade *kalja* (beer).

KARELIA IMATRA

Imatran Taidemuseo
GALLERY

(Virastokatu 1; ☺10am-7pm Mon-Fri Jun-Aug, 9am-7pm Mon-Fri, 10am-3pm Sat, 9am-4pm Sun Sep-May) FREE Attached to the public library, this bright white space has temporary exhibitions and a permanent collection of 1400 works concentrating on Finnish modernism, with works by Wäinö Aaltonen and Gallen-Kallela.

🏃 Activities

Imatra Express
FLYING FOX

(☎044-016-1096; www.imatraexpress.fi; basic/inverted/superman €35/50/70; ☺5-7pm Mon-Fri & Sun, noon-7pm Sat Jun-late Aug, or by arrangement) This flying fox over the gushing waters offers a death-defying upside-down option and a horizontal 'superman' option. Construction closed the attraction in 2017, but it's due to be operating again by summer 2018. Prices drop when there are no rapids.

Saimaa Adventures
OUTDOORS

(☎05-230-2555; www.saimaa-adventures.fi; Purjekuja 2) Adrenaline-charged summer activities include quad-bike safaris (two people per hour €145) and speedboat safaris to Saimaa island (€65 per two hours); winter options include ski or snowshoe rental (€8 per hour), ice-fishing trips (€50 per three hours), and one-hour tours floating in a drysuit along an icy stream (€48).

Vuoksen Kalastuspuisto
FISHING

(☎05-432-3123; www.vuoksenkalastuspuisto.fi; Kotipolku 4; fishing €5, equipment rental €5, plus per kg for fish caught €18-28; ☺9.30am-6pm May, 9am-10pm Jun-Sep) You can fish for salmon and trout in these stocked ponds in Mansikkala, use the on-site smoker, and purchase licences (€12/24 per day/week) for the surrounding waters. There's a seafood restaurant; it also rents out bikes, rowboats and kayaks (€20 per day), and offers camping (tent sites €17 plus €3 per person) and good-sized fishing cabins (from €65).

M/S Vuoksetar
CRUISE

(☎040-065-5848; www.vuoksenkalastuspuisto.fi; Kotipolku 4, Varpasaari; adult/child €15/8; ☺3pm late Jun-late Aug) Scenic one-hour river cruises along the Vuoski depart from the fishing park Vuoksen Kalastuspuisto.

🛏 Sleeping

Ukonlinna Hostel
HOSTEL €

(☎010-322-7711; www.hostelukonlinna.fi; Leiritie 8; dm €30, f €140-160; P🤶) With a prime position on the beach in Imatra's leisure area,

this cute little HI hostel books out quickly. Rooms all share bathrooms except the family room (room 8), which sleeps up to five people. Breakfast can be pre-ordered for €8. There are three lakeside saunas, and bikes and rowboats for hire. Staff are delightful.

Imatran Kylpylä Spa
SPA HOTEL €€

(☎020-500-7100; www.imatrankylpyla.fi; Purjekuja 2; s/d/f/ste/apt from €103/140/170/180/235, spa for nonguests adult/child €15/8; P@🤶🏊) The whopping flagship of Imatra's leisure area incorporates the family-oriented Promenade Hotel (with lake views), recently renovated Spa Hotel, and luxury apartments set on their own little hill sleeping up to eight people. There are cafes, restaurants, bars, a bowling alley, bike hire, badminton court and of course the spa itself, with several pools, Jacuzzis and treatments galore.

🍴 Eating & Drinking

Café Julia
CAFE €

(www.buttenhoff.fi; Koskenparras 4; dishes €7.50-13.50; ☺8am-5pm Mon-Fri, 9am-5pm Sat; 🤶) On the ground floor of the Buttenhoff restaurant, this charming cafe serves dishes like Finnish pancakes with smoked salmon and blackcurrants, but is best loved for cakes.

⭐ Ravintola Nuotta
FINNISH €€

(☎050-598-8932; www.ravintolanuotta.fi; Satamalaiturintie 13; mains €11.50-26.50; ☺noon-8.30pm Mon-Thu, to 9pm Fri, to 10pm Sat, to 7pm Sun late Apr-early Sep) Two sizes of *bliny* (Russian buckwheat pancakes), topped with hot or cold salmon, trout roe, crayfish tails, or sour cream, pickled cucumber, red onion and local herbs, are the speciality of this fabulous lakeside bar-restaurant, with a panoramic rooftop terrace. The bar opens until 2am on Friday and Saturday, when live bands play; dancing spills out into the car park.

Buttenhoff
FRENCH, RUSSIAN €€

(☎05-476-1433; www.buttenhoff.fi; Koskenparras 4; mains lunch €13.50-25, dinner €23-36; ☺11am-10pm Mon-Fri, noon-10pm Sat) Cooking up specialities from France (Burgundy escargot) and Russia (*bliny*), this 1st-floor restaurant also creates hybrid French-Russian dishes such as pan-fried perch *à la Russe*. At street level, and run by the same operator, casual Café Julia has fabulous cakes.

Kuohu
BAR

(Imatran Kaskentie 1; ☺2-10pm Mon & Tue, noon-11pm Wed & Thu, noon-midnight Fri & Sat, noon-8pm Sun; 🤶) Close to the rapids, in leafy

TRAVELLING TO RUSSIA

A boat cruise along the Saimaa Canal to Vyborg, 60km southeast, in Russia, is something of a spiritual journey to reunite Karelia.

Saimaan Matkaverkko (Map p176; ☑ 05-541-0100; www.saimaatravel.fi; Kipparinkatu 1) runs quick-and-easy 'visa-free' day cruises for all nationalities from Lappeenranta to Vyborg aboard the M/S *Carelia* (from €63, departs 7.45am four to six times weekly from late May to mid-September) that allow you around three hours to sightsee and shop. There's a Vyborg port fee of €8.80. It's also possible to stay overnight in Vyborg, with prices varying by season and usually costing more on weekends. You must provide the company with a copy of your passport at least three days before departure (and passports must be valid for at least a further six months from the end date of your trip). Book well in advance, as these cruises are heavily subscribed. The company can also organise a package (from €310, single supplement €145, meals and excursions extra, departing July to August) to St Petersburg that includes the cruise to Vyborg and a bus on to St Petersburg, with two nights' accommodation in Russia before returning to Lappeenranta.

If you want to travel independently (and you have a visa), several train and bus services pass through Lappeenranta on the way to St Petersburg and Moscow. For non-EU citizens who haven't organised a Russian tourist visa before leaving their country of residence, independent travel is difficult to impossible. If you can endure a long wait and complex bureaucracy, you could try the **Russian consulate** (☑ 05-872-0777; www.vfsglobal.com; Kievarinkatu 1A; ☺ 9am-3pm Mon-Fri) in Lappeenranta.

---

surrounds overlooking a splashing fountain, this stylish Arctic-white bar opens to an umbrella-shaded terrace (heated in winter) and hosts live music on weekends.

ℹ Information

Tourist Office (☑ 05-235-2330; www.imatra basecamp.com; Koskenparras; ☺ 5.30-6.30pm late Jun–mid-Aug) During the summer, Imatra's mobile tourist office visits various locations daily, including the pedestrianised area of Imatrankoski. If it's closed, the Lappeenranta tourist office (p178) can provide information on the town.

ℹ Getting There & Away

The **bus** and **train** stations are both 3km north of Imatrankoski on Koskikatu in Mansikkala, and are linked by frequent local buses (€3). Otherwise you'll need a **taxi** (☑ 020-016-464; www.imatrantaksi.fi).

Long-distance buses are operated by Matkahuolto (www.matkahuolto.fi) and budget company Onnibus (www.onnibus.com), but trains offer the speediest connections:

Helsinki €37, 2½ hours, seven daily
Joensuu €26, two hours, four daily
Lappeenranta €5, 25 minutes, two daily

NORTH KARELIA

Criss-crossed by dusty gravel roads, Finland's sparsely populated frontier has some of Finland's most abundant wildlife. Its strong Russian influence is evident in striking Orthodox churches: North Karelia was fought over for centuries by Sweden and Russia, with fierce fighting during the Winter and Continuation Wars. You'll often stumble across trenches, old battlegrounds and memorials to the fallen inside the quiet forests.

Just beyond North Karelia, Kuhmo, in central Finland, also has a Karelian heritage, though it's not strictly part of this province.

Outdoor activities abound in this region in both winter and summer. North Karelia's best trekking routes form the Karjalan Kierros (Karelian Circuit; www.vaellus.info; p191), a loop of 14 marked hiking trails (plus some canoe and cycling variants) with a total length of more than 1000km between Ilomantsi and Lake Pielinen.

Joensuu

☑ 013 / POP 75,557

At the egress of the Pielisjoki (Joensuu means 'river mouth' in Finnish), North Karelia's capital is a spirited university town, with students making up almost a third of the population. Joensuu was founded by Tsar Nikolai I and became an important trading port following the 1850s completion of the Saimaa Canal. During the Winter and Continuation Wars, 23 bombing raids flattened many of its older buildings, and today most of its architecture is modern. It's a lively place to spend some time before heading into the Karelian wilderness.

DON'T MISS

PIT STOP: PARIKKALA

What looks like an ordinary roadside rest stop adjoins a woodland area with 256 surreal life-size sculptures of figures in yoga poses. **Parikkalan Patsaspuisto** (www.patsaspuisto.net; Kuutostie 611, Parikkala; admission by donation; ⏲sunrise-sunset) is the work of sculptor Veijo Rönkkönen (1942–2010), who lived on the site and created 565 of them in his time. The site's current owner uses visitor donations (suggested €5) for its upkeep. Wandering the sculpture-lined trail is extraordinary, but mosquitoes and other biting insects are fierce in the warmer months so bring plenty of repellent. Before his death, Rönkkönen had planned to cover the site in sand, for the sculptures to be rediscovered far into the future like China's Terracotta Army.

On the shores of Simpelejärvi, **Laatokan Portti** (☎040-024-0557; www.laatokanportti.com; Kuutostie 722, Parikkala; d with/without bathroom €85/55, 1-/2-bedroom apt €130/160; P 📶), a welcoming lakeside property, has a private beach and boat dock, bike, canoe and motor boat hire, plus fishing equipment and guides. In winter you can rent snowmobiles. Rooms and apartments come with fridges; apartments have full kitchens, terraces and barbecues. Its restaurant serves hearty local specialities; there's also an adjacent fish shop, **Kalakauppa Parikkala** (☎040-024-0557; ⏲10am-6pm).

Sights

★Carelicum MUSEUM
(Map p184; www.joensuu.fi; Koskikatu 5; adult/child €5/3; ⏲10am-4.30pm Mon-Fri, 10am-3pm Sat & Sun) Themed displays – on the region's prehistory, its war-torn past, the Karelian evacuation, the importance of the sauna etc – cover both sides of Karelia's present-day border at this excellent museum. Highlights include a Junkers bomber engine, and local hunting and fishing equipment including a two-century-old crossbow.

Perhos-Botania GARDENS
(www.botania.fi; Heinäpurontie 70; adult/child €9/4; ⏲10am-5pm Mon, Tue, Thu & Fri, 10am-6pm Wed, 11am-4pm Sat & Sun Apr-Aug, shorter hours Sep-Mar) Founded in 1957, Joensuu's botanic gardens contain over 600 plant species in four separate areas: desert, tropical, sub-tropical and temperate. Highlights include a 570-sq-metre glass-paned greenhouse (with a butterfly enclosure and a resident sulphur-crested cockatoo, Juuso), a poison garden, a medicinal garden and kitchen garden as well as an apiary.

Taitokortteli ARTS CENTRE
(Map p184; ☎013-220-140; www.taitokortteli.fi; Koskikatu 1; ⏲10am-5pm Mon-Fri, 10am-3pm Sat year-round, plus noon-4pm Sun Jul) Dating back over a century, these charming wooden buildings are some of the few remaining. They now comprise an arts and crafts centre where you can see weavers at work, browse contemporary art and purchase clothing, toys and homewares by local designers. There's a gallery space as well as cafes and bars.

Orthodox Church of St Nicholas CHURCH
(Pyhän Nikolaoksen Kirkko; Map p184; ☎020-610-0590; www.joensuunortodoksit.fi; Kirkkokatu 32; ⏲10am-4pm Mon-Fri mid-Jun–mid-Aug or by appointment) Joensuu's most intriguing church is the wooden Orthodox church, built in 1887 with icons painted in St Petersburg during the late 1880s. Services are held at 6pm Saturday and 10am Sunday; visitors are welcome.

Joensuun Taidemuseo GALLERY
(Map p184; Kirkkokatu 23; adult/child €7/3; ⏲10am-4pm Tue & Thu-Sun, to 8pm Wed) The impressive collection at Joensuu's art museum spans Chinese pieces, examples of Finnish modernism and an intriguing selection of Orthodox icons.

Festivals & Events

Ilosaari Rock Festival MUSIC
(www.ilosaarirock.fi; Linnunlahdentie; ⏲mid-Jul) Founded in 1971, this massive three-day rock festival has a waterside location with its own beach, and attracts over 60 Finnish and international acts on its five stages. It has received awards for its environmental record.

Sleeping

Finnhostel Joensuu HOSTEL €
(Map p184; ☎050-408-4587; www.islo.fi; Kalevankatu 5B; s/d/q from €50/76/152; ⏲reception 3-8pm; P 📶) Great-value, sizeable rooms here come with bathroom and kitchen facilities as well as small balconies. Prices include breakfast, and access to a sauna and gym. Kids have indoor and outdoor play areas. HI discount.

Hotel GreenStar
HOTEL €

(Map p184; ☏ 010-423-9390; www.greenstar.fi; Torikatu 16; d from €59; ⏱ reception 7am-8pm Mon-Sat, 8am-1pm & 3-7pm Sun; ☏) ⚑ Eco-initiatives at this contemporary hotel include water heating rather than air-con and small communal areas to reduce heating. Clean, comfortable rooms sleep up to three for the same price (a pull-out armchair converts into a single bed). Breakfast (€9) is optional. Try to arrive when reception is staffed as the lobby's automatic check-in kiosk can be temperamental.

Linnunlahti
CAMPGROUND €

(Map p184; ☏ 040-033-3133; www.linnunlahti.fi; Linnunlahdentie 1; tent sites €8 plus per person €2, cottages €119-170; ☏) This bargain almost-lakeside campground is mobbed during the Ilosaari Rock Festival, when it's reserved for festival goers, but otherwise has sites to spare. Cottages sleeping two to six people have wi-fi. Depending on the season, you can rent different types of outdoors equipment.

Cumulus Joensuu
HOTEL €€

(Map p184; ☏ 020-048-118; www.cumulus.fi; Kirkkokatu 20; d from €130; P☀☏) The pick of Joensuu's central chain hotels has squeaky-clean rooms with powerful showers, a small gym, free parking, friendly staff and fast wi-fi. Breakfast is served in the cellar dining room.

✗ Eating

Kahvila & Konditoria Houkutus
CAFE, BAKERY €

(Map p184; www.houkutus.fi; Torikatu 24; small dishes €1.50-5.50, mains €8-17; ⏱ 7.30am-7pm Mon-Fri, 8.30am-5pm Sat) Houkutus does great coffee and even better cakes (the mint blackcurrant cake is a treat), along with savoury pastries such as quiches, meal-sized salads and filled bread rolls.

★ Teatteri
KARELIAN €€

(Map p184; ☏ 010-231-4250; www.teatteriravintola.fi; Rantakatu 20; lunch buffet €8.60-10.50, mains €18-32, menus €46-65; ⏱ 11am-10pm Mon & Tue, 11am-11pm Wed & Thu, 11am-midnight Fri, 11.30am-midnight Sat) ⚑ Locally sourced ingredients prepared in innovative ways are served in the town hall's art deco surrounds and on its beautiful summer terrace. Dishes span nettle ricotta with wild herb salad to liquorice-glazed goose with kale pesto; desserts like fennel and apple sorbet with blackberry panna cotta are the icing on the cake. Menus can be accompanied by wine or craft beer pairings.

Local Bistro
BISTRO €€

(Map p184; ☏ 010-323-4933; www.localbistro.fi; Koskikatu 9; lunch buffet €9.50, mains €16-28, 3-course menus €38-48; ⏱ 10.45am-9pm Mon-Thu, to 10pm Fri, noon-11pm Sat; ☏☀) Run by upbeat staff, this hip new bistro does a bargain lunch buffet but really comes into its own from 2pm, when its à la carte menu offers dishes like pike in citrus butter, buckwheat crumble-coated, and hazelnut-crusted chocolate mousse with rhubarb and raspberry coulis.

Ravintola Kielo
KARELIAN €€€

(Map p184; ☏ 013-227-874; www.ravintolakielo.fi; Suvantokatu 12; mains €20-29, tasting menu €46, with wine €75; ⏱ 4-10pm Mon-Sat) At the high end of Karelian cuisine, Kielo's artfully presented miniature starters such as whitefish escabeche with mussel mayo or sugar- and salt-cured Arctic char with smoked sour cream and fennel consommé set the stage for mains like pan-fried pike perch with sautéed forest mushrooms or braised pork belly with beetroot and roast Lapland potatoes. Wine pairings are superb.

🍸 Drinking & Nightlife

★ Kerubi
BAR, CLUB

(Map p184; ☏ 013-129-377; www.kerubi.fi; Siltakatu 1; ⏱ bar 11am-2pm Mon, 11am-11pm Tue-Thu, 11am-4am Fri, noon-4am Sat, 2pm-7pm Sun, club 10pm-4am Fri & Sat) Joensuu's best bar-club occupies its own island in the Pielisjoki, linked to the city centre by a bridge. DJs spin techno, trance and electronica on Friday and Saturday; live bands and stand-up comedy take place in the adjacent hall Tuesday to Saturday. Fantastic burgers, salads and steaks are served at its restaurant, which opens to a terrace overlooking the island's beach.

Romeo 1914
BAR

(Map p184; Matkustajasatama; ⏱ noon-midnight Jun-Aug, to 9pm May & Sep) Live music plays most nights aboard this former timber transporter built in 1914, now moored on the Pielisjoki. Wood-fired pizzas are cooked on the dockside terrace. Several other boat bars are located nearby.

Jokiasema
BAR

(www.jokiasema.fi; Hasanniementie 3; ⏱ 8am-midnight Jun-Aug; ☏) Sunsets are spectacular from this bar perched on the Pyhäselkä lake's edge, with a resident peg-leg pirate statue and seating on the terrace and pier, as well as a sauna in a rustic red timber building.

Joensuu

ⓘ Information

Karelia Expert (Map p184; ☑ 040-023-9549; www.visitkarelia.fi; Koskikatu 5; ⏱10am-5pm Mon-Fri; 🛜)

ⓘ Getting There & Away

AIR

The **airport** (JOE; www.finavia.fi; Lentoasemantie 30) is about 11km northwest of central Joensuu. An airport bus service (one way €5) meets all incoming flights, and departs from the **bus station** 65 minutes before flight departures and from the **corner of Koskikatu and Kauppakatu** (Map p184) (one hour before departures). A **taxi** (☑ 060-110-100; www.taksiitasuomi.fi) costs €25.

Finnair operates several flights a day between Helsinki and Joensuu.

BUS

The **bus station** (Map p184) is on the eastern side of the river.

Major **Matkahuolto** (www.matkahuolto.fi) services include the following:

Helsinki €30, 6½ hours, five express services daily

Jyväskylä €30, four hours, five daily

Kuopio €29.90, 2¼ hours, three express services daily

Lappeenranta €30, 4½ hours, two daily

Nurmes €20, two hours, three daily

Oulu €40, 6½ hours, two daily

Onnibus (www.onnibus.com) has cheaper but less frequent services to destinations including Helsinki (€15, 6¼ hours, two daily), Imatra (€5, 2½ hours, one daily) and Lappeenranta (€7, 3¼ hours, one daily).

TAXI

A *kimppakyyti* (shared taxi) route runs from Joensuu to Koli National Park. This **service** (☑ 020-741-4392) operates twice daily Sunday to Friday and three times on Saturdays year-round (one way/return €30/40). Book at least one day ahead. It also has an airport service (€5) on demand.

TRAIN

The **train station** (Itäranta) is east of the river, next to the bus station. Services include:

Helsinki €44, 4½ hours, four daily

Lieksa €14, 1¼ hours, two daily

Nurmes €21, two hours, one daily

Savonlinna €25, 2¼ hours, four daily; change at Parikkala

Ilomantsi

☑ 013 / POP 5316

The closest North Karelian town to the Russian border, Ilomantsi has an Orthodox religion and its own dialect. There is a handful of interesting sights here, but with little tourist infrastructure you're better off

Joensuu

◎ Top Sights
1 Carelicum C2

◎ Sights
2 Joensuun Taidemuseo B2
3 Orthodox Church of St Nicholas C1
4 Taitokortteli C2

🛏 Sleeping
5 Cumulus Joensuu C2
6 Finnhostel Joensuu............................. B3
7 Hotel GreenStar C2
8 Linnunlahti A3

🍴 Eating
9 Kahvila & Konditoria Houkutus C2
10 Local Bistro C2
11 Ravintola Kielo..................................... C2
12 Teatteri C2

🍷 Drinking & Nightlife
13 Kerubi D2
14 Romeo 1914 .... C3

visiting during the day and then heading for the national parks and scenic areas beyond.

Pyhän Elian Kirkko CHURCH
(www2.ort.fi; Kirkkotie 15; ⊙11.30am-5.30pm late Jun–mid-Aug) This beautiful wooden Orthodox church (the largest of its kind in Finland) has a striking Russian influence. Follow the *kalmisto* (graveyard) sign to the waterfront **Kokonniemi Cemetery**, where trees shade the graves of those lost in the many conflicts the town has endured.

Hermanni Winery WINERY
(☑020-778-9233; www.hermannin.fi; Käymiskuja 1; ⊙9am-4pm Mon-Fri, 10am-5pm Sat, noon-5pm Sun Jul, closed Sun Jun & Aug, closed Sat-Sun Sep-May) Finland's oldest winery was established in 1989. You can chat about the wine-making process and buy bottles, although due to Finnish alcohol laws, you'll need to visit an Alko liquor shop if you want buy the strongest apple and honey brandy to take home.

Parppeinvaara VILLAGE
(www.parppeinvaara.fi; Parppeintie 2; museum adult/child €8/6; ⊙museum 10am-6pm Jul, 11am-5pm Jun & Aug) Karelian traditions are celebrated at this little village 2km south of Ilomantsi. It's named for bard and *kantele* player Jaakko Parppei (1792–1885), whose songs inspired the *Kalevala* epic. Listen to the harpsichord-like sounds of this local stringed instrument at the small **cultural museum** on the hour from noon. Parppeinpirtti does

a wonderfully authentic Karelian buffet. The **Mesikkä Animal Museum** explores the relationship between Karelians and nature; there's a fascinating exhibition on the war years in the **Border General's Cabin**.

Hotelli Pogostan Hovi HOTEL €€
(☑040-196-4496; www.hotellipogostanhovi.fi; Kalevalantie 12; s/d/f from €63/84/150; 🅿🛜) If you need to stay in Ilomantsi, this recently renovated hotel, with 18 en suite rooms spruced up with patterned wallpaper, is your best bet. There's no in-house kitchen (so no breakfast), but family rooms have kitchenettes. Made from birch, pine and alder, its high-quality sauna is wonderfully aromatic.

★**Parppeinpirtti** KARELIAN €€
(☑010-239-9950; www.parppeinpirtti.fi; Parppeintie 4, Parppeinvaara; buffet adult/child €23.50/11.50; ⊙11am-6pm Jul, to 4pm Jun & Aug) Ilomantsi's one foodie highlight is this traditional house in the Parppeinvaara village, which does a real-deal *pitopöytä* (Karelian buffet) complete with a *kantele* soundtrack. Heap your plate with *vatruskoita* (salmon-stuffed pastry), swill down nonalcoholic *kotikalja* (a fermented drink that tastes like home-brewed beer) and finish with sticky berry soup.

★**Hermanni Wine Tower** WINE BAR
(Viintorni; ☑020-778-9233; www.hermannin.fi; Kappalaisentie; ⊙10am-11pm Jun–mid-Aug) Blackcurrants, crowberries and white currants from the fields and bogs around Ilomantsi are blended by Hermanni Winery (p185). At the top of the local 33m-high water tower, you can sample its local berry wines and liqueurs by the glass or tasting tray (€12 for five wines and one liqueur).

ℹ Information

Karelia Expert (☑040-024-0072; www.visit karelia.fi; Kalevalantie 13; ⊙9am-5pm Mon-Fri Jun-Aug, 8am-4pm Mon-Fri Sep-May) Reservations and information.

ℹ Getting There & Away

There's no public transport in the area; if you don't have your own wheels, you'll have to rely on **taxis** (☑013-88111).

Hattuvaara
☑013

About 40km northeast of Ilomantsi, Finland's most easterly settlement was famous for poem-singers, such as Arhippa Buruska-inen who is thought to have inspired tales in the *Kalevala*. The Poem and Border Rte runs through Hattuvaara as a tribute.

Taistelijan Talo HISTORIC BUILDING
(Heroes' House; ☑ 040-027-3671; www.taistelijan talo.fi; Hatuntie 387; museum €8; ☺ 10am-6pm Jun-Aug, 10am-6pm Mon-Fri, 10am-4pm Sat Sep) The striking wooden Taistelijan Talo was designed by Joensuu architect Erkki Helasvuo in 1988 to symbolise the meeting of East and West. On the ground floor, the **restaurant** (buffet €19) offers an excellent all-day Karelian buffet. The **WWII museum** downstairs has multimedia exhibits, photo exhibitions and weaponry displays relating chiefly to the Winter and Continuation Wars fought along the nearby border. Outside are artillery and vehicles as well as a **Big Hat sculpture** (the town's name translates as Hat Mountain).

❶ Getting There & Away

Hattuvaara is not served by public transport, so you'll need to make your own arrangements.

LAKE PIELINEN

At the heart of northern Karelia is Pielinen, Finland's fourth-largest lake. On its shores, precipitous Koli National Park has epic views and winter skiing. Bring your hiking boots because this is a place to be active; towns here are really just bases for getting into the great outdoors.

Koli National Park

The magnificent 347m-high Koli inspired Finland's artistic National Romantic era with artists including Pekka Halonen and Eero Järnefelt setting up their easels here. Koli was declared a national park in 1991 after intense debate between environmentalists and landowners. The area remains relatively pristine with over 90km of marked walking tracks and superb cross-county and downhill skiing.

🏃 Activities

Summer Chair Lift CHAIR LIFT
(one way/return €4/6; ☺ 11am-5.45pm mid–late Jun & early Aug, 10am-5.45pm Jul) Across from the Sokos Hotel Koli's upper car park, a summer chair lift sweeps you down the east side of Koli Hill to the shore of Lake Pielinen and back. The dizzying 212m descent/ascent, over

a distance of 770m each way, is definitely not for the vertigo prone, but vistas are sublime.

Koli Activ OUTDOORS
(☑ 040-085-7557; www.koliactiv.fi; ☺ Jun-Aug & Nov-Feb) During summer, Koli Activ rents out mountain bikes (€20/35 per three hours/day), canoes (€25/40 per two hours/day), kayaks and stand-up paddleboards (€25/50 per two hours) and rowboats (€15/30 per four hours/day) from its restaurant, Alamaja (p187). In winter it offers ski or snowshoe rental (€20/30 per three hours/day) from the Luontokeskus Ukko nature centre.

Matkailutila Paimentupa HORSE RIDING
(☑ 040-080-2709; www.paimentupa.fi; Kotaniemientie 1; 1-/3-hour rides €35/70, 15/45-min lesson €10/20) Treks and lessons on Icelandic horses are available from this operator based 3km south of town. Summer treks take place through the forest, while winter treks head along snowy trails and across frozen lakes.

From the **Luontokeskus Ukko** (☑ 020-639-5654; www.luontoon.fi/kolinluontokeskus; Ylä-kolintie 39; exhibition adult/child €5/2; ☺ 10am-5pm mid-Aug–mid-Apr, shorter hours mid-Apr–mid-Aug) nature centre, it's a brief walk to **Ukko-Koli**, Koli Hill's highest point; 200m further is **Akka-Koli**. On Akka-Koli's western slope is a 'Temple of Silence', an open space for contemplation, with a stone altar and wooden cross mounted in the rock. For a slightly longer walk, it's 2.6km from Ukko to Koli village or a steep 1.9km walk to Satama.

Koli Ski Resort SNOW SPORTS
(☑ 045-138-7429; www.koli.fi; lift ticket all areas per hour/day €23/37, ski/snowboard hire per day €32; ☺ 10am-6pm early Dec-Easter) Koli is one of the closest ski resorts to Helsinki. Its Ukko-Koli area has six steep, challenging slopes (three illuminated), the longest of which is 1500m, serviced by four lifts. Over 60km of cross-country trails include 22km of lit track. Ski-school lessons cost €46 per 50 minutes.

Koli Husky DOG SLEDDING
(☑ 040-876-6587; www.kolihusky.com; adult/child 10-minute ride €25/10, 2 hr €135/70; ☺ Nov-Feb) Winter husky trips take place on Lake Pielinen. Seasonal operating hours and departure points vary depending on weather conditions.

🛏 Sleeping

Future Freetime CAMPGROUND; RESORT €€
(☑ 010-322-3040; www.kolifreetime.fi; Kopravaarantie 27; tent site €16 plus per person €4, hostel s/d €40/60, guesthouse s/d €60/85, apt €80, cottages

WORTH A TRIP

EU'S EASTERNMOST POINT

If you want to add another tick to your 'superlative places' list and you've got your own wheels, you can take a trip to the EU mainland's easternmost point.

From the northern end of Hattuvaara, turn east on Polvikoskentie (it's initially sealed but quickly becomes rough gravel), from where it's a twisting, bumpy 19km drive through the forest to the end of the road. Park here and stay within the cobalt-coloured ropes marking the Finnish–Russian frontier zone as you walk for 100m, the last 40m of which are along a boardwalk, to the blue waters of Virmajärvi. By the lakeshore, a rustic 'monument' (made from a tree trunk and topped with a birdhouse-style wooden roof) marks the most easterly point in the EU that it's possible to reach.

The actual easternmost point is on a small island in the lake, where posts painted in the colours of the Finnish (blue-and-white) and Russian (red-and-green) flags sit either side of the shorter, plain-white border post. Border restrictions mean swimming and boating in the lake are forbidden, but it's a unique photo op.

€90-170; P) Situated 14km southwest of Koli village, just off Hwy 6 on Lake Valkealampi, this multipurpose place has a huge range of accommodation options – from camping through to fully kitted-out timber cottages (the biggest sleeps up to 16 people) – plus five saunas, a barbecue and smoker, and handy laundry and drying room.

Break Sokos Hotel Koli　　HOTEL €€
(☑ 020-123-4600; www.sokoshotels.fi; Ylä-Kolintie 39; d from €135; P🛜) At the top of Koli Hill, this modern hotel has some of Finland's finest views, two restaurants, two cafes, four saunas and a spa. You can hit the ski slopes from the front door; some rooms come with their own ski storage room. Extra beds for children start from €10 per night. Book well ahead for winter. It's linked to the lower car park by a free funicular. You can drive up to the hotel to drop off luggage.

Vanhan Koulun Majatalo　　GUESTHOUSE €€
(☑ 050-343-7881; www.vanhankoulunmajatalo. fi; Niinilahdentie 47; s/d/tr/q from €30/50/65/70, apt €80-120; P🛜) An old schoolhouse in the countryside 6km north of Koli village now houses this small, sociable guesthouse in the forest. Its eight rooms and two apartments sleeping two to six people are all simply decorated; linen costs an extra €10 per person. Facilities include a self-catering kitchen, laundry, ski maintenance room and smoke sauna.

🍴 Eating

⭐ Alamaja　　CAFE €
(www.koliactiv.fi; Ranatatie 12; lunch buffet €13, mains €16-19; ⊙11am-8pm Jun–mid-Aug, 11am-5pm mid-Aug–Sep & Dec-Easter) Right on the lake's shore at Koli harbour, this rust-red, double-storey timber building has two terraces overlooking the water (or, in winter, ice) and some of the best food for miles around: reindeer steaks with lingonberry jam, butter-fried vendace (whitefish) with sour cream and dill potatoes, delicious halloumi burgers and a different soup each day (plus, this being Finland, two saunas).

Kahvila Kolin Ryynänen　　GASTROPUB €€
(Ylä-Kolintie 1; mains €15-25; ⊙kitchen noon-8pm Tue & Wed, to 9pm Thu-Sat, bar to 2am Thu-Sat, to 10pm Sun-Wed; 🛜) In Koli village, this creative hub serves as an exhibition space and has an artist-in-residence as well as a sauna. Grilled lake fish and reindeer steaks are on the menu alongside gourmet burgers. Live music plays at weekends. Opening hours can vary.

ℹ Information

Koli's **summer tourist office** (☑ 045-138-7429; www.koli.fi; Ylä-Kolintie 2; ⊙Jun-Sep) has a comprehensive range of information and maps. It opens daily in July but shuts most weekends in June, August and September. If it's closed, the Luontokeskus Ukko (p186) nature centre has tourist information.

ℹ Getting There & Away

BOAT

In summer, the best way to arrive is by **lake ferry** (MF Pielinen; ☑ 040-088-9845; pielislaivat@ gmail.com; one way adult/child/car/bicycle €20/12/12/6; ⊙late Jun-late Aug) from Lieksa.

BUS

On weekends during the ski season, buses run to Koli *kylä* (village) from Joensuu (€10, 1½ hours, one daily Saturday and Sunday early December to Easter).

SANTA'S REINDEERS

At this delightful **farm** (☑ 050-592-4252; www.santasreindeers.fi; Haapalahdentie 171, Haapalahti; ⊙ 10am-9pm, activities by reservation) you can visit reindeer and husky puppies (€13), take a reindeer for a 90-minute forest walk (€40, minimum two people) or (Rudolph fans: look away now) dine on reindeer (in dishes from soup to sautéed steak; mains €15 to €20) or buy it vacuum packed. Cottage accommodation is available (two-/four-/10-person cottage from €60/95/200).

CAR

If you're coming by car follow Rd 6 and turn off at Rd 504. Koli Hill has road access with a short **funicular** (⊙ 7am-10pm) ride from the lower car park up to the Break Sokos Hotel Koli.

In winter, when the ice is thick enough, a 7km-long ice road crosses the lake from Vuonislahti to Loma-Koli, 8.5km east of Koli village, providing a shortcut of 60km.

TAXI

A shared taxi (p184) service operates twice daily Sunday to Friday and three times on Saturdays year-round between Joensuu and Koli National Park (one way/return €30/40). Book at least one day ahead.

Paalasmaa Island

Lake Pielinen's largest island, Paalasmaa, is the highest in Finland at 225m above sea level. The best view is from the 18m-high wooden observation tower, 3km along a marked trail from the Paalasmaan Lomamajat campground. From the mainland, first take the free summer chain-ferry, followed by bridges across four smaller islands to reach Paalasmaa. The mainland's ferry terminal is 6km east of the Nurmes–Koli road (Nurmes-sentie; Rd 6); the turn-off is 3.5km north of Juuka. In winter, an ice road runs via the island en route between Koli and Vuonislahti.

Paalasmaan Lomamajat　　CAMPGROUND €
(☑ 040-088-2008;　　www.paalasmaancamping.fi; Eteläpääntie 140, Paalasmaan; tent sites €25, cabins €40-50; ⊙ Jun-Aug; P) Paalasmaan Lomamajat is a campground at the eastern end of Paalasmaa island with a pretty lakeside setting. It rents canoes and rowboats (€20 per day) and has a small kid-pleasing mini-golf course. Cots can also be arranged for the cabins. Its cafe serves breakfast through to evening meals, as well as beer and wine to 11pm.

Vuonislahti

Little more than a train station in a field, this rural lakeside hamlet is a peaceful place to break your journey.

★**Kestikievari Herranniemi**　GUESTHOUSE €€
(☑ 013-542-110;　www.herranniemi.com; Vuonislahdentie 185, Vuonislahti; s/d/tr from €59/84/102, cabins €30-78, cottage €145; P) In an idyllic lakeside setting 2km south of Vuonislahti's train station, this quaint 200-year-old farm has a range of accommodation, home-cooked local dishes (€14 to €18), two saunas, canoes and rowboats for hire (€6/15 per hour/day), and bike hire (€3/15 per hour/day). Treatment therapies span herbal baths (€17) to *turve-sauna* (a sauna/mud bath; €30 per hour).

Hotelli Pielinen　　　　　HOTEL €€
(☑ 045-264-0303;　　　　www.hotellipielinen.com; Läpikäytäväntie 54; d/tr from €88/130, s/d/tr without bathroom from €50/72/75; P 🛜 🛋) Peacefully set near (but not on) Lake Pielinen in the tiny hamlet of Vuonislahti, Hotelli Pielinen has 17 modern, good-value rooms and a tiled indoor swimming pool. In winter the ice road across the lake to Koli's slopes makes this a handy base for skiers.

Lieksa

☑ 013 / POP 11,739
On the banks of Lake Pielinen, Lieksa is unlovely in itself, but from here you can easily explore Koli or go white-water rafting, horse riding, canoeing and bear-watching.

◉ Sights & Activities

Pielisen Museo　　　　　　MUSEUM
(☑ 040-104-4151; www.lieksa.fi; Pappilantie 2; adult/child €7/1.50; ⊙ 10am-6pm mid-May–mid-Sep) Over 70 Karelian buildings and open-air exhibits at this outdoor museum are organised by century or trade (such as farming, milling and fire-fighting). A fascinating insight into the forestry industry includes a look at a logging camp and floating rafts and machinery used for harvest and transport. In winter the only section open is the **indoor museum** (winter admission adult/child €3/1; ⊙ 10am-3pm Tue-Fri mid-Sep–mid-May) featuring photographs and displays on Karelian history.

★ Erä Eero WILDLIFE WATCHING
(☑040-015-9452; www.eraeero.com; €175; ☺4pm-6am) Erä Eero runs awesome overnight trips to its 18-person observation cabin, where you may see bears and beavers between April and October, as well as wolves, lynx, wolverines and birds of prey year-round. Coffee and snacks are included, along with sleeping bags (bunks are available). Breakfast costs €8. It's 27km southeast of Lieksa.

Ratsastustalli Ahaa HORSE RIDING
(☑040-525-7742; www.ahaatalli.fi; Nurmeksentie 54; 30-/45-min lesson €35/50; ☺9am-6pm) Situated 5.5km northwest of Lieksa, these stables offer riding lessons for all levels.

Lieksan Retkiaitta FISHING
(☑040-017-2226; www.retkikauppa.fi; Pielisentie 33; ☺9am-5pm Mon-Thu, to 6pm Fri, to 2pm Sat) Lieksan Retkiaitta sells permits for the Änäkäinen fishing area (€18/90 per day/week), and can advise on local fishing hot spots. It stocks a good range fishing, sports and camping equipment.

★ Festivals & Events

Lieksa Brass Week MUSIC
(☑045-132-4000; www.lieksabrass.com; tickets free-€25; ☺late Jul) During the last week of July, Lieksa Brass Week attracts international musicians. Competitions, concerts and lessons take place in venues throughout town.

🛏 Sleeping & Eating

Timitraniemi Camping CAMPGROUND €
(☑045-123-7166; www.timitra.com; Timitrantie 25; tent sites €15 plus per person €4.50, cabins €45-165; ☺mid-May–mid-Sep; ℗) At the mouth of the river, well-equipped Timitraniemi has 45 log cabins of varying sizes and plushness and plenty of grassy pitches. Facilities include a lakeside cafe, saunas, and bikes and boats for hire; rafting and fishing trips can be arranged.

Lieksan Leipomo BAKERY, CAFE €
(☑013-521-777; www.liekasnleipomo.fi; Pielisentie 31; dishes €3.50-8.50, lunch buffet €8.30; ☺7am-5pm Mon-Fri, 9am-2pm Sat) In a beautiful wooden building, this endearing bakery is a local favourite for filling lunch buffets featuring a daily soup (such as smoked reindeer) and fantastic cakes.

🛍 Shopping

Taito Pohjois-Karjala ARTS & CRAFTS
(www.taitopohjoiskarjala.fi; Pielisentie 23; ☺10am-5pm Mon-Fri, to 2pm Sat) Ceramics, art, jewellery, and knitted and woven garments (scarves, hats, gloves, blankets and more) in traditional designs are among the locally made Karelian crafts at this shop. Look out too for *Karjalainen suklaapiirakkarasia* – pastries with milk and dark-chocolate fillings that are a speciality of the region.

ℹ Information

Karelia Expert (☑040-017-5323; www.visitkarelia.fi; Pielisentie 20; ☺9am-5pm Mon-Fri Jun & Aug, to 5pm Mon-Fri, to 2pm Sat Jul, to 4pm Mon-Fri Sep-May) Books tours and accommodation.

ℹ Getting There & Away

The car ferry **M/F Pielinen** (p187) makes the 1¾-hour trip from Lieksa to Koli twice daily, departing from Lieksa at 10am and 3pm, and departing from Koli at noon and 5pm. Book ahead by phone as space is limited.

Buses (€18, 1¾ hours, one daily Monday to Friday) link Lieksa with Joensuu, but the train is faster and more frequent. Trains run from Helsinki to Lieksa (€56, six hours, two daily), via Joensuu (€14, 1¼ hours).

Patvinsuo National Park

This large marshland area between Lieksa and Ilomantsi is a habitat for swans and cranes, and if you're extremely lucky you might see bears. Using the *pitkospuu* (boardwalk) network, you can easily hike around; there are 80km of marked trails in all, including three marked nature trails (between 3km and 4.5km long), and several challenging hiking routes (mostly half-day walks).

It's an easy 3.5km stroll through forests and wetlands to a birdwatching tower at Teretinniemi on Suomunjärvi's southern shore.

In winter, cross-country skiing is possible on the unmaintained Mäntypolku and Nämänpuro Trails. Both start from Suomu car park. Suomu Information Hut rents out canoes and rowboats (€8/30 per hour/day; cash only).

🛏 Sleeping & Eating

Suomu Information Hut can direct you to the park's eight free camping areas. There are nine beds (€20 per night) in the information hut itself (cash only). Lomarengas (p298) can book cabins in and around the park. Foraging aside, no food is available in the park, so stock up in Lieksa, 50km northwest.

ⓘ Information

Suomu Information Hut (☑013-548-506; www.nationalparks.fi; Suomuntie 54; ⊙10am-5pm daily Jun-Aug, 10am-5pm Wed-Sun May & Sep) has a summer warden who can help with advice, permits, maps, and accommodation bookings.

ⓘ Getting There & Away

The only way to get to the national park is to drive. Or walk – if you're trekking, the Susitaival (Wolf's Trail) and Karhunpolku (Bear's Trail) meet at the park.

Ruunaa Recreation Area

Just 30km northeast of Lieksa, Ruunaa is an outdoor activities hub with 38km of waterways. Designated campsites (with fire rings) are also provided and maintained. Keep your eyes peeled as the area is home to otters, deer and sometimes bears.

🏃 Activities

Rafting & Canoeing

Above all, Ruunaa is synonymous with rafting. Within a 16km stretch, there are seven rapids (Class II–III) that you can shoot in wooden or rubber boats, the latter being more thrilling (and sometimes more spilling). Another way to ride the rapids is by canoe.

From May to October several launches depart daily from the Ruunaa Visitor Centre area or the rafting operators' wilderness camps. Most trips last around three hours. Advance reservations are definitely recommended. Transport can usually be arranged from Lieksa if you book a tour, and packages that include camp meals, smoke saunas or overnight accommodation are available. Nurmijärvi-based Erästely (p192) also offers various rafting and canoeing trips here.

Ruunaan Matkailu RAFTING
(☑013-533-130; www.ruunaanmatkailu.fi; Siikakoskentie 47; ⊙rafting trip wooden/rubber raft €30/32) In addition to three-hour rafting trips, Ruunaan Matkailu can organise cottages in the area, plus skiing, snowmobile safaris (from €120 for two hours), snowmobile rental (€50 for two hours excluding fuel), and ice fishing during winter. Trips depart from its summer-opening cafe opposite the Ruunaa Visitor Centre.

Koski-Jaakko RAFTING
(☑050-036-6033; www.koski-jaakko.fi; Yläviekintie 50; rafting trip €30; ⊙May-Oct) Rubber-raft trips lasting three hours leave from the Koski-Jaakko HQ around 7km along Siikakoskentie. Three-hour trips in wooden boats depart from the car park at Naarajoki.

Lieksan Matkakaverit RAFTING
(☑040-708-5726; www.ruunaa.eu; Ruunaantie 128; trips with/without lunch €55/36) This operator offers three-hour rafting and canoeing trips, as well as a smoke sauna.

Fishing

Ruunaa is a prized fly-fishing area. Trout and salmon fishing is exhilarating in the numerous rapids, with quieter areas accessible along a long wooden walkway. Fishing is permitted from June to early September and again from mid-November to late December. One-day/weekly fishing permits (€15/75) are available online at www.eraluvat.fi, at the Ruunaa Visitor Centre, and at Lieksan Retkiaitta (p189).

Trekking

The Karhunpolku (Bear's Trail) passes through Ruunaa. You can pick it up just 50m north of the Naarajoki bridge – the path is marked with round orange symbols on trees.

Around the river system and over two beautiful suspension bridges runs **Ruunaan Koskikierros**, a marked 29km loop along good *pitkospuu* (boardwalk) paths. If you have more time, there are another 20km of side trips you can take. Starting at the Naarajoki bridge, walk 5km along Karhunpolku to reach the trail. Another 3.3km brings you to the Ruunaa Hiking Centre.

🛏 Sleeping

There are 12 free *laavu* (basic lean-to sleeping shelters) in the hiking area. Campers are encouraged to pitch tents by the shelters, or at one of the 19 dedicated campfire sites. You can book national park accommodation via Lomarengas (p298), Karelia Expert (p189) and at the Ruunaa Visitor Centre.

Ruunaa Hiking Centre CAMPGROUND €
(☑013-533-170; www.ruunaa.fi; Neitikoskentie 47; tent sites €12 plus per person €3, cabins/cottages €35/100; P) Near the *pitkospuu* (boardwalk) to the Neitikoski rapids, this excellent hiking centre incorporates a large cafe serving breakfast, lunch and dinner, a camping area (May to September), a kitchen, a sauna, luxurious four- to six-bed cottages and simple cabins. Linen costs an extra €10 per person. Canoes, rowboats, snowshoes and fishing equipment is available for hire; you can also buy fishing licences here.

KARELIAN TREKS

North Karelia's best trekking routes form the **Karjalan Kierros**, a loop of 14 marked hiking trails (plus some canoe and cycling variants) with a total length of more than 1000km between Ilomantsi and Lake Pielinen. The best known are the Bear's Trail (not to be confused with the more famous Bear's Ring in Oulanka National Park) and Wolf's Trail, which link up in Patvinsuo National Park. They're described here from south to north; but you can walk in either direction. You'll need to arrange transport to the trailheads in advance.

Wilderness huts and lean-to shelters are scattered along the way, but it's advisable to carry a tent in case they're occupied. Much of the terrain is boggy marshland, so waterproof footwear is essential. Contact the **Lieksa** (p189) or **Ilomantsi** (p185) offices of Karelia Expert, or **Metsähallitus** (p192), the information office for the Forest & Park Service for information and advice on equipment rental. **Lomarengas** (p298) can book huts and cabins along the trail.

Susitaival (Wolf's Trail)

The 97km Wolf's Trail is a marked four- to six-day trek running north from Möhkö village to the marshlands of Patvinsuo National Park. The terrain consists mostly of dry heath, pine forest and swampy marshland, which can be wet underfoot – in places, you'll need to haul yourself over watercourses on a pulley-operated raft. This trail skirts the Russian border in areas where many of the battles in the Winter and Continuation Wars were fought. Early in the trek, at Lake Sysmä, you'll see a memorial and antitank gun. There are five lean-to shelters and three wilderness cabins along the route, and farm or camping accommodation is available in the village of Naarva. Around 100 bears and 50 wolves inhabit the area – the chances of running into one are slim but not impossible. If you do happen to meet a bear or wolf in the wild, back away slowly in the direction you came from.

Karhunpolku (Bear's Trail)

The Bear's Trail is a 133km marked trail of medium difficulty leading north from Patvinsuo National Park near Lieksa, through a string of national parks and nature reserves along the Russian border, including through the Ruunaa Recreation Area. This accessibility means the trail can be walked, or even mountain-biked, in relatively short stages. The trail ends at Teljo, about 50km south of Kuhmo. You'll need to arrange transport from either end.

From Patvinsuo, the trail crosses heathland and boardwalks for 17km to the first lean-to shelter at Ahokoski, then runs another 9km to a wilderness hut at Pitkäjärvi. Four kilometres further, a short trail detours to the WWII battleline of Kitsi. The trail then heads northwest to the Ruunaa Recreation Area.

Beyond Ruunaa it's around 30km to Änäkäinen, once a WWII battlefield but today a tranquil recreational fishing area. The trail follows the Jongunjoki through a peatland nature reserve on its final leg to the Ostroskoski wilderness hut, about 6km from Teljo. If you still have energy to burn, it's possible to canoe back to Nurmijärvi: contact canoe-rental outfit **Erästely** (p192) in advance.

Tapion Taival (Fighter's Trail)

The easternmost trekking route in Finland, Tapion Taival gives you the choice of a 13km wilderness track along the Koitajoki, an 8km northern extension across the Koivusuo Nature Park, or another extension north of Koivusuo to Kivivaara. The Koitajoki section through epic Karelian wilderness is a highlight. The path is marked by orange paint on tree trunks. You'll need your own transport and a good local map to reach the trekking area.

Ruunaan Matkailu COTTAGE €€
(☑ 013-533-130; www.ruunaanmatkailu.fi; Siikakoskentie 47; cottage from €90, with shared bathroom from €45; ℗) Situated 5km east of the Naarajoki bridge, these cottages sleeping up to eight people come with kitchenettes or full kitchens; some have fireplaces and their own saunas. Cheaper cottages share bath-

rooms. For all cottages, there's a €50 cleaning fee, as well as €7 per person for linen.

ℹ Information

Ruunaa Visitor Centre (☑ 020-564-5757; www.nationalparks.fi; Ruunaantie 129; ⊙10am-6pm May-Sep) Near the Naarajoki bridge, this friendly visitor centre has exhibitions, maps, a library and a short film about the area, and also sells fishing permits. It's a great place to research hiking trails.

Metsähallitus (☑ 020-639-4000; www.nation alparks.fi) The Forest & Park Service.

❶ Getting There & Away

If you're taking an organised trip, ask about transportation options from towns in the area. Otherwise a hire car is essential as no public transport runs here.

Nurmijärvi District

☑ 013

Renowned for its canoeing routes on the Jongunjoki, the Nurmijärvi area (also known Lieksan Nurmijärvi) is wild and remote. Nurmijärvi village has enough services to get you to the Jongunjoki or Lieksajoki, or to the Änäkäinen area for fishing and trekking.

✦ Activities

Canoe experts at Erästely run guided trips and offer canoe and kayak rental.

The circular **Pankasaari Route** from Nurmijärvi village can easily be done with a free route guide, available from Karelia Expert. It follows the Lieksajoki downstream to Pankajärvi, then rounds Pankasaari before returning to Nurmijärvi. There's almost no gradient and it's suitable for beginners – only the Käpykoski might present a challenge.

The beautiful wilderness river **Jongunjoki** has nearly 40 small rapids, none of them very tricky. Karelia Expert has a free route guide. You can start at either Jonkeri up north, further south at Teljo bridge, at Aittokoski, or even at Lake Kaksinkantaja. Allow four days if you start at Jonkeri and one day from Lake Kaksinkantaja.

Erästely CANOEING
(☑ 040-027-1581; www.erastely.fi; Kivivaarantie 1, Jongunjoki; 4-day packages from €135) Erästely organises all manner of guided and unguided multiday summer canoeing trips, staying in basic huts along the way. Canoe/kayak hire for extra days (from €15 per day) can be arranged. Prices include transport to and from the beginning or end of a route. Trips are popular so book well in advance.

The Metsähallitus Forest and Park Service controls fish quantities in three lakes in the Änäkäinen fishing area, 8km northeast of Nurmijärvi village, including some stocking of the waters.

Fishing is allowed year-round, except in the first three weeks of May. Permits are available from the Lieksan Retkiaitta (p189) outdoor shop in Lieksa. You can also buy them online at www.eraluvat.fi, which has a wealth of advice about local fishing areas and conditions, and downloadable maps showing target species.

🛏 Sleeping & Eating

Erästelyn Melontakeskus HOSTEL €
(☑ 040-027-1581; www.erastely.fi; Kivivaarantie 1, Jongunjoki; dm/d from €35/70) Canoe-trip company Erästely offers bed and breakfast accommodation at its headquarters – a 1920s-built former schoolhouse – with rooms sleeping four to 25 people. Linen costs an extra €10 per person. Rates include breakfast; there's a self-catering kitchen and two outdoor fireplaces for cooking, as well as a bonfire pit and a riverside smoke sauna.

Jongunjoen Matkailu B&B €€
(☑ 040-094-9215; www.jongunjoenmatkailu.com; Kivivaarantie 21, Jongunjoki; s/d €65/92, without bathroom €50/80; 🅿 🛜) This charming timber lodge is 2km east of the main road towards Änäkäinen. Two of its four sparingly decorated rooms have en suite bathrooms; three have lake views. Along with two saunas (including a traditional smoke sauna), there's a four-person, wood-heated hot tub. Breakfast is included; meals can be prearranged on request.

Kahvila Annukka CAFE, BAKERY €
(☑ 040-964-1083; www.kahvilaannukka.com; Nurmijärventie 154; dishes €1.50-7.50; ⊙ 8am-7pm Mon-Fri, 9am-7pm Sat, 10am-7pm Sun Jun-Sep) Breads, pastries and cakes are baked daily on site at this seasonally opening cafe, which also serves sandwiches and other light dishes along with pastries and coffee at tables inside the beautiful timber building and out on the terrace.

❶ Getting There & Away

Nurmijärvi is not served by public transport, but it may be possible to arrange a lift if you're taking an organised trip. Otherwise you'll need your own transport.

Nurmes

☑ 013 / POP 7983

On the northern shores of Lake Pielinen, Nurmes is a great base for activities such as snowmobiling, ice-fishing, dog-sledding and cross-country skiing tours in winter, and wildlife-watching, canoeing, hiking and more come summer. Founded in 1876 by Tsar Alexander II, the town is pleasant in its own right, with an Old Town area (Puu-Nurmes) of historical wooden buildings along Kirkkokatu.

◉ Sights & Activities

Karelia Expert takes bookings (at least 24 hours in advance) for most services; Bomba Action and Hyvärilä also offer a huge range of high-energy activities.

Bomba Village   VILLAGE
(☑010-783-0450; Tuulentie 10) The centrepiece of this re-created Karelian 'village' encompassing the Sokos Hotel Bomba is is the imposing **Bomba Talo**, with its high roof and ornate wooden trim. It's a replica of a typical 19th-century Karelian family house and was completed in 1978. It now houses the Bomban Talo restaurant and eating here is the only way to see inside. Outside are craft studios and a summertime market. Activities company Bomba Action is also located on the grounds.

Bomba Action   OUTDOORS
(☑040-087-9890; www.bomba-action.fi; Suojärventie 1, Bomba Village; ◷10am-2pm Mon-Fri, by appointment Sat & Sun) Based at Bomba Village, Bomba Action rents out canoes and rowboats (€10/30 per hour/day) in summer; and snowshoes and poles (€8/15 per three hours/day) in winter, as well as summer and winter fishing equipment (€10 per day from). It can also arrange quad bike trips, canoeing expeditions and snowmobile safaris, guided fishing and hiking trips, jet-skiing and water-skiing.

🛏 Sleeping & Eating

Hyvärilä   HOTEL, CAMPGROUND €
(☑040-104-5960; www.hyvarila.com; Lomatie 12; tent sites €10 plus per person €6, cabins €54-65, hostel dm €22, hotel s/d/f €85/103/170; ◷camping Jun–mid-Sep; 🅿🛜) Next door to a nine-hole golf course, and home to a golf simulator, this lakeside resort incorporates a campground, hostel accommodation, a 14-room hotel and a restaurant, all managed by cheerful staff. Golf aside, activities include a small swimming beach, tennis courts, and canoe and boat hire. Two saunas are by the lake. Wi-fi is available in the main hotel building.

Sokos Hotel Bomba   SPA HOTEL €€
(☑010-783-0450; www.sokoshotels.fi; Tuulentie 10; s/d/cabin from €119/131/168, spa for nonguests from €12.50; ◷spa 10am-10pm May-Aug, to 9pm Sep-Apr; 🅿✳@🛜♒) This sprawling complex has an enormous indoor pool and spa area

WORTH A TRIP

PAATERI

Between Vuonislahti and Vuonisjärvi, **Paateri** (☑040-104-4055; www.lieksa.fi; Paateri 21, Vuonisjärvi; adult/child €4/2.50; ◷10am-6pm mid-May–mid-Sep) was the home and workshop of Eva Ryynänen (1915–2001), Finland's most respected wood sculptor – as well as her greatest work, Paateri Wilderness Church (1991). Carved flowers and animals adorn the beams; the great tree-root altar is framed by a glass window that draws the living pine trees outside into the building. Every wooden surface in the home is embellished, and some beautiful sculptures are displayed in the workshop.

overlooking the lake and stylish modern rooms. There are also atmospheric Karelian-style log cabins (all with private bathrooms and several with their own saunas) amid the replica Karelian buildings of Bomba Village. On-site adventure company Bomba Action can arrange no end of outdoor activities.

Loma Sirmakka   APARTMENT €€
(☑013-480-455; www.lomasirmakka.com; Tavintie 6; 2-/4-person apt from €93/124; 🅿) Each of these simple but comfortable lakeside apartments has a full kitchen and laundry, making them ideal for larger families; some also have private saunas. Kids under six stay for free. Rates are cheaper for longer stays.

Bomban Talo   KARELIAN €€
(☑010-783-045; www.sokoshotels.fi; Suojärvenkatu 1; Karelian buffet €21, mains €19-29; ◷noon-9.30pm, buffet until 7pm) The wood cabin at Bomba Village contains the Sokos Bomba Hotel's restaurant serving a Karelian buffet, with *karjalanpiirakka* (rice-filled savoury pastry) designed to mop up *karjalanpaisti* (stew).

ⓘ Information

Karelia Expert (☑050-336-0707; www.visit karelia.fi; Kauppatori 3; ◷9am-5pm Mon-Fri; 🛜)

ⓘ Getting There & Away

Buses and trains depart from just by the main square. Up to three daily buses run to/from Joensuu (€20, two hours), Kajaani (€20, two hours) and Lieksa (€12, one hour).

Trains run to Joensuu (€21, two hours, three daily) via Lieksa (€8, 45 minutes). The train station is unstaffed; buy tickets online before you travel or on the train.

West Coast

Includes ➜

Uusikaupunki 196
Rauma 197
Pori 200
Kristinestad. 204
Närpes 205
Seinäjoki 205
Vaasa 206
Jakobstad 210
Kokkola 212
Kalajoki 213

Best Places to Eat

➡ Linds Kök (p205)
➡ Café Fäboda (p212)
➡ Gustav Wasa (p209)
➡ Lohilaakso (p214)

Best Places to Stay

➡ Kylmäpihlajan Majakka (p199)
➡ Huoneistomajoitus Krepelin (p204)
➡ Tankar Inn (p213)
➡ Hotel Alma (p206)
➡ Björkö Camping (p210)

Why Go?

Stretching for 500km, Finland's west coast harbours a cache of historic wooden towns such as Jakobstad, Kokkola and Unesco-protected Rauma, founded at the height of the Swedish empire. The area retains strong links with neighbouring Sverige (Sweden), with Swedish spoken almost everywhere.

Fantastic summer festivals in the region include the Nordic countries' biggest folk-music gathering in tiny Kaustinen, huge rock and tango festivals in Seinäjoki, and world-renowned jazz in Pori.

But the biggest attraction in western Finland is the coastline itself. Long beaches attract swimmers, surfers and birders around Pori and Kalajoki, where cosy cottages nestle into the dunes and forests. Enticing archipelagos pepper the coast around Vaasa and Uusikaupunki. Established in 2011, the Bothnian Sea National Park encompasses 160km of coastline, where rocky islets and sandy shorelines make up one of the country's most pristine and picturesque natural landscapes.

When to Go
West Coast

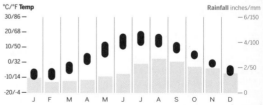

May Windsurfing season begins at the beautiful 6km-long Yyteri beach.

Jun Outdoor water parks open their slides and turn on the wave machines.

Jul Some of Finland's best music festivals take place.

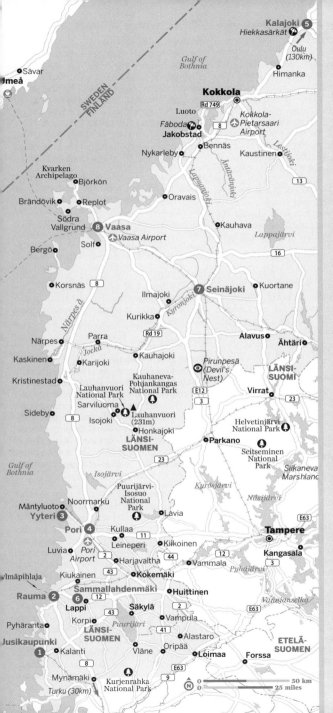

West Coast Highlights

1 **Velhoveden kierros** (p196) Cycling around the idyllic landscape and seascape of the archipelago near Uusikaupunki.

2 **Rauma** (p197) Wandering the narrow streets and admiring the colourful wooden houses in the Unesco-protected Old Town.

3 **Yyteri nature trails** (p203) Checking off your bird list while following the boardwalks through the Bothnian Sea National Park.

4 **Villa Mairea** (p109) Marvelling at Alvar Aalto's architectural masterpiece near Pori, along with the splendid collection of modern art therein.

5 **Seikkailupuisto Pakka** (p213) Testing your skills on the challenging rope courses strung through the trees in Kalajoki.

6 **Sammallahdenmäki** (p200) Surveying the stone cairns scattered through the forest at this Bronze Age burial site.

7 **Lakeuden Risti Kirkko** (p205) Viewing Seinäjoki's harmonious Aalto-designed town centre from the bell tower of its striking church.

8 **Pohjanmaan Museo** (p207) Taking in natural-history exhibits and international artworks at Vaasa's diverse museum.

Uusikaupunki

🎵 02 / POP 15,500

It was founded in 1617 and it's filled with historic wooden buildings, so it's ironic that 'Uusikaupunki' translates as 'New Town'. The treaty of 1721, which quelled hostilities between Sweden and Russia after the gruelling Great Northern War, was signed here. Straddling an inlet, the town's port was once a popular destination for smugglers...until the customs house was built in 1760.

Today Uusikaupunki draws a buzzing yachtie crowd in summer. There's a lovely riverside park and a few oddball museums, but the main attraction of Uusikaupunki is its lovely setting and laid-back charm. It's also a popular jumping-off point for the nearby Velhovesi archipelago, which is ideal for cycling and sailing.

◉ Sights

★ Bonk Museum
MUSEUM

(📞 02-841-8404; www.bonkcentre.fi; Siltakatu 2; adult/child €8/3; ⊙ 10am-6pm daily late Jun-early Aug, 11am-3pm Tue-Sat early-late Jun & mid-late Aug) The creation of local artist Alvar Gullichsen, this spoof museum–art installation is a classic display of oddball Finnish humour. In great detail, it traces the rise of the Bonk dynasty, which rose from humble fisherfolk beginnings to become the owner of a multiglobal industrial empire producing 'fully defunctioned machinery'.

Vanha Kirkko
CHURCH

(Old Church; www.ukisrk.fi; Kirkkokatu 2; ⊙ 11am-5pm Mon-Sat, noon-4pm Sun Jun–mid-Aug) The lovely 17th-century Vanha Kirkko is one of the highlights of Uusikaupunki. In keeping with the maritime roots of its parishioners, it has a star-spangled, barrel-vaulted roof that resembles a ship's hull. The interior has retained the original rustic pews and paintings, as well as wooden sculptures dating from the 15th and 16th centuries. Outside are the well-tended graves of young Finns who died during the 1939–40 Winter War.

Wahlberg House
MUSEUM

(📞 044-351-5447; Ylinenkatu 11; adult/child €4/free; ⊙ 10am-5pm Mon-Fri, noon-3pm Sat & Sun Jun-Aug, noon-3pm Tue-Fri Sep-May; 🔔) Wahlberg was a wealthy tobacco-factory owner, and his home contains the fine furnishings and other trappings of a 19th-century bourgeois family. The attic is given over to the story of Uusikaupunki's maritime history.

🏃 Activities & Tours

★ Velhoveden kierros
CYCLING

(Velhovesi Ring Rd; https://uusikaupunki.fi/velhovedenreitti) Circling the Velhovesi archipelago northeast of Uusikaupunki, the ring road is a 50km cycling route marked by orange circle signs (with side routes marked with green signs). The islands are connected by bridges and causeways, so you can cycle the whole way without worrying about ferry timetables. The picturesque route takes in fishing villages, harbours and plenty of swimming beaches.

MS Kerttu
CRUISE

(📞 040-186-6350; www.isokari.fi; adult/child €59/25; ⊙ 10:30am Wed-Sun Jul & early Aug) The MS *Kerttu* cruises out to Isokari lighthouse in Kustavi. Prices include lunch and a guided tour of the lighthouse. Other special events include birdwatching trips, midsummer cruises and singing cruises.

Galley Olga
CRUISE

(📞 050-420-5333; adult/child €58/28; ⊙ 10.30am Sat & Sun Jul & early Aug) The 130-year-old galley *Olga* makes the trip to Katanpää Fort Island in Kustavi.

🛏 Sleeping

Santtioranta Camping
CAMPGROUND €

(📞 02-842-3862; https://santtioranta-camping.fi; Kalalokkikuja 14; tent sites €15 plus per person €4, 2-/4-person cabins €59/69, linen €8; ⊙ Jun-early Sep) This peaceful beachside campground is 1.5km northwest of the town centre, halfway between the town and the archipelago. Simple, well-equipped cabins have fridge, microwave and coffee maker. You can hire bikes or rowing boats (€4/25 per hour/day) to explore the area.

Hotelli Aquarius
HOTEL €€

(📞 02-841-3123; www.hotelliaquarius.fi; Kullervontie 11; s/d/ste incl breakfast & sauna €117/137/207; @ 🛜 🏊) Set in a park on the edge of town, this large hotel offers straightforward rooms, most with sea views, as well as excellent recreational facilities such as tennis courts, minigolf and sauna. The hotel largely caters to business travellers, so prices drop at weekends.

Ranta Cafe & Bed
B&B €€

(📞 040-935-0644; www.caferanta.fi; Aittaranta 2; s/d/tr €95/129/169; ⊙ cafe 10am-6pm) In a prime location next to the vast riverside park (and next to the Bonk Museum), this darling red clapboard house has a cosy cafe downstairs and two spacious guest rooms upstairs.

There's no reception area, but the rooms have double beds and sofa beds, shiny wooden floors, kitchenettes and views of the city bay.

✖ Eating & Drinking

The row of restaurants along Aittaranta (on the south side of the city bay) have appealing waterfront bars – ideal places to enjoy a beer when the sun's out.

Kahveli INTERNATIONAL €€
(www.raflaamo.fi/en/uusikaupunki/ravintola-kahveli; Aittaranta 4; pizza & burgers €12-16, mains €16-29; ⊙11am-10pm) This welcoming spot has a cool, cosy interior and a sunny waterside terrace. Choose from a menu of classic Finnish dishes – including the signature platter of smoked, cured and pickled fish – or go for the international standards. Either way, the food is satisfying, the view is lovely and the service is spot on.

Gashaus Pooki INTERNATIONAL €€
(✑02-847-7100; www.ravintolapooki.fi; Ylinenkatu 21; mains €15-28; ⊙11am-10pm Mon-Fri, noon-10pm Sat, noon-6pm Sun) 𝄇 This restaurant and guesthouse has an award-winning Slow Food menu of seasonal dishes like beer-braised pork cheek, fried pike-perch with fennel, and smoked salmon with chanterelle sauce. The dining room is pleasant, but the multilevel courtyard is delightful. If you don't want to move far, there are four homey guest rooms upstairs (€85/120 per single/double).

❶ Information

Tourist Office (✑02-420-5333; http://matkailu.uusikaupunki.fi; Rauhankatu 10; ⊙9am-5pm Mon-Fri, to 3pm Sat Jun-Aug, 9am-4pm Mon-Fri Sep-May; 🛜) Offers bikes for hire.

❶ Getting There & Away

The bus station (Rauhankatu) is behind the kauppatori (market square). Note that fewer buses run at weekends. Services include the following:
Rauma €10.10, one hour, seven daily
Turku €13.70, 1½ hours, hourly

Rauma

✑02 / POP 39,700
Centred on its lively kauppatori (market square), Rauma's Old Town district, **Vanha Rauma**, is the largest preserved wooden town in the Nordic countries. The main pleasure here is simply meandering the quaint streets of this Unesco World Heritage Site.

In the Middle Ages Rauma's lacemakers ignored King Gustav Wasa's order to move to Helsinki to boost the capital's industry. By the 18th century Rauma was a thriving trade centre, thanks to the European fashion for lace-trimmed bonnets. Locals still turn out the delicate material, and celebrate their lacemaking heritage with an annual festival.

You might hear snatches of Rauman *giäl,* the local dialect that mixes English, Estonian, German and other languages that worked their way into the lingo from Rauma's intrepid sailors. Rauma remains an important shipping centre, transporting Finnish paper around the world.

❂ Sights

In the heart of modern Rauma, Vanha Rauma remains a living centre, with cosy cafes, shops and a few artisans working in small studios; try to visit between Tuesday and Saturday, when everything is open and the town hums with life.

There are over 600 18th- and 19th-century wooden buildings here, each with its own name – look for the small oval nameplate near the door. For a detailed history, pick up a free copy of *A Walking Tour in the Old Town* from the tourist office (p200).

Pyhän Ristin Kirkko CHURCH
(Church of the Holy Cross; Map p198; www.rauma.seurakunta.net; Luostarinkatu 1; ⊙10am-5pm Mon-Fri, 11am-3pm Sat, 10am-4pm Sun May-Sep) Sited picturesquely next to the little Rauma river, this stone beauty was built around 1520 as part of a Franciscan monastery on the site. The interior frescoes date from this era. The church was abandoned after the Reformation; it was re-established as a Lutheran church in 1640, after a fire destroyed the other church in town. The bell tower was constructed with the stones of the destroyed church.

Marela MUSEUM
(Map p198; ✑02-834-3528; Kauppakatu 24; adult/child €5/free; ⊙10am-5pm Tue-Sun Aug-Jun, daily Jul) Marela is arguably the most interesting of Rauma's museums and definitely one of its most elaborate buildings. The preserved home of a wealthy 19th-century merchant family, it's furnished with antiques, wall paintings and Swedish ceramic stoves.

Tammela MUSEUM
(Renovation Centre; Map p198; ✑02-834-4750; www.facebook.com/pg/VanhanRaumanTammela; Eteläpitkäkatu 17; ⊙11am-5pm) This quirky place

Rauma

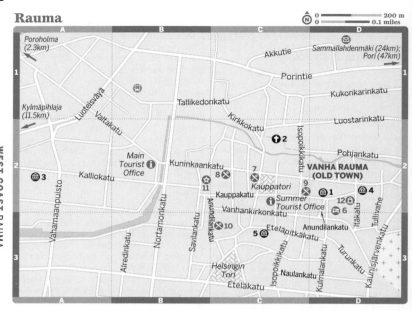

Rauma

◉ Sights
1 Marela D2
2 Pyhän Ristin Kirkko C2
3 Rauman Merimuseo A2
4 Rauman Taidemuseo D2
5 Tammela C3

🛏 Sleeping
6 Hotelli Vanha Rauma D2

✖ Eating
7 Goto C2
8 Kontion Kahvilat C2
9 Osteria da Filippo C2
10 Wanhan Rauman Kellari C3

✪ Entertainment
11 Iso Hannu B2

🛍 Shopping
Hellapuu Design House .... (see 7)
12 Pits-Priia D2
TaruLiina .... (see 7)

is part museum, part workshop and part historical-preservation lesson. Housed in a 19th-century building in the Old Town, Tammela demonstrates the history of the building through its renovations. For example, look for the 15 layers of wallpaper in one room.

Rauman Taidemuseo   GALLERY
(Map p198; ☎ 02-822-4346; www.raumantaide museo.fi; Kuninkaankatu 37; adult/child €6/3; ⊙ 11am-5pm Tue-Sun) Changing exhibitions of traditional and modern art stretch over two sides of a courtyard and two storeys.

Rauman Merimuseo   MUSEUM
(Maritime Museum; Map p198; ☎ 02-822-4911; www.rmm.fi; Kalliokatu 34; adult/child €9/3; ⊙ noon-4pm Sun-Fri May, daily Jun-Aug, Sun only Sep-Apr) Wandering around the Old Town, it's easy to forget that Rauma is a port, but its maritime museum is an engaging reminder of the town's seafaring livelihood. As well as old photos and displays, there's a thrilling navigation simulator of the M/S *Jenny,* which you can 'steer' into New York and San Francisco harbours.

🎉 Festivals & Events

Rauma Blues Festival   MUSIC
(www.raumablues.com; Kanavakatu; tickets €55-60; ⊙ mid-Jul) Finland's best blues musicians and international visitors perform over a July weekend.

Pitsiviikko   CULTURAL
(Rauma Lace Week; www.pitsiviikko.fi; ⊙ Jul) Beginning in the last week in July, Rauma's biggest event celebrates the town's lacemaking

history. From the turning of the first bobbin to the crowning of Miss Lace, the whole town comes to life, particularly for Mustan Pitsin Yö (Black Lace Night), when everyone dresses in – you guessed it – black lace.

Festivo   MUSIC
(www.raumanfestivo.fi; tickets free-€25; ⊗early Aug) Chamber music plays at venues throughout the Old Town over five days.

🛏 Sleeping

Poroholma   CAMPGROUND €
(🖉 02-533-5522; www.poroholma.fi; Poroholmantie 8; tent sites €15 plus per person €6, d €85, cottages €80-110; ⊗May-Aug) On beautiful Otanlahti bay, 2km northwest of Rauma, this five-star seaside holiday resort is crawling with sun-browned families. Accommodation ranges from old-fashioned inn rooms with shared bathroom to cosy log cabins, some with private terrace. Great facilities include sauna, laundry, kitchen, on-site restaurant, and bike and canoe hire, as well as sailing cruises.

★Kylmäpihlajan Majakka BOUTIQUE HOTEL €€
(🖉 045-175-0619; www.kylmapihlaja.com; s €99-119, d €135-155, ste €265; ⊗early Jun-Aug) Fall asleep to the sound of crashing waves in this authentic lighthouse, which rises 36m above the sea on the island of Kylmäpihlaja. Nautical-styled rooms are atmospherically furnished with wrought-iron beds. All bathrooms are shared, even the suite with fantastic four-way views. There's a restaurant. Catch a boat from Poroholma campground (adult/child return €20/10, 30 minutes).

Hotelli Vanha Rauma   BOUTIQUE HOTEL €€
(Map p198; 🖉 02-8376-2200; www.hotelvanharauma.fi; Vanhankirkonkatu 26; s/d €130/160; 📶) Once a warehouse in the old fish market, this is now the only hotel in the Old Town proper. Its 20 rooms embrace modern Scandinavian design, with lino flooring, leatherette chairs, flat-screen TV and views of the park or courtyard. Service is attentive, and the restaurant, SJ Nyyper, is well respected.

🍴 Eating

Kontion Kahvilat   CAFE €
(Kontion Cafe; Map p198; www.kontion.fi; Kuninkaankatu 9; dishes €4-8, mains €8-14; ⊗7.30am-5pm Mon-Fri, 8am-3pm Sat, 11am-4pm Sun) This 50-year-old bakery is a local institution – it even has its own cookbook. Breads, cakes and pastries are the main attraction, but light lunches such as soups and stews are also

available. And this is your chance to sample a local speciality: gingerbread cookies.

Osteria da Filippo   ITALIAN €
(Map p198; www.osteriafilippo.com; Kauppakatu 20; mains €12-14; ⊗11.30am-7.30pm Mon, Tue & Thu, to 10pm Wed, to 11pm Fri & Sat) Feast on simple pasta dishes and gourmet pizzas at this charming spot, filled with light, mismatched furniture and eclectic black-and-white photos.

★Wanhan Rauman Kellari   FINNISH €€
(Map p198; 🖉 02-866-6700; www.wrk.fi; Anundilankatu 8; mains €14.50-34; ⊗11am-10pm Mon, to 11pm Tue-Thu, to midnight Fri & Sat, noon-10pm Sun) A Rauma institution, this restaurant has served as a potato cellar and an air-raid shelter. Nowadays the atmospheric dining room and sun-drenched rooftop summer terrace are delightful settings for a sophisticated menu of Finnish faves.

Goto   INTERNATIONAL €€
(Map p198; 🖉 02-822-2750; www.ravintolagoto.fi; Kuninkaankatu 17; mains lunch €12-16, dinner €19-28; ⊗kitchen 11am-2pm & 5-10pm Mon-Fri, noon-3pm Sat) Watch the chefs work their magic in the open kitchen at this minimalist-chic restaurant. Look for enticing dishes like Gulf of Bothnia whitefish with cucumber and dill or barbecued Iberico pork with new potatoes. Find a seat in the shady courtyard and you might stay all day.

☆ Entertainment

Iso Hannu   CINEMA
(Map p198; 🖉 050-555-6644; www.isohannu.fi; Savilankatu 4; tickets Mon-Thu €10, Fri-Sun €11) This delightful independent cinema hosts its own mini film festival (www.blueseafilmfestival.net) in August.

🔒 Shopping

Rauma artisans have long been famed for their handiwork – not only in lacemaking but also in other fibre arts, woodworking, paper products and pottery. The Old Town is packed with boutiques selling unique, locally made products. See Rakastuneet Raumaan (In Love with Rauma; www.rakastunutraumaan.fi) for details. Or just wander the streets and see what you discover.

Pits-Priia   ARTS & CRAFTS
(Map p198; www.nyplaajat.net; Kauppakatu 29; ⊗10am-3pm Mon-Fri, to 2pm Sat) You can watch the town's distinctive bobbin lace being made at this venerable workshop. Exquisite examples of handmade lace are for sale.

DON'T MISS

SAMMALLAHDENMÄKI

The Unesco World Heritage–listed Bronze Age burial complex, **Sammallahdenmäki** (Lappi; ⊙dawn-dusk), dates back more than 3500 years. Thirty-six stone burial cairns of different shapes and sizes are spread over a kilometre of forest. The two biggest are **kirkonlattia** (church floor), a monumental quadrangle measuring 16m by 19m, and the **huilun pitkä raunio** (long cairn of Huilu). The moss-covered rocks and light-filtering forest create an evocative setting for the mysterious site.

Sammallahdenmäki is close to Lappi, 20km east of Rauma, signposted from Hwy 12. Buses run Monday through Friday only (€5.50, 30 minutes, four daily).

Hellapuu Design House   CLOTHING

(Map p198; www.hellapuu.com; Isokirkkokatu 7; ⊙10am-5pm Mon-Fri, to 2pm Sat, plus 11am-3pm Sun Jul) Here's a modern take on the Rauma lace tradition. Functional, solid-coloured knit dresses and tops are fancied up with an intricate (but durable) lace overlay. Also available: sustainable canvas bags with the same lacy embellishment. There are lots of other cute clothes here, featuring comfortable styles and bold patterns.

TaruLiina   FASHION & ACCESSORIES

(Map p198; www.taruliina.fi; Kuninkaankatu 17; ⊙10am-6pm Mon-Fri, to 3pm Sat) This brand-new boutique specialises in accessories and housewares made from recycled materials. The unique hand-crafted items include slippers, jewellery, handbags, children's clothing and household decorations; it's all 100% Finnish.

ℹ Information

Main Tourist Office (Map p198; www.visitrauma.fi; Valtakatu 2; ⊙9am-4pm Mon-Fri) Open year-round.

Post Office (Map p198; Porintie 4; ⊙10am-7pm Mon-Fri, to 3pm Sat)

Summer Tourist Office (Map p198; ☑02-834-3512; www.visitrauma.fi; Kauppakatu 13; ⊙9am-6pm Jun-Aug) In Vanha Raatihuone (the Old Town Hall) on the kauppatori.

ℹ Getting There & Away

Note that fewer buses run on Saturday and especially on Sunday. Direct services from the **bus station** (Map p198; Tehtaankatu 5):

Helsinki €25, four hours, eight daily

Pori €10, one hour, two hourly
Tampere €15, 2¾ hours, hourly
Turku €10, 1½ hours, hourly
Uusikaupunki €10.10, one hour, six daily

Pori

☑02 / POP 85,300

Try to get to Pori (Swedish: Björneborg) during its renowned jazz festival, which attracts 150,000 visitors annually and has the Finns scatting in the streets for a week in July. The whole town buzzes; even the local football team changed its name a couple of decades ago to FC Jazz. After the festival, Pori settles back down to business as an industrial centre and one of the most important deep-water harbours in Finland. It's a regional cultural centre), with a lively theatre scene, a contemporary art museum and an architectural landmark in nearby Noormarkku.

◉ Sights & Activities

Pori is one of Finland's oldest towns, founded in 1558 by Duke Johan (later King Johan III) of Sweden. Nonetheless, there are few historic buildings in town, due to a series of devastating fires, the most recent in 1852. The most distinctive edifices are the neo-Renaissance **Raatihuone** (Old Town Hall; Map p202; Hallituskatu 9) and the neo-Gothic **Keski-Porin kirkko** (Central Pori Church; Map p202; Hallituskatu 4; ⊙10am-1pm Mon-Fri) with its cast-iron steeple.

Pori Art Museum   MUSEUM

(Map p202; www.poriartmuseum.fi; Eteläranta; adult/child €5/2.50; ⊙11am-6pm Tue-Sun, to 8pm Wed) Founded by the celebrated art patron Maire Gullichsen (of Villa Mairea; p109), the city's art museum occupies the old customs house, in a prime riverfront location. The institution hosts rotating exhibits showcasing the work of contemporary local and regional artists. Exhibits especially focus on current social issues such as environmental awareness, multiculturalism and human rights.

Satakunnan Museo   MUSEUM

(Satakunta Museum; Map p202; ☑02-621-1078; www.pori.fi/satakunnanmuseo; Hallituskatu 11; adult/child €5/1.50; ⊙11am-6pm Tue & Thu-Sun, to 8pm Wed) Revamped for the Finnish centennial, this museum focuses on the nature, history and culture of the Satakunta region. Fascinating exhibits range from intact Viking skis to a display showing how a handbag's contents have changed over the centuries, as well as regional customs and traditions traced through a poignant journey from birth to death.

Kirjurinluoto
PARK

(Map p202; www.kirjurinluoto.fi; 🅿) FREE On the north bank of the Kokemäenjoki, this vast parkland offers something for everyone (especially kids). There are indoor and outdoor play areas, a petting zoo and a child-friendly swimming beach, as well as extensive gardens and 3.4km of walking trails.

✦✦ Festivals & Events

★ Pori Jazz Festival
MUSIC

(☑ 010-522-3200; www.porijazz.fi; Eteläranta; 1-/3-day pass €75/175; ⊘ mid-Jul) Established in 1966, the Pori Jazz Festival is one of Finland's biggest summer events, attracting international names in jazz, blues, funk and Latin rhythms, as well as 150,000 listeners each summer. More than 100 concerts take place over the course of nine days, plus many free jam sessions and children's events.

🛏 Sleeping

In town there are reliable chain hotels including Sokos and Scandic, as well as the excellent Hostel River. Other good accommodation options are at the beach at Yyteri, about 17km away. Jazz-festival accommodation in and around Pori books out up to a year in advance and prices skyrocket.

Hostel River
HOSTEL €

(Map p202; ☑ 02-534-0500; www.hostelriver.fi; Karjapaiha 2; s/d €50/70, breakfast €5.50; @ 🛜) A short walk from the riverside park (p201), this lemon-yellow wooden building houses a superb HI-affiliated hostel, where simple, light-filled rooms share bathrooms, kitchen and common area. Additional facilities include sauna and laundry. The super-friendly management makes this an excellent choice.

🍴 Eating & Drinking

Kauppahalli
MARKET €

(Market Hall; Map p202; www.porinkauppahalli.fi; Yrjönkatu 12; ⊘ 8am-5pm Mon-Fri, to 2pm Sat) At Pori's kaupahalli (covered market), look out for fresh-baked pastries, fresh produce and other local specialities, such as smoked river lamprey. This eel-like fish killed England's Henry I when he gorged on too many.

Borg Kitchen & Bar
GASTROPUB €€

(Map p202; ☑ 040-153-5640; www.ravintolaborg. fi; Eetu Salinin Aukio 6; mains €19-31; ⊘ 11am-10pm Mon-Thu, noon-midnight Fri & Sat, noon-4pm Sun)

Right in the centre of town, Borg is a classy place to go for a delightful meal in the dining room or lighter fare on the terrace. The place is beloved for its 'Borger': a little skewered sandwich of lamb and pork sausage.

Elba Cafè
MEDITERRANEAN €€

(Map p202; ☑ 040-908-300; www.elba.fi; Gallen -Kallelankatu 5; tapas €8-12, mains €16-26; ⊘ 11am-8pm Mon & Tue, to 10pm Wed-Sat, noon-10pm Sun) Fronted by a welcoming terrace, this classy yet cosy cafe–wine bar has light tapas dishes, substantial mains and luscious desserts, but the showstopper is the fantastic selection of wines with by-the-glass options. Service is spot on.

Bucco
ITALIAN €€€

(Map p202; ☑ 02-622-6185; www.bucco.fi; Hallituskatu 22; mains €25-37, 3-/4-/6-course menu €49/59/68; ⊘ 11am-11pm Tue-Fri, 4-11pm Sat) Once an old brewery workers' canteen, this stylish spot is now Pori's top restaurant. Look forward to Mediterranean dishes with a Finnish twist, such as roasted whitefish served on risotto with sautéed tomatoes and spinach; rosemary-glazed venison with truffle mashed potatoes and asparagus fricassée; and blueberry sorbet with Prosecco.

Raatihuoneen Kellari
FINNISH €€€

(Map p202; ☑ 02-633-4804; www.raatihuoneen kellari.fi; Hallituskatu 9; lunch buffet €11-13, dinner mains €24-38; ⊘ 11am-11pm Mon-Thu, to midnight Fri, 1pm-midnight Sat) Set in the atmospheric vaulted cellar of the Old Town Hall,

DON'T MISS

VILLA MAIREA

This fantastic **villa** (☑ 050-310-6442; www.villamairea.fi; Pikkukoivukuja 20, Noormarkku; adult/senior €20/12; ⊘ tours Tue-Sat) is considered one of the 20th century's architectural masterpieces and the pinnacle of Alvar Aalto's career. It is the former home of industrialists Harry and Maire Gullichsen, who were avid art collectors and tireless supporters of modern culture and social change. The house still contains the couple's museum-like collection of modern art.

Villa Mairea is located in Noormarkku, about 15km north of Pori. Noormarkku is the headquarters of Ahlström Corporation, the industrial giant that financed the Gullichsens' artistic endeavours.

Pori

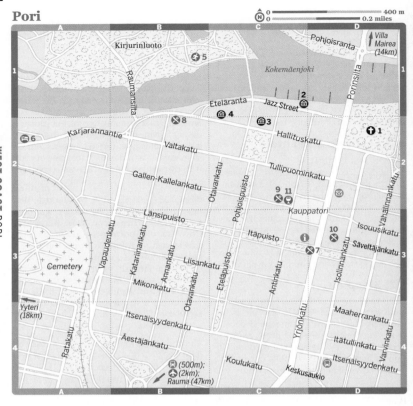

Pori

⊙ Sights
1 Keski-Porin kirkko.................................D2
2 Pori Art Museum...................................C1
3 Raatihuone...C2
4 Satakunnan Museo................................C1

⊕ Activities, Courses & Tours
5 Kirjurinluoto...B1

⊜ Sleeping
6 Hostel River..A2

⊗ Eating
7 Borg Kitchen & Bar................................D3
8 Bucco..B2
9 Elba Cafè...C2
10 Kauppahalli...D3
   Raatihuoneen Kellari......................(see 3)

⊖ Drinking & Nightlife
11 Beer Hunter's..C2

Raatihuoneen Kellari has mighty weekday lunch buffets and traditional dishes like grilled salmon and roasted reindeer fillet.

Beer Hunter's   MICROBREWERY
(Map p202; www.beerhunters.fi; Antinkatu 11; ⊙11am-2am) An ale-lovers' paradise, this distillery and microbrewery sells its own beer, cider and whisky along with a vast array of international brews.

❶ Information

Post Office (Map p202; Yrjönkatu 6; ⊙8am-7pm Mon-Fri, 10am-3pm Sat)
Tourist Office (Map p202; ☏ 02-621-7900; www.maisa.fi; Itäpuisto 7; ⊙9am-4.30pm Mon-Fri, plus 10am-3pm Sat Jun–mid-Aug)

❶ Getting There & Away

AIR
The little **Pori Airport** (www.finavia.fi/en/pori; Lentoasemantie 1) is about 2km south of

the town centre. Nextjet (www.nextjet.se) flies several times a day to Stockholm (Sweden) and Helsinki (50 minutes, from €54 one way).

BUS

Frequent direct services from the **bus station** (Map p202; cnr Isolinnankatu & Itsenäisyydenkatu):

Helsinki €25, four hours

Rauma €11.80, one hour

Tampere €15, 1¾ hours

Turku €15, two to three hours

Vaasa €20, 2½ to three hours

TRAIN

From Pori **train station** (Karjalankatu), just south of the town centre, there are six direct trains to Tampere (€16, 1½ hours), two of which continue on to Helsinki (€34, 3½ hours).

Around Pori

Yteri Beach

You probably don't think of Finland when you imagine your perfect beach holiday – but think again. Yteri Beach is a gorgeous 6km stretch of fine white sand, surrounded by dunes, sea grass and pine forest. The extensive sand flats attract dozens of species of wading bird – often visible from the 30km of boardwalks and walking trails.

It's not just birds that flock to these parts. The calm, shallow waters are perfect for families with small children; strong breezes attract windsurfers in the north; and naturists are drawn to the southern end of the beach. In short, there's something for everybody at Finland's most popular beach resort.

◉ Sights & Activities

Reposaari   ISLAND
(www.reposaari.net) Reposaari is a tiny island dotted with colourful wooden houses. Only 3km long and half a kilometre wide, the island village is as quaint as can be, with sweeping sea views all around. Räpsöö (as it's affectionately known) is about 12km north of Yteri and connected to the mainland by causeway. Bus 40 goes there hourly from the observation tower in Yteri village.

★ Yteri Nature Trails   BIRDWATCHING, WALKING
Between the beach and the Bothnian Sea, 30km of walking trails and boardwalks traverse the dunes and sand flats south of Yteri. They offer prime birdwatching, as do 15 observation towers along the way. Look for the marsh harrier, the common shelduck, the ringed plover and the ubiquitous sanderling. This is also an important nesting area for the endangered southern dunlin.

Seikkailupuisto Huikee   ADVENTURE SPORTS
(Huikee Adventure Park; ☑040-059-7722; www.seikkailupuistohuikee.fi; Hiekkarannantie 189; over/under 130cm €25/18; ⊙10am-8pm Mon-Sat, to 6pm Sun) A series of obstacle courses are strung between the treetops at this adventure park, and it's up to you to climb, swing, balance and zip your way through them. Various courses cater to different strengths and skill levels, including several that are designed for the smaller set (minimum height: 110cm).

Yterin Surfkeskus   WATER SPORTS
(Yteri Surf Centre; ☑050-512-1366; www.purje lautaliitto.fi/yyteri; Sipintie 1; SUP/windsurfer per hour €15/35; ⊙10am-6pm Jun-Aug) In summer, Yteri Beach is an excellent spot for novice windsurfers, while autumn winds create exciting conditions to challenge the experts. Yteri Surf Centre rents windsurfing equipment and stand-up paddle boards (SUPs).

🛏 Sleeping

Yteri Resort & Camping   CAMPGROUND €
(☑020-719-9773; www.suomicamping.fi; Yterinsantojentie 1; tent sites €15 plus per person €5, cottages €105-130) Surrounded by forest and just footsteps from the beach, this large campground has it all: an on-site restaurant, an Angry Birds–themed playground, a sauna, minigolf, tennis, volleyball and laundry facilities.

Yterin Kylpylähotelli   SPA HOTEL €€
(☑02-628-5300; www.yyterinkylpyla.fi; Sipintie 1; s/d/ste €120/158/295; 🅿🌊) The prime beachfront location attracts loads of families, who also appreciate the functional guest rooms, children's play areas and top-notch spa facilities. Nordic walking sticks and wintertime sledges and toboggans are also included.

ℹ Information

Bothnian Sea National Park (www.selkameri.fi) Some of the nature trails near Yteri run through this new national park (established 2011).

Visit Yyteri (www.visityyteri.fi) Managed by the Pori tourist office (p202), this site focuses exclusively on Yteri Beach and environs.

ℹ Getting There & Away

Local buses run from Pori bus station to the beach at Yteri (40 minutes, hourly Monday to Friday, four daily Saturday and Sunday).

Kristinestad

⏱ 06 / POP 6800

Named for Queen Kristina of Sweden, Kristinestad (Finnish: Kristiinankaupunki) was founded in the mid-17th century by maverick count Per Brahe. It was once a booming ship-building centre and a port for shipping tar and timber out of the Pohjanmaa region. These days, it's a sleepy little spot sustained by potato farming. But its maritime roots are still evident in the picturesque seaside town centre. Here, grand Empire-style merchant buildings adorn the grid-like roads, along with the 17th-century church and customs house. Around 300 historic wooden houses line the narrow lanes further inland.

In 2011 Kristinestad became Finland's first 'Cittaslow' town. An extension of the Slow Food movement, Slow Cities aims to rebalance the hectic pace of modern life – not only with 'ecogastronomy' but also with local arts, crafts, nature, cultural traditions and heritage.

Kristinestad's main draw is its charming town centre, crowded with colourful wooden houses. Look out for the 1700 **church** (Stakegatan; ⊘ 9am-4pm Mon-Sat mid-May–Aug) and the 1720 **Old Customs House**.

🛏 Sleeping

Kristinestad's lodging options are as old-fashioned and charming as the town itself, with several historic homes operating as unique guesthouses.

Bockholmens Camping CAMPGROUND €
(☑ 050-527-3356; www.facebook.com/Pukin saari-Camping-Kristiinankaupunki-Bockholmen -Camping-Kristinestad-361536740659629; Salavägen 32; tent sites €17 plus per person €4, cabins with/ without bathroom €79/48; ⊘ mid-May–early Sep) Just 1.5km southwest of the town centre, this small, friendly campground fronts a private beach. There's a variety of cabins for rent, all with kitchenette and some with en suite bathroom and even a sauna.

Huoneistomajoitus Krepelin B&B €€
(☑ 040-098-7978; www.krepelin.fi; Östra Långgatan 47; d €90, incl breakfast & sheets €110; 🐾) If you're curious about what it would be like to live in one of Kristinestad's little wooden houses, this former sea merchant's residence will give you a taster. The eight refurbished double rooms are tiny but ever so sweet, with maritime decor and in-room kitchenettes. Bikes available to hire and cat available to pet.

Hotel Leila HOTEL €€
(☑ 040-418-5185; www.hotelleila.fi; Västra Långgatan 39; s/d/ste €98/125/170; ❄🐾) Hotel Leila is a charming clapboard inn with darling rooms, wallpapered walls and an old-fashioned atmosphere. Basic breakfast provisions are supplied in your room. This is also the reception for the atmospheric, pistachio-painted **Hotel Alma** (www.hotelleila.fi; Parmansgatan; s/d/ste €98/125/170; 🐾) nearby.

🍴 Eating

There are lots of great places to eat in Kristinestad. As it's a Cittaslow town, many restaurants embrace the ideals of the Slow Food movement, and use local ingredients and traditional cooking methods.

Jungman FINNISH €€
(☑ 040-023-4389; www.jungman.fi; Sjögatan 8; lunch €10, pizza €12-13, mains €15-30; ⊘ 10am-9pm Mon-Thu, to 11pm Fri, 11am-2am Sat, noon-7pm Sun) Jungman is beloved for its unbeatable view of the sound and the bridge, visible through the glass walls (and enjoyable any time of year). The eating is also noteworthy, especially as the restaurant subscribes to the Slow Food philosophy. Don't miss the award-winning 'Cittaslow pastry' (in season), featuring locally grown rhubarb.

Pavis FUSION €€
(☑ 06-221-1215; www.facebook.com/Kesaravintola Pavis; Korkeasaarentie 16, Högholmen; lunch buffet €10-15, mains €17-29; ⊘ 11am-7pm Tue-Thu, noon-9pm Fri & Sat, noon-7pm Sun Jun-Aug) From Kristinestad centre, it's 3km south to the tiny island of Högholmen, where, beyond a picturesque patch of woodland, you'll find this fairy-tale eggshell-blue wooden summer pavilion with a terrace overlooking an idyllic little boat-filled harbour. The menu is an odd fusion of Finnish and Thai, but somehow it works. Try the exquisite salmon-mushroom soup or pike-perch with sweet-and-sour sauce.

ℹ Information

Tourist Office (☑ 040-740-2311; www.visitkris tinestad.fi; Östralånggatan 49; ⊘ 10am-4pm Mon-Fri year-round, to 5pm Jul)

ℹ Getting There & Away

Kristinestad is on Rd 662 off Hwy 8, 100km south of Vaasa. Buses run south to Pori (€10, 1½ hours, three daily) and north to Vaasa (€15 to €20, 1½ to two hours, seven daily).

Närpes

🗹 06 / POP 9400

The agricultural town of Närpes (Finnish: Närpiö) is officially bilingual (as of 2016), but it has one of the country's highest proportions of Swedish speakers (93% Swedophone). Most residents speak a unique local dialect known as Ostrobothnian Swedish, which is actually closer to Icelandic and unintelligible to other Finnish Swedes. Associated with farmers from this rural area, the dialect is often disparaged, but the local Närpes Teater celebrates this linguistic heritage by performing in the dialect – the country's first theatre to do so. Närpes is famous as Finland's tomato capital, and the countryside is dotted with greenhouses to prove it. The flat rural landscape is lovely – if uniform – and it's worth a stop for good eating and fascinating local culture.

Närpes Church   CHURCH
(🗹 040-836-4793; www.narpesforsamling.fi; Kyrkvägen 21; ⊘ 10am-noon & 1-3pm Mon-Fri Jun-Aug) Medieval Närpes Church, 1km south of Närpes' town centre, is surrounded by over 150 *kyrkstallar* (church stables), built in the 15th century for parishioners who rode in from rural farms to worship. Its altar dates from 1803 and was painted by the Swedish court painter Pehr Hörberg; the crucifix that lies upon it is from the 1400s.

Red & Green Hotel   HOTEL €€
(🗹 06-823-8400; www.hotelredgreen.fi; Närpesvägen 16; s/d from €103/128) There's nothing red or green about this slick new hotel, except that it's located in the tomato capital of Finland. Housed in a contemporary building, the hotel has 30 straightforward but elegant rooms, all decorated in subdued earth tones. There's an on-site restaurant, a sauna and conference facilities.

★**Linds Kök**   FINNISH €€
(🗹 040-510-8124; www.lindskok.fi; Bäcklidvägen 476; mains €24-32; ⊘ 11am-4pm late Jun–mid-Aug, by appointment rest of year; 🛋) 🍽 Dine amid mandarin and lime trees, strawberries, herbs and tomatoes growing inside this lush greenhouse. Fresh-as-it-gets Finnish specialities include creamy tomato soup, fried Arctic char with aioli and bananas and fried salmon with silky tomato sauce.

Närpes Teater   THEATRE
(Närpes Theatre; www.narpesteater.fi; Kyrkvägen 23; tickets adult/child €22/12; ⊘ 10am-6pm Mon-Fri, to 2pm Sat & Sun mid-Jun–Jul) Going strong for 50-plus years, this unique summer theater is special for two reasons. First, performances take place on a revolving stage, which certainly adds an element of unexpectedness. Second – an effect that's lost on most tourists – actors perform using the local Swedish dialect, the first professional theatre troupe to do so.

❶ Getting There & Away

Buses link Närpes with Kristinestad (€6.80 to €10, 25 minutes) and Vaasa (€10 to €17, 1¼ hours) up to 10 times daily.

Seinäjoki

🗹 06 / POP 61,200

Seinäjoki (Swedish: Östermyra) is often overlooked by visitors exploring the coast. But anyone interested in architecture shouldn't miss its striking town centre, designed by the country's most celebrated architect and designer, Alvar Aalto. Occupying two large city blocks, the centre consists of four municipal buildings and one church – each remarkable in its own right but also creating a uniquely integrated composite.

Seinäjoki enjoys a vibrant cultural life, with a city theatre, orchestra and art hall. Huge dance and music festivals, especially Tangomarkkinat (Tango Fair) and Provinssirock, draw crowds each summer.

◉ Sights

In 1951 Alvar Aalto won a competition to design Seinäjoki's civic and cultural heart from scratch, down to the last light fitting and door handle. The **Aalto Centre**, completed in the 1960s, is one of his most important works – a collection of icy-white structures and green spaces that exemplify his modernist style. The fan-shaped **Kaupunginkirjasto** (Public Library; Koulukatu 21) is a stunner, with rigid windows filtering the natural light. The **Kaupunginteatteri** (Theatre; http://seinajoenkaupunginteatteri.fi; Alvar Aallonkatu 12) foyer contains a series of Aalto's famous wooden reliefs. And the glittering blue-tiled, wave-like crest of the **Kaupungintalo** (City Hall; Kirkkokatu 6) incorporates the architect's 'signature' (*aalto* is Finnish for wave).

★**Lakeuden Risti Kirkko**   CHURCH
(Cross of the Plains Church; www.seinajoenseurakunta.fi; Koulukatu 24; lift €1; ⊘ 11am-6pm mid-May–mid-Aug, 2-6pm Mon-Fri mid-Aug–mid-May) Alvar

MOBILE SAUNA

An only-in-Finland experience, the two-day **Siirrettävien Saunojen** (Mobile Sauna Festival; www.sauna-ajot.com; Parra; ⊙ early Aug), held at lakeside Parra, 34km west of Närpes, sees entrants vie for the most unusual homemade mobile sauna. The only rules are that it must fit at least one person, and that it must be mobile.

Aalto's crowning achievement, Lakeuden Risti Church, is recognisable by its oddly secular steeple–clock tower (built with funds from a voluntary church tax, by the way). You'll get a great perspective on the Aalto town centre by taking the lift to the top.

The church itself, completed in 1960, was the first piece of Aalto's work on the Seinäjoki centre. It's a vast interior – with pine benches and marble floors – that exudes lightness and spirit. Aalto also designed most of the interior details, such as the textiles, the lamps and the communion silver, as well as the glorious stained-glass *Streams of South Ostrobothnia*.

✪ Festivals & Events

Provinssirock   MUSIC
(☑ 06-421-2700; www.provinssirock.fi; Törnävänsaari; 1-/3-day pass €85/145; ⊙ late Jun) This open-air rock festival sees international acts duel with top Finnish bands from across the musical spectrum (David Bowie and the Black Eyed Peas have held the same stage as HIM and the Rasmus). It's held over three days on five stages in Törnävä, 4km south of town. Festival buses run from Seinäjoki's train station.

Tangomarkkinat   DANCE
(☑ 06-420-1111; www.tangomarkkinat.fi; 1-/5-day pass €41/135; ⊙ early Jul) Seinäjoki is the undisputed tango capital of a country that is certifiably tango mad, and enormous crowds descend on this international festival. The first heels are kicked up at a huge open-air dance party in 'Tango St', followed by five days of dance competitions, tango classes and more.

🛏 Sleeping & Eating

Hotel Sorsanpesa   HOTEL €€
(☑ 020-741-8181; www.sorsanpesa.fi; Törnäväntie 27; d from €118; P ❄ @ 🛜 🌊) This riverside hotel looks like it's straight out of the Aalto-designed town centre, with its sleek white lines and unusual circular shape. Spacious rooms are decorated in cream and chocolate tones,

with modern furniture and big windows. The restaurant and bar open to a vast terrace overlooking the river.

Hotel Alma   BOUTIQUE HOTEL €€€
(☑ 06-421-5200; www.hotelalma.info; Ruukintie 4; d €168; @ 🛜) Next to the train station, this wooden hotel is a charmer. Its 13 generously sized rooms are decked out with art nouveau furnishings and named after steam trains. There's a quality restaurant and a terrace area for a tipple. Additional rooms are available in the nearby (though less atmospheric) annexe.

★ **Juurella**   FINNISH €€
(☑ 06-414-0720; www.juurella.fi; Keskustori 1; prix fixe €49-64; ⊙ 4-10pm Tue-Fri, 2-10pm Sat) 🍴 Juurella's award-winning chefs use seasonal local organic produce, with results that are nothing short of a masterpiece on a plate. These culinary inventions – such as beef with juniper-berry sausage or forest-mushroom pancakes – are pure bliss.

❶ Information

Tourist Office (☑ 06-420-9090; www.epmatkailu.fi; Valtionkatu 1; ⊙ 9am-4pm Mon-Fri Sep-Apr, to 5pm May-Aug) Located in the bus-and train-station complex. The office assists with booking accommodation in private homes during the festivals.

❶ Getting There & Away

The adjacent **bus and train stations** (Valtionkatu 1) are on the eastern edge of the town centre.

Seinäjoki is a rail hub; services include Helsinki (€38, three hours, 10 daily), Jyväskylä (€40, three hours, 10 daily) and Vaasa (€4.80, one hour, every two hours).

Regular buses go to Jyväskylä (€28 to €37, three to four hours, five daily) and Vaasa (€10, 1¼ hours, six daily); there are less frequent services to Helsinki (five hours, two daily), Jakobstad (two hours, one daily), Kokkola (2¾ hours, one daily), Oulu (six hours, one daily) and Tampere (2¾ hours, two daily).

Vaasa

☑ 06 / POP 67,500

Vaasa (Swedish: Vasa) sits above the 63rd parallel – southern Finns consider it 'The North'. Just 45 nautical miles from Sweden, the city has a significant Swedophone population, with a quarter of residents speaking Swedish as a first language.

The 17th-century town was named after Swedish royalty: the noble Wasa family. But

200 years later it was in Russian hands. The Old Town burned down in Vaasa's Great Fire of 1852 – caused by a careless visitor who fell asleep and dropped his pipe – and the new city was built from scratch, 7km away from the cinders. Vaasa has long been a family-holiday playground, with plenty of outdoor recreation and easy access to the Kvarken Archipelago. It's a cultural centre too, with three universities and a thriving arts scene, exemplified by its excellent museums.

◉ Sights

★ **Pohjanmaan Museo** MUSEUM
(Ostrobothnian Museum; Map p208; www.pohjanmaanmuseo.fi; Museokatu 3; adult/child €7/free; ⊙10am-5pm Tue-Sun) This dynamic, modern regional museum is divided into three sections. Downstairs, **Terranova** has a brilliant evocation of the region's natural history – complete with dioramas and storm-and-lightning effects. This is a great place to start if you're heading to the Kvarken Archipelago.

Kuntsin Modernin Taiteen Museo MUSEUM
(Kuntsi Museum of Modern Art; Map p208; ☑06-325-3920; http://kuntsi.vaasa.fi; Sisäsatama; adult/child €7/5; ⊙11am-5pm Tue-Sun) The beautiful former customs house now hosts changing exhibitions of pop art, kinetic art, surrealism and postmodernism. At its core is the collection of Simo Kuntsi, who gathered almost a thousand modern Finnish works from the 1950s onwards.

Tikanojan Taidekoti GALLERY
(Tikanoja Art Museum; Map p208; ☑06-325-3916; www.tikanojantaidekoti.fi; Hovioikeudenpuistikko 4; adult/child €7/free; ⊙10am-4pm Tue-Sun) Works by Degas, Gauguin, Matisse and Picasso are among this gallery's strong international collection.

🏃 Activities

Zip Adventure Park ADVENTURE SPORTS
(☑040-832-2221; www.zipadventurepark.fi; Niemeläntie 15, Vaskiluotu; over/under 120cm tall €20/15, archery tag €10; ⊙10am-8pm Mon-Sat, to 6pm Sun Jun-Aug, limited hours May, Sep & Oct) The five obstacle courses strung through the trees at this all-ages playground have challenges for all ages and skill levels (minimum height 100cm): there are tests of strength, balance, coordination and courage. The park also offers archery, axe throwing, slingshots and other primeval fun. It's on the island of Vaskiluoto, west of the centre and over the bridge.

Tropiclandia WATER PARK
(☑020-796-1300; www.tropiclandia.fi; Sommarstigen 1, Vaskiluoto; adult/child €17/12; ⊙10am-8pm Sun-Tue, to 9pm Wed-Sat; 🚼) Tropiclandia has enough water slides, wave machines, saunas and spa treatments to keep both kids and adults happy. It's on the island of Vaskiluoto.

MS Tiira CRUISE
(Map p208; ☑050-553-1236; www.jannensaluuna.com; adult/child €18/8; ⊙up to 2 departures daily late Jun–mid-Aug) Departing from Vaasa's inner harbour, MS *Tiira* cruises the Kvarken archipelago to Kuusisaari. Cruises last about 3½ hours, with a lunch stop (food not included) at **Janne's Saloon** (☑050-553-1236; Kuusisaari; light lunch €10-13.50, 3-course dinner €42-44; ⊙noon-8pm daily Jun-Aug, Fri-Sun only May & Sep), a restaurant owned by the same outfit.

🛏 Sleeping

Top Camping Vaasa CAMPGROUND €
(☑020-796-1255; www.topcamping.fi; Niemeläntie 1; tent sites €12.50 plus per person €8, 4-person cabins €70; ⊙mid-May–mid-Aug) This popular family getaway is 2km from town on the island of Vaskiluoto. There's loads of fun to be had at this place, including minigolf, pedal cars, a bouncy house, beach volleyball and various other diversions. Ask about discount packages with nearby Tropiclandia water park.

Hotel Astor HOTEL €€
(Map p208; ☑06-326-9111; www.astorvaasa.fi; Asemakatu 4; s/d €130/152; ⊙reception noon-midnight; @🛜) Handy for the bus and train station, this great little hotel has a historic interior and a personal feel, down to the freshly baked cakes at breakfast. Rooms in the older wing feature polished floors and dark-wood furnishings. Higher-priced doubles have their own sauna.

🍴 Eating

Sweet Vaasa CAFE €
(Map p208; www.sweetvaasa.fi; Hovioikeudenpuistikko 11; mains €9-12; ⊙9am-8pm Mon-Fri, 10am-6pm Sat; 🛜) The mainstays of this buzzing post-industrial-style cafe are the huge, healthy salads, such as the 'protein monster' (capsicum, bacon, egg, chicken, tuna, salmon, seeds and nuts). There's also a daily special (anything from Mediterranean chicken salad to goat's cheese salad with Parma ham).

Kauppahalli MARKET €
(Market Hall; Map p208; www.vaasankauppahalli.fi; Vasaesplanaden 18; ⊙8am-6pm Mon-Fri,

Vaasa

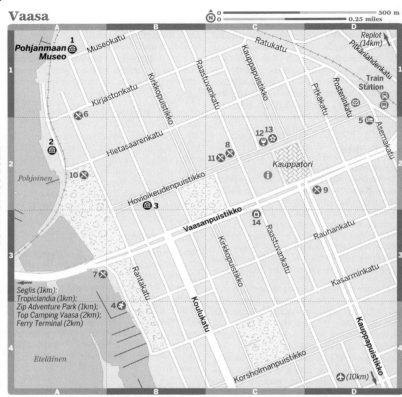

Vaasa

◎ Top Sights
1 Pohjanmaan Museo...................................A1

◎ Sights
2 Kuntsin Modernin Taiteen Museo.........A2
3 Tikanojan Taidekoti................................B2

✈ Activities, Courses & Tours
4 MS Tiira B4

🛏 Sleeping
5 Hotel Astor...D2

🍴 Eating
6 Bacchus...A1

7 Faros..A3
8 Gustav Wasa...C2
9 Kauppahalli..D2
10 Strampen...A2
11 Sweet Vaasa..C2

🍷 Drinking & Nightlife
12 Fontana C2

✪ Entertainment
13 Doo-bop Club C2

🛍 Shopping
14 Loftet...C3

9am-3pm Sat) Vaasa's covered market has stalls selling fresh pastries and market goodies.

Seglis FINNISH €€
(📞010-320-3779; www.seglis.fi; Niemeläntie 14; lunch buffet €12, mains €16-32; ⊘11am-2pm Mon-Fri May, 11am-10pm Mon-Fri Jun-Aug) On the island of Vaskiluoto, you can dine on Finnish classics on this wooden pavilion's waterside terrace overlooking the city.

Faros
INTERNATIONAL **€€**

(Map p208; ☑ 045-151-3007; www.faros.fi; Kalaranta Harbour; lunch €9.50-15.50, mains €15-29;
☺ 11am-11pm Mon-Sat, noon-9pm Sun Apr-Dec; ◉)
Moored in Kalaranta Harbour south of the
bridge, this revamped wooden ship has a
wide, sunny deck with magnificent views out
to sea. It's a prime spot for gourmet burgers
and sandwiches or more substantial dishes.

Bacchus
FINNISH **€€**

(Map p208; ☑ 010-470-6200; www.bacchus.fi; Rantakatu 4; mains €15-21; ☺ 6-11pm Tue-Fri, 4-11pm
Sat) In a rustic brick-vaulted cellar warmed
by animal skins, seasonally changing dishes
might include fried Arctic char with hollandaise sauce, duck confit with truffle risotto
or roasted polenta with root vegetables. The
wine cellar is exceptional.

Strampen
FINNISH **€€**

(Map p208; ☑ 041-451-4512; www.strampen.com;
Rantakatu 6; lunch buffet €12.80, dinner mains €20-
29; ☺ 11am-10pm Mon-Fri, noon-10pm Sat & Sun)
Right on the water, this perennial favourite
is housed in a formal 19th-century pavilion.
The place serves top-end meals inside and
affordable burgers and the like on the terrace.

★ Gustav Wasa
FINNISH **€€€**

(Map p208; ☑ 050-466-3208; www.gustavwasa.
com; Raastuvankatu 24; mains €19-33, 7-course
tasting menu €69, wine pairing €50; ☺ gastropub
5-10pm Mon-Fri, 3-10pm Sat, restaurant 6-10pm
Mon-Fri, 4-10pm Sat) A former coal cellar is
home to one of Finland's finest restaurants,
with sublime seven-course tasting menus
served in the intimate candlelit dining room.

 Drinking & Entertainment

Fontana
CLUB

(Map p208; www.fontanaclub.com; Hovioikeudenpuistikko 15; ☺ 10pm-4am Wed-Sat) With six bars,
two dance floors and a huge heated terrace,
this place is one of the biggest clubs in town.

Doo-bop Club
LIVE MUSIC

(Map p208; http://doobop.fi; Kauppapuistikko 12;
adult/student €8/5; ☺ 9pm-1am Fri & Sat) Run
as a nonprofit organisation, this lively club
serves up jazz, funk and soul in suitably
darkened surroundings.

 Shopping

Loftet
ARTS & CRAFTS

(Map p208; ☑ 06-318-5315; www.loftet.fi; Raastuvankatu 28; ☺ 10am-5pm Mon-Fri, to 3pm Sat) This
'house of crafts' occupies an actual wooden

house, its rooms packed with local wares.
Look for original clothing, jewellery, kitchenware, interior-design items and traditional
regional gifts. There are also some not-so-tra-
ditional options, such as boxer shorts bearing a Vaasa map. There's a cute cafe attached.

❶ Information

Main Post Office (Map p208; Hovioikeudenpuistikko 23A; ☺ 8am-7pm Mon-Fri) Opposite the
train station.

Tourist Office (Map p208; ☑ 06-325-1145;
www.visitvaasa.fi; Rewell Shopping
Center, Ylätori; ☺ 9am-5pm Mon-Fri year-
round, plus 10am-2pm Sat Sep-Apr)

❶ Getting There & Away

Accessible by local bus, the **airport** (www.
finavia.fi) is 12km southeast of the town centre.
Finnair (p80) flies several times daily to Helsinki
(from €125, 45 minutes).

From late June to early August **Wasaline**
(p304) runs daily ferries (adult/car/bicycle
€38/53/5, 4½ hours) between Vaasa and the
Swedish town of Umeå (Finnish: Uumaja). The
ferry terminal is on the western side of the island
of Vaskiluoto.

Up to five direct buses serve Helsinki (7½
hours) via Tampere (four hours). Frequent buses
run up and down the west coast. Services depart
from the **bus station** (Map p208).

Vaasa trains connect via Seinäjoki (€10, one
hour, up to 10 daily) to main-line destinations
such as Tampere (€31, two hours, five daily) and
Helsinki (€45, 3½ hours, five daily).

❶ Getting Around

Major car-hire companies have offices at the
airport and train station.

Rent bicycles from Top Camping Vaasa (p207)
or **Pyöräliike A Viertola** (☑ 06-317-1423; www.
pyoraviertola.fi; Kauppapuistikko 28; per day
€12; ☺ 10am-5pm Mon-Fri, to 1pm Sat).

The town has a **taxi** (☑ 06-100-411) service.

Around Vaasa

Kvarken Archipelago

Listed as a Unesco World Heritage Site in
2006, Kvarken stretches across to the Umeå
region of Sweden and includes the sea and
islands between the two countries. The
land here is rising at an astonishing rate –
around 8mm per year. During the last ice
age, the weight of the ice covering Kvarken
depressed the earth's crust by up to 1km.

Since the ice melted, the pressure has been released and new islands are emerging – it's estimated that by the year 4500, a land bridge will join Sweden and Finland. Vaasa's Terranova (p207) is a great place to learn more. Kvarken Archipelago (www.kvarkenworldheritage.fi) is also a great source of information about the World Heritage Site.

Kvarken's most accessible point is **Replot** (Finnish: Raippaluoto), a large island just off the Vaasa coast, linked by Finland's longest bridge (1.045km), which opened in 1997.

The Kvarken Archipelago is a fantastic destination for a cycle, with bridges connecting the smaller islands.

Kvarkenturer BOATING
(☑ 050-355-3924; www.kvarkenturer.fi; Skagbackvägen 27, Svedjehamnen; adult/child €55/45; ⊙11am Tue, Thu & Sat Jul & Aug) Frederic Sandvik offers boat trips from Svedjehamn harbour in Björköby out to Valsörarna in a quick 12-person boat. The four-hour trips include a guided 2km walk on the lighthouse island and lunch.

Björkö Camping CABIN €€
(☑ 050-526-2300; www.bjorkocamping.com; Raippaluodontie 1089, Björköby; 4-/6-person cabins €100/120; ⊙10am-8pm) Timber cabins at this beautifully situated site come with en suite bathrooms, kitchenettes equipped with fridges, microwaves and coffee makers, and covered terraces overlooking the private beach. Great facilities include a beach sauna, rowing boats and fishing equipment.

Cafe Arken CAFE €€
(☑ 06-352-0329; www.cafearken.fi; Byhamnvägen 194, Replot; lunch buffet €13, mains €15-24; ⊙noon-10pm Sun-Thu, to midnight Fri & Sat mid-May–Sep) This delightful timber summer pavilion has a terrace overlooking a small harbour. House specials include burgers, schnitzel and perch fillets. The delicious Toast Arken is a classic: breaded perch fillets, shrimp and hard-boiled egg on buttered, fried bread.

ℹ Information

By the Replot bridge, **Havets Hus** (☑ 050-378-5988; www.havetshus.fi; Raippaluodontie 2, Replot; ⊙10am-5pm Jun-Aug, to 7pm Mon-Fri Jul) has maps and information on activities including fishing, kayaking and canoeing.

ℹ Getting There & Away

There is no public transport to the Kvarken Archipelago, but the islands are accessible by car via the kilometre-long Replot bridge. It's about 30km (40 minutes) from Vaasa to the closest part of the islands. Alternatively, come from Vaasa aboard the MS Tiira (p207).

Jakobstad
☑ 06 / POP 19,500

In 1652 war widow Ebba Braha founded the town of Jakobstad in honour of her husband, Swedish war hero Jacob de la Gardie. The site was previously the harbour of the parish of the Pedersöre Kyrka. The church still stands today, lending its name to the town's Finnish name, Pietarsaari. But the Swedish identity runs deep, as more than half the population are Swedophone. Jakobstad is also the birthplace of Finland's (Swedish-speaking) national poet, JL Runeberg (1804–77).

Jakobstad's main attraction is its Skata (Old Town), which stretches for several blocks north of the centre. It contains some 300 of the best-preserved wooden houses in Finland.

◎ Sights

Skata OLD TOWN
(Old Town; Map p212) Originally the stamping ground of sailors and factory workers, Skata occupies several blocks north of the centre. The oldest street is Hamngatan, lined with 18th-century houses. But the prettiest street is Norrmalmsgatan, with a stunning clock tower bridging the street.

Pedersöre Kyrka CHURCH
(☑ 040-310-0447; Vasavägen 118; ⊙9am-4pm mid-May–mid-Aug) Dating from the 1400s, this is one of the region's oldest churches. King Gustav III of Sweden personally signed off on the plans to expand the church into the cruciform, though builders ignored his instruction to demolish the towering spire. The church is located about 2km south of the town centre.

Jakobstads Museum MUSEUM
(Malmska gården, Malm House; Map p212; ☑ 06-785-1371; www.jakobstad.fi; Storgatan 2; €4; ⊙noon-4pm Jul & Aug) Finland's richest man, shipping magnate Otto Malm, was the last person to live in Malm House, occupying it until 1898. Nowadays the house is the main building of the Jakobstads Museum, with period furnishings and interior decor. On the grounds are several farm buildings and other historic structures, some holding exhibits.

🛏 Sleeping & Eating

Hotel Epoque
HOTEL €€

(Map p212; ☎06-788-7100; www.hotelepoque.
fi; Jakobsgatan 10; s/d €125/143; ⊘reception
7am-10pm Mon-Fri, 8am-10pm Sat, 8am-4pm Sun;
🅿❄🛜) Housed in the elegantly restored
customs house, the Epoque is the town's best
place to stay, with 16 modern rooms and a refined, intimate atmosphere. Most rooms over-
look the nearby Skolparken botanic garden.

Stadshotellet Kaupunginhotelli
HOTEL €€

(Map p212; ☎06-788-8111; www.cfhotel.fi; Kana-
lesplanaden 13; s/d from €105/125) Prominently
placed on the main pedestrian thoroughfare,
this stately hotel offers super-easy access to
the town centre. The 100 rooms – all spruced
up after a recent renovation – feature contemporary furnishings, hardwood floors and
splashes of colour. There are also three restaurants, two nightclubs and two saunas.

After Eight
CAFE €

(Map p212; ☎06-781-6500; www.aftereight.fi; Storgatan 6; lunch €10; ⊘10am-4pm Mon-Fri) This
smashing cafe–cultural centre is the best
hang-out in town, with a relaxed atmosphere,
well-spaced tables, chilled-out music and a
grassy courtyard garden. Lunch (served from
10am to 1pm) offers simple but tasty dishes
such as salmon soup and Swedish meatballs, while homemade cakes are available
throughout the day. The place sometimes
opens in the evenings for special events.

Fiika Café & Interior
CAFE €

(Map p212; ☎044-998-8667; www.fiika.fi; Storgatan 13; mains €4-12; ⊘8am-8pm Mon-Sat, 2-6pm
Sun) This spacious cafe and cafeteria is a popular spot for a quick coffee or a light lunch.
Its terrace is particularly irresistible when
the sun's shining. The spacious interior also
includes a small store, selling crafty design
pieces, homemade sweets and scented soaps.

🍷 Drinking & Entertainment

Black Sheep
PUB

(Map p212; www.facebook.com/pubblacksheep;
Storgatan 20; ⊘4pm-2am) Live music is on
most weekends at this sociable pub, which
opens up to a huge beer garden.

Campus Allegro,
Schauman Hall
ARTS CENTRE

(Map p212; ☎06-822-9812; www.schaumanhall.fi;
Köpmansgatan 10) Facing the central market
square, Campus Allegro is a collection of old
and new buildings surrounding a historic
city street and covered with a glass roof. The
central foyer is home to a restaurant, cafe
and art gallery. But the centrepiece is Schauman Hall, a state-of-the-art concert hall with
a diverse line-up of classical, jazz and contemporary music.

ℹ Information

Post Office (Vasavägen 131; ⊘9am-6pm
Mon-Fri)

Tourist Office (Map p212; ☎044-785-1425;
www.jakobstad.fi; Salutorget 1; ⊘8am-6pm
Mon-Fri, 9am-3pm Sat Jun-Aug, 8am-4pm
Mon-Fri Sep-May) Next to the town square.

ℹ Getting There & Away

Kokkola-Pietarsaari airport (www.finavia.fi;
Kronoby) is 30km northeast of Jakobstad, with
flights from Helsinki, Tampere and Stockholm
(Sweden). **City Taxi Jeppis** (☎50-550-9866;
www.citytaxijeppis.fi) provides a taxi service
into town (€20 per person).

There are regular buses to Jakobstad's **bus
station** (Map p212) from Vaasa (€18, 1¾ hours),
Kokkola (€8.20, 45 minutes) and other west-
coast towns.

The closest train station is at Bennäs (Finnish:
Pännäinen), 11km away. A shuttle bus (€4, 15
minutes) meets arriving trains.

Around Jakobstad

Fäboda

About 8km west of Jakobstad, Fäboda's
small sandy beaches framed by rocky inlets
and thick forests offer idyllic swimming,
sunbathing, surfing and windsurfing. There
is no public transportation to Fäboda, but
it's a popular destination for a bike ride.
Rent bicycles from After Eight.

★Nanoq Arctic Museum
MUSEUM

(☎06-729-3679; www.nanoq.fi; Pörkenäsvägen 60,
Fäboda; adult/child €10/5; ⊘11am-6pm Jun-Aug)
About 8km west of Jakobstad, this gem of
a museum is the private achievement of
Pentti Kronqvist, who has made several expeditions to study the indigenous cultures of
the Arctic. Surrounded by forest, the open-
air museum includes reconstructions of
18 buildings, including a Greenlandic peat
house, a Lapland gold miner's camp and the
world's northernmost church. The collection
includes Inuit tools, fossils and other Arctic
souvenirs.

Jakobstad

N 0 ———— 200 m
0 ———— 0.1 miles

Jakobstad

◎ **Sights**
1 Jakobstads Museum A3
2 Skata...B1

🛌 **Sleeping**
3 Hotel Epoque B2
4 Stadshotellet Kaupunginhotelli B2

🍴 **Eating**
5 After Eight A3
6 Fiika Café & Interior A2

🍷 **Drinking & Nightlife**
7 Black Sheep A2

🎭 **Entertainment**
8 Campus Allegro, Schauman Hall B3

★ **Café Fäboda**   FINNISH €€

(☎ 06-723-4533; www.faboda.fi; Lillsandvägen 263; sandwiches €13.50, mains €22-32; ⊙ noon-9pm May-Aug; 🖊) On a picturesque rocky perch overlooking the beach, this breezy spot is the best place to dine for miles around. Specialities include gourmet cheeseburgers on brioche buns, freshly caught whitefish with white wine–butter sauce, and steaks such as Chateaubriand in thyme-Madeira sauce. Coffee and dessert are also divine, as is the glorious view of sea and forest.

Kokkola

☑ 06 / POP 46,600

The biggest attraction in Kokkola (Swedish: Karleby) is its charming Neristan (Lower Town; Old Town) where the town's sailors and fisherfolk once lived. Until the 1960s fishing boats could sail up the river to sell fish in the kauppatori, but you wouldn't believe it to look at the shallow water today. As with the Kvarken archipelago, the land around Kokkola is rising, which means that Kokkola is chasing its port as the sea gets further from the town. Nonetheless, it's a delightful place to stop for a day or two – to wander the dusty streets and admire the ancient wooden houses, or to catch a boat out to the lighthouse station at Tankar Island.

◎ Sights

Neristan   OLD TOWN

Neristan was once the working-class quarter of Kokkola, home to sailors, fisherfolk and artisans. The streets are lined with their colourful wooden cottages, which makes for a pleasant wander. Isokatu and Lätinen Kirkkokatu are the streets with the biggest collections of noteworthy homes. For a detailed walking tour, pick up the *Neristan Tourist Guide* from the tourist office.

Kieppi   MUSEUM

(Museum of Natural History; www.kokkola.fi/kieppi; Pitkänsillankatu 28; ⊙ 11am-4pm Tue-Sun Jun-Aug, noon-3pm Tue-Fri, 11am-4pm Sat & Sun Sep-May) **FREE** This little museum is a three-in-one deal. The dazzling mineral collection includes fragile crystals and meteorite fragments. The natural-history collection features stuffed mammals and birds (none of which were killed for the collection), as well as an extensive array of fossils. Finally there's a massive collection of butterflies, including almost all the butterfly species found in Finland.

🛏 Sleeping & Eating

Kokkola Camping   CAMPGROUND €

(☎ 06-831-4006; www.kokkola-camping.fi; Mentie 10; tent sites €14 plus per person €4, cottages €50-60, cabins from €90, exclusive cottages from €155) This small, super-friendly riverside campground is 2km north of the town centre at the harbour. There's a wide range of accommodation, from simple wooden cottages to swanky bi-level seaside 'exclusive cottages' with living area, terrace and kitchen.

WEST COAST KOKKOLA

Tankar Inn GUESTHOUSE €€
(☑040-806-5075; www.tankar.fi; Tankar Island; s/d without bathroom €80/110, additional r from €90) Here's your chance to experience the life of a lighthouse keeper. On the atmospheric Tankar lighthouse island, the old pilot station now houses the Tankar Inn, a simple hostelry with eight double guest rooms, as well as a shared kitchen, bathroom and living area. Additional (bigger) rooms are available in the lighthouse keeper's house and the guesthouse.

Vohevelikahvila CAFE €
(Waffle Cafe; www.vohevelikahvila.fi; Pitkänsillankatu 26; mains €5-8; ⊙10am-7pm Mon-Fri, to 6pm Sat, noon-6pm Sun) Behind the Kieppi natural-history museum, the sunny courtyard here is an ideal spot to drink coffee and feast on house-made waffles for breakfast or lunch. It's a perfect pit stop after a morning at the museum or while wandering around Neristan.

Villa Skogman INTERNATIONAL €€€
(☑06-834-9030; www.vanhankaupunginravintola.fi; Isokatu 28; mains €32-35; ⊙4pm-midnight Tue, noon-midnight Wed-Sat) Once a glazier's loghouse, this 1831 timber town house is now the elegant Villa Skogman. Here you'll find mouth-watering dishes with a French emphasis, such as lamb sirloin or garlic snails *au gratin,* with ingredients procured largely from local farms.

ⓘ Information

Tourist Office (☑040-806-5075; www.visit kokkola.fi; Tehtaankatu 3-5; ⊙8am-4pm Mon-Fri, plus 9am-1pm Sat Jun-Aug).

ⓘ Getting There & Away

Kokkola-Pietarsaari airport (p211) is 20km southeast of Kokkola, with flights to/from Helsinki, Tampere and Stockholm (Sweden).

Regular buses run to/from all coastal towns, especially Vaasa (€28.80, 2½ hours) and Jakobstad (€8.20, 45 minutes). The **bus station** is one block northwest of the train station.

Kokkola's **train station** is a main western-line stop to/from Helsinki (€51 to €59, four to five hours, six daily).

Kalajoki

☑08 / POP 12,600

Families flock here to spend their summer holidays in colourful timber cottages snuggled in the white sand dunes or in gleaming resorts overlooking the beach. Swimming, golf and Nordic walking (which was invented

WORTH A TRIP

TANKAR ISLAND

This lighthouse island, 18km northwest of Kokkola, offered safe passage through tangled waters, starting in 1889. Now **Tankar Island** (www.tankar.fi; cruise adult/child €20/10) makes a popular day trip for birdwatching, nature walks and salmon soup at the pierside **Café Tankar** (☑041-545-3432; mains €15; ⊙4-10pm Mon, 9am-10pm Tue-Sun May-Aug). The lighthouse itself isn't open to the public, but there's an 18th-century wooden chapel, a small sealing museum and other historic buildings to explore.

M/S *Jenny* makes the 1½-hour sailing eight or 12 times weekly from June to August, departing from Meripuisto: book with the **tourist office**. If you wish to spend the night, the old pilot station and lighthouse keeper's house are now the **Tankar Inn**.

here) keep visitors active in summer, along with water parks, adventure parks and all manner of outdoor fun. Winter offers great cross-country skiing.

Kalajoki village is just off the highway, with most of the facilities (bus station, banks). The resort area – with the beach, airfield and most accommodation – is 6km south of the village in the Kalajoen Hiekkasärkät (Kalajoki Dunes).

🏃 Activities

★**Seikkailupuisto Pakka** ADVENTURE SPORTS
(Pakka Adventure Park; ☑40-534-0837; www.seikkailupuistopakka.com; Tuomipakkaintie 19, Hiekkasärkät; rope course adult/child €25/20, rock climbing per 30min €15, zipline €20; ⊙10am-5pm Mon-Fri, to 6pm Sat & Sun) Summon your inner Tarzan at this treetop adventure park, where you can climb, swing, balance and zip your way through a series of obstacles. More than a dozen rope courses cater to various ages and skill levels (though 110cm is the minimum height).

Vihaslahti BIRDWATCHING
Commencing at the tourist office (p214), a 4km boardwalk runs through the sand dunes in the Vihas-Keihäslahti conservation area, terminating at a birdwatching tower. Keep your eyes peeled for species such as the red-backed shrike, red-necked phalarope, Slavonian grebe and wood sandpiper.

WEST COAST KALAJOKI

JukuPark
AMUSEMENT PARK

(☑ 08-469-2308; www.jukupark.fi; Jukupolku 3-5, Hiekkasärkät; €21; ☺ 11am-7pm mid-Jun–mid-Aug) SaniFani spa (p214) also owns JukuPark, an outdoor water park with loads of slides, splash pools, bouncy houses and saunas (for the mandatory warm-up). Get a second-day ticket for half-price.

🛏 Sleeping

Tapion Tupa
RESORT, HOSTEL €

(☑ 08-466-622; www.tapiontupa.fi; Matkailutie 3, Hiekkasärkät; d/q €90/108, apt €145-190; 🛜 🎏) Look for the happy dancing bears, who will lead you to this rambling holiday village with a range of red cottages amid the forest. Options include rooms in an Ostrobothnian house, basic log cabins and spiffy self-contained holiday apartments. Noise can be a problem. Tapion Tupa is 2km north of the main roundabout in Hiekkasärkät. It's the starting point for the **Siiponjoki nature trail**, a beautiful 20km walk that winds along the banks of the eponymous river.

Fontana Hotelli Rantakalla
HOTEL €€

(☑ 08-466-642; www.rantakalla.fi; Matkailutie 150, Hiekkasärkät; s/d/f hotel €105/135/179, annexe €70/99/129, s/d apt €130/169; ✳ 🛜 🎏) The spectacular views of the alluring Gulf of Bothnia are the selling point here. Perched on a dune overlooking the wide, glorious beach, the main building contains comfortable but dated rooms, while the new 'Diamond' apartments are classy indeed. The cheaper annexe is set back across the road (with no views), and breakfast is mediocre at best. But that view! The Rantakalla is 1.7km north of the main roundabout in Hiekkasärkät.

Spa Hotel Sani
SPA HOTEL €€€

(☑ 08-469-2500; www.kalajokiresort.fi; Jukupolku 5, Hiekkasärkät; s/d/f standard €122/167/198, superior €138/199/230; ✳ 🛜 🎏) Sani's conventional modern rooms have huge windows and amazing panoramic views from the balconies. Entrance to the **spa** (adult/child €15/9; ☺ 2-9pm Mon-Fri, 11am-8pm Sat, 11am-7pm Sun) and pools is included in the price. If that's not enough fun for your kids, there's also an indoor playground, with slides and a ball pit, as well as a bowling alley and a gym.

🍴 Eating

⭐ Lohilaakso
SEAFOOD €

(☑ 08-466-645; www.lohilaakso.fi; Tahkokorvantie 39, Hiekkasärkät; mains €16-20; ☺ 10am-9pm Jun-Aug) Smoked salmon and whitefish – served in salads or on platters – is the speciality of this stocked salmon-fishing pond and smokery. If you rent a rod (€5) and catch your own, they will smoke it (€5) and serve it whole (€18 per kilo), with potato salad and other sides (€9 per person). The smoking takes about an hour.

In case you're wondering, sitting at a pond-side picnic table, sipping a beer and feasting on warm smoked salmon that you caught yourself isn't a bad way to spend an afternoon. Lohilaakso is almost 3km north of the main roundabout in Hiekkasärkät.

Hotelli-Ravintola Lokkilinna
PIZZA €€

(☑ 08-469-6700; www.lokkilinna.fi; Matkailuttie 199, Hiekkasärkät; lunch buffet €14.50, pizzas €10.50-13, mains €16-29; ☺ 10.30am-3pm Mon & Tue, to 8pm Wed-Fri, noon-9pm Sat, to 4pm Sun) Overlooking the dunes, Lokkilinna has a fantastic summer terrace perfect for a beer and some pizza (toppings range from smoked reindeer to snails). The menu also features fancier fare, especially highlighting local produce and fresh fish. There's occasional live music. The attached hotel has 26 rooms, some with sea views and balconies (doubles from €120 to €150). The complex is 1km north of the main roundabout in Hiekkasärkät.

Pihvi tupa
STEAK €€€

(Steak House; ☑ 08-466-608; www.ravintolapihvi tupa.fi; Hilmantori 2, Hiekkasärkät; mains €23-33; ☺ 6-9pm Tue-Fri, 1-10pm Sat, 1-8pm Sun) They grill a mean steak at this simple but classy steakhouse in the heart of Hiekkasärkät. The glass-enclosed dining room is delightful on cool summer evenings, as are the perfect cuts of beef and lamb. All steaks come with house-cut potato wedges that might ruin French fries for you forever.

ℹ Information

Tourist Office (☑ 08-469-2500; www.visit kalajoki.fi; Jukupolku 3; ☺ 8am-4pm Mon-Thu, to 3pm Fri) At the SaniFani spa complex at Hiekkasärkät.

ℹ Getting There & Around

Several daily buses between Oulu (€20, 2¼ hours) and Kokkola (€14, one hour) stop at Kalajoki village and Hiekkasärkät.

Safaritalo (☑ 45-111-6633; www.hsop.fi; Merisärkäntie 10) has a big selection of bicycles for hire, including mountain bikes and road bikes, as well as child seats and trailers.

Oulu, Kainuu & Koillismaa

Includes ➜

Oulu 217
Kajaani 222
Sotkamo 223
Kuhmo 224
Hossa 225
Kuusamo & Ruka . . . 226
Juuma 232
Karhunkierros Trek
& Oulanka National
Park 232

Best Places to Eat

➡ Pekka Heikkinen & Kumpp (p223)

➡ Kitchen & Bar Oula (p219)

➡ Ravintola Hugo (p220)

➡ Rooster (p219)

➡ 1881 Uleåborg (p221)

Best Places to Stay

➡ Arctic Lighthouse Hotel (p222)

➡ Lapland Hotel Oulu (p218)

➡ Nallikari Camping (p218)

➡ Hotel Lasaretti (p218)

➡ Hotelli Kalevala (p225)

➡ Basecamp Oulanka (p232)

Why Go?

Stretching across Finland's waist from the Gulf of Bothnia to the long Russian border, this broad swath of territory takes in both Oulu's technology sector and brown bears patrolling the eastern forests. It offers some of the nation's most memorable outdoor experiences in both summer and winter, from birdwatching and beachcombing in the west to skiing, canoeing and trekking in the east.

The further you get from Oulu, the more remote things become. Kainuu is a heavily wooded wilderness and important animal habitat traversed by the famed UKK trekking route. Koillismaa, near the Russian border, is the transitional region between the south and Lapland, and includes Oulanka National Park, one of Finland's natural highlights, with tumbling rivers, isolated lakes and dense forests. The region is also home to Finland's most recent national park, Hossa National Park, established in 2017 to commemorate Finland's centenary of independence.

When to Go

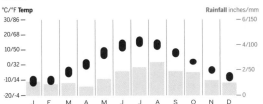

Oulu

Apr Still good snow cover for skiing, but with milder temperatures than winter and plenty of light.

Jul Bear watching in Kuusamo, canoeing in Oulanka National Park and chamber music in Kuhmo.

Sep The most beautiful time for hiking, with autumn *ruska* colours filling the forests.

Oulu, Kainuu & Koillismaa Highlights

1 Hossa National Park (p225) Viewing four-millennia-old rock art in Finland's newest national park, with canyons, lakes and a wealth of activities, including scuba diving.

2 Oulanka National Park (p233) Canoeing river routes or trekking the Karhunkierros trail through some of Finland's finest wilderness scenery.

3 Bear watching, Kuusamo (p227) Creeping into the evening forests around Kuusamo to spot brown bears.

4 Kauppatori, Oulu (p217) Lingering in the sunshine on the main square and discovering local specialities in the adjacent kauppahalli (market hall).

5 Kierikkikeskus (p222) Discovering what life was like

in Finland's Stone Age at the fascinating museum.

6 Marjaniemi Lighthouse, Hailuoto (p222) Scaling 110 steps inside the 19th-century Marjaniemi Lighthouse.

7 Kuhmon Kamarimusiikki, Kuhmo (p225) Catching superb chamber music concerts during this famous festival.

History

The region reflects its tar-producing history. In the 19th century the remote Kainuu and Koillismaa areas began producing tar from their many pine trees. They sent it on the precarious journey downriver to Oulu, from where it was shipped to the boat-building nations of Europe. The merchants prospered and Oulu still has a sleek, cosmopolitan vibe compared with the backwoodsy feel of the rest of its province.

Oulu

☑ 08 / POP 200,526

Prosperous Oulu (Swedish: Uleåborg) is one of Finland's most enjoyable cities to visit. In summer angled sunshine bathes the kauppatori (market square) in light and all seems well with the world. Locals, who appreciate daylight when they get it, crowd the terraces, and market stalls groan under the weight of Arctic berries. The city centre is spread across several islands, connected by pedestrian bridges and cycleways. Oulu is also a significant technology city; the university turns out top-notch IT graduates and the corporate parks on the city's outskirts employ people from all over the globe.

⊙ Sights

★ Kauppatori   SQUARE

(Map p220) Oulu has one of Finland's liveliest market squares, and its position at the waterfront makes it all the more appealing. The square is bordered by several old wooden storehouses now serving as restaurants, bars and craft shops. The squat *Toripolliisi* statue, a humorous representation of the local police, is a local landmark. Made from bronze, the lovable figure is the work of sculptor Kaarlo Mikkonen, and was installed here in 1987.

★ Tietomaa   MUSEUM

(Map p220; www.tietomaa.fi; Nahkatehtaankatu 6; adult/child €15/11, IMAX cinema €5.50/4; ☉10am-6pm, hours vary) This huge, excellent science museum can occupy kids for the best part of a day with a giant, 35m-high IMAX screen, hands-on interactive exhibits exploring planets and the human body, and an observation tower. An annually changing mega-exhibition is the focal point. Opening hours fluctuate; check the online calendar.

Oulun Tuomiokirkko   CHURCH

(Map p220; www.oulunseurakunnat.fi; Kirkkokatu 3A; ☉10am-8pm Jun & Aug, to 9pm Jul, noon-1pm Sep-May) Oulu's imposing cathedral was built in 1777, but then came the great fire of 1822, which severely damaged the structure. Prolific architect CL Engel rebuilt it in Empire style, adding a dome and Renaissance-style vaulting, which impart a powerful airiness to the fairly unadorned interior.

Hupisaaret Park   PARK

(Map p220) Just north of the city centre on the Hupisaaret Islands, connected by small bridges, this great park has bike paths, museums, greenhouses and a summer cafe. An observation deck looks out over the 750m-long fishway with 64 steps (a climb of 11m) built so that salmon can bypass the hydroelectric dam to reach the spawning grounds.

Pohjois Pohjanmaan Museo   MUSEUM

(Museum of Northern Ostrobothnia; Map p220; ☑08-5584-7150; www.ouka.fi/oulu/ppm; Ainolanpolku 1; adult/child €6/free; ☉10am-5pm Tue-Sun) The Museum of Northern Ostrobothnia in the city park has almost too much information to take in at first bite. It covers the earliest habitation of the region through to the 20th century, including plenty of coverage of the tar trade. Cameras allow you to zoom in on the impressive scale model of 1938 Oulu; a traditional pharmacy, paintings of the 1822 Great Fire and a schoolroom are included in the wide-ranging display.

Turkansaaren Ulkomuseo   MUSEUM

(www.ouka.fi/oulu; Turkansaarentie 165; adult/child €6/free; ☉10am-6pm late Jun–mid-Aug, to 5pm Apr-late Jun & mid-Aug–mid-Sep; ☑) Set across two river islands on the scenic Oulujoki, this open-air museum is a collection of traditional wooden buildings, from loggers' cabins to stables, and includes a handsome farmhouse. The 1694 church is an original from this former trading settlement. A working tar pit comes to the fore during **Tar-Burning Week** in late June. Turkansaari is 14km southeast of Oulu off Rd 22, served by one bus per day (€4.70, 20 minutes).

✦ Activities

Free maps from the tourist office (p221) detail Oulu's extensive network of bicycle paths. A good 3km walk or ride is from the kauppatori, across the bridge to Pikisaari and across another bridge to Nallikari, where there's a lovely beach facing the Gulf of Bothnia and activities including kitesurfing.

Kesän Sauna   SAUNA

(Map p220; www.kesansauna.fi; Koskitie 58; sauna €5; ☉5-9pm Mon-Fri, from 3pm Sat & Sun Jun-Aug) Built, maintained and run by volunteers, this floating wood-burning sauna sits 5m off the northern bank of the Oulujoki, reached by a hand-pulled punt. Unusually for a Finnish sauna, it's unisex, and bathing suits are mandatory. Fresh birch branches are available for a *vihta* (sauna whisk). Lockers are available, but bring your own towel. Winter openings are planned.

Lappis
KITESURFING

(☑ 041-433-8602; www.lappis.fi; Nallikari Majakka, Nallikari; 3hr kitesurfing/snow-kitesurfing lesson €150/250, kitesurfer/snow-kitesurfer hire per day €100; ⊙ by reservation) Based at Nallikari, Lappis offers summer kitesurfing on the Gulf of Bothnia's waters and winter snow-kitesurfing on the ice. You can also hire stand-up paddleboards and windsurfers as well as bikes (from €25 per day).

Oulu Wakepark
WATER SPORTS

(Map p220; ☑ 040-035-6565; www.ouluwakepark.com; Linnansaari; cable wakeboarding/waterskiing per hr €20; ⊙ 9am-7pm May-Sep) In the Gulf of Bothnia, this wakepark complete with ramps and rails is a scenic spot to try cable wakeboarding or waterskiing. The cable can be adjusted for speed and level of difficulty.

🖝 Tours

Salamapaja
OUTDOORS

(☑ 044-210-0033; http://salamapaja.fi; 4hr tour €120-175; ⊙ Sep-Mar) Professional photographer Thomas Kast leads fantastic aurora photography tours, teaching you how to capture the glowing skies at their most spectacular. He also has spare cameras if you need to borrow equipment. Prices include pick-up from your accommodation, and are cheaper for two or more people.

Summer Tours
BUS, WALKING

(Map p220; ☑ 08-4152-7770; www.oulunseudunoppaat.fi; Kirkkokatu 2A; ⊙ late Jun-late Aug) From late June to late August, bus tours, walking tours and cycling tours in English (many free) leave from the town hall, usually on Wednesdays and Saturdays: check the website for times. Reservations can be made online.

🎉 Festivals & Events

Tervahiihto
SPORTS

(Oulu Tar Ski Race; http://tervahiihto.fi; ⊙ late Feb-early Mar) Held in late February to early March, this 70km men's skiing race (40km for women) has been running since 1889.

QStock
MUSIC

(www.qstock.fi; Raatintie 4, Kuusisaari; ⊙ late Jul) Hip-hop, rock and – this being Finland – metal acts, play over six stages during this two-day festival in late July, which attracts more than 60 different artists and over 30,000 visitors. Most bands are Finnish, but past international performers have included Marilyn Manson, Megadeath, Twisted Sister and Alice Cooper.

Oulun Juhlaviikot
PERFORMING ARTS

(www.oulunjuhlaviikot.fi; ⊙ Aug) Jazz, blues, chamber and folk music feature alongside poetry, stand-up comedy, theatre, film and art exhibitions during this month-long festival at venues all over the city.

Air Guitar World Championships
MUSIC

(www.airguitarworldchampionships.com; ⊙ late Aug) Contestants from all over the world take the stage to show what they can do with their imaginary instruments during August's famous Air Guitar World Championships.

🛏 Sleeping

⭐ Nallikari Camping
CAMPGROUND €

(☑ 044-703-1353; https://nallikari.fi; Leiritie 10, Nallikari; tent site €15 plus per person €5, cottages €105-157, villas from €366; ⊙ campground & cottages May-Sep, villas year-round; 🅿 🛜; 🚌 15 from the city centre, 🚃 summer tourist train) Close to the lifeguard-patrolled beach at Nallikari, a 40-minute walk to the city centre via pedestrian bridges, this excellent campground has 150 tent pitches, 28 cottages sleeping up to five, and 24 luxurious villas with private saunas sleeping up to eight. It hires out bikes, cross-country skis and snowshoes.

⭐ Lapland Hotel Oulu
DESIGN HOTEL €€

(Map p220; ☑ 08-881-1110; www.laplandhotels.com; Kirkkokatu 3B; d/ste from €122/347; 🅿 @ 🛜 ⛱) Reindeer antlers above the beds, large prints of Lappish wildlife and carpets that evoke Lapland's forests are among the design elements of this striking contemporary hotel. Some of the 160 rooms have balconies and/or saunas, and baby cots are available. There's also a large lake-inspired free-form swimming pool and rental bikes. Kitchen & Bar Oula, its on-site restaurant, is superb.

⭐ Hotel Lasaretti
HOTEL €€

(Map p220; ☑ 020-757-4700; www.lasaretti.com; Kasarmintie 13; s/d/f from €108/125/155; 🅿 🛜 ⛱) In a tranquil parkside location, this inviting hotel sits in a group of renovated red-brick buildings that once housed a hospital. Stylish rooms have gleaming hardwood floors: ask for one with a water view. Excellent facilities include an indoor swimming pool with big windows overlooking the surrounding greenery and a busy bar-restaurant with a sunny terrace.

Hotel Scandic Oulu
HOTEL €€

(Map p220; ☑ 08-543-1000; www.scandichotels.com; Saaristonkatu 4; s/d from €132/149; 🅿 @ 🛜) This sleek hotel occupies half a city block right in the middle of town. From the space-opera lights in its spacious foyer to the high-ceilinged rooms with clean Nordic decor, it's a temple to efficiency, hygiene and modern design. Fantastic organic breakfasts include gluten-free options.

Sokos Hotel Eden SPA HOTEL €€
(🖉020-123-4603; www.sokoshotels.fi; Holstinsalmentie 29, Nallikari; s/d/f/ste from €94/119/144/304; 🅿❄@🛜✉; 🚌15 from the city centre, 🚆summer tourist train) This excellent spa hotel by the beach on Hietasaari offers great watery facilities – slides, intricate indoor pools, saunas – and massage treatments. Superior rooms on the new side of the building are bigger and have air-conditioning (handier than you may think) as well as a sea-view balcony. Nonguests can use the spa facilities for €18 per day (€12 for kids).

✖️ Eating

⭐**Rooster** CAFE €
(Map p220; 🖉020-711-8280; https://rooster.fi; Torikatu 26; mains €11-18, lunch buffet Mon-Fri/weekend €10.20/21; ⏱10.30am-2pm Mon-Fri, noon-4pm Sat & Sun, bar to midnight; 🍴) Inside a beautiful wooden building, Rooster has a minimalist Finnish-design interior. Burgers, such as its *Lohiburgeri* (salmon, marinated fennel and horseradish mayo), *Vuohenjuustoburgeri* (beef, grilled goat's cheese, watermelon and fig balsamic) and *Vegaanburgeri* (gado gado, mango, rocket and red-onion compote), are a speciality. Light lunch dishes include spicy sweet potato lasagne or nettle and pepper soup. Hours vary seasonally.

Oulun Kauppahalli MARKET €
(Map p220; www.oulunkauppahalli.fi; Kauppatori; ⏱8am-5pm Mon-Thu, to 6pm Fri, to 3pm Sat) On the square, the 1901-built kauppahalli has freshly filleted salmon glistening in the market stalls and plenty of spots to snack on anything from cloudberries to sushi.

Kauppuri 5 BURGERS €
(Map p220; 🖉020-749-5000; https://kauppuri5.fi; Kauppurienkatu 5; burgers €9-12; ⏱11am-1.30am) With a cosy interior and a great sunny terrace on the pedestrian strip, this casual spot is very popular for its delicious, decent-value handmade burgers. Specialities include Slaughterhouse (beef, pulled pork, bacon and barbecue sauce) or the Aura (Turku-made Aura blue cheese, red onion and tomato). It also stocks a great range of craft beers and ciders.

Pannukakkutalo CAFE €
(Map p220; http://pannukakkutalo.fi; Aittatori 9; dishes €4.90-12.40; ⏱11am-7pm Mon-Fri, to 6pm Sat, noon-6pm Sun; 🚲) Finland's distinctive *pannukakku* (salty oven-baked pancake) is the house speciality of this cafe in a rust-red former warehouse on the waterfront. Savoury varieties include warm- or cold-smoked reindeer, cured salmon, pickled whitefish, Aura blue cheese, fennel and mushrooms. Sweet options span wild lingonberries, blueberries, raspberries and cloudberries to apple, chocolate and cinnamon.

⭐**Kitchen & Bar Oula** FINNISH €€
(Map p220; 🖉040-671-0539; www.laplandhotels.com; Kirkkokatu 3; mains €17-32, 3-/5-course menu €56/65; ⏱5-10pm Mon-Sat Jun–mid-Sep, shorter hours mid-Sep–May) Beneath an igloo-inspired glass atrium, this restaurant inside the Lapland Hotel Oulu (p218) features outsized prints of Lapland scenes, such as spawning salmon. Gourmet Lappish dishes include cold-smoked Arctic perch soup with birch and fennel, chargrilled reindeer with redcurrant and moss jus, and smoked whitefish carpaccio with parsnip mayo and pickled dandelion, accompanied by an extensive wine list and Lapland-influenced cocktails.

Hella BISTRO €€
(Map p220; 🖉08-371-180; www.hellaravintola.fi; Isokatu 13; mains €20-34; ⏱4-10pm Mon-Thu, to 11pm Sat) This sweet little corner spot is a welcoming two-person show that offers excellent Italian-inspired fare. Attentive service is backed up by the food, which changes seasonally but features great salads, cannelloni stuffed with goat's cheese, and tender meats.

Puistola BISTRO €€
(Map p220; 🖉020-792-8210; www.ravintolapuistola.fi; Pakkahuoneenkatu 15; mains €15-32; ⏱bistro 2.30-9.30pm Mon-Thu, to 10.30pm Fri & Sat, noon-10.30pm Sun, cafe 9am-5pm Mon-Fri; 🕿) This curved-fronted, rose-pink, art nouveau place contains a deli-cafe that does great breakfasts and good-value lunches, plus a bistro that turns out steaks, grilled chicken, ribs, burgers and pasta from its open kitchen with plenty of flair. Try for a seat out on the terrace in fine weather. Service throughout is excellent.

Sokeri-Jussin Kievari FINNISH €€
(Map p220; 🖉08-376-628; www.sokerijussi.fi; Pikisaarentie 2; mains €20-38; ⏱11am-10pm Mon-Sat, noon-9pm Sun) An Oulu classic, this timbered inn on Pikisaari was once a sugar warehouse and has outdoor tables with good views of the

OULU, KAINUU & KOILLISMAA OULU

Oulu

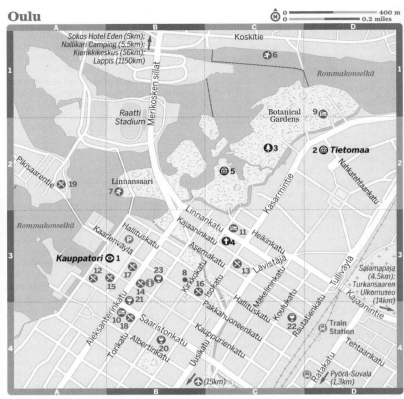

Oulu

⊙ Top Sights

1 Kauppatori B3
2 Tietomaa D2

⊙ Sights

3 Hupisaaret Park C2
4 Oulun Tuomiokirkko C3
5 Pohjois Pohjanmaan Museo C2

🎯 Activities, Courses & Tours

6 Kesän Sauna C1
7 Oulu Wakepark B2
8 Summer Tours B3

🛏 Sleeping

9 Hotel Lasaretti D1
10 Hotel Scandic Oulu B4
11 Lapland Hotel Oulu C3

🍴 Eating

12 1881 Uleåborg A3
13 Hella C3
14 Kauppuri 5 .... B3
   Kitchen & Bar Oula .... (see 11)
15 Oulun Kauppahalli B3
   Pannukakkutalo .... (see 12)
16 Puistola B3
17 Ravintola Hugo B3
18 Rooster B4
19 Sokeri-Jussin Kievari A2

🍸 Drinking & Nightlife

20 45 Special B4
21 Graali B3
   Potnia .... (see 15)
22 Snooker Time C4
23 Viinibaari Vox B3

centre. Traditional, no-frills dishes include elk stew. It's also a peaceful place for a beer a few steps away from the bustle of the city.

★ **Ravintola Hugo**   FINNISH €€€
(Map p220; ☎ 020-143-2200; www.ravintolahugo.fi; Rantakatu 4; 3-/5-course menus €45/65, with paired

wines €71/109; ☺5-9pm Tue-Thu, to 10pm Fri & Sat) Innovative cuisine using locally sourced products makes this elegant restaurant with white tablecloths and richly coloured walls a real Oulu highlight. Some outstanding flavour combinations feature in its menus (no à la carte), such as pike-perch with liquorice leaves and parsnip; lichen-smoked reindeer with wild mushrooms and powdered roast beetroot; and spruce and strawberry sorbet with clotted reindeer cream.

★ **1881 Uleåborg** FINNISH €€€
(Map p220; ☑08-881-1188; www.uleaborg.fi; Aittatori 4; mains €31.50-36.50, 3-course menu €54.50; ☺5-10pm Mon-Sat) In an old timber warehouse near the kauppatori, this classy spot combines a traditional setting with chic Finnish style and creative cooking (smoked reindeer and morel terrine, Åland lamb with spruce-smoked potatoes, lingonberry crème brûlée with cloudberry meringue). The awning-shaded, glassed-in terrace by the water is one of Oulu's loveliest summer spots.

🍷 Drinking & Nightlife

Viinibaari Vox WINE BAR
(Map p220; www.viinibaarivox.fi; Pakkahuoneenkatu 8; ☺3pm-midnight Mon-Thu, to 2am Fri & Sat) Hefty timber beams and low lighting give this wine bar a cosy, atmospheric ambience. A rotating menu of 30 to 40 wines are available by the glass each month, served with Finnish cheese and charcuterie plates. In summer, bentwood chairs are set up on the pavement terrace; the mulled wine is an instant winter warmer when it's snowing outside.

Potnia COFFEE
(Map p220; http://potniaroaster.business.site; Kauppahalli; ☺8am-5pm Mon-Thu, to 6pm Fri, to 4pm Sat) Hessian bags hang on the walls of this little coffee specialist inside the kauppahalli (p219), which roasts its own single-origin beans just outside Oulu. An ice drip produces iced coffee in summer. It also has oolong teas and home-baked cakes and pastries, including banana bread, walnut bread and cinnamon scrolls.

Graali PUB
(Map p220; www.graali.fi; Saaristonkatu 5; ☺2pm-2am) When it's cold and snowy outside, there's nowhere cosier than this pub, decorated with suits of armour and sporting trophies. Sink into a leather armchair by the open fire and feel the warmth return to your bones. A good whisky selection will help you along.

Snooker Time BAR
(Map p220; http://snookertime.net; Asemakatu 28; ☺4pm-1am Sun-Thu, to 2am Fri & Sat) With a bohemian clientele and a dive-bar feel, this characterful place is an Oulu favourite: locals describe it as the city's living room. Streetside seating and downstairs pool and snooker tables are the highlights.

45 Special CLUB
(Map p220; www.45special.com; Saaristonkatu 12; ☺8pm-4am) This grungy three-level club pulls a good mix of people for its downstairs rock and more mainstream top floor. There's a small cover charge on weekends and regular live gigs. It serves food until 3am.

ℹ Information

Tourist Office (Map p220; ☑08-5584-1330; www.visitoulu.fi; Torikatu 18; ☺9am-5.30pm Mon-Fri Jun, 9am-5.30pm Mon-Fri, 10am-4pm Sat Jul & Aug) Oulu's summer-opening tourist office has a good range of information on Oulu and other Finnish destinations. Free wi-fi is available throughout the city centre on the PanOulu network.

ℹ Getting There & Away

AIR

Oulu's airport (p303) is 14km southwest of the centre. Finnair and Norwegian have daily direct services to Helsinki; Arctic Airlink has several flights a week to Luleå, Sweden, and Tromsø, Norway. Buses 8, 9 and 56 link it to the city centre (€5.80, 25 minutes, half-hourly at least). A taxi costs around €45. There are car-hire desks and an ATM.

BUS

The **bus station** (Map p220; Ratakatu) is on the eastern side of the city centre, adjacent to the train station.

Matkahuolto (www.matkahuolto.fi) services include the following:

Helsinki €55, 9½ hours, up to 14 daily
Kajaani €20, 2¾ hours, four daily
Rovaniemi €24, 3½ hours, eight daily
Tornio €25.20, 2½ hours, six daily

Budget operator Onnibus (www.onnibus.com) has services to destinations including Helsinki (€23, eight hours, four daily) and Vaasa (€9, 4½ hours, two daily).

TRAIN

Direct trains (Rautatienkatu) run daily to Helsinki (€56, six hours, four daily) via Kajaani (€12.40, 2¾ hours). From Oulu, trains continue north to Rovaniemi (€14, 2¼ hours).

DON'T MISS

KIERIKKI STONE AGE CENTRE

This excellent museum, **Kierikkikeskus** (Kierikki Stone Age Centre; www.ouka.fi; Pahkal-antie 447, Yli-Ii; adult/child €8/5; ☺10am-4pm Mon-Fri early-late Jun & mid-late Aug, to 5pm Mon-Sat & noon-6pm Sun late Jun–mid-Aug), is by the Iijoki, whose banks are riddled with important Stone Age settlements. The informative display zeroes in on a handful of arte-facts, including preserved wooden fences to trap fish. A ponderous video gives excava-tion histories and a boardwalk leads to the picturesque riverbank, with re-created period buildings. In summer you can take potshots using a primitive bow and arrow, or send the kids paddling in a Stone Age canoe.

ⓘ Getting Around

There's a good network of local buses (www.oulunjoukkoliikenne.fi). Within the city centre (Zone A), a ride costs €1.50); across Zones A to D, it costs €3.30. Check route maps online and at bus stops.

Bicycles can be hired from locations including the central **Pyörä-Suvala** (☑08-338-175; www.pyorasuvala.fi; Lekatie 2; per hour/24hr/week €5/15/42; ☺9am-6pm Mon-Fri, 10am-2pm Sat).

Car-hire operators in town include **Budget** (☑020-746-6640; www.budget.fi; Kaarnatie 10), which offers cheap weekend deals.

Around Oulu

Hailuoto

☑08 / POP 996

A favourite Oulu beach escape, Hailuoto is a sizeable island of traditional red farmhous-es, venerable wooden windmills, modern wind farms and pines growing tall from the sandy soil. The largest island on the Gulf of Bothnia at 200.5 sq km, it's rising almost 1cm per year due to post-glacial rebound. At this rate, it's expected to join the mainland around the year 4000.

The road winds 30km from the ferry slip to the shallow-water beach (perfect for kids) at Marjaniemi at the island's opposite end, over-looked by a lighthouse. In the middle, Hai-luoto village has services including a petrol station, a bank, a library and grocery stores.

★ **Arctic Lighthouse Hotel**　　HOTEL €€
(☑030-650-2539; https://wildnordic.fi/arctic-light-house-hotel; Marjaniementie 783, Marjaniemi; small/standard/superior d €99/120/165, f €180; ☺early May-late Aug; ℗🤶) In the former **light-house** (Marjaniemen Majakka; www.hailuoto.fi; Marjaniementie 803, Marjaniemi; adult/child €5/3; ☺noon-2pm Jul) pilot station, this breezy place has rooms kitted out in blond wood and light fabrics. 'Small' rooms live up to their name:

it's worth upgrading to standard or superior rooms with marvellous sea views. Suites come with curved picture windows. The restaurant -cafe, with a sea-view terrace, serves a lunch buffet and à la carte evening dishes.

ⓘ Getting There & Away

From March to November, bus 59 travels from Oulu, running the length of the island to Mar-janiemi (€13.70, 1½ hours, three daily).

During the same months (conditions permit-ting), free **ferries** (www.finferries.fi; Luovontie; ☺Mar-Nov) run half-hourly to hourly. The main-land dock is 24km southwest of Oulu via Rd 816.

In winter there's a 7km-long ice road to the island (though it's not suitable for buses).

Haukipudas

Haukipudas, 21km north of Oulu at a scenic spot along the Kiiminkijoki, is renowned for its cream-painted, terracotta-roofed wooden **church** (www.oulunseurakunnat.fi; Kirkkotie 10, Haukipudas; ☺10am-6pm Mon-Fri early Jun-late Aug) FREE, one of Finland's most exquisite 'picture churches'. The interior is decorated with striking naive scenes painted in the 18th century, which depict biblical events including an unnerving Day of Judgement. Outside, by the separate belfry, stands an en-dearing wooden moustachioed *vaivaisukko* (pauper statue). Buses link Haukipudas with Oulu (€9.40, 30 minutes, three daily).

Kajaani

☑08 / POP 37,646

Capital of the Kainuu region, Kajaani is the major settlement in these parts. Apart from its pretty riverside and church at nearby Pal-taniemi, however, it's more stopover than destination.

Kajaani was a tar town; until the 19th cen-tury, the Kainuu region produced more than anywhere in the world. Other claims to fame are that Elias Lönnrot, creator of the *Kaleva-la,* worked here for a period, using it as a base for his travels, and long-reigning president Urho Kekkonen lived here as a student (at Kalliokatu 7).

◎ Sights

Paltaniemen kuvakirkko   CHURCH

(Paltamon Vanha Kirkko; www.paltamonseurakunta. fi; Paltaniementie 851, Paltaniemi; ☺10am-6pm mid-May–mid-Aug) **FREE** Paltaniemi's enchantingly weathered wooden church was built in 1726 and contains some of Finland's most interesting church paintings: rustic 18th-century works full of life and colour that enliven the roof and walls. Above the entrance, symbolically representing the dangers of life outside the church, is a vivid scene of hell that was covered for years to avoid offending parish sensibilities.

Eino Leino-Talo   MUSEUM

(www.einoleinotalo.fi; Sutelantie 28; ☺10am-6pm Sun-Fri mid-Jun–mid-Aug) **FREE** The Eino Leino-Talo is a re-creation of the place where Leino, one of Finland's foremost independence-era poets, was born in 1878. It's a lovely lakeside spot, with a cafe as well as photos and memorabilia. It's just 300m east of the Paltaniemen kuvakirkko.

🛏 Sleeping

Kartanohotelli Karolineburg   HOTEL €€

(☏010-230-5900; www.karolineburg.fi; Karoliinantie 8; s/d/f/ste from €90/100/195/135; **P �**) Set in a buttercup-yellow, white-trimmed wooden manor house and various outbuildings, this property on the eastern side of the river offers a wide range of vintage-style rooms, including suites with their own saunas and terraces. Elegant furnishings, leafy grounds and friendly staff make it a romantic choice.

✗ Eating & Drinking

As you head north, Finland's restaurant scene starts to worsen somewhere around Kajaani. There are a few decent lunch cafes on and around the main street, as well as a fabulous bakery/cafe (see below), but evening restaurants are minimal.

★Pekka Heikkinen & Kumpp   BAKERY, CAFE €

(www.pekkaheikkinen.fi; Välikatu 7; items €3-6.50; ☺7am-5.30pm Mon-Fri, to 4pm Sat, 11am-3pm Sun) Opened in 1913 and run by the fourth generation of the same family, Pekka Heikkinen's loaves are made from Finnish flour and baked in birch pans in its wood-fired oven. Savoury golden-brown pastries include *juustosarvi* (filled with cheese) and *pasteijat* (with veggie or meat fillings); *korvapuusti* (cinnamon scroll) and *kääremunkki* (rye pastry with fruit) are among the sweet varieties.

Sirius   FINNISH €

(☏08-612-2087; www.ravintolasirius.fi; Brahenkatu 5; lunch buffet €14; ☺11am-2pm Tue-Fri Jun–mid-Aug) Located above the rapids, with curved picture windows providing spectacular views, this striking 1940s villa was built as a residence for the local paper company's owner, It's now primarily a wedding and events venue, but during summer it serves the town's best lunch buffet, laden with dishes such as smoked salmon and fennel soup, and wild boar stew with cranberries.

Ulrika   BAR

(www.facebook.com/teemaravintolaulrika; Kauppakatu 21; ☺5pm-midnight Wed-Sat) In a central corner position, Ulrika has one of the town's sunniest terraces, strewn with wicker chairs, and a cinematic-themed interior with film reels, projectors and spotlights. Craft beer, cider and cocktails are served alongside Finnish street food such as salmon burgers on rye. Live music on weekends.

ℹ Information

Kajaani Info (☏08-6155-2555; www.kajaani.fi; Pohjolankatu 13; ☺9am-4.30pm Mon-Fri) Helpful tourist office in the town hall building.

ℹ Getting There & Away

The **airport** (KAJ; www.finavia.fi; Lentokentäntie 7) is 9km north of town. Finnair flies daily from Helsinki; a **bus** (www.akyllonen.fi; Lönnrotinkatu; ticket €5.50) runs from Lönnrotinkatu to coincide with flights. It's about €25 in a cab. Major car-hire companies have desks here.

Buses serve Helsinki (€34, 8½ hours, two daily), Joensuu (€25, 3½ hours, three daily), Kuopio (€27.50, 2½ hours, six daily) and Oulu (€20, 2¾ hours, four daily).

Trains (Asemakatu) run to/from Helsinki (€57, 6½ hours, three daily). The train station is on the southern side of the town centre.

Sotkamo

🗗08 / POP 938

The Sotkamo area, some 40km east of Kajaani, offers a typically beautiful Finnish land- and lakescape that's great fun to explore year-round, with plenty of family-friendly outdoor activities on offer, including a lake beach. It's especially well known as a winter-sports centre, with downhill and cross-country skiing at Vuokatti, 6.5km west.

Vuokatti SNOW SPORTS
(www.vuokatti.fi; Veikontie 5, Vuokatti; lift pass per day/week €39/170; ☉Dec–mid-Apr) The resort at Vuokatti has 13 slopes and nine lifts, as well as ski-jumping and cross-country trails criss-crossing the forest and frozen lakes.

Ski Tunnel SKIING
(www.vuokattisport.fi; Vuokatinhovintie 1, Vuokatti; adult/child €20/10; ☉9am-6pm Jun-early Oct) When the snow melts you can continue to ski in this 1.2km-long snow-filled tunnel, used by skiers to keep in shape over the summer. Ski hire costs €20.

⌂ Sleeping

There's a total of 8000 beds, both in Sotkamo and around the ski resort at Vuokatti, ranging from no-frills guesthouses to self-catering chalets and an enormous Sokos spa resort (www.sokoshotels.fi). Many places open only in winter. The tourist office can make bookings.

ⓘ Information

Located by the ski tunnel, the area's **tourist office** (☏08-619-410; www.vuokatti.fi; Opistontie 4, Vuokatti; ☉9am-6pm Jun-early Oct & Dec–mid-Apr) sells lift tickets, provides maps and can book accommodation.

ⓘ Getting There & Away

Sotkamo and Vuokatti are linked by bus to Kajaani (€8, 40 minutes, five daily December to mid-April, one daily mid-April to November); a trip between Sotkamo and Vuokatti on the same service costs €2.60.

Kuhmo

📞 08 / POP 8755
Surrounded by wilderness, Kuhmo makes a natural base for hiking and wildlife-watching. Vast taiga forests run from here right across Siberia and harbour wolves, bears and lynx. Kuhmo is also the unofficial capital of Vienan Karjala, the Karelian heartland now in Russia, explored by artists in the movement that was crucial to the development of Finnish national identity. Most of their expeditions set off from Kuhmo, as did one of Elias Lönnrot's, when he headed into

'Songland' to record the verses of bards that he later wove into the *Kalevala* epic. There's a fine *Kalevala* resource centre in the centre. This likeable little town also has a great chamber music festival in July.

◉ Sights

★**Juminkeko** CULTURAL CENTRE
(www.juminkeko.fi; Kontionkatu 25; adult/child €5/2; ☉noon-6pm Mon-Fri, daily in Jul) If you're interested in the *Kalevala* or Karelian culture, pay a visit to this excellent resource centre inside a beautiful hand-hewn timber building made using traditional methods and modern styling – its 24 wooden pillars support a roof covered with lingonberries and heather. Passionate staff are very knowledgeable; there are also themed art and photography exhibitions here each year.

Petola Luontokeskus NATURE CENTRE
(www.nationalparks.fi; Lentiirantie 342; ☉9am-4pm Mon-Fri early May–mid-Jun & mid-Aug–Oct, 9am-4pm mid-Jun–mid-Aug) On the main road 3.5km east of central Kuhmo, this centre has an informative exhibition in various languages on Finland's quartet of large carnivores, known hereabouts as *karhu* (bear), *ilves* (lynx), *ahma* (wolverine) and *susi* (wolf), as well as wild reindeer, locally present in small numbers, and golden eagles. There's a summer cafe, national park information and a cuddly-toy-filled gift shop.

Kuhmon Talvisotamuseo MUSEUM
(☏08-6155-5395; www.kuhmo.fi; Väinämöinen 11; adult/child €5/3; ☉9am-4pm Mon-Fri Jun, 9am-4pm Jul-Aug, to 3pm Mon-Fri Dec-Apr) Situated 4.5km southeast of central Kuhmo, by the Hotelli Kalevala, this Winter War museum documents that bitter conflict in the Kuhmo area, mostly through maps and excellent photographs (descriptions are available in English). The Finns were very successful on this front, inflicting enormous casualties on Russian divisions in frighteningly low temperatures.

⚐ Activities

Hiking is the big drawcard in Kuhmo – the eastern 'branch line' of the UKK route (p227) passes through here – but there are plenty of other ways to get active. The website www.wildtaiga.fi has details of activities offered in the region, including operators with hides for viewing bears, elk, flying squirrels, beavers, wolverines and wild reindeer.

Taiga Spirit   WILDLIFE WATCHING, OUTDOORS
(☑040-746-8243; www.taigaspirit.com; Lentiiran-
tie 4282, Lentiira; wildlife-watching/safaris from
€80/130) From its base in Lentiira, 43km
north of Kuhmo, close to the Russian border,
Taiga Spirit organises wildlife safaris and
bear- and wolverine-viewing from hides from
March to October. From November to April, it
runs multiday aurora tours; from February to
April there are multiday husky tours. B&B accommodation per single/double with shared
bathrooms at its base starts at €35/50.

Wild Brown Bear   WILDLIFE WATCHING
(☑040-546-9008; www.wildbrownbear.fi; Kost-
amustie 5644, Vartius; bear watching from €140;
☉Apr-Sep) With 26 hides, this operator's wildlife and photography excursions offer a high
chance of spotting bears (and possibly cubs
in September), wolverines, wolves and other
creatures. Accommodation is available in its
wooden lodge, with rooms sharing bathrooms
(from €60 per person including breakfast,
dinner and sauna). It's in a conservation area
63km north of Kuhmo by the Russian border.

✶✶ Festivals & Events

Kuhmon Kamarimusiikki   MUSIC
(Kuhmo Chamber Music Festival; www.kuhmo
festival.fi; concert tickets from €18.50; ☉mid-Jul)
This two-week festival in mid-July has a full
program performed by a variety of Finnish
and international musicians, many youthful.
Most concerts, usually five or six short pieces bound by a tenuous theme, are held in the
Kuhmo-Talo (☑08-6155-5451; www.kuhmotalo.
fi; Koulukatu 1) arts and cultural centre.

⌂ Sleeping

Book well ahead during July's Kuhmon
Kamarimusiikki festival, when prices rise.
Wildlife watching operators such as Taiga
Spirit and Wild Brown Bear have their own
lodges out in the surrounding wilderness.

Matkakoti Parkki   GUESTHOUSE €
(☑08-655-0271; www.matkakotiparkki.fi; Vienan-
tie 3; s/d €40/60; P🛜) Run by kind-hearted
hosts, this quiet little family guesthouse offers excellent value near the centre of town.
Its 19 rooms share bathrooms, which are
spotless. There's a kitchen you can use and a
home-cooked breakfast is included.

★ Hotelli Kalevala   HOTEL €€
(☑08-655-4100; www.hotellikalevala.fi; Väinämöinen 9; s/d/ste from €98/132/209; P@🛜) Built
in the shape of the *Kalevala kokko* (eagle),

this striking wood-and-concrete building
4.5km southeast of central Kuhmo is the
area's best place to stay. Most of its 47 warm-
hued rooms have lake views, and the hotel
takes full advantage of its gorgeous setting
with a relaxing Jacuzzi and sauna area with
vistas and plenty of activity options year-
round.

ⓘ Getting There & Away

Buses serve Kajaani (€20.40, 1¾ hours, one
daily) and Sotkamo (€13.70, one hour, one daily).

Hossa
☑08 / POP 40

This remote, strung-out settlement is wonderfully set up for fishing, hiking, snowmobiling
and cross-country skiing: there are many
marked trails and numerous lakes. The prize
draw here is newly minted Hossa National
Park, established in 2017 in honour of Finland's centenary of independence. It contains
spectacular natural and cultural features, including four-millennia-old rock art.

★ Hossa National Park   NATIONAL PARK
(www.nationalparks.fi) The country's 40th national park stretches over 11,000 hectares of
glittering lakes and dense forests. Highlights
include **Julma Ölkky**, a 3km-long lake-filled

canyon that narrows to just 10m wide; **Öllön**, a 40m-deep lake where scuba-diving will be possible; and **Värikallio**, a river canyon where 4000-year-old rock paintings can be viewed from a metal platform. Criss-crossing the park are canoeing and cross-country skiing routes, plus mountain-bike and hiking trails.

Hossa National Park
Visitor Centre
VISITOR CENTRE

(☎020-639-6041; www.nationalparks.fi; Jatkonsalmentie 6, Ruhtinansalmi; ⊙9am-8pm Jun-Sep, 10am-4pm Mar-May & Oct) FREE The visitor centre at Hossa National Park has a detailed exhibition on the Värikallio Stone Age rock paintings. Only discovered in 1977, the paintings of 61 figures depicting fishing, hunting, shamanic rituals and childbirth are unique in Finland. They're believed to have been painted by people aboard a boat or standing on the lake's ice. The centre sells fishing permits and maps, books huts, rents out equipment like canoes, kayaks and snowshoes, and can advise on activities, including scuba-diving at Öllön.

Hossan Poropuisto
FARM

(Hossa Reindeer Park; ☎040-755-9834; www.hossan poropuisto.fi; Mäntyniementie 10, Ruhtinansalmi; 1hr boat trip €20; ⊙9am-6pm mid-Jun–Sep or by appointment) Within Hossa National Park, this reindeer farm offers the opportunity to get to know these gentle, antlered beasts. You can feed the reindeer (€5 per bag); in summer, boat trips take you out to an island in the lake, while in winter, reindeer-pulled sleigh rides (€60 per 30 minutes) can be arranged. Its restaurant specialises in reindeer.

Raatteen Portti
MUSEUM

(www.raatteenportti.fi; Raatteentie 2, Suomussalmi; adult/child €10/5; ⊙10am-7pm late Jun–mid-Aug, 10am-4pm early May-late Jun & mid-Aug–Sep) Some

---

OFF THE BEATEN TRACK

RIISINTUNTURI

Consisting of fells and hillside bogs, **Riisitunturi** (www.nationalparks.fi), a 77-sq-km national park 58km northwest of Kuusamo, offers spectacular views and rewarding hiking, including several loop trails for day walks. A 29km trail crosses the park from one side to the other. In all there are 42km of hiking and snowshoeing trails, and 20km of cross-country ski trails. Details of huts and trails are listed on the website.

---

of the most bitter fighting of the Winter War took place 88km south of Hossa (23km east of the lakeside town of Suomussalmi) along the Raate road. The museum here screens a worthwhile audiovisual presentation and displays memorabilia. Outside, the moving **Avara Syli monument** is endowed with 105 bells, one for each day of the war, and surrounded by a field of stones, one for each dead soldier.

Karhunkainalo
CAMPGROUND €

(www.suomussalmi.fi; Jatkonsalmentie 8, Ruhtinansalmi; tent sites €14 plus per person €4, cottages from €75; ⊙camping Mar-Oct; P) Surrounded by pine forest, this campground within Hossa National Park is perfectly placed for fishing and hiking. Along with tent sites in season, it has cosy wooden cottages available year-round that sleep up to six and are equipped with bathrooms and kitchens. Good on-site facilities include a laundry and ski maintenance room.

Hossan Poropuisto Restaurant
FINNISH €€

(☎040-755-9834; www.hossanporopuisto.fi; Mäntyniementie 10; 3-course menu €34, mains €22-32; ⊙11am-6pm mid-Jun–Sep; ☝) At reindeer farm Hossan Poropuisto, this is the area's best place to eat. Hand-built wooden furniture, reindeer hides and an open fire make a atmospheric setting for smoked reindeer soup and roast reindeer with lingonberry jam. Children's dishes cost €8. The three-course menu must be booked three hours ahead; à la carte must be booked the day before.

Kuusamo & Ruka

☎08 / POP 15,673

Kuusamo is a remote frontier town 217km northeast of Oulu and close to the Russian border, while Ruka is its buzzy ski resort 30km north. Both make great activity bases.

⦿ Sights

Kuusamon Suurpetokeskus
WILDLIFE RESERVE

(www.kuusamon-suurpetokeskus.fi; Keronrannantie 31; adult/child €10/5; ⊙10am-5pm Apr-Sep) There's a great backstory to this bear sanctuary 35km south of Kuusamo on the Kajaani road. Rescued as orphans, the bears were nursed by their 'father' Sulo Karjalainen, who then refused to have them put down (they can't return to the wild) when government funding dried up. He casually takes them fishing and walking in the forest, but you'll meet them in their enclosures here. It's thrilling to see these intelligent

HIKING THE UKK

Pockets of pristine Finnish wilderness exist along the eastern border, best experienced along the **UKK route**. Named for Finland's president from 1956 to 1981, Urho Kaleva Kekkonen, this 400km trail is the nation's longest and greatest trekking route, starting at Koli in Karelia, and ending in Syöte. There are numerous possible access points, and alternative branches of the route, but the Kuhmo area offers some excellent portions of it: the Kuhmo to Hiidenportti leg and the Kuhmo to Lentiira leg. The superbly scenic trek east from Kuhmo to Lentiira via Iso-Palonen park takes at least four days. It's well marked and has simple *laavu* shelters at regular intervals, with campfires, firewood and pit toilets. Carry a sleeping bag and *plenty* of insect repellent. Pick up route maps at Petola in Kuhmo.

animals up close and appreciate their different personalities.

Hannun Luontokuvakeskus   GALLERY
(www.hannuhautala.fi; Rukatunturintie 9, Ruka; adult/child €5/2; ⊙9am-5pm Mon-Fri) In the tourist office (p232) building, this rotating exhibition displays the work of famous Finnish nature photographer Hannu Hautala with great accompanying information. There are some stunning shots; equally impressive is the patience that it required to get them.

🏃 Activities

★Rukatunturi   SNOW SPORTS
(www.ruka.fi; Rukatunturintie 9, Ruka; lift pass per day/week €41.50/202; ⊙Nov–mid-Apr) Busy Ruka fell has 34 ski slopes, of which 30 are illuminated; 26 lifts; a vertical drop of 201m; and a longest run of 1300m. Dedicated snowboard areas include a half-pipe. Cross-country trails total an impressive 500km, with 40km illuminated. Lift passes allow you to ski at Pyhä (p251) in Lapland too. In summer there's a toboggan run and several scenic chairlifts.

Head Ski Rent   SNOW SPORTS
(☑046-920-8231; www.headskirent.fi; Rukatunturintie 12, Ruka; ski/snowboard hire per day from €33/39; ⊙8am-7pm Mon-Sat, from 9am Sun Nov–mid-Apr) Ski shop Head Ski Rent hires out everything you need to hit the slopes, including top-of-the-line boots, skis and snowboards. At the end of the ski season, new equipment is sold at bargain prices.

RukaStore   CYCLING
(www.ruka.fi; Rukatunturintie 13, Ruka; mountain-bike hire per day from €30; ⊙10am-5pm Mon-Sat, to 6pm Sun) In the centre of Ruka, Ruka-Store has mountain bikes for hire and can advise on the best trails in both summer and winter. It also sells a good range of sports equipment and clothing.

👣 Tours

★Karhu-Kuusamo   WILDLIFE
(☑040-021-0681; www.karhujenkatselu.fi; Kitulantie 1, Mustaniemi; evening/overnight trips €120/140) Thrilling bear-watching trips spend the evening at a comfortable hide overlooking a meadow where bears regularly stop by: most of the summer you have a high chance of seeing a honeypaw. Evening trips return to town around midnight; overnight trips return the next morning. Tuomo, the knowledgeable guide, can also arrange birdwatching. It's 13km southeast of Kuusamo off Rd 866.

★Kota-Husky   DOG SLEDDING
(☑040-718-7287; http://kota-husky.fi; Jaksamontie 60, Karjalaisenniemi; 1hr husky visit €45, 2/6hr sleigh ride €95/210, 3½hour aurora tour €150) Kota-Husky has picturesque kennels in an old barn and runs excellent, great-value husky excursions for a maximum of 12 people. Most memorable are the aurora-watching tours in husky-pulled sleighs. It's 48km west of Ruka via Rd 9471.

Erä-Susi   DOG SLEDDING
(☑canoes 040-913-6652, huskies 040-570-0279; www.erasusi.com; Rukajärventie 30; husky farm visit €8, 2hr husky safari from €40; ⊙husky farm visit 10am-3pm Jun-Aug) Visit huskies at this farm 8km south of Ruka, or take them on a summer hike or winter safari. In summer, Erä-Susi also hires out canoes (from €50 per day) and kayaks (from €75 per day), from the Oulanka Visitor Centre (p234) in the middle of Oulanka National Park. Prices include pick-up or drop-off. It also offers guided trips.

Ruka Adventures   OUTDOORS
(☑08-852-2007; www.rukaadventures.fi; Rukanriutta 11, Ruka; quad-bike/snowmobile/ ice-fishing tours from €99/80/70) At the main-road turn-off, Ruka Adventures organises quad-bike

Native Wildlife

Finland's dense forests and extensive coastlines are home to prolific bird life and myriad impressive mammals. Keep your eyes peeled for elk, foxes and wild swans; or take a dedicated wildlife tour to spot bears, wolverines or the rare Saimaa ringed seal.

2

VLADISLAV T. JIROUSEK/SHUTTERSTOCK ©

4

TEEMU TRETJAKOV/SHUTTERSTOCK ©

1. Brown bear
The national animal of Finland (not the reindeer!), there are estimated to be over 1000 brown bears in the country.

2. Wolverine
Wildlife safari tours, run throughout the northeast, allow you to catch a glimpse of elusive animals such as the wolverine.

3. Elk
Elk are relatively common; increased fencing helps keep them off the roads.

4. Grey-headed woodpecker
Birdwatching is a typical outdoor activity in many of Finland's national parks.

3

CAMERIS/SHUTTERSTOCK ©

trips, canoeing and fishing, as well as winter activities including snowmobile tours and ice-fishing.

Stella Polaris
OUTDOORS

(☎040-843-3425; www.stellapolaris.fi; Rukanriutta 9, Ruka; rafting/fishing classes/snowmobile safaris from €34/17/75) Rafting trips are arranged by Stella Polaris in summer, along with fishing classes, which aim to improve your success rate. In winter it runs snowmobiling excursions.

Ruka Safaris
OUTDOORS

(☎08-852-1610; www.rukasafaris.fi; Rukarinteentie 1, Ruka; snowshoeing/snowmobile safaris/canoe trips from €89/155/73) Ruka Safaris run a wide range of summer and winter activities, including reindeer safaris, fishing and canoeing. A highlight is the five-hour sauna tour (€110), visiting various saunas in the area, and finishing with a meal made from foraged ingredients. It also rents mountain bikes (€40 per day), SUPs (stand-up paddleboards; €50 per day) and canoes (three hours €30).

RIVER ROUTES AROUND KUUSAMO

The Oulankajoki and Kitkajoki rivers, which meet close to the Russian border, offer canoeing and rafting in wilderness areas. You can do these trips as organised, guided adventures, or hire canoes or kayaks from one of many outfitters, who can arrange transport at either end.

Kitkajoki

The spectacular Kitkajoki offers some of Finland's best canoeing and rafting. There are two main sections: the family-friendly section from Käylä, on the Kuusamo–Salla road, to Juuma; and the challenging 'wild' section beyond Juuma, which includes plenty of tricky rapids.

KÄYLÄ TO JUUMA

The first 14km leg is suitable for families, involving no carrying. Start at the Käylänkoski, continue 3km to the easy Kiehtäjänniva, and a further kilometre to the Vähä-Käylänkoski: also Class I. Next come three Class II rapids spaced every 400m. A kilometre further is the trickiest: 300m Class III Harjakoski. The remaining 7km is mostly lakes.

JUUMA TO THE RUSSIAN BORDER

This 20km journey is one of Finland's most challenging river routes: you should be an expert paddler, and *must* carry your canoe at least once – around the 12m, Class VI Jyrävä waterfall. Ask for local advice and inspect the tricky rapids before you paddle into them. There's a minimum age of 18.

The thrill starts just 300m after Juuma, with the Class II Niskakoski. From here on, it's busy. Myllykoski, with a watermill, is a tricky Class IV waterfall. Right after Myllykoski, the 900m Class IV Aallokkokoski rapids mean quick paddling for quite some time. The Jyrävä waterfall comes right after this long section. Pull aside and carry your canoe; you might want to carry it from Myllykoski to beyond Jyrävä, skipping Aallokkokoski altogether.

After Jyrävä things cool down considerably, although there are some Class III rapids. When you meet the Oulankajoki, 13km further downriver, paddle upriver to Jäkälämutka or downriver to Kuusinkiniemi, by the border zone. Arrange return transport from these remote points in advance.

Oulankajoki

Shadowing the Karhunkierros much of the way, the Oulankajoki gives you a chance to see mighty canyons from a canoe or kayak. The first leg, a 20km trip, starts from Rd 950, north of Ristikallio. The first 7km or so is relatively calm paddling, until you reach the impressive Oulanka Canyon. The safe section extends for about 1km, after which pull aside and carry your canoe twice past dangerous rapids. You can overnight at Savilampi hut, also a popular starting point.

Some 3km after Savilampi are Taivalköngäs rapids (carry your canoe), where there's a hut. The next 9km are quiet, passing a couple of campgrounds before reaching Oulanka Visitor Centre (p234), which rents out canoes for this trip. Not far downstream are Kiutaköngäs rapids (carry your canoe). Below them the Lower Oulankajoki stretch is 25km of easy paddling, suitable for beginners, ending at Jäkälämutka parking area just short of the Russian border.

NorthTrek
OUTDOORS

(☑ 040-418-2832; www.northtrek.net; Erkkorannantie 1, Ruka; rafting/canoeing trips from €45, snowshoe tours/ husky safaris from €40/110) Based 7.5km southeast of Ruka, NorthTrek offers family-friendly rafting, canoeing and hiking trips. In winter there's snowshoeing, cross-country skiing and husky sleigh rides.

Rukapalvelu
OUTDOORS

(Tailored Adventures; ☑ 010-271-0500; http://rukapalvelu.fi; Rukakyläntie 13, Ruka; hiking tours/canoeing trips/snowmobile safaris from €69/119/195) The comprehensive range of activities organised by this operator spans winter husky and snowmobile safaris to summer fishing, canoeing and river-rafting. It also arranges trips to Russia (visa required) to see breathtakingly pretty Karelian villages.

🛏 Sleeping

Ruka has the lion's share of accommodation. Book well ahead for winter; in summer it's great value. There are numerous apartments in Ruka itself, and hundreds of cabins and cottages dotted throughout the surrounding area. For rentals, contact the tourist offices or booking services such as Lomarengas (p298), **ProLoma** (☑ 020-792-9700; www.proloma.fi), **Ski-Inn** (☑ 08-860-0300; www.ski-inn.fi) or **Ruka-ko** (☑ 020-734-4790; www.rukako.fi).

If you stay in Ruka in summer, accommodation providers offer a 'Summer Wristband', with discounts on dining and activities.

Willi's West
MOTEL €

(☑ 040-024-2992; www.wwsaloon.com; Rukanriutta 13, Ruka; s/d €66/99; P 🛜) At the Ruka turn-off on the main road, this friendly motel-style set-up offers good facilities, including a guest laundry. The 12 rooms are small apartments sleeping up to six, and have spacious bathrooms and small, equipped kitchens. The owners will take groups of walkers to the Karhunkierros trailheads.

Cumulus Rantasipi Rukahovi
HOTEL €€

(☑ 020-048-126; www.cumulus.fi; Rukankyläntie 15, Ruka; s/d/ste/apt from €86/96/160/186; P @ 🛜) Right by the major slopes in Ruka's centre, this huge 219-room complex draws everyone from conferencing execs to snowball-lobbing families. Standard rooms are a long hike from reception; spacious superiors have balconies. Both have drying cupboards. Duplex apartments are down the road. Its restaurant, bars and nightclub are the heart of Ruka nightlife in the ski and autumn *ruska* seasons.

Royal Hotel Ruka
BOUTIQUE HOTEL €€

(☑ 040-081-9840; https://royalruka.fi; Mestantie 1, Ruka; d/ste from €90/179; ⊘ Jul-Apr; P 🛜) At the foot of the fell at the turn-off to Rukajärvi, this intimate 16-room hotel looks like a children's fort waiting to be populated with toy soldiers. Rooms are plainer than the exterior suggests, but service is excellent. The classy restaurant offers such wild delicacies as hare, elk and bear; from July to November it only opens by reservation.

🍴 Eating & Drinking

Riipisen Riistaravintola
FINNISH €€

(☑ 08-868-1219; www.riipisen.fi; Rukaturintie 6, Ruka; mains €16-45; ⊘ 1-9pm Mon-Sat Sep-May) At the Kelo ski-lift area, 500m south of Ruka's main square, this log cabin has a rustic interior and attracts a convivial crowd. It specialises in game dishes, and you'll find Rudolf, Bullwinkle and, yes, poor Yogi on the menu here in various guises, depending on availability and season. Arctic hare, willow grouse and boar also feature.

Piste
INTERNATIONAL €€

(☑ 040-010-1620; www.ruka.fi; Rukankylätie 17, Ruka; mains €16-35.50, lunch buffet €23; ⊘ kitchen 11am-8pm, bar to 4am Sep-May, to 10pm Jun-Aug; 🛜 🚹) At the base of the lifts on Ruka's main square, this cavernous wooden hall has several attractive dining areas, including a large heated terrace, and good service. Dishes include burgers, steaks, fish, pasta dishes, soup and salads. Things get pretty lively at the bar, with regular bands during ski season. There's a play area for kids.

Zone
BAR

(www.ravintolazone.fi; Rukankyläntie 13, Ruka; ⊘ kitchen noon-9pm, bar to 4am; 🛜) The big glassed-in terrace at this year-round central bar packs out at night in the ski season and has its own fast-food kiosk. There's karaoke nightly (with 7000 song choices in various languages), regular live music (also nightly during the ski season) and a good-time vibe.

ℹ Information

Central Ruka has a free wi-fi network.

Kuusamo Info (☑ 040-860-8365; www.ruka.fi; Torangintaival 2, Kuusamo; ⊘ 9am-5pm Mon-Fri, 10am-2pm Sat, plus noon-4pm Sun Jun-Aug; 🛜) This large visitor centre is at the highway junction, 2km from central Kuusamo. It offers comprehensive tourist information, rental cottage booking and a cafe-shop. There's also a wildlife photography exhibition and national park information desk.

Ruka Info ([phone] 08-860-0250; www.ruka.fi; Rukatunturintie 9, Ruka; [clock] 9am-5pm early Jun & late Aug, 9.30am-7pm Sep & late Jun–mid-Aug, 10am-8pm daily Oct-May) Tourist information and accommodation booking in Ruka's village centre.

❶ Getting There & Away

Kuusamo airport (KAO; www.finavia.fi; Lentokentäntie, Kuusamo) is 4km northeast of town. Finnair has year-round services to/from Helsinki; winter services are much more frequent. Major car-hire companies have desks here. Buses serve incoming and outbound flights (€7, 10 minutes to Kuusamo, €10; 30 minutes to Ruka). Call [phone] 0100-84200 for a taxi.

Buses run to/from Kajaani (€25, 3½ hours, two daily), Oulu (€25, three hours, up to eight daily) and Rovaniemi (€34.50, three hours, three daily).

❶ Getting Around

Buses run between Kuusamo and Ruka twice daily (€6.80, 30 minutes). During the ski season there's a shuttle bus, which stops at major hotels.

Karhunkierros Bus ([phone] 040-722-2022; www.rukacharter.fi) operates buses to the Karhunkierros trailheads.

Juuma

Set on the beautiful lakeshore of Yli-Juumajärvi, Juuma is a popular base for Karhunkierros treks and rafting on the Kitkajoki. The surrounding wilderness offers opportunities to spot wildlife including bears, lynx and wolverines.

★**Basecamp Oulanka** RAFTING
([phone] 040-050-9741; http://basecampoulanka.fi; Myllykoskentie 30; rafting trips €39-95) Based at the lodge of the same name, this outfit is great for rafting trips on the Kitkajoki. The three-hour Käylä–Juuma trip is family-friendly, while the two-hour Wild Route and the 4½-hour trip to the border zone are for those aged 18 and over. Winter activities include snowshoeing and ice climbing. Conservation fees are included.

Juuman Leirintäalue CAMPGROUND €
([phone] 044-272-7872; www.juumanleirintaalue.fi; Riekamontie 1; tent sites €18, cottages €70-90; [clock] Jun-Sep; [P]) At the beginning of the Käylä road, this campground has a lovely lakeside location. There's a sauna, a laundry, and a cafe that can provide evening meals if you book the day before. It also arranges fishing licences and hires out boats. Heated cottages, with saunas and kitchens, sleep up to six and are open year-round.

Lomakylä Retki-Etappi CAMPGROUND €
([phone] 040-565-3474; www.retkietappi.fi; Juumantie 134; tent sites per person €14, additional person €6, cabins €30-80; [clock] Jun-Sep; [P]) At the start of the Little Bear's Ring and the Karhunkierros trailhead, this lakeside campground is a convenient place to stay. There are several cabins (some available in winter) and a daytime cafe. There's also a sauna, as well as boats and bikes to hire.

★**Basecamp Oulanka** LODGE €€
([phone] 040-050-9741; http://basecampoulanka.fi; Myllykoskentie 30; s/d from €69/100, lunch/half-board/full-board €11/25/36; [P]) Right on the Karhunkierros trail, this excellent wilderness lodge is a 1km walk from Juuma (5.5km by car). Rustic rooms smell of pine: larger rooms with sleeping lofts and charming forest-view balconies are great for families and groups. There's no internet or kitchen facilities, but it has a convivial bar and restaurant (reserve for dinner), sauna and Jacuzzi.

Karhunkierros Trek & Oulanka National Park

The Karhunkierros (Bear's Ring), one of the oldest and best-established trekking routes in Finland, offers some of the country's most breathtaking scenery. It is extremely popular in summer but it can be walked practically any time between late May and October.

Despite the name, it's not a circuit, rather a point-to-point walk of anything from 52km (Ristikallio to Juuma) to 82km (Hautajärvi to Ruka). There are four trailheads:

LITTLE BEAR'S RING

The Pieni Karhunkierros (Little Bear's Ring) is an easy-to-moderate 12km loop trail taking in some fantastic scenery as it follows the river valley far below. It begins by the Retki-Etappi cafe and traverses varying terrain; wet bits are all boardwalked. It's one of the most scenic short routes in Finland. There's a wilderness hut on this trail – Siilastupa – and a day hut at Myllykoski. It's well signposted and busy. You can do it with snowshoes in winter.

Karhunkierros Trek & Oulanka National Park

Trekking

the northern access point is from Hautajärvi visitor centre on the road to Salla; further south on Rd 950 the Ristikallio parking area is another access point. In the south you can start the walk at Ruka ski resort; or further northeast at Juuma village. Juuma also has a spectacular loop trail, the 12km Pieni Karhunkierros (Little Bear's Ring). Most people choose to walk north to south for transport-connection reasons. Much of the walk is through the **Oulanka National Park** (Oulangan; www.nationalparks. fi), also a great destination for canoeing and rafting.

The track is very well marked. While it's generally possible to walk it from late May, prior to mid-June the ground is often too soggy to make hiking enjoyable. Even if you don't intend to walk the whole route, a day walk can take you from Ristikallio to Oulanka Canyon and back, for example. It's also possible to drive to within 1km of Oulanka Canyon along a signposted dirt road about 12km north of Ristikallio. There are plenty of wilderness huts, so you can divide the route up according to your own pace. People tend to do Ristikallio to Juuma in two or three days, with a further long day to Ruka.

From Ristikallio

Start at the parking area at Ristikallio; you'll soon enter the national park. There's a wilderness hut (of use if you're coming the other way) about 2.5km in. Another 1km further on gets you to Puikkokämppä hut at a small lake. Continue another kilometre and a bit past the lake to Taivalköngäs (9km from the start, near the wilderness hut of the same name), with two sets of rapids and three suspension bridges.

From Hautajärvi

Another starting point is further north at the Hautajärvi visitor centre – this adds an extra 10km to the hike. The landscape is unimpressive until the path reaches the Savinajoki. The deep Oulanka Canyon is a highlight of this part of the trek. A wilderness hut is at the Oulanka riverfront near Savilampi, a lake 15km south of Hautajärvi. The distance from Savilampi to Taivalköngäs – where you'll join the Ristikallio trail – is 4km.

Taivalköngäs to Juuma

From Taivalköngäs the first stretch is through typical forest scenery enlivened by beautiful lakes. After 4km, you can camp at Lake Runsulampi; there's dry wood available. About 3.5km further east, there's **Oulanka Camping** (☑044-740-0001; www.national parks.fi; Liikasenvaarantie 137; tent sites per person €7.50, 4-person cabins €48; ☉Jun-Aug; ℗); another kilometre brings you to the Oulanka Visitor Centre (p234) and its welcome cafe. The rugged cliffs and muscular waters of the Kiutaköngäs rapids are a short way further on. From Oulanka it's 7km to Ansakämppä cabin, and a further 8km to Jussinkämppä wilderness hut on Kulmakkajärvi.

From here the trail is a little tougher. A hike through ridges and forests takes you to the Kitkajoki in another deep gorge. When you meet the Pieni Karhunkierros trail, you can turn right to head directly to Juuma via the bridge at Myllykoski, or turn left for the more scenic route via the Jyrävä waterfall (where you'll find Siilastupa hut, 16km beyond Jussinkämppä). Another 3.5km beyond here is Juuma, where there are campsites, and the Basecamp Oulanka (p232) lodge on the trail just outside it.

Ruka Extension

Juuma is one possible endpoint, but you can also walk 24km further to Ruka, which has a big choice of accommodation and better road connections to Kuusamo. There is one wilderness hut, Porontimajoki (often full), 9km down this trail, and several lean-to shelters. The first 15km are easy going, but then a series of ascents and descents mean that a posthike beer in Ruka will be very well earned.

🛏 Sleeping

There is a good network of wilderness huts along the Karhunkierros. All are similar and tend to be crowded in high season. A tent will come in handy, as someone often ends up sleeping outside. Dry firewood is generally available and there's a gas cooker in most huts, but carry a lightweight mattress with you. See www.nationalparks.fi for hut details.

ℹ Information

The website www.nationalparks.fi has comprehensive route information. The 1:50,000 *Rukatunturi-Oulanka* map is sold at park visitor centres and tourist offices. Map guides to the Karhunkierros are also available. The trail is so well signposted that you can easily make do with the free map on the website or from the Oulanka Visitor Centre.

Rukapalvelu (p231) in Ruka rents tents, packs and other hiking equipment. **Oulanka Visitor Centre** (☑020-639-6850; www.nationalparks. fi; Liikasenvaarantie 132; ☉10am-4pm Oct-May, 10am-6pm Jun-Sep; 🛜) in the middle of Oulanka National Park (p233), 20km north of Juuma, has an exhibition of photos and films with information on the national park, trekking supplies, a cafe, maps and fishing licences. An 800m walk (one way) takes you along the Oulankajoki to the Kiutaköngäs rapids. You can hire canoes and kayaks (from €50/75 per day) here through Erä-Susi (p227); prices include pick-up or drop-off and a safety lesson.

ℹ Getting There & Away

From early June to early August, a handy early-morning **bus** (p232; Kuusamo to trailheads €10, 1½ hours; Ruka to trailheads €6, 1¼ hours, two daily Monday to Friday) runs from Kuusamo to Salla via Ruka, Juuma, Ristikallio and Hautajärvi from Monday to Friday, and returns in the afternoon. On Monday, Wednesday and Friday, the same bus continues to the Oulanka Visitor Centre.

Outside these dates, there's a less convenient afternoon service, with no weekend buses.

For a taxi call **Rukan Taksipalvelu** (☑08-868-1222; www.rukataksi.fi).

Lapland

Includes ➜

Rovaniemi 241
Levi 253
Saariselkä 261
Saariselkä Wilderness
& Urho Kekkonen
National Park 263
Inari 266
Lemmenjoki
National Park 268
Inari to Norway 270

Best Places to Eat

➡ Restaurant Saaga (p253)

➡ Aanaar (p268)

➡ Aitta Deli & Dine (p247)

➡ Restaurant Sky Ounasvaara (p247)

➡ Mustaparran Päämaja (p241)

Best Places to Stay

➡ Arctic Light Hotel (p247)

➡ Lumihotelli (p239)

➡ Wilderness Hotel Nellim (p266)

➡ Hotel Mustaparta (p241)

➡ Porotila Toini Sanila (p272)

➡ Levi Panorama (p254)

Why Go?

Lapland casts a powerful spell: there's something lonely and intangible here that makes it magical. The midnight sun, the Sámi peoples, the aurora borealis (Northern Lights) and roaming reindeer are all components of this – as is Santa Claus himself, who 'officially' resides here – along with the awesome latitudes: at Nuorgam, the northernmost point, you have passed Iceland and nearly all of Canada and Alaska.

Spanning 30% of Finland's land area, Lapland is home to just 3% of its population. Its vast wilderness is ripe for exploring on foot, skis or sled. The sense of space, pure air and big skies are what's most memorable here, more so than the towns.

Lapland's far north is known as Sápmi, home of the Sámi, whose main communities are around Inari, Utsjoki and Hetta. Rovaniemi, on the Arctic Circle, is the most popular gateway to the north.

When to Go
Lapland

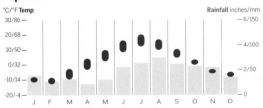

Apr The best month for sled treks and skiing, with reasonable temperatures and plenty of light.

Aug Lots of light and sunshine; trails are less crowded and biting insects fewer.

Dec Reindeer, snow and good old ho-ho-ho himself are guaranteed to inject Christmas spirit.

Lapland Highlights

1 Kilpisjärvi (p258) Hiking the lonely wildernesses in Finland's highlands around Kilpisjärvi in Fell Lapland.

2 Muonio (p255) Dashing through the snow pulled by a team of reindeer or huskies from the excellent Harriniva activities centre attached to the Arktinen Rekikoirakeskus (Arctic Sled-dog Centre).

3 Kemi (p238) Sailing on an ice-breaker, then sleeping in Kemi's ethereally beautiful snow castle, Lumilinna.

4 Lemmenjoki National Park (p268) Panning for gold in the beautiful Lemmenjoki river and walking in the national park.

5 Arktikum (p242) Learning about northern environments at Rovaniemi's superb arctic museum.

6 Siida (p266) Exploring Sámi culture at Inari's state-of-the-art museum.

7 Levi (p254) Skiing at Lapland's best-equipped resort, Levitunturi.

8 Aurora House, Sodankylä (p259) Catching a simulation of the aurora borealis if you miss the real thing.

9 Utsjoki (p271) Fishing the Tenojoki, Lapland's most beautiful stretch of river.

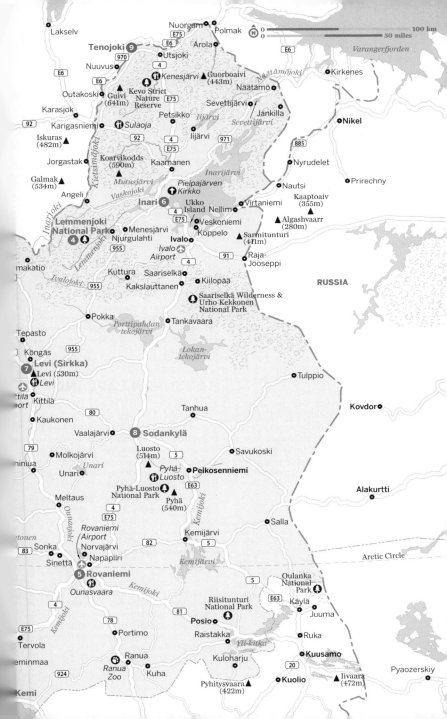

History

Sámi lived throughout Lapland, but during the 1600s Swedes increased their presence and in 1670 various cult sites and religious objects were destroyed by the Lutheran Church's Gabriel Tuderus (1638–1703). In the following centuries, more Finns came, adopted reindeer herding and were assimilated into Sámi communities (or vice versa).

The Petsamo area, northeast of Inari, was ceded to Finland in 1920 by the Treaty of Tartu. The Soviet Union attacked the mineral-rich area during the Winter War (1939–40), annexed it in 1944, and has kept it. Skolt Sámi from Petsamo were resettled in Sevettijärvi, Nellim and Virtaniemi.

The German army's retreat in 1944–45 was a scorched-earth affair; they burned all buildings in their path to hold off pursuit. Only a few churches, villages and houses in Lapland date from the prewar period.

Activities

Lapland's joy is the range of exciting outdoor activities year-round. Major settlements have plenty of tour operators. Rovaniemi, Lapland's capital, is a popular base, but Saariselkä, Levi and Muonio are closer to genuine wilderness.

Summer

Once the snow melts, there are fabulous multiday treks and shorter walks. The national-parks network offers everything from wheelchair-accessible nature trails to demanding wilderness routes for experienced hikers, but there are good walks almost everywhere. Lapland's surging rivers offer several excellent canoeing routes and spots for white-water rafting. Fishing is popular year-round: ice fishing is a memorable experience, and the beautiful Teno Valley offers superb salmon fishing.

Winter

There's good downhill skiing for six months of the year at several spots; Levi is the biggest resort, while smaller Pyhä-Luosto and Ylläs are more family- than party-oriented destinations. All have extensive cross-country trails.

Most memorable are sleigh safaris. Pulled by a team of huskies or reindeer, you cross the snowy wilderness, overnighting in log cabins with a relaxing wood sauna and eating meals cooked over a fire. You can organise trips of up to a week or more, or just head out for a jaunt for a couple of hours. Similar trips can be arranged on snowmobiles.

ℹ Information

DANGERS & ANNOYANCES

Lapland's dangers and annoyances relate to its natural environment.

➡ From mid-June to early August, Lapland is home to millions of biting insects, and during this *räkkä* season you'll need heavy-duty repellent. By early August most squadrons have dispersed.

➡ Parts of Lapland are real wildernesses; always consult national-park centres before attempting unmarked routes.

➡ Winter temperatures are seriously low: don't head outdoors without being properly equipped.

➡ Driving in Lapland calls for particular caution due to reindeer.

LANGUAGE

Three Sámi languages are spoken in Finnish Lapland: Northern, Skolt and Inari Sámi. Signs in Sámi areas are bilingual.

ℹ Getting Around

Considering the remoteness, bus connections are good, although there may only be one service a day, and often none on Sunday. Hiring a car from Rovaniemi, Levi or Saariselkä/Ivalo is a good option.

SOUTHERN LAPLAND

Right by the Arctic Circle, the city of Rovaniemi is a key draw for visitors, with various Santa Claus attractions (the red-suited saint officially resides here) and numerous tours and activities, ranging from reindeer-farm visits to snowmobiling safaris, dog sledding with huskies and various high-adrenaline adventures. Rovaniemi has a small ski area, but the best skiing is at Pyhä-Luosto. Elsewhere you can hike, take an ice-breaker cruise, stay in a winter snow castle and go berry picking in summer.

Kemi

✓ 016 / POP 21,766

Kemi is an important deep-water harbour and heavy-industry town. It's home to two of Finland's blockbuster winter attractions – a snow castle and an ice-breaker cruise – while summer diversions include a gem museum and a wide waterfront where you'll find a handful of kid-friendly activities at Santa's Seaside Office.

Sights & Activities

Lumilinna
CASTLE

(Snow Castle; 016-258-878; www.visitkemi.fi; Lumilinnankatu 15; adult/child €20/12; 10am-6pm late Jan-early Apr) Few things conjure fairy-tale romance like a snow castle. First built in 1996 as a Unicef project, this is a Lapland winter highlight and a favoured destination for weddings, honeymoons, and general marvelling at the ethereal light and sumptuously decorated interior. The design changes every year but always includes a chapel, a snow hotel, an ice bar and a restaurant (lunch menus €26, dinner menus €51 to €58; by reservation 11am to 2pm and 7pm to 9.30pm).

Santa's Seaside Office
VISITOR CENTRE

(040-637-0653; www.visitkemi.fi; Luulajantie 6; 10am-6pm early Jun-late Aug & mid-Dec–mid-Apr) Kemi's newest attraction, opened in 2017, is Santa's Seaside Office – a collection of cute red-painted timber buildings overlooking the waterfront, which house a gift shop, a cafe and, from Thursday to Saturday afternoons, Santa himself. Activities include writing a letter to Santa and sealing it in a bottle, elf sailor workshops and gingerbread decorating. Prices for individual activities vary.

Jalokivigalleria
MUSEUM

(Gemstone Gallery; www.visitkemi.fi; Kauppakatu 29; adult/child €9/5; 10am-4pm Mon-Fri) More than 3000 beautiful, rare stones and jewellery from 60 countries are displayed at the Gemstone Gallery, set in an old seaside customs house. Stones are on the ground floor; the upper floor contains exhibits such as replicas of famous diamonds. Interpretive information is in English and Finnish.

Sampo
CRUISE

(016-258-878; www.visitkemi.fi; Sampotie 137, Ajos Harbour; 4hr cruise €270, summer visit €10; cruises late Dec–mid-Apr, summer visits by reservation 10am-2pm Tue-Sat late Jun-late Aug) This retired ice-breaker runs memorable, though overpriced, excursions. The four-hour cruise includes a warming soup (a three-course meal is €32) and ice swimming in special drysuits. The best experience is when the ice is thickest, usually in March. Book well in advance. Kids under 12 aren't allowed to take part in ice swimming. Online bookings are cheapest.

Sleeping & Eating

Kemi's smattering of hotels includes a Cumulus (www.cumulus.fi) branch with a handy 24-hour reception if you're arriving

LAPLAND SEASONS

It's important to time your trip in Lapland carefully. In the far north there's no sun for 50 days of the year, and no night for 70-odd days. In June it's very muddy, and in July insects can be hard to deal with. If you're here to walk, August is great and September brings the spectacle of the *ruska* (autumn leaves). There's usually thick snow cover from mid-October to May; December draws charter flights looking for Santa, real reindeer and a white Christmas, but the best time for skiing and husky/reindeer/snow-mobile safaris is March and April, when you get a decent amount of daylight and less-extreme temperatures.

on a late flight (you'll still need to reserve ahead). From late January to early April, the standout place to sleep and eat is the Lumihotelli at the annual snow castle.

Hotelli Palomestari
HOTEL €€

(016-257-117; www.hotellipalomestari.com; Valtakatu 12; s/d/tr from €75/95/130; P) Near the train and bus stations on a pedestrian street, the 'fire chief' has 32 timber-floored rooms with trademark Finnish furniture, including a desk and sofa, and blackout curtains, friendly service and a downstairs bar with outside seating. Rates are cheapest at weekends and in summer.

Lumihotelli
HOTEL €€€

(016-258-878; www.visitkemi.fi; Lumilinnankatu 15; s/d/ste with shared bathroom from €220/350/400, apt from €230; late Jan-early Apr; P) The snow hotel's interior temperature is -5°C (23°F) – somewhat temperate when the outside temperate is closer to -30°C (-22°F) – but a woolly sheepskin and a sturdy sleeping bag keep you warm(ish) atop the ice bed. From late June to April, seaside glass villas with transparent walls and ceilings offer private bathrooms, kitchenettes and, conditions permitting, aurora-watching.

Panorama Cafe
CAFE €

(050-410-3605; www.panoramacafekemi.fi; Valtakatu 26; lunch buffet €9, dishes €4.50-9.50; 8am-3.30pm Mon-Fri) Panorama's great-value lunch buffet includes home-brewed beer. Dishes like arctic char and potato bake, wild-mushroom soup, reindeer meatballs with turnip mash, and elk sausages with cranberry sauce are delicious, but the ultimate reason to head up

EXPLORING THE ARCHIPELAGO

Off the Kemi–Tornio coast, **Perämeri National Park** (www.nationalparks.fi) is an archipelago of small islands that's an important conservation area for seals and a richly populated bird habitat. You'll need a boat (or snowmobile) to explore; ask at the Kemi (p240) or Tornio (p241) tourist offices about renting one.

to the 13th floor of Kemi's town hall is for its sweeping views over the Bay of Bothnia from the dining room and terrace.

ℹ Information

Tourist Office (☑ 016-258-878; www.visitkemi. fi; Valtakatu 26; ⊗8am-4pm Mon-Fri) In the town hall.

ℹ Getting There & Away

Kemi-Tornio Airport (KEM; www.finavia.fi; Lentokentäntie 75) is 6.5km north. Finnair has regular Helsinki flights. Airport **taxis** (☑ 020-068-000; www.merilapintaksit.fi) cost €20 and must be prebooked.

Buses departing from the **train station** (Rautatiekatu) serve Tornio (€6.80, 35 minutes, frequent), Rovaniemi (€22, 1½ hours, up to six daily) and Oulu (€20.40, 1¾ hours, up to 10 daily).

There's one direct train daily to Helsinki (€70, seven hours), and four daily services to Oulu (€14, one hour) and Rovaniemi (€15, 1½ hours).

Tornio

☑ 016 / POP 22,187

Situated on the impressive Tornionjoki, northern Europe's longest free-flowing river, Tornio is joined to its Swedish counterpart Haparanda by short bridges. After Russia claimed the Finnish trading centre in 1809, Haparanda was founded in 1821 across the river. Upon joining the EU, the twin towns reunited as a 'Eurocity'. Cross-border shopping has boomed here in recent years, with a vast Ikea on the Swedish side and new malls on the Finnish side. Finland is an hour ahead of Sweden (meaning double celebrations on New Year's Eve).

⊙ Sights

Tornionlaakson Maakuntamuseo   MUSEUM
(www.tornio.fi/museo; Keskikatu 22; adult/child €5/free, combination ticket with Aineen Taidemuseo

€8/free; ⊗11am-6pm Tue-Thu, to 3pm Fri-Sun) Tornio's local historical museum was founded in 1914 and has an interesting, recently renovated collection of old artefacts and costumes. Its Encounters on the Border exhibition traces the valley's history on the Finnish and Swedish sides from the last ice age to the present day. Interpretive touch screens are in English, Finnish and Swedish.

Aineen Taidemuseo   GALLERY
(www.tornio.fi/aine; Torikatu 2; adult/child €5/free, combination ticket with Tornionlaakson Maakuntamuseo €8/free; ⊗11am-6pm Tue-Thu, to 3pm Fri-Sun) Finnish art from the 19th and 20th centuries from the private collection of Veli Aine, a local business tycoon, is displayed at the attractive modern Tornio gallery. There are regular temporary exhibitions and a good cafe.

Tornion Kirkko   CHURCH
(www.tornio.seurakunta.net; Seminaarinkatu 2; ⊗10am-6pm Mon-Fri, 1.30-6pm Sat & Sun Jun & Jul, 10am-5pm Mon-Fri Aug) FREE Completed in 1686, this charming wooden church, visited by the king of Sweden, Charles XI, in 1694, is topped by a shingle roof.

🏃 Activities

The tourist office can book trips and handles fishing permits; there are several excellent spots along the Tornionjoki.

River rafting is popular in summer on the Kukkolankoski rapids north of town.

Green Zone Golf Course   GOLF
(☑ 016-431-711; http://torniogolf.fi; Näräntie; green fees €45, club rental €20; ⊗8am-10pm late Jun-late Jul, 9am-8pm May-late Jun & late Jul-Oct) Roamed by reindeer, this 18-hole golf course straddles Finland and Sweden (seven holes in Finland and 11 in Sweden). On the par 3 hole six, balls stay in the air for approximately an hour and three seconds (due to the countries' differing time zones).

Pohjolan Safarit   OUTDOORS
(Nordic Safaris; ☑ 040-069-2301; www.pohjolan safarit.fi; Koskitie 130) Rafting on the Tornionjoki takes place on inflatable rubber rafts or traditional wooden boats from June to October. The 90-minute rafting trips cost €40 per person, with a minimum of six people. From December to March the outfit runs four-hour snowmobile tours to a reindeer farm (€225 per person including lunch and a reindeer sleigh ride; single supplement €68). It's 15km north of Tornio.

✕✕ Festivals & Events

Kalott Jazz & Blues Festival MUSIC
(www.kalottjazzblues.net; ⏰ late Jun/early Jul) Established in 1983, this three-day festival takes
place in churches, parks, museums, shops,
bars and restaurants on both sides of the Finland–Sweden border. A free bus service travels
between venues. Many concerts are also free.

⏹ Sleeping & Eating

Options are fairly limited on both sides of
the border. Tornio has a good campground
and a brand-new boutique hotel; in Haparanda, you'll find hostel accommodation
and the central **Stadshotell** (☎ 0922-614 90;
www.haparandastadshotell.se; Torget 7; s/d from
1060/1295kr; P 🖥) on the main square.

Camping Tornio CAMPGROUND €
(☎ 016-445-945; www.campingtornio.com; Matkailijantie 9; tent sites €14 plus per person €4, cabins
€40-80, 2-bedroom chalets €90-200; ⏰ May-Aug;
P) Situated 3.5km southeast of the town
centre, off the road to Kemi, this 5.5-hectare
campground has a grassy riverside location
with a beach, boat and bike hire, a tennis
court and minigolf, and campfires. Other bo-
nuses include three saunas (one on the riverbank) and a laundry room. Its 15 cabins can
sleep up to six people. Bring insect repellent.

★**Hotel Mustaparta** BOUTIQUE HOTEL €€
(☎ 040-010-5800; http://mustaparta.fi; Hallituskatu 6; d/ste from €107/227; ✳ 🖥) Tornio's
best hotel by far tells the story of Iisakki
Mustaparta (Isaac Blackbeard), an 18th-
century leader of local farmers who defied
the ruling merchant class, in its bar-restaurant Mustaparran Päämaja, and themed
rooms stunningly decorated with wooden
floors reflecting his ship's decking, woven willow baskets, fur rugs, cushions and throws.
Some rooms open to French balconies.

★**Mustaparran Päämaja** FINNISH €€
(☎ 040-126-0222; http://mustaparta.fi; Hallituskatu 6; lunch buffet €10.50, mains €15.50-32.50;
⏰ 11am-9.30pm Mon-Fri, noon-9.30pm Sat, noon-
7.30pm Sun; 🖥 ♿) At the fabulous Hotel
Mustaparta, this atmospheric restaurant
styled after local hero Iisakki Mustaparta
has hefty timber beams, ships' wheels, wood-
en barrels and a buffet served on a skiff, and
inspired modern Finnish cuisine: smoked
arctic char with fennel sauce, beetroot-
marinated local lamb with blueberry jus,
and a reindeer burger with smoked cheese,
lingonberry pickle and tar-mustard mayo.

🛍 Shopping

Torniotar DESIGN
(Jääkärinkatu 6; ⏰ 10am-5.30pm Mon-Fri, to 3pm
Sat) A charming buttercup-coloured wooden
building houses this design shop. Most of the
homewares (ceramics, cushions, light fittings,
blankets and more), jewellery and women's
fashion are by Finnish designers; a handful
are from neighbouring Nordic countries.

ℹ Information

Tourist Office (☑ Finland 050-590-0562; www.
haparandatornio.com; Krannigatan 5, Haparanda, Sweden; ⏰ 8am-4pm Mon-Fri Swedish
time; 🖥) The tourist office for both towns in
located in the shared Tornio-Haparanda **bus
station** (Krannigatan 5, Haparanda, Sweden).

ℹ Getting There & Away

Kemi-Tornio airport, 22km east of town, has
regular flights to/from Helsinki. Bus 76 (€6.80,
20 minutes) drops off on Rd 926, 800m west
of the terminal, or it's a €40 **taxi** (☑ 020-068-
000; www.merilapintaksit.fi) ride.

From the shared Tornio-Haparanda **bus
station**, there are two direct daily services to
Rovaniemi (€23.50, 1¾ hours), and several
others that require a change (to a bus or train)
in Kemi (€6.80, 35 minutes, frequent). Swedish
buses run to Luleå, from where buses and trains
run to other destinations in Sweden.

Rovaniemi

☑ 016 / POP 62,231
Situated right by the Arctic Circle, the 'official' terrestrial residence of Santa Claus is
the capital of Finnish Lapland and a tourism boom town. Its wonderful Arktikum
museum is the perfect introduction to these
latitudes, and Rovaniemi is a fantastic base
from which to organise activities.

Thoroughly destroyed by the retreating
Wehrmacht in 1944, the town was rebuilt to
a plan by Alvar Aalto, with the major streets
in the shape of a reindeer's head and antlers
(the stadium near the bus station is the eye).
Its utilitarian buildings are compensated for
by its marvellous riverside location.

⦿ Sights

A Culture Pass combination ticket (adult/
child €20/10) offering unlimited access to
the three major sights – the Arktikum, Pilke
Tiedekeskus and Rovaniemen Taidemuseo –
is valid for a week. Pick it up from the museums or the tourist office (p248).

Rovaniemi's concert hall, Lappia-talo (p248), is one of several buildings in Rovaniemi designed by Alvar Aalto; others include the adjacent library and town hall.

★ Pilke Tiedekeskus   MUSEUM

(Map p246; www.tiedekeskus-pilke.fi; Ounasjoentie 6; adult/child €7/5; ⊙9am-6pm Mon-Fri, 10am-4pm Sat & Sun mid-Jun–Aug, shorter hours rest of year) Downstairs in the Metsähallitus (Finnish Forest and Park Service) building next to the Arktikum, this is a highly entertaining exhibition on Finnish forestry with a sustainable focus. It has dozens of interactive displays that are great for kids of all ages, who can clamber up into a bird house, build a timber-framed dwelling, get behind the wheel of a forest harvester or play games about forest management. Multilingual touch screens provide interesting background information.

★ Arktikum   MUSEUM

(Map p246; www.arktikum.fi; Pohjoisranta 4; adult/child €12/5; ⊙9am-6pm Jun-Aug, 10am-6pm Tue-Sun mid-Jan–May & Sep-Nov, 10am-6pm Dec–mid-Jan) With its beautifully designed glass tunnel stretching out to the Ounasjoki, this is one of Finland's finest museums. One half deals with Lapland, with information on Sámi culture and the history of Rovaniemi; the other offers a wide-ranging display on the Arctic, with superb static and interactive displays focusing on flora and fauna, as well as on the peoples of Arctic Europe, Asia and North America. Downstairs an audiovisual – basically a pretty slide show – plays on a constant loop.

Konttaniemen Porotila   FARM

(Napapiirin Porofarmi; ☑040-099-1530; https://porofarmi.fi; Tamsintie 76, Napapiiri; 2hr farm visit summer adult/child €20/10, with winter sleigh ride €50/37; ⊙by reservation) Meet reindeer (including adorable calves in season) and find out about their life cycle at this reindeer farm 7km northwest of Rovaniemi. Tours complete with lunch (of, yes, reindeer) are available year-round, and sleigh rides are available in winter.

Rovaniemen Kirkko   CHURCH

(Map p246; www.rovaniemenseurakunta.fi; Rauhankatu 70; ⊙9am-9pm mid-May–early Sep) Completed in 1950, this church replaced the one destroyed during WWII. The impressively large fresco behind the altar depicts a Christ figure emerging from Lappish scenery. Created by Lennart Segerstråle, the fresco has two sides: one populated by the faithful, the other by brawling drunkards and ravening wolves.

Rovaniemen Taidemuseo   GALLERY

(Korundi; Map p246; www.korundi.fi; Lapinkävijäntie 4; adult/child €8/4; ⊙11am-6pm Tue-Sun) A wide collection of contemporary Finnish art rotates in the clean white exhibition space of this gallery in an old brick truck depot. Performances by the Lapland Chamber Orchestra regularly take place in its concert hall.

⚡ Activities

Bear Hill Husky   DOG SLEDDING

(☑040-760-0020; www.bearhillhusky.com; Sinettäjärventie 22; kennel tours incl sled ride adult/child €59/29, expeditions from €119/59; ⊙Jul-Mar) Wintertime husky-pulled sled expeditions start at two hours' duration (prices include transport to/from Rovaniemi). Overnight tours run on Saturdays from late January to March, with accommodation in a traditional wilderness cabin with smoke sauna. If you just want a taster, kennel tours, where you meet the Alaskan huskies, include a 1km ride with their mushers (sled drivers).

Husky Point   DOG SLEDDING

(☑040-079-0096; www.huskypoint.fi; Kittiläntie 1638, Sinettä; 90min kennel tour incl sled ride €125, 2-day sled tour from €350) Brilliant winter excursions with husky sleds range from short rides to multiday treks. It also does summer dog trips and reindeer visits.

Safartica   OUTDOORS

(Map p246; ☑016-311-485; www.safartica.com; Koskikatu 9; ⊙3hr reindeer sled tour €148, 4hr mountain-bike tour €121) In addition to reindeer-pulled sled tours and mountain-bike tours, this superb outfit runs river activities such as summer berry-picking trips (three hours; €75), midnight-sun lake floating in special flotation suits (three hours; €92), ice fishing

---

ARCTIC ANIMALS

Places to visit animals include **Konttaniemen Porotila**, a reindeer farm 8km north of Rovaniemi. **Husky Point** at Sinettä offers guided reindeer visits and sled rides in both summer and winter. **Arctic Circle Husky Park** (☑040-824-7503; www.huskypark.fi; Joulumaantie 3, Napapiiri; adult/child €10/5; ⊙11am-4pm Jun-Aug, 10am-4pm Sep-May) is near Santa's grotto and allows you to meet dogs and go on sled trips. The **zoo** (p248) at Ranua is an easy day trip from Rovaniemi.

(2½ hours; €89), snowshoe hiking (two hours; €69) and a snowmobile adventure (six hours; €192).

Ounasvaara   OUTDOORS
(☑ 044-764-2830; https://ounasvaara.fi; Taunontie 14; winter lift ticket per day €38, ski hire per day €38; ☺ winter activities early Nov–late Mar, summer activities late Jun–mid-Aug) This long fell across the river to the east of town is a place to get active. In winter there's a ski centre with 10 slopes, five lifts and 200km of cross-country trails. Come summer it offers mountain-biking (bike hire €20 per day) and a toboggan run (€10); walkers can take advantage of the cross-country skiing tracks.

Lapland Welcome   OUTDOORS
(Map p246; ☑ 020-735-2942; www.laplandwelcome. fi; Rovakatu 26; 5hr aurora tours from €89, hiking tours from €69, 3hr cross-country ski trips from €80) Aurora tours, hiking and cross-country skiing are among the excursions offered by this company, which has a good attitude to customer service and personable guides.

Lapland Safaris   OUTDOORS
(Map p246; ☑ 016-331-1200; www.laplandsafaris. com; Koskikatu 1; ☺ 4hr/overnight snowmobile tours €99/680) Lapland Safaris is the largest and best-established of Rovaniemi's tour operators, with a huge variety of options. Snowmobiling is big in winter; in summer there are hiking trips (six hours; from €99) and fishing excursions (three hours; from €89).

Rovaniemi Food Walk   FOOD
(Map p246; ☑ 040-488-7173; www.aittadeli.com; €50, with drinks €75; ☺ by reservation) Offering a taster of Lapland cuisine, these three-hour tours are a moveable feast, starting at streetfood restaurant Roka (p247), followed by a contemporary Finnish main course (such as slow-cooked reindeer or whitefish with pickled cucumber) at Aitta Deli & Dine (p247), and finishing with dessert and a cocktail at Cafe & Bar 21 (p247).

✨ Festivals & Events

Napapiirin Hiihto   SPORTS
(Arctic Circle Ski Marathon; www.napapiirinhiihto. fi; ☺ mid-Mar) The Arctic Circle Ski Marathon has events spanning 1km to 8km backpack cross-country skiing to marathon routes ranging from 20km to 70km.

Jutajaiset   CULTURAL
(www.jutajaiset.fi; ☺ late Jun/early Jul) Held over three days in late June and/or early July,

ARCTIC SNOW HOTEL

On Lehtojärvi's lakeshore, this **hotel** (☑ 040-769-0395; www.arcticsnowhotel .fi; Lehtoahontie 27, Sinettä; s/d/ste €180/260/350, glass-igloo tw €499; ☺ Nov–Mar; P) offers the complete snow-hotel experience and also has a snow restaurant as well as warmer eating choices. Alongside the snow hotel is an array of glass igloos (available from the beginning of December), ideal for aurora-watching. It's 26km northwest of Rovaniemi; pick-ups can be arranged.

The temperature of the ice-hotel rooms never gets above 5°C, but reindeer furs and sleeping bags keep you warm.

You can visit the complex (adult/child €15/8) even if you're not a guest.

Jutajaiset is a celebration of Lapland folklore, with music, dance and theatre at venues around town.

🛏 Sleeping

Rovaniemi's opportunities for aurora-borealis viewing, particularly in October, November and March, and its 'Christmas capital' status see prices peak at these times, when you'll need to book well ahead. Summer brings the cheapest rates.

Guesthouse Borealis   GUESTHOUSE €
(Map p246; ☑ 044-313-1771; www.guesthouse borealis.com; Asemieskatu 1; s/d/tr/apt from €58/68/99/175; P🕾) Friendly owners and proximity to trains make this family-run spot a winner. Rooms are simple, bright and clean, and guests can use a kitchen. Breakfast, served in an airy dining room, features Finnish porridge. The two apartments each have their own entrance and full kitchen; one has a private balcony and private sauna.

Santasport   HOTEL €€
(☑ 020-798-4202; http://santasport.fi; Hiihtomajantie 2; s/d/q from €84/104/174, s/d with shared bathroom from €50/68; P🕾🏊) A 15-minute stroll from the town centre at the base of Ounasvaara, this sports complex offers great value. Functional, modern rooms offer heaps of space and include fridge, microwave and drying cupboard; cheaper 'hostel' rooms share bathrooms. On site are a large swimming pool, spa facilities, bowling, gym, indoor play-park, and bike and cross-country ski hire.

Snow Sports

With snow on the ground for some six months a year, Finns know the best way to beat the long winter is to get out there and play in it. Skiing – both downhill and cross-country – is the most popular winter sport, but there are also dog-sledding and snowmobile tours.

1. Winter wonderland
Winter is Finland at its best. Embrace the cold with outdoor activities, set against a stunning backdrop of snow and ice.

2. Cross-country skiing
A pleasant way to see the landscape. For Finns, it's also a method of transport and a way to stay fit.

3. Huskies
Crossing the snowy wilderness on a sleigh safari pulled by a team of energetic huskies is a memorable experience.

4. Snowmobile safaris
If you prefer a motorised excursion, consider a snowmobile safari in Lapland.

Rovaniemi

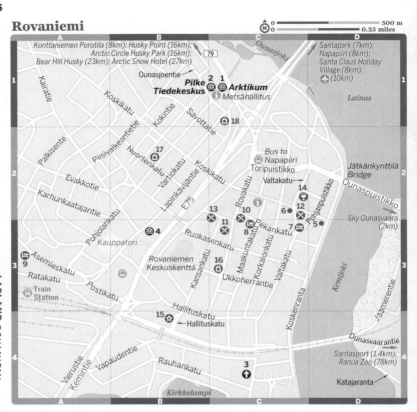

Rovaniemi

◎ Top Sights
1 Arktikum	C1
2 Pilke Tiedekeskus	C1

◎ Sights
3 Rovaniemen Kirkko	C4
4 Rovaniemen Taidemuseo	B3

⊕ Activities, Courses & Tours
5 Lapland Safaris	D3
Lapland Welcome	(see 10)
Rovaniemi Food Walk	(see 13)
6 Safartica	C2

🛏 Sleeping
7 Arctic Light Hotel	C3
8 City Hotel	C3
9 Guesthouse Borealis	A3

⊗ Eating
10 Aitta Deli & Dine	C2
11 Cafe & Bar 21	C3
Monte Rosa	(see 8)
12 Nili	C2
13 Roka	C2

⊜ Drinking & Nightlife
14 Kauppayhtiö	C2
Paha Kurki	(see 12)

✪ Entertainment
15 Lappia-talo	B4

⌂ Shopping
16 Katijuu	C3
17 Lauri Tuotteet	B2
18 Marttiini	C1

City Hotel HOTEL **€€**
(Map p246; ☎016-330-0111; www.cityhotel.fi;
Pekankatu 9; s/d/ste from €96/126/236; ☐⦿)
Epicentral City Hotel has 90 compact, stylish rooms with large windows and plush
maroon and brown fabrics, but it retains
an intimate feel. Luxe rooms offer proper
double beds (rather than two singles joined

together), while smart suites have a sauna. There are also two free saunas on the top floor and free summertime bike hire.

Sky Ounasvaara   HOTEL €€

(☑ 016-323-400; www.laplandhotels.com; Juhan-nuskallientie; d/tr/f/apt from €101/126/135/143; ☺ Jun-Apr; ℗ 🐾) Rooms here are functional, if plain, but most have private saunas; family rooms have a pull-out sofa bed. Snazzier apartments also come with saunas, as well as full kitchens, washing machines and living areas with fireplaces. Winter activities such as sledding and snowshoeing are on the doorstep. The excellent restaurant (p247) also opens to nonguests.

★ Arctic Light Hotel   BOUTIQUE HOTEL €€€

(Map p246; ☑ 020-171-0100; www.arcticlighthotel. fi; Valtakatu 18; d/apt from €150/349; ℗ ❄ 🐾) In Rovaniemi's former 1950s town hall, with original fixtures including wood panelling, a vintage lift and wrought-iron balustrades, Lapland's top hotel has handcrafted artworks adorning individually designed rooms (some with private saunas). Loft rooms have skylights for aurora borealis views; the two apartments sleep four, with separate living rooms. Buffet breakfasts are designed by Finnish-American TV chef Sara La Fountain. Breakfast highlights include superfood-powered energy shots, smoothies, traditional Finnish cakes, fresh local berries, homemade jams and locally smoked salmon, plus cooked-to-order bacon and eggs and pancakes..

🍴 Eating

Cafe & Bar 21   CAFE €

(Map p246; www.cafebar21.fi; Rovakatu 21; dishes €10-14; ☺ 11am-8.30pm Mon & Tue, to 9.30pm Wed & Thu, to 11pm Fri, noon-11pm Sat, noon-8.30pm Sun; 🐾) A reindeer-pelt collage on the grey-concrete wall is the only concession to place in this artfully modern designer cafe-bar. Black-and-white decor makes it a stylish haunt for salads, superb soups, tapas and its house-speciality waffles, along with creative cocktails. The bar stays open late.

★ Aitta Deli & Dine   FINNISH, DELI €€

(Map p246; ☑ 040-488-7173; www.aittadeli.com; Rovakatu 26; lunch buffet €10, platters €10-30, 4-course dinner menu €44, with paired wine or beer €69; ☺ restaurant 11am-4pm Mon & Tue, to 10pm Wed-Sat, to 3pm Sun, deli 11am-6pm Mon-Fri, to 3pm Sat) 🌿 Locally sourced, organic food at Aitta includes sharing platters piled high with reindeer heart and tongue, lingonberry and elk

stew, bear and nettle sausages, and rye and barley breads. Two- and three-course menus are available at lunch and dinner, but the pick of the dinner offerings is the four-course Taste of Lapland menu paired with natural wines or craft beers.

Nili   FINNISH €€

(Map p246; ☑ 040-036-9669; www.nili.fi; Valtakatu 20; mains €19-35, 4-course menu €56, with paired wines €100; ☺ 5-11pm Mon-Sat) A timber-lined interior with framed black-and-white photos of Lapland, kerosene lamps, traditional fishing nets, taxidermied bear and reindeer heads, and antler chandeliers gives this hunting-lodge-style spot a cosy, rustic charm. Local ingredients are used in dishes such as zandar lake fish with tar-and-mustard foam and reindeer with pickled cucumber and lingonberry jam, accompanied by Finnish beers, ciders and berry liqueurs.

Roka   INTERNATIONAL €€

(Map p246; ☑ 050-311-6411; www.ravintolaroka.fi; Ainonkatu 3; lunch buffet €9.90, street-food dishes €8.50-12, mains €15.50-23; ☺ 10.30am-9pm Mon-Thu, to 11pm Fri, noon-11pm Sat, noon-9pm Sun) With its exposed-brick walls, communal tables and blackboard-chalked menus, this post-industrial-style bistro is Rovaniemi's hippest eatery. Street food – such as sandwiches on homemade bread (beef brisket and horseradish mayo); grilled halloumi with red-onion compote and tzatziki), fish and chips, and braised pork belly – is its signature; mains include reindeer with roast beetroot and game sauce, and pan-fried pike.

Monte Rosa   STEAK €€

(Map p246; ☑ 016-330-0111; www.monterosa.fi; Pekankatu 9; mains restaurant €23-37, bar €10-28; ☺ 11am-11pm Mon-Fri, 5-11pm Sat & Sun; 🐾) Inside the City Hotel (p246), Monte Rosa goes for the romance vote with a low, candlelit interior and intimate booth seating. Char-grilled steaks are cooked to order; reindeer and local fish are also on the menu. Downstairs, the Bull Bar serves ribs and huge burgers out of the same kitchen.

★ Restaurant Sky Ounasvaara   FINNISH €€€

(☑ 016-323-400; www.laplandhotels.com; Juhan-nuskalliontie; mains €24-36, 5-course menu €69, with wine €127; ☺ 6-9.30pm Mon-Sat, to 9pm Sun Jun-Apr) For a truly memorable meal, head to the 1st floor of the Sky Ounasvaara hotel, where wraparound floor-to-ceiling glass windows onto the forest outside create the impression of dining in a tree house. Specialities include Lappish potato dumplings with local mushrooms, and reindeer tartare.

Drinking & Entertainment

Paha Kurki BAR
(Map p246; www.pahakurki.com; Koskikatu 5; 4pm-3am;) Dark yet clean and modern, this rock bar has a fine variety of bottled beers, memorabilia on the walls and a good sound system. A Finnish rock bar is what other places might call a metal bar: expect more Pantera than Pixies.

Kauppayhtiö BAR
(Map p246; www.kauppayhtio.fi; Valtakatu 24; 11am-9pm Tue-Thu & Sun, to 3.30am Fri, 1pm-3.30am Sat;) Almost everything at this oddball gasoline-themed bar-cafe is for sale, including colourful plastic tables and chairs, and retro and vintage toys, as well as new streetwear and Nordic clothing at the attached boutique. DJs play most evenings and there are often bands at weekends – when it's rocking, crowds spill onto the pavement terrace. Bonus: pinball machines.

Lappia-talo CONCERT VENUE
(Map p246; 040-028-2484; www.rovaniementeatteri.fi; Hallituskatu 11; box office 1-5pm Tue-Fri, 11am-1pm Sat & 1hr prior to performances) Concerts (mostly classical) and theatre productions (often with an Arctic theme) take place across the three stages of Rovaniemi's Alvar Aalto–designed concert hall.

Shopping

★**Lauri Tuotteet** ARTS & CRAFTS
(Map p246; www.lauri-tuotteet.fi; Pohjolankatu 25; 10am-5pm Mon-Fri) Established in 1924, this former knife factory in a charming log cabin at the northwestern edge of town still makes knives today, along with jewellery, buttons, felt boots and traditional Sámi items like engraved spoons and sewing-needle cases. Everything is handmade from local materials, including reindeer antlers, curly birch and goats willow timbers, and Finnish steel.

Katijuu FASHION & ACCESSORIES
(Map p246; http://katijuu.fi; Rovakatu 11; 10am-4pm Mon-Fri) Reindeer and elk leather, lambskin, and red fox, mink and marten fur are used by Lapland designer Kati Juujärvi to create hats, gloves and mittens, belts and fur collars, as well as clothing for men, women and children such as vests, jackets, dresses and trousers. Seasonal collections are named for places along the Kemijoki river.

Marttiini ARTS & CRAFTS
(Map p246; www.marttiini.fi; Vartiokatu 32; 10am-6pm Mon-Fri, to 4pm Sat Sep-May, plus noon-3pm Sun Jun-Aug) This former factory of Finland's famous knife manufacturer Marttiini is now a shop open to visitors with a small knife exhibition, and cheaper prices than you can get elsewhere. It's near the Arktikum (p242); there are branches at Santa Claus Village and at the Rinteenkulma shopping centre in the town centre, as well as one in Helsinki.

Information

Metsähallitus (Map p246; 020-564-7820; www.metsa.fi; Pilke Tiedekeskus, Ounasjoentie 6; 9am-6pm Mon-Fri, 10am-4pm Sat & Sun mid-Jun–Aug, shorter hours rest of year) Information centre for the national parks; sells maps and fishing permits.

Tourist Information (Map p246; 016-346-270; www.visitrovaniemi.fi; Maakuntakatu 29; 9am-5pm Mon-Fri mid-Aug–mid-Jun, plus 10am-3pm Sat mid-Jun–mid-Aug;) On the square in the middle of town.

Getting There & Away

AIR

Rovaniemi's airport (p303), 8km northeast of the city, is the 'official airport of Santa Claus' (he must hangar his sleigh here) and a major winter destination for charter flights. Finnair and Norwegian have several flights daily to/from Helsinki. There are car-hire desks, cafes, ATMs, money changers, a children's playground and a Santa Claus Post Office outpost.

Airport minibuses (016-362-222; http://airportbus.fi) meet arriving flights, dropping off at hotels in the town centre (€7, 15 minutes). They pick up along the same route about an hour before departures. A taxi to the city centre costs €20 to €30 depending on the time of day and number of passengers.

BUS

Express buses go south from the **bus station** (Matkahuolto Rovaniemi; Map p246; 020-710-5435; www.matkahuolto.fi; Lapinkävijäntie 2) to Kemi (€22, 1½ hours, up to six daily) and Oulu (€24, 3½ hours, up to eight daily). Night buses serve Helsinki (€83.90, 12¾ hours, up to four daily). Daily connections serve just about everywhere else in Lapland. Some buses continue north into Norway.

TRAIN

One direct train per day runs from Rovaniemi to Helsinki (€80, eight hours), with two more requiring a change in Oulu (€14, 2¼ hours). There's one train daily northeast to Kemijärvi (€11, one hour).

ⓘ Getting Around

Major car-hire agencies have offices at the airport and in town; book vehicles well ahead at peak times.

Bus 8 (Rovakatu P; Map p246; Poromiehentie) to the attractions at Napapiiri runs from the train station via the city and airport (€3.90, 25 minutes, up to five hourly 6.30am to 6.30pm).

Many hotels offer bike rental in summer for around €20 per day; sports complex **Santasport** (p243) also rents bikes to nonguests.

For a taxi, call **Taksi Rovaniemi** (☑ 020-088-000; www.rovaniemenaluetaksi.fi).

Around Rovaniemi

Santa Claus Village

The southernmost line at which the sun doesn't set on at least one day a year, the Arctic Circle (Napapiiri in Finnish) crosses the Sodankylä road 7.5km north of Rovaniemi (although the Arctic Circle can actually shift several metres daily). There's an **Arctic Circle marker** here; surrounding it is the 'official' **Santa Claus Village** (www.santaclausvillage. info; Tarvantie 2, Napapiiri; ⊙9am-6pm Jun-Aug, 10am-5pm mid-Jan–May, Sep & Nov, 9am-7pm Dec–mid-Jan) FREE, a touristy complex of shops, activities and accommodation including the **Santa Claus Holiday Village** (☑ 040-159-3811; www.santaclausholidayvillage.fi; Tähtikuja 2, Napapiiri; d from €109; P ☎) cabins, and the new **Snowman World** (http://snowmanworld.fi), with glass-sided apartments and a winter-only ice hotel complete with restaurant and bar.

The **Santa Claus Post Office** (www.santaclausvillage.info; Sodankyläntie, Napapiiri; ⊙9am-6pm Jun-Aug, 10am-5pm mid-Jan–May, Sep & Nov, 9am-7pm Dec–mid-Jan) FREE receives over half a million letters yearly from children all over the world. Your postcard sent from here will bear an official Santa stamp, and you can arrange to have it delivered at Christmas. For €7.95, Santa will send you a Christmas card.

At the tourist-information desk you can get your Arctic Circle certificate (€4.20).

But the top attraction for most is, of course, Santa himself, who sees visitors year-round in a rather impressive **grotto** (www.santaclausvillage.info; Sodankyläntie, Napapiiri; visit free, photographs from €20; ⊙9am-6pm Jun-Aug, 10am-5pm mid-Jan–May, Sep & Nov, 9am-7pm Dec–mid-Jan) FREE, with a huge clock mechanism (it slows the earth's rotation so that Santa can visit the whole world's children on Christmas

Eve). A private chat (around two minutes) is absolutely free, but you'll need to pay for official photographs (no other photography is allowed). You can also get a certificate of 'niceness' or of meeting Santa (each €7.95).

Other attractions include a husky park (p242); reindeer-pulled sleigh rides (on wheels in summer, traditional runners in snow; from €17/13 per adult/child for 400m); ice sculpting; and varying Christmassy exhibitions. Bus 8 heads here from the train station, via the city and airport.

Closer to Rovaniemi town centre, the separate Christmas theme park **Santapark** (https://santaparkarcticworld.com/santapark; Tarvantie 1; adult/child winter €33/27.50, summer €17.50/15; ⊙10am-6pm late Nov–mid-Jan, to 5pm Mon-Sat mid-Jun–mid-Aug) is linked by bus 8.

Rautiosaari

Also known as the Devil's Cauldrons, these 14 **glacial potholes** (Hiidenkirnut; Sukulanrakka, Rautiosaari; ⊙sunrise-sunset Jun-Oct) FREE were created some 10,000 years ago by melt water from frozen glaciers and polished smooth by rotating rocks. Three of the potholes, including the largest, the Devil's Soup Bowl (15m deep with an 8m diameter), are the biggest of Finland's hundred-plus such formations. Metal staircases let you descend into several of the holes. The site is 25km southwest of Rovaniemi off Rd 926 on the slopes of Sukulanrakka at Rautiosaari.

Ranua

Ranua's excellent **zoo** (Ranuan Eläinpuisto; www.ranuazoo.com; Rovaniementie 29, Ranua; adult/child €17/14; ⊙9am-7pm Jun-Aug, 10am-4pm Sep-May) focuses almost entirely on Finnish animals, although there are also polar bears and musk oxen. A boardwalk runs past all the creatures, which include minks and stoats, impressive owls and eagles, wild reindeer, elk, bears in a big paddock (they hibernate from November to March), lynx and wolverines. Kid-pleasing attractions include horse rides, mini-karts, pettable domestic animals and adventure courses. Ice-cream stops dot the route, and there's a cafe and lunch restaurant.

In November and from January to May, prices per adult/child drop to €15/13.50; in December, they rise to €18.50/16. The zoo is 78km southeast of Rovaniemi on Rd 78. Up to six daily buses serve Rovaniemi (€17.30, one hour).

Kemijärvi

📞 016 / POP 7749

Peaceful Kemijärvi sits on a spectacular lake and makes a good stop on your way north or south. The lake and the creations of the town's sculpture festival are the main attractions.

◎ Sights & Activities

Puustelli   GALLERY
(www.visitkemijarvi.fi; Lepistöntie 19; €5; ⊙ noon-6pm Tue-Sun early Jun-Jul) On the western side of town (take the path past the campground and keep going), this noble old building displays many of the wooden sculptures from past years of the Kuvanveistoviikko festival. Follow signs for 'Taidekeskus'.

Off-Piste Adventures   HORSE RIDING
(📞 040-963-9807; www.offpisteadventures.com; Sodankyläntie 1007, Kallela; 2hr trek €78, 20min sleigh ride €20; ⊙ 8am-8pm) Sleighing excursions pulled by well-loved reindeer or sturdy Finnhorses operate in winter; you can also ride the latter year-round. The stables are 14km north of town off the E63.

✲ Festivals & Events

Kuvanveistoviikko   ART
(www.kemijarven-kuvanveistoviikot.fi; ⊙ late Jun/early Jul odd-numbered years) Watch artists from numerous countries create their works at this wood-sculpting festival.

Ruska Swing   MUSIC
(www.ruskaswing.fi; ⊙ early Sep) Plenty of dancing takes place during this festival of swing, jazz and blues music.

⊨ Sleeping

★ Uitonniemi   GUESTHOUSE €€
(📞 016-320-7700; www.uitonniemi.fi; Uitonniementie 1; d from €105; 🅿 🛜) On Kemijärvi's lakeshore, with its own pier, this charming log cabin built in 2009 using traditional Finnish techniques has six rooms with exposed timber walls, kitchenettes and lake views. It has a cosy guest lounge and sauna, as well as a guest-only restaurant serving Lappish specialities. Ask about lake cruises crossing the Arctic Circle in summer.

Mestarin Kievari   HOTEL €€
(📞 016-320-7700; www.mestarinkievari.fi; Kirkkokatu 9; s/d/f from €88/105/210; 🅿 🛜) The 21 rooms are comfortable if fairly unadorned at this central inn. Some are in a newer wing, while others have a private sauna; spacious family rooms with sloping ceilings sit at the top. Its **restaurant** (📞 016-320-7700; www.mestarinkievari.fi; Kirkkokatu 9; mains €15-26, pizza €12-13.50, lunch buffet €12; ⊙ 6.30am-9pm Mon-Fri, 8am-8pm Sat, 8am-10am & 2-8pm Sun) is the best place to eat in town.

ℹ Information

Tourist Office (📞 040-189-2050; www.visitkemijarvi.fi; Vapaudenkatu 8; ⊙ 9am-3.30pm Mon-Fri) Helpful information desk in the town centre.

ℹ Getting There & Away

There are three buses on weekdays (one at weekends) to destinations including Pyhä (€10.10, one hour) and Rovaniemi (€17.30, 1¼ hours). One train runs daily to Helsinki (€87, 14 hours), via Rovaniemi (€11, one hour).

Pyhä-Luosto

The area between the fells of Luosto (514m) and Pyhä (540m) forms a popular winter sports centre. Most is part of Pyhä-Luosto National Park, and is excellent for trekking. Pyhä and Luosto both have ski slopes and are fully serviced resort 'villages'. They make value-packed, if quiet, places to stay in summer, with bargain modern apartments and log cottages available. Pyhä is 16km northwest of the main Kemijärvi–Sodankylä road, while Luosto is the same distance east of the Rovaniemi–Sodankylä road. A good road connects the two resorts, which are 25km apart.

◎ Sights

Pyhä-Luosto National Park   NATIONAL PARK
(www.nationalparks.fi) This park's core is the line of fells stretching 35km from Pyhä to beyond Luosto. It preserves old-growth forest with endangered plant species, the southern Lapland fell ecosystem, and *aapa* (open bog) areas harbouring snipe, bean geese, swans and golden eagles. Walkers are well provided for, with several marked trails, together with the resorts' network of ski trails.

Luontokeskus Naava   NATURE CENTRE
(📞 020-564-7302; www.nationalparks.fi; Luontotie 1, Pyhä; ⊙ 10am-6pm mid-Feb–late Apr & Jun-Sep, 9am-5pm Mon-Fri, 10am-5pm Sat & Sun Oct–mid-Feb) 𝗙𝗥𝗘𝗘 By the roundabout in Pyhä, this modern nature centre has a good exhibition on the geology and ecosystem of the area, information on Pyhä-Luosto National Park, and activities such as hiking and fishing. There's a decent cafe too.

Kopara
FARM

(☏ 040-840-9199; www.kopara.fi; Luostontie 1160; farm entry €5, sled rides from €35; ☺ 11am-3pm Mon-Fri early Jun-Sep, to 4pm daily Jan-Apr) Between Pyhä and Luosto (15km northwest of Pyhä and 8km southeast of Luosto), this farm is a good place to meet reindeer. You can go on a short walk that has information boards on the creatures, and tempt them closer with a feed bucket. In winter various sledding trips are on offer. Quality handicrafts are sold at its cafe, which specialises in blueberry pie in summer and, er, smoked-reindeer soup in winter.

Lampivaara
MINE

(☏ 016-624-334; www.amethystmine.fi; adult/child €18/10; ☺ 11am-5pm Jun–mid-Aug, to 4pm mid-Aug–Sep, to 3pm Tue-Sat Oct, to 2pm Mon-Sat Dec–mid-Apr) Situated 3km south of Luosto up on the hillside, this amethyst mine focuses on small-scale production for jewellery, using low-impact mining methods. Guided tours (English available) depart on the hour, and you get to dig for your own piece of amethyst. The mine is a 2.5km walk from Ukko-Luosto parking. In winter you can ski here or take the snow train from Ukko-Luosto parking (including admission adult/child €55/25; from Luosto €68/30).

🏃 Activities & Tours

Pyhätunturi & Luostotunturi
SNOW SPORTS

(www.pyha.fi; Kultakeronkatu, Pyhä; lift tickets per day/week €44/213; ☺ Dec–mid-Apr) At Pyhä there are eight lifts and 14 ski runs – the longest is 1.8km, with a vertical drop of 280m. At Luosto there are three lifts and seven runs, plus a half-pipe and snowboard slopes. Between them, Pyhä and Luosto have around 200km of trails for cross-country skiers, some 40km of which are lit. Lift passes are also valid for Ruka (p227).

Pyhä Safaris
OUTDOORS

(☏ 040-778-9106; www.pyhasafaris.com; Sädetie 1, Pyhä; snowmobile rental per 4hr/day €160/210, snowmobile safari per 2/6hr €75/175; ☺ Dec–mid-Apr) At the Pyhä roundabout, this outfit offers snowmobile trips, including two- and four-day expeditions as far as the Arctic Ocean in Norway on request, along with 30-minute reindeer sleigh rides (€75) and 30-minute husky-sledding rides (€85).

Lapland Safaris
OUTDOORS

(☏ 016-624-336; www.laplandsafaris.com; Orresokantie 1, Luosto; 3½hr snowmobile tour incl reindeer sleigh ride €151; ☺ Dec–mid-Apr) In

WATERFALL WALK

The highlight of this protected old-growth forest, 80km southeast of Rovaniemi off Rd 81, is the 16m-high **Auttiköngäs waterfall** (www.national parks.fi; Auttiköngääntie). It's reached by a 3.5km nature trail, which winds from the car park and traverses a suspension bridge above the Auttijoki. Bird life here includes black woodpeckers, redstarts and crossbills, and, if you're lucky, grey wagtails and golden eagles. Next to the car park, a small hut has displays on log floating and the timber industry and a summer-opening cafe. In summer you can forage for blueberries and lingonberries growing along the trail. Come winter, you'll need snowshoes to explore here.

winter, Lapland Safaris runs various jaunts on snowmobiles, along with husky-sledding excursions (two hours; €149) and snowshoe aurora tours (2½ hours; €68).

🛌 Sleeping

Along with some excellent hotels, the Pyhä-Luosto area has hundreds of cottages, cabins and apartments; local agencies **Pyhähippu** (☏ 016-882-820; www.pyhahippu.fi; Kultakeronkatu 4, Pyhä; ☺ 11am-7pm) and **Pyhä-Luosto Matkailu** (☏ 020-730-3020; www.pyha-luostomatkailu.fi; Laukotie 1, Luosto; ☺ noon-5pm Mon-Fri) offer online bookings. Rates at all properties spike during winter.

⭐ Santa's Hotel Aurora
HOTEL €€

(Aurora Chalet; ☏ 040-010-2200; www.santashotels.fi; Luppokeino 1, Luosto; d from €126, glass igloos from €362; ☺ Aug–mid-Apr; 🅿 🛜) At the Luosto slope, this is one of Lapland's most original and stylish hotels and a great winter hideaway. All rooms have their own sauna and many have an open fireplace; the wide floorboards and warm colours create a rustic, romantic ambience combined with modern comforts. From its 10 glass-roofed igloos, you can view the aurora borealis from your bed.

Otherwise, reception will text you when the aurora is visible – a nice touch that saves unnecessary shivers. The hotel's activity company can arrange snowmobiling and other expeditions.

Hotelli Pyhätunturi
HOTEL €€

(☏ 088-600-500; www.ski-inn.fi; Kultakeronkatu 21, Pyhä; d/chalets from €135/145; ☺ Jul-Apr; 🅿 @ 🛜)

Ski in and out of Pyhä's major hotel, located part of the way up the chairlift at the top of the road. Some of its 51 rooms and self-contained chalets have great views, as does the restaurant, which is romantically candlelit at night. A sauna, gym and Jacuzzi ease ski-tired muscles. Bike hire is available. Kids can be accommodated with cots or small beds.

Hotelli Luostotunturi
HOTEL €€

(☑ 016-620-400; www.laplandhotels.com; Luostontie 1, Luosto; d/tr/f/apt from €89/99/109/115; P @ 🛜 🏊) The rounded design of this 176-room hotel is supposed to resemble a reindeer's earmark. Most of the spacious rooms have a log-built balcony, and some have an extra loft-style sleeping space; apartments come with kitchenettes and saunas. Excellent facilities include an indoor pool, spa treatments, bike hire, three restaurants, a bar and the area's only nightclub.

❶ Getting There & Away

Two daily buses (four in winter) link Rovaniemi with Luosto (€28, 1¾ hours) and Pyhä (€31, 2¼ hours); these are the only buses connecting Pyhä and Luosto (€7.30, 30 minutes).

Buses also link Pyhä with Kemijärvi (€10.10, 45 minutes, three daily) and Sodankylä (€17.30, 1¼ hours, two daily).

FELL LAPLAND

Lapland's northwestern corner has some of the region's most breathtaking scenery. In winter its snowscapes are straight off a Christmas card, while in summer the mountainous terrain takes in green forests and icy-blue lakes, and the *ruska* (autumn leaves) season brings a kaleidoscope of colours. Finland, Norway and Sweden converge at the tip of the westernmost arm. Further south are the big winter resorts of Ylläs and Levi, which offer some of Finland's best skiing.

Ylläs

Amid breathtaking mountain scenery, Ylläs is Finland's highest skiable fell. On either side are the villages **Äkäslompolo**, in a pretty lakeside setting, and smaller **Ylläsjärvi**. Both are typical ski-resort towns with top-end hotels, holiday cottages, charter flights and winter activities. They shut down substantially in summer, when reindeer roam with impunity. Both villages are about 5km from their respective slopes.

◉ Sights & Activities

Skiing, snowboarding and other snow sports are the big draw in winter, while summer brings horse riding and mountain biking. The Yllästunturi Visitor Centre can advise on activities, as can hotels.

Yllästunturi Visitor Centre
NATURE CENTRE

(☑ 020-564-7039; www.nationalparks.fi; Tunturintie 54; ◷ 9am-5pm Jun-Oct, shorter hours rest of year) At the foot of the fell's western slopes, 2.5km from Äkäslompolo, this nature centre has a good downstairs exhibition on the local environment and way of life, as well as a cafe, maps, tourist information and advice on hiking in the park. It sells fishing licences and hires out snowshoes.

★ Sauna Gondola
SAUNA

(Gondoli Sauna; ☑ 040-738-5307; http://gondoli sauna.fi; Ylläs 1 Gondoli; up to 12 people €1350; ◷ 5-9pm late Sep-Apr) This four-person, timber-lined sauna is the world's only one in a cable-car gondola, which takes a 20-minute, 4km circuit from the top of the fell to the base (with a brief stop) and back again. The package, for up to 12 people, includes two hours' worth of trips, as well as the use of a mountaintop sauna and hot tub.

Ylläksen Vaellushevoset
HORSE RIDING

(☑ 050-436-1921; www.yllaksenvaellushevoset.fi; Kuerlinkantie 2, Äkäslompolo; 1/2hr trek €40/60; ◷ by reservation) Treks on Icelandic horses through the forest and along the lakes are organised year-round by this operator, which provides helmets, jackets and winter clothing. From June to October, when there's no snow, there are also eight-hour treks (€140) with picnic €160) either during the day or under the midnight sun. The stables are 9.2km southwest of Äkäslompolo off Rd 940.

Skiing

Finland's **highest skiable fell** (www.yllas. fi; Iso-Ylläsksentie 44; lift pass per day/week €39.50/188; ◷ late Oct-early May) has 63 downhill slopes and 28 lifts, including special areas for snowboarders. The vertical drop is 463m and the longest run is 3km. Cross-country skiing trails total 250km. Equipment hire and lessons are available.

Hiking

There are excellent hiking possibilities in this underrated area. Check the Pallas-Yllästunturi pages on www.nationalparks. fi for a list. A couple of long-distance treks head to Olos or Levi (54km and 50km);

there are several shorter trails, including the 12km **Kiirunankieppi (Ptarmigan Trail)** from the Yllästunturi visitor centre. Longer routes lead all the way to Pallastunturi (72km; p257) and on to Hetta.

Mountain Biking

In summer Ylläs is popular with mountain bikers, and you can take your bike up in the gondola lift to the top of the downhill trails (430m vertical descent).

Sport Shop CYCLING
(☑ 016-569-099; www.akaslompolosportshop. fi; Tunturintie 15, Ylläsjärvi; bikes per day €20-40; ☺ 10am-6pm Mon-Fri, to 1pm Sat & Sun) In the Taiga building at the base of the lifts on the Ylläsjärvi side, Sport Shop rents out bikes of all types.

🛏 Sleeping & Eating

In winter, the Ylläs area has 23,000 beds, but it's advisable to book well ahead. Most accommodation shuts in summer, but a few of the larger hotels stay open and there are plenty of cottages around. **Destination Lapland** (☑ 016-510-3300; www.destinationlapland. com) is the major booker.

Saaga HOTEL, CHALET €€
(☑ 016-323-600; www.laplandhotels.com; Iso-Ylläksentie 42; d/chalets from €110/124; ☺ hotel late Sep-Apr, chalets year-round; P ☎) Next to Ylläs' gondola lift, this ski-in hotel is the highest on the fell, and sells lift tickets and hires out ski equipment from its on-site shop. Most of its 84 modern hotel rooms have a balcony or terrace, and all have drying cupboards, and pull-out sofa beds accommodating an extra two people. Self-catering chalets sleep up to six.

★ Hotel Ylläshumina HOTEL €€€
(☑ 020-719-9820; www.yllashumina.com; Tiura-järventie 27, Äkäslompolo; s/d from €146/185, 2-/4-person apt from €250/327; ☺ mid-Aug–Sep & early Nov–mid-Apr; P ☎) Ski and hiking trails fan out from this complex of log cabins in Äkäslompolo, near the lake. Even the standard rooms, set in separate raised buildings, fit a whole family, with a loft sleeping area and kitchenette. Facilities include a full ski service, restaurant and pub; the sauna and outdoor hot tub are great after a day on the slopes.

Lainio Snow Village ICE HOTEL €€€
(☑ 040-589-0858; www.snowvillage.fi; Lainiotie 99; d/ste with shared bathroom from €260/387, cottages from €280; ☺ mid-Dec–mid-Apr; P)

Every winter, this ice hotel is built 16km east of Ylläsjärvi off Rd 80. It's a spectacular complex of buildings in a huge igloo with sumptuous rooms where you sleep in heavy-duty sleeping bags atop your icy bed. There's a neon-lit ice bar-restaurant (three-course dinner €60). Nonguests can tour the snow village (adult/child €8/4) from 10am to 9pm.

★ Restaurant Saaga FINNISH €€
(☑ 016-323-600; www.laplandhotels.com; Iso-Ylläksentie 42; mains €17-34; ☺ 4-10pm late Sep-Apr; ☎ ♿) Inside the Saaga hotel at the base of the ski slopes, this restaurant is Ylläs' best. Lapland specialities include buckwheat *blini* with white lake-fish roe from Inarijärvi, reindeer tartare with pickled mushrooms, roast arctic char with smoked-birch butter, and blueberry crème brûlée with cloudberry ice cream. Its kids' menu includes 'laughing frankfurters' and 'happy reindeer'.

❶ Getting There & Around

During the ski season, a shuttle heads from **Kittilä airport** (KTT; www.finavia.fi; Levintie 259, Kittilä) to Ylläsjärvi (€21) and Äkäslompolo (€24). Reservations are essential; book at http://yllasexpress.fi.

Local buses connect Äkäslompolo and Ylläs-järvi during the ski season (€7, 25 minutes, frequent). A **gondola lift** (www.yllas.fi; Iso-Ylläksentie 44; 1 trip/day pass €6/23; ☺ late Jun-Sep & Nov-early May) provides access to the top of the downhill trails.

Levi

One of Finland's most popular ski resorts, Levi has a compact centre, top-shelf modern facilities and a large accommodation capacity. It hosts many high-profile winter events and is also a very popular destination for hiking during the *ruska* (autumn leaves) season. There's enough going on here in summer that it's not moribund, and great deals on smart modern apartments make it an excellent base for exploring western Lapland, particularly for families.

Levi is actually the name of the fell, while Sirkka is the village, but most people refer to the whole place as Levi. The ski season runs from around late October to early May, depending on conditions; in December overseas charter flights descend at nearby Kittilä, bringing families in search of reindeer and a white Christmas.

◉ Sights

Samiland MUSEUM
(www.samiland.fi; Tunturitie 205; adult/child €12/9;
☉10am-8pm May-Nov, to 6pm Dec-Apr) Attached
to the Levi Panorama hotel at the top of the
main ski lift, this museum is a Unesco project. The illuminating exhibition gives plenty of good multilingual information on the
Sámi, including details about their traditional beliefs and reindeer herding, accompanied
by past and present photographs. Outdoors
on the hillside is a collection of traditional
kota huts and storage platforms.

🏃 Activities

Winter brings a full complement of snowy
activities, from husky, reindeer and snowmobile trips to snowshoeing and ice fishing. In summer, canoeing on the Ounasjoki
is popular, as is the mountain-biking park
(p254) on the ski slopes. The tourist office
can book most activities.

★Levitunturi SNOW SPORTS
(www.levi.fi; Hissitie; lift pass per day/week
€43.50/202.50; ☉late Oct-early May) Levi's
ski resort has 43 downhill slopes, many lit,
and 28 lifts. The vertical drop is 325m and
the longest run 2.5km. There are two snow
parks with half-pipes and a superpipe for
snowboarders, and several runs and free lifts
for children. Equipment hire and lessons are
available. Cross-country skiing is also superb
here, with 230km of trails, some illuminated.

PerheSafarit SNOW SPORTS
(☎016-643-861; www.perhesafarit.fi; Leviraitti
1; 2hr snowmobile or motor-sled safari from €115;
☉mid-Dec–Apr) Snowmobile and motor-sled
excursions take place around Levi Fell; some
include a visit to a reindeer farm.

Kinos Safaris OUTDOORS
(☎050-403-2000; www.kinossafaris.com; Myllyjoentie 1; 2hr snowmobile safari from €119) Kinos'
winter safaris include snowmobile trips
around Levi; other options include safaris to
reindeer and husky farms, ice fishing, aurora
tours and a sauna safari. Summer activities
range from stand-up paddleboarding and
jet-skiing tours to quad-bike safaris, fly fishing and canoeing. Snowmobile rental starts at
€160 per day; you can also hire fishing equipment, jet skis, canoes, kayaks and quad bikes.

Lapland Safaris OUTDOORS
(☎016-654-222; www.laplandsafaris.com; Kesk-
uskuja 2; 2hr snowmobile safari from €99; ☉Dec-

early Apr) Winter excursions run by Lapland
Safaris include snowmobile safaris, full-day
husky safaris (€417) and snowshoe hikes
(€66 for two hours).

Mountain-biking Park MOUNTAIN BIKING
(www.levi.fi; Hissitie; lift €4, bike hire per day €47;
☉10am-6pm Jun-Sep) The mountain-biking
park on the ski slopes is a popular summer
option. There are decent rigs available for
hire and you can take your bike up in the
gondola lift. Trails have a descent of 310m.

🛌 Sleeping

Levi is one of Finland's most popular winter
holiday centres, with 24,000 beds.

In addition to hotels, the town essentially
consists of holiday apartments and cottages;
Levin Matkailu Keskusvaraamo (☎016-
639-3370; www.levi.fi; Myllyjoentie 2; ☉9am-6pm
Mon-Fri, 10am-4pm Sat Jun-Apr, 9am-6pm Mon-Fri
May), in the tourist office, is the best place
to book these. Prices peak in December, and
from February to May.

Hullu Poro Hostel HOSTEL €
(☎016-651-0100; www.hulluporo.fi; Sivulantie 2;
dm €30-35; ☉Sep-Apr; Ⓟ) A well-equipped
budget option, this staff-less complex offers
rooms that have two single beds and a desk;
they share a decent bathroom, lounge area
and proper kitchen between two. Linen costs
an extra €18 per stay. It's more convenient
if you've got transport, as you must check in
and out at Hullu Poro hotel, 2km southeast.

★Levi Panorama HOTEL €€
(☎016-336-3000; www.golevi.fi; Tunturitie 205; d/
ste/chalets from €72/129/126; Ⓟ@🛜) High up
on the fell, with a great ski-in-ski-out area,
this stylish hotel has brilliant rooms with
lots of space, streamlined Nordic furniture,
big photos of Lapland wildlife and views
over the pistes. Superiors add a balcony, although most face the forest. There are several in-house restaurants and bars; you can
nip up and down to town on the gondola.

K5 Levi HOTEL €€
(☎016-639-1100; www.golevi.fi; Kätkänrannantie 2;
d/chalets from €132/154; ☉Nov–mid-Aug; Ⓟ@🛜)
Directly opposite the tourist office, this sleek,
modern hotel has spacious rooms with
checked fabrics in warm shades of red; most
come with a sauna and glassed-in balcony, or
a Jacuzzi. All have drying cupboards. There
are also good family rooms and two-storey
chalets. Numerous facilities include a bistro-
style restaurant, a bar and a gym.

Hullu Poro   HOTEL €€

(☑ 016-651-0100; www.hulluporo.fi; Rakkavaaran-
tie 5; d/f/apt from €102/154/182; P ☏) Friendly and informal, the 'Crazy Reindeer' is an
enormous complex of 146 rooms and 11
apartments, including family suites with
balconies, two-storey apartments sleeping
up to six that have full kitchens, and rooms
with private saunas. There are three restaurants (Finnish, Italian and pub fare) and a
spa complex. Cots for babies are available
free of charge.

 Eating

Jängällä   FINNISH €€

(☑ 044-086-0090; www.jangalla.fi; Tähtitie 4;
mains €19-34; ◷ 4-10pm Sep-Apr) Amazing
flavour combinations at this rustic-contem-
porary restaurant with rough-hewn timber
tables span roast wild boar with blackcurrant sauce, reindeer shank with lingonberry
hollandaise and an elk burger with tar mayo
on a rye bun to blueberry pudding with
salted-caramel cloudberries. Local produce
is also used in its craft cocktails, like Kettu
(birch-infused vodka, bilberry, soda, egg
white and bitters).

Panimo & Pub   FINNISH €€€

(www.levinpanimo.fi; Levinraitti 1; mains €19.50-
36.50, tapas plate €14; ◷ kitchen noon-10pm; ☏)
The atmospherically candlelit downstairs
Kellari restaurant cooks inventive dishes
such as gooseberry-stuffed reindeer, wild
boar and elk sausages or roast whitefish
with cranberry sauce. For a taster, order
the Lapland tapas platter. Upstairs, the bar
serves house-brewed beers and homemade
tar-wood liqueur, and opens to a terrace that
catches the evening sun.

ℹ Information

Tourist Office (☑ 016-639-3378; www.levi.fi;
Myllyjoentie 2; ◷ 9am-6pm Mon-Fri, 10am-4pm
Sat Jun-Apr, 9am-6pm Mon-Fri May; ☏) Behind
the tepee-like building on the roundabout in the
centre of the resort.

ℹ Getting There & Away

Levi is on Rd 79, 170km north of Rovaniemi.
Buses from Rovaniemi (€32.80, 2½ hours, four
daily) continue to Muonio (€13.70, 50 minutes).
A bus (www.tunturilinjat.fi; €8, reservations
essential) meets all incoming flights at Kittilä
airport (p253), 15km to the south.

Major car-hire franchises are at Kittilä airport;
they will deliver to Levi free of charge.

Muonio

☑ 016 / POP 2362

The last significant stop on Rd 21 before
Kilpisjärvi and Norway, Muonio sits on the
scenic Muonionjoki that forms the border
between Finland and Sweden. It's a fine base
for summer and winter activities, including
low-key skiing at nearby Olos. Most of the
town was razed during WWII, but the 1817
wooden church escaped that fate.

★**Harriniva**   OUTDOORS

(☑ 040-015-5100; www.harriniva.fi; Harrinivantie
35) Attached to the Arktinen Rekikoirakeskus, this excellent set-up has a vast program of
activities. In summer these include canoe and
boat trips (three hours; €50), midnight-sun
rafting trips (1½ hours; €45), foraging tours
(four hours; €50), and fishing (five hours;
€80) on the salmon-packed Muonionjoki.
In winter, try reindeer sledding (five hours;
€140) and snowmobiling (two hours; €110).

Arktinen Rekikoirakeskus   DOG SLEDDING

(Arctic Sled-dog Centre; ☑ 040-015-5100; www.har
riniva.fi; Harrinivantie 35; ◷ guided tour adult/child
€8/5, dog-sledding safaris 1½hr/2 days €90/580)
At Harriniva, the Arktinen Rekikoirakeskus
has over 400 lovable dogs, all with names and
their own personalities. A great guided tour
of their town departs up to two times daily. In
winter wonderful dog-sledding safaris range
from 1½-hour trips to excursions of two days,
a week or more. Multiday trips include meals
and hut accommodation.

Lomamaja Pekonen   GUESTHOUSE €

(☑ 040-550-8436; www.lomamajapekonen.fi; La-
henrannantie 10; s/d €45/60, cabins €40-50, cottages €75-95, apt from €95; P ☏) In the centre of
town, this appealing spot has cute red wood-
en cabins running up a slope just across from
the Muonionjoki, and more upmarket apartments and cottages behind them. There's
space for vans but not tents. It has canoes,
fishing equipment and bikes for hire, and organises guided trips on the river in summer.

★**Harriniva**   HOTEL, CAMPGROUND €€

(☑ 040-015-5100; www.harriniva.fi; Harrinivantie
35; s/d from €88/98, cabins d/q from €41/56,
tent sites €12 plus per person €5, glamping dome
€150; P @ ☏) Activities operator Harriniva
offers a wide range of accommodation. Hotel rooms are simple but attractively done
out in wood and have plenty of space; some
have their own sauna. There are also cabins
and tent sites by the river and, best of all,

LAPLAND MUONIO

state-of-the-art perspex glamping domes for aurora-watching; these have their own open fireplaces.

Swiss Cafe Konditoria CAFE €

(www.swisscafemuonio.com; Puthaanrannantie 5; dishes €2-6; ⊙10am-6pm May-Sep, to 5pm Oct-Apr; 🛜) Run by a Swiss confectioner, this cafe has great lattes, delectable hot chocolate, and sweet and savoury pastries such as smoked-reindeer pie, blueberry and apple pie, or white-chocolate truffle cake with almond brittle. It also sells his fantastic Lapland photographs and local arts and crafts.

❶ Information

Muonio has no tourist office, but information is online at www.tosilappi.fi.

❶ Getting There & Away

Muonio is at the junction of western Lapland's main two roads: Rd 21, which runs from Tornio to Kilpisjärvi, and Rd 79, which runs northwest from Rovaniemi via Kittilä.

Buses connect Muonio with Rovaniemi (€43.90, 3½ hours, three daily) and Kittilä (€15.50, 1½ hours, up to five daily).

Hetta

🗐 016 / POP 202

The spread-out village of Hetta, usually signposted as Enontekiö (the name of the municipal district), is an important Sámi town and a good place to start trekking and exploring the area. It's also the northern end of the popular Hetta–Pallastunturi Trek.

◉ Sights & Activities

There's a small **ski resort** (www.hettahii htomaa.fi; Peuratie 23; 1-day lift pass €25; ⊙1-7pm Tue-Fri, noon-5pm Sat & Sun Feb–mid-Apr) here in winter, and various guides offering husky, snowmobile and ski-trekking excursions.

Fell Lapland Visitor Centre NATURE CENTRE

(🗐020-564-7950; www.nationalparks.fi; Peuratie 15; ⊙9am-5pm Mar, Apr & Jun-late Sep, to 4pm Mon-Fri late Sep-Feb & May) This nature centre at the eastern end of town provides information about Pallas-Yllästunturi National Park (p257) and the Enontekiö region. There's an interesting exhibition on the Sámi and their nomadic history, lots of audiovisual presentations, as well as nature displays on the park and a cafe.

Hetta Huskies DOG SLEDDING

(🗐016-641-590; http://hettahuskies.com; Hetantie 211; 1/3hr safari €65/145) Based 2km west of town on Hetantie (Rd 93), Hetta Huskies runs reliably good husky-sledding excursions. You can meet the dogs at any time of year (adult/child €25/15) and go hiking with a posse of them (snowshoes €10 per person). Multiday tours, including hut accommodation and meals, range from a two-day journey (€475) to an epic eight-day adventure (€1775).

✨ Festivals & Events

Marianpäivät RELIGIOUS

(www.marianpaivat.fi; ⊙late Mar) Hetta's big festival is for three days around the feast day of the Annunciation. There are Sámi dances and parties, reindeer races, reindeer-lassoing competitions, sleigh rides and concerts, and the town buzzes with activity.

🛏 Sleeping & Eating

The main street, Ounastie, has several fast-food eateries, and from June to late September the Lapland Hotel Hetta has an evening restaurant. The petrol station has a shop and there's also a small supermarket.

Hetan Lomakylä CAMPGROUND €

(🗐040-020-5408; www.hetanlomakyla.fi; Ounastie 23; tent sites €14 plus per person €5, cabins €35-60, cottages €65-105; ⊙Mar-Oct; P 🛜) On the banks of the Närpistöjoki, with two riverside smoke saunas and a communal kitchen, this campground has grassy tent pitches, smart painted wooden cabins that share terraces with their neighbours, and cottages that come with kitchen, sauna and loft sleeping area.

★Ounasloma COTTAGE €€

(🗐016-521-055; www.ounasloma.com; Ounastie 1; cottages €73 plus per person €12; P @ 🛜) This family-run, riverside place has a series of wooden cottages in a well-kept area with a lake beach. The standard cottages are great for families; bigger ones are suitable for large groups. Some have an open fireplace. Linen costs €7 per person. Rowboats, bikes and sleds are free to use. In winter it arranges snowmobile safaris and ice fishing.

Hetan Majatalo GUESTHOUSE, HOTEL €€

(🗐016-554-0400; www.tosilappi.fi; Riekontie 8; d/tr/q hotel €104/126/148, d/q guesthouse €78/120; P @ 🛜) In the town centre, but set back in its own garden away from the road, this welcoming place offers two types of accommodation in facing buildings: clean, simple guesthouse rooms sharing bathrooms, and spacious wood-clad hotel rooms, some sleeping six, with private bathrooms and pyramid-shaped skylights. Rates include hearty breakfasts and use of the sauna.

Lapland Hotel Hetta HOTEL €€
(☎016-323-700; www.laplandhotels.com; Ounastie 281; d/ste/apt from €92/122/155; ☉hotel Jun-late Sep, apt by reservation year-round; P@☎≋) While Hetta feels old-fashioned, it has good facilities, including an indoor pool and straightforward but spacious renovated rooms – ask for one facing the lake. Two rooms are accessible for guests with disabilities. Apartments in the adjacent building have covered terraces and sleep up to six. Its restaurant serves evening meals involving reindeer, char and other Lapland staples.

🛍 Shopping

Hetta Silver JEWELLERY
(www.hettasilver.com; Ruijantie 15; ☉10am-5pm Mon-Fri) ✍ At the junction of the westbound and northbound roads, this local silversmith's workshop also produces pieces from antlers, horn, stone and gems.

ℹ Information

Head to the Fell Lapland Visitor Centre for information on the national park and trekking routes.
Tourist information (www.tosilappi.fi; Ounastie 165; ☉9am-4.30pm Mon-Fri) is available in the municipal building on the main road.

ℹ Getting There & Away

Enontekiö airport (ENF; www.finavia.fi; Hetantie 775) is 7km west of Hetta. It's mainly used for winter charters; scheduled services to Helsinki are infrequent.

Buses travel to Rovaniemi (€56.90, 4¾ hours, up to two daily) and Kilpisjärvi (€29.20, 3½ hours) via a swap-over at Palojoensuu. There are also buses to Hetta from Muonio (€15.50, 1¼ hours, one daily).

Pallas-Yllästunturi National Park

Covering 102,000 hectares, Finland's third-largest **national park** (www.nationalparks.fi) forms a long, thin area running from Hetta in the north to the Ylläs ski area in the south.

There are 350km of hiking trails, 80km of mountain-bike trails and 500km of cross-country skiing trails. The main attrac-

tion is the excellent 55km trekking route from the village of **Hetta to Pallastunturi** in the middle of the park, where there's a hotel, the Pallastunturi Luontokeskus nature centre and transport connections. You can continue from here to Ylläs, although there are few facilities on that section. In winter Pallastunturi Fell is a small but popular place for both cross-country and downhill skiing.

🏃 Activities

The 55km trek/ski from **Hetta to Pallastunturi** (or vice versa) is a Lapland classic and offers some of the best views in the country from the top of the fells. While there's plenty of up and down, it's not a difficult route, though long stretches of it are quite exposed to wind and rain – pack weatherproof gear. The route is well marked, and there are several wilderness huts along the way. The popularity of the trek means huts get pretty crowded at peak times. See www.nationalparks.fi for the route and wilderness huts.

The Hetta trailheads are separated from town by the lake. Various operators in town will run you across (around €10 to €15). Some can also drive your car to Pallastunturi while you are doing the trek (around €100). Contact the Fell Lapland Visitor Centre for operators. From Pallastunturi you can extend your trek a further 72km to the park's southernmost border, by the ski resorts at Ylläs. Good shorter walks include a 9km loop across the tops of Taivaskero and Laukukero.

🛏 Sleeping

The park has wilderness huts; Pallastunturi Luontokeskus (p258) and the Fell Lapland Visitor Centre in Hetta make reservations and provide keys for the lockable huts (€12 per person). At Pallastunturi the seasonally opening Hotelli Pallas has a wonderful natural setting.

Hotelli Pallas HOTEL €€
(☎016-323-355; www.laplandhotels.com; Pallastunturintie 560, Pallastunturi; d/q from €67/150, d with shared bathroom from €55; ☉mid-Feb–Apr & mid-Jun–late Sep; P☎) Built in 1938, this old wooden place up in the fells is just what a weary trekker wants to see. The upstairs rooms are the most modern. Connecting rooms are good for families; cheaper rooms have a toilet but share a shower. There's a good Finnish restaurant, a lakeside sauna (with winter ice-hole), and walks and skiing on the doorstep.

❶ Information

Pallastunturi Luontokeskus (☑ 020-564-
7930; www.nationalparks.fi; Pallastunturintie
557, Pallastunturi; ⊙ 9am-5pm Jun-Sep & mid-
Feb–Apr, to 4pm rest of year; 🛜) This nature
centre at Pallastunturi Fell sells trekking maps,
makes hut reservations and offers advice about
the region. The Hetta route leaves from here.

❶ Getting There & Away

From Monday to Friday, one bus runs from
Muonio (€7.40, 30 minutes) via Pallastunturi to
Kittilä (€18.70, 1¾ hours). In summer a return
service runs in the other direction. Otherwise,
you'll have to call a local taxi on ☑ 016-538-582.

Kilpisjärvi

☑ 016 / POP 114

The remote village of Kilpisjärvi, the northernmost settlement in the 'arm' of Finland,
sits on the doorstep of both Norway and
Sweden. At 480m above sea level, this small
border post, wedged between the lake of
Kilpisjärvi and the magnificent surrounding
fells, is also the highest village in Finland.
The main reason to venture out here is for
brilliant summer and *ruska* (autumn colour) trekking or spring cross-country skiing.

Kilpisjärvi consists of two small settlements 5km apart – the main (southern) centre has most services; the northern knot has
the hiking centre and trailheads.

🥾 Activities

Hiking is the big draw here. For aerial access
to remote hiking and fishing locations, take
a float plane or helicopter flight. Summer
lake cruises take you to within 3km of the
point where Finland, Norway and Sweden
converge, with a couple of hours to walk to
the tri-border marker.

Walking

The Kilpisjärvi area offers fantastic long
and short hikes. All trekking routes and
wilderness huts around the area are clearly
displayed on the 1:100,000 *Halti Kilpisjärvi*
map. See also www.nationalparks.fi.

Saana   HIKING

From the Retkeilykeskus, the ascent to slate-
capped Saana Fell (1029m) begins with a
gentle climb through woodland ending
abruptly in a thigh-straining 742 wooden
steps up the steeper part. From the top, it's
an easier gradient up the angled slate cap
to the highest point. When you come down,

you can continue right around the base of
the fell to make a long loop trail (10km plus
the ascent/descent of 3km each way).

Kolmen Valtakunnan Raja   HIKING

This route heads through Malla Nature Park
to Kolmen Valtakunnan Raja, a concrete
block in a lake that marks the treble border of Finland, Sweden and Norway. From
the car park 2.5km north of the **Kilpisjärven Retkeilykeskus** (Kilpisjärvi Hiking Centre;
☑ 016-537-771; www.kilpisjarvi.info; Käsivarrentie
14663; tent sites €12 plus per person €4, s/d €65/75,
2-/4-person cottages €82/92; ⊙ mid-Mar–late Sep;
Ⓟ 🛜) hiking centre, it is 11km, with a climb
through birch forest rewarded with an easy
but spectacular route along the hillside, with
great lake views below. A summer boat service leaves from below the Kilpisjärven Retkeilykeskus three times daily, dropping you
a 3km stroll from the border marker. This
allows an easy visit, or walking one way and
cruising the other. Near the border marker is
a free wilderness hut for overnighting.

Halti   HIKING

The 50km hike to Halti Fell (1324m), the
highest point in Finland, is a rewarding, reasonably well-marked trip. There are several
wilderness cabins along the route with res-
ervable sections. You can get close to the fell
by road through Norway.

Scenic Flights & Cruises

M/S Malla   CRUISE

(☑ 040-848-5494; www.mallalaiva.com; Lentosatama; single/return €20/30; ⊙ 10am, 2pm & 6pm
Jun-Sep) In summer, cruises depart three
times daily from Kilpisjärvi, sailing across
the lake to a dock 3km from the treble border marker at the meeting point of Finland,
Norway and Sweden. The return trip takes
three hours, with a 30-minute crossing each
way and two hours on the ground.

Polar-Lento   SCENIC FLIGHTS

(☑ 040-039-6087; www.harriniva.fi; Lentosatama;
10min scenic flight from €180) Polar-Lento runs
scenic flights in the Kilpisjärvi area in a floatplane, and can also provide chartered transport to remote lakes for fishing or hiking.
Flights to Halti and Sweden start at €480.

Heliflite   SCENIC FLIGHTS

(☑ 040-015-5111; www.heliflite.fi; Lentosatama;
⊙ 30min scenic flights from €310) Heliflite runs
scenic helicopter flights in the Kilpisjärvi area,
and can also be chartered for transport to remote lakes for fishing or hiking possibilities.

🛏 Sleeping

Lining the main road are several camp-grounds with cabins. Many places are open only during the hiking season (around mid-June to September).

★ Tundrea   CHALET, APARTMENT €€
(Kilpisjärven Lomakeskus; ☑ 040-039-6684; www.tundrea.com; Käsivarrentie 14188; chalet/apt from €93/149; P 🛜) Alongside the tumbling Tsahkaljoki, this riverside spot is the best of the clutch of cabin complexes in the centre of Kilpisjärvi. In addition to beautifully furnished wooden chalets and apartments with their own sauna, loft bedroom and fully equipped kitchen, there's a wood-and-stone restaurant (mains €13.50 to €32; open June to September) with an open fire.

ℹ Information

Kilpisjärven luontokeskus Visitor Centre
(☑ 020-564-7990; www.nationalparks.fi; Käsivarrentie 14145; ⊙ 9am-5pm late Mar-Sep, to 4pm Mon-Fri early-late Mar; 🛜) At the southern end of the village, this national-park centre is effectively the tourist information office. It has maps, advice on trekking and a nature display, and it sells fishing permits.

ℹ Getting There & Away

Buses connect Kilpisjärvi with Rovaniemi (€72.90, six hours, two daily) via Muonio (€34.50, three hours), Levi (€43.60, 5¼ hours) and Kittilä (€46.60, 5½ hours). In summer one heads on to Tromsø, Norway (€33.20, 3¾ hours).

It's a spectacular 196km drive between Muonio and Kilpisjärvi. There are petrol stations in Kaaresuvanto (where there's a border crossing into Sweden) and Kilpisjärvi itself.

NORTHERN LAPLAND

Sparsely populated and extraordinarily beautiful, with fells, lakes and forests, Lapland's north is a magical place for hiking, snow sports and learning about Sámi culture. At these latitudes, your chances of seeing the aurora borealis (Northern Lights) are high when skies are clear and dark.

Sodankylä

☑ 016 / POP 8739

Sodankylä is the main service centre for one of Europe's least populated areas, with a density of just 0.75 people per square kilometre. It's at the junction of Lapland's two main highways and makes a decent staging post between Rovaniemi and the north; even if you're just passing through, stop to see the humble but exquisite wooden church Vanha Kirkko. A contrast is provided by the high-tech observatory Aurora House just outside town, an important collection point for data on the atmosphere and the aurora borealis.

◉ Sights

Vanha Kirkko   CHURCH
(☑ 040-019-0406; www.sodevl.fi; Kirkkotie 1; ⊙ 9am-6pm Jun-Aug) FREE One of the few buildings in Lapland to survive the Nazis' scorched-earth retreat in WWII is this, the region's oldest church, dating from 1689. It stands in a graveyard encircled by a low wooden fence and is noteworthy for its decorative shingles and prominent prong-like standards. The interior is simple and charming, with gnarled wooden benches and pulpit, and a simple altar made from leftover beams. The stone church nearby was built in 1859.

Alariesto Galleria   GALLERY
(www.visitsodankyla.fi; Jäämerentie 3; adult/child €5/3; ⊙ 9am-4pm Mon-Fri) Above the tourist office, this gallery displays paintings by famous local artist Andreas Alariesto (1900–89), who depicted traditional Sámi life in an attractive naive style. It also has temporary exhibitions. There are good-value prints for sale.

Aurora House   VISITOR CENTRE
(Revontulikota Pohjan Kruunu; ☑ 040-514-2858; www.arcticacademy.fi; Välisuvannontie 13; up to 4 people €88; ⊙ by reservation) If you miss witnessing the aurora borealis, this 45-minute simulation in a purpose-built riverside tepee is the next best thing. Lean back on a reclining chair to watch images gathered over three decades projected on the ceiling while a local guide explains the science and folklore. You'll also hear radio signals as they hit the ionosphere. The centre is 11km south of Sodankylä.

🎪 Festivals & Events

Midnight Sun Film Festival   FILM
(https://msfilmfestival.fi; ⊙ mid-Jun) Dubbed the 'anti-Cannes', this four-day festival in mid-June sees the village's population double, with round-the-clock screenings in three venues, often attended by high-profile directors.

🛏 Sleeping & Eating

Sodankylä lacks standout sleeping options, so consider staying in Kemijärvi or Rovaniemi instead.

LAPLAND SODANKYLÄ

NORTHERN LIGHTS

The aurora borealis, an utterly haunting and exhilarating sight, is often visible to observers above the Arctic Circle, which is where a large portion of Lapland lies. The phenomenon is particularly striking during the dark winter; in summer the sun more or less renders it invisible. The aurora appears as curtains of greenish-white light stretching east to west across the sky for thousands of kilometres. At its lower edge, the aurora typically shades to a crimson-red glow. Hues of blue and violet can also be seen. The lights seem to dance and swirl in the night sky.

These auroral storms, however eerie, are quite natural. They're created when charged particles (protons and electrons) from the sun bombard the earth. These are deflected towards the North and South Poles by the earth's magnetic field. There they hit the earth's outer atmosphere, 100km to 1000km above ground, causing highly charged electrons to collide with molecules of nitrogen and oxygen. The excess energy from these collisions creates the colourful lights.

The ancient inhabitants of Lapland believed the aurora borealis was caused by a giant fox swishing its tail above the Arctic tundra. One of the Finnish words for the aurora is *revontulet* (fires of the fox).

To see the lights, you'd best have a dark, clear night with high auroral activity. October, November and March are often optimal for this. Then it's a question of waiting patiently outside, preferably between the hours of 9pm and 2am, and seeing if things kick off. If you've got a vehicle, don't bother paying for an aurora-watching trip. There are several useful websites for predicting auroral activity:

Geophysical Institute (www.gi.alaska.edu/AuroraForecast) Change the map view to Europe to view activity levels.

University of Oulu (http://cc.oulu.fi/~thu/Aurora/forecast.html) Finland-based page with links so you can make your own prediction.

Service Aurora (www.aurora-service.eu) Daily and hourly forecasts and text-message notification service; also runs excellent multiday **aurora-watching tours** (☎040-726-3534; http://tours.aurora-service.eu; 3-/4-night tours €995/1195; ⌚late Oct-late Mar).

Majatalo Kolme Veljestä GUESTHOUSE €
(☎040-053-9075; www.majatalokolmeveljesta.fi; Ivalontie 1; s/d with shared bathroom from €55/69; P@ᯤ) Situated 500m north of the town centre, this family-run guesthouse has small but spotless rooms with Ikea-style furniture such as wire storage units. Guests share decent bathrooms and have the use of a lounge and kitchen facilities (there's a big supermarket across the road). Prices include breakfast, sauna, tea and coffee.

Hotelli Karhu HOTEL €€
(Hotel Bear Inn; ☎040-122-8250; http://hotel-bearinn.com; Lapintie 7; s/d/tr from €105/115/125; Pᯤ) This central hotel offers old-fashioned but decent rooms with modern bathrooms. Some single rooms come with a cute mini-sauna. There's an on-site restaurant, but there are better options elsewhere.

Päivin Kammari FINNISH €€
(www.paivinkammari.fi; Jäämerentie 11; lunch buffet €10.80, mains €15-28; ⌚10am-9pm Mon-Sat, noon-6pm Sun; ᯤ) Cosy and homelike, this is the best eating spot in town, with a good-value lunch buffet, soups, quiches and cakes, along with hearty mains incorporating local *muikku* (vendace, or whitefish; a small lake fish) and reindeer. Tables set up on the street-side terrace in warm weather.

Shopping

Taigakoru JEWELLERY
(www.taigakoru.fi; Sompiontie 4; ⌚10am-6pm Mon-Fri, to 3pm Sat) In the centre of town, this jewellery shop is famous hereabouts for the gold and silver works of goldsmith Seppo Penttinen.

Information

Tourist Office (☎040-746-9776; www.visitsodankyla.fi; Jäämerentie 3; ⌚9am-4pm Mon-Fri) At the intersection of the Kemijärvi and Rovaniemi roads.

Getting There & Away

Sodankylä is on the main Rovaniemi–Ivalo road (E75), and the E63 from Kemijärvi and Karelia ends here.

Buses serve Rovaniemi (€27.10, two hours, four daily), Ivalo (€31.40, two hours, four daily) and Kemijärvi (€20.40, two hours, three daily Monday to Friday, one Saturday and Sunday).

Saariselkä

📞 016 / POP 354

The bustling, touristy village of Saariselkä (Sámi: Suolocielgi), 250km north of the Arctic Circle, is more resort than community, as it's basically a collection of enormous hotels and holiday cottages, but it's a great spot to get active. It's a major winter destination for Christmassy experiences, sled safaris and skiing, and in summer it serves as the main base for trekkers heading into the awesome Saariselkä Wilderness (p263).

🏃 Activities

Saariselkä bristles with things to do year-round. Things are most active in winter, with numerous snowy excursions, such as husky and reindeer sledding, snowmobiling and ice-fishing trips, organised by the many companies in town. In summer options include visiting the gold-panning settlement of Tankavaara (p262), reindeer farms, canoeing, fishing, white-water rafting and various guided walks.

Ski Saariselkä   SNOW SPORTS
(http://skisaariselka.fi; Kullanhuuhtojantie; ski pass per day/week €37/132; ⊙late Nov-May) Ski Saariselkä's 15 downhill slopes are served by six lifts; the longest run is 1300m and the vertical drop is 180m. There's also a freestyle park and some 240km of cross-country trails, some lit. Saariselkä is known for snow-kiting; lessons are available.

Husky & Co   DOG SLEDDING
(📞044-729-0006; www.huskyco.fi; Hirvaspirtti 1; 1hr summer farm tour adult/child €40/20, 2½hr summer husky hike €80/40, 3/5hr winter safari €135/170) Husky & Co has more than 250 dogs and offers great-value sledding safaris in winter, and farm tours and hikes with huskies (one dog per person) in summer. Other activities include reindeer sleigh rides, quad-bike tours and aurora tours.

LuontoLoma/Pro Safaris   RAFTING
(📞016-668-706; www.lapinluontolomat.fi; Lutontie 3; 3hr rafting trip €90; ⊙by reservation) Ride the rapids on a three-hour rafting jaunt organised by this outfit. In summer it also rents canoes and kayaks (€50 per day) and mountain

bikes (from €35 per day); in winter you can hire skis or snowshoes (each €15 per day) and snowmobiles (€200 per day).

Lapland Safaris   OUTDOORS
(📞016-668-901; www.laplandsafaris.com; Saariseläntie 13) Based at the Lapland Hotel Riekonlinna (p261), this is one of Saariselkä's major activity operators, with a full summer and winter program. Summer options include a 2½-hour mountain-bike ride (€71) and a five-hour hiking and fishing trip (€125); in winter highlights include a two-hour reindeer safari (€118) and a four-hour aurora-spotting snowmobile tour (€144). Children under 12 pay half-price.

🎉 Festivals & Events

Polar Night Jazz   MUSIC
(Kaamosjazz; www.inarisaariselka.fi/kaamosjazz; ⊙late Nov) Since 1982, this three-day jazz festival during the *kaamos* (polar night) has seen evening concerts and jam sessions take place in venues throughout Saariselkä and Inari, often under the aurora borealis.

🛏 Sleeping

Prices in Saariselkä's hotels are highest during the ski season and *ruska* (autumn-leaves season; late August to mid-September). Many rural cabins and cottages are available for rent. Ask at the Kiehinen (p262) nature centre, or browse the Lomarengas (p298) website. Accommodation service **Saariselän Keskusvaraamo** (📞016-554-0500; www.saariselka.com; Honkapolku 2; ⊙9am-4.30pm Mon-Thu, to 4pm Fri) can book a wide range of cabins, cottages and apartments in and around the village.

Saariselkä Inn   INN €
(📞044-729-0006; www.saariselkainn.com; Saariseläntie 10; d/tr/apt from €66/128/138; 🅿🛜) In the heart of Saariselkä, this friendly village pub brews its own beer and offers good accommodation in a variety of neighbouring buildings. Rooms are spacious and warm, with en suite bathrooms and comfortable mattresses; they're an absolute steal in summer. Apartments are equipped with saunas. A simple breakfast is served in winter only.

Lapland Hotel Riekonlinna   HOTEL €€
(📞016-559-4455; www.laplandhotels.com; Saariseläntie 13; d/ste/apt from €114/128/150; 🅿@🛜) Some of the spacious rooms at this central 232-room hotel come with saunas and all have balconies. Apartments sleeping up to six people are in a separate building 100m

away and are great for families, with fully equipped kitchens, drying cupboards, saunas and private parking with heating. Top-notch amenities include two restaurants and activities operator Lapland Safaris (p261).

Santa's Hotel Tunturi
HOTEL €€€

(☑016-681-501; www.santashotels.fi; Lutontie 3; d/ste from €166/283, 2-/4-person apt €222/350; ☺Jun-Apr; P@☎) With 266 rooms, this vast complex sprawls across six buildings, but it hasn't lost its traditional roots or excellent service. There are numerous grades of room and apartment; all but the standards come with their own sauna, and many also have a balcony. The most modern are the enticing superiors and suites. Prices drop in summer.

✕ Eating

Restaurant Kaunispään Huippu
CAFE €€

(☑016-668-803; www.kaunispaanhuippu.fi; Kaunispää; mains incl salad buffet €21-32.50; ☺10am-5pm, closed May & Oct) Attached to the Kaunispään Huippu arts-and-crafts shop, this panoramic restaurant on top of Kaunispää fell has views across to Russia. Smoked-reindeer mousse with blackcurrant sauce, willow-grouse breast with Inarijärvi vendace roe, roast elk with morel sauce, and oatmeal pie with salmon and arctic char are among the savoury dishes; afterwards, don't miss the crowberry jam–filled doughnuts.

Laanilan Kievari
FINNISH €€

(☑040-023-9868; www.laanilankievari.fi; Sateenkaarenpääntie 9; lunch buffet €7.90, dinner mains €27-39.50; ☺11am-3pm, dinner by reservation early Jun–mid-May) Off the main road 2.5km south of Saariselkä, this cute wooden hut with a roaring open fire has good-value lunch buffets. It's well worth booking in for dinner, though, when the game-oriented mains might include wood pigeon or elk fillet. In winter a small pond is cut into the ice for you to brave after you use the on-site sauna.

Petronella
FINNISH €€€

(☑016-668-930; http://ravintolapetronella.fi; Honkapolku 5; mains €17-43; ☺3-11pm Sep-late Apr) A wood-and-stone-decorated dining room sets the stage for artfully presented Lappish food such as roast snow grouse with thyme-nettle jus, arctic char flambéed in brandy, or reindeer sirloin with lingonberry -pepper sauce.

🛍 Shopping

Kaunispään Huippu
ARTS & CRAFTS

(www.kaunispaanhuippu.fi; Kaunispää; ☺10am-5pm, closed May & Oct) Inside this timber-lined shop, beautifully displayed traditional arts and crafts include jewellery made from gold, silver and local gemstones (Lemmenjoki garnet, Luumäki beryl, Luosto amethyst), knives handmade from Finnish steel, and handstitched clothing. There's also Sámi literature and local specialities such as crowberry juice, cloudberry sweets and tar liquorice.

ℹ Information

Kiehinen (☑020-564-7200; www.national parks.fi; Siula Centre, Kelotie 1; ☺9am-9pm Mon-Fri, to 4pm Sat & Sun mid-Jun–Aug, shorter hours rest of year) In the Siula building, just off the main road near the petrol station, this nature centre offers hiking information, cabin reservations, fishing permits, maps and a small nature display. It also contains Saariselkä's **tourist information desk** (☑040-168-7838; www.inarisaariselka.fi; Siula Centre, Kelotie 1; ☺9am-9pm Mon-Fri, to 4pm Sat & Sun mid-Jun–Aug, shorter hours rest of year).

ℹ Getting There & Around

Buses run from Rovaniemi to Saariselkä (€50.10, 4¼ hours, four daily), continuing to Ivalo (€7.40, 30 minutes).

From mid-November to early May a ski bus connects Ivalo, the major hotels, Saariselkä ski slopes, Kakslauttanen and Kiilopää several times daily (all-day ticket €5).

Four buses daily run to/from Kiilopää (€4.70, 10 minutes) for the Saariselkä Wilderness hiking trails, and Tankavaara (€7.40, 25 minutes).

Around Saariselkä

Tankavaara

Kultamuseo
MUSEUM

(www.kultamuseo.fi; Tankavaarantie 11C; adult/child €12/6, gold panning per hour/day €12/45; ☺9am-5pm Jun-Sep, 10am-4pm Mon-Fri Oct-May) In 1868 the remote area of Tankavaara on the Ivalojoki, 32km south of Saariselkä, experienced a gold rush, with a community of up to 500 panners seeking their fortune. The story is related in this museum, which also covers gold production around the world. A cubic metre of sand is on display, along with the sobering 2g of gold it normally contains here. In summer try your luck and pan for gold. There's an original smoke sauna and octagonal hut.

Tankavaara Nature Centre
NATURE CENTRE

(Tankavaaran Luontokeskus; ☑020-564-7251; www.nationalparks.fi; Tankavaarantie 11B; ⊙10am-5pm Mon-Fri Jun-Aug, 9am-4pm Mon-Fri Sep) FREE
Next door to Tankavaara's gold-panning museum, Kultamuseo, this nature centre has advice on activities and trekking in Urho Kekkonen National Park. Good exhibitions cover the local environment, including a display on raptors; you can also watch a half-hour audiovisual presentation. It sells maps and fishing permits, and has keys to the huts in the national park. Circular **nature trails** (1km to 6km) arc out from the centre.

Wanha Waskoolimies
CAFE €

(☑016-626-158; www.tankavaara.fi; Tankavaarantie 11B, mains €12-19; ⊙9am-9pm) By the entrance to gold-panning museum Kultamuseo at Tankavaara, this atmospheric cafe-restaurant actually predates the museum and serves typical Lapland dishes incorporating ingredients like Inarijärvi lake fish, Kittilä wild boar, Vuotso reindeer, and locally foraged berries and mushrooms. The attached Wild West Saloon has regular live music, billiards, darts and Finnish craft beers. You can also stay here in rooms (two/four people €98/118) or cabins (two/four people €70/80), or camp (€13).

Saariselkä Wilderness & Urho Kekkonen National Park

Saariselkä Wilderness, incorporating the 253,800-hectare Urho Kekkonen National Park and large tracts of protected forest, extends to the Russian border. It's a fabulous slice of Finland, home to bears, wolverines and golden eagles, plus thousands of free-grazing reindeer. This is a brilliant trekking area, with a large network of wilderness huts amid the unspoilt beauty of this huge expanse of forest, marshland and low fells.

◉ Sights

Saariselkä (p261) sits in the area's northwestern corner, while the gold-panning settlement of Tankavaara is in the southwestern corner.

Natural attractions in the wilderness area include **Rumakuru Gorge**, near the hut of the same name. **Luirojärvi** is the most popular trekking destination, including a hike up the nearby **Sokosti summit** (718m), the highest in the park. **Paratiisikuru** (Paradise Gorge), a steep descent from the 698m

Ukselmapää summit, and nearby **Lumikuru** (Snow Gorge), are popular day trips between Sarvioja and Muorravaarakka huts. Two historical **Skolt Sámi settlements**, with restored old houses, lie 2km south of Raja-Jooseppi, and 2km west of Snelmanninmaja hut, respectively.

🏃 Activities

There's some great hiking to be done on well-defined trails in the Saariselkä–Kakslauttanen–Kiilopää area. It's is divided into several zones, each with different rules. Although fires (using dead wood) are allowed in certain areas, take a camp stove, as fire bans are common in summer. A map and compass are *essential* for the most remote areas of the park.

Kiilopää, 17km southeast of Saariselkä, is the best launch pad; marked trails head directly into the wilderness from here. The *Saariselkä-Kiilopää* hiking map gives you a wealth of day-walk options. Short walks from here include the boardwalked ascent of Kiilopää Fell (one hour return), rewarded by great views.

For longer adventures, use wilderness huts as bases and destinations, and create your own itinerary according to your ability: an experienced, fit hiker can cover up to 4km per hour, and up to 28km per day. You will need to carry all food; water in rivers is drinkable.

The four- to six-day loop from the main road to Luirojärvi is the most popular, and can be extended beyond the lake. To reach areas where few have been, take a one-week walk from Kiilopää to Kemihaara campground.

The most remote route follows old roads and walking routes through the fells all the way from Raja-Jooseppi in the north to Kemihaara or Tulppio in the southeast.

🛏 Sleeping

There are 200 designated free camping areas as well as some 40 free wilderness huts, some with locked bookable sections. Book these (€12 per bed; shared sleeping), and private cabins, at any of the park visitor centres.

You'll need a sleeping bag and mat for the wilderness huts; bookable ones have mattresses. Visitor centres supply maps and details of huts, as does the www.nationalparks.fi website.

Suomen Latu Kiilopää
HOTEL, HOSTEL €€

(Fell Centre Kiilopää; ☑016-670-0700; www.kiilopaa.fi; Kiilopääntie 620; s/d from €74/82, apt from €107, dm €30, tent sites €25; P☎) Right at Kiilopää's trailheads 17km south of

Saariselkä Wilderness & Urho Kekkonen National Park

Saariselkä, this excellent facility has outlying buildings with simple, comfortable hotel rooms, a hostel (offering HI discount) with a small kitchen, as well as a variety of cottages and apartments. It also rents out bikes, and camping and skiing equipment (best to book), and can arrange guided treks.

There's a cafe-restaurant (packed lunch €9; dinner €23) and a traditional smoke sauna that's fired up regularly; it's free for guests and costs €10 for nonguests.

ℹ️ Information

There are national-park nature centres in **Saariselkä** (p262) and **Tankavaara** (p263).

The website www.nationalparks.fi has extensive information on the area.

MAPS

Three Karttakeskus maps are available for the area. The western part of the park is shown on the 1:50,000 *Saariselkä-Kiilopää* map; the 1:50,000 *Sokosti-Suomujoki* map will take you beyond Luirojärvi; the entire park is shown on the 1:100,000 *Koilliskaira* map. Visitor centres also sell a simpler map for day walks in the Saariselkä-Kiilopää area.

ℹ️ Getting There & Away

The easiest trailheads to reach are Saariselkä (p261) or Kiilopää. Buses link Kiilopää with

0 — 10 km
0 — 5 miles

714m ⊹

RUSSIA

Jaurujoki

Peskihaara
Mantoselkä
Korvatunturi Fell (483m)
Manto-oja
Vieriharju
Naltiojoki
Nuorttijoki
Kemihaara
⊹429m
Reindeer
Round-up Site
352m ⊹
Karhuoja
Nuortti
Recreational
Fishing Area
Tikkasen
Vieriharju
Mettopalo
Nuortti
Marjarova
Kärkekeoja
Sokli
Savukoski
(60km)
Tulppio

Ivalo (€11.80, 50 minutes, up to two daily) and Roveniemi (€47.20, four hours, one daily).

Buses to/from Ivalo (€6.80, 25 minutes, up to two daily) stop at Raja-Jooseppi border station. It's another starting point for treks, as it takes you directly into real wilderness.

Ivalo

☏ 016 / POP 3080

A small town by most standards, Ivalo (Sámi: Avvil) is a metropolis in these latitudes. With plenty of services and an airport that's particularly busy in winter, it's a useful place, though with few attractions. However, Inari's Sámi culture and Saariselkä's plentiful activities are close by.

Guesthouse Husky   DOG SLEDDING
(☏ 040-510-7068; www.guesthousehusky.fi; Hirviniementie 65; 1hr/4hr/day €106/187/293) Over 140 huskies live on this farm 5.5km southwest of Ivalo, which offers a variety of day trips and overnight or multiday safaris and winter sleigh rides. On guaranteed departure dates, couples won't have to pay for a minimum number of people. Longer excursions include your own husky team; this costs extra on shorter ones. You can also stay here.

Kamisak   HORSE RIDING
(☏ 050-570-7871; http://kamisak.com; Rovaniementie 915; 2/4hr ride €100/150) Year-round, Kamisak offers riding on native Finnish horses, from short treks to a five-day expedition costing €1250 including meals and accommodation. From November to April it also runs two-hour guided tours of its husky kennels that include a short sleigh ride. The property is 7km south of Ivalo.

★ **Guesthouse Husky**   B&B €€
(☏ 040-510-7068; www.guesthousehusky.fi; Hirviniementie 65; s/d/f from €78/98/121; ☉ Jun-Sep & Nov-Apr; ℗ ✳ @ 🛜) Surrounded by forest, this friendly, family-run husky farm offers great accommodation in a large rust-red wooden house built in traditional Finnish style. Spotless timber-lined rooms have bright fabrics and good showers; guests can use the small kitchen area and sauna, and meet the huskies and play with the puppies. In winter, home-cooked evening meals (two-/three-course menus €21/25) can be arranged.

Hotelli Kultahippu   HOTEL €€
(☏ 016-320-8800; www.hotellikultahippu.fi; Petsamontie 1; s/d/f from €89/104/175; ℗ 🛜) In the riverside 'Speck of Gold' pub (Kultahippu), rooms are unexpectedly stylish, with big windows (and, mercifully, mosquito netting). Several have private saunas; some have balconies overlooking the Ivalojoki. Bike rental is available for guests. The restaurant and bar are excellent, but try to avoid a room above the nightclub at weekends.

Kultahippu   FINNISH €€
(☏ 016-320-8800; www.hotellikultahippu.fi; Petsamontie 1; lunch buffet €11.50, mains €16-35; ☉ kitchen 11am-9pm, bar to midnight Sun-Thu, to 3am Fri & Sat) The cavernous, gleaming dark-wood dining room at the Hotelli Kultahippu

opens to a 120-seat sun terrace overlooking the river in summer. Finnish specialities include creamy salmon soup with house-made rye bread, Inarijärvi whitefish with sour-cream sauce, and reindeer fillet with roast wild mushrooms. The pub and club (11pm to 4am Friday and Saturday) are the main local nightspots.

❶ Information

Metsähallitus (☑ 040-168-9668; www.inari saariselka.fi; Ivalontie 10; ⊙ 9am-4pm Mon-Fri) Local and national park information.

❶ Getting There & Around

Ivalo's small airport (p268) is 9.5km southwest of the town. Finnair has direct flights year-round to Helsinki, and a new, direct seasonal winter service to London Gatwick; Norwegian also serves Helsinki. Some routes stop at small regional airports. Buses (€3.60, five minutes) serve inbound and outbound flights. There are car-hire desks and wi-fi but no ATMs or money changers.

Buses link Ivalo with Inari (€8.20, 30 minutes, up to four daily), some continuing to Norway; and Rovaniemi (€53.50, four hours, up to four daily).

Nellim
☑ 016 / POP 156

Situated on the shores of Inarijärvi 42km northeast of Ivalo, this tiny, tucked-away village is one of the major Skolt settlements and worth a visit for anyone interested in Sámi culture. There's also a significant Inari Sámi and Finnish population, and Nellim likes to dub itself the meeting point of three peoples.

On the last Friday in August, the Orthodox festival of St Triphon (p272) kicks off here. There's no bus service to Nellim, so you'll need your own transport.

Safari Service   CRUISE
(☑ 040-773-9142; www.safariservice.fi; Nellimintie 4204; 3hr cruise €250) Safari Service can take you out from Nellim for three-hour boat trips on vast Inarijärvi.

★ **Wilderness Hotel Nellim**   LODGE, CABIN €€
(☑ 050-430-7600; http://nellim.fi; Nellimintie 4230; s/d/f from €80/98/120, cabins from €120, 2-/3-bedroom apt €240/360; ℗) At this wonderfully remote lakeside property, the pick of the options are the 'aurora bubbles': perspex-domed cabins where you can watch the spectacle of the aurora borealis from the warmth of your bed from September to mid-April. Year-round there are timber lodge

rooms, log cabins and self-catering apartments. The buffet-only restaurant and bar serves craft cocktails and beers.

Inari
☑ 016 / POP 565

The tiny village of Inari (Sámi: Anár) is Finland's most significant Sámi centre and the ideal starting point to learn something of Sámi culture. Home to the wonderful Siida museum and Sajos (cultural centre and seat of the Finnish Sámi parliament), it also has a string of superb handicrafts shops. It's a great base for forays into Lemmenjoki National Park and the Kevo Strict Nature Reserve.

The village sits on Lapland's largest lake, Inarijärvi, a spectacular body of water with more than 3000 islands in its 1084-sq-km area.

❍ Sights

★ **Siida**   MUSEUM
(www.siida.fi; Inarintie 46; adult/child €10/5; ⊙ 9am-7pm Jun-Aug, to 6pm Sep, 10am-5pm Wed-Mon Oct-May) One of Finland's most absorbing museums, state-of-the-art Siida offers a comprehensive overview of the Sámi and their environment. The main exhibition hall consists of a fabulous nature exhibition around the edge, detailing northern Lapland's ecology by season, with wonderful photos and information panels. In the centre of the room is detailed information on the Sámi, from their former semi-nomadic existence to modern times.

Pielpajärven Kirkko   CHURCH
(⊙ 24hr) FREE This *erämaakirkko* (wilderness church) is accessible by a marked walking track (7.5km one way) from the parking area at Siida. If you're driving, there's another trailhead beyond here, from where it's 4.3km. In winter you'll need snowshoes. The area has for centuries been an important marketplace for the Sámi; the first church was erected in 1646. The present church was built in 1760 and restored in the 1970s. Open the shutters to get the full benefit (close them before leaving).

Sajos   CULTURAL CENTRE
(www.samediggi.fi; Siljotie 4; ⊙ 9am-5pm Mon-Fri) FREE The spectacular wood-and-glass Sámi cultural centre stands proud in the middle of town. It holds the Sámi parliament as well as a library and music archive, a restaurant, exhibitions and a craft shop.

🏃 Activities

Hiking opportunities in the area include the walk to the wilderness church Pielpajärven Kirkko, and a 9km trail from the Siida museum to the top of Otsamo fell. Other summer activities include lake cruises, scenic flights and horse riding; in winter there are snowmobiling safaris as well as aurora-watching trips.

Visit Inari — CRUISE

(☑ 040-179-6069; www.visitinari.fi; Inarintie 38; 3hr cruise adult/child €35/15; ☺ cruises Jun-Sep) From June (as soon as the ice melts) to late September, cruises on Inarijärvi sail to Ukko Island (Sámi: Äjjih), which is sacred to the Sámi. During the brief (20-minute) stop, most people climb to the top of the island, but there are also cave formations at the island's northern end. There are one or two daily departures from Siida car park.

Tuula Airamo — WILDLIFE

(http://visitinari.fi; Tulvalahdentie 235; 3hr visit per person €110; ☺ by reservation 2pm Mon, Wed & Fri) Friendly Tuula offers a great experience: over three hours, you visit her typical Lapland home, meet and feed reindeer, and learn traditional Sámi handicrafts. Advance online bookings are essential; there's a minimum of two people. It's 18km northwest of Inari via the Angeli road (Rd 9553).

Petri Mattus — WILDLIFE

(☑ 040-019-3950; Kittiläntie 3070; ☺ 2-4hr per 1/2 people €140/240) Head out on snowmobiles to feed the reindeer or, in May, watch calving and earmarking – depending on conditions, this could be an overnight trip. It's 30km southwest of Inari off Rd 995.

RideNorth — HORSE RIDING

(☑ 040-081-4424; www.ridenorth.fi; Koskelantie 70; horse riding/husky sledding from €65/115) Treks on beautiful, hardy Norwegian fjord horses take place year-round, while in winter you can take sled excursions with well-cared-for huskies. In summer you can go hiking with the huskies.

Ivalon Lentopalvelu — SCENIC FLIGHTS

(☑ 040-570-8369; www.lentopalvelu.fi; Inarintie 38; flights for up to 3 people from €200; ☺ Jun-Sep) The seaplanes parked in the lake do scenic flights and chartered trips around Inarijärvi.

✨ Festivals & Events

Skábmagovat — FILM

(http://skabmagovat.fi; ☺ late Jan) This indigenous-themed film festival (with many films in English) sees collaborations with groups from other nations.

King's Cup — SPORTS

(www.siida.fi; ☺ late Mar/early Apr) Held over the last weekend in March or the first weekend in April, this is the grand finale of Lapland's reindeer-racing season. It's a great spectacle as the beasts race around the frozen lake, jockeys sliding like waterskiers behind them. The semifinals are on Saturday and the finals on Sunday; plenty of betting livens things up.

Inari Viikot — CULTURAL

(www.inariviikot.fi; ☺ Jul) Over two weeks in the second half of July, cultural events include traditional village parties and markets, concerts and dancing, along with hiking trips, water sports and kids' activities.

Ijahis Idja — MUSIC

(Nightless Night; www.ijahisidja.fi; ☺ Aug) Over a weekend, usually in August, this excellent music festival features groups from all spectra of Sámi music.

🛏 Sleeping

Uruniemi Camping — CAMPGROUND €

(☑ 050-371-8826; www.uruniemi.fi; Uruniementie 7; tent sites €16, d with shared bathroom from €25, cabins €28-120; ☺ Jun–mid-Sep; P 🐾) The most pleasant place to pitch a tent hereabouts is this well-equipped lakeside campground 2km south of town. Along with campsites, there are basic rooms and cottages; facilities include a cafe and a sauna, and kayaks, boats and bikes for hire. Heated cottages are available year-round.

Tradition Hotel Kultahovi — HOTEL €€

(☑ 016-511-7100; www.hotelkultahovi.fi; Saarikoskentie 2; d with/without sauna from €140/110; P 🐾) This cosy Sámi family–run place overlooks the Jäniskoski rapids and has 45 spruce-furnished rooms, some with a great river view. All have been freshly renovated. Many have a drying cupboard and riverside balcony or terrace; some also contain a sauna. There's a fantastic riverside sauna too. The hotel's restaurant, Aanaar, serves delicious Lappish specialities.

Villa Lanca — GUESTHOUSE €€

(☑ 040-748-0984; www.villalanca.com; Kittilänratsuie 2; s/d/apt from €75/95/110; P 🐾) Atmospheric rooms at this central guesthouse are decorated with Asian fabrics, feather charms and real artistic flair. The cute attic rooms are spacious and cheaper; but lack a bit of headroom. Breakfast includes delicious homemade bread. It's a great place to learn about Sámi culture.

Hotelli Inari   HOTEL €€
(☑040-179-6069; http://visitinari.fi; Inarintie 40; s/d/apt from €119/130/180; P🐾🛜) On the lakeshore in Inari's village centre, this well-run hotel has spacious rooms with powerful showers. Those in the annexe have stylish grey-and-black decor and private saunas or glassed-in balconies for viewing the aurora. From December to April there's a two-night minimum stay. The restaurant (mains €15 to €28) serves local fish and reindeer alongside pizza and burgers.

🍴 Eating

The best restaurants are attached to hotels, but there are cafes in many of the main tourist sights, including the Sajos cultural centre and Siida museum. The village has a supermarket for self-caterers, as well as a small shop at the petrol station.

★ Aanaar   FINNISH €€
(☑016-511-7100;   www.hotelkultahovi.fi; Saarikoskentie 2; mains €13.50-31.50, 3-/5-course menu €43.50/62, with paired wines €62/85; ⊙11am-2.30pm & 5-10.30pm) 🐾 A panoramic glassed-in dining room overlooks the Juutuanjoki's Jäniskoski rapids at Inari's best restaurant, situated in the Tradition Hotel Kultahovi (p267). Seasonal local produce is used in dishes such as morel and angelica-root soup, smoked reindeer heart with pine-needle vinaigrette, grilled Inarijärvi lake trout with bilberry sauce and smoked beetroot, and Arctic king crab with nettle butter.

🛍 Shopping

Inari is the main centre for Sámi handicrafts, including silversmithing, antler carving and clothing, and there are several studios and boutiques in the village.

Inarin Hopea   JEWELLERY
(☑016-671-333; www.inarinhopea.fi; Inarintie 61; ⊙10am-7pm mid-Jun–Aug, to 5pm Sep, to 5pm Mon-Fri Nov–mid-Jun) You can watch gold- and silversmith Matti Qvick at work in his studio, which is filled with his traditional handmade jewellery (rings, bracelets, pendants, earrings and more, at all price points) based on Sámi designs and local wildlife such as Arctic foxes and Scandinavian lynx. He's been crafting here since 1982. Pieces can be custom fitted while you wait.

Sámi Duodji Ry   ARTS & CRAFTS
(www.duodjishop.fi; Siljotie; ⊙10am-5pm Mon-Fri) 🐾 In the Sajos (p266) building, this is the main shop of the Finnish association of Sámi craftspeople. It has a good range of Sámi books and CDs, as well as beautifully crafted silverware and handmade clothing.

Samekki   JEWELLERY
(☑016-671-086; www.saariselka.fi/samekki; Lehtolantie 5; ⊙10am-4pm mid-Jun–Aug, Mon-Fri only Sep–mid-Jun) 🐾 Down a small lane behind the library is the studio of Petteri Laiti, a famous Sámi artisan. The silverwork and handicrafts are very highly regarded; you'll often see the artist at work here.

❶ Information

Inari's **tourist office** (☑040-168-9668; www. inarisaariselka.fi; Inarintie 46; ⊙9am-7pm Jun-Aug, to 6pm Sep, 10am-5pm Wed-Mon Oct-May; 🛜) is in the Siida museum (p266) and is open the same hours. There's also a nature information point here.

❶ Getting There & Away

Inari is 38km northwest of Ivalo on the E75. Up to four daily buses run here from Ivalo (€8.20, 30 minutes). Shuttle buses serving **Ivalo Airport** (IVL; ☑020-708-8610; www.finavia.fi; Lentokentäntie 290; €30, 45 minutes) can be booked through Inari's tourist office website (www.inarisaariselka.fi).

Two direct daily buses serve Inari from Rovaniemi (€60.10, five hours). Both continue to Norway: one to Karasjok (€23.70, three hours) and, in summer, on to Nordkapp (€77.90, 5½ hours); and another to Tana bru (€37.60, three hours, up to four per week).

Lemmenjoki National Park

At 285,550 hectares, Lemmenjoki (Sámi: Leammi) is Finland's largest national park, covering a remote wilderness area between Inari and Norway. This is prime hiking territory, with desolate wilderness rivers, rough landscapes and the mystique of gold, as solitary prospectors slosh away with their pans in the middle of nowhere. Boat trips on the river allow more leisurely exploration of the park.

The launch pad is **Njurgulahti**, an Inari Sámi community by the river; it's often simply referred to as Lemmenjoki. It's 11km down a turn-off signposted 34km southwest of Inari on the Kittilä road.

◉ Sights

Sallivaara
HISTORIC SITE

(www.nationalparks.fi) Accessed off the Inari–Kittilä road, 70km southwest of Inari, this reindeer round-up site was used by Sámi reindeer herders twice yearly until 1964. Round-ups were an important social event, lasting several weeks and involving hundreds of people and animals. The corrals and cabins have been reconstructed, and you can overnight in one of the free huts (bring a tent in case they're full). There's top-quality birdwatching on nearby wetlands. From the parking area it's a 6km signposted walk.

Kaapin Jouni
HISTORIC SITE

(www.nationalparks.fi) This historic farm on the other side of the river from Njurgulahti was once the home of the 'reindeer king' Jouni Aikio. You can visit by organising boat trips from places to stay such as Ahkun Tupa.

🏃 Activities

Most trails start from Njurgulahti, including a family-friendly 4.5km marked nature trail. Marked trekking routes are in the relatively small 'basic area' between the rivers Lemmenjoki and Vaskojoki; a 20km loop between Kultahamina and Ravadasjärvi huts takes you to some of the most interesting gold-panning areas. Another route heads over Látnjoaivi Fell to Vaskojoki hut and back, taking you into the 'wilderness area', which has fewer restrictions on where to camp but no trail markings. For any serious trekking, you will need the 1:100,000 *Lemmenjoki* map. From Kultahamina, it's a 21.5km walk back to Njurgulahti along the river, via Ravadas, 6.5km closer. You can get the boat one way and walk the other.

Cruises

In summer a scheduled boat service operated by Ahkun Tupa runs from Njurgulahti village to the Kultahamina wilderness hut at Kultasatama (Gold Harbour) via the Ravadas falls. There are departures at 10am and 5pm from mid-June to mid-August; in early June and from mid-August to mid-September, only the evening one runs (one way/return €20/30, 1½ hours to Kultasatama).

🛌 Sleeping

Ahkun Tupa
CABIN, GUESTHOUSE €

(☏ 016-673-435; www.ahkuntupa.fi; Rd 9551, Njurgulahti; 2-/4-person cottages with shared bathroom from €40/50, d/q with shared bathroom from

---

BEAR'S NEST

At the edge of Myössäjärvi, 16km south of Inari, look out for the Karhunpesäkivi rest stop. From here, a 300m timber boardwalk (mainly comprising steps) leads through the forest to Finland's largest **tafone** (Karhunpesäkivi; www.inarisaarelka.fi; Myössäjärvi; ⊙ sunrise-sunset), a cave-like formation found in granular rock, and the only one in the world known to have shifted from its original base during the last ice age. You can enter the hollow boulder; although you have to crawl. The honeycomb-like structure is high enough to stand upright.

€30/40; ⊙ Jun-late Sep; P) This rustic waterside property 46km southwest of Inari has rooms, cottages and some farther-flung log cabins. All share bathroom facilities. It offers river cruises (from €10 for a runabout to €45 for a seven-hour day including gold panning) with commentary in English, and rents out canoes. The restaurant does lunch specials and salmon and reindeer mains (€8 to €28), including reindeer tongue.

Paltto
CABIN €

(☏ 040-028-7544; www.lemmenjoki.org; Lemmenjoen Kylätie 100; cabins from €65; ⊙ Jun–mid-Oct; P) This home of an active Sámi family has a felt studio (p270) selling some extraordinary works of art, as well as comfortable accommodation in log cabins, with access to a sauna and a boat. Excellent boat trips (from €70; minimum two people) range from half-day to full-day trips that can include Sámi yoiks (chants), meeting reindeer, gold panning and a traditional lunch.

Valkeaporo
CAMPGROUND, COTTAGE €

(☏ 040-039-4682; www.valkeaporo.fi; Lemmenjoentie 134; tent sites 1 person/2 person or family €10/20, cottages €50-120; ⊙ Mar-Sep) With splendid water frontage on spectacular Menesjärvi, this campground has smart cottages, good facilities, and boat and canoe hire (from €50 per day). You can also camp here. It offers four-hour boat trips (€30) and six-hour gold-panning boat trips (€50) on the Lemmenjoki. It's 1km northwest of the Lemmenjoki turn-off from the main Inari–Kittilä road.

Hotel Korpikartano
LODGE €€

(☏ 040-777-4339; www.korpikartano.fi; Meneskartanontie 71, Menesjärvi; s/d/apt from €85/96/157;

OFF THE BEATEN TRACK

FINLAND'S COLDEST COFFEE STOP

A great coffee-and-petrol stop between eastern and western Lapland, 105km from Inari on the road to Kittilä, **Tieva-Baari** (☎016-657-635; Inarintie 6595; dishes €3-11; ⏰9am-10pm Mon-Fri, 10am-10pm Sat & Sun), is located in Pokka, which is proud to be Finland's coldest place, having once registered a chilly -51.5°C (-60.7°F). The interior features stuffed birds, tropical plants, great doughnuts and a charismatic owner who isn't happy until the mercury hits -30°C (-22°F). It has simple cabins (€40 to €80) and camping (€10; June to August only), and can organise winter excursions.

P 📶) On the shores of one of the region's most beautiful lakes, 3.5km northeast of the Lemmenjoki turn-off from Rd 955, this remote wilderness lodge has colourful rooms (some with kitchenettes), rental equipment including skis, canoes and kayaks, and a flexible attitude that makes staying here a delight. Lunch is available for €18; a three-course evening meal is €29.

Shopping

Kammigalleria JEWELLERY

(☎040-744-3763; www.kammigalleria.fi; Lemmenjoentie 650; ⏰noon-6pm Tue-Sat Jun-Sep & by appointment) Male reindeer drop their heavy antlers in November: see beautiful jewellery and handicrafts that Kikka Laakso makes from them – and leather and bone – at this workshop on a reindeer farm on the Lemmenjoki road.

Paltto ARTS & CRAFTS

(☎040-028-7544; www.lemmenjoki.org; Lemmenjoen Kylätie 100; ⏰10am-5pm early Jun-late Sep & by appointment) Felt artworks and handicrafts are of extremely high quality at this artist's studio 1km west of Njurgulahti. It's also possible to stay in cabins (p269) here.

Getting There & Away

No public transport serves the area – some accommodation options can arrange transport for guests. Otherwise your own vehicle is essential (make sure you've fuelled up beforehand, as there are no petrol stations).

Inari to Norway

Norway stretches right across the top of Finland, and there are three main routes north from Inari: to the west via Karigasniemi (the most common Nordkapp route); north to Utsjoki; and east to Sevettijärvi. From Utsjoki, you can turn east along the fabulous Tenojoki to Nuorgam, the EU's northernmost village. The Kevo Strict Nature Reserve stretches between the western route and the northern one.

Karigasniemi

☎016 / POP 300

Right on the Norwegian border, the village of Karigasniemi (Sámi: Gáregasnjárga) sits on the picturesque banks of the Inarijoki, which becomes the Tenojoki 4km to the north when it joins the Karasjoki, and is popular with anglers fishing for the river's renowned salmon. It makes a handy refuelling stop for petrol as well as supplies. Locals speak Fell Sámi, the main Sámi language of northern Norway.

Tenon Eräkievari GUESTHOUSE, CABIN €€

(☎040-679-5320; http://tenonerakievari.com; Rovisuvannontie 59; s/d/tr €75/100/115, cabins €75-115; P 📶) In a great spot 8.5km north of town up the Utsjoki road on the banks of the Tenojoki, this peaceful property makes a good base for river fishing. Rooms and cabins all share bathrooms; there's an on-site cafe serving local delicacies like roast salmon and reindeer stew (mains €24 to €32). It often hosts events, so advance reservations are required.

Kalastajan Majatalo PUB, CABIN €€

(☎040-484-8171; www.hansabar.fi; Ylätenontie 32; d/cabins/apt from €122/100/70, tent or caravan sites €28; P 📶) In the village centre, Kalastajan Majatalo offers comfortable rooms, including 12 in a 2016-opened annexe, as well as apartments equipped with full kitchens, and simple cabins that share kitchen and bathroom facilities. The restaurant (mains €15 to €34) serves salmon, steaks, burgers and stews and has a small kids' menu.

Getting There & Away

Buses link Karigasniemi with Ivalo (€28.80, two hours, one daily) via Inari (€22, 1½ hours). Buses also run from Rovaniemi (€63.20, six hours, two daily) via Karigasniemi to Karasjok in Norway

(€17.30, 40 minutes). In summer that service continues to Nordkapp (€63.20, five hours).

The 100km drive northeast to Utsjoki is stunningly beautiful, but you'll need your own wheels.

Kevo Strict Nature Reserve

Some of Finland's most breathtaking scenery is within the 712-sq-km **Kevo Strict Nature Reserve** (www.nationalparks.fi) along the splendid 40km gorge of the Kevojoki (off-limits from April to mid-June). The main trail is 63km long (four days one way) and runs through the canyon, from the Sulaoja parking area 11km east of Karigasniemi on the road westbound from Kaamanen, to Kenesjärvi, on the Kaamanen–Utsjoki road. Be aware that hikers cannot hunt, fish or collect plants or berries, and must stay on marked trails.

The trek is rough with several fords – ask about water levels before heading off. The Guivi trail separates from the main trail and loops through fell scenery before rejoining the main trail further along: it's a 77km journey. You can also walk a return trip from Sulaoja. Use the 1:100,000 *Utsjoki Kevo* outdoor map.

Bring a tent if you plan to hike the canyon, as there's only one wilderness hut on the main route (there are another two on the Guivi leg). Camping is permitted within the reserve at 20 designated sites.

Ruktajärvi wilderness hut is at the gorge route's southern end near where the Guivi trail branches off, and Njávgoaivi and Kuivi are on the Guivi loop. There's also a simple turf hut between these two. There are cabins on the main road 500m south of the trailhead.

Catch the Karigasniemi-bound bus from Inari (€18.70, 1¼ hours, two daily) and ask the driver to drop you off at the clearly marked Sulaoja trailhead. From Kenesjärvi, buses run to Inari (€23.50, 1¾ hours, one daily) or Utsjoki/Nuorgam (€6.80, 45 minutes, two daily).

Utsjoki

📘 016 / POP 170

The border village of Utsjoki (Sámi: Ohcejohka) is strung out along the main road that crosses the Tenojoki into Norway over a handsome bridge. It's an important Sámi community. The river is the main attraction in these parts; head along its banks towards Nuorgam or Karigasniemi and you'll find several picturesque spots with cabins catering to families or groups of friends going fishing.

The tourist office can provide advice and maps for the Kevo trail and the various lessused trails that fan out from Utsjoki – the best is a 35km circular route with a wilderness hut at Koahpelásjärvi to overnight in.

Kylätalo Giisá   VISITOR CENTRE

(📞 040-822-8889; Utsjoentie 9; ⊗ 8am-6pm Mon-Fri, 10am-3pm Sat mid-Jun–Aug, 8am-4pm Mon-Fri Sep–mid-Jun) 🖋 The village hall, Kylätalo Giisá, has a handicraft shop and cafe.

Camping Lapinkylä   CAMPGROUND, CABIN **€**

(📞 040-559-1542; www.arctictravel.fi; Ringinvatro 14C; tent sites per 2 people €12, cabins €48-70, apt from €130; ⊗ Jun-Sep; P 🛜) Opposite the Kylätalo Giisá, the area's most central campground has a sauna, neat wooden cabins, and plenty of grass on which to pitch your tent. It also does terrific fishing trips and rents out boats (rowboats €25 per hour; €50 per hour with motor), and has heated apartments, which are also available in winter.

ℹ️ Information

Tourist office (📞 040-181-0263; www.nationalparks.fi; ⊗ 10am-5pm mid-Jun–mid-Sep).

ℹ️ Getting There & Away

Two buses daily link Utsjoki with Ivalo (€29.20, 2¼ hours) via Inari (€23.50, 1¾ hours). One continues to Tana bru (€16.80, 10 minutes).

Nuorgam & Teno Valley

📘 016 / POP 167

The 44km road from Utsjoki northeast to Nuorgam (Sámi: Njuorggan), the northernmost village in Finland (N 70°04'), is one of Lapland's most spectacular. It follows the Tenojoki, one of Europe's best salmon-fishing rivers, and a spectacular sight as its broad waters cut through the undulating dune-like landscape and across sandy spits and rocky banks. Most anglers gather near Boratbokcankoski and Alaköngäs Rapids (7km southwest of Nuorgam), but there are good spots right along this stretch, and the other way from Utsjoki, towards Karigasniemi, which is another beautiful drive following the Tenojoki and the Norwegian border.

Apart from fishing, there's not a great deal to do in Nuorgam, but it's a relaxing spot, and is the northern end of a great trekking route from Sevettijärvi.

There are many campgrounds and cabins catering to fishing parties scattered between Nuorgam and Utsjoki, and several more on the Karigasniemi road. The National Parks website (www.nationalparks.fi) has a full list.

Nuorgamin Lomakeskus CAMPGROUND, CABIN €
(📞 040-029-4669; www.nuorgaminlomakeskus.
fi; powered sites €20 plus per adult/child €5/3,
cabins €60-95, apt €90-170; ⊘ cafe & reception
Mar–mid-May, mid-Jun–mid-Aug & Sep–mid-Oct;
🅿 @ 🛜) The heart of village life, Nuorgamin Lomakeskus offers camping, cabins
and cottage apartments with the works. It
sells fishing permits, has a cafe-restaurant,
and sells the 'Nuorgam: Top of EU' T-shirt.
Book ahead for cabins, as anglers fill them
fast. It's possible stay here outside the
opening times if you make arrangements
in advance.

ℹ️ Getting There & Away

There are two evening buses from Rovaniemi
(€85.50, seven hours, two Sunday to Friday, one
Saturday) via Inari (€37.20, three hours), Inari
(€29.20, 2½ hours) and Utsjoki (€9.30, 30 minutes). The same service continues to Tana bru in
Norway (€6.80, 1¼ hours, daily in summer, four
times weekly in winter).

Sevettijärvi

📞 016 / POP 280

The road east from Kaamanen heads along
the shore of spectacularly beautiful Inarijärvi to the village of Sevettijärvi (Skolt Sámi:
Ce'vetjäu'rr), in the far northeast of Finland.
It's a remote area that merits exploration.

About 300 Skolt live in and around Sevettijärvi, which has a church (Orthodox, as the
Skolt were evangelised by the Russians back
in the 15th century), a shop and bar, and a
school, whose dozen-odd pupils are taught in
the Skolt language.

⊙ Sights

Kolttien Perinnetalo MUSEUM
(Sevettijärventie 9041; ⊘ 10am-5pm early Jun–early
Sep) FREE Kolttien Perinnetalo is a delightful little museum with photos, crafts and
memorabilia of the poignant Skolt history.
The Skolt traditionally used a system of four
seasonal camps, and other nearby buildings
show some of this way of life.

🏃 Activities

Sevettijärvi's namesake lake offers good fishing, as does the Näätämöjoki and, of course,
Inarijärvi; Porotila Toini Sanila sells licences. Sevettijärvi also has some excellent, remote, long-distance hiking trails. Winter
skiing trails are marked with blue poles.

There's fantastic trekking in this lake-
spangled wilderness. Though trails are easily followed, this is a remote area, so you'll
need a compass and the 1:50,000 trekking
maps for the area, available at tourist offices
throughout the region. Midsummer to early
October is the best time to trek due to swol-
len rivers and streams from winter melt water; trails close from December to May.

The **Sevettijärvi to Pulmanki trek** (60km
to 70km) is the most popular. The better of
two trailheads is just north of Sevettijärvi,
at Saunaranta. There are several mountain
huts along the route; after the last one, you
emerge onto a road at Arola by Pulmankijär-
vi, along which you can walk 20km to Nuorgam, or call 📞 016-678-356 for a taxi (it's best
to pre-arrange it so you're not stranded).

Other marked routes from Sevettijärvi
include the **Saamenpolku** (Sámi trail), a
circular trail of 90km that loops around to
Näätämö and the Norwegian border and
back. Expect plenty of river crossings. The
Inarinpolku is a 100km trek to the fjords of
the Arctic Ocean in Norway.

✨ Festivals & Events

St Triphon CULTURAL
(⊘ late Aug) The Orthodox festival of St Triphon is celebrated by the Skolt Sámi on the
last weekend of August. It starts in Nellim on
the Friday, then moves to Sevettijärvi, with celebrations and dances on the Saturday evening
and Sunday morning. Visitors are welcome.

🛏️ Sleeping & Eating

★ **Porotila Toini
Sanila** GUESTHOUSE, COTTAGE €
(📞 016-672-509; www.sanila.fi; Sanilantie 36; d
with shared bathroom €40-57, 2-/4-/8-person cottages €160/200/280; 🅿 🛜) 🌱 Run by a rein-
deer-owning family who taught at the local
school, Porotila Toini Sanila is a great place
to learn about the Skolt way of life. A series
of rooms across a few central buildings offer
simple, attractive comfort with shared bathrooms. Self-contained cottages also available.

ℹ️ Getting There & Away

Sevettijärvi has a bus service to Ivalo (€27.80,
2¾ hours, one daily Monday to Friday) via Inari
(€22, two hours).

There is no petrol station in Sevettijärvi; the
nearest is in the border village of Näätämö,
30km northeast.

Understand
Finland

FINLAND TODAY.............................274
One hundred years of independent Finland; see how things stand today.

HISTORY 276
A long-time battleground between Sweden and Russia, Finland has gone from strength to strength since WWII.

THE SÁMI 284
Reindeer, herded with all the latest technology, are still a big part of life for Finland's remarkable indigenous groups.

FINNISH LIFESTYLE & CULTURE 286
Saunas, summer cottages and long silences: Finns are an intriguing bunch.

FINNISH DESIGN 289
A byword for excellence, Finnish design has its roots in practicality and in the natural landscape.

THE ARTS 292
From epic bards' tales and the golden age of Finnish painting to the symphonic metal of Nightwish.

FOOD & DRINK 295
Stunning summer produce and new Suomi cuisine make for an exciting gastronomic landscape.

Finland Today

As Finland enters its second century as an independent nation, the country is engaged in domestic projects, including sweeping initiatives to combat climate change, and cross-border initiatives such as the Helsinki–Tallinn tunnel. The tech industry is also going from strength to strength, with Nokia relaunching under the new ownership of former employees. Since the start of the decade, it has been a legal requirement for Finns to have access to broadband, which now extends to 93% of the population.

Best in Print

Kalevala (Elias Lönnrot; 1835) Readable 'national epic' compiled from the songs of bards.

The Year of the Hare (Arto Paasilinna; 1975) Offbeat tale of hare-y travels.

Seven Brothers (Aleksis Kivi; 1870) Nineteenth-century Finnish classic.

Let the Northern Lights Erase Your Name (Vendela Vida; 2007) A New Yorker travels to Lapland in search of her Sámi origins.

101 Very Finnish Problems (Joel Willans; 2017) Hilarious examination of Finnish idiosyncrasies by a long-time Helsinki resident.

Tove Jansson, Life, Art, Words: the Authorised Biography (Boel Westin; 2014) Biography of author and illustrator Tove Jansson, creator of the Moomins.

Best on Film

Man Without a Past (2002) The second part of producer, writer and director Aki Kaurismäki's *Finland* drama trilogy, preceded by *Drifting Clouds* (1996) and followed by *Lights in the Dusk* (2006).

Miesten Vuoro (Steam of Life; 2010) Brilliant documentary of men sharing the stories of their lives in the sauna.

Tuntematon Sotilas (The Unknown Soldier; 1955) Considered Finland's greatest film about the Winter War, traditionally screened on Independence Day (6 December).

Century of Success

Since its independence from Russia in 1917, remote, forested, cold, sparsely populated Finland has had a hell of a century. It has propelled itself from agricultural backwater of the Russian empire to one of the world's most prosperous nations, with great standards of living and education, low crime, a practical, deep-rooted sense of environmentalism, strong cultural output and a muscular technology industry. During the centenary in 2017, Finns toasted a remarkable success story. Commemorative projects included the reopening of the Eduskunta (Finnish Parliament House) in Helsinki, and the creation of the country's 40th national park, the sprawling wilderness of Hossa National Park.

Climate Change

Southern Finland has encountered dramatically changed weather patterns, with much milder winters. The once-unthinkable prospect of a non-white Christmas in Helsinki is now a reality. Scientists in the Arctic are producing increasingly worrying data and it seems that northern nations such as Finland may be some of the earliest to be seriously affected. Though Finland will reap corn sown by bigger nations, its people and government are very environmentally conscious. Finland's own commitment to combating climate change is strong, having set a legally binding target in 2014 of 80% emissions reduction by 2050, and ratifying the Paris Agreement in 2016. A large nuclear-power sector is backed by an increasing percentage of renewable energy, and by 2030 the country will have a ban on diesel vehicles.

Economy

Once dominated by forestry, which has lessened in importance in line with the decrease in demand for paper due to digital reading habits, Finland's economy is now as much or more about technology and services. Although Finnish company Nokia initially failed to crack the smartphone market and was sold to Microsoft, it has bounced back. In 2016 the Nokia brand was bought by former Nokia employees, and next-generation Nokia phones launched in 2017.

The long-term economic outlook is positive, with a well-balanced economy built on strong foundations with a highly skilled workforce.

Helsinki–Tallinn Tunnel

Ambitious plans continue to formulate in Finland today. Most ambitiously of all, planning is progressing for the construction of a 92km-long tunnel beneath the Gulf of Finland linking Helsinki with Tallinn in neighbouring Estonia. In 2016 the EU provided additional money for the project, which will see travel times reduced from the current two-hour ferry trip to a 45-minute trip by road. It's expected to be completed by 2035.

Russia

The enormous eastern neighbour has been one of the main talking points in Finland since some time in the 12th century, when Russian power began to loom large over the land. Long experience with the Bear has stood Suomi in good stead, and the two countries have a strong relationship, with much exchange of commerce and tourism. It's a very important market for both import and export of goods and services, and any Russian counter-sanctions against the EU could cost Finland dearly. To that end, Finland, although a member of the EU, is not a member of NATO to keep onside with Russia. Nevertheless, Finns on the street are understandably nervous of a nationalistic Moscow, exacerbated by events such as the annexation of Crimea. Memories of bitter fights for freedom are too painful for national service and the army not to be taken seriously here.

Society

Finns are rightly proud of the strong foundations of their society. Famously high tax rates mean the nation is well equipped to look after its citizenry with some of the world's best health care and education. Despite the high excise on alcohol, Finns appreciate the reliable public transport and world-class universities, libraries and other infrastructure these same taxes afford. Like much of the world, the country is holding its breath as ageing baby boomers retire and it attempts to maintain high pensions.

In 2017 Finland became the first country in Europe to trial a basic universal income. The two-year pilot scheme provides unemployed Finns aged 25 to 58 involved in the trial with a guaranteed sum in place of their existing social benefits, which is paid even if they find work.

POPULATION: **5.5 MILLION**

AREA: **338,145 SQ KM**

PERCENTAGE OF FINLAND MADE UP OF WATER: **10%**

GDP: **€240 BILLION**

UNEMPLOYMENT RATE: **8.8%**

ANNUAL COFFEE CONSUMPTION PER CAPITA: **12KG**

if Finland were 100 people

91 would speak Finnish
6 would speak Swedish
1 would speak Russian
3 would speak other languages

electricity generation
(% of power sources)

Nuclear — 28
Fossil Fuels — 24
Hydro — 16

Imported Electricity — 15
Renewable Wood — 12
Peat — 5

population per sq km

FINLAND   DENMARK   UNITED KINGDOM

≈ 16 people

History

Finland's extensive history stretches from its pre-ice-age days through to its contemporary reputation as a tech hub. For centuries this cold northern land was used as a wrestling mat between two heavyweights, Sweden and Russia. Following its eventful emergence from their grip, it has gone on to become one of the world's most progressive and prosperous nations, which celebrated its centenary of independence in 2017.

Early Days

What is now Finland was inhabited way back: pre-ice-age remains have been found dating from some 120,000 years ago. But the big chill erased most traces and sent folk scurrying south to warmer climes. Only at the retreat of the formidable glaciers, which had blanketed the country 3km deep, was human presence re-established.

The first post-thaw inhabitants had spread over most of Finland by about 9000 BC. The people used stone tools and hunted elk and beaver.

One of the best places to learn about the Stone Age in Finland is the excellent Kierikkikeskus museum near Oulu.

Pottery in the archaeological record shows that a new influence arrived from the east to southern Finland about 5000 years ago. Because Finland was the furthest point west that this culture reached, it's suggested that these new people brought a Finnic language with them from Russia. If so, those who lived in Finland at this time were the ancestors of the Finns and the Sámi.

In the 1st century AD, the Roman historian Tacitus mentioned a tribe called the Fenni, whom he described as wild savages who had neither homes nor horses. He might have been referring to the Sámi or their forebears, whose nomadic existence better fits this description. Studies indicate that today's Sámi are descended mostly from a small original group, and some claim that a divergence of pre-Finnish and Sámi cultures can be seen as far back as 700 BC. Nomadic cultures leave little archaeological evidence, but it seems the Sámi gradually migrated northwards, probably displaced by the southerners and the advance of agriculture into former hunting lands. Verses of the *Kalevala*, which is derived from ancient oral tradition, seem to refer to this conflictive relationship.

TIMELINE	125,000 BC	9000 BC	3000 BC
	Present-day Finland is inhabited, as finds at Susiluola cave, near Kristinestad, indicate, but its residents, of whom little is known, are eventually evicted by the last ice age.	The retreat of the ice age's glaciers reopens the northern lands to human habitation. The forests and lakes that replace the ice provide tempting hunting and fishing grounds.	The appearance of distinctive 'Comb Ware' pottery indicates the presence of a new culture that seems to come from the Volga region to the east, perhaps bringing a pre-Finnish language with it.

Swedish Rule

The nascent kingdom of Sweden saw Finland as a natural direction for extending its influence in the Baltic and countering the growing power of Novgorod (later to become Russia) in the east. Missionary activity began in the 12th century, and legend tells of an Englishman, Bishop Henry, leading an expedition of baptism that ended stickily when he was murdered by Lalli, a disgruntled peasant.

Things started to heat up in the 13th century. The Pope called a crusade against the Häme tribe, which was increasingly influenced both religiously and politically from Novgorod, and Russian and Swedish forces clashed several times in the first battles of what became an ongoing saga.

Swedish settlement began in earnest around the middle of the century when Birger Jarl established fortifications at Häme and Turku, among other places. The cathedral at Turku was also under construction and this city was to be Finland's pre-eminent centre for most of its history. The Swedish knights and nobles in charge of these operations set a pattern for a Swedish-speaking bourgeoisie in Finland, which lasted well into the 20th century. Other Swedes, including farmers and fishers, gradually settled, mainly along Finland's Baltic coast. A number of incentives such as land grants and tax concessions were given to encourage new settlers, many of whom were veterans of the Swedish army.

Sweden's squabbles with Novgorod continued for two centuries. Treaties drawn up by the two powers defined the spheres of influence, with Sweden gaining control of southwest Finland and much of the west coast, while Novgorod controlled Karelia, spreading the Orthodox faith and Byzantine culture in the region.

In 1527 King Gustav Vasa of Sweden adopted the Lutheran faith and confiscated much of the property of the Catholic Church. The Finnish Reformation was ushered in by Mikael Agricola, who studied with Luther in Germany and returned to Finland in 1539 to translate parts of the Bible into Finnish. His hard-line Protestant attitudes meant that most of the frescoes in medieval churches were whitewashed (to be rediscovered some 400 years later in relatively good condition).

Sweden started another chess game with Russia in Savo and Kainuu, using its Finnish subjects as pawns to settle areas well beyond the agreed boundaries. Russia retaliated, and most of the new settlements were razed in the bloody Kainuu War of the late 16th century.

The 17th century was Sweden's golden age, when it controlled much of the Baltic. Finland was put under the control of various governors.

During the Thirty Years' War in Europe, political power in Finland was exercised by Count Per Brahe, who travelled around the country and founded many towns. He was a larger-than-life figure who made his own

Duke Karl, regent of Finland, didn't care much for the family business. Campaigning against his nephew the king, he encouraged a peasant mutiny in 1596 and finally deposed him, exacting brutal revenge on his opponents.

HISTORY SWEDISH RULE

As well as being the biggest landowner in Sweden, Per Brahe the Younger was a gourmet and wrote his own cookbook, which he took with him on his travels and insisted was followed to the letter.

AD 100	1155	1323	1527
The Roman historian Tacitus refers to the 'Fenni', most likely the Sámi, in the first known historical mention of the area. He isn't complimentary about their lack of permanent housing.	The first Christianising expedition is launched from Sweden against the pagan Finns. Further expeditions follow, and Finland is effectively under Swedish dominion for the next six centuries.	The Peace of Oreshek, signed by Sweden and Novgorod at Pähkinäsaari, establishes a frontier in the Karelian Isthmus, and delineates permitted spheres of influence still evident in present-day Finland.	King Gustav Vasa of Sweden adopts the Lutheran faith and confiscates much of the property of the Catholic Church. Finland's main Reformation figure, Mikael Agricola, returns from Germany in 1539.

rules: once censured for having illegally bagged an elk, he responded curtly that it had been on its last legs and he had killed it out of mercy.

Although Finland never experienced feudal serfdom to the extent seen in Russia, ethnic Finns were largely peasant farmers forced to lease land from Swedish landlords.

In 1697 the Swede Karl XII ascended the throne. Within three years he was drawn into the Great Northern War (1700–21) between Sweden and allied forces of Russia, Denmark and other Baltic powers, which marked the beginning of the end of the Swedish empire.

Tar, used to caulk sailing ships, was a major 19th-century Finnish export, produced by burning pine trees in a tar pit. Bark was removed from the trees four years earlier to stimulate resin production.

From Sweden to Russia

Peter the Great took advantage of Sweden's troubles and, though losing early engagements, soon stormed through Finland, which had been recently decimated by famine. From 1714 to 1721 Russia occupied Finland, a time still referred to as the Great Wrath, when several thousand Finns were killed and many more taken into slavery. The 1721 Treaty of Uusikaupunki brought peace at a cost – Sweden lost south Karelia to Russia.

Finland again paid the price for thwarted Swedish ambitions in the war of 1741–43, with Russia again occupying the country, a period called the Lesser Wrath.

Tsar Alexander I signed a treaty with Napoleon and then attacked Finland in 1808. Following a bloody war, Sweden ceded Finland to Russia in 1809. Alexander pledged to respect Finnish customs and institutions. Finland kept its legal system and its Lutheran faith, and became a semi-autonomous grand duchy. At first Russia encouraged development, and Finland benefited from the annexation. The capital was transferred from Turku to Helsinki in 1812.

Finland was still very much an impoverished rural society in the 19th century, and travel to the interior, especially in Lapland, could be an arduous journey of weeks by riverboat and overland. The tar and paper industries produced revenue from the vast forests, but were controlled by magnates in Baltic and Bothnian ports such as Oulu, which flourished while the hinterland remained poor.

A Nation Born

Early stirrings of Finnish nationalism could be heard in the 19th century. Dissatisfaction with the Swedish administration came to a head with a letter written from officers of the Finnish army to the queen of Sweden questioning the legality of the war they were pursuing against Russia. Meanwhile academic studies of Finnish cultural traditions were creating a base on which future nationalistic feelings could be founded.

1637	1640	1700	1714
Per Brahe the Younger becomes governor of Finland and goes on to found many towns. Meanwhile Finnish cavalry earns a fearsome reputation in the Thirty Years' War.	Finland's first university is founded in Turku, which is the country's principal city until Helsinki is made capital in 1812.	Karl XII of Sweden is drawn into the Great Northern War, which is to mark the beginning of the end for the Swedish empire.	Russia occupies Finland, marking the beginning of the seven years known as the Great Wrath. When peace is made, Russia retains southern Karelia.

The famous phrase 'Swedes we are not, Russians we will not become, so let us be Finns', though of uncertain origin, encapsulated the growing sense of Finnishness. Artistic achievements such as Elias Lönnrot's *Kalevala* and Johan Ludvig Runeberg's poem *Our Land,* which became the national anthem, acted as standards to rally around. As Russia tightened its grip with a policy of Russification, workers, and artists such as Jean Sibelius, began to be inspired against the growing oppression and the nation became emotionally ripe for independence.

In 1906 the Eduskunta parliament was introduced in Finland, with universal and equal suffrage (Finland was the first country in Europe to grant women full political rights). Russian political oppression continued, however, and poverty was endemic. In search of work and a better life, many Finns moved south to Helsinki, or emigrated to North America in the first decades of the 20th century.

The Russian Revolution of October 1917 enabled the Finnish parliament to declare independence on 6 December of that year. Although Russia recognised the new nation, it hoped for a parallel workers' uprising, and it fomented dissent and supplied arms to that end.

Following an attack by Russian-armed Finnish Reds on the civil guards in Vyborg, the Finnish Civil War flared in late January 1918. During 108 days of heavy fighting, approximately 30,000 Finns were killed. The Reds, comprising the rising working class, aspired to a Russian-style

LENIN IN FINLAND

One man who spent plenty of time in Finland was Vladimir Ilyich Lenin, father of the Russian Revolution. Having had a Finnish cellmate during his exile in Siberia, he then regularly visited the country for conferences of the Social Democratic Party, meeting Stalin for the first time at one of them. Lenin lived near Helsinki in 1907 before he was forced to flee the Russian Empire. In a Hollywood-style escape, he jumped off a moving train to avoid tsarist agents, and was then sheltered in Turku before being moved to remote island communities in the southwest. Lenin found shelter on Parainen, but fearing capture he walked across thin ice with a local guide to Nauvo (there's a famous painting of this in the Hermitage in St Petersburg), from where he finally jumped on a steamer to Stockholm.

Lenin entered Finland again via Tornio in 1917. After the abortive first revolution, he lived in a tent for a while in Iljitsevo, before going back to Russia and his date with destiny.

Lenin, even before having visited Finland, had agitated for Finnish independence, a conviction that he maintained. In December 1917, he signed the declaration of Finnish independence. Without his support, it is doubtful that the nation would have been born at that time. You can learn more about Lenin in Finland at the **Lenin Museum** (Map p136; ☑010-420-9222; www.lenin.fi; 1st fl, Hämeenpuisto 28; adult/child €8/free; ◷11am-6pm Jun-Aug, to 5pm Tue-Sun Sep-May) in Tampere.

1741–43	1808	1812	1827
Russia again occupies Finland. The Treaty of Turku ends what becomes known as the Lesser Wrath, but cedes parts of the Savo region of Finland to Russia.	Finland is invaded and occupied by Russia, becoming a grand duchy of the Russian Empire in 1809; at the Diet of Porvoo, Tsar Alexander I promises to respect its autonomy.	Helsinki becomes the capital, replacing the Swedish-rule capital of Turku.	Elias Lönnrot makes the first of his song-collecting journeys into remote Karelian forests, which culminate in the publication of *Kalevala*, the national epic.

socialist revolution while retaining independence. The nationalist Whites, led by CGE Mannerheim, dreamed of monarchy and sought to emulate Germany.

The Whites, with substantial German help, eventually gained victory and the war ended in May 1918. Friedrich Karl, Prince of Hessen, was elected king of Finland by the Eduskunta on 9 October 1918, but the defeat of imperial Germany a month later made Finland choose a republican state model, under its first president, KJ Ståhlberg.

Though internal struggles continued, and despite the crushing blows of WWII, Finland gained fame internationally as a brave new nation. Significant events included Finland's Winter War heroics, Paavo Nurmi's distinguished career as a long-distance runner, Ester Toivonen's Miss Europe title in 1933, Artturi Virtanen's Nobel Prize for Chemistry in 1945, the Helsinki Olympics of 1952 and plaudits won by Finnish designers in international expositions. These achievements fostered national confidence, helped Finland to feel that it belonged at the table of nations, and gave it strength to survive the difficult Cold War period that followed.

The Winter War & Its Continuation

Diplomatic manoeuvrings in Europe in the 1930s meant that Finland, inexperienced in the sinuous negotiations of Great Power politics, had a few difficult choices to make. The security threat posed by the Soviet Union meant that some factions were in favour of developing closer ties with Nazi Germany, while others favoured rapprochement with Moscow. On 23 August 1939, the Soviet and German foreign ministers, Molotov and Ribbentrop, signed a nonaggression pact, which gave the Soviet Union a free hand in Finland. The USSR argued that its security required a slice of southeastern Karelia and the right to build bases on Finnish soil. Finland refused, and on 30 November 1939 the Winter War between Finland and the Soviet Union began.

This was a harsh winter – temperatures reached -40°C (-40°F) and soldiers died in their thousands. Despite a lack of artillery and planes, Finland resisted the Red Army, with mobile skiing troops conducting successful guerrilla-style assaults in small groups. Stalin was forced to send more and more divisions to the front, with some 600,000 soldiers eventually being committed. Several Russian divisions were destroyed, with an estimated 130,000 dead as the Finns stopped the Russian advance by early January. But this was an unwinnable war, and after 105 days of fighting in the harshest imaginable conditions, Finland conceded. In the Treaty of Moscow (March 1940), Finland was forced to cede the Karelian Isthmus, together with the eastern Salla and Kuusamo regions and some islands: in total nearly one-tenth of its territory. More than 400,000 Karelian refugees flooded across the new border into Finland.

Mannerheim had a fascinating life divided into several distinct phases. Check out www.mannerheim.fi for an extremely comprehensive online biography, or visit his former home, the Mannerheim-Museo, in Helsinki.

Though still part of Russia, Finland issued its first postage stamps in 1856 and its own currency, the markka, in 1860.

1853	1865	1899	1917
As part of the Russian Empire, Finland is involved in the Crimean War, with British troops destroying fortifications at Loviisa, Helsinki and Bomarsund.	Finland's most famous composer Jean Sibelius is born in Hämeenlinna. His 1899 *Finlandia* symphony becomes a symbol of the Finnish independence movement.	The tsar implements a policy of Russification in Finland and attempts to impose the Russian language on the country. Widespread protests result and campaigns for independence gain strength.	Finland declares independence from the Soviet Union. Shortly afterwards the Finnish Civil War breaks out between the communist Reds and the establishment Whites.

In the following months, the Soviet Union attempted to persuade Finland to cede more territory. Isolated from the Western Allies, Finland turned to Germany for help and allowed the transit of German troops. When hostilities broke out between Germany and the Soviets in June 1941, German troops were already on Finnish soil, and the Continuation War between Finland and the Red Army followed. In the subsequent fighting, the Finns advanced, reaching their old borderline in December. Finns began to resettle Karelia. When Soviet forces staged a huge comeback in the summer of 1944, Finnish president Risto Ryti, who had promised Ribbentrop that Finland would not negotiate peace with Russia without German agreement, resigned, with Mannerheim taking his place. Mannerheim negotiated an armistice with the Russians, ceding Finland's 'other arm', the Petsamo area of the Kola Peninsula, and ordered the evacuation of German troops. Finland waged a bitter war in Lapland to oust the Germans, who staged a 'scorched earth' retreat from the country until the general peace in the spring of 1945.

Against the odds, Finland had remained independent, but at a heavy price. The territorial losses of 1940 and 1944 were ratified at the Peace of Paris in February 1947, and heavy war reparations were ordered to be paid to the Soviet Union. Many in Finland are still bitter about the loss of these territories. Nevertheless, the resistance against the might of the Red Army is something of which Finns are still proud.

In the first elections in 1907, 19 female members were elected to the Eduskunta, making them the first female MPs in the world. Finland has been a trailblazer for equality in politics ever since.

HISTORY THE COLD WAR

The Cold War

The year of the Helsinki Olympics, 1952, was also the year that Finland completed paying its heavy war reparations to the Soviet Union. Mostly paid in machinery and ships, they in fact had a positive effect, as they established the heavy engineering industry that eventually stabilised the Finnish postwar economy.

Finnish society changed profoundly during this period. In the 1940s the population was still predominantly agricultural, but the privations of the war, which sent people to the towns and cities in search of work, as well as the influx of nearly half a million Karelian refugees, sparked an acute housing crisis. Old wooden town centres were demolished to make way for apartment blocks, and new suburbs appeared almost overnight around Helsinki. Conversely, areas in the north and east lost most of their young people (often half their population) to domestic emigration.

From the end of the war until the early 1990s, the overriding political issue was a familiar one: balance between East and West. Stalin's 'friendship and cooperation' treaty of 1948 was used by the USSR throughout the Cold War as coercion in an attempt to limit Finland's interaction with the West.

A *kotiryssä* (Russian contact) was crucial for politicians of ambition in Cold War Finland, when much career advancement was under Moscow's control. But those friendly dinners on the Kremlin's tab could look a little treasonous if the vodka loosened your tongue...

1920	1939	1948	1950
Relations with the Soviets are normalised by the Treaty of Tartu, which sees Finnish territory expand to its largest point ever, including the Petsamo region in the far northeast.	The Winter War sees the Soviet Union invade Finland. After 15 weeks of fighting in subzero conditions, Finland is forced to cede a substantial amount of territory.	The 'friendship and cooperation' treaty is signed between Finland and the Soviet Union.	Urho K Kekkonen becomes prime minister for the first time. In 1956 he is elected to the position of president, which he holds for 25 years.

A savvy political head was needed to negotiate these choppy waters, and Finland found it in the astute if controversial figure of Urho K Kekkonen, president from 1956 to 1981 and a master of diplomacy.

Canny and unorthodox, Kekkonen realised that he was the devil the Kremlin knew, and he used this to his advantage. Similarly, he did so with the West's fear that Finland would fall completely under the sway of the USSR. He signed a free-trade agreement with the European Free Trade Association (EFTA) in 1961, which brought Finland closer to a European orbit, but also signed a parallel agreement for preferential trade with the Soviets.

Kekkonen and his government had a close relationship with many of the KGB's big men in Finland, and political nominations were submitted to Moscow for approval within a framework of 'friendly coexistence'. Many Finns regard his era with embarrassment, believing that Kekkonen abased the country by such close contact with the Bear, and that his grip on power and web of behind-the-scenes manoeuvrings were uncomfortably reminiscent of the Kremlin itself. Nevertheless, Kekkonen presided over a period in which the nation moved from an impoverished agricultural state to a modern European democracy with a watertight welfare system and healthy economy, all in the shadow of a great power whose actions in Eastern Europe had given ample reason for Finland to tread with extreme caution.

After Kekkonen's resignation due to ill health at 81, the Soviets continued to dabble in Finnish politics, mostly with the aim of reducing US influence and preventing Finland joining what is now the EU. That particular chapter of Finland's long and complicated relationship with its eastern neighbour came to a close with the collapse of the USSR.

For an in-depth look into Finnish history, head to the website http://finland.fi, which has excellent essays written by experts on various periods.

Modern Finland

Following the collapse of the Soviet Union, a load was lifted from Finland, but the early 1990s were not the easiest of times. The bubble of the 1980s had burst, the Soviet Union disappeared with debts unpaid, the markka was devalued and unemployment jumped from 3% to 20%.

However, Finland could finally integrate itself fully with Europe. Since joining the EU in January 1995, Finland has largely prospered, and was a founding member of the euro in 2002.

Balancing power between the president and the parliament had long been on the agenda since Kekkonen's monarch-like presidency, and in 1999 a new constitution was approved limiting certain presidential powers. The first to take the wheel under the new order was Tarja Halonen of the Social Democratic Party, elected in 2000. Referred to affectionately as Muumimamma (Moominmamma), she was well loved by many Finns and was re-elected for a second (and, by law, final) six-year term in 2006

1952	1971	1973	1995
Helsinki hosts the summer Olympic Games. Finland completes war reparation payments of US$300 million to the USSR as decreed by the Peace of Paris in 1947.	For the first time, urban dwellers outnumber rural dwellers in Finland.	The Delegation for Sámi Affairs, the beginnings of the Sámi parliament, convenes for the first time. Finland signs a trade agreement with the EEC despite Soviet pressure not to.	After a referendum with a 57% 'yes' vote in October 1994, Finland joins the EU.

before being succeeded in 2012 by the National Coalition Party's Sauli Niinistö. Finland's next presidential elections will be held in 2018.

Parliamentary politics have twisted and turned in recent years. In 2015's general election, Juha Sipilä led his Centre party to victory. Sipilä formed a centre-right coalition and was appointed prime minister by the Finnish Parliament. In 2017, however, one of the three coalition parties, the nationalist Finns Party, elected anti-immigration hardliner Jussi Halla-aho as its leader, and Sipilä and the leader of third coalition partner, Minister of Finance Petteri Orpo of the National Coalition Party, announced that they would no longer govern with the Finns Party. The government averted collapse when 20 members of parliament defected from the Finns Party, forming the breakaway New Alternative party. Sipilä's government retained a parliamentary majority as the New Alternative continued as a coalition partner, and the Finns Party was relegated to the opposition. The next parliamentary elections are due in 2019.

The country's relationship with post-Soviet Russia remains high on the agenda, and though Finland has experienced far less immigration than most European countries – and despite the Finns Party's decline – immigration continues to be a contentious issue.

Finland's own indigenous people, the Sámi, have been afforded greater recognition in the last 50 years, with the establishment of a Finnish Sámi parliament and the enshrinement of their languages in regional laws. However, disputes between reindeer herders and forestry firms in the north have ignited debate as to whether Sámi interests continue to come second to those of the country's timber industry.

Despite the challenges ahead, Finland can feel just a wee bit pleased with itself. It continues to boom on the back of the technology sector along with the traditionally important forestry industry, design, manufacturing and, increasingly, tourism. The country consistently ranks highly in quality-of-life indices and has in recent years outperformed its traditionally superior neighbour Sweden in many areas. For a cold, remote, sparsely populated forest nation, it's doing rather well.

2000	2002	2011	2017
Finland elects Tarja Halonen as its first female president. She proves a popular figure and holds the post for the maximum 12 years.	Along with several other European countries, Finland adopts the euro, bidding farewell to the markka after 142 years.	The rise of the anti-immigration Finns Party reflects increasingly ambivalent attitudes towards Finland's role in the EU.	Finland celebrates its centenary of independence.

The Sámi

Sámi are the indigenous inhabitants of Lapland and are today spread across four countries from the Kola Peninsula in Russia to the southern Norwegian mountains. About half of Finnish Sámi live in the Sámi region called Sápmi. Archaeological evidence suggests this region was first settled soon after the last ice age around 9000 years ago, but it wasn't until the beginning of the Christian era – the early Iron Age – that Finns and Sámi had become two distinct groups with diverging languages.

Traditions & Beliefs

The early inhabitants were nomadic people – hunters, fishers and food gatherers – who migrated with the seasons. Early Sámi society was based on the *siida* – small groups comprising a number of families who controlled particular hunting, herding and fishing grounds. Families lived in a *kota,* a traditional dwelling resembling the tepee or wigwam of native North Americans. Smaller tents served as temporary shelters while following the migrating reindeer herds; a 'winter village' system also developed, where groups came together to help survive the harsh winter months. Mechanisation in the 1950s meant reindeer herders could go out on snowmobiles and return home every night. This ended the need for nomadism and the Sámi became a settled people.

The natural environment was essential to Sámi existence: they worshipped the sun (father), earth (mother) and wind, and believed all things in nature had a soul. There were many gods, who dwelled in *seita* places (holy sites): fells, lakes or sacred stones. The link with the gods was through the *noaidi* (shaman), the most important member of the community.

Traditional legends, rules of society and fairy tales were handed down through the generations by storytelling. A unique form of storytelling was the yoik, a chant in which the singer would use words, or imitate the sounds of animals and nature to describe experiences or people. It's still used by the Sámi today, sometimes accompanied by instruments.

For more information, visit the excellent Siida museum in Inari, Samiland in Levi or the Arktikum in Rovaniemi. Hidden away via the 'web exhibitions' page on the Siida website (www.siida.fi), you can access a series of excellent pages on the Inari and Skolt Sámi cultures.

Sámi Groups

More than half of the 70,000 Sámi population are in Norway, while around 9000 reside in Finland; there are close cross-border cultural ties. Five distinct Sámi groups with distinct cultural traditions live in Finland. Vuotso Sámi live around Saariselkä and are the southernmost group. Enontekiö Sámi dwell around Hetta in the west and, with Utsjoki Sámi, who settled from Finland's northernmost tip along the Norwegian border to Karigasniemi, have the strongest reindeer-herding heritage. Inari Sámi live around the shores of Inarijärvi and have a strong fishing tradition. Skolt Sámi originally inhabited the Kola Peninsula around Petsamo, and fled to Finland when the Soviet Union took back control of that area. They number around 600, live around Sevettijärvi and Nellim, and are of Orthodox religion.

Sámi languages are related to Finnish and other Finno-Ugric languages. There are three Sámi languages, not very mutually intelligible, used in Finland today. There are another seven Sámi languages in Norway, Sweden and Russia.

Role of the Reindeer

Reindeer have always been central to the Sámi existence. Sámi consumed the meat and milk, used the fur for clothing and bedding and made fish hooks and harpoons from the bones and antlers. Today a significant percentage of Sámi living in Sápmi are involved in reindeer husbandry. Tourism is another big employer.

Originally the Sámi hunted wild reindeer, usually trapping them in pitfalls. Hunting continued until around the 16th century, when the Sámi began to domesticate entire herds and migrate with them. Towards the end of the 19th century, Finland's reindeer herders were organised into *paliskunta* cooperatives, of which there are now 56 in northern Finland. Reindeer wander free around the large natural areas within each *paliskunta,* which are bordered by enormous fences that cross the Lapland wilderness. Each herder is responsible for his stock and identifies them by earmarks – a series of distinctive notches cut into the ear of each animal. GPS collars now help owners to track their animals.

Handicrafts

The colourful Sámi costumes, featuring jackets, pants or skirts embroidered with bright red, blue and yellow patterns, are now mostly worn on special occasions and during Sámi festivals.

Sámi handicrafts (including bags and boots made from reindeer hide, knitted gloves and socks, textiles, shawls, strikingly colourful Sámi hats, jewellery and silverware) are recognised as indigenous art. Genuine handicrafts carry the name 'Sámi duodji'. Inari is one of the best places to buy them.

Never ask a Sámi how many reindeer he or she owns. It's a very personal matter, like someone's bank balance. It's something they wouldn't even necessarily reveal to their closest friends.

THE SÁMI ROLE OF THE REINDEER

Finnish Lifestyle & Culture

Despite the magnificent lakescapes, enchanting forests and plethora of outdoor activities, Finland's greatest highlight is the Finns. Isolated in this corner of Europe and inhabiting an extreme land with extended periods of light and dark, warmth and bitterly cold temperatures, they do their own thing and have developed a strongly independent, self-reliant streak, coloured by a seriously offbeat sense of humour.

Sisu

Finland is not Scandinavia, nor is it Russia. Nevertheless, Finnish tradition owes something to both cultures. But the modern Finn is staunchly independent. The long struggle for emancipation and the battle to survive in a harsh environment have engendered an ordered society that solves its own problems in its own way. They have also given birth to the Finnish trait of *sisu*, often translated as 'guts', or the resilience to survive prolonged hardship. Even if all looks lost, a Finn with *sisu* will fight – or swim, or run, or work – valiantly until the final defeat. This trait is valued highly, with the country's heroic resistance against the Red Army in the Winter War usually thought of as the ultimate example.

Despite its proximity, Finland is generally considered not to be part of Scandinavia, culturally or geographically. Many Finnish-speaking Finns are insistent on this point, and prefer the less specific term 'Nordic countries' to describe Finland and its western neighbours.

Love of Nature

Finns have a deep and abiding love of their country's forests and lakes. In July Finland is one of the world's most relaxing, joyful places to be – a reason Finns traditionally have not been big travellers. After the long winter, why miss the best their country has to offer? Finns head en masse for the *mökki* (summer cottage) from midsummer until the end of the July holidays. Most Finns of any age could forage in a forest for an hour at the right time of year and emerge with a feast of fresh berries, wild mushrooms and probably a fish or two. City-dwelling Finns are far more in touch with nature than most of their European equivalents.

Sauna

No matter where you are in Finland, you'll never be far from a sauna (pronounced *sah*-oo-nah, not *saw*-nuh). With over two million in homes, hotels, summer cottages, campgrounds and numerous other unlikely places, saunas are prescribed to cure almost every ailment, used to seal business deals, or just to socialise in over a few beers.

Traditionally saunas were used as a family bathhouse as well as a place to smoke meat and even give birth. The earliest references to the Finnish sauna date from chronicles of 1113 and there are numerous mentions of their use in the *Kalevala*.

Most saunas are private, in Finnish homes, but public saunas are common and most hotels have one. An invitation to a family's sauna is an honour, just as it is to be invited to a person's home for a meal.

Finland hits the headlines every now and then for the fact that its speeding fines are based on income. You're a multimillionaire doing 80km/h in a 50km/h zone? Expect a fine of €100,000 or more...

SUMMER COTTAGES

Tucked away in Finland's forests and lakelands are half a million *kesämökkejä* (summer cottages). Part holiday house, part sacred place, the *mökki* is the spiritual home of the Finn and you don't know the country until you've spent time in one. The average Finn spends less than two days in a hotel per year, but several weeks in a cottage.

These are places where people get back to nature. Amenities are often basic – the gloriously genuine ones have no electricity or running water – but even the highest-flying Euro-techno-executives are in their element, chopping wood, DIYing, picking chanterelles and blueberries, rowing and selecting young birch twigs for the *vihta* (sauna whisk). There's no better sauna than a *mökki* one: the soft steam of the wood stove caresses rather than burns, and the nude dash for an invigorating spring into the chilly lake is a Finnish summer icon. As is the post-sauna can of beer, new potatoes with fresh dill, and sausages grilled over pine cones on the barbecue. It's hard not to feel at peace when gazing out at the silent lake, trees perfectly reflected in it by the midnight sun, and anything of consequence miles away.

The best way to experience a *mökki* is to be invited to one by a Finnish friend, but failing that there are numerous ones you can rent, particularly in the Lakeland area.

The sauna is taken naked. While a Finnish family will often take the sauna together, in mixed gatherings it is usual for the men and women to go separately.

Public saunas are generally separated by gender and if there is just one sauna, there are usually different hours for men and women. In unisex saunas you will be given some sort of wrap or covering to wear. Finns strictly observe the nonsexual character of the sauna and this point should be respected. The sauna was originally a place to bathe and meditate.

The most common sauna is the electric sauna stove, which produces a fairly dry, harsh heat compared with the much-loved chimney sauna, driven by a log fire and the staple of life at summer cottages. Even rarer is the true *savusauna* (smoke sauna), without a chimney. The smoke is let out just before entry and the soot-blackened walls are part of the experience. Although the top of a sauna can reach more than 120°C (248°F), many Finns consider the most satisfying temperature for a sauna to be around 80°C (178°F). At this temperature you'll sweat and, some Finns claim, feel the wood smoke in your lungs.

Proper sauna etiquette dictates that you use a *kauha* (ladle) to throw water on the *kiuas* (sauna stove), which then gives off the *löyly* (sauna steam). At this point, at least in summer in the countryside, you might lightly strike yourself with the *vihta* (*vasta* in eastern Finland) – a bunch of fresh, leafy birch twigs. This improves circulation, has cleansing properties and gives your skin a pleasant smell. When you are sufficiently warmed, you'll jump in the sea, a lake, river or pool, then return to the sauna to warm up and repeat the cycle several times. If you're indoors, a cold shower will do. The swim and hot-cold aspect is such an integral part of the sauna experience that in the dead of winter Finns cut a hole in the ice and jump right in.

While suicide rates are a problem, it's a myth that Finns have the highest rate of it in the world. It actually only comes in ninth in Europe, between Serbia and Belgium.

Sadness

There's a definite depressive streak in Finns, more so than in their western neighbours. While they aren't among Europe's biggest drinkers per capita, the incidence of alcoholism is high. The winter darkness can strain even the most optimistic soul – seasonal affective disorder (SAD) is significant here and suicide levels are higher than the comfortable standard of living would predict. The melancholic trend is reflected in

DRIVIN' WHEELS

Few countries have such an obsession with cars as Finland. The interest goes right down the scale, from watching Formula One to changing the oil in the old Datsun parked outside.

You won't be in Finland for long before you'll hear a baritone bellow and see a glint of fins and whitewall tyres as some American classic car rolls by, immaculately polished and tuned. You probably never knew that so many Mustangs, Chargers or Firebirds existed this side of the Atlantic. Even non-classics long since dead elsewhere are kept alive here with loyal home maintenance.

Rally driving sends Finns wild – the exploits of legends such as Tommi Mäkinen and Marcus Grönholm are the latest of a long line in a sport in which Finland has excelled. In Formula One, too, Suomi punches well above its weight, with Keke Rosberg, Mika Häkkinen and Kimi Räikkönen all former world champions. In small towns, often the only entertainment for the local young is trying to emulate them by doing blockies around the kauppatori...

Finland's oldest automotive magazine, *Moottori* (www.moottori.fi), has extensive coverage on vehicles you might see here, and lists rallies, vintage and classic-car shows and other events.

Finns' love of darkly themed music and lyrics of lost love – even the cheeriest summer Suomi-pop hits sound like the singer's just backed over his or her dog, and Finnish tango takes lugubriousness off the chart.

Silence

While the 'silent Finn' concept has been exaggerated over the years, it's certainly true that Finns believe in comfortable silences, so if a conversation dies off naturally there's no need to jump-start it with small talk. Finns quip that they invented text messaging so they didn't have to talk to each other, and sitting in the sauna for 20 minutes with your best friend, saying nothing, is perfectly normal. Finns generally have a quirky, dark, self-deprecating sense of humour and may just be saving their words for a well-timed jibe.

That's not to say Finns don't talk. They do, and once they get a couple of pints of lager in them, they really do, as that reserve goes out the window to be replaced by boisterous bonhomie.

Cosy Finland (http://cosyfinland.com) offers an interesting chance to meet Finns in their own habitat. It will set you up with a dinner invitation at a multilingual host's home, where you'll try local specialities and get to know Finland away from the tourist beat.

Religion

The Lutheran church dominates the religious scene here, with some 78% of Finns describing themselves as such on a census form. The next religious group, Finnish Orthodox, makes up only 1.5% of the population. Nevertheless, Finns have one of the lowest rates of church attendance in the Christian world.

Various Lutheran revivalist movements are seeking to combat this and are often in the news. The ultra-conservative Laestadian movement, many of whose members frown on such evils as dancing and earrings, has many adherents, as does the charismatic church Nokia-Missio. Almost one in 10 Finns belongs to a revivalist movement.

Finnish Design

The rustle of the birch or waterbird's splash on a lake are never far below the surface of a Finn's soul and they have taken this closeness to nature and melded it to a solid Nordic practicality to create a unique design tradition. Finnish designers evoke both the colourful optimism of summer and winter's austere minimalism in work that ranges from traditional Suomi design icons to avant-garde modern creations testing the limits of 3D printing.

The Roots of Creativity

Its inhabitants' almost mystical closeness to nature has always underpinned design in Finland, and it's rarely been a self-conscious art. However high Finland may climb on the lifestyle indexes these days, its design still has its roots in practicality. Indeed, it is a practicality originally born of poverty: the inventiveness of a hand-to-mouth rural population made life easier in very small steps.

Finland's location and its historical role as a pawn in a long-running Russia-Sweden chess game have given it a variety of influences and a certain flexibility. As a meeting point between East and West, it has traditionally been a place of trade, a point of tension and, therefore, a point of change and innovation. Its climate, too, is a key factor, as it has meant that efficiency has always been the primary requisite for design of everyday objects. In bald terms, if that axe didn't chop enough wood for the winter, you wouldn't survive it.

The forest is ever-present in Finnish life, so it's no surprise to find that nature is the dominant and enduring motif in the country's designs, from Lapland's sheath knives to the seasonal flower-and-forest colours of Marimekko's palette. Timber remains an important material, and reassuringly chunky wooden objects adorn almost every Finnish home and summer cottage.

SUITCASE-FRIENDLY SOUVENIRS

→ One of Sami Rinne's engagingly quirky ceramics – maybe that mug with a handle like a reindeer's antlers?

→ A set of Verso's colourful, original felt mats and coasters to brighten up your dinner table.

→ A pair of Minna Parikka's shoes – 21st-century style straight from a smoky 1930s nightclub.

→ One of Jani Martikainen's birch trivets (pot-plant bases) from his Majamoo company. The only trouble is that the plant hides it.

→ Whatever the versatile Harri Koskinen has just designed – from lighting to glassware.

→ Edgy, humorous streetwear from Daniel Palillo.

→ Cushion covers, duvet sets and more by Aino-Maija Metsola.

Alvar Aalto

Alvar Aalto was for many the 20th century's number-one architect. In an era of increasing urbanisation, postwar rebuilding and immense housing pressure, Aalto found elegant solutions for public and private edifices that embraced functionalism, but never at the expense of humanity. Viewed from the next century, his work still more than holds its own, and his huge contributions in other areas of art and design make him a mighty figure indeed.

Aalto had a democratic, practical view of his field. He saw his task as 'a question of making architecture serve the wellbeing and prosperity of millions of citizens, where it had previously been the preserve of a wealthy few. But he was no utilitarian. Beauty was always a concern, and he was adamant that a proper studio environment was essential for the creativity of the architect to flower.

Born in 1898 in Kuortane near Seinäjoki, Aalto worked in Jyväskylä, Turku and Helsinki before gaining an international reputation for his pavilions at the World Fairs of the late 1930s. His 1925 marriage to Aino Marsio created a dynamic team that pushed boundaries in several fields, including glassware and furniture design. Their work on bending and laminating wood revolutionised the furniture industry, and the classic forms they produced for their company, Artek, are still Finnish staples. Aalto's use of rod-shaped ceramic tiles, undulated wood, woven cane, brick and marble was particularly distinctive.

Aalto's notable buildings are dotted throughout Finland. A comparison of the Aalto Centre in Seinäjoki with the Ristinkirkko in Lahti highlights the range of his work. Charmingly, Aalto's favourite design was his own wooden boat (on show at his summer house near Jyväskylä), which he planned and built with great love, but little knowledge of boatbuilding. It was barely seaworthy at the best of times, and regularly capsized and sank.

Best Aalto Buildings

Finlandia Talo, Helsinki

Otaniemi University, Espoo

Workers' Club Building, Jyväskylä

Aalto Centre, Seinäjoki

Villa Mairea, Pori

The Classics

If the early 21st century is a new golden age for Finnish design, the original one was in the 1950s and 1960s. The freelance designers producing marvels in glass for Iittala, ceramics for Arabia, cookware for Hackman and furniture for Artek won international recognition and numerous prestigious awards, particularly at the Triennale di Milano shows. Though times were still tough after the war, and the country was struggling to house refugees from occupied Karelia, the successes of these firms, together with the Helsinki Olympic Games of 1952, helped put a still-young nation on the map and build confidence and national pride, which had been weakened after the gruelling battles with Russia and Germany.

FINNISH DESIGN CLASSICS

➡ Artek's Aalto chairs. To think that we take bent wood for granted in our furniture today.

➡ The Iittala vase (also known as the Savoy vase or Aalto vase). Yes, Aalto again. Whether or not it actually resembles an Inuit woman's leather pants, it's undeniably a classic.

➡ An Unikko bed sheet from Marimekko. Who doesn't dream better under those upbeat red poppies?

➡ 1930s ringed tumblers designed by Aino Aalto, inspired by the circles created by throwing rocks in the water – you'll drink your breakfast juice out of one of them within a couple of days of your arrival.

➡ Marttiini knives, first made at Rovaniemi in Lapland in 1928 and still the first choice for outdoors folk.

The story of the Iittala glass company could be a metaphor for the story of Finnish design. Still producing from models imported from Sweden in the early 20th century, the company began to explore more homegrown options. Glass design competitions were an outward-looking source of ideas: from one of these came Alvar Aalto's famous Iittala vase, which he described as 'an Eskimo woman's leather trousers'. Then two giants of postwar design, Tapio Wirkkala (1915–85) and Timo Sarpaneva (1926–2006), began to explore textures and forms gleaned from Finnish lakescapes. Coloured glass fell from use and the classic Iittala ranges were born, with sand-scouring creating the appearance of cut ice, and Wirkkala's impossibly fluid forms seemingly melting away. The opaque look, which resembled ceramics, was a later creation as a new generation took to the field. Harri Koskinen (b 1970) and Annaleena Hakatie (b 1965) were among the leading lights, though the company has never been afraid to commission foreign designers. Iittala is today under the same ownership as Hackman, the long-established cutlery and cookware producers, and Arabia, which roughly paralleled Iittala's glassware trajectory with ceramics.

Clothing has been another area of success. Finland, unlike its Nordic neighbours, has tended to beat its own fashion path. It's traditionally been a place where teenagers can wear a jumper knitted by granny to school, and though new and exciting ideas are constantly created here, they tend to be built on solid, traditional foundations.

The godfather of Finnish design, Kaj Franck (1911–89), took ideas from traditional rustic clothing for his pared-back creations, but it was the birth and rapid rise to prominence of Marimekko, founded in 1951, that made an international impact. Optimistic, colourful and well made, it bucked contemporary trends, focusing on a simple and unashamed beauty. Though the company went through a difficult period, it's back at the top these days, as the retro appeal of its classic shirts, bags, curtains and fabrics fills wardrobes with flowers once again.

Other well-established Finnish names include Aarikka, with its wooden jewellery and other accessories that have always had a cheerily reassuring solidity and honesty, and Kalevala Koru, a byword for quality silver and gold jewellery. Pentik's wide range of interior-design and homeware products includes the recent Saaga range, inspired by the designs of Sámi shaman drums.

The Newcomers

A strong design tradition tends to produce good young designers and Finland's education system is strong on fostering creativity, so Suomi is churning them out at a fair rate. New names, ranges and shops crop up in Helsinki's Design District like mushrooms overnight, and exciting contemporary design is being produced on all fronts. Fennofolk is the name for one broad movement that seeks, like the original giants of Finnish design, to take inspiration from Suomi's natural and cultural heritage, adding a typically Finnish injection of weirdness along the way.

There are exciting things continuing to happen across all fields of design. Paola Suhonen's IVANAhelsinki clothing label combines innovation with practicality and sustainability, while Hanna Sarén's clothing continues to go from strength to strength since being referenced in *Sex and the City*. Julia Lundsten and Minna Parikka are head-turning young stars of the footwear world.

In industrial design, Harri Koskinen is a giant. His clean-lined minimalism produces objects that are always reassuringly practical, but quite unlike anything you've ever seen before. Helsinki bristles with high-quality graphic-design studios that are leading lights in their field.

The website www.finnishdesign.com mostly sticks to the well-established names, but it's a good introduction. Design Forum Finland's webpage www.designforum.fi has useful links; its awards are another good way to keep tabs on the scene. Helsinki's Design Museum is also a superb source of information.

One of the biggest and most versatile names on the Finnish design scene is Stefan Lindfors, whose reptile- and insect-inspired work has been described as a warped update of Aalto's own nature-influenced work.

The Arts

Finland has a flourishing cultural scene and puts a high priority on the arts, especially music, in its education system. Writers and artists typically looked to the Finnish wilderness for their inspiration, and their creations went on to evoke a strong sense of pride in Finland that became an important part of the movement that eventually led to Finnish independence in 1917.

Literature

Finland had a rich oral tradition of folklore, but written Finnish was created by the Reformation figure Mikael Agricola (1510–57), who wrote the first alphabet. Although written Finnish was emerging in schools, the earliest fiction was written in Swedish.

All that changed in the early 19th century with the penning of the *Kalevala* and the beginning of a nationalistic renaissance. Poet JL Runeberg wrote *Tales of the Ensign Stål,* capturing Finland at war with Russia, while Aleksis Kivi wrote *Seven Brothers,* the nation's first novel, about brothers escaping conventional life in the forest, allegorising the birth of Finnish national consciousness.

This theme continued in the 1970s with *The Year of the Hare,* a look at a journalist's escape into the wilds by the prolific, popular and bizarre Arto Paasilinna. Other 20th-century novelists include Mika Waltari, who

FINLAND'S NATIONAL EPIC

It's hard to overestimate the influence on Finland of the *Kalevala,* an epic tale compiled from the songs of bards that tells everything from the history of the world to how to make decent home brew. Intrepid country doctor Elias Lönnrot trekked eastern Finland during the first half of the 19th century in order to collect traditional poems, oral runes, legends, lore and folk stories. Over 11 long tours, he compiled this material with his own writing to form what came to be regarded as the national epic of Finland.

The mythology of the book blends creation stories, wedding poems and classic struggles between good and evil. Although there are heroes and villains, there are also more nuanced characters that are not so simply described. The main storyline concentrates on the events in two imaginary countries, Kalevala (characterised as 'our country') and Pohjola ('the other place', or the north). Many commentators feel that the epic echoes ancient territorial conflicts between the Finns and the Sámi. Although impossible to accurately reproduce the Finnish original, the memorable characters are particularly well brought to life in poet Keith Bosley's English translation of the *Kalevala,* which is a fantastic, lyrical read.

The first version of *Kalevala* appeared in 1833, with another following in 1835 and yet another, the final version, *Uusi-Kalevala* (New Kalevala), in 1849. Its influence on generations of Finnish artists, writers and composers was and is immense, particularly on painter Akseli Gallen-Kallela and composer Jean Sibelius, who repeatedly returned to the work for inspiration.

Beyond Finland the epic has influenced the Estonian epic *Kalevipoeg* and American poet Henry Wadsworth Longfellow. Indeed, JRR Tolkien based significant parts of his mythos on the *Kalevala.*

MODERN SÁMI MUSIC

Several Finnish Sámi groups and artists have created excellent modern music with the traditional yoik (chant; also *joiks* or *juoiggus*) form. The yoik is traditionally sung a capella, often invoking a person or place with immense spiritual importance in Sámi culture. Wimme is a big name in this sphere, and Angelit produce popular, dance-floor-style Sámi music. One of their former members, Ulla Pirttijärvi, releases particularly haunting solo albums, while Vilddas are on the trancey side of Sámi music, combining it with other influences. Look out too for rockier offerings from SomBy and Tiina Sanila, Sámi hip-hop artist Ailu Valle and electro-acoustic compositions from Niko Valkeapää.

gained international fame with *The Egyptian,* and FE Sillanpää, who received the Nobel Prize for Literature in 1939. The national bestseller during the postwar period was *The Unknown Soldier* by Väinö Linna. The seemingly endless series of autobiographical novels by Kalle Päätalo and the witty short stories by Veikko Huovinen are also very popular. Finland's most internationally famous author is Tove Jansson, whose books about the fantastic Moomin family have long captured the imagination.

Along with Paasilinna, notable living writers include the versatile Leena Krohn, Mikko Rimminen, who has attracted attention for both novels and poetry, and Leena Lehtolainen, the author of prize-winning crime novels.

Music

Finland's music scene is one of the world's richest and the output of quality musicians per capita is amazingly high, whether a polished symphony orchestra violinist or a headbanging bassist for the next big death-metal band. Summer is all about music festivals of all conceivable types.

Classical Music

Composer Jean Sibelius' work dominates Finland's music, but some contemporary composers are also turning heads. Partly thanks to Helsinki's Sibelius Academy, Finnish musical education is among the best in the world, with Finnish conductors, singers and musicians performing with some of the world's top orchestras. There are some excellent classical-music festivals in Finland.

Popular Music

Finland has one of the most storming metal scenes around. The biggest exports are HIM with their 'love metal' and darkly atmospheric Nightwish, whose former vocalist Tarja Turunen is also pursuing a solo career. Catchy light-metal rockers the Rasmus continue to be successful. All genres of metal are represented, including Finntroll's folk metal (blending metal and humppa), the 69 Eyes' Gothic metal, Apocalyptica's classical metal, Children of Bodom's melodic death metal, Sonata Arctica's and Stratovarius' power metal, Eternal Tears of Sorrow's symphonic metal and Impaled Nazarene's black metal.

Local hip-hop, known as Suomirap, also has a dedicated following, thanks to artists such as Elastinen and Pyhimys.

Lighter music includes surf-rockers French Films, pop-rockers Sunrise Avenue, the Von Hertzen Brothers, indie band Disco Ensemble, emo-punks Poets of the Fall and melodic Husky Rescue. Past legends (still going in some cases) include Hanoi Rocks, the Hurriganes and the unicorn-quiffed Leningrad Cowboys. Several groups sing in Finnish, including Eppu Normaali, Zen Café, Kotiteollisuus, Apulanta and mellow folk rockers Scandinavian Music Group.

As well as compiling and writing the *Kalevala,* Elias Lönnrot's work in creating a standard Finnish grammar and vocabulary by adopting words and expressions from various dialects was of great importance. Finnish has remained very much the same ever since, at least in written form.

The website Music Finland (https://musicfinland.com) is a fantastic resource for Finnish music across all genres, with articles, information on artists and event listings.

Jazz is also very big in Finland, with huge festivals at Pori and Espoo. Finns have created humppa, a jazz-based music that's synonymous with social dances. One of the biggest names in humppa are the Eläkeläiset, whose regular albums are dotted with tongue-in-cheek covers of famous rock songs.

Painting & Sculpture

Modern Finnish art and sculpture plays with disaffection with technological society (think warped Nokias) and reinterprets the 'Finnishness' (expect parodies of sauna, birches and blonde stereotypes).

Although contemporary art enjoys a high profile in Finland, the National Romantic era is considered Finland's 'golden age' of art. The main features of these artworks are virgin forests and pastoral landscapes. Following is a list of the best-known artists of this era. The most comprehensive collections are displayed by the Ateneum and Kansallismuseo in Helsinki, and the Turun Taidemuseo in Turku.

Fanny Churberg (1845–92) One of the most famous female painters in Finland, she created landscapes, self-portraits and still lifes using ahead-of-her-time techniques.

Albert Edelfelt (1854–1905) Among the most appreciated of Finnish artists. Was educated in Paris and a number of his paintings date from this period. Many paintings are photo-like depictions of rural life.

Akseli Gallen-Kallela (1865–1931) An important figure in the National Romantic movement, drinking companion of composer Jean Sibelius and perhaps Finland's most famous painter. Had a distinguished and prolific career as creator of *Kalevala*-inspired paintings.

Pekka Halonen (1865–1933) A popular artist of the National Romantic era. Thought of as a 'nature mystic', his work, mostly devoted to ethereal winter landscapes, is largely privately owned.

Eero Järnefelt (1863–1937) A keen visitor to Koli, where he created more than 50 paintings of the 'national landscape'. His sister married Sibelius.

Juho Rissanen (1873–1950) Depicted life among ordinary Finns, and his much-loved paintings are displayed at the Ateneum and at Turun Taidemuseo.

Tyko Sallinen (1879–1955) The greatest of the Finnish expressionists, Sallinen is often considered the last of the golden-age artists.

Helene Schjerfbeck (1862–1946) Probably the most famous female painter of her age, she is known for her self-portraits, which reflect the situation of Finnish women more than 100 years ago. Considered Finland's greatest artist by many contemporary observers.

Hugo Simberg (1873–1917) Most famous for his haunting work in Tampere's cathedral, which employs his characteristic folk symbolism. Unusual and well worth investigating. Also well represented in Helsinki's Ateneum.

Ville Vallgren (1855–1940) A notable golden-age sculptor, Vallgren is most famous for creating the Havis Amanda statue in Helsinki.

von Wright, Magnus (1805–68), Wilhelm (1810–87) and Ferdinand (1822–1902) The brothers von Wright are considered the first Finnish painters of the golden age, most famous for their paintings of birds. They worked in their home near Kuopio and in Porvoo.

Emil Wickström (1864–1942) Was to sculpture what Gallen-Kallela was to painting, and he sculpted the memorial to Elias Lönnrot in Helsinki. Many of his works are at his studio in Visavuori.

Best Painted Churches

....

Pyhän Ristin Kirkko, Hattula

....

Keuruun Vanha Kirkko, Keuruu

....

Pyhän Laurin Kirkko, Lohja

....

Sankta Maria Kyrka, Kvarnbo

....

Sankt Mikael Kyrka, Finström

....

Paltaniemen kuvakirkko, Paltaniemi

Food & Drink

Finland's food scene has flourished in the last few years, as a wave of gourmet restaurants in the major cities has added gastronomic innovation to the exceptional fresh local produce.

Staples & Specialities

Finnish cuisine has been influenced by both Sweden and Russia and draws on what was traditionally available: fish, game, meat, milk and potatoes, with dark rye used to make bread and porridge, and few spices employed.

Soups are a Finnish favourite and one common in homes and restaurants. Heavy pea, meat or cabbage soups are traditional workers' fare, while creamier fish soups have a more delicate flavour.

One light snack that you'll see everywhere is the rice-filled savoury pastry from Karelia, the *karjalanpiirakka*. These are tasty cold, heated, toasted or with egg butter, and have several variations.

Fish is a mainstay of the Finnish diet. Fresh or smoked salmon *(lohi)*, marinated herring *(silli), siika* (lavaret, a lake whitefish), *kuha* (pike-perch or zander) and delicious Arctic char *(nieriä* or *rautu)* are common, and the tiny lake fish *muikku* (vendace, or whitefish) is another treat.

Two much-loved favourites that you'll see in many places are grilled liver, served with mashed potatoes and bacon, and meatballs. Finns have been known to fight over whose granny cooks the best ones.

Reindeer has always been a staple food for the Sámi. The traditional way to eat it is sautéed with lingonberries. Many restaurants also offer it on pizza or as sausages. It also comes in fillet steaks, which, though expensive, is the tastiest way to try this meat. Elk is also eaten, mostly in hunting season, and you can even get a bear steak – or more commonly, a potted or preserved meat – in some places, although the latter is very expensive, as only a small number are hunted every year.

> Late in the summer, it's a tradition to have crayfish parties, where the succulent little creatures are consumed by the dozen.

Meals

Most hotels offer a free buffet breakfast. Finns tend to eat their biggest meal of the day at lunchtime, so many cafes and restaurants put on a *lounas* special (of buffet) from Monday to Friday. Weekend *brunssi* (brunch) has become a big deal in the cities. Finns have dinner as early as 5pm. It's often just a light meal, but will eat much later if it's an organised, 'going out for dinner' affair.

For a sweet snack at any time of day, hit a cafe for a *pulla* (cardamom-flavoured bun), *korvapuusti* (cinnamon whirl) or *munkki* (doughnut).

Markets

Big towns all have a kauppahalli (covered market), which is the place to head for all sorts of Finnish specialities, breads, cheeses, deli produce, meat and a super variety of both fresh and smoked fish. It's also a top place for a cheap feed, with cafes and stalls selling sandwiches and snacks. The summer kauppatori (market square) also has food stalls, coffee stops and market produce, particularly vegetables and fruit.

Dining Websites

Eat.fi (www.eat.fi) Finland-wide site.

Heleats.com (www. heleats.com) Articles and reviews of Helsinki restaurants.

Ravintola.fi (www. ravintola.fi) Finland-wide listings site and app.

NOT-SO-SWEET SWEETS

Finns love their sweets, although some of them make the unsuspecting visitor feel like the victim of a novelty-shop joke. Salty liquorice, fiery 'Turkish peppers' and tar-flavoured gumdrops may sound like punishments rather than rewards, but are delicious after the first few times. Finnish chocolates, particularly those made by Fazer, are also excellent.

New Suomi Cuisine

Riding the wave of new Nordic cuisine is a new breed of Finnish chef experimenting with traditional ingredients such as lake fish, berries, wild mushrooms, reindeer and other seasonal produce in decidedly untraditional fashion. Especially in Helsinki, you'll find a number of gourmet restaurants offering exquisite multicourse tasting menus that make a great contrast to the heavier, sauce-laden typical cuisine.

Foraging

The forage ethos is one of the principal drivers of new Nordic cuisine, but it's not a new concept. Finns head out gleefully all summer to pick berries and mushrooms: blueberries, jewel-like wild strawberries, peppery chanterelles and the north's gloriously tart, creamy cloudberries, so esteemed that they feature on the €2 coin. People here are enthusiastic kitchen gardeners too, with tender new potatoes and fresh dill featuring heavily. The variety and quality of fresh produce means that summer is by far the best time to eat in Finland.

Vegetarians & Vegans

Most medium-sized towns in Finland will have a vegetarian restaurant *(kasvisravintola)*, usually open weekday lunchtimes only. It's easy to self-cater at markets, or take the salad/vegetable option at lunch buffets (which is usually cheaper). Many restaurants also have a salad buffet. The website www.vegaaniliitto.fi has a useful listing of vegetarian and vegan restaurants; follow 'ruoka' and 'kasvisravintoloita' (the Finnish list is more up to date than the English one).

Brewpubs

Panimoravintola Plevna, Tampere

Teerenpeli, Lahti and elsewhere

Birri, Helsinki

Beer Hunter's, Pori

Panimoravintola Koulu, Turku

Drinking

The Finns lead the world in *kahvi* (coffee) consumption. While the distinctive standard Finnish brew can be found everywhere, smarter cafes and restaurants will have espresso machines. Cafes are ubiquitous, ranging from 100-year-old imperial classics to trendy networking joints and simple country caffeine stops.

Finns drink plenty of *olut* (beer). Among the major local brews are Karhu, Koff, Olvi and Lapin Kulta. The big brands are all lagers, but you'll also find speciality brewers including Malmgård, a 1614-established, hydropowered estate. Its beers can be found around Finland. Craft breweries and microbreweries produce excellent light and dark beers: look for the word *panimo* or *panimo-ravintola*. Cider is also popular, as is *lonkero*, a ready-made mix of gin and fruity soft drink, usually grapefruit. Finns don't tend to drink in rounds; everybody pays their own.

Beer, wine and spirits are sold by the state network, Alko. There are stores in every town. The legal age for drinking is 18 for beer and wine, and 20 for spirits.

Other uniquely Finnish drinks include *salmiakkikossu,* which combines dissolved liquorice sweets with the iconic Koskenkorva vodka (an acquired taste); *fisu,* which does the same but with Fisherman's Friend pastilles; *sahti,* a sweet, high-alcohol beer; and cloudberry or cranberry liqueurs.

Survival Guide

DIRECTORY A-Z 298

Accommodation........ 298

Customs
Regulations............ 299

Electricity 299

Food 299

Health................. 300

Insurance.............. 300

Internet Access......... 300

Legal Matters 300

LGBT Travellers......... 300

Money................. 300

Opening Hours 301

Post...................301

Public Holidays.........301

Safe Travel.............301

Taxes & Refunds........301

Telephone 301

Time 301

Toilets.................301

Tourist
Information............301

Travellers with
Disabilities............ 302

Visas.................. 302

Volunteering 302

Work.................. 302

TRANSPORT.......303

GETTING THERE
& AWAY 303

Entering Finland........ 303

Air 303

Land 303

Sea 304

GETTING AROUND.......305

Air 305

Bicycle 305

Boat 305

Bus 305

Car & Motorcycle....... 306

Hitching............... 306

Local Transport......... 306

Taxi 308

Train 308

LANGUAGE 309

Directory A-Z

Accommodation

Many rural accommodation options open only in summer, and ski areas book out in winter – reserve well ahead. Most properties don't have 24-hour reception.

➡ **Hotels** Chains such as Sokos and Scandic dominate, but boutique and/or designer hotels are emerging. Most rooms have twin beds that can be pushed together rather than double beds.

➡ **Camping** Campgrounds open throughout the countryside in the warmer months.

➡ **Cottages** In Finnish tradition, lakeside and coastal cabins are popular in the warmer months.

➡ **Hostels** Typically basic, even in larger cities.

➡ **Student residences** During the summer break, student residences often rent rooms to travellers. Facilities vary widely.

SLEEPING PRICE RANGES

The following price ranges refer to a double room in high season.

€ less than €70

€€ €70–160

€€€ more than €160

Camping

Finland's campgrounds are a delight, and have much to offer to all types of travellers.

Most campgrounds are open only from June to August, and popular spots are crowded during July and the midsummer weekend.

Almost all campgrounds have cabins or cottages for rent, which are usually excellent value – from €40 for a basic double cabin to €120 for a cottage with kitchen, bathroom and sauna.

The Camping Key Europe (http://campingkeyeurope. com) offers useful discounts. You can buy it at most campgrounds for €16 per year, or online at www.camping. fi, where you'll also find an extensive listing of campgrounds across the country.

Finland's *jokamiehenoikeus* (everyman's right; p30) allows access to most land, and means you can pitch a tent almost anywhere on public land or at designated free campsites in national parks.

Farmstays

A growing, and often ecologically sound, accommodation sector in Finland is that of farmstays. Many rural farms, particularly in the south, offer B&B accommodation, a unique opportunity to meet local people and experience their way of life. Plenty of activities are also usually on offer. Home-cooked breakfasts are typically included; evening meals are also usually available. Your hosts may not speak much English; if you have difficulties, the local tourist office will be happy to help arrange the booking.

ECEAT (www.eceat.fi) lists a number of organic, sustainable farms in Finland that offer accommodation. Local tourist offices keep lists of farmstay options in the surrounding area; the website www.visitfinland.com links to a few, and Lomarengas (www.lomarengas.fi) also has many listed on its website.

Guesthouses

A Finnish *matkakoti* (guesthouse) is a no-frills spot offering simple but usually comfy accommodation with shared bathroom, typically for travelling salespeople. It can be pretty good value, usually includes breakfast and sometimes rises well above the norm: check out places such as Naantali and Hanko for some exceptional options in this class.

Hostels & Summer Hotels

For solo travellers, hostels generally offer the cheapest bed and can be good value for twin rooms. Finnish hostels are invariably clean, comfortable and very well equipped, though most are in somewhat institutional buildings.

Some Finnish hostels are run by the Finnish Youth Hostel Association (SRM), and many more are affiliated.

BOOK YOUR STAY ONLINE

For more accommodation reviews by Lonely Planet authors, check out http://lonelyplanet.com/hotels. You'll find independent reviews, as well as recommendations on the best places to stay. Best of all, you can book online.

It's worth being a member of HI (Hostelling International; www.hihostels.com), as members save 10% per night at affiliated places. You'll save money with a sleep sheet or your own linen, as hostels tend to charge extra for this.

From June to August, many student residences are made over as summer hostels and hotels. These are often great value, as you usually get your own room, with kitchen (bring your own utensils, though) and bathroom either to yourself or shared between two people.

Hotels

The majority of hotels in Finland belong to one of a few major chains, including the following:

Cumulus (www.cumulus.fi)

Scandic (www.scandichotels.com)

Sokos (www.sokoshotels.fi)

Omenahotelli (www.omena.com) Offers good-value unstaffed hotels booked online.

Hotels in Finland are designed with the business traveller in mind and tend to charge robustly. But on weekends and during the July summer holidays, prices in three- and four-star hotels tend to drop by 40% or so.

Superior rooms vary in value. In many places they are identical to the standard and your extra cash gets you only a bathrobe and a fancier shampoo. In others an extra €20 can get you 50% more space, views over the town and a private sauna. It's worth asking. The discount for singles is marginal at all times, so you may prefer to pay the little extra for a twin room, which is usually much larger.

Most hotel rooms have tiny Nordic bathrooms. If you want a bathtub, this can usually be arranged. Many hotels have 'allergy rooms', which have no carpet and minimal fabric.

Nearly all Finnish hotels have a plentiful buffet breakfast included in the rate and many include a sauna session.

Self-Catering

One of Finland's joys is its plethora of cottages for rent, ranging from simple camping cabins to fully equipped bungalows with electric sauna and gleaming modern kitchen. These can be remarkably good value and are perfect for families. There are tens of thousands of cabins and cottages for rent in Finland, many in typical, romantic forest lakeside locations. Local booking agents are mentioned under individual destinations. Local tourist offices and town websites also have lists. By far the biggest national agent for cottage rentals is **Lomarengas** (☑030-650-2502; www.lomarengas.fi).

Customs Regulations

Travellers arriving from outside the EU by air or sea can bring duty-free goods up to the value of €430 without declaration (€300 if arriving from outside the EU by bus, car or train). You can also bring in up to 16L of beer, 4L of wine, 2L of liquor not exceeding 22% vol or 1L of spirits, or 200 cigarettes or 250g of tobacco.

If you're coming from another EU country, there's no restriction on the value of gifts or purchases for personal use.

Electricity

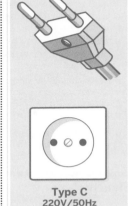

Type C
220V/50Hz

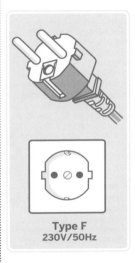

Type F
230V/50Hz

Food

See p295 for information on Finland's eating scene.

As a guide, the following price ranges refer to a standard main course:

€ less than €17

€€ €17–27

€€€ more than €27

PRACTICALITIES

➡ **Newspapers & magazines** *Helsingin Sanomat* (www. hs.fi/english) is the main daily paper in Finland. The *Helsinki Times* (www.helsinkitimes.fi) is an English-language weekly. Foreign newspapers and magazines are widely available.

➡ **Radio** The national radio broadcaster is YLE (www. yle.fi), which has a number of stations offering news and various types of music.

➡ **TV** National TV networks broadcast plenty of English-language programs, subtitled in Finnish.

➡ **Smoking** Forbidden in all enclosed public places in Finland.

➡ **Weights & measures** Finland uses the metric system. Decimals are indicated by commas.

Health

Travel in Finland presents very few health problems. The standard of care is extremely high and English is widely spoken by doctors and medical-clinic staff, the level of hygiene is high and there are no endemic diseases.

The main health issues to be aware of are extreme climates (with the potential for nasties such as hypothermia and frostbite, or viral infections such as influenza) and biting insects such as horseflies and mosquitoes, though they're more an annoyance than a real health risk.

Health care is widely available and standards are excellent. The 'Health services in Finland' page of the website www.infopankki. fi is an excellent source of information, with links to clinics and price-comparison websites.

Insurance

Citizens of the European Economic Area (EEA) are covered for emergency medical treatment on presentation of a European Health Insurance Card (EHIC), though they will be liable to pay a daily or per-appointment fee as a Finn would. Enquire about EHICs at your health centre, travel agency or (in some countries) post office well in advance of travel. Citizens from other countries should find out if there is a reciprocal arrangement for free medical care between their country and Finland. If not, health insurance is strongly recommended. Make sure your policy covers you for any activities you plan to do, such as skiing.

Worldwide travel insurance is available at www. lonelyplanet.com/travel -insurance. You can buy, extend and claim online any time – even if you're already on the road.

Internet Access

Wireless internet access is widespread. Several cities have extensive free networks and nearly all hotels, as well as many restaurants, cafes and bars, offer free access to customers and guests.

Data is very cheap. If you have an unlocked smartphone, you can pick up a local SIM card for a few euros and charge it with a month's worth of data at a decent speed for under €20. Ask at R-kioski shops for the latest deals.

Legal Matters

Finnish police have the power to impose a fine or arrest you; you're entitled to a interpreter. If you are arrested, you can be detained for three days (longer if the matter is serious) and you should face court within four days.

Police must notify your consulate if you're not a Finnish citizen. You can request they contact a family member or other designated person, but this may be refused if it's considered to jeopardise the investigation. You're presumed innocent until proven guilty.

LGBT Travellers

Finland's cities are open, tolerant places. Helsinki has a small but welcoming gay scene and the country's largest pride festival. Tampere and Turku also host pride festivals. Same-sex marriage became legal in Finland on 1 March 2017.

The tourist board website, www.visitfinland.com, is a good starting point for information.

Money

Finland adopted the euro (€) in 2002. Euro notes come in five, 10, 20, 50, 100, 200 and 500 denominations and coins in five, 10, 20 and 50 cents and €1 and €2. The one- and two-cent coins used in most other Eurozone nations are not accepted in Finland.

Credit Cards

Credit cards are widely accepted and Finns are dedicated users of plastic, even to buy a beer or cup of coffee.

Using ATMs with a credit or debit card is by far the easiest way of getting cash in Finland. ATMs have a name, Otto, and can be found even in small villages.

Moneychangers

Currency can be exchanged at banks and, in the big cities, independent exchange facilities such as Forex (www.forex.fi).

Travellers cheques are very rarely used but can usually be changed at the same places.

Tipping

➡ Service is considered to be included in bills, so there's no need to tip at all unless you want to reward exceptional service.

➡ Doormen in bars and restaurants expect a cloakroom tip (around €2) if there's no mandatory coat charge.

Opening Hours

Many attractions in Finland only open for a short summer season, typically mid-June to late August. Opening hours tend to shorten in winter in general.

Alko (state alcohol store) 9am–8pm Monday to Friday, to 6pm Saturday

Banks 9am–4.15pm Monday to Friday

Businesses and Shops 9am–6pm Monday to Friday, to 3pm Saturday

Nightclubs 10pm–4am Wednesday to Saturday

Pubs 11am–1am (often later on Friday and Saturday)

Restaurants 11am–10pm, lunch 11am–3pm. Last orders are generally an hour before closing.

Post

Post offices can be found in cities, towns and some villages. The website www.posti.fi lists locations.

Public Holidays

Finland grinds to a halt twice a year: around Christmas and New Year, and during the midsummer weekend.

National public holidays:

New Year's Day 1 January

Epiphany 6 January

Good Friday March/April

Easter Sunday & Monday March/April

May Day 1 May

Ascension Day May

Whitsunday Late May or early June

Midsummer's Eve & Day Weekend in June closest to 24 June

All Saints Day First Saturday in November

Independence Day 6 December

Christmas Eve 24 December

Christmas Day 25 December

Boxing Day 26 December

Safe Travel

Finland is a safe country and travellers exercising common sense shouldn't experience any problems. The natural environment poses the main issues.

➡ Winter temperatures can be seriously low; it's vital to make sure you're well equipped with suitable clothing if you're heading outdoors.

➡ Parts of Finland are very remote; if you're hiking in the wilderness, have a map and compass (and know how to use them) and inform someone of your plans.

➡ After the snowmelt, rivers can be prone to flooding.

➡ Mosquitoes and other biting insects are especially fierce around July; strong repellent is essential.

➡ Watch out for reindeer on roads.

Taxes & Refunds

Value-added tax (VAT) is levied at 10% for books, medicines, passenger transport, accommodation services and cultural and entertainment events, 14% for restaurants and 24% for most other items. It should already be included in stated prices.

Non-EU residents may be able to claim a refund on a minimum €40 spent per shop per day. The website www.vero.fi has details.

Telephone

Public telephones basically no longer exist in Finland.

The country code for Finland is ☎358. To dial abroad first dial ☎00.

Mobile Phones

The cheapest and most practical solution is to purchase a Finnish SIM card and pop it in your own phone. First make sure your phone is blocked from doing this by your home network. You can buy a prepaid SIM card at any R-kioski shop. You can also top up credit at R-kisoki or online or at ATMs. Roaming charges within the EU have been abolished.

Time

Finland is on Eastern European Time (EET), an hour ahead of Sweden and Norway. In winter it's two hours ahead of UTC/GMT; from 3am on the last Sunday in March to 3am on the last Sunday in October the clocks go forward an hour to three hours ahead of UTC/GMT.

Toilets

Public toilets are widespread in Finland, but expensive – often €1 a time. On doors, 'M' is for men, while 'N' is for women.

Tourist Information

The main website of the Finnish Tourist Board is www.visitfinland.com. Cities, large towns and major tourist destinations have tourist offices.

Travellers with Disabilities

By law, most Finnish institutions must provide ramps, lifts and special toilets for travellers with limited mobility, and all new hotels and restaurants must install disabled facilities. Trains and city buses are also accessible by wheelchair. Some national parks offer accessible nature trails, and Helsinki and other cities have ongoing projects in place designed to maximise access for people with disabilities in all aspects of urban life.

Before leaving home, get in touch with your national support organisation. The website www.finlandforall.fi has a searchable database of accessible attractions, accommodation and restaurants. Download Lonely Planet's free Accessible Travel guide from http://lptravel.to/AccessibleTravel.

Visas

A valid passport or EU identity card is required to enter Finland. Most Western nationals don't need a tourist visa for stays of less than three months. South Africans, Indians and Chinese, however, are among those who need a Schengen visa. For more information, contact the nearest Finnish embassy or consulate, or check the website www.formin.finland.fi.

Volunteering

Check first with the Finnish embassy or consulate in your home country to find out whether volunteering affects your visa status.

Go Abroad (www.go abroad.com) lists volunteering opportunities in Finland.

Work

In most cases a residence permit is required to work in Finland, but there are exceptions, such as fruit- and berry-picking jobs of no more than 90 days. Comprehensive information is available at www.migri.fi. Contact the Finnish embassy or consulate in your home country well in advance of travelling.

Australian citizens aged between 18 and 30 and New Zealand citizens aged between 18 and 35 can apply for a 12-month working-holiday visa under a reciprocal agreement – contact the Finnish embassy in your home country.

Transport

GETTING THERE & AWAY

Finland is easily accessed from the rest of Europe and beyond. There are direct flights from numerous destinations, while Baltic ferries are another good option.

Flights, cars and tours can be booked online at www.lonelyplanet.com/bookings.

Entering Finland

Entering Finland is a breeze and you'll experience no problems if your papers are in order.

Finland has no issues with any previous visas or stamps you may have in your passport.

Air

Finland is easily reached by air, with direct flights to Helsinki from many European, North American and Asian destinations. It's also served by budget carriers from several European countries. Most other flights are with Finnair, Norwegian or Scandinavian Airlines (SAS).

Most flights land at **Helsinki-Vantaa airport** (www.helsinki-vantaa.fi), 19km north of the capital. Winter charters serve **Rovaniemi** (RVN; ✆020-708-6506; www.finavia.fi; Lentokentäntie), Lapland's main airport, and other smaller regional airports. Other international airports include **Tampere** (TMP; ✆020-708-5521; www.finavia.fi; Tornikaari 50), **Turku** (TKU; www.finavia.fi; Lentoasemantie 150) and **Oulu** (OUL; Lentokentäntie 720; ☎). The website www.finavia.fi includes information for Finnish airports.

Land

Finland can be reached by land directly from Russia, Norway and Sweden.

Border Crossings

There are several border crossings from northern Sweden and Norway to northern Finland, with no passport or customs formalities.

There are nine main border crossings between Finland and Russia, including several in the southeast and two in Lapland. They are more serious frontiers; you must already have a Russian visa.

Bus

Buses link Finland with Sweden, Norway and Russia.

SWEDEN

The linked towns of Tornio (Finland) and Haparanda (Sweden) share a **bus station** (Krannigatan 5, Haparanda, Sweden) from where you can get onward transport into their respective countries. A possible, if remote, crossing point is the Lapland villages of Kaaresuvanto (Finland)

and Karesuando (Sweden), separated by a bridge and both served sporadically by domestic buses.

NORWAY

Three routes link Finnish Lapland with northern Norway, some running only in summer. These are operated by Eskelisen Lapin Linjat (www.eskelisen.fi), whose website has detailed maps and timetables, as does the Finnish bus website Matkahuolto (www.matkahuolto.fi).

All routes originate or pass through Rovaniemi. The two northeastern routes continue via Inari to Tana Bru/Vadsø or Karasjok. The Karasjok bus continues in summer to Nordkapp (North Cape). On the western route, a Rovaniemi–Kilpisjärvi bus continues to Tromsø in summer.

RUSSIA

Daily express buses run to Vyborg and St Petersburg from Helsinki and Lappeenranta. These services appear on the website of Matkahuolto (www.matkahuolto.fi).

Car & Motorcycle

Vehicles can easily be brought into Finland on ferries or overland, provided you have registration papers and valid insurance (Green Card).

Train

The only international trains are to Russia. Fares fluctuate; book well in advance for the best deals.

The Man in Seat Sixty-One (www.seat61.com) is an up-to-date source of information for train travel. Eurail (www.eurail.com) and InterRail (www.interrail.eu) are also good resources.

RUSSIA

Finland's only international trains are to/from Moscow and St Petersburg in Russia.

High-speed Allegro train services (known as Sapsan trains in Russia) run daily from Helsinki to the Finland Station in St Petersburg (3½ hours, four daily). The evening train is usually cheaper. The Tolstoi sleeper runs from Helsinki via St Petersburg (Ladozhki station) to Moscow (14½ hours, one daily). Fares include a sleeper berth, with upmarket sleeper options available.

All trains go via Lahti, Kouvola, Vainikkala (26km south of Lappeenranta) and the Russian city of Vyborg. At Helsinki station tickets are sold at the international ticket counter.

You must have a valid Russian visa; immigration procedures are carried out on board.

There are significant discounts for families and small groups. See www.vr.fi.

Sea

Arriving in Finland by ferry is a memorable way to begin your visit, especially if you dock in Helsinki. Baltic ferries are big floating hotels/shopping plazas, with duty-free stores, restaurants, bars, karaoke, nightclubs and saunas. Many people use them simply for boozy overnight cruises, so they can get pretty rowdy on Friday and Saturday nights.

Services are year-round between major cities. Book ahead in summer, at weekends and if travelling with a vehicle. The boats are amazingly cheap if you travel deck class (without a cabin) – they make their money from duty-free purchases. Many ferry lines offer 50% discounts for holders of train passes. Some offer discounts for seniors, and for ISIC and youth-card holders. There are usually discounts for families and small groups travelling together.

Ferry companies have detailed timetables and fares on their websites. Fares vary widely according to season.

Operators include the following:

Eckerö Line (☎06000-4300; www.eckeroline.fi) Finland–Sweden, Finland–Estonia

Finnlines (☎010-343-4810; www.finnlines.com) Finland–Sweden, Finland–Germany

Linda Line (☎0600-066-8970; www.lindaline.fi) Finland–Estonia

St Peter Line (☎09-6187-2000; https://stpeterline.com) Finland–Russia

Tallink/Silja Line (☎0600-15700; www.tallinksilja.com) Finland–Sweden, Finland–Estonia

Viking Line (☎0600-41577; www.vikingline.fi) Finland–Sweden, Finland–Estonia

Wasaline (☎020-771-6810; www.wasaline.com; Laivanvarustajankatu 4, Helsinki) Finland–Sweden

Sweden

The daily Stockholm–Helsinki, Stockholm–Turku and Kapellskär–Mariehamn (Åland) routes are run by **Tallink/Silja** (☎0600-15700; www.tallinksilja.com) and **Viking Line** (☎0600-41577; www.vikingline.fi). Tallink/Silja doesn't offer deck tickets on the Helsinki run, but shared cabins are available. The cheapest crossings are typically to/from Turku (11 to 12 hours). Note that Åbo is Swedish for Turku.

Eckerö Line (☎06000-4300; www.eckeroline.fi) sails from Grisslehamn, north of Stockholm, to Eckerö in Åland. It's by far the quickest option, at just two hours. There's a connecting bus from Stockholm and some other Swedish towns.

Finnlines (☎010-343-4810; www.finnlines.com) runs a cargo ferry connecting Naantali, near Turku, with Kapellskär via Långnäs in Åland two to three times daily (nine hours).

Wasaline (☎020-771-6810; www.wasaline.com; Laivanvarustajankatu 4, Helsinki) sails

---

CLIMATE CHANGE & TRAVEL

Every form of transport that relies on carbon-based fuel generates CO_2, the main cause of human-induced climate change. Modern travel is dependent on aeroplanes, which might use less fuel per kilometre per person than most cars but travel much greater distances. The altitude at which aircraft emit gases (including CO_2) and particles also contributes to their climate change impact. Many websites offer 'carbon calculators' that allow people to estimate the carbon emissions generated by their journey and, for those who wish to do so, to offset the impact of the greenhouse gases emitted with contributions to portfolios of climate-friendly initiatives throughout the world. Lonely Planet offsets the carbon footprint of all staff and author travel.

from late June to early August from Vaasa in Finland to Umeå, Sweden (4½ hours).

Russia

St Peter Line (☑09-6187-2000; https://stpeterline.com) connects Helsinki with St Petersburg three to four times weekly. A significant added benefit of arriving in Russia this way is a visa-free stay of up to three days in St Petersburg. Canal cruises from Lappeenranta also allow you to do this.

Estonia

Several ferry companies zip between Helsinki and Tallinn in Estonia. In winter there are fewer departures and the crossing is slower due to the ice.

Eckerö Line (☑0600-4300; www.eckeroline.fi; Länsiterminaali (West Terminal), Helsinki) runs car and passenger ferries (two to 2½ hours, up to three daily), as do **Tallink/Silja Line** (☑0600-15700; www.tallinksilja.com) (two hours, eight daily) and **Viking Line** (☑0600-41577; www.vikingline.fi) (1¾ hours, five daily). **Linda Line** (Map p60;☑0600-066-8970; www.lindaline.fi; Makasiiniterminaali, Helsinki; ☺Apr-Oct) runs small passenger-only hydrofoils (1½ hours, three daily).

Germany

Finnlines (☑010-343-4810; www.finnlines.com) runs six to seven ferries a week from Helsinki to Travemünde (29 hours).

GETTING AROUND

A useful combined journey planner for Finland's public-transport network is online at www.journey.fi.

Air

Finnair (www.finnair.com) runs a fairly comprehensive domestic service out of Helsinki. Standard prices are expensive, but check the

ROAD DISTANCES (KM)

	Helsinki	Jyväskylä	Kuopio	Kuusamo	Lappeenranta	Oulu	Rovaniemi	Savonlinna	Tampere	Turku
Jyväskylä	272									
Kuopio	383	144								
Kuusamo	804	553	419							
Lappeenranta	223	219	264	684						
Oulu	612	339	286	215	551					
Rovaniemi	837	563	511	191	776	224				
Savonlinna	338	206	160	579	155	446	671			
Tampere	174	148	293	702	275	491	712	355		
Turku	166	304	448	848	361	633	858	446	155	
Vaasa	419	282	377	533	501	318	543	488	241	348

website for offers. Multitrip journeys can be significantly cheaper than one-way flights. Some Lapland destinations are winter only.

Bicycle

Finland is as bicycle friendly as any country you'll find, with plenty of paths and few hills. Bikes can be taken on most trains, buses and ferries. Åland is particularly good for cycling. Helmets are recommended but no longer required by law.

Hire

You can hire a bike in nearly every Finnish town. Most campgrounds and many urban hotels offer bikes for a small fee or for free, but these are mainly for cycling around town, not for ambitious road trips. Better bikes are available at dedicated outlets. Expect to pay around €15 per day or €90 per week for a good-quality road bike and €45/120 for a mountain bike.

Boat

Lake boats were once important summer transport. These services are now largely kept on as cruises, and make a great, leisurely way to

journey between towns. The most popular routes are Tampere–Hämeenlinna, Tampere–Virrat, Savonlinna–Kuopio and Lahti–Jyväskylä.

Coastal routes include Turku–Naantali, Helsinki–Porvoo and ferries to the Åland archipelago.

The website http://lautta.net is handy for domestic lake-boat and ferry services.

Bus

Bus is the main form of long-distance transport in Finland, with a far more comprehensive network than the train system. Buses run on time and are rarely full.

Intercity buses fall into two main categories: *vakiovuoro* (regular), stopping frequently at towns and villages; and slightly pricier *pikavuoro* (express). Because there are few motorways, even express buses aren't that fast, averaging about 60km/h.

Ticketing is handled by Matkahuolto (www.matkahuolto.fi), which has an excellent website with all the timetables. Matkahuolto offices work normal business hours, but you can always just buy the ticket from the driver.

Towns have a *linja-autoasema* (bus terminal), with local timetables displayed (*lähtevät* is departures, *saapuvat* arrivals).

Separate from the normal system (though its timetables appear on the Matkahuolto website), Onnibus (www.onnibus.com) runs a variety of budget inter-city routes in comfortable double-decker buses. Most of these radiate from Helsinki and can be much cheaper than normal fares if booked in advance.

Departures between major towns are frequent, but reduce substantially at weekends. In more remote areas there may be no weekend buses at all. Schedules change during the summer holidays, when it can be much harder to move around isolated regions.

Prices

Prices refer to express services where available. There are some online advance-purchase offers, and return tickets are 10% cheaper than two one-way fares, provided the trip is at least 60km each way.

Discounts Children aged four to 16 pay half-fare. Student discounts require full-time study in Finland; there's a 50% discount on journeys longer than 60km. If booking three or more adult tickets together, a 25% discount applies.

Car & Motorcycle

Finland's road network is excellent, although there are few motorways. When approaching a town or city, *keskusta* on signs indicates the town centre. There are no road tolls but *lots* of speed cameras.

Petrol is expensive in Finland; check current prices at www.fuel-prices-europe.info. Many petrol stations are unstaffed, but machines take cash and most (but not all) chip-and-PIN-enabled credit

and debit cards. Change for cash is not given.

Hire

Car rental is expensive, but rates can work out reasonably with advance booking or with a group. A small car costs from €65/205 per day/week with 300km free per day, not including insurance. One-way rentals attract a surcharge and are not always possible. Book ahead at peak times to ensure a car is available. Most cars have manual transmission; automatic cars may be available but at a premium and should be reserved well in advance of travel. As ever, the cheapest deals are online.

In larger towns, look out for weekend rates. These can cost little more than the rate for a single day, and you can pick up the car early afternoon on Friday and return it late Sunday or early Monday.

Car-hire franchises with offices in many Finnish cities include the following:

Avis (www.avis.com)

Budget (www.budget.com)

Europcar (www.europcar.com)

Hertz (www.hertz.com)

Sixt (www.sixt.com)

Road Conditions & Hazards

Wildlife Beware of elk and reindeer, which don't respect vehicles and can dash onto the road unexpectedly. This sounds comical, but elk especially constitute a deadly danger. Notify the police if there is an accident involving these animals. Reindeer are very common in Lapland; slow right down if you see one, as there will be more nearby.

Conditions Snow and ice on the roads, potentially from September to April, and as late as June in Lapland, make driving a serious undertaking. Snow chains are illegal: people use either snow tyres, which have studs, or special all-weather tyres. The website http://liikennetilanne. liikennevirasto.fi has road webcams around Finland that

are good for checking conditions. Select *kelikamerat* on the map.

Road Rules

➡ Finns drive on the right.

➡ The speed limit is 50km/h in built-up areas, from 80km/h to 100km/h on highways, and 120km/h on motorways.

➡ Use headlights at all times.

➡ Seat belts are compulsory for all.

➡ Blood alcohol limit is 0.05%.

An important feature of Finland is that there are fewer give-way signs than most countries. Traffic entering an intersection from the right has right of way. While this doesn't apply to highways or main roads, in towns cars will often nip out from the right without looking: you must give way, so be careful at smaller intersections in towns.

Hitching

Hitching is never entirely safe, and we don't recommend it. Travellers who hitch should understand that they are taking a small but potentially serious risk.

In Finland hitching is possible, but expect long waits. It's more common in remote areas where bus services are fewer, but still unusual. Your greatest friend will be your insect repellent. Mosquitoes can't believe their luck that such a large juicy mammal would stand in one place for such a very long time.

Local Transport

Helsinki has Finland's only metro and trams. All Finnish cities and towns have a bus network, with departures every 10 to 15 minutes in large towns, and every 30 to 60 minutes in smaller towns. Fares are around €2.50 to €3.50; pay the driver.

Train Routes

Taxi

The taxi (taksi) in Finland is an expensive creature, particularly for short rides. There's a flagfall of €5.90 in Helsinki (often more elsewhere) and a per-kilometre charge of €1.57. These fares increase if there are more than two passengers, and there's a surcharge for night and weekend service.

Hail taxis on the street or at bus and train stations, or call or book one online.

Train

State-owned Valtion Rautatiet (VR; www.vr.fi) runs Finnish trains. It's a fast, efficient service, with prices roughly equivalent to buses on the same route.

VR's website has comprehensive timetable information. Major stations have a VR office and ticket machines. Tickets can also be purchased online, where you'll also find discounted advance fares. You can also board and pay the conductor, but if the station where you boarded had ticket-purchasing facilities, you'll be charged a small penalty fee (€2 to €5).

Types of Trains

The main types of trains are the high-speed Pendolino (the fastest and most expensive class), fast Intercity (IC), Express and 2nd-class-only Regional trains (H on the timetable).

On longer routes there are two types of sleeping carriage. Traditional blue ones offer berths in one, two or three-bed cabins, while newer sleeping cars offer single and double compartments in a double-decker carriage. There are cabins with bathroom, and one equipped for wheelchair use. Sleeper trains transport cars.

Cost

Fares vary slightly according to the type of train, with Pendolino the priciest. A one-way ticket for a 100km express train journey costs approximately €25 in 2nd ('eco') class. First-class ('extra') tickets cost around 35% more than a 2nd-class ticket. A return fare gives a 10% discount.

Children under 17 pay half-fare; those under six years travel free (but without a seat). A child travels free with every adult on long-distance trips, and there are also discounts for seniors, local students and any group of three or more adults travelling together.

Train Passes

Various passes are available for rail travel within Finland, or in European countries including Finland. There are cheaper passes for students, people aged under 26 and seniors. Supplements (eg for high-speed services) and reservation costs are not covered, and terms and conditions change – check carefully before buying. Always carry your passport when using the pass.

EURAIL

Eurail (www.eurail.com) offers a good selection of passes available to residents of non-European countries, which should be purchased before arriving in Europe. Most of the passes offer discounts of around 25% for under-26s, or 15% for two people travelling together.

The Eurail Country Pass, valid for a single country, costs €286/387 for five/eight days' 2nd-class travel in a one-month period within Finland.

A Eurail Select Pass, covering four countries of your choosing, costs €389 for five days within a month.

Eurail Global Passes offer a variety of options for travel in 28 European countries, from €488 for five days' travel within a one-month period to €803 for one month's continuous travel. The Global Passes are much better value for under-26s, as those older have to buy a 1st-class pass.

On most Eurail passes, children aged between four and 11 get a 50% discount on the full adult fare.

Eurail passes give a 30% to 50% discount on several ferry lines in the region; check the website for details.

INTERRAIL

If you've lived in Europe for more than six months, you're eligible for an InterRail pass (www.interrail.eu). The InterRail Finland pass offers travel only in Finland for three/four/six/eight days in a one-month period, costing €119/150/201/241 in 2nd class. The Global Pass offers travel in 30 European countries and costs from €267 for five days' travel in any 15-day period, to €632 for a month's unlimited train travel. On both passes, there's a 33% discount for under-26s.

InterRail passes give a 30% to 50% discount on several ferry lines in the region; check the website for details.

Language

Finnish is a distinct national icon that sets Finland apart from its Scandinavian neighbours. It belongs to the exclusive Finno-Ugric language family, which also counts Estonian and Hungarian as members. There are around six million Finnish speakers in Finland, Sweden, Norway and Russian Karelia. In Finnish, Finland is known as Suomi and the language itself as suomi.

If you read our coloured pronunciation guides as if they were English, you shouldn't have problems being understood. Note that a is pronounced as in 'act', ai as in 'aisle', eu as the 'u' in 'nurse', ew as the 'ee' in 'see' with rounded lips, oh as the 'o' in 'note', ow as in 'how', uh as the 'u' in 'run', and the r sound is rolled. The stressed syllables are indicated with italics in our pronunciation guides.

BASICS

Hello.	*Hei.*	hayn
Goodbye.	*Näkemiin.*	na·ke·meen
Yes.	*Kyllä.*	kewl·la
No.	*Ei.*	ay
Please.	*Ole hyvä.*	o·le hew·va
Thank you (very much).	*Kiitos (paljon).*	kee·tos (puhl·yon)
You're welcome.	*Ole hyvä.*	o·le hew·va
Excuse me.	*Anteeksi.*	uhn·tayk·si
Sorry.	*Anteeksi.*	uhn·tayk·si

How are you?
Mitä kuuluu?   mi·ta koo·loo

Fine. And you?
Hyvää. Entä itsellesi?   hew·va en·ta it·sel·le·si

What's your name?
Mikä sinun nimesi on?   mi·ka si·nun ni·me·si on

My name is ...
Minun nimeni on ...   mi·nun ni·me·ni on ...

Do you speak English?
Puhutko englantia?   pu·hut·ko en·gluhn·ti·uh

I don't understand.
En ymmärrä.   en ewm·mar·ra

ACCOMMODATION

Where's a cheap/nearby hotel?
Missä olisi halpa/ lähin hotelli?   mis·sa o·li·si huhl·puh/ la·hin ho·tel·li

I'd like a single/double room.
Haluaisin yhden/ kahden hengen huoneen.   huh·lu·ai·sin ewh·den/ kuh·den hen·gen hu·o·nayn

How much is it per night/person?
Paljonko se on yöltä/hengeltä?   puhl·yon·ko se on ew·eul·ta/hen·gel·ta

I want a room with a ...	*Minä haluan huoneen ...*	mi·na huh·lu·uhn hu·o·nayn ...
bathroom	*kylpy- huoneella*	kewl·pew- hu·o·nayl·luh
window	*jossa on ikkuna*	yos·suh on ik·ku·nuh

DIRECTIONS

Where's the ...?	*Missä on ...?*	mis·sa on ...
bank	*pankki*	puhnk·ki
market	*kauppatori*	kowp·pa·to·ri
post office	*postitoi- misto*	pos·ti·toy- mis·to

Can you show me (on the map)?
Voitko näyttää sen minulle (kartalta)?   voyt·ko na·ewt·ta sen mi·nul·le (kar·tuhl·tuh)

EATING & DRINKING

I'd like ..., please.   *Saisinko ...*   sai·sin·ko ...

LANGUAGE EMERGENCIES

SIGNS

Sisään	Entrance
Ulos	Exit
Avoinna	Open
Suljettu	Closed
Kielletty	Prohibited
WC	Toilets

a table for (four)	*pöydän (neljälle)*	peu·ew·dan (nel·yal·le)
the non-smoking section	*savutto-malta puolelta*	suh·vut·to-muhl·tuh pu·o·lel·tuh

Do you have vegetarian food?
Onko teillä kasvisruokia? — on·ko teyl·la kuhs·vis·ru·o·ki·uh

What would you recommend?
Mitä voit suositella? — mi·ta voyt su·o·si·tel·luh

I'll have a ...	*Tilaan ...*	ti·laan ...
Cheers!	*Kippis!*	kip·pis

I'd like (the) ..., please.	*Saisinko ...*	sai·sin·ko ...
bill	*laskun*	luhs·kun
drink list	*juoma-listan*	yu·o·muh-lis·tuhn
menu	*ruokalistan*	ru·o·kuh-lis·tuhn
that dish	*tuon ruokalajin*	tu·on ru·o·kuh-luh·yin

breakfast	*aamiaisen*	aa·mi·ai·sen
lunch	*lounaan*	loh·naan
dinner	*illallisen*	il·luhl·li·sen

bottle of (beer)	*pullon (olutta)*	pul·lon (o·lut·tuh)
(cup of) coffee	*(kupin) kahvia*	(ku·pin) kuh·vi·uh
glass of (wine)	*lasillisen (viiniä)*	luh·sil·li·sen (vee·ni·a)
(cup of) tea	*(kupin) teetä*	(ku·pin) tay·ta
(mineral) water	*(kivennäis-) vettä*	(ki·ven·na·is·) vet·ta

EMERGENCIES

Help!	*Apua!*	uh·pu·uh
Go away!	*Mene pois!*	me·ne poys

Call ...!	*Soittakaa paikalle ...!*	soyt·tuh·kaa pai·kuhl·le ...
a doctor	*lääkäri*	la·ka·ri
the police	*poliisi*	po·lee·si

I'm lost.
Olen eksynyt. — o·len ek·sew·newt

Where are the toilets?
Missä on vessa? — mis·sa on ves·suh

SHOPPING & SERVICES

I'm looking for ...
Etsin ... — et·sin ...

How much is it?
Mitä se maksaa? — mi·ta se muhk·saa

Can you write down the price?
Voitko kirjoittaa hinnan lapulle? — voyt·ko kir·yoyt·taa hin·nuhn luh·pul·le

That's too expensive.
Se on liian kallis. — se on lee·uhn kuhl·lis

There's a mistake in the bill.
Laskussa on virhe. — luhs·kus·suh on vir·he

Do you accept ...?	*Voinko maksaa ...?*	voyn·ko muhk·saa ...
credit cards	*luotto-kortilla*	lu·ot·to-kor·til·luh
travellers cheques	*matka-sekillä*	muht·kuh-se·kil·la

I'd like ..., please.	*Saisinko ...*	sai·sin·ko ...
a receipt	*kuitin*	ku·i·tin
my change	*vaihto-rahat*	vaih·to-ruh·huht

I'd like ..., please.	*Haluaisin ...*	huh·lu·ai·sin ...
a refund	*vaihtaa tämän*	vaih·taa ta·man
to return this	*palauttaa tämän*	puh·lowt·taa ta·man

TIME & DATES

What time is it?
Paljonko kello on? — puhl·yon·ko kel·lo on

It's in the ...	*Kello on ...*	kel·lo on ...
morning	*aamulla*	aa·mul·luh
afternoon	*iltapäivällä*	il·tuh·pa·i·val·la
evening	*illalla*	il·luhl·luh

Monday	*maanantai*	*maa*·nuhn·tai
Tuesday	*tiistai*	*tees*·tai
Wednesday	*keskiviikko*	*kes*·ki·*veek*·ko
Thursday	*torstai*	*tors*·tai
Friday	*perjantai*	*per*·yuhn·tai
Saturday	*lauantai*	*low*·uhn·tai
Sunday	*sunnuntai*	*sun*·nun·tai

WEATHER

What's the weather like?

Millainen ilma siellä on?	*mil*·lai·nen *il*·muh *si*·el·la on

It's ...	*Siellä ...*	*si*·el·la ...
cold	*on kylmä*	on *kewl*·ma
hot	*on kuuma*	on *koo*·ma
raining	*sataa*	*suh*·taa
snowing	*sataa lunta*	*suh*·taa *lun*·tuh

TRANSPORT

Can we get there by public transport?

Pääseekö sinne julkisella liikenteellä?	*paa*·see·keu *sin*·ne *yul*·ki·sel·luh *lee*·ken·teel·la

Where can I buy a ticket?

Mistä voin ostaa lipun?	*mis*·ta voyn *os*·taa *li*·pun

One ... ticket, please.	*Saisinko yhden ... lipun.*	*sai*·sin·ko *ewh*·den ... *li*·pun
one-way	*yksi-suuntaisen*	*ewk*·si-*soon*·tai·sen
return	*meno-paluu*	*me*·no-*pa*·loo

My luggage has been ...	*Matkata-varani ...*	*muht*·kuh·tuh·vuh·ruh·ni ...
lost	*ovat kadonneet*	*o*·vuht *kuh*·don·nayt
stolen	*on varastettu*	on *vuh*·ruhs·tet·tu

Where does this ... go?	*Minne tämä ... menee?*	*min*·ne *ta*·ma ... *me*·nay
boat	*laiva*	*lai*·vuh
bus	*bussi*	*bus*·si
plane	*lentokone*	*len*·to·*ko*·ne
train	*juna*	*yu*·nuh

NUMBERS

1	*yksi*	*ewk*·si
2	*kaksi*	*kuhk*·si
3	*kolme*	*kol*·me
4	*neljä*	*nel*·ya
5	*viisi*	*vee*·si
6	*kuusi*	*koo*·si
7	*seitsemän*	*sayt*·se·man
8	*kahdeksan*	*kuhk*·dek·suhn
9	*yhdeksän*	*ewh*·dek·san
10	*kymmenen*	*kewm*·me·nen
20	*kaksi-kymmentä*	*kuhk*·si·*kewm*·men·ta
30	*kolme-kymmentä*	*kol*·me·*kewm*·men·ta
40	*neljäkymmentä*	*nel*·ya·*kewm*·men·ta
50	*viisikymmentä*	*vee*·si·*kewm*·men·ta
60	*kuusikymmentä*	*koo*·si·*kewm*·men·ta
70	*seitsemän-kymmentä*	*sayt*·se·man·*kewm*·men·ta
80	*kahdeksan-kymmentä*	*kuhk*·dek·suhn·*kewm*·men·ta
90	*yhdeksän-kymmentä*	*ewh*·dek·san·*kewm*·men·ta
100	*sata*	*suh*·tuh
1000	*tuhat*	*tu*·huht

What time's the ... bus?	*Mihin aikaan lähtee ... bussi?*	*mi*·hin *ai*·kaan *lah*·tay ... *bus*·si
first	*ensimmäinen*	*en*·sim·mai·nen
last	*viimeinen*	*vee*·may·nen
next	*seuraava*	*se*·u·raa·vuh

I'd like a taxi ...	*Haluaisin tilata taksin ...*	*huh*·lu·ai·sin *ti*·luh·tuh *tuhk*·sin ...
at (9am)	*kello (yhdeksäksi aamulla)*	*kel*·lo (*ewh*·dek·sak·si *aa*·mul·luh)
tomorrow	*huomiseksi*	*hu*·o·mi·sek·si

How much is it to ...?

Miten paljon maksaa matka ...?	*mi*·ten *puhl*·yon *muhk*·saa *muht*·kuh ...

Please take me to (this address).

Voitko viedä minut (tähän osoitteeseen).	*voyt*·ko *vi*·e·da *mi*·nut (*ta*·han o·*soyt*·tay·sayn)

Please stop here.

Pysähdy tässä.	*pew*·sah·dew *tas*·sa

Behind the Scenes

SEND US YOUR FEEDBACK

We love to hear from travellers – your comments keep us on our toes and help make our books better. Our well-travelled team reads every word on what you loved or loathed about this book. Although we cannot reply individually to your submissions, we always guarantee that your feedback goes straight to the appropriate authors, in time for the next edition. Each person who sends us information is thanked in the next edition – the most useful submissions are rewarded with a selection of digital PDF chapters.

Visit **lonelyplanet.com/contact** to submit your updates and suggestions or to ask for help. Our award-winning website also features inspirational travel stories, news and discussions.

Note: We may edit, reproduce and incorporate your comments in Lonely Planet products such as guidebooks, websites and digital products, so let us know if you don't want your comments reproduced or your name acknowledged. For a copy of our privacy policy visit lonelyplanet.com/privacy.

OUR READERS

Many thanks to the travellers who used the last edition and wrote to us with helpful hints, useful advice and interesting anecdotes:

Ad de Jong, Aurora & Davide Camisa, Bryony Retter, Carla de Beer, Christian Lukasczyk, David Wille, Gerlinde Konrad, Robert Mitchell, Roberta Palen, Stella-Maria Thomas, Suzanne Richter, Tamara Mehl, Ulla Nielsen

WRITER THANKS

Mara Vorhees

Kiitos a million times over to my Finnish family, Outi and Kauko Ojala, for their in-depth knowledge of Finland, for their never-ending hospitality and for so many laughs over the course of 30 years. Here's to 30 more! *Kiitos* another million times to my American family – to my parents, who keep coming back for more; to my kiddos, for their ever-adventurous spirits, and to my favourite travel companion of all time, for accompanying me on this fabulous journey.

Catherine Le Nevez

Kiitos paljon/tack så mycket first and foremost to Julian, and to all of the locals, tourism professionals and fellow travellers who provided insights, inspiration and good times. Huge thanks too to destination editor Gemma Graham, my Finland and Scandinavia co-authors, and all at Lonely Planet. As ever, *merci encore* to my parents, brother, *belle-sœur* and *neveu*.

Virginia Maxwell

Greatest thanks to my travelling companion and navigator, Max Handsaker. Thanks also to Peter Handsaker for holding the fort at home, and to the extremely helpful staff at the tourist offices in both of the Finnish regions that I researched.

ACKNOWLEDGEMENTS

Climate map data adapted from Peel MC, Finlayson BL & McMahon TA (2007) 'Updated World Map of the Köppen-Geiger Climate Classification', *Hydrology and Earth System Sciences*, 11, 1633–44.

Cover photograph: Traditional Sámi dress and drinking cup, Inari, Lapland, Doug Pearson/Alamy ©

THIS BOOK

This 9th edition of Lonely Planet's *Finland* guidebook was researched and written by Mara Vorhees, Catherine Le Nevez and Virginia Maxwell. The previous two editions were written by Andy Symington, Catherine Le Nevez and Fran Parnell. This guidebook was produced by the following:

Destination Editor
Gemma Graham

Product Editor
Rachel Rawling

Senior Cartographers
Valentina Kremenchutskaya, David Kemp

Book Designer
Clara Monitto

Assisting Editors Sarah Bailey, Andrew Bain, Lucy Cowie, Pete Cruttenden, Sarah Reid, Gabrielle Stefanos, Simon Williamson

Assisting Cartographer
Michael Garrett

Cover Researcher
Naomi Parker

Thanks to Hannah Cartmel, Kate Chapman, Bruce Evans, Kate Mathews, Genna Patterson, Martine Power, Kirsten Rawlings, Tony Wheeler, Amanda Williamson

Index

A

Aalto, Alvar 161, 164, 167-8, 201, 205-6, 290
accommodation 19, 298-9, *see also individual locations*
  camping 30-1, 59, 298
  internet resources 299
  snow hotels 15, 243, **15**
  summer cottages 13, 287, **13**
activities 22-4, 28-35, *see also individual activities & locations*
air travel
  to/from Finland 303
  within Finland 305
Åland Archipelago 10, 38, 114-31, **115**, **11**
  accommodation 114
  climate 114
  festivals & events 116
  food 114
  highlights 115
  history 115-16
  tourist information 116
  travel seasons 114
  travel to/from 116-17
  travel within 117
amusement parks
  JukuPark 214
  Muumimaailma 91
  Santapark 249
  Särkänniemi 134
  Serena water park 65
  Tropiclandia 207
animals, *see* wildlife
aquariums
  Maretarium 111
  Sea Life 65
Archipelago National Park 97-9
Archipelago Trail 88

Map Pages **000**
Photo Pages **000**

architectural sites
  Helsinki 49
  Muuratsalon Koetalo 167
  Säynätsalon Kunnantalo 167
  Seinäjoki 205-6
  Villa Mairea 201
architecture 20-1
area codes 17
Arktikum 242
art galleries 19, *see also museums*
  Aineen Taidemuseo 240
  Ålands Kulturhistoriska & Konstmuseum 118
  Alariesto Galleria 259
  Amos Andersonin Taidemuseo 53
  Ateneum 48
  Didrichsen Taidemuseo 53
  Espoo Museum of Modern Art 74
  Gallen-Kallelan Museo 74
  Hämeenlinnan Taidemuseo 144
  Hannun Luontokuvakeskus 227
  Joensuun Taidemuseo 182
  Kiasma 48
  Kuopion Taidemuseo 169
  Pori Art Museum 200-1
  Rauman Taidemuseo 198
  Rovaniemen Taidemuseo 242
  Serlachius Museum Gösta 142
  Sinebrychoffin Taidemuseo 52
  Taidetehdas 106
  Tikanojan Taidekoti 207
  Turun Taidemuseo 85
  Villa Gyllenberg 53
  Walter Runeberg Sculpture Collection 106
arts 292-4, *see also* design
arts centres
  Juminkeko 224
  Kaapelitehdas 77
  Konepahalli 53

  Sibeliustalo 146
  Sajos 266
  Taitokortteli 182
  Tennispalatsi 53
ATMs 125
aurora borealis 260
Auttiköngäs waterfall 251

B

bears 10, 20, 191, 224-5, 226-7, 229, **10**, **228**
beer 296
Bengtskär Lighthouse 98
birdwatching 35, **229**
bicycle travel, *see* cycling
boat travel, *see also* cruises
  to/from Finland 304-5
  within Finland 205
Bomarsund Fästningsruin 126
Bomba Village 193
books 274, *see also* literature
border crossings 303
Brändö 129-30
breweries
  Beer Hunter's 202
  Birri 72
  Huvila 154
  Malmgård Brewery 111
  Stallhagen Brewery 128
  Suomenlinnan Panimo 69
budgeting 17, 298, 299
bus travel
  to/from Finland 303
  within Finland 305-6
business hours 17, 301

C

camping 30-1, 59, 298
canoeing & kayaking 34
  Eckerö 123
  Kitkajoki 230
  Nurmijärvi District 192
  Oulankajoki 230
  Raseborg 102
  Ruunaa Recreation Area 190

  Squirrel Route 159
car travel 288, 303, 306
castles & fortresses
  Bomarsund Fästnings-ruin 126
  Hämeenlinna 143-4
  Kastelholms Slott 125-6, **11**
  Linnoitus 175
  Lumilinna 239
  Örö Fortress 18, 97-8
  Olavinlinna 152, **163**
  Raseborg Castle 103
  Suomenlinna 46-7, **46**
  Svartholma Sea Fortress 109
  Turun Linna 84
cell phones 16, 301
ceramics 76, 289
chapels
  Kamppi Chapel 53, **20**
  Taidekappeli 85
children, travel with 36-7, 65
churches 294
  Dragsfjärdin Kirkko 98
  Ekenäs Church 102
  Hattulan Pyhän Ristin 143
  Hollolan Kirkko 147
  Johanneksenkirkko 51
  Kerimäen Iso Kirkko 156
  Keuruun Vanha Kirkko 141
  Korpo kyrka 95
  Kotkan Kirkko 111
  Lakeuden Risti Kirkko 205
  Lappee Church 175
  Naantalin Kirkko 91
  Nagu kyrka 94
  Orthodox Church of St Nicholas 182
  Orthodox Church of Sts Peter & Paul 113
  Oulun Tuomiokirkko 217
  Paltaniemen kuvakirkko 223
  Pargas Church 94
  Pedersöre Kyrka 210
  Petäjäveden Vanha Kirkko 168
  Pielpajärven Kirkko 266

Pyhän Elian Kirkko 185
Pyhän Laurin Kirkko 105
Pyhän Ristin Kirkko 197
Ristinkirkko 147
Rovaniemen Kirkko 242
Sankt Göran's Kyrka
117-18
Sankt Johannes Kyrka 126
Sankt Mikael Kyrka 127
Sankt Olof Kyrka 122
Sankta Catharina
Kyrka 122
Sankta Maria Kyrka 125
Suomenlinnan Kirkko 47
Temppeliaukion Kirkko 54
Tornion Kirkko 240
Tuomiokirkko (Helsinki)
49, **2**, **45**
Tuomiokirkko (Porvoo) 106
Tuomiokirkko
(Tampere) 134
Turun Tuomiokirkko
(Turku) 84
Uspenskin Katedraali 49
Vanha Kirkko,
(Sodankylä) 259
Vanha Kirkko
(Uusikaupunki) 196
climate 16, 22-4, *see also*
individual locations
climate change 274, 304
coffee 275, 296
costs 306
credit cards 300
cross-country skiing 33-4,
146, **245**
cruises, *see also* boat travel
Hämeenlinna 145
Hanko 100
Helsinki 55
Inari 267
Jyväskylä 164
Kemi 239
Kilpisjärvi 258
Kuopio 169-70
Lakeland 11, **11**
Lappeenranta 176
Lemmenjoki National
Park 269
Raseborg 103
Russia 181
Turku 85
Uusikaupunki 196
Vaasa 207
culture 286-8
currency 16
customs regulations 299
cycling 18, 32-3, 305
Åland Archipelago 10,
122, 127
Archipelago Trail 88

Levi 254
Mail Road 122
Mänttä 142
Uusikaupunki 196
Ylläs 253

D
dangers, *see* safety
departure tax 303
design 289-91, **9**
Design District (Helsinki) 9
Design Museum 51
disabilities, travellers
with 302
discount cards 48
dog sledding 12, 23, 33,
12, **245**
Hetta 256
Koli National Park 186
Kuusamo 227
Muonio 255
Rovaniemi 242
Saariselkä 261
drinking & nightlife 14, 296,
14, *see also individual*
locations
driving, *see* car travel

E
Eckerö 123-4
economy 274-5
Ekenäs, *see* Raseborg
Ekenäs Archipelago
National Park 105
electricity 275, 299
emergencies 17, 310
environmental issues
274, 304
Espoo 74
events, *see* festivals &
events
exchange rates 17

F
Fäboda 211-12
factories
ceramics 76
glass 143
farmstays 298
Fasta Åland 117-28
Fell Lapland 252-9
ferry travel 304-5
festivals & events 22-4, *see*
also individual festivals
& events, music festivals
films 274
Finström 127
fishing 34, 35
Eckerö 123
Föglö 130

Imatra 180
Kotka 111
Lieksa 189
Mariehamn 118-19
Nurmijärvi District 192
Ruunaa Recreation Area
190-1
Fiskars 104-5
Föglö 130
food 21, 295-6, 299, **15**
forest food 33
internet resources 295
language 309-11
lemin särä 179
markets 15, 295
Runeberg torte 107
sweets 296
foraging 296
fortresses, *see* castles &
fortresses

G
galleries, *see* art galleries
gay travellers 73, 300
Geta 124-5

H
Hailuoto 222
Häme 38, 132, 143-9, **133**
accommodation 132
climate 132
food 132
highlights 133
travel seasons 132
Hämeenlinna 143-6, **144**
Hamina 112-13
Hammarland 122-3
handicrafts 285
Hanko 15, 99-102, **100**, **15**
Hattulan Pyhän Ristin 143
Hattuvaara 185-6
Haukipudos 222
health 300
Helsinki 38, 42-81, **43**, **50-1**,
60-1, **72**
accommodation 42, 47,
58-9, 62-3
activities 54-5
children, travel with 65
climate 42
discount cards 48
drinking & nightlife
72-6, **14**
entertainment 75-6
festivals & events 58
food 42, 64, 67-72
highlights 43, 46-7
history 48
itineraries 49

LGBT travellers 73
neighbourhoods 44-5, **44**
shopping 9, 77-9
sights 48-9, 51-4
tourist information 79
tours 55
travel seasons 42
travel to/from 79-81
travel within 81
walking tours 55, 66, **66**
Helvetinjärvi National
Park 141
Hetta 256-7
Hiekkalinna 175
hiking 10, 28, 30-1
Geta 124
Helvetistä Itään Nature
Trail 141
Karelia 191
Karhunkierros Trek 232-4
Karhunpolku (Bear's
Trail) 191
Kilpisjärvi 258
Koli National Park 186
Kuhmo 225
Oravareitti 159
Pallas-Yllästunturi
National Park 257, **10**
Pieni Karhunkierros 232
Pirkan Taival 135
Pyynikki 135
Riisintunturi 226
Ruunaa Recreation
Area 190
Sevettijärvi 272
Squirrel Route 159
Susitaival
(Wolf's Trail) 191
Tapion Taival
(Fighter's Trail) 191
Ylläs 252-3
UKK route 227
history 274, 276-83
hitching 306
holidays 301
homewares 290
horse riding
Eckerö 123
Inari 267
Koli National Park 186
Lieksa 189
Ylläs 252
Hossa 225-6
Hossa National Park 18,
225-6
Houtskär 96

I
ice-fishing 34
Iittala 143

Ilomantsi 184-5
Imatra 179-81
Inari 266-8
Iniö 96
insurance 300
internet access 300
internet resources 17, 293
islands 19
  Hailuoto 222
  Kobba Klintar 121
  Kotkan Saaret 111
  Kuusisaari 53
  Reposaari 203
  Tankar Island 213
  Tervasaari 49
itineraries 25-7, **25**, **26**, **27**, see also individual locations
Ivalo 265-6

J

Jakobstad 210-11, **212**
Joensuu 181-5, **184**
jokamiehenoikeus 30
Jomala 122
Juuma 232
Jyväskylä 161-7, **166**, **163**

K

kahvi (coffee) 275, 296
Kainuu 40, 215, 222-5, **216**
  accommodation 215
  climate 215
  food 215
  highlights 216
  history 216
  travel seasons 215
Kajaani 222-3
Kajsaniemi 48
Kalajoki 213-14
Kalevala 292
Kansallismuseo 53
Karelia 38, 173-93, **174**, 13
  accommodation 173
  climate 173
  food 173
  highlights 174
  travel seasons 173
Karhunkierros Trek 232-4, **233**
Karigasniemi 270-1
Karl, Duke 277
Kauppatori 49
kayaking, see canoeing & kayaking

Map Pages **000**
Photo Pages **000**

Kemi 238-40
Kemijärvi 250
Kenkävero 158
Kerimäen Iso Kirkko 156
Kerimäki 156
kesämökkejä 287
Keuruu 141
Kevo Strict Nature Reserve 271
Kiasma 48
Kilpisjärvi 258-9
Kimito Island 97-9
Kobba Klintar 121
Koillismaa 40, 215, 225-34, **216**
  accommodation 215
  climate 215
  food 215
  highlights 216
  history 216
  travel seasons 215
Kökar 131
Kokkola 212-13
Koli National Park 186-8
Kolovesi National Park 157-8, **163**
Korpo 95-6
Kotka 109-12, **110**
Kotkan Saaret 111
Kristinestad 204
Kuhmo 224-5
Kultaranta 91
Kumlinge 129
Kuopio 168-72, **170**
Kustavi 97
Kuusamo 226-32
Kuusisaari 53
Kvarken Archipelago 209-10

L

Lahti 146-9, **148**
Lake Pielinen 186-93
Lakeland 11, 38, 150-72, **151**, 11, **162-3**
  accommodation 150
  climate 150
  food 150
  highlights 151
  travel seasons 150
lakes 162-3
Langinkoski Imperial Fishing Lodge 112
language 16, 285, 309-11
Lapland 12, 40, 235-72, **236-7**, 12
  accommodation 235
  activities 238
  climate 235, 239
  food 235
  highlights 236

  history 238
  language 238
  safety 238
  travel seasons 235, 239
  travel within 238
Lappeenranta 175-9, **176**
legal matters 300
Lemi 179
Lemland 127-8
Lemmenjoki National Park 268-70
Levi 253-5
LGBT travellers 73, 300
Lieksa 188-9
lifestyle 286-8
Linnansaari National Park 157, **162**
Linnoitus 175
literature 292-3, see also books
Lohja 104
Loviisa 108
Lumilinna 239
Lumparland 128

M

Mänttä 142-3
Mariehamn 117-22, **118**
Marimekko 9, 289, 290-91, **9**
markets 15, 295, **15**
matkakoti 298
measures 300
metal music 293
Mikkeli 158-60
mobile phones 16, 301
money 16, 17, 300-1
Moomins 91, 92, 134, 293
motorcycle travel 303, 306
Muonio 255-6
museums, see also art galleries
  Aboa Vetus & Ars Nova 84
  Ainola 70
  Ålands Jakt och Fiske-museum 123
  Ålands Kulturhistoriska & Konstmuseum 118
  Alvar Aalto Museo 161
  Amurin Työläis-museokortteli 134
  Arkkitehtuurimuseo 51
  Arktikum 242
  Bomarsund Museum 126
  Bonk Museum 196
  Carelicum 182
  Design Museum 51
  Eino Leino-Talo 223
  EKTA Museum 102

  Fängelsemuseet Vita Björn 126
  Fiskars Museum 104
  Forum Marinum 84-5
  Halosenniemi 70
  Helsingin Kaupunginmuseo 49
  Heureka 65
  Hiihtomuseo 146
  Jakobstads Museum 210
  Jalkaväkimuseo 159
  Jalokivigalleria 239
  Jan Karlsgårdens Friluftsmuseum 126
  Kansallismuseo 53
  Karelia Aviation Museum 175
  Keski-Suomen Museo 161
  Kieppi 212
  Kierikkikeskus 222
  Kolttien Perinnetalo 272
  Kuhmon Talvisotamuseo 224
  Kultamuseo 262
  Kuntsin Modernin Taiteen Museo 207
  Kuopion Korttelimuseo 168-9
  Kuopion Museo 168
  Lahden Historiallinen Museo 147
  Lottamuseo 70
  Luonnontieteellinen Museo 65
  Luostarinmäen Käsityöläismuseo 84
  Lusto Suomen Metsämuseo 156
  Mannerheim-Museo 52
  Marela 197
  Merikeskus Vellamo 109
  Moomimuseo 18, 134
  Museo Militaria 145
  Museo Skogster 145-6
  Museumship Pommern 117
  Naantali Museum 91
  Nanoq Arctic Museum 211
  Önningeby Museo 122
  Päämajamuseo 159
  Palanderin Talo 144-5
  Pargas Hembygdsmuseum 94
  Pielisen Museo 188
  Pilke Tiedekeskus 242
  Pohjanmaan Museo 207
  Pohjois Pohjanmaan Museo 217
  Raatteen Portti 226
  Rauman Merimuseo 198-9
  Rintama Museo 102
  Rosala Viking Centre 98

Runebergin Koti 106
Sagalunds Museum 98
Samiland 254
Satakunnan Museo 200
Serlachius Museum
    Gustaf 142
Seurasaaren
    Ulkomuseo 54
Sibeliuksen
    syntymäkoti 145
Sibelius Museum 85
Siida 266
Sjöfartsmuseum 117
Sjökvarteret 118
Suomen Lasimuseo 143
Suomenlinna 47
Suomen Ortodoksinen
    Kirkkomuseo 169
Tammela 197
Tietomaa 217
Tornionlaakson
    Maakuntamuseo 240
Turkansaaren
    Ulkomuseo 217
Vakoilumuseo 134
Vapriikki 134-5
Wahlberg House 196
Werstas 134
Wolkoff Home Museum
    175
music 293-4
music festivals 12
    Air Guitar World
        Championships 218
    Festivo 199
    Hamina Tattoo 113
    Ilosaari Rock Festival 182
    Kalott Jazz & Blues
        Festival 241
    Kuhmon
        Kamarimusiikki 225
    Lemin Musiikkijuhlat 177
    Lieksa Brass Week 189
    Polar Night Jazz 261
    Provinssirock 206
    QStock 218
    Rauma Blues Festival 198
    Ruisrock 86, **12**
    Savonlinna 155
    Sibelius Festival
        (Lahti) 147
    Sibelius Festival
        (Loviisa) 109
    Tampere 135
Muuratsalo 167

N
Naantali 91-3
Nagu 94-5
Närpes 205

national parks & reserves
    10, 28, 30, **29**
    Archipelago National
        Park 97-9
    Ekenäs Archipelago
        National Park 105
    Helvetinjärvi National
        Park 141
    Hossa National Park 18,
        225-6
    Kevo Strict Nature
        Reserve 271
    Koli National Park 186-8
    Kolovesi National Park
        157-8, **163**
    Kuusamon
        Suurpetokeskus 226-7
    Lemmenjoki National
        Park 268-70
    Linnansaari National Park
        157, **162**
    Luontokeskus Naava 250
    Nuuksio National Park 74
    Oulanka National Park
        232-4, **233**
    Pallas-Yllästunturi
        National Park 257-8, **10**
    Patvinsuo National Park
        189-90
    Perämeri National
        Park 240
    Petola Luontokeskus 224
    Pyhä-Luosto National
        Park 250
    Riisitunturi National
        Park 226
    Saariselkä Wilderness
        263-5, **2**
    Syöte National Park 225
    Tankavaara Nature
        Centre 263
    Urko Kekkonen National
        Park 263-5, **2**
    Yllästunturi Visitor
        Centre 252
Nellim 266
New Suomi cuisine 296
New Valamo 160-1
newspapers 300
Nordic walking 31
North Karelia 181-6
Northern Lapland 259-72
Northern Lights 260
Nuorgam 271-2
Nurmes 192-3
Nurmijärvi District 192
Nuuksio National Park 74

O
opening hours 17, 301
opera 155
Örö Fortress 18, 97-8

Oulanka National Park
    232-4, **233**
Oulankajoki 230
Oulu 38, 215, 217-22 **216**,
    220
    accommodation 215,
        218-19
    activities 217-18
    climate 215
    drinking & nightlife 221
    festivals & events 218
    food 215, 219-21
    highlights 216,
    history 216
    sights 217
    tourist information 221
    tours 218
    travel seasons 215
    travel to/from 221
    travel within 222

P
Paalasmaa Island 188
Paateri 193
Pallas-Yllästunturi National
    Park 257-8, **10**
Pargas 94
parks & gardens
    Aulanko 145
    Esplanadin Puisto 48-9
    Hupisaaret Park 217
    Kaivopuisto 52
    Kajsaniemi 48
    Kirjurinluoto 201
    Kruununpuisto 179
    Perhos-Botania 182
    Sapokka Vesipuisto 110
    Tervasaari 49
Parliament House 53
Parppeinvaara 185
Patvinsuo National Park
    189-90
Perämeri National Park 240
permits, fishing 35
Petäjävesi 168
Pilke Tiedekeskus 242
Pirkanmaa 38, 132, 140-3,
    133
    accommodation 132
    climate 132
    food 132
    highlights 133
    travel seasons 132
planning, see also individual
    regions
    calendar of events 22-4
    children, travel with 36-7
    Finland basics 16-17
    Finland's regions 38-
        40, 63

itineraries 25-7, **25**,
    26, **27**
repeat visitors 18
travel seasons 16
politics 282-3
population 275
Pori 200-3, **202**
Porvoo 106-8, **108**
postal services 301
public access 30
public holidays 301
Punkaharju 155-6
Pyhä-Luosto 250-2
Pyhä-Luosto National
    Park 250

R
radio 300
rafting 34
    Juuma 232
    Kitkajoki 230
    Ruunaa Recreation
        Area 190
    Saariselkä 261
    Tornio 240
Ranua 249
Raseborg 102-4
Rauma 14, 197-200, **198**, **14**
Rautiosaari 249
reindeer 20, 285, **5**
reindeer farms
    Konttaniemen Porotila 242
    Kopara 251
    Santa's Reindeers 188
religion 288
Reposaari 203
Riisitunturi National
    Park 226
road distances 305
Rte 66 140
Rovaniemi 241-9, **246**
    accommodation 243-7
    activities 242-3
    drinking 248
    entertainment 248
    festivals & events 243
    food 247-8
    shopping 248
    sights 241-2
    tourist information 248
    travel to/from 248
    travel within 249
Ruka 226-32
Ruovesi 141
Russia, travel to/from 80,
    181, 187
Russian influence 275, 278
Ruunaa Recreation Area
    190-2

INDEX S–Y

S
Saariselkä 261-2
Saariselkä Wilderness 263-5, **264-5**
safety 301, 206
Sallivaara 269
Saltvik 125
Sámi music 293
Sámi people 13, 284-5, **13**
Sammallahdenmäki 200
Santa Claus Village 249
Santa's Seaside Office 239
saunas & spas 9, 21, 32, 56-7, 286-7, **8-9, 56-57**
  festivals 206
  Hanko 100
  Helsinki 54
  Kuopio 169
  Naantali 92
  Oulu 217
  Regatta Spa 18
  Tampere 135
  Ylläs 252
Savonlinna 151-5, **152, 11**
Savonlinna Opera Festival 155
Säynätsalo 167
sceneic flights
  Inari 267
  Kilpisjärvi 258
sculpture 294
Seal Lakes 157-8
seals 20, 157, **20**
Seinäjoki 205-6
Serlachius Museum Gösta 142
Seurasaaren Ulkomuseo 54
Sevettijärvi 272
shipwrecks 120
shoes 289
shopping 289, 290, see also individual locations
Sibelius, Jean 292, 293
Siirrettävien Saunojen 206
skiing & snowboarding 33-4, **245**
  Koli National Park 186
  Levi 254
  Pyhä-Luosto 251
  Riisitunturi 226
  Rovaniemi 242-3
  Rukatunturi 227
  Saariselkä 261
  Sotkamo 223
  Syöte 225
  Ylläs 252

ski-jumping 146
sledding, see dog sledding
smoking 300
snow hotels 15, 243, **15**
snowmobiling 33, **245**
Sodankylä 259-61
Sotkamo 223-4
South Coast 38, 82, 97-113, **83**
  accommodation 82
  food 82
  highlights 82
  east of Helsinki 105-13
  west of Helsinki 97-105
South Karelia 175-81
Southern Archipelago 128-9, 130-1
Southern Lapland 238-52
souvenirs 289
spas, see saunas & spas
sports events
  Finlandia Ski Marathon 147
  Paavo Nurmi Marathon 86
  Ski Games 147
  Sulkavan Suursoudut 158-9
Squirrel Route 159
St Petersburg, travel to/from 80
Stone Age 276
Sulkava 158
summer cottages 13, 287, **13**
Sund 125-6
Suomenlinna 46-7, **46**
Syöte National Park 225

T
Taidekappeli 85
Tampere 38, 132, 133-40, **136-7, 8**
  accommodation 132, 135-7
  activities 135
  climate 132
  drinking & nightlife 139
  entertainment 139
  festivals & events 135
  food 132, 137-9
  highlights 133
  history 134
  shopping 140
  sights 134-5
  tourist information 140
  travel seasons 132
  travel to/from 140
  travel within 140

Tankar island 313
Tankavaara 262-3
taxes 301, 303
taxis 308
telephone services 301
Tennispalatsi 53
Teno Valley 271-2
Tervasaari 49
theme parks, see amusement parks
Tiketti 75
time 16, 301
tipping 301
toilets 301
Tornio 240-1
tourist information 301
tours 18
train travel
  to/from Finland 304
  within Finland 308, **307**
travel to/from Finland 17, 303-5
travel within Finland 17, 305-8
trekking, see hiking
Turku 38, 84-91, **86**
  accommodation 82, 86-7
  activities 85
  drinking & nightlife 89
  entertainment 89-90
  festivals & events 86
  food 82, 88-9
  highlights 83
  history 84
  shopping 90
  sights 84-5
  tourist information 90
  travel to/from 90
  travel within 90-1
Turku Archipelago 93-7
Tuusulanjärvi 70
TV 300

U
UKK route 227
Unesco World Heritage Sites
  Kvarken Archipelago 209-10
  Sammallahdenmäki 200
  Suomenlinna 46-7, **46**
  Vanha Rauma 14, **14**
Urho Kekkonen National Park 263-5, **264-5, 2**
Utsjoki 271
Uusikaupunki 196-7

V
Vaasa 206-9, **208**
vacations 301
Vanha Porvoo 106
Vanha Rauma 14, 197, **14**
Vårdö 126-7
vegan travellers 296
vegetarian travellers 296
visas 16, 302
Visavuori 142
vihta 32, 287, **57**
volunteering 302
Vuonislahti 188-9

W
walking tours
  architecture 55
  Helsinki 66, **66**
  Suomenlinna 47
water parks, see amusement parks
water sports 34
weather 16, 22-4, see also individual regions
websites 17, 293
weights 300
West Coast 38, 194-214, **195**
  accommodation 194
  climate 194
  food 194
  highlights 195
  travel seasons 194
Wife-Carrying World Championships 168
wildlife 20, 228-9, **228-9**
wildlife reserves, see national parks & reserves
wildlife watching 10
  Eckerö 123
  Erä Eero 189
  Inari 267
  Kuhmo 225
  Kuusamo 227
  Rovaniemi 242
  Yyteri Nature Trails 203
winter sports 33-4, **244-245**
wolverines 20, **229**
work 302

Y
Ylläs 252-3
Yyteri Beach 203

Map Pages **000**
Photo Pages **000**

Map Legend

Sights

- Beach
- Bird Sanctuary
- Buddhist
- Castle/Palace
- Christian
- Confucian
- Hindu
- Islamic
- Jain
- Jewish
- Monument
- Museum/Gallery/Historic Building
- Ruin
- Shinto
- Sikh
- Taoist
- Winery/Vineyard
- Zoo/Wildlife Sanctuary
- Other Sight

Activities, Courses & Tours

- Bodysurfing
- Diving
- Canoeing/Kayaking
- Course/Tour
- Sento Hot Baths/Onsen
- Skiing
- Snorkelling
- Surfing
- Swimming/Pool
- Walking
- Windsurfing
- Other Activity

Sleeping

- Sleeping
- Camping
- Hut/Shelter

Eating

- Eating

Drinking & Nightlife

- Drinking & Nightlife
- Cafe

Entertainment

- Entertainment

Shopping

- Shopping

Information

- Bank
- Embassy/Consulate
- Hospital/Medical
- Internet
- Police
- Post Office
- Telephone
- Toilet
- Tourist Information
- Other Information

Geographic

- Beach
- Gate
- Hut/Shelter
- Lighthouse
- Lookout
- Mountain/Volcano
- Oasis
- Park
- Pass
- Picnic Area
- Waterfall

Population

- Capital (National)
- Capital (State/Province)
- City/Large Town
- Town/Village

Transport

- Airport
- Border crossing
- Bus
- Cable car/Funicular
- Cycling
- Ferry
- Metro station
- Monorail
- Parking
- Petrol station
- S-Bahn/Subway station
- Taxi
- T-bane/Tunnelbana station
- Train station/Railway
- Tram
- Tube station
- U-Bahn/Underground station
- Other Transport

Routes

- Tollway
- Freeway
- Primary
- Secondary
- Tertiary
- Lane
- Unsealed road
- Road under construction
- Plaza/Mall
- Steps
- Tunnel
- Pedestrian overpass
- Walking Tour
- Walking Tour detour
- Path/Walking Trail

Boundaries

- International
- State/Province
- Disputed
- Regional/Suburb
- Marine Park
- Cliff
- Wall

Hydrography

- River, Creek
- Intermittent River
- Canal
- Water
- Dry/Salt/Intermittent Lake
- Reef

Areas

- Airport/Runway
- Beach/Desert
- Cemetery (Christian)
- Cemetery (Other)
- Glacier
- Mudflat
- Park/Forest
- Sight (Building)
- Sportsground
- Swamp/Mangrove

Note: Not all symbols displayed above appear on the maps in this book

OUR STORY

A beat-up old car, a few dollars in the pocket and a sense of adventure. In 1972 that's all Tony and Maureen Wheeler needed for the trip of a lifetime – across Europe and Asia overland to Australia. It took several months, and at the end – broke but inspired – they sat at their kitchen table writing and stapling together their first travel guide, *Across Asia on the Cheap*. Within a week they'd sold 1500 copies. Lonely Planet was born.

Today, Lonely Planet has offices in Franklin, London, Melbourne, Oakland, Dublin, Beijing and Delhi, with more than 600 staff and writers. We share Tony's belief that 'a great guidebook should do three things: inform, educate and amuse'.

OUR WRITERS

Mara Vorhees

Turku & the South Coast; Åland Archipelago; West Coast Mara Vorhees writes about food, travel and family fun around the world. Her work has been published by *BBC Travel*, *Boston Globe*, *Delta Sky*, *Vancouver Sun* and more. For Lonely Planet, she regularly writes about destinations in Central America and Eastern Europe, as well as New England, where she lives. She often travels with her twin boys in tow, earning her an expertise in family travel. Follow their adventures and misadventures at www.havetwinswilltravel.com.

Catherine Le Nevez

Helsinki; Karelia; Oulu, Kainuu & Koillismaa; Lapland Catherine's wanderlust kicked in when she roadtripped across Europe from her Parisian base aged four, and she's been hitting the road at every opportunity since, travelling to around 60 countries and completing her Doctorate of Creative Arts in Writing, Masters in Professional Writing, and postgraduate qualifications in Editing and Publishing along the way. Over the past dozen-plus years she's written scores of Lonely Planet guides and articles covering Paris, France, Europe and far beyond. Her work has also appeared in numerous online and print publications. Topping Catherine's list of travel tips is to travel without any expectations. Catherine also wrote the Plan and Understand features, as well as the Survival Guide content.

Virginia Maxwell

Tampere, Pirkanmaa & Häme; The Lakeland Although based in Australia, Virginia spends at least half of her year updating Lonely Planet destination coverage in Europe and the Middle East. Though the Mediterranean is her major area of interest – she has covered Spain, Italy, Turkey, Syria, Lebanon, Israel, Egypt and Morocco for Lonely Planet guidebooks – Virginia has also written Lonely Planet guides to *Armenia*, *Iran*, *Australia* and the previous edition of *Finland*. Follow her @maxwellvirginia on Instagram and Twitter.

Published by Lonely Planet Global Limited
CRN 554153
9th edition – May 2018
ISBN 978 1 78657 467 1
© Lonely Planet 2018   Photographs © as indicated 2018
10 9 8 7 6 5 4 3 2 1
Printed in China